CompTIA Authorized Quality Curriculum

The logo of the CompTIA Authorized Quality Curriculum (CAQC) program and the status of this or other training material as "Authorized" under the CompTIA Authorized Quality Curriculum program signifies that, in CompTIA's opinion, such training material covers the content of CompTIA's related certification exam.

The contents of this training material were created for the CompTIA Linux+ exam covering CompTIA certification objectives that were current as of June 2007. CompTIA has not reviewed or approved the accuracy of the contents of this training material and specifically disclaims any warranties of merchantability or fitness for a particular purpose. CompTIA makes no guarantee concerning the success of persons using any such "Authorized" or other training material in order to prepare for any CompTIA certification exam.

How to Become CompTIA Certified

This training material can help you prepare for and pass a related CompTIA certification exam or exams. In order to achieve CompTIA certification, you must register for and pass a CompTIA certification exam or exams.

In order to become CompTIA certified, you must:

1. Select a certification exam provider. For more information please visit www.comptia.org/certification/general_information/exam_locations.aspx.

2. Register for and schedule a time to take the CompTIA certification exam(s) at a convenient location.

3. Read and sign the Candidate Agreement, which will be presented at the time of the exam(s). The text of the Candidate Agreement can be found at www .comptia.org/certification/general_information/candidate_agreement.aspx.

4. Take and pass the CompTIA certification exam(s).

For more information about CompTIA's certifications, such as its industry acceptance, benefits, or program news, please visit www.comptia.org/certification.

CompTIA is a not-for-profit information technology (IT) trade association. CompTIA's certifications are designed by subject matter experts from across the IT industry.

Each CompTIA certification is vendor-neutral, covers multiple technologies, and requires demonstration of skills and knowledge widely sought after by the IT industry.

To contact CompTIA with any questions or comments, please call (1) (630) 678-8300 or e-mail questions@comptia.org.

Robb H. Tracy (CNA, CNE, CNI, A+, Network+, Linux+) has designed and implemented technical training products and curricula for major hardware and software vendors including Novell, Micron Technology, TestOut, Messaging Architects, Caselle, MoveNetworks, Makau, Cymphonix, and NextPage. Robb has also served on industry-wide certification committees, and is a co-founder of Nebo Technical Institute, Inc., a leading provider of information technology training and consulting. Robb is also the author of *Novell Certified Linux Engineer (Novell CLE) Study Guide* (Novell Press, 2005) and *Novell Certified Linux Engineer 9 (CLE 9) Study Guide* (Novell Press, 2006). Robb was also a contributing author to *SUSE Linux 10 Unleashed* (Sams Publishing, 2006).

About the Technical Editor

Brian Barber (Linux+, MCSE, MCSA, MCP+I, MCNE, CNE, CNA-GW) is a consultant with Sierra Systems Consultants Inc., specializing in IT service management and infrastructure architecture design and implementation. He first started using Linux at home with Red Hat 5.1 and since then he has been a staunch advocate of open source software, belonging to the Ottawa Canada Linux User Group (OCLUG) since 2001. His primary areas of interest are operating systems, multiplatform integration, directory services, and enterprise messaging. In the past he has held the positions of Senior Technical Analyst at MetLife Canada and Senior Technical Coordinator at the LGS Group Inc. (now a part of IBM Global Services). Brian was a contributing author to six books and the technical editor for three others.

About LearnKey

LearnKey provides self-paced learning content and multimedia delivery solutions to enhance personal skills and business productivity. LearnKey claims the largest library of rich streaming-media training content that engages learners in dynamic media-rich instruction complete with video clips, audio, full motion graphics, and animated illustrations. LearnKey can be found on the Web at www.LearnKey.com.

This book is dedicated to all the individuals who have made a difference in my life. To my Dad, for instilling in me a love of teaching and all things mechanical. To my Mom, for teaching me the value of hard work and devotion. To my mentor, Dennis Simmons, for teaching me to strive for excellence in all I do. To my wife and best friend, for supporting and loving me through the process of writing this book.

CONTENTS AT A GLANCE

CONTENTS

ACKNOWLEDGMENTS

The title page of this book lists Robb H. Tracy as its author. However, this attribution is deceiving. By no means was this a one-person job. Behind every book is a team of people who rarely get the credit they deserve. They are the unsung heroes who make sure the job gets done.

First, I would also like to acknowledge the efforts of the production team behind this book. These folks were the glue that kept everything together. Thanks to Timothy Green for giving me the opportunity to write this book. I appreciate your confidence in me! Thanks to Jennifer Housh for managing the development process. No matter the time of day, Jenni was always there with the information I needed. Thanks, Jenni!

Finally, a huge thank you to Brian Barber. Brian reviewed each and every word and exercise step in this book for technical accuracy. His efforts kept me honest and were absolutely invaluable, dramatically increasing the overall quality of this title. Brian spent many late nights testing the lab exercises in this book, ensuring that you have a successful experience. Thanks, Brian!

INTRODUCTION

Congratulations on your decision to become Linux+ certified! By purchasing this book, you've taken the first step toward earning one of the hottest certifications around. Being Linux+ certified provides you with a distinct advantage in today's IT job market. When you obtain your Linux+ certification, you prove to your employer, your co-workers, and to yourself that you truly know your stuff with Linux.

This is a big issue. Over the years, I've had the opportunity to interview a number of job applicants for open positions in my organization. I learned early on that you can't rely on the Skills and Knowledge section of an applicant's résumé to get an accurate picture of what they can and can't do. Case in point: Back in the late 1990s my group had a position open that required an exceptionally strong background in computer hardware and networking. The job posting listed "extensive background with computers and networking" as one of the requirements for the position.

One of the candidates I interviewed claimed in her résumé to have an extensive background in these areas. In fact, during the interview she claimed to be an expert in the field. I have to admit, her résumé did look impressive.

However, as the interview progressed I began to have some doubts. This person just didn't speak or act like a true techie, so I decided to give a little test. I asked her to connect an Iomega Jazz drive to the external SCSI port on a workstation. A pretty easy task for an expert, right? Well, she couldn't do it. In fact, she didn't even know where to begin.

To make a long story short, upper management eventually hired this applicant in spite of my objections. It wasn't a good situation. She didn't have the background required and subsequently performed very poorly on the job and eventually quit after only a year. The key problem in this situation was conflicting definitions of a "computer and networking expert." We define this as someone who could install expansion cards, hard drives, and operating systems as well as set up a computer network.

This applicant, on the other hand, had a very different definition. She considered herself to be an expert because she knew how to use Microsoft Word, Excel, and PowerPoint. She also knew how to log into a network using her username and password. In essence, she was an expert end user, but she was not an expert system administrator, which was what we were looking for.

All this could have been avoided if my company had listed specific certifications in the job requirements instead of just asking for an "extensive background with computers and networking." Certifications help everyone involved in the hiring process. By requiring Linux+ certification, prospective employers can weed out applicants who really don't have the skills and knowledge required for a particular position. Having your Linux+ certification also helps you demonstrate to potential employers that you truly have the Linux background you claim on your résumé, giving you an advantage over other job applicants who aren't certified.

With this in mind, we need to introduce you to this book and the Linux+ certification program. We'll cover the following topics:

- Who this book is for
- How this book is organized
- The Linux+ certification exam
- Tips for succeeding on the Linux+ certification exam

Let's begin by discussing whom this book is for.

Who This Book Is For

Before you start this book, you need to be aware that I have two primary goals in mind as I write:

- To help you prepare for and pass the Linux+ exam offered by CompTIA.
- To provide you with the extra skills and knowledge you need to be successful on the job after you are certified.

Essentially, when we're done here I want you to be able to do more than just recite facts. I want you to be able to walk the walk and talk the talk. I want you to be able to actually do the job once hired.

To accomplish this, we're going to focus heavily on the core Linux knowledge and skills in this book required by the Linux+ certification. That means you need to already have a strong computing background before starting. You need to have a strong set of basic computer skills, such as:

- Knowing how to power your system off and on
- Knowing how to use a mouse and keyboard
- Knowing how to use end-user applications, such as word processors, spreadsheets, Web browsers, and e-mail clients

In addition to these skills, you also need to be very familiar with computer hardware and basic networking concepts and technologies. As we progress through this book, I'll try to provide background information where needed, but I'm going to assume that you already know your stuff with PC hardware and computer networking. You should be familiar with the following:

- PC cases and power supplies
- Motherboards
- Expansion slots and expansion boards
- CPUs and memory
- Storage devices such as hard drives, floppy drives, and optical drives
- Video boards and monitors
- Peripheral devices such as printers, scanners, and digital cameras
- Basic networking principles
- Common networking topologies (such as the star, bus, and ring)
- Common networking components such as NICs, cables, routers, and hubs/switches
- Common networking protocols (such as IP, IPX, TCP, UDP, and NetBIOS)
- Common networking services, such as FTP servers, Web servers, and mail servers

If possible, I strongly recommend that you have your A+ certification and your Network+ certification under your belt (or have equivalent experience in the field) before starting this book. These two certification programs will provide you with the hardware and networking background you need to be successful in your Linux+ certification program.

If you have this background, you're ready to roll! Let's next discuss how this book is organized to accomplish its two main goals.

How This Book Is Organized

I love CompTIA certification programs. They go the extra mile to make sure their certifications truly reflect current trends in the information technology industry, and the Linux+ certification is no exception. They define their certification programs by publishing objectives that list the skills and knowledge that a certified person should have.

However, these objectives, as currently published, are organized by topic. They aren't organized into a logical instructional flow. As you read through this book, you'll quickly notice that I don't address the Linux+ objectives in the same order as they are published by CompTIA. All of the objectives are covered; however, I've reorganized them such that we start with the most basic Linux concepts first. Then, as we progress through the course, we'll address increasingly more advanced Linux+ objectives, building upon the skills and knowledge covered in preceding chapters.

In addition, I've included information to emphasize important points, supply real-world examples, and provide tips for taking the Linux+ exam. Each chapter contains the following:

- ■ **Certification Objectives**   Each chapter begins with a list of Linux+ objectives that will be covered in the chapter. After completing each chapter, you should revisit the list of certification objectives and ask yourself "Can I actually do that now?"

- ■ **Exam Watch**   Exam Watch notes point out gotchas to watch for on the Linux+ exam. While I can't legally disclose exact questions from the exam, I can emphasize key concepts and skills that you should pay special attention to.

- ■ **Certification Exercises**   Each chapter has one or more certification exercises. Just about anyone can memorize a bunch of facts and pass an exam. This isn't enough for me. I would consider myself a failure as an instructor if that's all you could do after reading this book. Instead, I want you to be able to actually *perform* the tasks we cover in each chapter.

   To accomplish this, I've included many hands-on exercises in the book that will help you practice the skills and knowledge presented in the text. Don't pass over these exercises! If you want to do well on your Linux+ exam and perform well on the job, you need to practice. The more you practice the longer you will retain your newfound Linux knowledge.

- ■ **On the Job**   In addition to certification exercises, I've also included On the Job notes throughout each chapter. The goal is to provide you with knowledge beyond that which is required to pass the Linux+ exam. I've worked in the IT industry for a long time and I try to share real-world tips, tricks, and experiences that I've learned over the years in these notes.

- ■ **Scenario & Solution**   Each chapter also includes Scenario & Solution tables that present you with hypothetical scenarios and ask you to determine the correct way to address them. These also help you advance your knowledge and skills from the "pass the exam" level to the "perform well on the job" level.

on the
Øob

SCENARIO & SOLUTION

You're installing a Linux system that will function as a Web application server. Which packages should you install?	To provide Web application services, you will need Apache Web server, Tomcat servlet container, and a database application such as MySQL.

- **Certification Summary** At the end of each chapter, you will find a Certification Summary section that will review the key concepts and skills covered in the chapter.

✓ - **Two-Minute Drill** In addition to the Certification Summary, you will also find a Two-Minute Drill at the end of each chapter that contains a list of the most salient points from the chapter. This is an excellent review tool that you can use to prepare for your Linux+ exam.

Q&A - **Self Test** Each chapter includes a Self Test that you can use to prepare for your Linux+ exam. The Self Test contains test items that are similar to those found on the actual exam.

- **Lab Questions** A key aspect of moving from the memorization learning level to the application learning level is the ability to synthesize multiple ideas and skills together and apply them to an unencountered situation. That's the role of the Lab Question at the end of each Self Test. In the Lab Question, you are presented with a hypothetical scenario. To solve the problem presented, you must design a solution using multiple concepts and skills that will work together correctly. Be warned that the Lab Questions are intentionally difficult. Again, my goal is to help you pass the Linux+ exam *and* be proficient on the job. If you can correctly solve the Lab Questions, then you are on your way!

e x a m

ⓦatch *When taking the Self Tests, you should record your answers on a separate piece of paper. This will allow you to go through the items multiple times as you prepare for your Linux+ exam without giving away the correct answer.*

Once you've finished reading this book, you should take some time to meditate on and synthesize what you've learned. The reason for doing this is that the human brain has two main memory areas:

- Short-term memory
- Long-term memory

When you read this book, the information is first stored in your short-term memory. Your short-term memory is much like the cache on your PC's CPU. It's really fast, providing you with instant access to the information it contains. However, it's also very small. It just doesn't hold very much. The average person can only store between five and nine pieces of information in their short-term memory at a time.

When your short-term memory is full and new information needs to be loaded, one of two things happens:

- The existing information gets moved into your brain's long-term memory.
- The information gets dumped.

Obviously, you want the former and not the latter. The key to making this happen is meditation, practice, and application. If you just read this book, you probably won't remember many specific details when you're done. If you read this book and meditate about what you've read, you will remember many more details. Meditation gives your brain a chance to move information from your short-term memory into your long-term memory.

If you read this book, meditate on what you've learned, and then practice the skills and concepts you learned, using the Self Tests and Certification Exercises, you will retain considerably more. When you practice, you exercise your brain, making it easier to find and recall the information from your long-term memory. Then, if you take what you know and apply it to an unencountered circumstance in the real world, you ensure that the information is retained for a very long period of time.

The point is, don't just read this book and expect to remember everything. Utilize the resources included in this book to help reinforce the ideas and skills you learn. Later in this Introduction, we'll discuss test-preparation and test-taking strategies in more depth.

With this in mind, let's now spend some time familiarizing you with the Linux+ certification exam.

The Linux+ Certification Exam

Now that you understand how this book is organized, it's time for you to become familiar with the Linux+ certification program and its associated exam. You need to know the following:

- About the Linux+ certification
- Taking the Linux+ exam
- Exam makeup

About the Linux+ Certification

The Linux+ certification is an excellent program! Linux+ is a vendor-neutral certification designed and administered by the Computing Technology Industry Association, affectionately known as CompTIA. It's considered *vendor-neutral* because the exam isn't based on one particular vendor's hardware or software. This is somewhat unique in the information technology industry. Many IT certification programs are centered on one particular vendor's hardware or software, such as Microsoft's Certified System Engineer (MCSE) certification, Novell's Certified Novell Engineer (CNE) certification, or Red Hat's Certified Engineer (RHCE) certification.

The Linux+ certification, on the other hand, is designed to verify your knowledge and skills with the Linux operating system in general, not on any one particular distribution. According to CompTIA:

> *Professionals holding the CompTIA Linux+ credential can explain fundamental management of Linux systems from the command line, demonstrate knowledge of user administration, understand file permissions, software configurations, and management of Linux-based clients, server systems, and security.*

To verify your knowledge, CompTIA requires you to take the Linux+ exam to earn your certification. By passing this exam, you demonstrate that you have the skills and knowledge equivalent to a Linux system administrator who has 6–12 months of on-the-job experience.

CompTIA has published a set of objectives that define the Linux+ certification. These objectives specify what a Linux system admin with 6–12 months of experience should know and be able to do. You can view the Linux+ objectives at http://certification.comptia.org/linux/. All of the test items on the Linux+ exam are based on these objectives.

To define the Linux+ objectives, CompTIA organized a volunteer committee made up of representatives from the IT industry occupying a variety of positions in their respective organizations. They then asked these individuals "What does a Linux administrator with 6–12 months of experience have to know and be able to do to be effective on the job?" Using the responses from the committee members, CompTIA was able to craft a profile that they used to write a series of objectives. Some sample Linux+ objectives include

- Configure file systems (for example, ext2 or ext3 or Reiser file system).
- Manage packages after installing the operating system (for example, install, uninstall, update, RPM, tar, gzip).
- Select appropriate parameters for a Linux installation (for example, language, time zones, keyboard, mouse).

If you're going to be Linux+ certified, then you have to be able to do the tasks contained in these objectives. As we go through this book, you'll see that the complete list of Linux+ objectives is quite extensive. I love Linux+!

Let's now talk about the exam itself.

Taking the Linux+ Exam

The Linux+ exam is a timed exam that is delivered electronically on a computer. It's composed of 98 questions that you will have 90 minutes to complete. The exam interface is fairly straightforward. Each item is displayed one at a time on the screen, as shown in Figure I-1.

As you can see in Figure I-1, the Linux+ exam presents you with a question along with a series of responses. You use the mouse to mark the appropriate response and then select Next to go to the next question. If you need to go back to a prior question, select Previous.

The exam is composed of several types of questions:

■ **Multiple Choice**   The multiple-choice question format presents you with a question and asks you to mark the correct answer from a list of choices. The bulk of the questions on the Linux+ exam are multiple-choice questions.

Most multiple-choice questions require only one answer; some will require you to select multiple correct responses from the list displayed. If this is the case, the test question will end with the text (Choose *x*.) where *x* is the number of responses you should mark.

exam

⍵atch   *If you run into a particularly difficult question on the exam, don't spend too much time on it! I've known numerous students who have fallen into this trap. They encounter a very hard question on the exam and become obsessed with finding the answer. They accomplish the task, but burn up so much time in the process that they can't complete the rest of the exam.*

If you run into a really difficult question on your Linux+ exam, skip it and move on. After you have finished the rest of the test, come back to your skipped questions and use the remainder of your exam time to figure them out.

FIGURE I-I The Linux+ exam interface

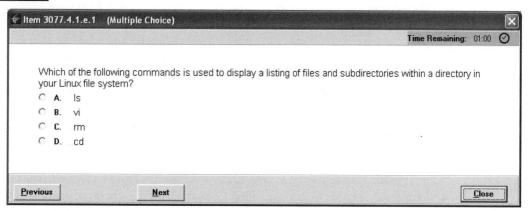

> **Exhibit** The exhibit question is a variation on the multiple-choice question type. In an exhibit question, you are presented with an Exhibit button. When you click it, a diagram, image, or scenario is displayed on the screen. You use the information in the exhibit to determine the correct answer to the multiple-choice question in the item.
>
> **Point and Click** Point and click questions display an image on the screen along with a question about the image. You then click on the appropriate location on the image to answer the question.

After you complete your exam, the computer will immediately evaluate it and your score will be printed out. To pass, you need a minimum score of 675 points out of a possible 900. Hopefully, you will pass your exam on the first try. However, if you don't, your score printout will list the objectives where you missed questions. You can use this information to review and prepare yourself to retake the exam. We'll discuss this in more detail later in this Introduction.

To make the exam globally available, CompTIA administers the Linux+ exam through two testing partners:

> **Thompson Prometric** www.prometric.com/default.htm
>
> **Pearson VUE** www.vue.com/

To sign up for your Linux+ exam, choose one of these testing partners and visit their Web site. There you will find a link that will help you locate a testing center near you. Most community and technical colleges are authorized testing centers.

Just specify the exam you want to take and your locale information. You will then be provided with a list of testing centers near you, as shown in Figure I-2.

You can then use the Prometric or the VUE Web site to schedule your exam and pay your fees. You can also call either provider directly and schedule your exam over the phone. Be aware that they will need to verify your identity before they can sign you up, so be prepared to share your Social Security number when you call or log on. The test provider will send you a confirmation e-mail listing the date, time, and location of your exam.

On the day of the test, be sure you allow adequate travel time. You never know when you will run into a traffic jam. In addition, you should try to show up early enough to find a parking spot and walk to the testing center. If you're taking your exam at a community college or a trade school, you may find that you have to walk a very long distance to get from the parking lot to the building where the exam is delivered. The last thing you need right before your exam is to feel rushed and stressed!

FIGURE I-2	Locating a testing center near you

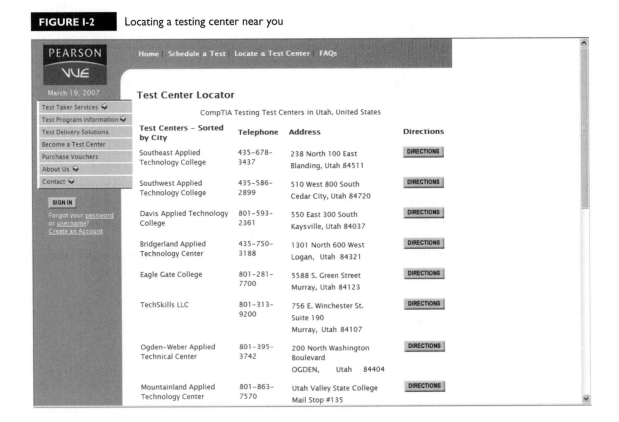

When you check in at the testing center, you will be required to show two forms of identification, one of which must have your photo on it. The following are acceptable forms of ID:

- Driver's license
- Social Security card
- Credit card
- Student ID card
- Military ID card
- State-issued ID card

Be warned that, when you check in, you must surrender your cell phone, iPod, PDA, laptop, or any other electronic devices to the test proctor. You're not allowed to take any reference materials into the exam room, including blank paper. Most testing centers will provide you with note-taking materials that must remain in the room where the test is being administered. Some testing centers will provide you with paper and a pencil; others may provide a small whiteboard slate with an erasable pen.

Let's now look at the composition of the Linux+ exam itself.

Exam Makeup

The Linux+ certification is composed of a single exam containing 98 questions. The exam is divided up into six categories, which CompTIA calls *domains*. These are shown in Table I-1.

As you can see in the table, some domains are tested more heavily than others. When studying, be sure to pay special attention to those domains with the highest percentage of exam questions!

With this in mind, let's now discuss how to prepare for the Linux+ exam.

TABLE I-1 Linux+ Domains	Domain	Percentage of Exam Questions
	Installation	19 percent
	Management	26 percent
	Configuration	20 percent
	Security	21 percent
	Documentation	6 percent
	Hardware	8 percent

Tips for Succeeding on the Linux+ Certification Exam

I'll never forget the first time I took an IT certification exam back in the early 1990s. I was so nervous that I almost couldn't function. Fortunately, the exam went very well and I passed it handily. Over the last decade, I've helped a number of individuals prepare themselves for a variety of certification exams. I've even written a number of industry certification exams myself. As a result, I've learned a number of things that you can do to increase the likelihood that you will pass your exam. We'll discuss the following here:

■ Preparing for the exam
■ Taking the exam

Let's begin by learning how you can prepare yourself for the Linux+ exam.

Preparing for the Exam

The most important thing you can do to prepare for your Linux+ exam is to thoroughly study. No tip, no trick, no strategy can compensate for a lack of study. Remember, the goal is to move the information you need to pass the exam into your long-term memory. Following are some suggestions for studying that can help you prepare for your certification exam.

One to Two Months Before Your Exam

■ Schedule your Linux+ exam. Ideally, you should schedule it to take place about 30–60 days after you begin this book. If you don't give yourself a deadline, you probably will never "get around" to studying for and taking the exam.

■ Pace yourself. Don't try to cram for the exam the night before. This is a very common mistake made by many students. (I did this myself in college.) Cramming rarely works because your short-term memory can only hold a limited amount of information. All that stuff you're trying to cram into your short-term memory gets lost. Instead, successful test-takers spend a good deal of time loading information into their long-term memory. You can do this by setting a goal to read a certain number of pages or chapters each day and sticking to it.

■ Take notes! As you read each chapter, write down important information that stands out to you. Writing this down helps reinforce the information, moving it from short-term memory into long-term memory in your brain. It also provides you with a valuable review resource.

■ Do the lab exercises, even the simple ones. Doing the lab exercises helps you learn the practical implementation of the conceptual skills and knowledge presented in each chapter.

■ Take the Self Tests at the end of each chapter. After you read a chapter, get a blank piece of paper and run through the Self Test, recording your responses on the paper. (Don't write in the book!) Check your answers and review the topics you missed.

■ Review the Certification Summary and Two-Minute Drill after you complete each chapter.

Two to Three Days Before Your Exam

■ Review your notes.

■ Retake the Self Tests at the end of each chapter. Review any topics that you are still struggling with.

■ Repeat the lab exercises for each chapter. This time, however, try to complete the exercises without looking at the steps in the book.

The Night Before Your Exam

■ Relax! Being well rested is a key to performing well on your exam. Don't get so worked up and nervous that you can't sleep the night before your exam. Get to bed at a reasonable hour.

■ Review your notes.

■ Review the Certification Summary and Two-Minute Drill again for each chapter. Repetition is the key to retention!

The Morning of Your Exam

■ Eat a good breakfast. Your brain requires a tremendous amount of calories to operate. Give it what it needs!

■ Review your notes.

■ Review the Certification Summary and Two-Minute Drill once again for each chapter. Did I mention that repetition is the key to retention?

■ Retake the Self Tests one more time at the end of each chapter.

■ Allow yourself plenty of time to get to the testing center. Don't get stressed out by being late.

What we're trying to do in this process is upload the information you need to pass your test into your long-term memory through repetition and practice. Then, shortly before the exam, we're exercising the brain by retrieving that stored information and bringing it to the forefront of your thoughts (kind of like loading data from a hard drive into system RAM) so that it is ready and available when you take the test.

Next, let's talk about some strategies you should keep in mind when actually taking the exam.

Taking the Exam

As I mentioned earlier, I've written a number of industry certification exams in addition to developing training materials for them. Because I've done this, I have some insights as to what goes on inside the devious minds of test item writers. I'm going to share them with you here:

■ *Carefully read the text of each question (called the* stem*)*. Some of the information in the stem is superfluous and intended to distract you. However, the question stem usually contains one or two critical pieces of information that influence the correct answer. If your testing center provides you with writing materials (and they should), I suggest you quickly jot down the key points from the stem.

■ *Carefully read each response*. Don't just skim them. Test item authors deliberately include responses that are *almost* correct, but not quite. (We call them *red herrings*.) The intent is to distract you away from the real answer. I know it sounds sneaky, but the intent is to make the exam such that you can't divine the correct answer without really knowing your stuff.

■ *Eliminate responses that are obviously wrong*. Each item will have one or more responses that are blatantly wrong. (Usually it's because the test author couldn't think of anything better to include as a response.) Eliminate these answers and focus only on the responses that could be correct.

■ *Make your best choice and move on*. My experience has been that your first impression is usually the correct one. If you agonize over the answers, you can over-think the question and end up picking the wrong response. You also waste valuable time. After carefully reading the question and each response, go with your intuition and then go on to the next item.

■ *If you get stuck on a particularly difficult item, don't waste a lot of time trying to figure out the right answer.* You can skip the item and come back to it later. Many students get obsessed with finding the right answer to a particularly difficult question and end up with insufficient time to answer the rest of the items on the exam. Answer the questions that you can and then come back to the difficult questions that will require more time.

After you finish your exam, your results will be automatically printed out for you. The report will be embossed by your test proctor to certify the results. Don't lose your report; it's the only hard copy you will receive. I've heard of many candidates who had to send a copy of their test report back to the testing company when technical problems prevented their test results from being recorded correctly.

The report will display your performance on each section of the exam. The Linux+ exam is a pass-fail exam. If you score 675 or better, you pass! A candidate with a score of 677 is every bit as certified as a candidate with a score of 898.

If you didn't pass, you can use the information on your report to identify the areas where you need to study. You can retake the exam immediately, if you wish. However, there are two things you need to keep in mind before you do this:

■ You have to pay full price for the retake.

■ The second exam probably won't be the same as the first. CompTIA publishes multiple forms of the Linux+ exam. You could actually score worse on the second exam than on the first.

If you fail, I suggest that you step back, take a deep breath, go home, and study up on the items you missed. Then schedule your retake within a day or two. If you wait any longer than that, your mind will probably go "cold" and you may need to go through the entire preparation process again from scratch.

Basically, you're better off if you pass the first time. It can be done if you properly prepare yourself. I've personally taken around 20 IT certification exams and I've always passed on the first try. If you follow the advice I've given you here, you should be well prepared for your Linux+ exam.

---

exam

ⓦatch *If you don't pass, you can retake the Linux+ exam as soon as you want, even the same day. However, if you don't pass again, you must wait at least 30 days before you will be allowed to take the exam a third time.*

Exam XK0-002

Exam Readiness Checklist

Official Objective	Study Guide Coverage	Ch #	Pg #	Beginner	Intermediate	Expert
Installation (1.0)						
Identify all system hardware required (for example, CPU, memory, drive space, scalability) and check compatibility with Linux distribution (1.1)	Installing Linux	3	113			
Determine appropriate method of installation based on environment (for example, boot disk, CD-ROM, network (HTTP, FTP, NFS, SMB)) (1.2)	Installing Linux	3	134			
Install multimedia options (for example, video, sound, codecs) (1.3)	Configuring Hardware	12	671			
Identify purpose of Linux machine based on predetermined customer requirements (for example, appliance, desktop system, database, mail server, Web server, etc.) (1.4)	Introducing Linux Installing Linux	1 3	12 103			
Determine what software and services should be installed (for example, client applications for workstation, server services for desired task) (1.5)	Installing Linux	3	126			
Partition according to pre-installation plan using fdisk (for example, /boot, /usr, /var, /home, swap, RAID/volume, hot-spare, lvm) (1.6)	Installing Linux	3	118			
Configure file systems (for example, ext2 or ext3 or Reiser) (1.7)	Installing Linux	3	119			
Configure a boot manager (for example, LILO, ELILO, GRUB, multiple boot options) (1.8)	Managing the Linux Boot Process	11	618			
Manage packages after installing the operating systems (for example, install, uninstall, update, RPM, tar, gzip) (1.9)	Installing and Managing Software on Linux	8	421			

Exam Readiness Checklist

Official Objective	Study Guide Coverage	Ch #	Pg #	Beginner	Intermediate	Expert
Select appropriate networking configuration and protocols (for example, inetd, xinetd, modems, Ethernet) (1.10)	Configuring Network Boards	13	750			
Select appropriate parameters for Linux installation (for example, language, time zones, keyboard, mouse) (1.11)	Installing Linux	3	142			
Configure peripherals as necessary (for example, printer, scanner, modem) (1.12)	Configuring Hardware	12	839			
Management (2.0)						
Manage local storage devices and file systems (for example, fsck, fdisk, mkfs) using CLI commands (2.1)	Managing the Linux File System	6	298			
Mount and unmount varied file systems (for example, Samba, NFS) using CLI commands (2.2)	Managing the Linux File System	6	307			
Create files and directories and modify files using CLI commands (2.3)	Managing the Linux File System	6	281			
Execute content and directory searches using find and grep (2.4)	Managing the Linux File System	6	292			
Create linked files using CLI commands (2.5)	Managing the Linux File System	6	287			
Modify file and directory permissions and ownership (for example, chmod, chown, sticky bit, octal permissions, chgrp) using CLI commands (2.6)	Working with Linux Users and Groups	7	380			
Identify and modify default permissions for files and directories (for example, umask) using CLI commands (2.7)	Working with Linux Users and Groups	7	388			
Perform and verify backups and restores (tar, cpio) (2.8)	Managing the Linux File System	6	320			

Exam Readiness Checklist

Official Objective	Study Guide Coverage	Ch #	Pg #	Beginner	Intermediate	Expert
Access and write data to recordable media (for example, CD RW, hard drive, flash memory devices) (2.9)	Configuring Hardware	12	314			
Manage runlevels and system initialization from the CLI and configuration files (for example, /etc/inittab and init command, /etc/rc.d, rc.local) (2.10)	Managing the Linux Boot Process	11	641			
Identify, execute, manage, and kill processes (for example, ps, kill, killall, bg, fg, jobs, nice, renice, rc) (2.11)	Managing Linux Processes and Services	10	549			
Differentiate core processes from non-critical services (for example, init, [kernel processes], PID, and PPID values) (2.12)	Managing Linux Processes and Services	10	554			
Repair packages and scripts (for example, resolving dependencies, repairing, installing, updating applications) (2.13)	Installing and Managing Software on Linux	8	453			
Monitor and troubleshoot network activity (for example, ping, netstat, traceroute) (2.14)	Configuring Linux Network Services	14	763			
Perform text manipulation (for example, sed, awk, vi) (2.15)	Using the Linux Shell	9	512			
Manage print jobs and print queues (for example, lpd, lprm, lpq, CUPS) (2.16)	Configuring Linux Network Services	14	843			
Perform remote management (for example, rsh, ssh, rlogin) (2.17)	Configuring Linux Network Services	14	869			
Perform NIS-related domain management (yp commands) (2.18)	Configuring Linux Network Services	14	862			
Create, modify, and use basic shell scripts (2.19)	Using the Linux Shell	9	518			

Exam Readiness Checklist

Official Objective	Study Guide Coverage	Ch #	Pg #	Beginner	Intermediate	Expert
Create, modify, and delete user and group accounts (for example, useradd, groupadd, /etc/passwd, chgrp, quota, chown, chmod, grpmod) using CLI utilities (2.20)	Working with Linux Users and Groups	7	349			
Manage and access mail queues (for example, sendmail, postfix, mail, mutt) using CLI utilities (2.21)	Configuring Linux Network Services	14	873			
Schedule jobs to execute in the future using at and cron daemons (2.22)	Managing Linux Processes and Services	10	582			
Redirect output (for example, piping, redirection) (2.23)	Using the Linux Shell	9	508			
Configuration (3.0)						
Configure client network services and settings (for example, settings for TCP/IP) (3.1)	Configuring Network Boards	13	752			
Configure basic server network services (for example, DNS, DHCP, Samba, Apache) (3.2)	Configuring Linux Network Services	14	793			
Implement basic routing and subnetting (for example, /sbin/route, IP forward statement) (3.3)	Configuring Network Boards	13	770			
Configure the system and perform basic makefile changes to support compiling applications and drivers (3.4)	Installing and Managing Software on Linux	8	430			
Configure files that are used to mount drives or partitions (for example, fstab, mtab, Samba, nfs, syntax) (3.5)	Managing the Linux File System	6	309			
Implement DNS and describe how it works (for example, edit /etc/hosts, edit /etc/host.conf, edit /etc/resolv.conf, dig, host, named) (3.6)	Configuring Linux Network Services	14	802			
Configure a network interface card (NIC) from a command line (3.7)	Configuring Network Boards	13	750			

Exam Readiness Checklist

Official Objective	Study Guide Coverage	Ch #	Pg #	Beginner	Intermediate	Expert
Configure Linux printing (for example, CUPS, BSD LPD, Samba) (3.8)	Configuring Linux Network Services	14	839			
Apply basic printer permissions (3.9)	Configuring Linux Network Services	14	843			
Configure log files (for example, syslog, remote log file storage) (3.10)	Documenting and Troubleshooting the System	16	977			
Configure the X Window System (3.11)	Configuring Hardware	12	712			
Set up environment variables (for example, $PATH, $DISPLAY, $TERM, $PROMPT, $PS1) (3.12)	Using the Linux Shell	9	483			
Security (4.0)						
Configure security environment files (for example, hosts.allow, sudoers, ftpusers, sshd_config, PAM) (4.1)	Configuring Linux Security	15	922			
Delete accounts while maintaining data stored in that user's home directory (4.2)	Working with Linux Users and Groups	7	368			
Given security requirements, implement appropriate encryption configuration (for example, blowfish 3DES, MD5) (4.3)	Configuring Linux Security	15	925			
Detect symptoms that indicate a machine's security has been compromised (for example, review log files for irregularities or intrusion attempts) (4.4)	Configuring Linux Security	15	936			
Use appropriate access level for login (for example: root level vs. user level activities, su, sudo) (4.5)	Configuring Linux Security	15	908			
Set process and special permissions (for example, SUID, GUID) (4.6)	Working with Linux Users and Groups	7	392			

Exam Readiness Checklist

Official Objective	Study Guide Coverage	Ch #	Pg #	Beginner	Intermediate	Expert
Identify different Linux Intrusion Detection Systems (IDS) (for example, Snort, PortSentry) (4.7)	Configuring Linux Security	15	939			
Given security requirements, implement basic IP tables/chains (note: requires knowledge of common ports) (4.8)	Configuring Linux Security	15	926			
Implement security auditing for files and authentication (4.9)	Configuring Linux Security	15	940			
Identify whether a package or file has been corrupted/altered (for example, checksum, Tripwire) (4.10)	Installing and Managing Software on Linux Configuring Linux Security	8 15	426 940			
Given a set of security requirements, set password policies to match (complexity/aging/shadowed passwords) (for example, identify systems not shadow passwords) (4.11)	Configuring Linux Security	15	943			
Identify security vulnerabilities within Linux services (4.12)	Configuring Linux Security	15	903			
Set up user-level security (for example, limits on logins, memory usage, and processes) (4.13)	Configuring Linux Security	15	907			
Documentation (5.0)						
Establish and monitor system performance baseline (for example, top, sar, vmstat, pstree) (5.1)	Documenting and Troubleshooting the System	16	969			
Create written procedures for installation, configuration, security, and management (5.2)	Documenting and Troubleshooting the System	16	962			
Document installed configuration (for example, installed packages, package options, TCP/IP assignment list, changes, configuration, and maintenance) (5.3)	Documenting and Troubleshooting the System	16	960			

Exam Readiness Checklist

Official Objective	Study Guide Coverage	Ch #	Pg #	Beginner	Intermediate	Expert
Troubleshoot errors using system logs (for example, tail, head, grep) (5.4)	Documenting and Troubleshooting the System	16	976			
Troubleshoot application errors using application logs (for example, tail, head, grep) (5.5)	Documenting and Troubleshooting the System	16	982			
Access system documentation and help files (for example, man, info, readme, Web) (5.6)	Getting Help	4	173			
Hardware (6.0)						
Describe common hardware components and resources (for example, connectors, IRQs, DMA, SCSI, memory addresses) (6.1)	Working with PC Hardware	2	45			
Diagnose hardware issues using Linux tools (for example, /proc, disk utilities, ifconfig, /dev, live CD rescue disc, dmesg) (6.2)	Documenting and Troubleshooting the System	16	987			
Identify and configure removable system hardware (for example, PCMCIA, USB, IEEE 1394) (6.3)	Working with PC Hardware	2	82			
Configure Advanced Power Management and Advanced Configuration and Power Interface (ACPI) (6.4)	Configuring Hardware	12	684			
Identify and configure mass storage devices and RAID (for example, SCSI, ATAPI, tape, optical recordable) (6.5)	Working with PC Hardware Configuring Hardware	2 12	71 700			

1
Introducing Linux

Congratulations on your decision to become Linux+ certified! By obtaining your Linux+ certification from CompTIA, you will show the world that you really know your stuff about one of the hottest new operating systems in the information technology industry today.

The introduction and adoption of Linux has been an interesting drama to observe. When Linux was first introduced back in the early 1990s, it was greeted with a collective yawn. The big operating system vendors of the day, including Microsoft, IBM, and Novell, barely even noticed. At the time, Linux was considered a hobbyist's plaything, reserved for only the geekiest of geeks.

Since that time, however, Linux has made slow but steady progress into the server room in an increasing number of organizations around the world. So much so, in fact, that everyone is starting to pay attention, including the big three mentioned above.

on the
Job

Novell has gone so far as to actually buy out SUSE Linux, headquartered in Germany, and market their own Linux distribution. Novell saw Linux and open source as the way of the future and bought SUSE and other open source companies, such as Ximian, to eventually replace its NetWare operating system.

Linux has even started making inroads into the desktop market, slowly replacing the Microsoft Windows operating system used by employees in many organizations. Since its introduction in the early '90s, Linux has gone from a programmer's pet project to a major force for change in the information technology industry.

As such, there is a growing demand for network administrators who can implement, maintain, and support the Linux operating system. If you've had any experience with Linux, you know that it is very different than the operating systems most users are familiar with, such as Microsoft Windows and Mac OS. Migrating from either of these systems to Linux requires a degree of expertise. By the time we're done with this book, you will have the knowledge and skills required to make this happen.

Before we can launch into a discussion of how to install and configure Linux, you need to have a solid understanding of where Linux came from, how you can get it, the roles it can play in your network, and the tools you can use to interact with the operating system. In this chapter, the following topics will be covered:

- Introducing Linux
- Using the Linux user interface

Let's begin by introducing you to the Linux operating system.

CERTIFICATION OBJECTIVE 1.01

Describe the Background and History of Linux

In this part of this chapter we're going to spend some time getting acquainted with Linux. Specifically, we're going to discuss:

- The role and function of Linux
- The historical development of Linux
- Linux distributions
- Common Linux roles

The first topic we need to review is the role Linux plays in a computer system.

The Role and Function of Linux

Linux is an *operating system*. All operating systems, including Linux, provide four key functions in a computer system:

- **Application Platform**   An operating system provides applications with a platform where they can run, managing their access to the CPU and system memory.
- **Hardware Moderator**   The operating system also serves as a mediator between running applications and the system hardware. Most applications are not written to directly address a computer's hardware. Instead, most operating systems include pre-written code that can be called from an application to access system hardware, such as memory, hard drives, and communication ports. This feature makes life much easier for programmers. Instead of having to write code for doing these tasks in each and every program, they can simply reuse this existing code provided by the operating system. It also ensures that one application running on the system doesn't try to use memory already in use by another application, and that applications don't use an inordinate amount of CPU time.
- **Data Storage**   The operating system is also responsible for providing an efficient and reliable means for storing information. Usually this is done using some type of storage device, such as a hard disk drive, that has been formatted with a particular type of file system that organizes the information in an easily retrievable format.

■ **Security**   The operating system is responsible for providing a degree of security for the data it hosts. The system administrator can create rules and grant rights that determine who can access what information. Some operating systems, such as Linux and Windows 2000/XP, do this job very well. Others, such as DOS or Windows 98, provide only a very minimal level of security.

■ **Connectivity**   The operating system manages connectivity between computer systems using a variety of network media and interfaces, including infrared, Ethernet, RS-232, and wireless.

Believe it or not, I frequently encounter people who don't understand the role Linux plays in a computer system. They are under the mistaken impression that Linux is some kind of killer application that they can run under Windows on their workstation.

This is mainly due to the fact that most users in recent years have grown up using Microsoft Windows on their computers. Their home computer came with Windows bundled on it; their computer at work probably runs Windows as well. Because of this, they perceive the operating system and the hardware of their computer as being married together in an inseparable union. You may have heard someone refer to his or her computer as a "Windows computer."

Actually, the computer hardware and the operating system are independent of each other. That's because the modern PC is modular in nature. The Windows operating system can be easily removed from the system and any compatible operating system can be installed in its place, including DOS, Windows, Linux, Solaris, and even Mac OS (if you install a special expansion board with the appropriate ROM chip).

The Linux operating system is composed of the following components:

■ **The Linux Kernel**   This is the heart of Linux; hence it is called the *kernel*. The kernel is the actual operating system itself. It's the component that fulfills the key operating system duties discussed above.

■ **Libraries**   Libraries are pre-written code "pieces" that application programmers use in their programs. As we discussed earlier, this can be a huge time saver. Imagine what would happen if you were a programmer and you had to include code in your applications that would allow it to work with every type of hard disk drive interface currently on the market. What a task! With libraries, the programmer doesn't care whether a SCSI or an IDE hard drive is installed in the system. He or she simply calls the appropriate library and tells the operating system that data is to be written or read from the drive. The operating system takes care of the rest.

■ **Utilities**   Linux includes a wide variety of utilities that you can use to complete operating system management tasks, such as maintaining the file system, editing text files, managing running processes, and installing new software packages.

■ **User Interface**   Of course, you as the end user need some means of interacting with the operating system. Linux includes both a command-line interface (CLI) and a graphical user interface (GUI). We'll explore both of these interfaces later in this chapter.

Let's next review how Linux came into being.

The Historical Development of Linux

Linux is somewhat of an anomaly in the software development industry. Most software products, whether they are applications or operating systems, are developed as a part of a well-organized design and development effort. I've personally worked

SCENARIO & SOLUTION

How does an operating system manage applications?	Operating systems manage applications by allocating each application a memory range it can use. The operating system manages memory access to ensure that one application doesn't try to use memory that's being used by another application. The operating system also controls access to the CPU.
You've just purchased a new computer that uses a dual-core Intel CPU. The computer came pre-bundled with Windows XP Home. Can you use Linux on this system?	Yes. Because the operating system and computer hardware are modular, you can remove Windows and install Linux. Likewise, you could also repartition the hard disk drive and install Linux on it, creating a dual-boot system.
You are a computer programmer. You need to access the hard disk drive to write data to a file. What is the most efficient way to do this?	You can link to an operating system library in your programming code and call functions from it that will allow you to easily create a file, write data to it, and close the file when you're done.

for many years in the software development industry and I've seen how it works first hand. Here's what happens in most companies:

1. The software company identifies a customer need.
2. A design team is put together, usually composed of programmers, project managers, and marketers.
3. The design team hashes out a Product Requirements Document (PRD) that specifies exactly what the product will do.
4. The tasks identified in the PRD are assigned to teams of programmers who write their assigned part of the code.
5. When complete, the code is checked in and the product is tested through a series of testing cycles.
6. When the product has its bugs worked out (or at least most of them), the finished product is shipped to the customer.
7. The customer uses the product for a period of time and usually identifies bugs that were missed in the initial testing. In addition, they usually identify new features and functionality that they would like to see added.
8. The software company receives feedback from the customers and the cycle begins all over again.

This is how most commercial software products are developed. Linux, on the other hand, didn't conform to this cycle when it was originally developed. Instead, one person, a graduate student at the University of Helsinki in Finland, initially developed the Linux kernel. This was Linus Torvalds.

In the early 1990s, Torvalds became interested in a freeware product called *Minix*. Developed by Andrew S. Tanenbaum, Minix was a clone of the commercial UNIX operating system. Tanenbaum was a university professor who taught computer programming in the Netherlands. At the time, there were three main operating systems that were generally available:

- DOS
- Mac OS
- UNIX

Windows was also on the horizon at the time. However, it was simply a shell that ran on top of DOS. It really wasn't a true operating system yet. Each of these operating systems was commercially developed. As such, patents and copyrights carefully protected the source code for each product.

At one point the source code to the UNIX operating system had actually been made available to universities for teaching purposes. However, this practice had been stopped. This left Tanenbaum without an effective tool to teach his students about the inner workings of an operating system.

Undaunted, Tanenbaum set out to make his own operating system to use in class. He developed a small clone of the UNIX kernel called Minix. His goal was to provide students with a real operating system and its accompanying source code. Tanenbaum even included the source code to Minix in his textbook, *Operating Systems: Design and Implementation* (Prentice Hall, 2006).

Inspired by Tanenbaum and Minix, Torvalds developed his own UNIX clone in 1991, which he dubbed *Linux*. Now, this first version of Linux was extremely minimal in nature. It wasn't a full-blown operating system complete with applications and utilities. Instead, Linux version 0.02, released on October 5, 1991, consisted of only the Linux kernel and three utilities:

- **bash**   A command-line interface
- **update**   A utility for flushing file system buffers
- **gcc**   A C++ compiler

In an unprecedented move, Torvalds posted the source code for his Linux operating system on the Internet and made it freely available to anyone who wanted to download it. The corporate software development model had been completely broken.

Torvalds took things one step further and invited other programmers to take the Linux source code and enhance it. Linux took on a life of its own and became a worldwide collaborative development project. No secrecy; no tightly guarded copyrights. Access to the Linux source code was open to anyone who wanted it.

This collaborative development project on Linux continued for several years. In 1994, Linux version 1.0 was ready for release. The results since have been nothing short of amazing.

So why did Torvalds "give away" Linux to anyone who wanted it? Why didn't he follow the standard corporate development model and make a mountain of money? To understand this, you need to be familiar with the *GNU's Not UNIX* (GNU) movement. In the early 1980s a programmer named Richard Stallman at the Massachusetts Institute of Technology proposed an alternative to the standard corporate software development model. He objected to the proprietary nature of the process and the product.

In 1983, Stallman launched the *GNU Project*. GNU is centered around the idea that the source code for applications and operating systems should be freely distributable to anyone who wants it. He felt that the source code for programs should be free from all restrictions that prevent copying, modification, and redistribution. Stallman hoped that allowing programmers around the world to modify an application's source code would result in higher-quality software.

The GNU Project slowly took hold. Many useful applications, such as the GNU C Compiler (gcc) were developed under GNU. Torvalds was heavily influenced by the GNU Project and released the source code for his Linux operating system kernel to the world as a result.

Today, many powerful applications are available, via GNU, that run on Linux. This array of powerful applications has been a key factor that has helped take Linux from a programmer's pet project to a robust tool suitable for wide deployment in the modern organization.

Linux itself is licensed under the *GNU General Public License* (GPL). The key thing to remember about the GPL is that it requires that the source code remain freely available to anyone who wants it. As a result, anyone can download the Linux kernel's source code, modify it, recompile it, and run it.

This is a very unusual aspect of Linux. Most modern operating system vendors do not make their products' source code freely available. To the contrary, most operating systems have a section in their End User License Agreement (EULA) that prevents the user from reverse-compiling the operating system.

on the
ⓘob
There are applications available that can reverse-compile a binary program file. This process re-creates the program's source in a text file. The source code generated isn't an exact duplicate of the original source code, but an approximation that can be very close to the original source code.

Because Linux is distributed under the GPL, anyone can download the source code and create a custom version of Linux.

Let's next discuss Linux distributions.

SCENARIO & SOLUTION

You've downloaded the source code for the Linux kernel. You made several modifications to make the kernel handle Web site hosting tasks better. You've recompiled the kernel and it runs great. Can you legally give a copy of your new kernel to a coworker?	Yes, you can. Under the GPL, anyone can modify the Linux kernel and create their own custom Linux distribution. As long as you abide by the particulars of the GPL, such as making your source code freely available, you can redistribute your version of Linux.

Linux Distributions

The concept of a Linux *distribution* can be confusing to those new to Linux. Perhaps the best way to think of a distribution is to compare Linux to ice cream. Ice cream comes in a variety of flavors; however, the basic formula of the ice cream itself is the same. Most ice cream is made from:

- Cream
- Milk
- Sugar
- Eggs

Companies that sell ice cream take this basic ice cream recipe and customize it by adding additional ingredients, such as chocolate, vanilla, fruit, cookies, nuts, and candy. By doing this, they create their own flavors of ice cream.

Linux distributions work in much the same way. Because the source code for the Linux kernel is freely distributable, software vendors are free to download it. This kernel source code is similar to the basic recipe for ice cream. The kernel is the core of the operating system around which everything else runs.

Like ice cream companies, the software company can then modify and enhance the source code and create a customized kernel. They can also add tools, utilities, and applications to the operating system to enhance its usefulness, just as ice cream companies add additional ingredients to the basic ice cream recipe.

The result is a Linux distribution. You may already be aware that there are many different Linux distributions available. This is yet another unique characteristic of Linux that differentiates it from other operating systems.

Nearly every other operating system is developed and marketed by a single vendor. For example, the only vendor who develops and sells OS X is Apple, Inc. You can't go to Novell for their version of the Mac OS nor can you go to Microsoft for their version of the Mac OS. Likewise, you can't get a copy of Windows from Apple or Novell.

Imagine what the world would be like if other operating systems were developed in the same manner as Linux. Suppose you wanted to purchase a copy of the latest version of Windows. If Windows were licensed under the GPL, you would visit your local computer store and find that there were many different Windows distributions available from a variety of different software vendors, only one of which would be Microsoft.

Each distribution would be slightly different from the others, although they would still be based on the same kernel. One may be optimized as a high-power Web server. Another may be optimized for graphics, music, and video. You would be able to browse through the different distributions and find the one that is best for you.

This scenario is unlikely as far as Windows is concerned. However, with Linux that's exactly what is available to you. Many different software developers have taken the basic Linux kernel and modified it to suit some particular purpose. They may have also bundled many powerful applications with it. Some distributions may be customized to provide file and print services in a network. Others may be customized to provide excellent productivity applications on end users' desktops. Either way, the result is a customized Linux distribution.

Today there are hundreds of different distributions available. Some of the more popular Linux distributions include

- SUSE Linux
- Fedora Linux
- Red Hat Enterprise Linux
- Debian Linux
- ALT Linux
- Gentoo Linux
- Slackware Linux

- TurboLinux
- Mandrake Linux
- Lycoris Linux
- Linspire
- CentOS
- Ubuntu

on the
Öob
A great table providing an overview and comparison of most Linux distributions is available at http://en.wikipedia.org/wiki/Comparison_of_Linux_distributions.

So which distribution is best? That is a dangerous question. Normally pacifist network administrators and programmers can come to blows once they start debating which distribution is the best. That's because the distribution that works the best for you may not meet the needs of someone else. The key here is to try out several distributions and pick the one you like.

Personally, I have grown to love SUSE Linux from Novell. You can download a copy of this distribution from **http://www.opensuse.org**. It has become my Linux distribution of choice. Likewise, I really like Red Hat Enterprise Linux and Fedora from Red Hat. You can download a copy of Fedora from **http://fedora.redhat.com**. Because of this, most of the screenshots you will see in this book will be from OpenSUSE. Anywhere that there's a significant difference between OpenSUSE and other distributions, I'll make a note of it in the text.

Let's now discuss the varied roles a Linux system can fill in your computer network.

Common Linux Roles

Because Linux is distributed under the GPL, software vendors have been able to tweak and customize the operating system to operate in a variety of roles. While the number of these roles is virtually limitless, for your Linux+ exam you need to be familiar with the following roles:

- Linux on the desktop
- Linux as a server
- Linux as a firewall

Let's begin by discussing Linux on the desktop.

Linux on the Desktop

Linux can be optimized to function extremely well on the desktop. However, Linux has been somewhat slow to make inroads into this market. There are two important reasons for this.

First, there has been a historical lack of desktop productivity applications available for Linux. Users need word processing, spreadsheet, and presentation software on their desktops to do their day-to-day work. In the past, these types of applications haven't been readily available. This situation has been getting better recently. The introduction of the OpenOffice.org productivity suite has really helped make Linux a viable option for the desktop.

The second issue is that the average user tends to find Linux somewhat intimidating. For you and I, this isn't a problem. We're comfortable with Linux. We know how to use it effectively. Unfortunately, the average user in most organizations first learned how to run a computer using some version of Windows. They are comfortable with Windows and they don't want to learn a new operating system.

The key to making Linux viable on the desktop is to first provide users with the applications they need to get their work done. The second is to make the user

INSIDE THE EXAM

Distributions on the Linux+ Exam

One of the wise decisions made by the industry experts who developed the Linux+ certification was to make it vendor-neutral. You will not be tested on one particular distribution. The tasks you will be tested on should be generic in nature. Therefore, you can use the distribution of your choice when studying for your exam.

However, I strongly recommend that you opt for one of the more widely implemented distributions. The test writers at CompTIA appear to have used distributions such as OpenSUSE, Fedora/Red Hat Linux, and Debian when they created the Linux+ exam. You should probably elect to use one of these distributions as well when you study.

interface easy and intuitive such that a migration from Windows to Linux is as painless for the end user as possible.

Several vendors have been working on Linux distributions that do just this. They optimize Linux to run productivity applications as efficiently and as fast as possible. They also bundle application suites, such as OpenOffice.org, with the operating system and have them installed by default. Additionally, they rework their Linux window managers to provide the end user with an easy-to-use graphical interface.

Two of the more popular desktop Linux distributions include the following:

- SUSE Linux Enterprise Desktop
- Red Hat Desktop

One of the key advantages of using Linux on the desktop is the fact that Linux systems are immune to most of the viruses circulating today. If you've ever been responsible for managing a computer network, you know what a daunting task virus protection can be. Using Windows-based e-mail clients and browsers exposes your network to a wide variety of virus, worm, and spyware threats. You must spend large amounts of money and time deploying anti-virus software to keep your network systems from becoming infected.

However, most viruses, worms, and spyware apps won't run on Linux. By deploying Linux on the desktop, you can conserve valuable time and money by eliminating the need for anti-virus software.

In addition to a desktop operating system, Linux can also be deployed as a server operating system.

Linux as a Server

Linux works great as a server. In fact, Linux is experiencing widespread acceptance in the server room, much more so than on the desktop. That's because Linux can assume a variety of server roles, including the following:

- **File Server**   Using the Network File System (NFS) or Samba service, Linux can be configured to provide network storage of users' files.
- **Print Server**   Using the Common UNIX Printing System (CUPS) and Samba services together, Linux can be configured to provide shared printing for network users.
- **Database Server**   Linux works great as a database server. There are a variety of database services available for Linux servers, including MySQL and PostgreSQL.

- ■ **Web Server** Linux is also widely deployed as a Web server. The most popular Web service currently used on Linux is the Apache Web server.
- ■ **E-Mail Server** There are a variety of different e-mail services available for Linux that can turn your system into an enterprise-class e-mail server.

The widespread popularity of Linux as a server is due to a number of reasons. First of all, Linux is extremely stable. Simply put, a Linux server rarely crashes. It just keeps running and running. Other server operating systems have had a notorious reputation for crashing on a regular basis.

Second, Linux servers are very fast. Many benchmark tests have been run pitting Linux servers against other server operating systems. Each time, Linux servers have performed as well, if not much better, than other comparable operating systems.

Third, Linux servers are much less expensive. Most other server operating systems charge expensive per-seat licensing fees, making them very expensive to deploy in large networks. Depending upon the distribution you choose, a Linux server may cost little or even nothing at all.

The cool thing about Linux servers is that you don't necessarily have to use a special version of Linux. Almost any distribution can be configured to provide network services (and perform that service extremely well). In fact, the server in my office runs on SUSE Linux 10.0, which is not specifically designed to be a network server. However, because of the robust nature of Linux, it works great.

If you are going to deploy Linux as a server in a larger organization, then you may want to consider using a distribution specifically optimized to function in the server role. Red Hat offers the Red Hat Enterprise Server AS and ES distributions that have a proven track record as enterprise-class servers. Likewise, Novell offers the SUSE Linux Enterprise Server (SLES) distribution that is also optimized for the server role.

Finally, Linux can also be used as a firewall. Let's discuss this next.

Linux as a Firewall

In today's networked world, you must be constantly vigilant against threats coming into your network from the outside. Most organizations implement network firewalls to protect their internal computer network from threats on the external public network (such as the Internet).

So what exactly is a firewall? A firewall is a special computer system that sits between your network and another network. It usually has two or more network interfaces installed. One network interface is connected to the internal network and the second interface is connected to the public network. This is shown in Figure 1-1.

FIGURE 1-1

Using Linux as
a firewall

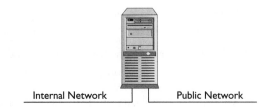

Internal Network   Public Network

The job of a firewall is to analyze all of the network traffic that flows between
the internal networks and the external network, including inbound and outbound
traffic. The firewall is configured with rules that define what kind of traffic is allowed
through and what kind isn't. Any network traffic that violates the ruls is not allowed
through, as shown in Figure 1-2.

Linux can be customized and configured to operate as a firewall in your network.
Using netfilters and iptables, you can create rules that filter network traffic at the
packet level. Using Squid, you can create an application-level gateway on a Linux
system as well.

Now that you understand the various roles that a Linux system can fill on your
network, we need to shift gears and actually start working with the Linux user
interface. Let's do that next.

FIGURE 1-2

Firewalls block or
allow traffic based
on rules.

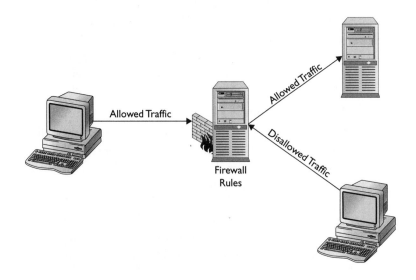

SCENARIO & SOLUTION

You need to implement Linux as a file server in your network. What software should be installed to make it fill this role?	You have two choices. You can install and use NFS to provide Network File System access. NFS works great for Linux or UNIX client systems. However, it doesn't work as well for Windows clients. Samba is a better choice for these systems.
You want to start using Linux on your users' desktops. What issues should you consider before doing so?	First of all, Linux can be intimidating to the average end user. You may want to consider implementing an extensive training program. Second, you should make sure you install software packages that will allow them to complete their day-to-day tasks.

CERTIFICATION OBJECTIVE 1.02

Use the Linux User Interface

For an operating system to be useful, it must provide some means for the user to communicate with it. Users need a way to tell the operating system what it should do, such as running a program, copying a file, or shutting down. These tasks are done using a *user interface*. Linux provides two types of user interfaces:

- **Command-Line Interface (CLI)** With the command-line interface, the user communicates with the Linux operating system by typing commands at a command prompt, as shown in Figure 1-3.

- **Graphical User Interface (GUI)** In addition to a command-line interface, Linux also offers users an easy-to-use graphical user interface. While most network administrators are at ease with the Linux CLI, most end users aren't. They are much more comfortable with a GUI. Because of the dominance of Windows in the home computer market, most end users have never even used a command-line type of interface. To make life easier, the XFree86 project developed a free windows system that provides a GUI on the Linux operating system. Using X Windows along with a window manager and a desktop environment (such as GNOME or KDE), users can interact with the Linux kernel using a mouse instead of the keyboard. The KDE graphical interface is shown in Figure 1-4.

FIGURE 1-3 The Linux command-line interface

Welcome to SUSE LINUX 10.1 (i586) - Kernel 2.6.16.13-4-default (tty3).
mylinux login: rtracy
Password:
Last login: Thu Aug 31 10:40:52 MDT 2006 on tty1
Have a lot of fun...
rtracy@mylinux:~> _

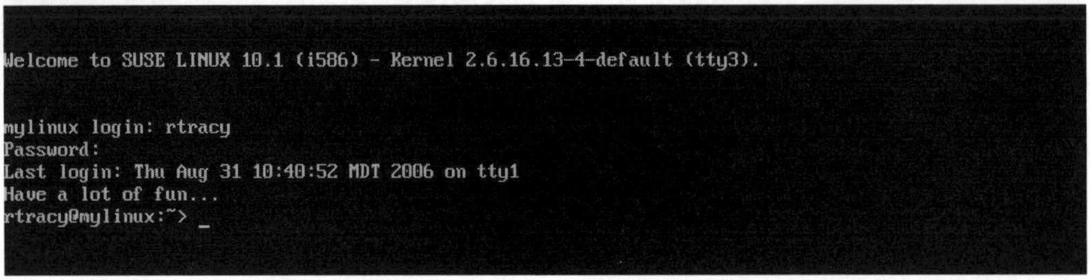

Next, let's spend some time getting acquainted with both of these user interfaces beginning with the command line.

Using the Linux Command-Line Interface

While graphical user interfaces are generally easier to use, many, if not most, of the tasks you must perform to administer and support a Linux system must be done from the command line. Basically, end users use the GUI; administrators use the command line.

Therefore, we will spend a great deal of time working with the Linux command-line interface in this book. In this chapter, we will give you a brief introduction to

FIGURE 1-4 The Linux graphical user interface

Trash
SUSE
Firefox
Office
My Computer
Network Browsing
Printer
1
2
10:53 am
08/31/06

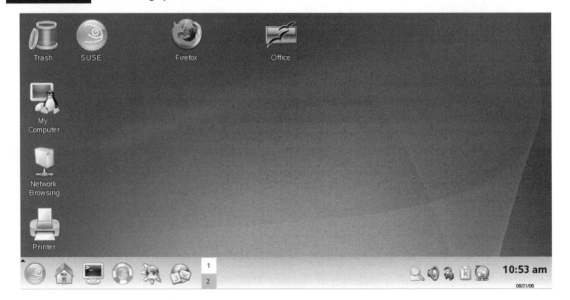

the command line. In later chapters, we will investigate the Linux CLI in more depth. In this chapter, we will discuss the following topics:

- Linux shells
- Running commands at the shell prompt
- Commonly used CLI commands and utilities

Let's begin by discussing Linux shells.

Linux Shells

To fully understand how the command-line interface works under Linux, you need to understand the concept of a *shell*. A shell is a command interpreter that allows you to type commands from the keyboard to interact with the operating system kernel.

Back in the days before Windows, most computer users had no choice but to be familiar with command-line shells. In the various versions of DOS that were in use back then, the only way you could communicate with the operating system was to enter commands through a command-line shell called COMMAND.COM.

Linux also uses command-line shells. However, unlike DOS, you have a choice of which shell you want to use. As with many other aspects of Linux, you can try out several of different command-line shells and choose the one that you like the best. Some of the more popular shells include the following:

- **sh (Bourne Shell)**   The sh shell was the earliest shell, being developed for UNIX back in the late 1970s. While not widely used on Linux systems, it is still very widely used on UNIX systems.
- **bash (Bourne-Again Shell)**   The bash shell is an improved version of the sh shell and is one of the most popular shells today. It's the default shell used by most Linux distributions. If you're using the command line on a Linux system, more than likely you're using the bash shell.
- **csh (C Shell)**   The csh shell was originally developed for BSD UNIX. It uses a syntax that is very similar to C programming.
- **tsch**   The tsch shell is an improved version of the C Shell. It is the default shell used on FreeBSD systems.
- **zsh (Z Shell)**   The Z Shell is an improved version of the bash shell.

When you first boot your Linux system and log in, your default shell is loaded. You can identify which shell you're using by entering **env** at the current shell prompt. The env command lists all the environment variables for the currently logged-in user. One of the variables is the shell in use, as shown next.

```
LESSKEY=/etc/lesskey.bin
NNTPSERVER=news
INFODIR=/usr/local/info:/usr/share/info:/usr/info
MANPATH=/usr/local/man:/usr/share/man:/usr/X11R6/man:/opt/gnome/share/man
HOSTNAME=mylinux
GNOME2_PATH=/usr/local:/opt/gnome:/usr
XKEYSYMDB=/usr/X11R6/lib/X11/XKeysymDB
HOST=mylinux
TERM=linux
SHELL=/bin/bash
PROFILEREAD=true
HISTSIZE=1000
MORE=-sl
GROFF_NO_SGR=yes
JRE_HOME=/usr/lib/jvm/jre
USER=rtracy
```

In the figure above, the bash shell is the default shell for the rtracy user account, as indicated by the SHELL variable.

However, you're not stuck with the default shell. If you want to switch to a different shell, simply enter the shell command at the prompt. For example, if you are currently using the bash shell and want to use zsh instead, simply enter **zsh** at the prompt. This is shown in the following illustration.

```
rtracy@mylinux:~> zsh
rtracy@mylinux:~> _
```

To stop using the new shell and revert back to the original shell, simply enter **exit**, as shown next.

```
rtracy@mylinux:~> zsh
rtracy@mylinux:~> exit
rtracy@mylinux:~> _
```

Back in the "old days" of DOS, you could only run one command-interpreter session at a time. Even though all CPUs since the 80286 were capable of running in Protected mode, MS-DOS ran the CPU in Real mode. This was done to preserve backward-compatibility with the old 8086 and 8088 CPUs.

In Protected mode, the CPU can run multiple virtual 8086 emulation sessions at the same time. In Real mode, the CPU emulates a fast 8086, which only allows one session to run at a time.

Unlike DOS, Linux is fully capable of running an x86 CPU in Real mode, which allows it to run multiple command-line sessions at once. Each session can run its own programs, all simultaneously. This can be very useful if you have one program running and then need access to the command prompt. Simply press ALT-FX (where X is a number from 2 to 6) to open a new session. For example, to switch to the third alternate console screen, press ALT-F3. You can then return to your original session by pressing ALT-F1.

As with Windows, you can also run terminal sessions within the Linux GUI. This is done by running a terminal program such as Konsole. To run multiple command-line sessions, simply open two or more terminal windows. Each session can run programs independently of the other sessions. This is shown in Figure 1-5.

This can also be accomplished in a second way. While you're within the Linux GUI, press CTRL-ALT-FX (where X is a number from 2 to 6). This will switch you to a text-based shell prompt. To switch back to your GUI environment, press ALT-F7.

FIGURE 1-5   Running multiple command-line sessions within the Linux GUI

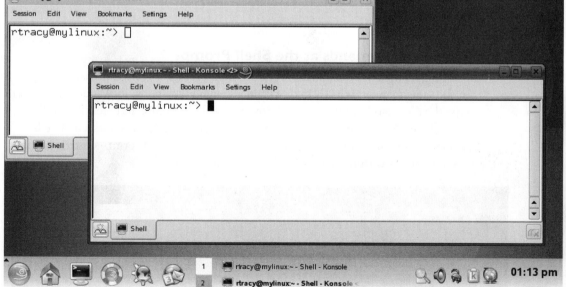

EXERCISE 1-1

Working with Linux Shells

In this exercise, you learn how to access the shell prompt, change shells, and access alternate console screens. Complete the following:

1. Boot your Linux system to a shell prompt (run-level 3). If your system booted into a graphical system, log in and then press CTRL-ALT-F1.

2. At your login prompt, authenticate to the system.

3. View your default shell by entering **echo $SHELL** at the prompt. Your default shell is displayed. On most systems, this will be /bin/bash.

4. Open an alternate console window by pressing ALT-F2. A new login prompt is displayed.

5. Authenticate again to the system.

6. Return to the first console screen by selecting ALT-F1.

7. Load the zsh shell by entering **zsh** at the prompt.

8. Return to your default shell by entering **exit** at the prompt.

Now that you know how to access your shell, let's talk about how you use it to run programs.

Running Commands at the Shell Prompt

Running a program or command from the shell prompt is relatively easy. It is done in the same manner as in DOS or within a command window in Windows. You just type the command or program file name at the shell prompt and press ENTER. For example, in the illustration shown next the ls command has been issued. The ls command is equivalent to the DIR command under DOS. It prints a listing of files and directories within the current directory on screen.

```
Welcome to SUSE LINUX 10.1 (i586) - Kernel 2.6.16.13-4-default (tty3).


mylinux login: rtracy
Password:
Last login: Thu Aug 31 13:16:18 MDT 2006 on tty1
Have a lot of fun...
rtracy@mylinux:~> ls
bin  Desktop  Documents  grep  public_html
rtracy@mylinux:~> _
```

There is one issue here you need to be aware of. That is the fact that Linux handles the path to the executable you want to run in a different manner than Windows or DOS.

on the

!

Öob

This is the one issue that I see new Linux administrators struggle with the most. Be sure you know how Linux handles the PATH variable.The PATH variable is an environment variable that contains a list of directories.

Within DOS or a Windows command window, the command interpreter first looks for the file name you specify at the prompt in the current directory. If the file isn't located in the current directory, the command interpreter reads the PATH environment variable. It searches each directory listed in the PATH variable, looking for the file name that was entered at the command prompt. If the file is found, it will then run the executable. If not, an error message is displayed on the screen for the user.

Linux also employs a PATH environment variable. However, Linux does *not* check the current directory the way DOS does when executing a file. This can be a real stumbling block to new Linux administrators and users. Because of prior experience with other operating systems, they expect to be able to switch to the directory where an executable resides and run it from the command line.

Under Linux, this doesn't work. Instead, Linux only searches for the file being run within the directories in the current user's PATH variable. A typical Linux PATH environment variable is shown in the next illustration.

```
MINICOM=-c on
MAIL=/var/mail/rtracy
PATH=/home/rtracy/bin:/usr/local/bin:/usr/bin:/usr/X11R6/bin:/bin:/usr/games:/opt/gnome/bin:/opt/kde
3/bin:/usr/lib/jvm/jre/bin:/usr/lib/mit/bin:/usr/lib/mit/sbin
CPU=i686
JAVA_BINDIR=/usr/lib/jvm/jre/bin
INPUTRC=/home/rtracy/.inputrc
PWD=/home/rtracy
JAVA_HOME=/usr/lib/jvm/jre
LANG=en_US.UTF-8
PYTHONSTARTUP=/etc/pythonstart
TEXINPUTS=:/home/rtracy/.TeX:/usr/share/doc/.TeX:/usr/doc/.TeX
SHLVL=1
HOME=/home/rtracy
LESS_ADVANCED_PREPROCESSOR=no
OSTYPE=linux
LS_OPTIONS=-N --color=tty -T 0
XCURSOR_THEME=crystalwhite
WINDOWMANAGER=/usr/X11R6/bin/kde
```

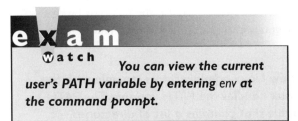

Even if the executable in question resides in the current directory, Linux won't be able to find it if the current directory is not in the PATH variable. Instead, the shell will return an error. For example, in the next illustration, an executable file named runme.pl is located in the home directory of the rtracy user. This has been verified using the ls command.

```
rtracy@mylinux:~> ls
bin  Desktop  Documents  grep  public_html  runme.pl
rtracy@mylinux:~> runme.pl
-bash: runme.pl: command not found
rtracy@mylinux:~>
```

However, when runme.pl is entered at the shell prompt, the shell can't find the file because rtracy's home directory (/home/rtracy) is not listed within the PATH environment variable.

There are two ways to deal with this. First, you can enter the full path to the executable file. For the example shown above, you could enter **/home/rtracy/ runme.pl** at the shell prompt to execute the file.

Second, you can switch to the directory where the executable file resides. Then add **./** to the beginning of the command. In the above example, you would first verify that the current directory is /home/rtracy; then you could enter **./runme.pl** at the shell prompt. The ./ characters denote the current directory. By adding them to the beginning of a command, you tell the shell to look for the specified file in the command in the current directory.

There's one other issue that you need to be aware of when working with Linux shells. Linux file names and directory names are case-sensitive! That means Linux commands are also case-sensitive. If the executable file you are going to run is runme.pl, then you must enter **runme.pl** at the shell prompt. Runme.pl, RUNME.PL, or Runme.PL won't work. The shell interprets each of those as different files.

This applies to directory names as well. If you're calling /home/rtracy/runme.pl, then you must enter the command using the exact case. /Home/Rtracy/Runme.pl will point the command interpreter to a completely different place in the file system.

Now that you know how to enter commands at the shell, let's review some commonly used Linux commands and utilities.

Commonly Used CLI Commands and Utilities

As you gain experience with Linux you'll discover that it includes some very powerful commands and utilities that you will use over and over. These include the following:

- **halt** This command shuts down the operating system, but can only be run by the root user.
- **reboot** This command shuts down and restarts the operating system. It also can only be run by root.
- **init 0** This command also shuts down the operating system, and can only be run by your root user.
- **init 6** This command also shuts down and restarts the operating system. It also can only be run by root.
- **man** This command opens the manual page for the command or utility specified. The man utility is a very useful tool. If you are unsure how to use any command, use man to access its manual page. For example, you could enter **man ls** at the shell prompt to learn how to use the ls utility. This is shown in Figure 1-6.
- **info** The info utility also displays a help page for the indicated command or utility. The information displayed tends to be more in-depth than that displayed in the man page for the same command. For example, the info utility has been used to display information about ls in Figure 1-7.

- **su** This command switches the current user to a new user account. For example, if you're logged in as rtracy and need to change to user account dcoughanour, you can enter **su dcoughanour** at the shell prompt. This command is most frequently used to switch to the superuser root account. In fact, if you don't supply a username, this utility assumes that you want to change to the root account. If you enter **su -**, then you will switch to the root user account and have all of root's environment variables applied.

FIGURE 1-6   Using the man utility to learn how to use ls

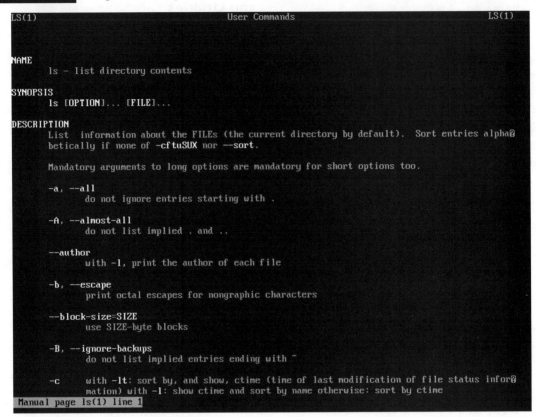

```
LS(1)                            User Commands                            LS(1)



NAME
       ls - list directory contents

SYNOPSIS
       ls [OPTION]... [FILE]...

DESCRIPTION
       List  information about the FILEs (the current directory by default).  Sort entries alpha@
       betically if none of -cftuSUX nor --sort.

       Mandatory arguments to long options are mandatory for short options too.

       -a, --all
              do not ignore entries starting with .

       -A, --almost-all
              do not list implied . and ..

       --author
              with -l, print the author of each file

       -b, --escape
              print octal escapes for nongraphic characters

       --block-size=SIZE
              use SIZE-byte blocks

       -B, --ignore-backups
              do not list implied entries ending with ~

       -c     with -lt: sort by, and show, ctime (time of last modification of file status infor@
              mation) with -l: show ctime and sort by name otherwise: sort by ctime
Manual page ls(1) line 1
```

exam

w a t c h   *The su command is many times mistakenly thought to stand for "super user." It doesn't. It stands for "switch user."*

■ **env**   This command displays the environment variables for the currently logged-in user.

■ **echo**   This command is used to echo a line of text on the screen. It's frequently used to display environment variables. For example, if you wanted to see the current value of the PATH variable, you could enter **echo $PATH**.

FIGURE I-7   Using the info utility to learn about ls

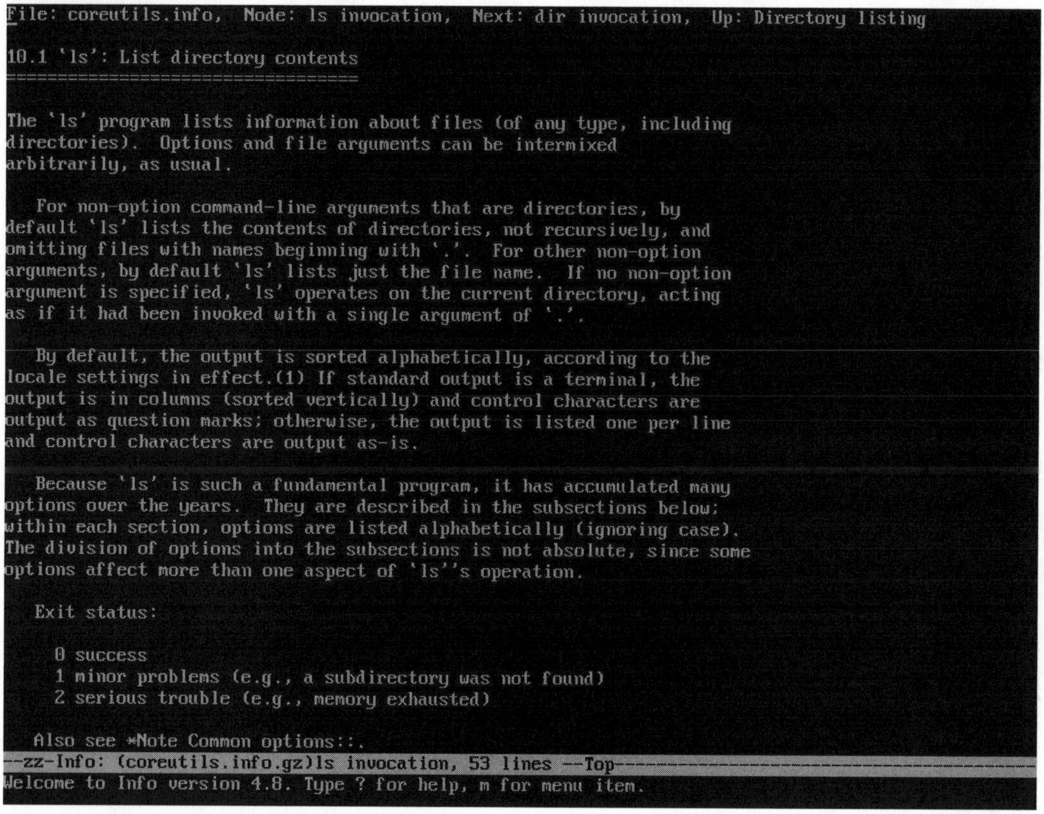

```
File: coreutils.info,  Node: ls invocation,  Next: dir invocation,  Up: Directory listing

10.1 'ls': List directory contents
===================================

The 'ls' program lists information about files (of any type, including
directories).  Options and file arguments can be intermixed
arbitrarily, as usual.

    For non-option command-line arguments that are directories, by
default 'ls' lists the contents of directories, not recursively, and
omitting files with names beginning with '.'.  For other non-option
arguments, by default 'ls' lists just the file name.  If no non-option
argument is specified, 'ls' operates on the current directory, acting
as if it had been invoked with a single argument of '.'.

    By default, the output is sorted alphabetically, according to the
locale settings in effect.(1) If standard output is a terminal, the
output is in columns (sorted vertically) and control characters are
output as question marks; otherwise, the output is listed one per line
and control characters are output as-is.

    Because 'ls' is such a fundamental program, it has accumulated many
options over the years.  They are described in the subsections below;
within each section, options are listed alphabetically (ignoring case).
The division of options into the subsections is not absolute, since some
options affect more than one aspect of 'ls''s operation.

    Exit status:

      0 success
      1 minor problems (e.g., a subdirectory was not found)
      2 serious trouble (e.g., memory exhausted)

    Also see *Note Common options::.
--zz-Info: (coreutils.info.gz)ls invocation, 53 lines --Top--------------------
Welcome to Info version 4.8. Type ? for help, m for menu item.
```

exam
watch   *The $ character tells echo that the text that comes after it is a variable, not a literal string, and that it should use the current value of that variable. If you were to leave off the $, the echo command would simply display PATH on the screen.*

■ **top**   This command is a very useful command that displays a list of all applications and processes currently running on the system. You can sort them by CPU usage, memory usage, process ID number, and which user owns them. A sample top screen is shown in Figure 1-8.

Using top to view active processes

```
top - 13:50:22 up 38 min,  5 users,  load average: 0.00, 0.01, 0.00
Tasks:  53 total,    1 running,  52 sleeping,    0 stopped,    0 zombie
Cpu(s):  1.4% us,  1.5% sy,  0.0% ni, 95.9% id,  0.0% wa,  0.9% hi,  0.3% si
Mem:    256724k total,   210180k used,    46544k free,    37296k buffers
Swap:   514040k total,        0k used,   514040k free,   138340k cached

  PID USER      PR  NI  VIRT  RES  SHR S %CPU %MEM    TIME+  COMMAND
    1 root      16   0   720  288  244 S  0.0  0.1  0:00.96 init
    2 root      34  19     0    0    0 S  0.0  0.0  0:00.02 ksoftirqd/0
    3 root      10  -5     0    0    0 S  0.0  0.0  0:00.06 events/0
    4 root      11  -5     0    0    0 S  0.0  0.0  0:00.02 khelper
    5 root      11  -5     0    0    0 S  0.0  0.0  0:00.00 kthread
    7 root      10  -5     0    0    0 S  0.0  0.0  0:00.14 kblockd/0
    8 root      20  -5     0    0    0 S  0.0  0.0  0:00.00 kacpid
   92 root      15   0     0    0    0 S  0.0  0.0  0:00.00 pdflush
   93 root      15   0     0    0    0 S  0.0  0.0  0:00.58 pdflush
   95 root      16  -5     0    0    0 S  0.0  0.0  0:00.00 aio/0
   94 root      15   0     0    0    0 S  0.0  0.0  0:00.02 kswapd0
  301 root      11  -5     0    0    0 S  0.0  0.0  0:00.00 cqueue/0
  302 root      11  -5     0    0    0 S  0.0  0.0  0:00.01 kseriod
  342 root      11  -5     0    0    0 S  0.0  0.0  0:00.00 kpsmoused
  707 root      11  -5     0    0    0 S  0.0  0.0  0:00.00 scsi_eh_0
  764 root      10  -5     0    0    0 S  0.0  0.0  0:00.66 reiserfs/0
  857 root      16  -4  4344  720  340 S  0.0  0.3  0:00.38 udevd
 1283 root      11  -5     0    0    0 S  0.0  0.0  0:00.00 kgameportd
 1291 root      10  -5     0    0    0 S  0.0  0.0  0:00.00 khubd
 1361 root      20   0     0    0    0 S  0.0  0.0  0:00.00 shpchpd_event
 2120 root      16   0  1516  504  428 S  0.0  0.2  0:00.00 acpid
 2121 messageb  17   0  6812 2180  952 S  0.0  0.8  0:00.32 dbus-daemon
 2149 root      15   0  4404  768  432 S  0.0  0.3  0:00.04 syslog-ng
 2152 root      16   0  1656  524  324 S  0.0  0.2  0:00.00 klogd
 2199 root      16   0  4720 1764 1292 S  0.0  0.7  0:00.02 resmgrd
 2237 root      16   0  4348 2948 1440 S  0.0  1.1  0:01.66 hald
 2284 root      22   0  1820  604  524 S  0.0  0.2  0:00.00 hald-addon-acpi
 2676 root      15   0  1616  504  404 S  0.0  0.2  0:00.06 vmware-guestd
 2815 root      16   0  1816  616  532 S  0.0  0.2  0:00.82 hald-addon-stor
 2961 mdnsd     16   0  4720 2012 1400 S  0.0  0.8  0:00.00 mdnsd
```

- **which**   This command is used to display the full path to a shell command or utility. For example, if you wanted to know the full path to the ls command, you would enter **which ls**. The full path to ls is displayed on screen, as shown in the next illustration.

```
rtracy@mylinux:~> which ls
/bin/ls
rtracy@mylinux:~>
```

- **whoami**   This command displays the username of the currently logged-in user.
- **netstat**   This command displays the status of the network, including current connections, routing tables, etc.

FIGURE 1-9   Viewing network board parameters with ifconfig

```
mylinux:~ # ifconfig
eth0      Link encap:Ethernet  HWaddr 00:0C:29:71:59:D2
          inet addr:192.168.1.36  Bcast:192.168.1.255  Mask:255.255.255.0
          inet6 addr: fe80::20c:29ff:fe71:59d2/64 Scope:Link
          UP BROADCAST NOTRAILERS RUNNING MULTICAST  MTU:1500  Metric:1
          RX packets:157 errors:0 dropped:0 overruns:0 frame:0
          TX packets:23 errors:0 dropped:0 overruns:0 carrier:0
          collisions:0 txqueuelen:1000
          RX bytes:21694 (21.1 Kb)  TX bytes:2577 (2.5 Kb)
          Interrupt:177 Base address:0x1080

lo        Link encap:Local Loopback
          inet addr:127.0.0.1  Mask:255.0.0.0
          inet6 addr: ::1/128 Scope:Host
          UP LOOPBACK RUNNING  MTU:16436  Metric:1
          RX packets:256 errors:0 dropped:0 overruns:0 frame:0
          TX packets:256 errors:0 dropped:0 overruns:0 carrier:0
          collisions:0 txqueuelen:0
          RX bytes:13408 (13.0 Kb)  TX bytes:13408 (13.0 Kb)

mylinux:~ # _
```

- **route**   This command is used to view or manipulate the system's routing table.
- **ifconfig**   This command is used to manage network boards installed in the system. It can be used to display or modify your network board configuration parameters. This command can only be run by the root user. Sample output from ifconfig is shown in Figure 1-9.

Let's practice using common Linux commands in the following exercise.

EXERCISE 1-2

Using Linux Commands

In this exercise, you learn how to use common Linux commands from the shell prompt. Complete the following:

1. Boot your Linux system to a shell prompt (run-level 3). If your system booted into a graphical system, log in and then press CTRL-ALT-F1.

2. At your login prompt, authenticate to the system.

3. At the shell prompt, determine your current directory by entering **pwd**. What is the current directory?

4. Determine the current user by entering **whoami**. Who is the current user?

5. Create a directory listing of the files in the current directory by entering **ls**.

6. Get more information about the ls utility by entering **man ls** at the shell prompt.
7. Use the PGDN key to scroll through the man page. Which option can you use with ls to use a long listing format?
8. Press q.
9. Create a long listing with the ls command by entering **ls –l** at the shell prompt.

With this information in mind, we'll now learn how to use the graphical user interface on Linux.

Using the Linux Graphical User Interface

In addition to the shell prompt, most Linux systems also offer a graphical user interface (GUI). In this part of this chapter, we will discuss the following topics:

- How the Linux GUI works
- Using the Linux GUI

Let's begin by discussing how the Linux GUI works.

How the Linux GUI Works

As we mentioned earlier, the GUI on a Linux system is created using the X Window System software.

on the **job**

Many times you will hear the X Window System referred to as "X Windows," "XI I," or just "X."

The X Window System provides the base system for the graphical interface on Linux. It allows programmers to run applications in windows. It also allows users to move windows around on the screen as well as click on items with the mouse.

However, the X Window System alone isn't enough. You have to have three additional components to create a fully functional Linux GUI system:

- **Window Managers**   The role of the window manager is to control the appearance of the windows on the screen. It also determines how they are arranged on the screen. Commonly used window managers include the following:
  - Enlightenment
  - fvwm
  - twm
  - Window Maker
  - IceWM
  - Sawfish
  - Xfwm

- **GUI Toolkits** GUI toolkits are libraries used by programmers to create X Window applications. On Linux, the GTK+, Motif, and Qt toolkits are commonly used.

- **Desktop Environments** The desktop environment is used to actually present the GUI desktop to the end user. It allows you to place icons on the desktop, customize the appearance of your windows, add wallpaper to the desktop background, and so on. Two very popular Linux desktop environments include the K Desktop Environment (KDE) and GNOME.

Using the Linux GUI

When you put these three components together, you create a graphical user interface on your Linux system that works in a very similar manner as Microsoft Windows. You will find many of the desktop components you may be familiar with on Windows in the Linux GUI. For example, within the KDE desktop environment, there are Trash, My Computer, and Network Browsing icons, as shown in Figure 1-10.

These three desktop elements correspond to the Recycle Bin, My Computer, and My Network Places elements in Microsoft Windows. To use these elements, simply click on them.

on the job *Not all desktop environments appear as shown in these figures. Some will include the Trash, My Computer, and Network Browsing icons; others won't. In addition, some desktop environments require you to double-click these icons; others, such as KDE, only require a single click.*

We don't have nearly the time or space required to investigate all desktop environments in this book. We'll focus our discussion on KDE and GNOME.

For example, clicking My Computer will display information about your system and show the contents of the file system on your computer, as shown in Figure 1-11.

FIGURE 1-10 Trash, My Computer, and Network Browsing icons on the KDE desktop

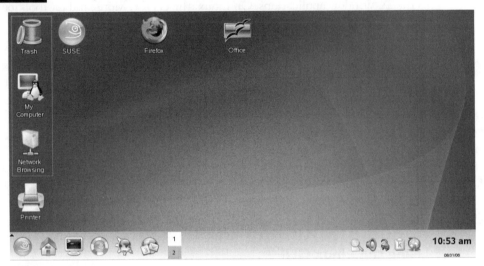

FIGURE 1-11 Viewing My Computer in KDE

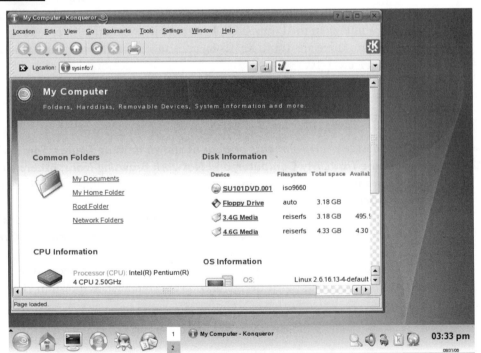

Whenever you delete a file from within the desktop environment, it is moved to the Trash. You can empty the Trash by right-clicking on it and selecting Empty Trash Bin. You can also restore deleted files by doing the following:

1. Select Trash.
2. Right-click the file or directory you want to restore.
3. Select Restore in the pop-up menu shown in Figure 1-12.

You can browse other computers on the network by selecting Network Browsing. The screen in Figure 1-13 is displayed.

In addition, the desktop has shortcut icons that can be used to launch applications. In Figure 1-14, you can visit the SUSE Web site, launch the Firefox Web browser, or run OpenOffice.org by selecting the appropriate desktop shortcut.

The Linux GUI also includes a taskbar across the bottom of the desktop. This is shown in the next illustration.

The taskbar includes a menu button on the far left side of the screen. This is the equivalent of the Start button on a Windows system. It contains menu items that allow you to run applications by pointing and clicking with your mouse. This is shown in the next illustration.

Restoring deleted
files in KDE

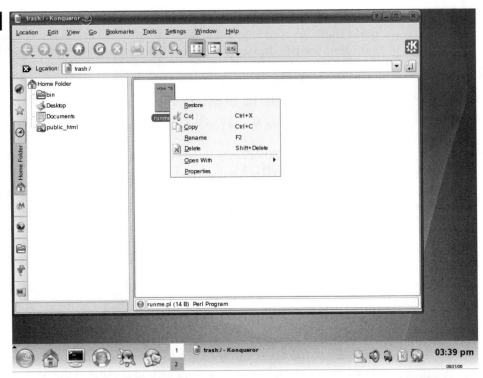

Viewing network
services in KDE

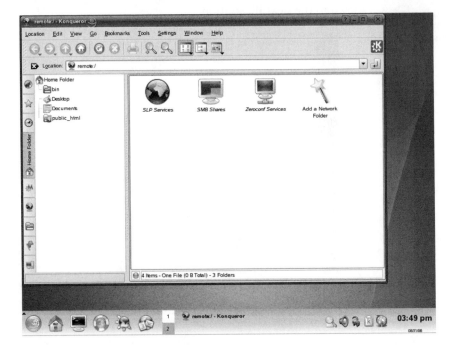

FIGURE 1-14

Desktop
shortcuts in KDE

On the right side of the menu button, the taskbar also includes shortcut icons used to launch commonly used applications. Next to these buttons is a panel where icons for active applications are displayed. In Figure 1-15, OpenOffice.org has been launched on the desktop. A corresponding icon appears in the taskbar.

On the far right side of the taskbar are system applets that allow you to control such things as the audio volume level and update downloads. The system clock is also displayed.

FIGURE 1-15

Application
icons in the KDE
taskbar

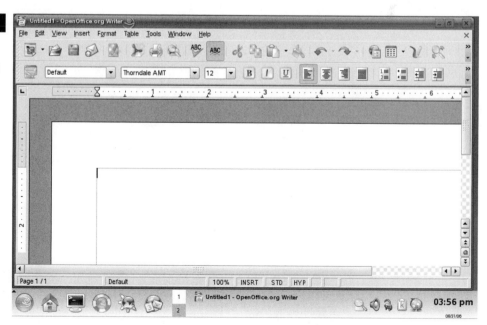

CERTIFICATION SUMMARY

In this chapter, you were introduced to the Linux operating system. We first discussed what an operating system is. We also discussed the components that comprise the Linux operating system. We emphasized the fact that modern computer systems and operating systems are modular. You can install Linux on any compatible computer.

We then spent some time reviewing the historical development of Linux. We reviewed the typical corporate software development model and related how Linux was developed outside this norm. We talked about GNU and the GPL. We discussed the fact that Linux is developed under the GPL, allowing anyone free access to the source code.

We reviewed how Linux distributions are created and reviewed several of the more popular distributions. We also discussed the different roles that Linux can play in a typical organization, including servers, desktops, and firewalls.

We finished this chapter by reviewing the two user interfaces provided by most Linux distributions: the command-line interface and the graphical user interface.

✓ TWO-MINUTE DRILL

Describe the Background and History of Linux

❑ Linux is an operating system.

❑ Operating systems provide four key functions:

  ❑ Application platform

  ❑ Hardware moderator

  ❑ Data storage

  ❑ Security

❑ Linux is composed of the following components:

  ❑ Kernel

  ❑ Libraries

  ❑ Utilities

  ❑ User interfaces

❑ Linus Torvalds first developed Linux in the early 1990s.

❑ Linux is licensed under the GPL.

❑ Anyone can download and modify the Linux kernel source code.

❑ Different software companies develop unique Linux flavors called distributions.

❑ Linux can function as a server, desktop system, or firewall in a computer network.

Use the Linux User Interface

❑ Linux offers a command-line and a graphical user interface.

❑ The Linux command-line interface is created by shells.

❑ The bash shell is the default shell for most distributions.

❑ Linux shells do not search the current directory when running a file from the command prompt.

❑ The Linux GUI is composed of the following components:

  ❑ X Window System

  ❑ Window manager

  ❑ GUI toolkit

  ❑ Desktop environment

SELF TEST

Describe the Background and History of Linux

1. Which of the following are applications? (Choose two.)
   - A. Linux
   - B. MySQL
   - C. VMware
   - D. DOS
   - E. Active Directory

2. Your company recently purchased 12 new computer systems. The computers have Intel Pentium IV 2.5 GHz CPUs and 40MB hard drives. Your supervisor wants to install Linux on them, but is concerned that it can't be done because they already have Windows XP Professional installed. Can this be done?
   - A. Yes, but you must install a new hard drive for Linux.
   - B. No, Windows is embedded in the system hardware. You must purchase systems without an operating system installed.
   - C. No, modern motherboards are hard-coded to recognize your Windows Certificate of Authority. If it doesn't find this, the system won't boot.
   - D. Yes, you can erase the hard drive and install Linux.

3. Which of the following is the true operating system component within Linux?
   - A. Linux libraries
   - B. Linux kernel
   - C. X Window System
   - D. bash shell

4. Which of the following provides pre-written code that programmers can use in Linux programs?
   - A. Linux kernel
   - B. X Window System
   - C. bash shell
   - D. Linux libraries
   - E. Window manager

5. What was the name of the UNIX clone written by Andrew Tanenbaum?
   - A. CPM
   - B. DR-DOS

    C. Linux

    D. Minix

    E. Solaris

    F. AIX

6. What did Linus Torvalds do with the source code for Linux?

    A. He sold it to IBM.

    B. He gave it to Microsoft for free.

    C. He developed Minix.

    D. He patented and copyrighted it.

    E. He posted it on the Internet for anyone who wanted a copy.

7. Who initiated the GNU Project?

    A. Richard Stallman

    B. Andrew Tanenbaum

    C. Linus Torvalds

    D. Richard Berkley

8. You are a computer programmer. Your supervisor wants you to download the source code for the latest Linux kernel and modify it to support a custom application your company is developing for use in-house. Can you do this?

    A. No, the source code for Linux is no longer available on the Internet.

    B. No, the copyright on the source code won't permit it.

    C. Yes, but you must pay a royalty to the GNU Project.

    D. Yes, you can create a new Linux flavor and even redistribute it as long as the source code remains freely available.

9. You have been tasked with setting up an e-mail server for your organization of 150 people. You're considering using a Linux system to do this. Is this possible?

    A. Yes, Linux can be configured to provide e-mail services.

    B. No, while Linux can be configured to provide e-mail services, it's not recommended for more than 25 users.

    C. Yes, but you'll have to purchase special e-mail software that's compatible with Linux.

    D. No. E-mail software is not currently available for Linux.

10. Which Linux services can be used to provide network printing? (Choose two.)

    A. MySQL

    B. NFS

    C. CUPS

    D. Samba

    E. NIS

    F. OpenPrint

11. Which Linux services could be used to provide network file storage for users? (Choose two.)

    A. MySQL

    B. NFS

    C. PostgreSQL

    D. Samba

    E. NIS

    F. FileManager

12. Which Linux services could be used as a database server? (Choose two.)

    A. MySQL

    B. NFS

    C. PostgreSQL

    D. Samba

    E. NIS

    F. Access

13. Which Linux service can be used to turn a Linux system into an application-level gateway?

    A. MySQL

    B. NFS

    C. PostgreSQL

    D. Samba

    E. NIS

    F. Squid

Use the Linux User Interface

14. Which shell is the default shell for most Linux distributions?

    A. sh

    B. csh

    C. bash

    D. zsh

15. Which shell is the default shell for most FreeBSD systems?

    A. sh

    B. csh

    C. zsh

    D. tsch

16. You are working with a bash shell on a Linux system. You are in the middle of installing an application on the system when you discover that the installation program needs to access a license diskette in the floppy drive. You need to mount the floppy so this can happen, but this requires access to the shell prompt. You don't want to halt the installation to do this. What can you do?

    A. Nothing, you must halt the installation, mount the floppy, then restart the installation.

    B. You can press CTRL-PAUSE on the keyboard. This will pause the installation while you mount the floppy.

    C. You can press ALT-F2 to open an alternate console screen and mount the floppy.

    D. Insert the floppy and press CTRL-SHIFT-F6. This will automatically mount the floppy without pausing the program.

17. Which x86 processor mode allows the Linux kernel to run multiple shell sessions at the same time?

    A. Real

    B. Protected

    C. 486 Enhanced

    D. 586 Emulation

18. You've downloaded an executable file named updatedb.sh from your company's FTP server to /tmp on your Linux system. You open a shell and change to the /tmp directory. When you enter **updatedb.sh**, the shell indicates that it can't find the file. What can you do?

    A. Enter the file name in all capital letters.

    B. Add a ./ before the file name when entering it at the prompt.

    C. Enter the file name without the .sh extension.

    D. Move the file to your home directory and then execute it.

19. You need to find out what directories in the Linux file system are parts of the path. What command can you use? (Choose two.)

    A. env

    B. show $PATH

  C. man path

  D. echo $PATH

  E. writeln PATH

20. You've downloaded an executable file named updatedb.sh from your company's FTP server to /tmp on your Linux system. You open a shell and change to the /tmp directory. When you enter **./Updatedb.sh**, the shell indicates that it can't find the file. What can you do?

  A. Enter the file name in all lower-case letters.

  B. Add a **.** before the file name when entering it at the prompt.

  C. Enter the file name without the .sh extension.

  D. Move the file to your home directory and then execute it.

21. Which Linux utility can be used to display a list of all running processes on your system?

  A. env

  B. procman

  C. processes

  D. top

  E. echo $PROCESSES

22. Which Linux utility can be used to display your network board configuration?

  A. netstat

  B. route

  C. ifconfig

  D. ipconfig

  E. echo $NETWORK_CONFIG

23. Which Linux utility can be used to change to a different user account at the shell prompt?

  A. user

  B. chuser

  C. swuser

  D. su

SELF TEST ANSWERS

Describe the Background and History of Linux

1. ☑ **A and D.** These are true operating systems because they fill the four operating system roles.
☒ **B, C,** and **E** are incorrect. They are applications. They may fill one or more of the four operating system roles, but none of these fill all four.

2. ☑ **D.** Hardware and operating systems are modular. As long as the hardware is compatible, you can install any operating system designed for the CPU.
☒ **A, B,** and **C** are incorrect. A computer's hardware is not tied in any way to a particular operating system.

3. ☑ **B.** The Linux kernel is the component that handles operating system functions.
☒ **A, C,** and **D** are incorrect. Each of these components is part of the operating system, but they don't fill the four operating system roles.

4. ☑ **D.** Libraries contain pre-written code that programmers can reuse in their applications.
☒ **A, B, C,** and **E** are incorrect. The kernel doesn't contain pre-written code nor does the X Window System, the bash shell, or the window manager.

5. ☑ **D.** Andrew Tanenbaum wrote the Minix operating system when universities were no longer allowed access to the UNIX source code.
☒ **A, B, C, E,** and **F** are incorrect. They are operating systems that were written by commercial software developers.

6. ☑ **E.** Linus Torvalds posted the source code for his Linux kernel on the Internet and invited other programmers to modify and enhance it.
☒ **A, B, C,** and **D** are incorrect. A and B are wrong because he did not give it to IBM or Microsoft. C is wrong because Minix was developed before Linux. D is wrong because Torvalds did not patent Linux.

7. ☑ **A.** Richard Stallman came up with the freely distributable source code concept behind GNU.
☒ **B, C,** and **D** are incorrect. Although they have been involved in the GNU Project, these other figures were not the founders.

8. ☑ **D.** Under the GPL, you are free to download the Linux source code and modify it.
☒ **A, B,** and **C** are incorrect. A is incorrect because the source code remains freely available. B is incorrect because the source code isn't copyrighted. C is incorrect because the GPL doesn't require royalties.

9. ☑ **A.** A variety of powerful e-mail packages are available for Linux that make it highly suitable for large organizations.
   ☒ **B, C,** and **D** are incorrect. **B** is incorrect because Linux can support very large numbers of users. **C** and **D** are incorrect because many free e-mail services are available for Linux.

10. ☑ **C and D.** The CUPS service can be used alone to provide network printing to other Linux systems. When combined with Samba, network printing can be extended to Windows systems as well.
    ☒ **A, B, E,** and **F** are incorrect. These are not printing services.

11. ☑ **B and D.** The NFS service can be used to provide file sharing for systems running an NFS client. The Samba service can also be used for Samba clients, such as Windows.
    ☒ **A, C, E,** and **F** are incorrect. These are not file sharing services.

12. ☑ **A and C.** MySQL and PostgreSQL are both very powerful Linux database servers.
    ☒ **B, D, E,** and **F** are incorrect. These are not database servers.

13. ☑ **F.** The Squid service can turn any Linux system into an application-level gateway device.
    ☒ **A, B, C, D,** and **E** are incorrect. **A** and **C** are a database services. **B** and **D** allow you to share local directories and files with remote computers. **E** allows multiple Linux systems to share a common set of configuration files.

Use the Linux User Interface

14. ☑ **C.** bash is the default shell used with most Linux distributions.
    ☒ **A, B,** and **D** are incorrect. While these shells are available on most Linux distributions, they are usually not the default shell.

15. ☑ **D.** tsch is the default shell used with FreeBSD.
    ☒ **A, B,** and **C** are incorrect. They are not used as the default shell on FreeBSD.

16. ☑ **C.** Pressing ALT-F2 will open an alternate console. You can use this console to mount the floppy without stopping the installation program in the first console screen. You can switch back by pressing ALT-F1.
    ☒ **A, B,** and **D** are incorrect. **A** is incorrect because you don't have to halt the installation. **B** is incorrect because pressing CTRL-PAUSE will not pause the running program. **D** is incorrect. This key sequence will not automatically mount the floppy.

17. ☑ **B.** An x86 CPU running in Protected mode can run multiple shell sessions.
    ☒ **A, C,** and **D** are incorrect. **A** is incorrect because Real mode only emulates a fast 8088 CPU. **C** and **D** are incorrect. These modes don't exist.

18. ☑ **B.** Adding **./** before the file name tells the shell that the file resides in the current directory.
☒ **A, C,** and **D** are incorrect. **A** is incorrect because Linux is case-sensitive. **C** is incorrect because the shell still doesn't know that the file resides in the current directory. **D** is incorrect for the same reason.

19. ☑ **A** and **D.** Both of these commands will print the PATH variable on the screen.
☒ **B, C,** and **E** are incorrect. **B** is incorrect because show is not a valid utility. **C** is incorrect because the man utility only displays a help page. **E** won't work from a shell prompt.

20. ☑ **A.** Linux is case-sensitive. The command in the question uses an uppercase "U."
☒ **B, C,** and **D** are incorrect. **B** is incorrect because it uses incorrect syntax. **C** is incorrect because it doesn't solve the issue of case sensitivity. **D** is incorrect because it won't solve the case sensitivity issue either.

21. ☑ **D.** The top utility displays running processes.
☒ **A, B, C,** and **E** are incorrect. **A** is incorrect because it only displays your environment variables. **B** is incorrect because it doesn't display running processes. **C** is incorrect. It isn't a valid command. **E** is likewise an invalid command.

22. ☑ **C.** The ifconfig command is used to view and modify your network board configuration.
☒ **A, B, D,** and **E** are incorrect. **A** displays information about your network connections, but not your network board. **B** is incorrect because it displays route information. **D** is actually used on a Windows system, not Linux. **E** is an invalid command.

23. ☑ **D.** The su utility will change your current user account. It is frequently used to change to the root account.
☒ **A, B,** and **C** are incorrect. **A** is an invalid command. **B** is also an invalid command. **C** is an invalid command.

2

Working with
PC Hardware

I n order for you to become Linux+ certified, the folks at CompTIA expect you to have a solid understanding of PC hardware. While you don't have to have the depth of knowledge required to be A+ certified, you do need to know how to install an expansion board in an expansion slot, configure system memory, and manage system resources.

You might be asking "Why do I need to know about PC hardware to be Linux+ certified? Isn't this certification about operating systems?" Yes, Linux+ is all about setting up and managing a Linux system.

However, to be a really good Linux system administrator, you must be proficient with PC hardware. Why? Linux expects a lot more out of the user and the system administrator. Other operating systems hide a lot of their functionality behind the scenes. Their mission statement can be summed up as "Don't ask how it works; you don't need to know."

Linux, on the other hand, *expects* you to ask how it works. The operating system was designed by geeks for geeks. It provides you with an extensive set of tools to customize and configure how things work. In essence, Linux provides you with the tools and the parts; it's up to you to put it all together to function the way you want.

Because Linux operates on this model, you are expected to thoroughly understand how the underlying system works, including the hardware itself. Therefore, in this chapter, I'll provide you with an overview of how the hardware in a typical PC system works. The following topics will be covered:

- Personal computer components
- Removable hardware interfaces

Let's begin by discussing the components found in a personal computer.

CERTIFICATION OBJECTIVE 2.01

Describe Personal Computer Components

In this part of this chapter we're going to spend some time discussing the various parts that comprise a typical PC computer system. For your Linux+ exam, you need to understand the following pieces and parts:

Power supplies	CPUs
Motherboards	Memory

- Expansion slots
- Video adapters

- Expansion boards
- Storage devices

The first topic we need to review is the role and function of the power supply in a PC system.

Power Supplies

One of the most important components in any PC system (and probably the most overlooked) is the power supply. To understand the need for the power supply, you need to understand that the various components inside your PC operate using direct current (DC). However, the wall outlet that you plug your PC system into uses alternating current (AC). Somehow, we need to transform the wall AC current into DC current that our computer system components can use.

That's the job of the power supply. It converts 110-volt AC current from your wall outlet into DC current. Without a good power supply, nothing else in the system works. I always tell my students that the power supply is kind of like the battery and tires on your car. Batteries and tires aren't glamorous. In fact, they are downright boring. However, nothing will stop your car faster than a bad battery or a bad tire. The same principle holds with power supplies. A bad power supply results in a dead system.

INSIDE THE EXAM

Hardware on the Linux+ Exam

Just as the Linux+ exam doesn't require you to know any particular Linux distribution, it is also vendor-neutral with respect to hardware. You don't have to know any particular hardware make or model; you just need to know the general role and function of each component in the system.

Notice that the CompTIA objectives listed at the beginning of this chapter specify that we cover a wide range of devices. We'll cover most of them here in this chapter. However, several devices, such as RAID arrays and tape drives, will be covered later in this book when we cover related Linux concepts.

Be prepared to answer a fairly large number of hardware questions on the exam. About 8–10 percent of the items will be hardware-centric.

A typical power supply is shown in Figure 2-1.

In Figure 2-1 you can see that there is a black socket into which you plug a standard electrical cord that plugs into a wall outlet. This is the AC side of the power supply. The back of the power supply has a series of wires and plugs that carry DC current to the various components in the PC system.

on the **Job**

Never _open a power supply to work on it. If it's plugged into the wall outlet,_ you will be exposed to 110-volt AC wall current. It could kill you!

The various components inside your PC need different voltage levels of DC current. In most modern systems, the power supply provides three different voltages:

- 3.3 volts
- 5 volts
- 12 volts

When working with power supplies, it's important to remember that not all power supplies are created equal. Power supplies come in a variety of wattages, ranging from 200 watts on the low end to 500 or more watts on the high end. Simply put, the more wattage a power supply offers, the more components inside the PC that it can deliver power to at the same time.

FIGURE 2-1

The PC power supply

The power supply has one wire coming off of it that plugs into your motherboard called the POWER_GOOD wire. If, at any time, the power supply fails to supply the appropriate level of current on this wire, the system will immediately shut off.

Power supplies also have one other key job. They are responsible for cooling the system. Notice in Figure 2-1 that the power supply includes a built-in fan. This fan is responsible for cooling all of the components running inside your system. This is a very important job. Your system generates a great deal of heat. Without some way to dissipate all that heat, your components would quickly degrade and eventually fail. As you can see, the power supply is a very important part of the PC!

With this in mind, let's next review the role and function of the motherboard in a PC system.

Motherboards

The motherboard is really the heart of the PC system. Its job is to create electrical pathways that connect everything together. A typical motherboard is shown in Figure 2-2.

The motherboard connects the CPU with the system RAM. It also connects the CPU and the RAM with the expansion slots. It provides connectors that allow you to connect a mouse and a keyboard to the system as well as parallel and serial devices (such as printers).

SCENARIO & SOLUTION

What are the two key roles played by a power supply in a personal computer?	The power supply is responsible for converting AC current into DC current for internal PC components. It is also responsible for cooling the components with a fan.
You're working on a PC system and it spontaneously shuts down several times each day. What could be causing this to happen?	It's very likely that the power supply is starting to fail. When it gets too hot or the internal components need more current than it can supply, the voltage on the POWER_GOOD wire drops and the motherboard shuts down.

FIGURE 2-2

A PC
motherboard

The motherboard also contains a very important chip call the BIOS. The BIOS contains a series of very small programs that allow the system to function. For example, have you ever wondered how the system knows what letter you've pressed on the keyboard? The BIOS provides the software that allows the keyboard to send data to the CPU.

The BIOS has many parameters that you can configure. You do this by accessing the CMOS setup program. When you boot most PC systems, you will see a message stating something to the effect of "Press F1 to enter setup." The actual keystroke varies from system to system. When you press the key indicated the CMOS setup program (which is actually one of the small programs that reside in the BIOS) is run, allowing you to configure various parameters. A typical CMOS setup program is shown in Figure 2-3.

As you can see, you can use the CMOS setup program to configure:

■ The system date and time
■ The type of floppy drive installed in the system
■ The type of hard drive(s) installed in the system
■ Power management features of the motherboard
■ The order of boot devices in the system

The motherboard also includes a socket into which you can insert the system CPU. Let's review the role and function of the CPU next.

SCENARIO & SOLUTION

You power on your computer one morning and it fails to boot. A message is displayed on the screen that says "NTLDR Missing." What's causing this problem?	Most likely, you've left a non-bootable floppy diskette in the floppy diskette drive. Usually, the BIOS on most motherboards are configured by default to boot from the floppy diskette drive before the hard drive. When the system found the floppy, it tried to boot off of it instead of booting from the hard drive. You can fix this by simply removing the diskette or by changing the system boot device order using the CMOS setup program.

CPUs

If the motherboard is the heart of a PC, then the central processing unit (CPU) is the brains of the system. The motherboard itself doesn't have any intelligence. It simply provides the pathways necessary for data to get from one part of the system to another. The intelligent part of the PC is the CPU.

on the job

You may hear the CPU referred to by a variety of names in the industry, including logic chip, processor, or microprocessor. If you hear any of these terms, we're talking about the CPU.

FIGURE 2-3

The CMOS setup program

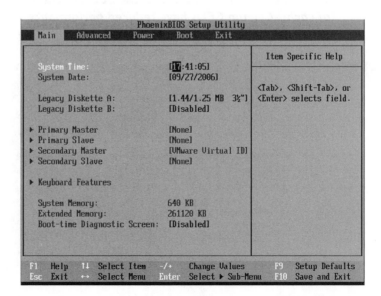

The CPU is an integrated circuit built on a slice of silicon. A typical CPU is shown in Figure 2-4.

Have you ever wondered how a PC can calculate a spreadsheet or render a 3-D gaming scene on the screen? It's all done with electricity. The CPU contains millions of transistors connected by hairline traces of aluminum. These transistors work together to store and manipulate data. By manipulating the electrical charges in these transistors, the CPU can perform arithmetic and logical operations. To do this, each CPU has sets of instructions designed into the processor itself.

Over the years, the CPUs used by computers have evolved from relatively slow CPUs in the original IBM PC to the speed demons we use today. Two primary manufacturers have produced them: Intel and Advanced Micro Devices (AMD). The main families of CPUs that have been produced by Intel include the following:

- Pentium
- Pentium Pro
- Pentium II
- Pentium III

- Pentium IV
- Pentium D (64-bit)
- Pentium Extreme (64-bit)
- Celeron

on the **Job**

Celeron CPUs are scaled-down versions of the Intel Pentium CPU. When the first Pentiums came out, they were priced beyond the reach of many home users. To capture this market, Intel took the standard Pentium CPU and reduced the amount of Level 2 cache installed, reducing production costs and making them more affordable. In fact, the first generation of Pentium II Celeron CPUs had no Level 2 cache at all. Because of the reduced amount of cache, Celeron CPUs have reduced performance compared to a standard Pentium CPU of the same clock speed.

FIGURE 2-4

The CPU

CPUs produced by AMD include the following:

- K6
- Athlon (K7)
- Athlon XP
- Sempron
- Athlon 64
- Athlon 64 FX (for graphics and games)
- Athlon 64 X2 Dual-Core

When working with CPUs, there are a variety of factors you need to be aware of:

- **Socket**   Motherboards provide a socket that the CPU fits into. Different CPUs have different physical dimensions and must, therefore, use different types of sockets to connect to the motherboard. A variety of socket sizes and shapes have been used over the years, including the following:
  - Socket A (Used with AMD Athlon)
  - Socket 7
  - Socket 8
  - Socket 370
  - Socket 423
  - Socket 478

  A Socket 478 motherboard connector for a Pentium IV CPU is shown in Figure 2-5.

- **Speed**   All motherboards use a clock. This clock isn't the system clock you're probably familiar with. Instead, the motherboard clock is an oscillator that generates a certain number of electrical pulses every second. These pulses set the tempo for the CPU and are measured in megahertz (MHz) or millions of pulses per second. The number of pulses per second is determined by a quartz crystal and is referred to as the *clock speed*.

FIGURE 2-5

A Pentium IV
CPU socket

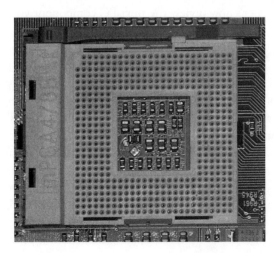

Older CPUs ran at the speed of the motherboard clock. However, newer CPUs use a function called a *multiplier* to run at a clock speed that is a multiple of the motherboard clock speed.

- **Cache** In addition to speed, you also need to be concerned with cache. Most CPUs have their own memory built into the CPU itself called *cache RAM*. This isn't the same memory as your system RAM. Instead, cache is made of *static* RAM, which is much faster than regular system RAM. The CPU can store frequently needed data in its cache. This dramatically increases system performance. There are two types of cache you should be aware of:

  - **Level 1 (L1)** L1 cache is a small SRAM chip built into the CPU. The CPU loads upcoming program code into the L1 cache. Instead of stopping and waiting for a time-consuming task to be completed, such as writing data to disk, the CPU can keep processing code from the L1 cache.

  - **Level 2 (L2)** Adding L1 cache to the CPU dramatically increases its performance, so why not add even more? Most modern CPUs have additional SRAM cache incorporated into the chip to further increase performance.

on the **Ĵob** *The more cache a CPU has, the faster it runs, even if the clock speed isn't increased. In fact, many high-end CPUs designed for servers (such as Intel's Xeon CPU) incorporate huge amounts of cache.*

The important point here is that if you want to install a CPU in a motherboard, you must ensure that it uses the correct socket and the correct motherboard speed. If it doesn't, it won't work. (It may even start to smoke!)

Let's now review the next PC component you need to be aware of: RAM.

System Memory

If you've worked with computers, you're probably already familiar with the concept of random access memory (RAM). No matter how much RAM we install in any PC system, it never seems to be enough. Let's spends some time discussing what RAM is and how it works.

RAM is the place in a computer where programs and data currently in use on the system are stored. RAM is very fast. Information in RAM can be accessed very quickly because the CPU can directly access data in any memory location at any time. This makes it an ideal storage device for data that needs to be manipulated by the CPU.

SCENARIO & SOLUTION

You want to upgrade your computer's processor and have purchased a new AMD Athlon CPU. Upon opening your system case, you see that your motherboard uses a Socket 370 CPU socket. It appears to have the correct number of pins in the correct orientation for your new CPU. Should you install it?	No. The Socket 370 socket is for Intel CPUs. You should only install Intel CPUs in Intel sockets and AMD CPUs in AMD sockets. Even though the pin-outs may appear to be correct, the electrical connections are different. If you put the AMD CPU in the Intel socket, it will destroy the CPU.
You're trying to decide which CPU you should purchase for your computer. One is a Pentium IV 2.5 GHz CPU; the other is a Pentium IV Celeron 2.5 GHz CPU. The Celeron CPU is considerably less expensive. Which is the best choice?	The answer depends on what you want the CPU to do. If performance is the most important factor in your decision, then you will probably be disappointed with the Celeron. Even though the clock speed is the same, it won't perform as fast as the standard Pentium IV because it has much less cache. If you're more concerned about cost than performance, then the Celeron CPU might be the best choice.

For example, suppose you need to create a word-processing document. The first thing you do is open your word-processing application. When you do, the program code for the application is loaded from your hard disk drive into RAM. When you open a word-processing file in the application, the data you are working on is also loaded into RAM.

This brings up a very important point that you are probably already painfully aware of. That is the fact that RAM is non-persistent. The programs and data in RAM stay there only as long as your computer is running. That's because system RAM is made up of a type of memory called dynamic RAM (DRAM). DRAM must be constantly refreshed every few milliseconds with electrical current. If this doesn't happen, the programs and data in RAM disappear! When you shut down your computer system, your system RAM is no longer refreshed and, hence, all the data is gone. That's why you always (hopefully) save your files to the hard drive before shutting down. When you power the system back on again, the programs and data you were working on must be reloaded again from persistent storage on the hard drive.

DRAM stores data one bit at a time in a storage cell. Each storage cell is composed of a capacitor and a transistor. The transistor regulates current or voltage flow and acts as a switch or gate for electronic signals. The capacitor stores an electrical charge. The absence or presence of a charge in the capacitor can be used by the system to represent binary data (a 0 or a 1). These capacitors lose their charge rather quickly and must be constantly recharged (or *refreshed*) every few milliseconds.

DRAM, in modern PCs, is implemented as a series of DRAM chips soldered to an interface board called a "stick" of memory. A typical stick of memory is shown in Figure 2-6.

Let's review the types of memory you may encounter.

Memory Technologies

Over the years, memory sticks have been manufactured using a variety of technologies. Some of the more common technologies include the following:

- **Fast Page Mode (FPM) RAM**   FPM RAM was first introduced in 1987. For the first ten years of the PC's existence, we used FPM RAM almost exclusively. The significant aspect of FPM RAM that you should remember is that it didn't use any kind of clocking to synchronize the RAM chips with the motherboard clock. Instead, FPM RAM required the CPU to wait a specified amount of time (called the *access time*) to access data in the memory chips. The access time was measured in nanoseconds. If you've ever used 70ns or 60ns memory modules, then you've used FPM RAM. The 70ns or 60ns designation indicates the access time of the module.

on the **Job**   *At one time, I was under the impression that memory manufacturers designed their memory chips to use a specific access time. However, I went to work for a major memory manufacturer after college in the '90s and I learned otherwise. It turns out that chips from the same die could have radically different access times. We would run memory through an access time test after they came off the dies and sort them according to their tested access speed.*

- **Extended Data Out (EDO) RAM**   EDO RAM was introduced in 1995. Essentially, it was an improved version of FPM RAM. EDO RAM needed to be refreshed less frequently, providing the CPU with a longer window when it could read or write data to the chips on the module.

FIGURE 2-6   A "stick" of memory

■ **Synchronous Dynamic RAM (SDRAM)**   SDRAM was introduced in late 1996. SDRAM was an entirely new type of memory module. FPM RAM could no longer keep up with faster and faster CPUs. To accommodate these faster systems, SDRAM implements a clock on each memory module and uses this clock to synchronize the memory module with the motherboard clock and the CPU. SDRAM was dramatically faster than FPM or EDO RAM. The important point to remember when working with SDRAM is the fact that you *must* use memory modules whose clock speed is exactly the same as the clock speed of the motherboard. For example:

■ 66 MHz bus requires PC66 SDRAM

■ 100 MHz bus requires PC100 SDRAM

■ 133 MHz bus requires PC133 SDRAM

■ **Double-Data Rate Synchronous DRAM (DDR-SDRAM)**   DDR-SDRAM is one of the more commonly used types of memory in use today. DDR-SDRAM is similar to SDRAM; however, it runs two processes for every clock cycle. This effectively doubles your memory throughput. Like SDRAM, you must use the correct clock speed on your memory module for the motherboard clock and CPU you're using in the system. The following are common speed designations:

■ PC-1600: 100 MHz   ■ PC-2700: 166 MHz

■ PC-2100: 133 MHz   ■ PC-3200: 200 MHz

■ **DDR2-SDRAM**   DDR2-SDRAM is an improved version of DDR-SDRAM. The key advantage of DDR2-SDRAM is that it supports the higher clock speeds used in the latest motherboards. As with all other types of SDRAM, you must use the correct speed module for your particular motherboard. The following are DDR2-SDRAM speed designations:

■ PC2-4200: 266 MHz

■ PC2-5300: 333 MHz

■ PC2-6400: 400 MHz

Let's next review the types of memory modules you may encounter.

Memory Module Packages

In addition to technology, memory modules have been manufactured in a variety of different packages over the years. Some of the more common types include the following:

- **72-Pin SIMM**   SIMM stands for single inline memory module. In the 1990s 72-pin SIMMs were used for a very long time, primarily with FPM, EDO, or BEDO RAM chips. SIMMs are keyed, so they can't be inserted backwards. The important thing to remember when working with 72-pin SIMMs is that they usually had to be installed in pairs. We called this *banking*. That's because SIMM modules had be installed in banks of two. The issue at hand is the fact that the width of the memory module has to match the width of the data bus on your motherboard; 72-pin SIMMs were 32 bits wide (that is, they could process data 4 bytes at a time). If your data bus was also 32 bits wide, then you could install a single SIMM at a time. However, if the data bus on your motherboard was 64 bits wide, such as on a Pentium system, then you had to install two SIMMs at a time (32 + 32 = 64).

- **168-Pin DIMM**   DIMM stands for dual inline memory module. DIMMs are used with SDRAM. A DIMM is simply a bigger, wider SIMM. It uses two sets of memory chips, one on each side of the module. By using two sets of memory chips, DIMMs are 64 bits (8 bytes) wide. Because most of the motherboards that use DIMMs use a 64-bit data bus, you usually don't have to worry about banking issues. You can install one DIMM at a time in most systems.

- **184-Pin DIMM**   A 184-pin DIMM is very similar to a 168-pin DIMM. The key differences are the number of pins and the fact that 184-pin DIMMs are used with DDR-SDRAM.

- **240-Pin DIMM**   240-pin DIMMs are used with DDR2-SDRAM.

With this review of system RAM in mind, let's now turn our attention to the expansion slots on your motherboard.

SCENARIO & SOLUTION

How does DRAM store binary PC data?	DRAM uses a capacitor to store a small electrical charge. The absence of a charge can be represented as a binary 0; the presence of a charge can be represented as a binary 1.
You have an empty memory slot on your motherboard that requires PC-2100 DDR-SDRAM. You have a PC133 SDRAM module; can you use it in the empty memory slot?	No. Even though PC133 SDRAM and PC2100 DDR-SDRAM operate at the same clock speed, they use different module packages. SDRAM uses a 168-pin module. DDR-SDRAM uses a 184-pin module.

Expansion Slots

One of the key revolutions introduced by the IBM PC was the fact that it was a modular computer system. Early computer systems built in the 1950s and 1960s were custom manufactured for a specific purpose. These computers were very expensive and not very flexible. You couldn't add or remove parts to modify or upgrade the functionality of the system.

The original PC changed all that. IBM designed the IBM PC to be very modular. For the first time, you could purchase a basic PC system and then install additional components to add the functionality you needed.

To make this possible, IBM designed their original PC motherboards with an extension to the data bus called the expansion (or I/O) bus. The expansion bus allowed you to install expansion boards in expansion slots and have these devices be able to communicate with other critical system components, including the system memory, the CPU, and other expansion boards. Today, all PC motherboards use an expansion bus. In fact, most include several different types of expansion buses.

Over the years, a variety of different types of expansion buses have been implemented in personal computer systems. In this topic, we're going to discuss the following:

- The ISA bus
- The PCI bus
- The AGP bus
- Working with system resources

The ISA Bus

The Industry Standard Architecture (ISA) bus was the earliest type of expansion bus used in the PC. In fact, it was introduced in the first IBM PCs. The earliest version of the ISA bus was 8 bits wide. You probably won't see any motherboards that use an 8-bit ISA bus any more. They were obsolete by the late 1980s. However, you probably will still run into systems that use the 16-bit version of the ISA expansion bus.

The 16-bit ISA bus was introduced in the mid-1980s with the Intel 80286 CPU. It ran at a clock speed of 8.33 MHz. The 16-bit ISA bus used a 98-pin expansion slot. Three 16-bit ISA expansion slots are shown in Figure 2-7.

The 16-bit ISA bus was very widely implemented and a very large number of expansion boards were developed for it. You could purchase sound boards, network boards, MIDI boards, SCSI boards, and many other types of boards that used the 16-bit ISA expansion bus. A typical 16-bit ISA board is shown in Figure 2-8.

on the

iob

The ISA bus worked relatively well. However, it had two shortcomings. First of all, it was not exactly a speed demon. Throughput was quite slow, around 8 MB/s. Second, ISA boards weren't self-configuring. You had to manually configure interrupts, port addresses, and DMA channels. We'll discuss these parameters in more detail later in this chapter.

FIGURE 2-7 The 16-bit ISA expansion slot

FIGURE 2-8 A 16-bit ISA expansion board

The 16-bit ISA expansion bus was with us for many years. However, in the late 1990s, motherboards and CPUs began to quickly outpace the performance offered by ISA. Several other expansion buses were developed as a result. However, most of them quickly became obsolete. The one that made the cut is the PCI bus. Let's discuss PCI next.

The PCI Bus

In the mid-1990s a new type of expansion bus was introduced for personal computers that far outclassed the ISA bus. This was the Peripheral Component Interconnect (PCI) bus. PCI was designed and developed by an industry group called PCI-SIG. Most of the motherboards you will work with for the foreseeable future will probably have a PCI bus implemented. Typical PCI expansion slots are shown in Figure 2-9.

A PCI hard disk drive controller expansion board is shown in Figure 2-10.

The PCI bus offers some distinct advantages over the older ISA bus that make it indispensable to us today. First of all, the PCI bus is much, much faster than the ISA bus. The PCI bus is 32 bits wide and runs at 33 MHz. This allows it to transfer data at a rate around 66 MB/s. That is much faster than ISA!

FIGURE 2-9

PCI expansion
slots

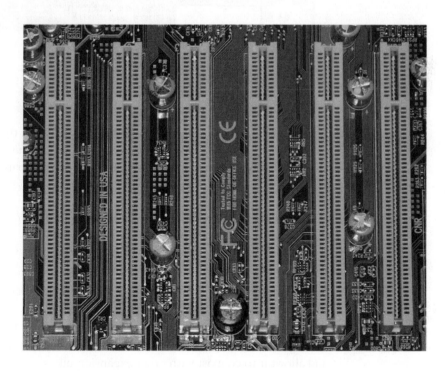

A PCI expansion board

In addition, PCI implements a new bus that resides between the data bus and the I/O bus on your motherboard. This new bus is called the *local bus* or the *mezzanine bus*. To do this, PCI uses a new type of chipset on the motherboard. It's composed of two parts:

- **Northbridge** The Northbridge is the chip that actually controls and manages the PCI expansion bus. Its job is to manage the devices installed in your PCI expansion slots and to connect them to the CPU, to the system memory, and to other PCI expansion cards.

- **Southbridge** The Southbridge chip acts as an intermediary between the PCI bus and other expansion buses (such as the ISA bus) on the motherboard. The Southbridge is sometimes referred to as the *PCI bridge*. The Southbridge allows the PCI bus to function independently of the CPU and allows it to co-exist with other expansion buses.

These features are all pretty cool. However, the thing I like the best about the PCI bus is the fact that PCI cards are self-configuring. Unlike an ISA card, you can simply plug a PCI board into an expansion slot and let the motherboard BIOS, the operating system, and the board itself negotiate and assign an interrupt, a port address range, and a DMA channel.

on the

ᵢob

Not only can a PCI expansion board configure itself, but also multiple boards can share interrupts. We'll discuss this in more detail later in this chapter. In addition, an updated version of the PCI bus has been recently introduced called PCI Express, which can transfer a lot of data very, very quickly. PCI Express is usually reserved for video boards in most motherboards. Other types of boards, such as sound boards and network boards, are still implemented on the standard PCI bus.

With PCI under our belt, let's next discuss AGP.

The AGP Bus

The Accelerated Graphics Port (AGP) is a specialty type of bus originally developed by Intel. Other buses, such as ISA and PCI, are used with a variety of different devices. You can have ISA video boards, network boards, sound boards, etc. You can also have PCI video boards, network boards, soundboards, USB adapters, and so on.

However, AGP implements only video expansion boards. A typical AGP expansion slot is shown in Figure 2-11.

An AGP video board is shown in Figure 2-12.

Many PC technicians argue that AGP really isn't a true expansion *bus*. Other expansion buses, such as ISA and PCI, can accommodate many different expansion boards all at the same time. Not so with AGP. You can only have a single AGP expansion slot and a single AGP expansion board installed in the system at a time.

AGP is well suited to video applications. The base throughput for an AGP card is about 266 MB/s. Now that is dramatically faster than ISA; it's also much

FIGURE 2-11

An AGP
expansion slot

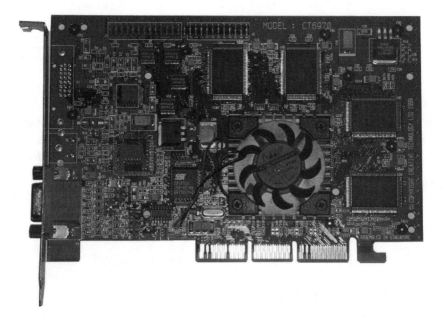

FIGURE 2-12

An AGP
expansion board

faster than PCI. However, this is only the base rate. AGP is available in a variety of modes that multiply this base rate. These modes include the following:

- 1x AGP: 266 MB/s
- 2x AGP: 533 MB/s
- 3x AGP: 1066 MB/s

The fastest AGP mode currently available is 8x AGP. That's fast!

on the *AGP has been the primary means for implementing video boards in most PC*
Job *systems for many years. However, AGP is actually starting to be phased out in*
favor of PCI Express. As fast as AGP is, PCI Express is even faster!

Before we end this topic, we need to spend some time discussing system resources.

Working with System Resources

As we've reviewed the various types of expansion buses, we've frequently mentioned the term *system resources*. Every device in a PC system has to be configured with a set of system resources that tell the device what communication channels and addresses it can use. To effectively manage a Linux system, you must have a solid understanding of what these system resources are and how they work. In this part of this chapter, we'll discuss the following:

- ■ Interrupt request channels
- ■ Input/output ports
- ■ DMA channels
- ■ Plug-n-play

Let's begin by discussing interrupts.

Interrupt Request Channels   The first system resource you need to be familiar with is the interrupt request channel.

Interrupt request channels are also referred to as **IRQs** *or just* **interrupts.**

When a device is installed in a PC system, it needs some means of letting the CPU know when it needs attention. Many devices in your PC need lots of CPU time; other devices only need the CPU on occasion. We need a way to make sure the busy devices get the attention they need without wasting time on devices that don't need as much. This is done through interrupts.

The CPU in your system has one wire on it called the interrupt (INT) wire. If current is applied to this wire, the CPU will stop what it is doing and service the device that placed current on the wire. If no current is present on the wire, then the CPU will continue working on whatever processing task has been assigned to it.

The interrupt system in a PC is very similar to a typical classroom. In a classroom setting, the instructor usually presents the material she has prepared to the students. If a student has a question, he can raise his hand and interrupt the instructor's presentation. After the question is answered, the instructor resumes the presentation.

PC interrupts work in much the same manner. Like the instructor, the CPU goes about its business until it is interrupted. Once interrupted, the CPU diverts its attention to the device that raised the interrupt. Once the device's request has been satisfied, the CPU goes back to what it was doing before.

The advantage to using interrupts is that the CPU only services system devices when they need it. It doesn't waste processing time on devices that are idle.

However, the scenario we've just discussed presents a problem. In a typical classroom, there are many students, not just one. Likewise, a PC system has many different devices that all need to get the CPU's attention from time to time. Unlike the hypothetical instructor we discussed above, the CPU only has a single INT wire. That would be sufficient if there were only a single device installed in the system. But this isn't the case. We need some way to allow many different devices to use that same INT wire. This is done using a programmable interrupt controller (PIC) chip.

The PIC chip has nine leads. One is connected to the INT wire on the CPU. The other eight are connected to interrupt wires in your motherboard's expansion slots. When a device in an expansion slot needs attention, it applies current to its interrupt wire. The PIC is alerted by this event and applies current to the CPU's INT wire. The CPU acknowledges the interrupt and the PIC then tells the CPU which interrupt number was activated. The CPU can then service the device.

Early PCs only had 8 interrupts and a single PIC, as related above. However, a modern PC has 16 interrupts. To get the extra interrupts, two PIC chips are actually cascaded together. That is, the wire that would normally be connected to the CPU INT wire on one PIC is connected instead to the second interrupt wire on the first PIC chip (whose INT wire is connected to the CPU). The second interrupt wire on the second PIC, which should be numbered INT 9, is actually wired to INT 2 in the expansion slots. Have you ever heard someone say that INT 2 and INT 9 are the same interrupt? Now you know why!

When working with interrupts, there are some important facts that you should keep in mind:

- Every device in the PC must be assigned an interrupt.
- Two ISA devices cannot share an interrupt.
- Two PCI devices can share interrupts.
- A PCI device cannot share an interrupt with an ISA device.
- Because INT 2 and INT 9 are actually the same wire on the PIC chips, you assign either one to a device in the system, but you can't assign both at the same time.
- Some system devices have interrupts assigned to them by default. Some of these can be changed or disabled; many cannot:
  - IRQ 0 – System Timer
  - IRQ 1 – Keyboard
  - IRQ 3 – COM 2
  - IRQ 4 – COM 1
  - IRQ 5 – LPT 2
  - IRQ 6 – Floppy Drive
  - IRQ 7 – LPT 1
- Interrupts 0, 1, and 8 are hard-wired. Under no circumstances can you use these interrupts for any other device in the system.
- If a device with a default interrupt assignment isn't installed in the system or it is disabled, you can use its interrupt for another device.

In addition to interrupts, devices also require an I/O address to function in a PC system. Let's talk about I/O addresses next.

Input/Output Addresses   Input/output (I/O) addresses go by a variety of names in a PC system. You may hear them referred to as I/O ports, port addresses, or simply as ports.

I/O addresses allow communications between the devices in the PC and the operating system. I/O addresses are very similar to mailboxes. To send a letter to someone, you must know his or her mailing address. You write their address on the letter and the mail carrier delivers it to the box with that address. Likewise, the person you wrote to can respond to your letter and leave it in their mailbox for the mail carrier to pick up.

I/O addresses work in much the same manner. They serve as mailboxes for the devices installed in the system. Data can be left for a device in its I/O address. Data from the device can be left in the I/O address for the operating system to pick up.

On a personal computer, there are only 16 interrupts available for assignment to system devices (which can sometimes represent a serious constraint). With I/O addresses, however, there are plenty to go around. A PC has 65,535 port addresses for devices to use.

When working with I/O addresses, there are a number of important facts to keep in mind:

- All devices must have an I/O address assigned.
- Most devices will use a range of I/O addresses.
- Devices must use unique I/O ports.

- Default I/O port assignments:
  - 0000h – DMA Controller
  - 0020h – PIC 1
  - 0030h – PIC 2
  - 0040h – System Timer
  - 0060h – Keyboard
  - 0070h – CMOS Clock
  - 00C0h – DMA Controller
  - 00F0h – Math Co-processor
  - 0170h – Secondary IDE Hard Disk Controller
  - 01F0h – Primary IDE Hard Disk Controller
  - 0200h – Joystick
  - 0278h – LPT2
  - 02E8h – COM4
  - 02F8h – COM2
  - 0378h – LPT1
  - 03E8h – COM3
  - 03F0h – Floppy Disk Drive Controller
  - 03F8h – COM1

Direct Memory Access Channels   In addition to interrupts and I/O addresses, some devices also require that you configure it with a direct memory access (DMA) channel. DMA channels are used by high-throughput devices to communicate directly with RAM *without* involving the CPU. Bypassing the CPU can dramatically increase the device's data transfer rate.

Not all devices need DMA. Other devices, however, would be severely handicapped if they couldn't use DMA. These devices include

- Sound boards
- Floppy diskette drives
- Hard disk drives

DMA is implemented on the motherboard using the DMA controller chip (DCC). The DCC is very similar to the PIC chip we reviewed earlier. The DCC has four leads that connect it to the memory controller chip (MCC) and the expansion bus slots. Each of these leads is referred to as a DMA channel. Data from an expansion slot is routed through the DCC to the MCC, allowing direct access to the system memory.

When working with DMA, you should keep the following points in mind:

- No two devices can use the same channel.
- Modern systems use two cascaded DMA controllers. Just as we cascade two PICs together to get 16 interrupts, we can also cascade two DCCs together to get 8 DMA channels. Just as interrupt 2 and 9 are really the same interrupt due to cascading, DMA channels 0 and 4 are actually the same DMA channel.
- The floppy diskette drive in your system is assigned DMA channel 2 by default.

Before we finish talking about system resources, we need to discuss how they are configured on an expansion board. Let's do that next.

Plug-n-Play   In the "old days" of ISA, we had to manually configure the system resources used by an expansion board in an expansion slot. Most ISA boards had a series of jumpers or DIP switches that you would use to configure the board's interrupt, I/O address, and DMA channel. This doesn't sound too difficult in theory, but in practice it could be very difficult.

The problem lay with the fact that most expansion boards, to cut manufacturing costs, couldn't be configured to any of the 16 interrupts or 65,536 port addresses available on the system. Instead, most boards offered the choice of two or three interrupts and I/O address ranges. The issue was that most board manufacturers chose the exact same choice of interrupts and I/O address ranges. You could easily run out of resources. For example, you may have had interrupts 2 and 3 available in your system, but the board you wanted to install could only be configured to use interrupts 4, 5, or 7. To implement the board, you would have to manually reconfigure other devices in the system in an attempt to free up an interrupt it could use.

In the mid-1990s, manually configured boards began to be replaced by software-configured boards. With these boards, you first installed it in an available expansion slot. Then you ran a program from a floppy diskette that came with the board and used it to specify what system resources it would use. This was better, but we still had to deal with a shortage of resources.

This was all fixed when the plug-n-play (PnP) standard was introduced in the late 1990s. PnP is great! In fact, it's still in use today. The PnP standard is designed to automatically configure the system resources used by your expansion boards for you every time you boot the system. It makes life so much easier for a system administrator. All you have to do is install the board in an available slot and turn the system on. No jumpers, no DIP switches, no misplaced configuration diskettes.

A PnP system requires three components to be present in your system:

- A PnP-compatible BIOS
- A PnP-compatible device
- A PnP-compatible operating system

When the system is powered on, the PnP BIOS negotiates with the PnP expansion board to determine what interrupt, I/O addresses, and DMA channels it will use. If necessary, the operating system can also add its input as to what resources it thinks should be assigned.

on the
Job

In the earliest version of PnP, the system didn't always operate correctly.
System administrators called it "plug-n-pray."

PnP is used for all PCI and AGP expansion boards. In the late 1990s, there were even some 16-bit ISA motherboards and cards that also supported PnP.

With system resources behind us, we now need to look at the storage devices used in PC systems.

SCENARIO & SOLUTION

You're working with an older PC system that uses a serial port mouse connected to COM1. You've installed a 16-bit ISA network board in the system and configured it to use INT 4. When you try to use the system, it frequently locks up. What's causing this problem?	The issue here is that COM1 uses INT 4 by default and 16-bit ISA devices, including your COM ports, can't share interrupts. When the network board and the serial mouse try to use the same interrupt at the same time, the CPU doesn't know which device to service and the system halts.
You need to install four PCI expansion boards in a PC system. You check your interrupt usage and find that only one interrupt is available. Can you still install these boards, or will you have to just select one of them?	You can install all of the boards. PCI cards can share interrupts. Your PnP system will work out the details for you when the system boots. If you check interrupt usage after installing the boards, you'll see that many boards will be configured to use the same interrupt number.

Storage Devices

Recall our earlier discussion of system RAM. Do you remember the key drawback to DRAM? It has to be constantly refreshed with electricity every few milliseconds. If the system fails to do this, then the data and programs stored in RAM are forever lost. The DRAM we use for system memory is really fast, but it isn't persistent. To make a PC system truly usable, we need some kind of long-term, persistent storage medium that will retain data even if the power to the system is shut off.

In this topic, we're going to review several storage devices that can do just that. We'll cover the following:

- Floppy diskettes
- Hard disk drives
- Optical drives
- Flash memory drives

Let's begin with floppy diskette drives.

Floppy Diskettes

One of the oldest persistent storage devices used in PC systems is the floppy diskette drive. Floppy disks have changed very little since the first PC. Back then, computers didn't have hard disk drives. Instead, they booted off of floppy disks, they loaded programs from floppy disks, and they saved data on floppy disks. In fact, if you were a true computer geek, you would install a second floppy disk drive in your system so you wouldn't have to swap floppy disks as frequently.

Today, floppy disks are quickly disappearing from computer systems. They have persisted as long as they have because they are extremely useful. They provide an easy means for moving files between systems and they can be used to boot a malfunctioning system for repair. In spite of these benefits, the days of the floppy diskette drive are numbered. It won't be long before floppy drives are no longer supported.

Until then, you still need to be familiar with floppy diskettes for your Linux+ exam. Floppy diskettes use an oxide-coated Mylar disk to store data. This is shown in Figure 2-13.

This Mylar disk is the "floppy" part of the floppy diskette. The disk is actually encased in a rigid plastic sheath that protects it. The sheath has a hole on both sides, covered by a metal slide that allows the heads in a floppy diskette drive to access the surface of the disk to read or write data. These heads can read or write both sides of the disk surface simultaneously. A motor in the floppy diskette drive moves the heads forward and backward while a spindle motor spins the disk itself, allowing different areas of the disk surface to be accessed.

FIGURE 2-13

Floppy diskette
construction

Floppy disks have been produced in a variety of sizes and capacities over the years. These include the following:

- 5.25" Single Sided, Double Density: 180 KB
- 5.25" Double Sided, Double Density: 360 KB
- 5.25" Double Sided, High Density: 1.2 MB
- 3.5" Double Sided, Double Density: 720 KB
- 3.5" Double Sided, High Density: 1.44 MB (This is the type most commonly used today.)

Floppy disks have three key disadvantages:

- They are very slow.
- They don't hold very much.
- Diskettes degrade and lose data after a short amount of time.

Hard Disk Drives

Because of the limitations associated with floppy diskette drives, hard disk drives have become the primary type of persistent storage used in PC systems. Hard disk drives are much faster, store huge amounts of data, and are much more reliable than floppy diskettes.

Hard disk drives read and write magnetic information to and from spinning aluminum disks called *platters*. These are shown in Figure 2-14.

Most hard disk drives use multiple platters. The platters are coated with a magnetic surface material that allows the hard disk drive heads to read and write magnetic information to and from drive.

on the **Öob**

Don't open a hard disk drive as we did in Figure 2-14. Hard drives are sealed units that contain exceptionally pure air. If you open the drive, you allow dust into the system that can scratch the surface of the platters, rendering them useless.

Each platter has two heads. One reads the top side of the platter; the other reads the bottom side. The heads themselves don't actually touch the surface of the platters. As the platters spin, a thin cushion of air is created on their surface. The heads actually rest on this cushion of air.

Hard disk platters spin very fast. A low-end drive spins at about 5400 RPMs. Most workstation hard drives spin at 7200 RPMs. High-end server drives spin at 10,000 RPMs or faster. The faster the platters spin, the faster the drive can read or write data.

Every hard disk drive has several parameters that are collectively called the drive's geometry. These parameters are used by your system BIOS (or by the BIOS on a

FIGURE 2-14

Hard disk drive platters

hard disk interface board) to determine how the drive is to be accessed and where data can be stored. The parameters that compose the drive geometry include the following:

- **Heads**   The heads parameter refers to the number of read/write heads in the drive.
- **Cylinders**   A cylinder refers to the concentric parallel tracks on all sides of all platters in the hard disk drive. Imagine a hollow cylinder that penetrates down through all of the platters in a hard drive. Depending on how wide the cylinder is you can fit a certain number of progressively wider cylinders, beginning in the center of the platters and working your way outward to the edge, within the drive platters.
- **Sectors Per Track**   In addition to creating imaginary cylinders in the drive, you can also slice each platter up into imaginary pie-shaped wedges. The sectors per track parameter refers to the number of wedges the platters have been divided into.

Many times, you will hear the drive geometry parameters referred to as simply CHS (cylinders, heads, and sectors per track). Back in the "old" days, we had to manually configure these parameters in the CMOS setup program whenever we added a new drive to the system. Today, this isn't as much of an issue. Your BIOS still needs to know these parameters to be able to address the disk. However, most CMOS setup programs come configured by default to query the hard drive each time the system boots and automatically update the BIOS with the drive's geometry.

Currently, you have two choices of hard disk drive families that you can use in PC systems: IDE and SCSI. Let's briefly review IDE first.

IDE Hard Disk Drives   If you own a computer, more than likely you have some type of IDE hard disk drive installed. IDE drives are the most widely used type of hard disk drive and are very commonly implemented in desktop computer systems. IDE drives are inexpensive, can store a lot of data, and are relatively fast, making them ideal for most systems.

on the
ⓘob   *There have been many different versions of IDE hard drives used over the years. The original drives were called IDE. Later drives were called Enhanced IDE (EIDE). The current generation of IDE drives are called ATA drives. However, everyone simply refers to all of these drives as "IDE."*

IDE stands for Integrated Drive Electronics. This name is derived from the fact that IDE drives implement the hard disk drive controller hardware on the drive itself instead of a separate expansion board. A single controller on one drive can control a total of two different IDE devices.

Most desktop motherboards available today include two separate IDE channels called the Primary and the Secondary channels. Because one controller can manage two IDE devices, you can install a maximum of two IDE drives on each channel. Each channel is configured using a 40-pin, 80-wire ribbon cable that connects each device to the motherboard.

on the
Ø o b
Older IDE drives used a 40-pin, 40-wire connector. Be sure you don't use one of these older cables in a newer ATA system.

IDE devices on the same channel operate in a master/slave relationship. If an IDE hard drive is set to be a master drive on the IDE channel, then its integrated drive controller is enabled and will take control of all IDE devices on the channel. If an IDE drive is set to be a slave, its controller is disabled and must be controlled by a controller on a different drive on the channel. The master/slave relationship is usually established by setting or removing a jumper from a set of pins on the drive itself.

Each IDE channel in a system can have one master and one (optional) slave drive.

e x a m

w a t c h *The number one mistake made by PC technicians when working with IDE drives is forgetting to set the master/slave relationship correctly.*

You can't configure two masters on the same channel nor can you configure two slaves. It is acceptable, however to implement a single master drive on the Primary IDE channel in the system and a second master drive on the Secondary IDE channel.

Most desktop systems today use the latest generation of IDE hard drives called ATA. ATA drives are much faster than older IDE hard drives. They are available in four different speeds:

- ATA 33
- ATA 66
- ATA 100
- ATA 133

Lately, a new type of IDE drive called Serial ATA (SATA) has been introduced and it is quickly becoming very popular. SATA drives are much faster than the fastest ATA drives. In addition, SATA drives are not subject to the master/slave configuration rules that ATA drives are. Instead, each SATA drive in your system has its own dedicated hard disk channel that greatly enhances speed and throughput.

In addition to ATA drives, you can also use SCSI drives in a PC. Let's talk about SCSI next.

SCSI Hard Disk Drives   SCSI stands for Small Computer System Interface. However, in the industry, we just call it "skuzzy." SCSI is a general-purpose interface that can be used to connect a variety of different types of devices to a PC system, including:

- Hard disk drives
- CD/DVD drives
- Tape drives

- Scanners
- RAID arrays
- Printers

SCSI is very powerful and very flexible. However, you probably won't encounter many SCSI hard drives in desktop PC systems. That's because SCSI hard disk drives are considerably more expensive than comparable IDE drives. SCSI hard disks are usually implemented in high-end server systems instead.

SCSI implements a communications chain that connects a series of devices together. The SCSI chain runs cabling from device to device to device. These devices can be implemented inside the server and connected together using a ribbon cable or they can be implemented externally using cables. Either way, the SCSI controller controls all devices in the chain. The SCSI controller is usually

SCENARIO & SOLUTION

Curiosity has gotten the best of you and you have decided to open up a hard disk drive to see the parts inside. You have reassembled the disk and want to install it back into your computer. Is this a good idea?	No. By opening the case, you have introduced fine dust particles into the interior of the disk. Because the space between the heads and the platters is so small, these particles can get stuck between them and actually mar the surface of the platters, destroying data. If you open a disk, throw it away when you're done.
You've decided to install a second IDE hard disk drive on the Primary IDE channel in your PC. You've connected the drive to the cable, connected power, and booted the system. However, the drive isn't recognized by the system BIOS. In fact, the first hard drive in the system is no longer recognized either. What's causing this?	Most IDE hard drives are shipped from the manufacturer preconfigured as master drives. When you connected it to the Primary IDE channel, you added a second master drive to the channel. To fix the problem, look for a jumper on the drive that will configure it to be a slave drive.

implemented as an expansion board in an expansion slot in the motherboard. It usually has two connectors:

- **Internal**   The internal connector is used to connect internal SCSI devices using a SCSI ribbon cable.
- **External**   The external connector is used to connect external SCSI devices to the controller.

Older SCSI controllers supported up to eight devices (including the SCSI controller itself) in the SCSI chain. Many newer SCSI controllers support up to 16 devices (again, including the SCSI controller). The controller determines what data should be sent to which device in the chain using the SCSI ID. Each device in the SCSI chain must have a unique ID number between 0 and 7 (0 and 15 on newer controllers).

Whenever I teach a class that covers SCSI, I always emphasize at this point that the SCSI ID assigned to a device has nothing to do whatsoever with its physical location in the SCSI chain. It's simply a logical number we assign. However, the SCSI ID does perform a crucial function. It defines the priority of the device in the SCSI chain. The lower the SCSI ID assigned to a device, the higher its priority. By default, SCSI controllers are assigned a SCSI ID of 7. SCSI hard disk drives are usually assigned a high-priority ID of 0 or 1. CD/DVD drives are usually assigned a lower priority SCSI ID of 4 or 5.

The way you set the SCSI ID varies from device to device. Most hard disk drives use three jumpers to set the ID value. These three jumpers have the following values:

- Jumper 1 = 1
- Jumper 2 = 2
- Jumper 3 = 4

The SCSI ID is determined by adding together the values of all jumpers with shunts installed. For example, if you use no shunts at all (in other words, no jumpers are closed), then the SCSI ID is set to $0 + 0 + 0 = 0$. If you put a shunt on jumper 2, then the SCSI ID is set to $0 + 2 + 0 = 2$. If you put a shunt on jumpers 2 and 3, then the SCSI ID is set to $0 + 2 + 4 = 6$.

In addition to SCSI ID, you also need to be concerned with *termination* when setting up a SCSI chain. Each end of the SCSI chain must have a terminating resistor installed to absorb data signals. This prevents the signal from reflecting back down the bus.

Termination can be implemented in a variety of ways on the SCSI chain. Some terminators are implemented by attaching a terminator to the end of the SCSI ribbon cable for internal devices. For external devices, the terminator may be a special plug that is inserted in the second SCSI port on the last external device in the SCSI chain.

Termination can also be implemented on the SCSI devices themselves. This can be done in the following ways:

- **Resistor Packs** Resistor packs are inserted in the SCSI device's circuit board to enable termination.

- **Jumpers** A shunted jumper is frequently used to enable termination on the device.

- **Software** SCSI controller boards usually include a software setup program run from the controller board's BIOS that can be used to turn termination off and on.

- **Active Termination** Many SCSI devices use active termination. With active termination, the device checks to see if it's the last device on the chain. If it is, it automatically enables the terminating resistor.

e x a m

ⓦ a t c h   *My experience has been that about 95 percent of problems encountered when working with SCSI are due to misconfigured SCSI IDs or terminators.*

When configuring SCSI termination, it's important to remember that *both* ends of the SCSI bus must be terminated, but nothing in the middle can be terminated. Any devices after the terminator in the SCSI chain will not be visible to the controller.

Over the years, a wide variety of SCSI standards have been introduced. A thorough review of all of the standards is beyond the scope of this topic. It would take an entire chapter devoted to the various SCSI standards to cover all the different flavors of SCSI available. For our purposes here, just make sure that all of the devices in your SCSI chain, including the SCSI controller, use the same SCSI standard. For example, if you're using Wide Ultra SCSI III hard disk drives, then you need to use a Wide Ultra SCSI III controller.

Now that you understand how hard disk drives are implemented, we next need to talk about optical storage devices.

SCENARIO & SOLUTION

You're configuring a SCSI chain in your PC. You've connected an external SCSI scanner to the external port on your SCSI adapter. You've connected an internal hard drive and DVD drive to the controller's internal ribbon connector. The DVD drive is the last device on the cable. You've enabled termination on the controller and on the DVD drive. When you boot the system, the controller doesn't detect the SCSI scanner. Why is this happening?	You have termination configured incorrectly. Remember that the controller card is part of the SCSI chain. By enabling termination on the card, you cut the scanner off of the chain. To fix this, disable termination on the controller and enable it on the SCSI scanner.
You're configuring a SCSI chain in your computer system. You've configured your SCSI controller to use ID 7, your SCSI hard drive to use ID 6, and your SCSI DVD drive to use ID 1. Will this configuration work?	Yes. This configuration will work. However, it isn't configured correctly. Because the hard drive will be the most heavily utilized device on the SCSI chain, it needs to have a higher priority. It should be set to ID 0 or 1. The DVD drive should be set to ID 5 or 6.

Optical Storage Devices

In addition to floppy diskettes and hard disks, you can also use optical storage media to store data in a PC system. Currently, you can use CD or DVD optical devices in your computer.

Optical storage media stores binary data just like any other storage device. However, the way it stores that data is very different. Unlike floppy diskettes and hard disks, optical drives do not use magnetism. Instead they store data in the form of reflected light. The bottom surface of a CD or a DVD is encoded using a series of pits and lands. Pits don't reflect light; lands do. By bouncing a laser beam off the bottom surface of a CD or a DVD, we can reconstruct binary computer data in the form of 0's and 1's by capturing the reflections and non-reflections created by the pits and lands.

Compact discs (CDs) are 120 mm in diameter and are 1.2 mm thick. A CD can store 650–700MB of binary computer data or 74 minutes of digital audio. Digital versatile discs (DVDs) have the same dimensions as a CD. However, because the tracks on a DVD are thinner and closer together, a DVD can store dramatically more data than a CD (4.7 GB).

The key advantages of using optical media to store data in a PC are as follows:

- They can store a relatively large amount of data.
- They are highly portable.
- They are very inexpensive to manufacture.

CDs and DVDs were originally introduced for use in PCs as a read-only media. To encode the pits and lands that store binary PC data, a CD or DVD had to be pressed at a manufacturing facility. Once pressed, no more data could be added to the disc.

Today, that has all changed. In a modern PC system, you can implement writable and re-writable CD and DVD drives (usually called *burners*). Optical burner drives implement a second, high-intensity laser in addition to the standard read laser. This second laser is used to write information to the bottom side of a burnable CD or DVD. Once-writable CDs or DVDs use a special photo-reactive dye on the bottom side of the disc. When the high-intensity laser in an optical burner strikes this dye, it changes the pigment to a darker color. By doing this, we can encode binary data on the disc using light and dark spots that operate much like the pits and lands found on a factory-pressed CD or DVD.

With a CD-R or DVD-R optical burner, the data becomes fixed as soon as it is burned. You can't erase or modify the data after that. To be able to do this, you need to use a re-writable optical burner (called a CD-RW or DVD-RW). A re-writable burner uses a high-intensity secondary laser just like a CD-R or DVD-R. However, the bottom surface of a CD-RW disc uses a photo-reactive crystalline coating. These discs can be encoded with light and dark spots just like a CD-R disc. They can also be erased. Using the right intensity and frequency in the laser, a CD-RW drive can reset the crystals on the bottom surface of the disc back to their original state, allowing you to burn new data.

CD burners are available in two varieties:

- **CD-R** CD-Rs can write data once to a CD-R disc. They can also read standard CD-ROMs as well as burned CD-Rs.

- **CD-RW** CD-RWs can write data to write-once CD-R discs or to erasable CD-RW discs. They can also read CD-RWs, CD-Rs, and CD-ROMs.

DVD burners are available using a much wider array of standards:

- **DVD-R** DVD-R discs use organic dye technology like a CD-R. DVD-Rs are compatible with most DVD drives and players.

- **DVD+R** DVD+R is a write-once variation of DVD+RW.

- **DVD-RW** DVD-RWs use a crystalline phase change coating, allowing them to be erased and re-written. DVD-RWs are playable in many DVD drives and players.

- **DVD+RW** DVD+RW is an erasable disc format based on CD-RW technology. DVD+RW discs are readable in many existing DVD drives and players.

Flash Drives

The last type of storage device we need to discuss in this chapter are flash drives. Instead of using magnetically encoded platters or optical discs to store data, flash drives use a memory chip. You may recall from our earlier discussion of system memory that one of the problems with DRAM is the fact that it isn't persistent. If you turn off the power, you lose all of your data. You might be wondering how we can use a memory chip, then, to store persistent PC data.

This is done using a different type of memory chip. Instead of DRAM, a flash drive uses flash memory. Flash memory can be electronically erased and reprogrammed. Flash memory is also persistent. Once written, it retains its contents even if the electrical current is turned off.

This combination makes flash drives a very useful and very powerful storage solution for PCs. They can store large amounts of data in a very small package. In fact, most flash drives are so small that they can be carried on a keychain. Many times you will hear flash drives referred to as *thumb drives* due to their small size.

Essentially, a flash drive is little more than a printed circuit board with a flash memory chip installed that is connected to a USB interface. Once plugged into a USB port on your computer, your system can read information from or write information to the flash drive as if it were a small hard disk drive.

That's it for this topic. We've covered a wide range of PC components. Before we end this chapter, we need to cover one more topic: removable hardware.

CERTIFICATION OBJECTIVE 2.02

Describe Removable Hardware Interfaces

In recent years, new hardware interfaces for PCs have been introduced that have revolutionized the way we connect external devices to the system. Prior to these interfaces, we could still connect external devices to the system using serial ports, parallel ports, keyboard ports, and mouse ports. However, for most of these external devices to work correctly, you had to make sure they were properly connected and turned on (if applicable) before you powered on the PC system itself. If you didn't, the system usually wouldn't recognize that the device was attached. In addition, you couldn't unplug one external device and connect a new one while the system was running. That kind of change usually required a full system reboot.

With removable hardware interfaces, all of that has changed. Now, we can add or remove external devices while the system is running and have the PC automatically recognize the change. In this topic we're going to review the following removable hardware interfaces:

- Universal serial bus
- FireWire IEEE1394
- PCMCIA

Let's begin by discussing USB.

Universal Serial Bus

Universal serial bus (USB) is a high-speed removable hardware interface that has pretty much replaced serial, parallel, mouse, and keyboard ports on the PC. Most PC systems today include an integrated USB interface in the motherboard. USB can be used to connect a wide variety of external devices, including:

- External hard drives
- External CD and DVD drives
- Printers
- Scanners
- Digital cameras
- Mice
- Keyboards
- Flash drives

USB connects these devices into a bus. A single USB bus can include up to 127 external devices. All devices on the bus are grouped into one of three categories:

- **Hubs**   USB hubs are central connecting points for USB devices. USB uses a star topology. All devices on the bus connect to a USB hub. The USB interface in your PC, whether it is an expansion board or is built into the motherboard, functions as the root hub in your USB bus. The cool thing about USB is the fact that you can cascade multiple USB hubs together to connect additional devices to the bus. Simply plugging one USB hub into a USB port on another hub does this. This makes USB extremely scalable.
- **Functions**   Functions are individual external USB devices such as printers, scanners, hard drives, keyboards, and mice.
- **Hub and Function**   Some USB devices are both a function and a hub at the same time. For example, many USB keyboards include several USB ports that you can use to connect additional USB devices. This type of device is both a function and a hub.

Because all USB devices eventually connect to the PC through the root hub in your USB interface, USB eliminates the need for multiple interfaces to support multiple external devices. This is a really cool feature of USB. Back in the "old" days of serial and parallel ports, you had to implement a separate interface for each device you wanted to connect. For example, if you wanted to connect two parallel printers to the same PC, you had to purchase and install an additional parallel port interface for the second printer. This isn't an issue with USB. A single USB interface can support many USB devices. Some USB devices, such as a flash drive, can even draw the power they need to run directly from the USB bus. Other USB devices, such as external DVD drives, need their own power supply unit that is plugged into a wall outlet.

In addition, USB devices are self-configuring, self-identifying, and hot-swappable. You can attach a USB device to the system while it is running. When you do, the device will advertise its presence to the PC, which will assign the necessary resources for it to function. When you're done using the device, you can stop the device and disconnect it without halting the system.

USB has been implemented in two different versions:

■ **USB 1.1**   This version of USB is the oldest. It transfers data at a rate of 12 Mbps.

■ **USB 2.0**   This is the current version of USB. It is much faster than earlier versions. It can transfer data at 480 Mbps.

The important thing to remember is that the overall speed of the entire bus is set to the speed of the slowest device. For example, if you have a USB 2.0 interface and connect a USB 1.1 hard drive to it, the entire system slows down to 12 Mbps.

Now that you understand the function of USB in a computer system, here is a possible scenario question and answer.

SCENARIO & SOLUTION

Your PC system provides only a single USB port in the root hub. However, you need to connect five different USB devices to the bus. To make this work, you've purchased two three-port USB hubs. You've connected the first hub to one of the root hub ports in the PC. You've connected the second hub to a port in the first hub. This leaves you with five open USB ports to which you will connect the various devices needed by the system. Will this work?	Yes. USB hubs can be cascaded together in this manner. This allows you to dramatically increase the number of USB devices that can be connected to a single system.

In addition to USB, a second removable hardware interface called FireWire is commonly used with PCs. Let's review this standard next.

FireWire IEEE 1394

FireWire is very similar to USB. It is designed to support high-speed data transfers between external devices and your PC system. FireWire isn't as widely implemented as USB. Most PC systems sold today do not include a FireWire interface. To use FireWire devices, you will probably have to install a FireWire expansion board in an expansion slot in your system's motherboard.

on the **Job**

FireWire is also referred to as IEEE 1394 or i.Link.

Like USB, FireWire devices are PnP-compatible and hot-swappable. It is frequently used for:

- External hard drives
- External CD and DVD drives
- Digital cameras
- Digital video cameras

FireWire is extremely fast. It can transfer data at 400 Mbps. Unlike USB, FireWire does not use a star topology. Instead, FireWire connects devices in true bus fashion by running a cable from device to device to device, forming a chain. A maximum of 63 devices can be connected together in this manner.

The last removable hardware interface we're going to discuss in this chapter is PCMCIA.

PCMCIA

PCMCIA stands for Personal Computer Memory Card International Association. This association is a consortium of 300 industry manufacturers that has defined a set of standards for credit card-sized expansion boards used in notebook PCs.

Notebook computer systems face a special challenge. We want notebooks to be modular just like a desktop PC system. However, their small size makes this very difficult to accomplish. Standard-sized expansion boards just don't fit inside a notebook PC.

To keep notebooks small and modular at the same time, the PCMCIA consortium has defined specifications for PC Cards. These cards function much like expansion boards in a desktop PC system. For example, if you wanted to add wireless networking capabilities to a notebook PC, you could install a wireless network PC Card in a PCMCIA slot.

Like USB and FireWire devices, PC Cards are PnP-compatible and-hot swappable. If you plug in a PCMCIA card in a notebook PC, the card will advertise itself to the system. The card will have the resources it needs to function assigned to it and it becomes available for use. When you're done, you can stop the card and remove it without halting the system.

Version 2.1 of the PCMCIA standard was released in 1995 and is commonly implemented in modern notebook computer systems. This version of PCMCIA is referred to as *CardBus*. CardBus devices are 32 bits wide and run at 33 MHz. They offer many of the same features found on PCI expansion boards, such as bus mastering.

CERTIFICATION SUMMARY

In this chapter, you were introduced to the basic components that comprise a PC system. We began by emphasizing that a significant portion of the Linux+ exam is focused on PC hardware. We then reviewed the role and function of the power supply in a PC system. We related that the power supply's job is to convert AC wall current into DC current that the PC can use. It's also responsible for cooling the internal PC components with a cooling fan.

Next, we talked about the motherboard. We related that the primary function of the motherboard is to tie all of the components in the PC together, including the CPU, RAM, and expansion boards. We also pointed out that the motherboard includes a chip called the BIOS that contains many software programs that allow the CPU to communicate with the hard drive, the keyboard, the system memory, and so on.

After looking at the motherboard, we next discussed the CPU. We related that the primary function of the CPU is to perform arithmetic and logical functions with the data we supply. We discussed the fact that the motherboard clock sets the tempo for the CPU. We also discussed the importance of L1 and L2 cache on a CPU. We also reviewed the various CPU families that have been produced by Intel and AMD.

We then turned our attention to the system memory. We first discussed how DRAM stores data using transistors and capacitors. We emphasized that DRAM must be frequently refreshed to keep the data it stores intact. We then reviewed the various memory technologies that have been used over the years. We also reviewed the memory module packages that have been used to implement memory technology. We pointed out that most systems today use either DDR-SDRAM or DDR2-SDRAM.

After discussing memory, we turned our attention to the expansion bus. We emphasized that the expansion bus makes the modern PC modular in nature. We then reviewed the ISA, PCI, and AGP expansion buses. We emphasized that ISA boards must be manually configured while PCI and AGP boards can be automatically configured using PnP. We also reviewed the role and function of interrupts, I/O addresses, and DMA channels. We emphasized that you need to be very familiar with these system resources for your Linux+ exam. We also reviewed how the PnP system works, emphasizing that PCI expansion cards use PnP and can be configured to share interrupt channels.

Next, we discussed the various types of storage devices used in a PC system, beginning with the floppy diskette drive. We then reviewed how IDE and SCSI hard disk drives work and how they are configured. We emphasized that most hard drive troubleshooting issues can be traced back to incorrect master/slave settings with IDE drives and termination/ID settings with SCSI drives. We ended this topic by discussing how optical and flash memory storage devices work.

We finished this chapter by discussing removable hardware interfaces that are used to connect external devices to a PC. We first looked at USB. We noted that USB uses hubs to create a cascaded star topology that can connect up to 127 external devices. We then reviewed how IEEE 1394 accomplishes a similar task using a daisy-chained bus topology. We finished by reviewing the PCMCIA standard that is used to create credit card-sized expansion boards for notebook PC systems.

✓ TWO-MINUTE DRILL

Describe Personal Computer Components

- ❑ Power supplies convert AC current to DC current and keep the PC system cool.
- ❑ The motherboard interconnects all of the PC devices, allowing them to communicate together.
- ❑ The BIOS contains many small programs that allow the CPU to communicate with basic system devices such as RAM, keyboards, floppy diskette drives, and hard disk drives.
- ❑ The BIOS is configured using the CMOS setup program.
- ❑ CPUs perform arithmetic and logical functions.
- ❑ Primarily Intel and AMD manufacture PC CPUs.
- ❑ Intel CPUs include the following:
  - ❑ Pentium Pro
  - ❑ Pentium II
  - ❑ Pentium III
  - ❑ Pentium IV
  - ❑ Pentium D
  - ❑ Pentium Extreme
  - ❑ Celeron
- ❑ AMD CPUs include the following:
  - ❑ K6
  - ❑ Athlon
  - ❑ Athlon XP
  - ❑ Sempron
  - ❑ Athlon 64
  - ❑ Athlon 64 FX
  - ❑ Athlon 64 X2 Dual-Core
- ❑ You must use the right CPU in the right CPU socket in the motherboard.
- ❑ The motherboard clock is used to drive the CPU.

- ❏ CPUs use integrated cache memory to speed it up.
- ❏ DRAM is fast, but isn't persistent.
- ❏ System memory technology includes the following:
  - ❏ FPM
  - ❏ EDO
  - ❏ SDRAM
  - ❏ DDR-SDRAM
  - ❏ DDR2-SDRAM
- ❏ System memory is packaged in the following types of modules:
  - ❏ 72-pin SIMM
  - ❏ 168-pin DIMM
  - ❏ 184-pin DIMM
  - ❏ 240-pin DIMM
- ❏ The ISA bus is 16 bits wide and runs at a clock speed of 8.33 MHz.
- ❏ ISA cards must be manually configured.
- ❏ ISA cards can't share interrupts.
- ❏ The PCI bus is 32 bits wide and runs at a clock speed of 33 MHz.
- ❏ PCI cards are self-configuring and can share interrupts.
- ❏ The AGP bus is used only for video boards.
- ❏ AGP is beginning to be replaced by PCI Express.
- ❏ Interrupts are used to alert the CPU that a device needs attention.
- ❏ Every device in the PC must have an interrupt assigned.
- ❏ Two ISA devices cannot share an interrupt.
- ❏ Two PCI devices can share interrupts.
- ❏ A PCI device cannot share an interrupt with an ISA device.
- ❏ I/O addresses are like mailboxes for PC devices.
- ❏ I/O addresses are written in hex.
- ❏ All devices must have an I/O address assigned.
- ❏ Most devices will use a range of I/O addresses.
- ❏ Devices must use unique I/O ports.

❏ DMA channels allow a device to communicate directly with the system RAM without using the CPU.

❏ Devices must use unique DMA channels.

❏ PnP allows devices to be automatically configured with system resources when the PC is booted.

❏ A PnP system requires three components:

  ❏ A PnP-compatible BIOS

  ❏ A PnP-compatible device

  ❏ A PnP-compatible operating system

❏ Floppy diskettes save data on a coated Mylar disk.

❏ Floppy drives are being phased out.

❏ Hard disks use coated aluminum platters to store data.

❏ Drive geometry consists of the following parameters:

  ❏ Heads

  ❏ Cylinders

  ❏ Sectors Per Track

❏ IDE hard drives have the disk controller integrated into the drive itself.

❏ IDE uses master and slave drives.

❏ An IDE channel can only have one master drive.

❏ Most PCs provide two IDE channels (Primary and Secondary).

❏ SCSI hard drives are used mostly in server systems.

❏ SCSI devices are connected in a chain.

❏ Each SCSI device in the chain is assigned a SCSI ID.

❏ The lower the SCSI ID, the higher the device's priority.

❏ Both ends of the SCSI chain must be terminated and nothing in between.

❏ Optical drives use pits and lands to represent binary 0's and 1's.

❏ Writable optical discs use a special photo-reactive coating that can be used to encode binary data.

❏ Flash drives used flash memory to persistently store data.

Describe Removable Hardware Interfaces

- ❑ USB allows you to connect up to 127 external devices to the PC.
- ❑ USB devices are self-configuring and hot-swappable.
- ❑ USB hubs can be cascaded.
- ❑ FireWire allows you to connect up to 63 devices.
- ❑ FireWire devices are self-configuring and hot-swappable.
- ❑ FireWire devices are daisy-chained together.
- ❑ PCMCIA defines small expansion boards and slots for notebook computers.
- ❑ PCMCIA devices are self-configuring and hot-swappable.

SELF TEST

Describe Personal Computer Components

1. What DC voltage levels does a power supply provide? (Choose two.)
- A. 3.3 volts
- B. 24 volts
- C. 6 volts
- D. 5 volts
- E. 18 volts

2. You need to install Linux on a workstation. The hard drive has been wiped and is ready for the new operating system. You insert your first Linux installation CD in the CD drive and boot the system. Instead of starting the installation routine, the screen displays an error message indicating that an operating system couldn't be found. What's causing the problem?
- A. Your Linux CD is damaged.
- B. The hard drive is failing and needs to be replaced.
- C. The CD drive is malfunctioning.
- D. The boot device order is set incorrectly in the BIOS.

3. Which of the following is an Intel CPU?
- A. Celeron
- B. Athlon
- C. Sempron
- D. Opteron

4. Which of the following CPU sockets is used for the AMD Athlon CPU?
- A. Socket 370
- B. Socket 423
- C. Socket 478
- D. Socket A
- E. Socket AMD

5. What type of memory is used to create the CPU cache?
- A. DRAM
- B. SDRAM
- C. SRAM

    D. FPM RAM

    E. EDO RAM

6. Which type of memory is used in 72-pin SIMM modules? (Choose two.)

    A. SDRAM

    B. SRAM

    C. FPM RAM

    D. EDO RAM

    E. DDR-SDRAM

7. Which type of memory is used in 184-pin DIMM modules? (Choose two.)

    A. SDRAM

    B. SRAM

    C. FPM RAM

    D. EDO RAM

    E. DDR-SDRAM

8. How wide is the ISA expansion bus? (Choose two.)

    A. 8 bits

    B. 16 bits

    C. 24 bits

    D. 32 bits

    E. 64 bits

9. How wide is the standard PCI expansion bus?

    A. 8 bits

    B. 16 bits

    C. 24 bits

    D. 32 bits

    E. 64 bits

10. What is the clock speed of a standard PCI expansion bus?

    A. 4.77 MHz

    B. 8.33 MHz

    C. 16 MHz

    D. 24 MHz

    E. 33 MHz

11. Which PCI component functions as an intermediary between the PCI bus and other expansion buses on the motherboard?

- **A.** Northbridge
- **B.** Southbridge
- **C.** PCI Gateway
- **D.** ISA Bridge

12. Your motherboard has a built-in AGP video board as well as an available AGP slot. You've heard that you can implement a dual-monitor system by installing two video boards in the PC. Can you do this with the open AGP slot and the integrated video adapter?

- **A.** Yes, you can install a second adapter in the open AGP slot.
- **B.** No, Linux doesn't support dual-monitor systems.
- **C.** Yes, but you'll have to configure your BIOS to enable both devices.
- **D.** No, only a single adapter can function on the AGP bus at any given time.

13. You're installing two ISA expansion boards in an older PC system. One is a sound board, the other a network board. The system has INT 2 and INT 9 available. Can you assign these interrupts to these two boards?

- **A.** Yes, either board can use either interrupt.
- **B.** Yes, but the sound board must use INT 2 and the network board must use INT 9.
- **C.** No, sound boards can't use INT 2 or INT 9.
- **D.** No, network boards can't use INT 2 or INT 9.
- **E.** No, INT 2 and INT 9 can't be used at the same time.

14. You're installing an ISA board in a system that includes both ISA and PCI expansion slots. INT 5 is currently in use by a PCI board. However, you've heard that PCI cards can share interrupts. Can you configure the ISA board to use INT 5 too?

- **A.** Yes, PCI cards can share interrupts.
- **B.** Yes, but you must enable the PCI Bridge in the CMOS setup program.
- **C.** No, ISA boards can't use INT 5. They are reserved for PCI boards.
- **D.** No, PCI cards can't share interrupts with ISA boards.

15. Which of the following hard drive parameters refers to a set of concentric, parallel tracks on all sides of all platters in a hard disk drive?

- **A.** Cylinders
- **B.** Heads

    C. Sectors Per Track

    D. Write Precompensation

    E. Landing Zone

16. How many slave drives can be configured on the Secondary IDE channel? (Choose two.)

    A. 0

    B. 1

    C. 2

    D. 4

    E. 6

    F. 8

17. If there are two hard drives on a Primary IDE channel, how many master drives must be configured on the channel?

    A. 0

    B. 1

    C. 2

    D. Unlimited

18. Suppose you have an IDE DVD drive and an IDE hard drive connected to the Secondary IDE channel. The DVD drive is connected to the first connector on the ribbon cable; the hard drive is connected to the second connector. Which drive must be set to be the master drive?

    A. The DVD drive.

    B. The hard drive.

    C. Either device can be the master.

    D. Neither device can be the master if dissimilar devices are connected to the same IDE channel.

19. Which SCSI ID has the highest priority?

    A. 0

    B. 1

    C. 3

    D. 5

    E. 7

20. Suppose you have a SCSI chain with four devices connected on an internal ribbon cable: An internal hard drive (hd0) at the end of the cable followed by a second hard drive (hd1), an internal CD drive (cd0), and then the SCSI controller (sc0). Which devices should have termination enabled? (Choose two.)

    A. Hd0

    B. Hd1

    C. Cd0

    D. Sc0

Describe Removable Hardware Interfaces

21. Which USB category includes devices such as printers, scanners, and hard drives?

    A. Hub

    B. Function

    C. Hub and Function

    D. Terminal Device

22. What is the maximum number of USB devices that can be connected to a single USB bus?

    A. 8

    B. 24

    C. 63

    D. 127

    E. 256

23. How fast does FireWire transfer data?

    A. 12 Mbps

    B. 64 Mbps

    C. 400 Mbps

    D. 480 Mbps

24. You currently have an external FireWire hard drive connected to the FireWire port in your computer. You need to disconnect the hard drive and connect a FireWire digital video camera to your FireWire port. Can you do this without rebooting the system?

    A. No, you must bring the system down to do this.

    B. No, you can't connect a FireWire digital video camera to a FireWire port used by an external hard drive.

    C. Yes, you can shut down the hard drive and connect the camera.

    D. Yes, but you must use a different port for each device.

SELF TEST ANSWERS

Describe Personal Computer Components

1. ☑ **A** and **D.** The power supply provides 3.3v, 5v, and 12v DC current.
   ☒ **B, C,** and **E** are incorrect. The power supply provides only the three voltage levels listed above.

2. ☑ **D.** The most likely cause of this problem is that the system is set to boot off the hard drive first. When it can't find the operating system on the hard drive, the error message is displayed.
   ☒ **A, B,** and **C** are most likely incorrect. While these options are remotely possible, the most likely cause is simply a misconfigured boot order in the BIOS.

3. ☑ **A.** The Celeron CPU is manufactured by Intel.
   ☒ **B, C,** and **D** are incorrect. Each of these CPUs is manufactured by AMD.

4. ☑ **D.** Socket A is used for the Athlon CPU.
   ☒ **A, B, C,** and **E** are incorrect. These sockets are used for Intel CPUs.

5. ☑ **C.** Cache memory uses a special type of RAM called static RAM.
   ☒ **A, B, D,** and **E** are incorrect. They are memory technologies used for system RAM.

6. ☑ **C** and **D.** SIMM modules used FPM, EDO, and BEDO memory technologies.
   ☒ **A, B,** and **E** are incorrect. SDRAM and DDR-SDRAM are used in DIMM modules. SRAM is only used for cache.

7. ☑ **E.** 184-pin DIMM modules use DDR-SDRAM memory.
   ☒ **A, B, C,** and **D** are incorrect. 184-pin DIMM modules do not use SDRAM, SRAM, FPM RAM, or EDO RAM.

8. ☑ **A** and **B.** The ISA bus came in 8-bit and 16-bit variations.
   ☒ **C, D,** and **E** are incorrect. Other expansion buses use these bus widths.

9. ☑ **D.** The standard PCI bus is 32 bits wide. However, there are 64-bit versions of the PCI bus used in high-end server systems.
   ☒ **A, B, C,** and **E** are incorrect. No PCI bus used an 8-, 16-, or 24-bit wide data path. One could argue that **E** is correct because there are 64-bit variations of PCI available. However, these are not used in standard desktop PCs.

10. ☑ **E.** The PCI bus operates at 33 MHz, although there are 66 MHz variations available in server systems.
    ☒ **A, B, C,** and **D** are incorrect. The PCI bus is not available in these clock speeds.

11. ☑ **B.** The Southbridge functions as an intermediary between the PCI bus and other expansion buses on the system, such as the ISA bus.

   ☒ **A, C,** and **D** are incorrect. **A** is incorrect because the Northbridge is responsible for managing the PCI bus itself. **C** and **D** are simply fabricated distracters.

12. ☑ **D.** Even if you have a built-in video adapter and an AGP slot, you can only use one or the other because AGP only allows one device at a time on the bus.

   ☒ **A, B,** and **C** are incorrect. **A** is incorrect because if you install a board in the AGP slot, the on-board video adapter will be disabled. **B** is incorrect because Linux supports multiple monitors. **C** is incorrect because both devices can't be enabled at the same time.

13. ☑ **E.** Because of the way the system's PIC chips are cascaded, INT 2 and INT 9 are actually the same interrupt.

   ☒ **A, B, C,** and **D** are incorrect. **A** is incorrect because both interrupts can't be used at the same time. The same is true for **B**. **C** is incorrect because as long as only one of the two interrupts is used, a sound board can use either INT 2 or INT 9. The same is true of **D**.

14. ☑ **D.** PCI cards can only share interrupts with other PCI cards. They can't share interrupts with ISA boards.

   ☒ **A, B,** and **C** are incorrect. **A** and **B** are incorrect because PCI cards can only share interrupts with other PCI cards. **C** is incorrect because ISA or PCI cards can use INT 5.

15. ☑ **A.** Cylinders are composed of concentric, parallel tracks on all sides of all platters in a hard disk drive.

   ☒ **B, C, D,** and **E** are incorrect. **B** refers to the number of heads in the drive. **C** refers to the number of pie-shaped wedges created in each track on the drive. **D** and **E** are obsolete parameters only used in very old hard drives.

16. ☑ **A and B.** Any IDE channel can have either 0 or 1 slave drive on the channel. If no master is implemented on the channel, then no slave drives can be implemented. If a master drive is implemented, then the channel can have one slave drive.

   ☒ **C, D, E,** and **F** are incorrect. **C** is incorrect because a maximum of one slave drive can be configured on any IDE channel. **D, E,** and **F** are incorrect because an IDE channel can have a maximum of only two drives installed.

17. ☑ **B.** If there are two hard drives on an IDE channel, one of them has to be set to be a master drive. The other must be a slave drive.

   ☒ **A, C,** and **D** are incorrect. **A** is incorrect because there must be one master if one or more drives are installed on the channel. **C** is incorrect because there can only be one master drive on any IDE channel. **D** is incorrect for the same reason.

18. ☑ **C.** The location on the IDE cable has no bearing on whether a drive is a master device or a slave device.
    ☒ **A, B,** and **D** are incorrect. **A** or **B** could be correct, but they don't *have* to be set as the master. **D** is incorrect. Any IDE device can be a master or a slave.

19. ☑ **A.** The lower the SCSI ID, the higher the device priority.
    ☒ **B, C, D,** and **E** are incorrect. Because they have a higher ID value, they have lower priority in the SCSI chain.

20. ☑ **A** and **D.** Because the first hard drive and the SCSI controller are located at the ends of the SCSI chain, they must have termination enabled. No devices in between should have termination enabled.
    ☒ **B** and **C** are incorrect. Because these devices reside in the middle of the chain, they must not have termination enabled.

Describe Removable Hardware Interfaces

21. ☑ **B.** USB functions include end devices, such as printers, scanners, and hard drives, that don't include USB hub functionality. Be aware that manufacturers of some of these devices do include hub functionality, making them a Hub and Function.
    ☒ **A, C,** and **D** are incorrect. **A** and **C** are incorrect if the device doesn't include additional USB ports that other devices can be plugged into. **D** is a fabricated distracter.

22. ☑ **D.** By cascading multiple USB hubs together, you can create a USB bus that can accommodate up to 127 devices. Be aware that the hubs used to create the bus, including the root hub, each count as one device.
    ☒ **A, B, C,** and **E** are incorrect. While you could have 8, 24, or 63 devices on a USB bus, these numbers do not represent the maximum number of USB devices on the bus. **E** is incorrect because 256 is twice the number of possible devices on a USB bus.

23. ☑ **C.** A FireWire bus transfers data at 400 Mbps.
    ☒ **A, B,** and **D** are incorrect.

24. ☑ **C.** FireWire devices are self-identifying, self-configuring, and hot-swappable.
    ☒ **A, B,** and **D** are incorrect. **A** is incorrect. While you could bring the system down to switch devices, you don't have to. **B** and **D** are incorrect because any compatible FireWire device can be connected to any FireWire port.

3

Installing Linux

To be Linux+ certified, you need to know how to perform a clean installation of a Linux distribution. If you've already had experience installing other operating systems, you may be tempted to jump right in and starting installing Linux without any forethought. After all, installing operating systems such as Microsoft Windows is a relatively straightforward process. All you have to do is step through a series of screens presented by the Installation Wizard, as shown in Figure 3-1.

Operating systems such as Windows are designed to be installed by novice users. Most of the decisions are made automatically for you. All you need to do is click Next.

Linux, on the other hand, isn't as simple to install. Linux is extremely flexible. It can fill a wide variety of roles in your organization. Therefore, you have to make a number of decisions as the operating system is installed. In the previous chapter, you learned that most Linux distributions expect you to have a solid understanding of the internal components that comprise a PC system. The same is true with respect

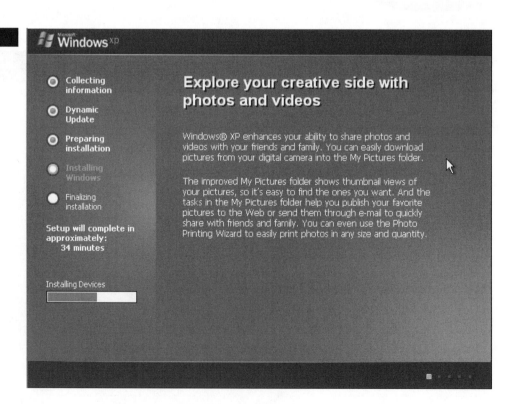

FIGURE 3-1

Installing
Microsoft
Windows

to the installation process. Most Linux distributions expect you to have a solid understanding of the Linux system before you start installing.

Linux has actually become dramatically easier to install in the last ten years. The distributions available in the mid-1990s were quite challenging to install. Hardware support was limited; the installation wizard, if one existed at all, was very primitive. The first time I installed a Linux distribution in 1995, it required two full days to work through all the problems, issues, and quirks that I encountered.

Today, most Linux distributions use some type of graphical installation wizard, similar to that used by Windows, to facilitate the installation process. The Installation Wizard used by SUSE Linux, called YaST (Yet Another Setup Tool) is shown in Figure 3-2.

FIGURE 3-2   The SUSE Linux Installation Wizard

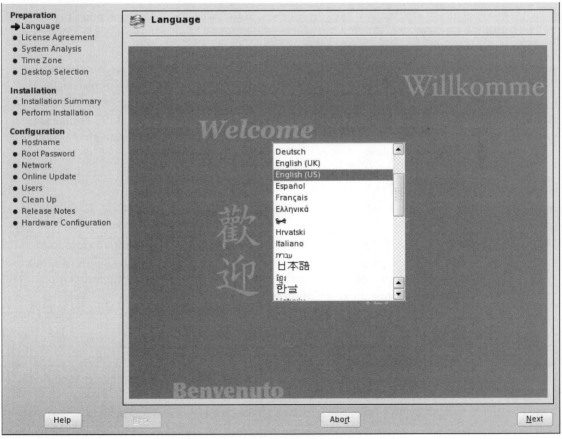

INSIDE THE EXAM

Installing Linux

Because there is a right way and a wrong way to implement a new Linux system, you will be tested extensively on Linux installation topics on the Linux+ exam. Be aware that roughly 20 percent of the exam questions will be related to installation. Also be aware that the exam will test you heavily on deployment planning topics, not just on the installation process itself.

One of the problems encountered by the Linux+ certification committee and test authors is the wide variety of installation processes used by the various Linux distributions. There's no way for the Linux+ exam to address them all. It's not reasonable for the exam to expect you to be familiar with them all either. There are just too many distributions. Therefore, CompTIA has specified that you need to pick one of the following distributions and become familiar with how to install it:

- SUSE Linux
- Red Hat Fedora
- Mandrake
- TurboLinux

You don't need to know all four of these distributions. Just pick one from the list above and then learn how to install it. We don't have time and space in this book to cover all four distributions. Instead, we're going to focus on installing one of the most widely used distributions: SUSE Linux (also called OpenSUSE). The principles you learn here by installing SUSE Linux can be applied to other distributions without much difficulty.

Even though most Linux distributions use some type of intuitive graphical installation wizard, you are still expected to have a solid understanding of Linux. To install Linux properly, you need to spend some time planning the installation *before* you actually start the installation process.

In this chapter, we're going to spend some time learning how to implement a new Linux system. The following topics will be covered:

- Planning a Linux installation
- Installing Linux

Let's begin by discussing how to plan a new Linux installation.

CERTIFICATION OBJECTIVE 3.01

Plan a Linux Installation

If you're reading this book, you're probably a "techie." You love computers and you're not intimidated by new technologies. You love to investigate new innovations in hardware and software and experiment with them. The brightest spot in your week is when the delivery van arrives at your place of work with a load of new technology. You happily work overtime for days on end getting everything set up and running.

Being a techie can be a lot of fun. However, techies are notorious for sharing a common set of traits, including the following:

- Techies never read the documentation for any piece of software or hardware. It's much more fun to experiment and figure it out on our own.
- Techies hate to plan out any hardware or software deployment. It takes the fun out of playing with all that cool new stuff.
- Techies hate to document anything they do when working with technology. All of the information we need is in our heads anyway, right?

When working with Linux, you absolutely must overcome these tendencies and do things the right way. If you don't you'll be spending a lot of time fixing your mistakes later.

on the
ዕo b

If you're working on a test system at home or in a lab environment, you can probably get away with implementing Linux the "techie way." There's usually no real risk in making mistakes. In fact, it can be a great learning experience. I highly recommend it when time permits.

However, when working with a system that will be used in your organization's production environment, the techie approach is completely unacceptable. Mistakes on your part can lead to system outages. Any kind of outage costs your organization time and money. Mistakes of this nature will probably cost your job.

Instead of installing a Linux system in a haphazard, unstructured manner, you should develop a deployment plan before you start the installation process. Doing so will help you prevent a litany of costly errors (and probably save your job).

Being a confessed techie myself, I know how painful this process can be. When tasked with deploying new Linux systems, your first impulse is to get on the phone with your hardware vendor and starting ordering. Resist this urge! If you will instead follow the process laid out in this chapter and actually plan the implementation before you start ordering hardware and software, you will make life a lot easier for yourself and for those who will follow in your job after you.

Let me give you an example of what I'm talking about. Years ago, I worked for a major networking software vendor. One of the functional groups in my department wanted to implement a new software package that would make their jobs easier. When reviewing the system requirements, they found that the software required a Windows NT 4 server. Rather than develop a plan for the new server deployment, this group bypassed the planning process. They ordered a new server and set up the software themselves without telling anyone.

All of the critical data from that group as well as the group I worked in was saved on this Windows NT 4 server. This information represented hundreds of thousands of hours of work and was worth millions of dollars. No one on my team gave it a second thought until several years later when we discovered that our company's Information Systems team had no idea that server even existed on the network. No one had ever run a single backup of the data on that server. No one had implemented an uninterruptible power supply (UPS) on the system. No one was responsible for patching the operating system. Millions of dollars' worth of information was completely unprotected. One simple power spike coming in through the power lines could have completely destroyed everything we'd been working on for years with no way to recover it. In addition, only one person had the Administrator password. If he had quit or been laid off, we would have lost administrative access to the system as well.

Where was the point of failure in this story? No implementation plan was developed for this new server. Had someone planned the deployment, they would have noted these issues before the server was installed and planned for them accordingly.

In this part of this chapter, we'll discuss how to go about planning a Linux installation. The following topics will be addressed:

- Conducting a needs assessment
- Selecting a distribution
- Verifying system requirements and hardware compatibility
- Planning the file system

- Selecting system software packages
- Specifying user accounts
- Gathering network information
- Selecting an installation source

The first step in any Linux deployment plan is to conduct a needs assessment. Let's discuss this topic first.

Conducting a Needs Assessment

Conducting a needs assessment is one of the most important aspects of creating a Linux deployment plan. It's also the most frequently skipped step. Even when it is done, it's usually done poorly.

What exactly is a needs assessment? It's the process of determining why the Linux deployment is being undertaken and what outcomes are expected when it is complete. Completing a needs assessment will require you to step out of your technician role and step into the role of a project manager. In this role, you will need to meet with a variety of different individuals and gather data about the deployment. Your findings should be recorded in a word processing document that can be easily distributed and reviewed by others. When you're done, the needs assessment portion of your deployment plan should contain the following information (at a minimum):

- *What are the goals of the project?* You should find out why the implementation is being requested. What problem will this installation fix? What will be the final result of the implementation? What organizational objectives will be met by the implementation? When you list the goals of the project, be sure to use language that is clear and measurable.

on the
Job

When determining goals, be sure to talk to everyone involved. If you don't you won't be getting a clear picture of what is expected and will probably fail to meet a particular goal. Let me give you an example. About a year ago, I was contracted by a financial organization to install a new Linux server in their main office. I spent a considerable amount of time interviewing one of the owners when I conducted the needs assessment. I felt that I had a pretty solid understanding of what they wanted.

To make a long story short, I installed and configured the Linux server in the office and was feeling very good about the smoothness of the deployment. As I was packing up to leave, the owner walked into the server room and handed me a CD containing a popular network-based financial accounting software package. He indicated that his administrative staff needed to use this software to complete their day-to-day jobs. I cringed when I looked at the system requirements and discovered that it required a Windows server.

Where did I go wrong? I didn't talk to other employees in the office. Talking to just one person wasn't enough. The owner didn't know this particular software package was needed when I initially interviewed him during the needs assessment. If he had, I could have accounted for this software in our plan.

- *Who are the stakeholders in this project?* As a part of your needs assessment, you should identify all individuals who will be impacted by the project in any way. You should ask the following questions:
    - Who requested the new system?
    - Who will use the system after it's installed?
    - Who has the authority to approve funds for the project?
    - Who has authority to allocate your time to the project?
    - Who must give final approval to this project before it can begin?
    - Who will maintain and support the system after it is implemented?
    - Is the new system a fit with our current technology environment and strategy direction?

    These are absolutely critical questions that must be answered before you begin any project. You'll be surprised at how many employees in the company you work for will try to circumvent established policies and try to get you to do something for them without the proper approval.

    Don't make the mistake of assuming that a new system has been approved and funded simply because someone asked for it. (Trust me, it happens all the time.) If you identify all the stakeholders in the project, you can be sure that the project has been approved and that the necessary funds have been allocated before you place your first order.

- *When is the system needed?* A key question you should ask is when the project should be completed. Before you can create a schedule for your project, you need to know when it is your stakeholders expect it to be complete.

Here is a possible scenario question and its answer.

SCENARIO & SOLUTION

You're responsible for managing the Linux systems in your organization's computer network. The lead tech writer in your organization stopped by your office and asked you to install a database server for her team. Who else should you talk to before ordering hardware and software?	You should probably talk to the lead tech writer's team members and determine exactly what they need the system to do. You should also meet with the lead tech writer's supervisor and make sure funds are available to purchase the necessary equipment. You should meet with your supervisor as well to make sure she will allocate you the time necessary to complete the project. Finally, you should meet with your Information Systems group and make sure the new system will use approved software.

By gathering this data in your needs assessment, you can define one of the most critical components in your installation plan: the project *scope*. The project scope defines exactly *what* to do, *when* to do it, and *who* will do it. If you've ever managed a project before, you know that every project is a three-way tug-of-war between:

- Schedule
- Resources
- Scale

This delicate balancing act is shown in Figure 3-3.

To successfully manage any project, you must keep these three elements in balance. If the schedule is excessively short, then you will need to either increase the number of resources assigned to the project or you will need to decrease the

FIGURE 3-3

Balancing schedule, resources, and scale in the project scope

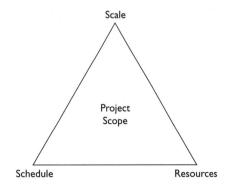

scale of the project. For example, suppose your installation project involves rolling out Linux across the desktops of 300 users and you are the only resource assigned to the project. As long as the schedule allows enough time, you can complete this task. However, if the schedule specifies that the project be done in a week, you will probably need to add more resources to the project or you will need to decrease the number of desktops included in the project.

on the *I call this relationship the "Three-Legged Stool of Project Management."*
Job *If all of the legs on a three-legged stool aren't the same length, the stool will be unbalanced. The same holds true with project management. If your schedule, scale, and resources aren't in balance, the project will probably fail in some way.*

I've been responsible for managing projects for most of my career and this analogy has come in very handy on many occasions. The issue here is that your project sponsor will probably want you to do way more than is feasible in a unrealistic amount of time with too few resources.

Early in my career, I wanted to impress my managers and I frequently agreed to take on projects using impossible parameters. This was not a wise thing to do. The relentless stress and long hours can take an awful toll on your health.

I've learned that you must push back to get these three parameters in balance. I've found that using a simple diagram such as that shown in Figure 3-3 or using the "Three-Legged Stool" analogy can be a very effective tool to communicate the need for balance to project sponsors.

Using project management software can be extremely helpful in helping you calculate exactly how long a project will take. Using project management software, you can assign specific tasks to specific resources and assign durations. In addition, you can define *dependencies*. Dependencies are used to specify which tasks must be completed before others can begin. A sample project with dependencies is shown in Figure 3-4.

The great thing about project management software is that it can calculate your schedule for you. By entering tasks and durations and then associating them with specific resources, you can easily see how long a project is going to take. You can also adjust various parameters (remember the three-legged stool) to see what the effect will be. For example, you can add an additional resource to the project and see the effect it has on your overall schedule. You can also see the effect of specifying nine-hour days instead of eight-hour days.

Using project management software to plan a project and define dependencies

ID	Description	Start	End	
1	⊟**Design Phase**	**6/05/06**	**6/15/06**	
2	Research Existing Content	6/05/06	6/06/06	
3	Set Up Equipment and Software	6/07/06	6/07/06	
4	Set Up Document Template	6/08/06	6/08/06	
5	Create Design Document	6/09/06	6/15/06	
6	⊟**Alpha Development**	**6/16/06**	**8/16/06**	
7	Develop Alpha Draft of Administration Guide	6/16/06	7/27/06	
8	SME Review of Alpha Draft	7/28/06	8/03/06	
9	Input SME Review Changes	8/04/06	8/10/06	
10	Edit Alpha Draft	8/11/06	8/16/06	

However, be sure to use common sense when manipulating your project. I've worked with many project managers who get very excited when they see that they can pull their project's schedule in by a significant amount of time by manipulating various parameters. However, the adjustments they make aren't realistic. For example, you can really shorten a project schedule by specifying 18-hour working days for all resources involved. However, most people can't handle working that many hours for long stretches of time. Family life suffers, personal health suffers, burnout sets in, and productivity plummets. In short, do a reality-check against your schedule. Remember that what looks good on paper may not work in real life.

With your project scope defined, you're ready to move on to the next component in your project plan. Let's next discuss selecting a distribution.

SCENARIO & SOLUTION

You're responsible for implementing 60 new Linux systems in your organization. Your manager has asked to you to cut the schedule for the deployment in half. How can you respond?	Based on what we've talked about in this chapter, you should inform your manager that cutting the schedule in half will require adjustments elsewhere in the project scope. For example, you may need to hire a temporary employee to help you complete the implementation. Alternatively, you could also request that the number of systems being deployed be reduced. Simply saying "yes" to the request will probably cause the project to fail.

Selecting a Distribution

As we discussed in Chapter 1 of this book, Linux is available in a wide variety of flavors called *distributions*. One of the key parts of your deployment plan is specifying which of these distributions you will use on your system. Which one is best? That depends on your preferences and what you want to the system to do. Here are some guidelines you can use to select the right distribution:

- *Will the system function as a workstation or a server?* One of the cool things about Linux is the fact that you can implement just about any distribution as either a workstation or as a server. This is unique among operating systems. Most operating systems are designed to function either as a server or as a workstation, but not both. Most Linux distributions, on the other hand, can be used in either role.

  However, be aware that there are Linux distributions available that are specifically designed and optimized to function as servers, and others as workstations. For example, Red Hat provides two distributions that are designed for providing network services:

  - **Red Hat Enterprise Linux ES**   This distribution is designed for servers in medium organizations that will be placed under moderate workload.

  - **Red Hat Enterprise Linux AS**   This distribution is designed for very large organizations that will place a very heavy load on their server systems.

  Red Hat also provides two distributions that are designed specifically for use in desktop systems:

  - **Red Hat Desktop**   This distribution is designed for use by the average end user on desktop systems used to complete day-to-day work.

  - **Red Hat Enterprise Linux WS**   This distribution is intended for use by high-end users, such as engineers or graphic designers, who use high-end desktop hardware to complete more advanced computing tasks.

  Likewise, Novell sells two versions of SUSE Linux:

  - **SUSE Linux Enterprise Server**   This distribution is designed for use in high-end server systems in very large organizations.

  - **SUSE Linux Enterprise Desktop**   This distribution is designed for use by end users on their desktop workstations.

There are also purpose-specific distributions to create Linux-based appliances using standard PC hardware. For example, you can create a powerful network firewall using distributions such as SmoothWall, IPCop, or Coyote Linux.

- *Does the distribution offer support?* Some vendors offer technical support for their Linux distributions while others offer limited support or no support at all. If the system will be used in a corporate environment, you should seriously consider implementing a well-supported distribution. If a problem occurs at some point after the system has been installed, you need to be able to resolve the issue and get the system back into production as fast as possible. You're not going to have time to search the Internet to find a solution. You need to be able to call someone and get an answer immediately.

    Be aware that, while the distribution itself may be free or nearly free, you will be required to pay for technical support. The price charged for support varies from vendor to vendor, so it pays to shop around.

on the

Job

There's a lot of confusion in the industry right now about the difference between Linux distributions from the same vendor. One version is free; the other requires a fee to be paid to download. For example, you can purchase a copy of Red Hat Desktop or you can download a copy of Fedora for free. The difference is support. If you purchase a copy of Red Hat Desktop, you are entitled to tech support from Red Hat. In fact, the more you pay, the better the level of support you receive.

The same holds true with SUSE Linux. You can either purchase a copy of SUSE Linux Enterprise from Novell or download a free copy of SUSE Linux from http://www.opensuse.org. Once again, the difference is the level of support. If you purchase a copy, you have access to tech support. If you download a free copy, you must support yourself using forums and newsgroups.

To save money on your part, we're going to be using Fedora and SUSE Linux in this book. However, I strongly recommend that you purchase a supported version of Linux if you're going to deploy it in a production environment.

- *Will the applications you want to install run on the distribution?* Before selecting a specific distribution, you should evaluate the software you want to run and verify that it is supported by the operating system.

Now that you understand distributions, some possible scenario questions and their answers follow.

SCENARIO & SOLUTION	
You've been tasked with implementing a Linux system in your organization that will run a network-based database application. What type of distribution should you choose?	Because the system will be used to provide a network-based service to client systems, you should consider using a distribution that has been optimized to function as a network server.
You've been tasked with implementing a new Linux server in your network that will host mission-critical applications. You've downloaded an obscure distribution from the Internet that doesn't offer technical support. It appears to function properly in your lab. Should you use it for your new server?	It's probably not a good idea to use an obscure, unsupported distribution for a mission-critical server. A well-known, well-supported distribution would be a better choice.

In addition to these considerations, you should also verify that the distribution you want to use runs on your system hardware. Let's discuss this factor next.

Verifying System Requirements and Hardware Compatibility

As a techie, you probably love ordering hardware. It's even more fun when your employer pays for it! Because of this, you may be strongly tempted to start browsing vendor Web sites and order your new systems before your Linux deployment plan is complete.

You should resist this urge at all costs! Before you download or purchase your Linux distribution, you need to make sure it will run on your hardware. Many system administrators frequently ignore this process. In fact, I'll admit to having done this myself. It's a very poor practice because you run the risk of ordering hardware that isn't compatible with your hardware. If this happens, it's likely that your project schedule will be put at risk. It can take a considerable amount of time to return and reorder hardware. If this happens, you'll probably spend some tense moments in your supervisor's office explaining why the project is behind schedule.

In this topic, we're going to discuss two things you can do to keep this from happening:

- Checking hardware compatibility
- Verifying system requirements

Let's begin by discussing hardware compatibility.

Checking Hardware Compatibility

Back in the early days of Linux, hardware compatibility was a real problem, especially if you were trying to install Linux on a notebook system. There just weren't enough developers writing Linux drivers. If you were installing Linux on a generic system using common hardware components, you usually could get Linux installed and working correctly. However, if your system used non-typical or proprietary hardware, such as a high-end video board, then you may or may not have been able to get Linux running correctly.

The problem centered on drivers. Back then, most hardware vendors didn't provide Linux device drivers for their devices. They didn't perceive Linux as a serious operating system and didn't want to waste time and money developing device drivers for it. Instead, you had to rely on the good will of a developer somewhere in the world to write a driver for your particular piece of hardware. If a driver didn't exist for your device, you were out of luck.

Fortunately, this is less of an issue today. It's been a long time since I've had to scour the Internet trying to find a driver for my hardware. Most vendors now offer a Linux version of the drivers for their hardware. In fact, most of the drivers for common PC hardware are actually included in the various Linux distributions.

To be safe, however, it is still a very good idea to check the Web site for your distribution and verify that your system's hardware is listed on the distribution's Hardware Compatibility List (HCL). Even though hardware support for Linux has become much better in the last decade, there are still devices that aren't supported. You can use your distribution's HCL to check and see if it will support your system's devices.

HCLs are usually available in two locations. First, most distributions include a list of supported hardware in a text file on the first installation CD or DVD. However, I rarely use this version of the HCL. Because it's a static document on disc, it hasn't been updated since the disc was burned. If a device in your computer was released at some point after the disc was burned, you have no idea if it's supported or not.

Instead, I much prefer using the HCL maintained on most distributions' Web sites. This version of the HCL contains the most current data on supported hardware. For example, if you choose to install the SUSE Linux distribution on your system, you can use a Web browser to access its HCL at http://hardwaredb.suse.de/. Once there, you can search for your particular system hardware and see if it is supported. In Figure 3-5, we've used the SUSE Linux HCL to see if a particular nVidia video card is supported by the distribution.

FIGURE 3-5	SUSE LINUX: hardware compatibility list

Using the SUSE
Linux HCL

↘ SUSE Linux component database - CDB v3.0

Result for express search: **239 products found (page 11 of 12)** 🖨 printable page

!Important!: Always read the details of the product entries in the hardware database. The
Supportstatus displayed in the overview here is probably not adeqate for the SUSE LINUX
product version you are using. Informations for the single products of the SUSE LINUX AG can
only be found in the detail view of the particular hardware component.

◀ 3 4 5 6 7 8 9 10 **11** 12 ▶ Page size: [20 ▼] [OK]

Vendor	Product (=chipset)	Details	Status
nVidia Corporation	Quadro FX 700 *	🔍	☑ full
nVidia Corporation	Quadro FX Go1000 *	🔍	☑ full
nVidia Corporation	Quadro FX Go1400 *	🔍	☑ full
nVidia Corporation	Quadro FX Go700 *	🔍	☑ full
nVidia Corporation	Quadro FX1000 DH	🔍	☑ full
nVidia Corporation	Quadro FX2000 DH	🔍	☑ full
nVidia Corporation	Quadro NVS *	🔍	☑ full
nVidia Corporation	Quadro NVS 110M *	🔍	☑ full
nVidia Corporation	Quadro NVS 120M *	🔍	☑ partially
nVidia Corporation	Quadro NVS 280 PCI-E/Quadro FX 330 *	🔍	☑ full
nVidia Corporation	Quadro NVS 300M *	🔍	☑ partially
nVidia Corporation	Quadro NVS 440 *	🔍	☑ full

Notice in Figure 3-5 that most nVidia video cards are fully supported. However, some nVidia cards are not. For example, the Quadro NVS 120M is only partially supported. This would be a very good thing to know before starting your installation!

If you choose to use a Red Hat distribution, you can likewise check the HCL on Red Hat's Web site (http://hardware.redhat.com) to verify that your system hardware is supported. This site is shown in Figure 3-6.

Most distributions include some kind of HCL on their Web site. However, not all of them do. Some distribution vendors simply don't have the time or resources to conduct extensive hardware testing to verify the myriad of PC devices available on the market.

FIGURE 3-6	**Red Hat Hardware Catalog**

Using the Red
Hat HCL

Welcome to the Red Hat Hardware Catalog, the database containing certified and compatible hardware for Red Hat products.

Browse Red Hat Enterprise Linux Certified and Compatible Hardware

Operating System Version	Compatible	Certified and Supported
Red Hat Enterprise Linux 4:	Compatible Systems and Peripherals	Certified Systems
Red Hat Enterprise Linux 3:	Compatible Systems and Peripherals	Certified Systems
Red Hat Enterprise Linux 2.1:	Compatible Peripherals	Certified Systems

Quick Search

[   ] [Search] [Clear] Advanced Search

on the **Job**

Driver availability is one of the reasons I prefer to stick with big-name, well-supported Linux distributions when I'm setting up a system that will be used in a production environment. Only if I'm experimenting with a system at home or in a lab environment at work am I comfortable working with a poorly supported distribution. If something goes wrong in this situation, nothing is lost.

However, one of my key roles as a Linux system administrator in a production environment is to protect data and run at maximum efficiency. I need to know for a surety that my hardware is supported by the operating system. I can't afford to spend hours scouring the Internet trying to find a driver nor do I want to waste time troubleshooting a system that functions erratically.

In addition to checking the HCL, you also need to check your distribution's system requirements. Let's discuss this issue next.

Verifying System Requirements

Back in the early days of Linux, we didn't worry much about system requirements for the various distributions. That was because the early versions of Linux would run on relatively minimal hardware. They didn't require much memory, disk space, or processing power.

However, as Linux has matured over the years, most distributions are now beginning to require much more robust system hardware to provide an acceptable degree of performance. How do you know what the system requirements are? Once again, check your distribution vendor's Web site. For example, if you visit http://www.novell.com/products/suselinux/sysreqs.html, you can view the system requirements for SUSE Linux, as shown in Figure 3-7.

When formulating your deployment plan, be sure to specify the hardware needed by the distribution you've selected.

A key aspect of your system requirements is your PC's CPU architecture. When downloading your Linux distribution, be sure you select the correct architecture for your system's CPU. For years, we didn't worry much about this issue because we really only worked with a single architecture: Intel's 32-bit x86 architecture. Although most distributions were available for the x86 architecture and the Alpha architecture, the average system administrator didn't have many Alpha machines. Nearly every system we worked with ran on some variation of the x86 architecture

Today, however, there are many more hardware options available to us as system administrators. We still have the venerable x86 and Alpha architectures, but we also have the newer 64-bit x86 architecture. In addition, Intel has recently introduced the IA-64 architecture used by their Itanium CPUs. Each of these architectures requires a different version of your Linux distribution. In fact, many Linux distributions have even been ported to run on the Power PC (PPC) architecture from Apple Computer.

The important point is to be sure that you select the appropriate architecture for your distribution. For example, if you selected SUSE Linux as your distribution and accessed the SUSE download page on the Internet, you would see the options displayed in Figure 3-8.

Notice that you can choose from the x86, x86-64, PPC, or IA64 architectures. Similar options are available when downloading Fedora, as shown in Figure 3-9.

FIGURE 3-7	
SUSE Linux system requirements	**SUSE Linux 10.1** Hardware Requirements SUSE Linux supports most PC hardware components. The following requirements should be met to ensure smooth operation of SUSE Linux 10.1: • Processor: Intel Pentium 1-4 or Xeon; AMD: Duron, Athlon, Athlon XP, Athlon MP, Athlon 64, Sempron or Opteron • Main memory: At least 256 MB; 512 MB recommended • Hard disk: At least 500 MB for minimal system; 3 GB recommended for standard system • Sound and graphics cards: Supports most modern sound and graphics cards

FIGURE 3-8

SUSE Linux
architectures

Regardless of which distribution you choose, make sure you download the correct version for your system's architecture. For example, if you are going to install Linux on a Pentium IV CPU, then you need the x86 version of your distribution. If your hardware uses an AMD Athlon 64 CPU, then you need x86-64 version of the distribution. If you pick the wrong one, most Linux installers will generate an error and you won't be able to complete the installation.

With hardware issues out of the way, you can now move on to the next component of your plan where you will specify how the Linux file system will be configured. Let's discuss this topic next.

Fedora
architectures

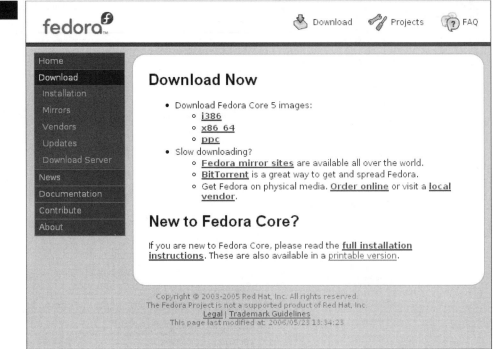

Planning the File System

When planning a Linux implementation, you need to include specifications for how the file system will be created and maintained on the system's hard disk drive. This is yet another unique aspect of the Linux operating system. When implementing other operating systems, such as Microsoft Windows, you usually create only a single disk partition and format it using the NTFS file system.

SCENARIO & SOLUTION

You're installing SUSE Linux on a PC that uses a Pentium III 700 MHz CPU. Which SUSE Linux distribution architecture should you download?	The Pentium III CPU uses the 32-bit x86 CPU architecture. Therefore, you should download the x86 version of the distribution.
You're installing SUSE Linux on a PC that uses an AMD Turion 64 CPU. Which distribution architecture should you download?	The Turion 64 uses the 64-bit x86 architecture. Therefore, you should download the x86-64 version of the distribution.

Technically, you do have the option of selecting from the NTFS or FAT 32 file systems when installing a Windows 2000 or XP system. However, FAT 32 has so many limitations, such as a lack of support for permissions, that very few system administrators use it.

With Linux, however, you have many more choices to make. You can customize how your disk will be partitioned and what file system will be used. In this part of the chapter, we'll discuss the following:

- Choosing a file system
- Planning your partitions

Let's begin by discussing file systems.

Choosing a File System

Back in Chapter 2, we discussed how a hard disk drive works. We related that the drive is made up of multiple aluminum platters each with two read-write heads that are used to read and write data. When conducting disk I/O operations, the operating system needs to know where data is stored, how to access it, and where it is safe to write new information.

This is the job of the *file system*. Its role is to reliably store data on the hard drive and organize it in such a way that it is easily accessible. When you use a file browser to navigate through the directories on a hard disk drive and open a file, it's the file system that makes the entire process possible.

Most Linux distributions offer a wide variety of file systems that you can choose from. In this topic, we'll review three of the most widely used types:

- ext2
- ext3
- Reiser

Let's begin by discussing the ext2 file system.

ext2   The ext2 file system is one of the oldest Linux file systems still available. The acronym *ext2* stands for *Second Extended File System*. It was originally introduced back in 1993. It stores data in the standard hierarchical fashion used by most other file systems. Data is stored in files; files are stored in directories. A directory can contain either files or other directories called subdirectories.

The maximum file size supported in the ext2 file system is 2 terabytes (TB). An ext2 volume can be up to 4TB. File names can be up to 255 characters long. The ext2 file system supports Linux file system users, groups, and permissions (called POSIX permissions). It also supports file compression.

The ext2 file system is a fantastic file system. It's been around a long time, long enough for most of its bugs to be worked out. In fact, it's probably the most widely used Linux file system ever implemented. It's also reputed to be the fastest Linux file system available.

However, ext2 has one key weakness that has led to the development of other file systems. This is the fact that ext2 takes a long time to recover if the system shuts down abruptly. When shutting down the Linux system, the operating system first cleanly dismounts the file system. During the dismount, the operating system makes sure all pending file system transactions are written to disk before the system shuts off.

The problem arises when the system is shut down without completing this clean dismount procedure. For example, suppose a power outage occurs and the Linux system shuts off suddenly without going through the proper shutdown procedure. When this happens, it is possible that pending disk transactions weren't completed.

To clean up the file system, the ext2 file system will automatically run a program called e2fsck the next time the system is booted. This utility tries to fix any problems that were created when the system went down without properly dismounting the disk. If it finds non-allocated files or unclaimed blocks of data, it will write this information in a directory called lost+found. By doing this, ext2 tries to ensure that data integrity is maintained in spite of the improper shutdown.

The issue here is that e2fsck will analyze the entire file system when this happens, not just the last few files that were in the process of being modified. On a basic Linux system, this can take from 10 to 15 minutes. On an extensive system that has a lot of file system data (such as a network file server), this process can take several hours. It's bad enough that the system went down unexpectedly in the first place; now you have to wait hours for it to start back up again!

Because of this issue, two other Linux file systems have started replacing ext2. The first of these is ext3. Let's discuss this file system next.

ext3   The ext3 file system is an updated version of ext2. In fact, *ext3* stands for *Third Extended File System*. In fact, most of the file system utilities used by ext2 are also used by ext3. You can easily upgrade disks using the ext2 file system to ext3. You can even downgrade an ext3 disk to ext2.

However, the ext3 file system offers one key advantage that makes it highly preferable over ext2: journaling. Remember that the key disadvantage of ext2 is the fact that it must check the entire file system if the system goes down uncleanly; this can take a great deal of time. Journaling eliminates this problem.

Before committing a transaction to the hard disk drive, the ext3 file system records the transaction to a journal and marks it as incomplete. After the disk transaction is complete, the ext3 file system marks the transaction as complete in the journal. By doing this, the ext3 file system can keep a log of the most recent file transactions and whether or not they were actually completed.

If an event such as a power outage occurs that causes the system to shut down without properly dismounting the disk, the ext3 file system will replay the journal when the system comes back up. This allows the file system to verify the data on the disk and bring it back to a consistent state (if possible) using the information stored in the journal. However, unlike ext2, the ext3 file system doesn't need to check the entire file. Because it has a log of the most recent transactions in the journal, the ext3 file system simply checks the transactions that are listed as incomplete.

Using journaling, disk recovery time after an improper shutdown takes dramatically less time than that experienced using ext2. Instead of taking hours, the ext3 file system can replay the journal in only a few seconds, even if the file system is very large. For this reason, the ext3 file system is the default file system for many of the Linux distributions currently available.

The disadvantage to ext3 is the fact that the journaling process uses up more system memory and slows down disk I/O operations. However, because it does a better job of ensuring data integrity and does it faster, most system administrators prefer ext3 over ext2 in spite of the decreased performance.

In addition to ext3, you can also choose from a second journaling file system called Reiser. Let's discuss this file system next.

Reiser   The Reiser file system is an alternative to the ext3 file system. Like ext3, Reiser utilizes journaling to make crash recovery very fast. However, Reiser is a completely different file system from ext2 and ext3, using a dramatically different internal structure. This allows the Reiser file system to support a larger maximum file size of 8TB and maximum volume size of 16TB. In addition, the different structure of Reiser allows it to perform much faster than ext2 or ext3.

Because of these advantages, the Reiser file system is the default file system used by Linux distributions such as SUSE Linux and Linspire.

Most distributions will allow you to choose which file system you want to implement when you partition your system's hard disk drives during the installation process.

You should already know what file system you want to use before you reach that point. Therefore, when planning your Linux implementation, you should specify which of these file systems you want to use in your deployment plan.

on the **Ĵ o b**

So which file system should you use? It depends upon your personal preferences. My choice is the Reiser file system.

In addition to specifying which file system you will use on your Linux system's hard disk drive, you also need to specify how to partition it. Let's talk about how this is done next.

Planning Your Partitions

A *partition* is a logical division of your hard disk drive. Using the read-write heads inside the hard disk drive, an operating system can create magnetic divisions on the drive platters to divide it into separate sections. A hard drive can have a single partition that encompasses the entire hard drive or it can have many partitions. Each partition on the disk appears logically to the operating system as if it were a separate hard disk drive.

When you install other operating systems, such as Microsoft Windows, you generally don't worry much about partitioning. A single partition encompassing the entire hard drive is usually sufficient.

With Linux, however, this is not the case. With a Linux system, you will use many partitions. These partitions need to be created during the initial installation of the system. Changing your disk partitioning after the system is installed can be done, but it is very difficult and time consuming. Therefore, you should plan out how you will partition your system hard drive before you start the installation process.

SCENARIO & SOLUTION

You're installing a new Linux system. This system will host mission-critical applications. This system must perform as fast as possible. It must protect the integrity of the server data if the system goes down unexpectedly. If it does go down, the system needs to be back up and running as quickly as possible. Which file system would be the best choice?	Because of the requirements specified, the Reiser file system would be the best choice. Reiser is considered to be the fastest Linux file system. It also uses journaling to protect data and to speed up crash recovery.

By default, most Linux distributions propose two partitions by default during the installation process, as shown in Figure 3-10.

- **swap** This partition is used for virtual memory by the Linux operating system. Essentially, Linux will use the hard disk space contained in the swap partition as though it were system RAM. When the system RAM is under heavy load, the operating system can move data and programs that are loaded into RAM but not currently in use into memory addresses mapped to the swap partition.

  When the data is needed again, it is moved from the swap partition back into RAM. Essentially this allows the system to simultaneously run more programs than it has enough physical RAM to support.

  In early versions of Linux, the standard recommendation was that the swap partition be at least as big as the amount of system RAM installed. Today, however, we need much more virtual memory. Therefore, you should create a swap partition that is at least twice as large as your installed RAM. If the system will be heavily utilized, you should consider using a swap partition that is even larger.

- **/** This partition is mounted at the root directory (/) of the Linux file system. All user data, programs, log files, and configuration files are contained in this single disk partition.

Even though this is the default partitioning proposal made by most Linux distributions during installation, you should consider creating more partitions than these two. To understand why we do this, you need to first understand that Linux uses a single file system structure to represent all of the storage space used by the Linux system. This is shown in Figure 3-11.

FIGURE 3-10
Default Linux partitioning

Expert Partitioner

Device	Size	F	Type	Mount	Mount By	Start	End
/dev/sda	8.0 GB		VMware,-VMware Virtual S			0	10
/dev/sda1	502.0 MB		Linux swap	swap	K	0	
/dev/sda2	5.6 GB		Linux native	/	K	64	79

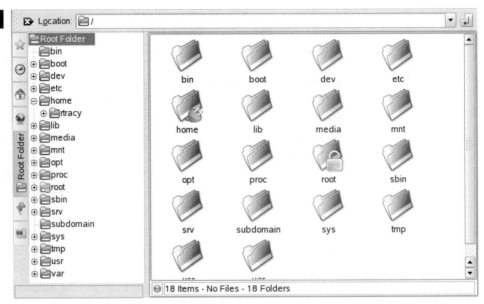

FIGURE 3-11

The Linux file system hierarchy

Different partitions can be mounted at different points in this hierarchy. For example, in Figure 3-12, an extra partition (/dev/sda3) has been created on the first SCSI hard disk drive in the system (/dev/sda), which is mounted at the /home directory.

When you navigate through the Linux file system hierarchy and double-click on the /home directory, you are actually redirected to a different partition on the hard drive. If you had multiple hard drives in the system, you could even put the partition mounted in /home on a completely different hard drive. The partitioning is completely transparent to the end user.

FIGURE 3-12

Mounting /dev/sda3 in /home

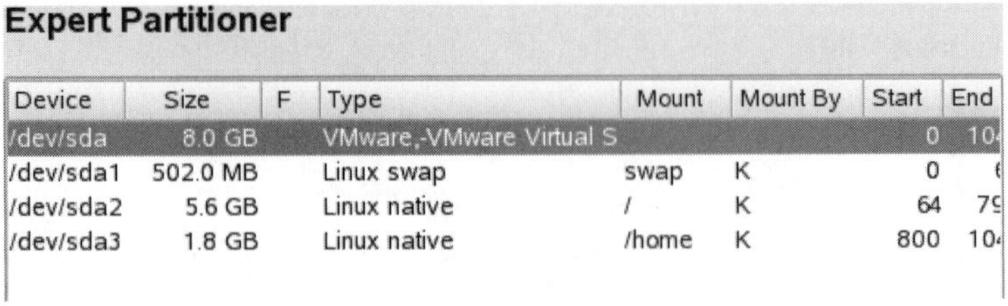

Expert Partitioner

Device	Size	F	Type	Mount	Mount By	Start	End
/dev/sda	8.0 GB		VMware,-VMware Virtual S			0	104
/dev/sda1	502.0 MB		Linux swap	swap	K	0	6
/dev/sda2	5.6 GB		Linux native	/	K	64	79
/dev/sda3	1.8 GB		Linux native	/home	K	800	104

When planning your Linux partitions, I encourage you to create many partitions on your hard drives. Doing this can add a degree of fault tolerance to your Linux system. Problems encountered in one partition are isolated from the other partitions in the system. For example, suppose you used the default partitioning proposal when installing Linux and had your entire file system mounted at the root directory (/). If a user were to consume all of the available space on the partition by copying huge files to his home directory in /home, it could cause the entire system to crash.

If, on the other hand, you were to create a separate partition for /home and the user were to again consume all the available disk space on the /home partition by copying very large files to his home directory, the system will remain running. The partitions containing your system files, log files, and application files are not affected because the issue is isolated to a single partition.

on the
Oob

Doing this also protects your user data in the event that something happens to the system files. About two years ago, I had a Linux server go down hard after a massive power spike and subsequent power outage. In a fit of laziness during the initial installation, I had opted to use the default partitioning scheme and all the server data was saved in a single partition mounted at /. To make a long story short, the power spike mangled the partition on the disk and made all of the data unreadable. If I had used a separate partition for /home, there's a chance that this extra partition may not have been mangled and I could have recovered user data from it. Instead, I had to reinstall from scratch and restore data from backup.

When planning your Linux partitions, you should consider creating separate partitions for the directories listed in Table 3-1.

Using these recommended partitions will add a degree of stability to your system. Unfortunately, this partitioning scheme doesn't use disk space efficiently. For example, your /home partition may run out of space and users won't be able to save additional data, even though there may be plenty of extra space available in other partitions on the disk. However, the added stability is worth the inefficiency. I've often heard it said that hard disks are cheap while data is priceless.

Once you've planned out your partitions, the next task you need to complete is to specify the software you want to install on your Linux system. Let's discuss how this is done next.

| TABLE 3-1 | Recommended Linux Partitions |

Mount Point	Recommendation
/	Create a partition for the root directory. This partition should be about 4GB or larger in size.
/boot	Create a partition for the /boot directory, which contains your Linux system files. This partition should be 100–200MB in size.
/home	Create a partition for users' files. You should allocate as much space as necessary to accommodate users' data.
/opt	Create a partition for application files installed into /opt. You should allocate as much space as necessary to accommodate applications that use this directory.
/tmp	Create a partition for your system's temporary files stored in /tmp. You should allocate at least 1GB or more for this partition.
/usr	Create a partition for your system utilities stored in /usr. You should allocate at least 5GB to this partition. You may need to allocate more depending on what packages you choose to install.
/var	Create a partition for the log files stored in /var. Because log files can become quite large, it's a good idea to isolate them in their own partition. You should allocate at least 3GB of space for this partition.

Selecting Software Packages

One of the things that I absolutely love about Linux is the wide array of open source software available. Your Linux distribution probably includes a fairly extensive sampling of packages that you can specify be installed along with the operating system.

SCENARIO & SOLUTION

You're installing Fedora on a PC that has 512MB of RAM installed. How big should your swap partition be?	On a modern Linux system, the swap partition should be at least twice the size of the system RAM. In a system with 512MB of RAM, you should have a swap partition that is at least 1GB in size.
You're planning a Linux system that will host an application that creates very large log files. It will also provide file storage for a number of network users. Which directories should you create separate partitions for?	Obviously, you have to create a partition for the / directory. Because the application creates large log files, you should be sure to create a separate partition at the /var directory. Also, because users will store files in /home, you should also create a separate partition for this directory as well.

In fact, it's the inclusion of this extra software that makes your installation set so big. Most distributions require 6–8 CDs or a DVD to store all the packages that you can choose from to install.

If you're a true techie, you'll be mesmerized the first time you see the list of available software. For example, SUSE Linux offers about 30 different games alone that you can install, as shown in Figure 3-13.

More than likely, you'll be tempted to install just about everything. This may be a perfectly acceptable approach for a lab system or a home system. However, if you're going to use the Linux system in a production environment, you should probably not do this. You could be installing software that you really don't want the end user to have access to. For example, you probably don't want your end users hosting their own Web site from their desktop because you installed the Apache Web server on their system.

FIGURE 3-13   Installing software packages in SUSE Linux

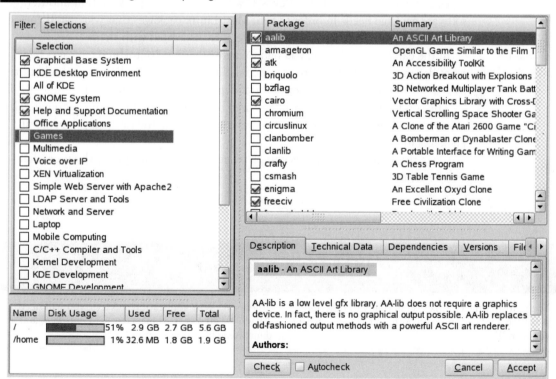

A much better approach is to use your deployment plan to identify the role the system will play. (We discussed how to do this earlier in the chapter.) With this information in hand, review the packages available with your distribution and specify exactly which packages you need to include in the installation.

For example, if the system is going to function as a network server providing file and print services, you will need to install the Samba and cups (Common UNIX Printing System) packages. If it is a network server that will function as a Web, e-mail, and news server, then you may need to install the Apache, Tomcat, imap, and inn (Internet News) packages. If the system is going to be used as a desktop system, then you may want to install OpenOffice.org to provide end users with word processing, spreadsheet, and presentation software.

The point is this: Make sure you install the packages that are needed and avoid installing software that isn't. If, after installing the system, you determine you need additional packages, you can easily install them after the fact. I'll show you how to do this in a later chapter.

One of the nice features of most installers is that they automatically calculate *dependencies* for you. A dependency is a particular software package that another software package needs in order to run. Most Linux packages that you install during installation will have a variety of dependencies associated with them.

In the early days of Linux, you had to manually figure out which packages had what dependencies and be sure you included them in the installation. It could turn into quite a mess with layer upon layer of dependencies, as shown in Figure 3-14.

The good news is that the installers used by most distributions now automatically calculate package dependencies for you and will include the necessary dependent packages in the installation.

Once this part of your plan is complete, you next need to specify the users that will be created on the system.

SCENARIO & SOLUTION

You're installing a Linux system that will function as a Web application server. Which packages should you install?	To provide Web application services, you will need Apache Web server, Tomcat servlet container, and a database application such as MySQL.

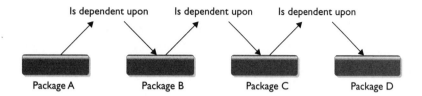

Layered package
dependencies

Is dependent upon   Is dependent upon   Is dependent upon

Package A   Package B   Package C   Package D

Specify User Accounts

Linux is a true multi-user operating system. This means that a single system can include multiple user accounts. In fact, multiple users can use the same system at the same time using a network connection.

Therefore, when planning to install your Linux system, you should determine the user accounts that will be needed on the system. The installation utilities used by most Linux distributions provide you with the ability to create these accounts during the installation process. No matter what distribution you use, you will always create the root user account during the installation.

The root user account is the superuser account for a Linux system. The root account can do anything it wants on the Linux system.

on the
Job

The root user account is very powerful and must be used judiciously. Put bluntly, you can really make a mess of your system if you do something wrong. Because you're logged in as root, the system assumes you know what you're doing and will let you do it. For safety and security reasons, you should not use the root account for day-to-day work. Instead, you should create a standard user account for these tasks. When you actually need superuser privileges to complete a task, you can switch to the root user account. When the task is complete, you should switch back to your standard user account.

When you install Linux, you'll be prompted to provide a password for the root user account. You'll also be given the opportunity to create additional user accounts on the system. In your deployment plan, specify which user accounts you plan on creating. As with software packages, it's not a problem if you need to add or remove user accounts later on after the installation is complete. Linux provides an extensive set of tools to manage user accounts and passwords. I'll show you how to do this in a later chapter.

Once this information is in your plan, you're ready to move on to the next step: gathering network information. Let's review how this is done next.

Gathering Network Information

In today's networked world, it is very likely that most of the Linux systems you will be working with will be connected to some type of computer network. You need to gather the network information necessary for your system to connect to the network before you start the installation and include it in your deployment plan. Here's a list of questions you need to answer:

■ *Will the system have its networking configuration dynamically assigned or will it need to be manually configured?* Most IP networks today use a Dynamic Host Configuration Protocol (DHCP) server to dynamically assign IP addresses and various other networking parameters to a workstation when it is booted on the network. Most Linux systems that will function as a desktop workstation will use this option. In this case, you don't need to do much to configure your networking parameters. The information will be dynamically assigned to the system every time it boots up.

However, if the Linux system is going to function as a server in the network, you shouldn't use DHCP to dynamically assign network configuration information. The problem is that the system could receive a different IP address each time it's booted. While this won't hurt a workstation, it can cause a host of problems with servers. Hence, network servers are usually assigned a static IP address.

If your system needs to have a static IP address assigned, then you need to gather the following parameters:

■ IP address   ■ Router address

■ Subnet mask   ■ DNS server address(es)

■ *What hostname will be assigned to the system?* Every Linux system needs to have a hostname assigned. Ideally, this hostname should be unique on your network, meaning no other system on the network should have the same hostname assigned. During the installation process, you will be prompted to provide a hostname.

- *What is the name of the DNS domain the system will reside in?* More than likely, your organization has its own DNS domain, such as *mycorp.com*. You will be asked to provide your organization's domain name during the installation process.

- *Will the system need a host firewall configured?* Most Linux distributions include a host firewall that can be enabled during the installation process. A host firewall can be an invaluable asset to your organization's security. Essentially, the host-based firewall prevents other systems on the network from connecting to the system.

  For workstation systems, you should enable this firewall and block all of your IP ports and services. You should also enable the host firewall on server systems. However, most server systems run applications that provide network-based services to other hosts on the network. Therefore, you will need to open up the necessary IP ports in the firewall to allow network hosts to connect to the associated services.

  If you're installing a server system, you should list the network services it will provide in your deployment plan along with their associated port numbers. This list will provide you with the information you need to make the necessary exceptions in your firewall configuration.

With your network configuration information specified, you're ready to move on to the last part of your deployment plan: selecting an installation source. Let's discuss how this is done next.

SCENARIO & SOLUTION

You're installing a Linux system that will function as a Web server. Which IP ports need to be opened in your host firewall?	By default, Web servers use IP ports 80 and 443. These ports should be opened on the host firewall to allow clients to connect to the httpd service running on the system.
You're implementing a Linux system that will function as a desktop workstation. Should you use static or dynamic IP addressing?	You can actually use either method. However, for ease of management, using DHCP to assign IP addresses would probably be the best option in most situations.

Selecting an Installation Source

Most Linux distributions provide you with many different options for installing the system. These options include the following:

- Installing from a CD or DVD
- Installing from a network server
- Completing a remote installation using VNC

Let's first discuss how to complete an installation from a CD or DVD.

Installing from a CD or DVD

The most common method for installing Linux is to use a set of installation CDs or DVDs. Using this method, you simply insert the first CD in the set (or the DVD) into the system's optical drive and boot the system from the disc.

You have two different options for obtaining your installation discs. First, some Linux vendors create retail boxes for their distribution that can be purchased from a computer store. For example, you can currently purchase SUSE Linux in this manner. This is a great option if you don't have a high-speed Internet connection and want printed documentation.

However, most Linux administrators simply download a copy of Linux from the vendor's Web site. For example, if you wanted to install Fedora, you could open a Web browser and navigate to http://fedora.redhat.com and select the download link. After selecting your system architecture, you are connected to a mirror site on the Internet that contains the distribution, as shown in Figure 3-15.

Notice in Figure 3-15 that you can either download a single DVD containing all of the distribution files or you can download five separate CDs. You can choose one or the other, but you don't need both. If you're using a fast, reliable Internet connection and have a DVD drive installed in the target system, I recommend the DVD option. You only have to download a single file and you don't have to swap discs during the installation process. When I'm performing a Linux deployment, many times I need to install multiple systems at once. In this situation, I want to be able to start the installation and leave the system while I work on another system. I don't want to have to constantly swap out discs on multiple machines to get them installed.

Also notice that the files shown in Figure 3-15 all have an .iso extension. These are called *ISO images*. Once you've downloaded the appropriate .iso file or files, you can use CD- or DVD-burning software to burn the ISO image to an actual CD or DVD. I prefer a package called PrimoDVD from Veritas to burn ISO images to a CD or DVD, as shown in Figure 3-16.

FIGURE 3-15

Downloading ISO images

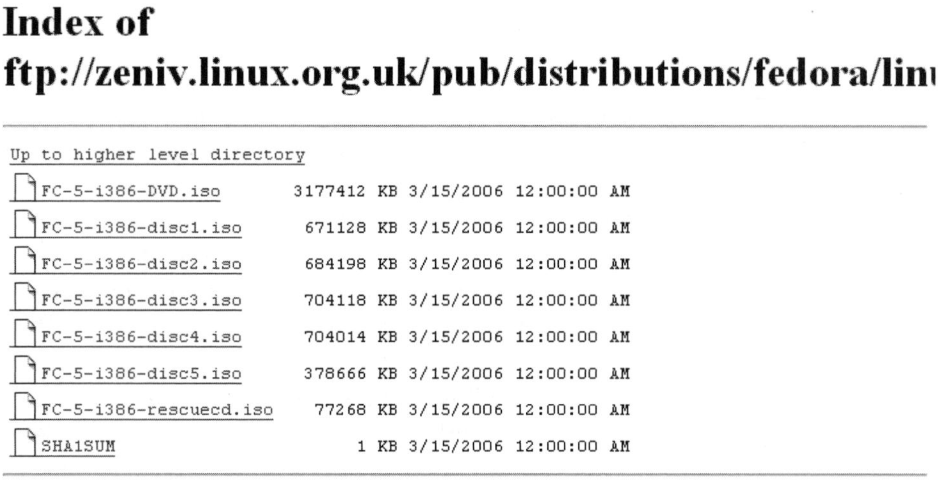

Index of ftp://zeniv.linux.org.uk/pub/distributions/fedora/lin
Up to higher level directory
FC-5-i386-DVD.iso 3177412 KB 3/15/2006 12:00:00 AM
FC-5-i386-disc1.iso 671128 KB 3/15/2006 12:00:00 AM
FC-5-i386-disc2.iso 684198 KB 3/15/2006 12:00:00 AM
FC-5-i386-disc3.iso 704118 KB 3/15/2006 12:00:00 AM
FC-5-i386-disc4.iso 704014 KB 3/15/2006 12:00:00 AM
FC-5-i386-disc5.iso 378666 KB 3/15/2006 12:00:00 AM
FC-5-i386-rescuecd.iso 77268 KB 3/15/2006 12:00:00 AM
SHA1SUM 1 KB 3/15/2006 12:00:00 AM

FIGURE 3-16 Burning an ISO image to disc

File Edit Drive Robotics View Tools Window Help
Disc Publisher
Drive
Status
Publisher Drive (G:)
Host:1 ID:1 (F:)
1 Recorder(s)
Copies: 1
Speed: Max
Record and Verify
Verify every round
Print
Disc Image file: C:\Documents and Settings\rtracy\Desktop\FC-5-i386-DVD.iso
.ISO Track Image
Job
Status
Action / Resu
Job 1 - Image...
1 Job(s) opened
PxHelper
Auto Insert Notification ON
Autorun shield ON

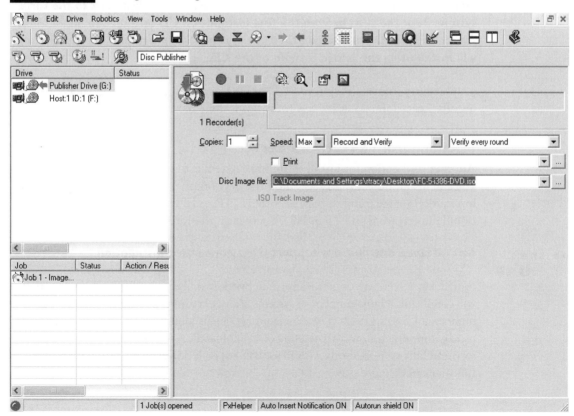

Most optical burning software supports the burning of ISO images to CD. Check your documentation to see how it's done with your particular package.

After downloading a very large ISO file from the Internet, it's a very good idea to check the md5sum checksum value to make sure it arrived intact without any corruption. See Chapter 8 to learn how to do this.

In addition, if you're installing Linux into a VMware virtual machine, you don't actually have to burn the ISO image to disc. Instead, you can configure the virtual machine to connect directly to the ISO image itself. The virtual machine will think that the image is actually a real CD or DVD and install from it. Installing Linux using this method is much faster because the data is stored on a hard drive instead of an optical disc.

In addition, if you're installing Fedora, you can actually install directly from the ISO images without using VMware. To do this, first move the hard drive from the system you want to install Linux on to a different computer that already has an operating system installed. Create a 4GB partition on the disk and copy the ISO image file to this partition. Move the disk back to the target system. Boot the system from the first installation CD and set the installation source to Hard Drive. You can then specify the ISO image and the installation will install using the image instead of the CD.

In addition to installing from a CD or DVD, you can also perform a network installation of Linux. Let's discuss how this is done next.

Installing from a Network Server

Another cool option for installing a Linux system is to install from a network server. You can install from a Linux server on the network that has been installed as an installation source using the SMB, NFS, HTTP, or FTP protocols. You can even install directly from an FTP or HTTP server on the Internet.

Not all Linux distributions support a network-based installation.

The key advantage of performing a network installation of Linux is the fact that you can install a large number of systems at once without having to burn a large number of CDs or DVDs. The disadvantage of this method is that the installation usually runs much slower than a CD or DVD install. An installation from a network server usually runs at a somewhat reasonable speed; however, an installation over the Internet can be quite slow.

To complete a network installation, you must complete several preparatory steps. First of all, if you intend to install over the network from a local server, you need to copy the Linux installation files from all CDs (or from the DVD) to a directory on the server. Alternatively, you could also mount the CD or DVD in the file system where network clients can access it. Then you need to select the protocol that will be used to access it. For example, if you want to use the SMB protocol to access the installation files, you must install and configure the Samba service on the server. Once done, you must create a share for the directory where the installation files reside. You could also configure the HTTP, NFS, or FTP service on the server to accomplish the same task.

Once the source server is set up, you next need to download a basic installation CD image. For example, if you wanted to complete a network installation of SUSE Linux, you would use a browser to navigate to http://en.opensuse.org and select the Download link. In the page that is displayed, you can download a Net Boot Image, as shown in Figure 3-17.

FIGURE 3-17

Downloading a
Net Boot Image

Downloads SUSE Linux 10.1   [edit]

BEFORE YOU INSTALL READ THIS:

The package manager in SUSE 10.1 is regrettably broken on most systems. To correct this problem, you should follow these steps after installing SUSE:

- Open Yast choose "online update configuration", click next, and wait until finished.
- Press the updater icon on your taskbar/panel.
- If it updates -- congratulations -- all is well.
- If it throws up an error, close it.
- Follow the instructions in this SDB article or this mail 🔗.

You probably also want to read about Using 10.1 and the Most Annoying Bugs.

Architecture	CD 1	CD 2	CD 3	CD 4	CD 5	Addon CD[1]	DVD [2]	Net Boot Image
x86	🔘	🔘	🔘	🔘	🔘	🔘	🔘	🔘
	Torrent 🔗					Torrent 🔗	Torrent 🔗	
x86-64	🔘	🔘	🔘	🔘	🔘	🔘	🔘	🔘
	Torrent 🔗					Torrent 🔗	Torrent 🔗	
ppc	🔘	🔘	🔘	🔘	🔘	🔘	Not Available	🔘
	Torrent 🔗					Torrent 🔗		
Checksums	MD5SUMS 🔗					MD5SUMS 🔗	MD5SUMS 🔗	MD5SUMS 🔗

You will need to burn this image to disc and then boot the system from it.

on the
①ob
If you're installing the Fedora system, you can burn a disc from the /images/ boot.iso image located on the first installation CD and boot the system from it. You can then select your alternate installation source.

In the first installation screen, press F3 to access other options and then press F4 to specify the installation source, as shown in Figure 3-18.

FIGURE 3-18   Selecting an installation source

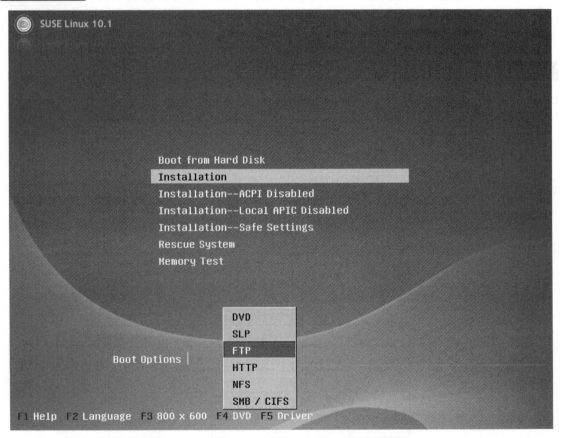

If you select SMB/CIFS, you must specify the parameters shown in the next illustration to connect to the remote server.

```
SMB (Windows Share) Installation
Server
[                                    ]

Share
[                                    ]

Directory
[                                    ]

Domain
[                                    ]

User (using "guest" if empty)
[                                    ]

Password
[                                    ]

        [    OK    ]      [  Cancel  ]
```

If you select FTP, you must specify the server IP address or domain name, directory, username, and password to access the FTP service on the remote server. The remote server could be a server on the local network or an FTP server on the Internet. Check your distribution's Web site for a list of FTP-based network installation repositories on the Internet. The FTP installation screen is shown in the next illustration.

```
FTP Installation
Server
[                                    ]

Directory
[                                    ]

User (anonymous login if empty)
[                                    ]

Password
[                                    ]

        [    OK    ]      [  Cancel  ]
```

If you select HTTP, you must specify the server IP address or domain name and directory on the remote server. This is shown in the next illustration.

As with an FTP installation, the HTTP installation source can reside on the local network or on the Internet. Check your distribution's Web site for a list of HTTP-based network installation repositories on the Internet.

```
HTTP Installation
Server
[                                    ]

Directory
[                                    ]

        [    OK    ]      [  Cancel  ]
```

If you select NFS, you must specify the server IP address or domain name and directory on the remote server. This is shown in the next illustration.

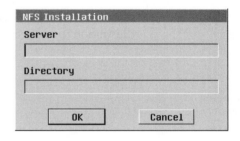

Once you select the installation source, select Installation from the main menu and the installation will proceed using the installation files from the remote server.

You can also complete an installation using a VNC connection. Let's review how this is done next.

Completing a Remote Installation Using VNC

VNC stands for Virtual Network Computing. Essentially, VNC allows you to "project" the video output from one system to another system. Using the VNC protocol, you can start the installation on your target system, but then use a Web browser on another system to view the installation screens.

On a SUSE Linux system, you can enter **vnc=1** in the boot options field in the first installation screen, as shown in Figure 3-19.

After starting the installation, you'll be prompted to provide various network parameters needed to create a VNC connection. After doing so, you can access the Installation Wizard screens by opening a Web browser on another system and navigating to http://*IP_address_of_system*:5801. For example, if I assigned my system an IP address of 192.168.1.10 in the initial VNC configuration screens, I could access it by opening http://192.168.1.10:5801 in a browser, as shown in Figure 3-20.

Using this VNC connection, you can complete the installation process from the comfort of your own office.

For your deployment plan, you need to determine which installation source you are going to use and prepare the prerequisite systems, if necessary.

Once you've completed this step, your Linux deployment plan is complete. You should now have the data you need to complete the installation in an organized, efficient manner. You file your deployment plan in a safe place once your installation is complete. This information can be an invaluable help for other system administrators who may need to work on your system at some point.

In my line of work, I work for a variety of different companies under contract. When they have a problem, they call me and I go on-site to fix their systems. Most of the time, this works out very well for everyone involved. However, from time to time, I have to go on-site for a company that hasn't documented their network

FIGURE 3-19   Configuring a VNC installation

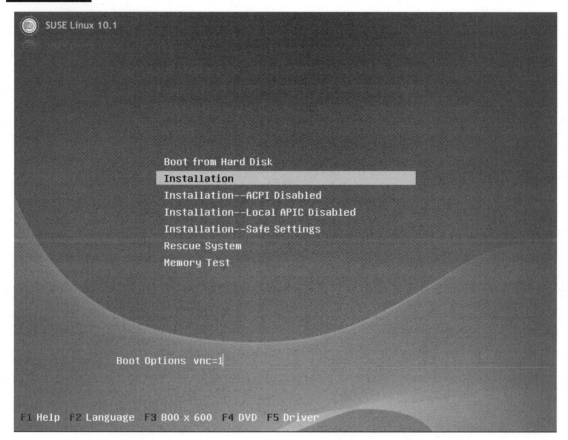

or their computer systems. It can be an extremely frustrating experience. As a consultant, I have no idea how the system has been set up nor do I know why. What may have been obvious to the original implementer is not obvious at all to someone else working on the system later on. A job that should take two or three hours to complete ends up taking two or three days instead. That costs my clients a lot of extra money and it dramatically increases my blood pressure.

At this point, you're ready to order your hardware, download your distribution, and actually start installing a Linux system. Let's review how this is done next.

FIGURE 3-20   Completing the installation using VNC

Install Linux

It's finally time to start installing a Linux system! After spending hours creating a Linux deployment plan, most techies breathe a sigh of relief when they finally get their hands on their new software and start installing. This is what we live for!

When installing new systems, I strongly recommend that you set up an isolated lab environment and install your systems there. This will give you a chance to observe the systems and ensure that everything is working properly before turning your users loose with them.

Once you're sure everything is working correctly, you can move them from the lab environment to your users' production environment.

As I mentioned at the beginning of this chapter, there are simply too many different Linux distributions available to include them all on the Linux+ exam or in this chapter. You are expected to choose one of the following distributions and learn how to install it:

- SUSE Linux
- Red Hat Fedora
- Mandrake
- TurboLinux

In this chapter, we're going to review how to perform an installation of SUSE Linux 10.1. To complete this exercise, I strongly recommend that you do one of two things:

- Purchase a lab system that you can experiment with. This should be a system with no important data on it. The exercises in this chapter will require you to wipe your hard drive clean and install Linux on top of it. Don't do this without backing up any important data first! If you don't, the data will be forever gone.

- Purchase a copy of VMware Workstation from http://www.vmware.com. This will allow you install multiple virtual Linux systems without repartitioning your hard drive. VMware Workstation offers a 30-day free evaluation period, but if its price tag is too steep, you can also download a copy of VMware Server. This version of VMware is free. It isn't officially supported on Windows XP or 2000 Professional, but I've seen it install correctly on many such systems.

Once you have a system prepared to install Linux on, you're ready to get started. Let's begin by discussing how to install SUSE Linux.

EXERCISE 3-1

Installing SUSE Linux

In this exercise, we're going to install SUSE Linux. At the time this book was written, SUSE Linux 10.1 was the most current version available. By the time you read this, a newer version may have been released. If so, you may need to adjust the steps presented here to accommodate the updated software.

To complete these exercises, you'll need a system that meets the following requirements:

- CPU: Pentium II 266 or later
- Memory: 256MB
- Hard disk: 8GB or larger
- Optical drive: CD or DVD drive
- Mouse and keyboard
- Sound board (optional)
- Network board (optional)

If the system has already had an operating system installed, you will need to use a disk partitioning tool, such as fdisk, to remove all partitions. Be sure to back up any important data before you do so!

Alternatively, you can choose to use VMware Workstation to host your virtual Linux system. If you do, you will need to use a VNC connection to complete the installation from a Web browser on either the host system or a remote system.

Installing SUSE Linux

1. On a workstation with a CD or DVD burner, open a Web browser and navigate to http://en.opensuse.org/Download.

2. Follow the instructions on the Web page to download the latest SUSE Linux release. If your system has a CD drive, be sure to download the CD images. If your system uses a DVD drive, you may want to opt for the DVD image.

3. Using your burning software, burn your image(s) to disc. Follow the directions in your burning software documentation for burning ISO images.

4. Insert your first installation CD or DVD into your target system's optical drive.

5. Configure your target system to boot from the CD/DVD drive first.

    a. Boot your target system and access the CMOS setup program. Your start-up screen should display a message indicating which keystroke is required to access the setup program.

    b. Use your CMOS setup program to configure your system to boot from the CD or DVD drive first.

    c. Save your changes and reboot the system. The computer should now boot from the SUSE Linux installation disc. The screen in Figure 3-21 is displayed.

6. Select Installation. Wait while the Installation Wizard starts.

7. In the Language screen, select your *language*, then select Next.

FIGURE 3-21   Starting the SUSE Linux installation

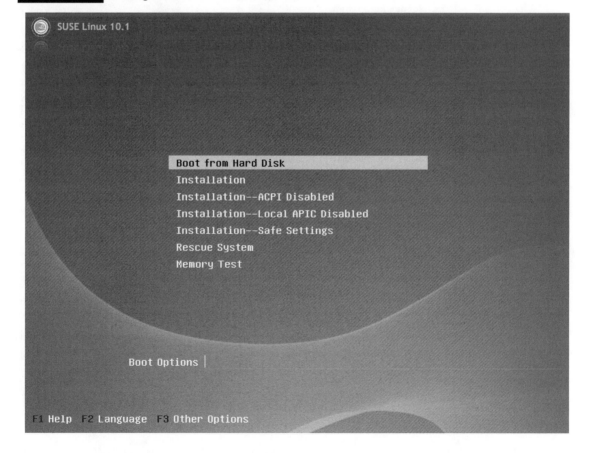

8. In the Media Check screen, select Start Check. Wait while the media is checked.

9. When the media check is complete, select Next. The License Agreement screen is displayed, as shown in Figure 3-22.

10. Read the license agreement.

11. Select Yes, I Agree to the License Agreement; then select Next. The Installation Mode screen is displayed, as shown in Figure 3-23.

12. Verify that New Installation is marked; then select Next.

13. In the Clock and Time Zone screen, select your *region* and your *time zone*.

FIGURE 3-22   Accepting the license agreement

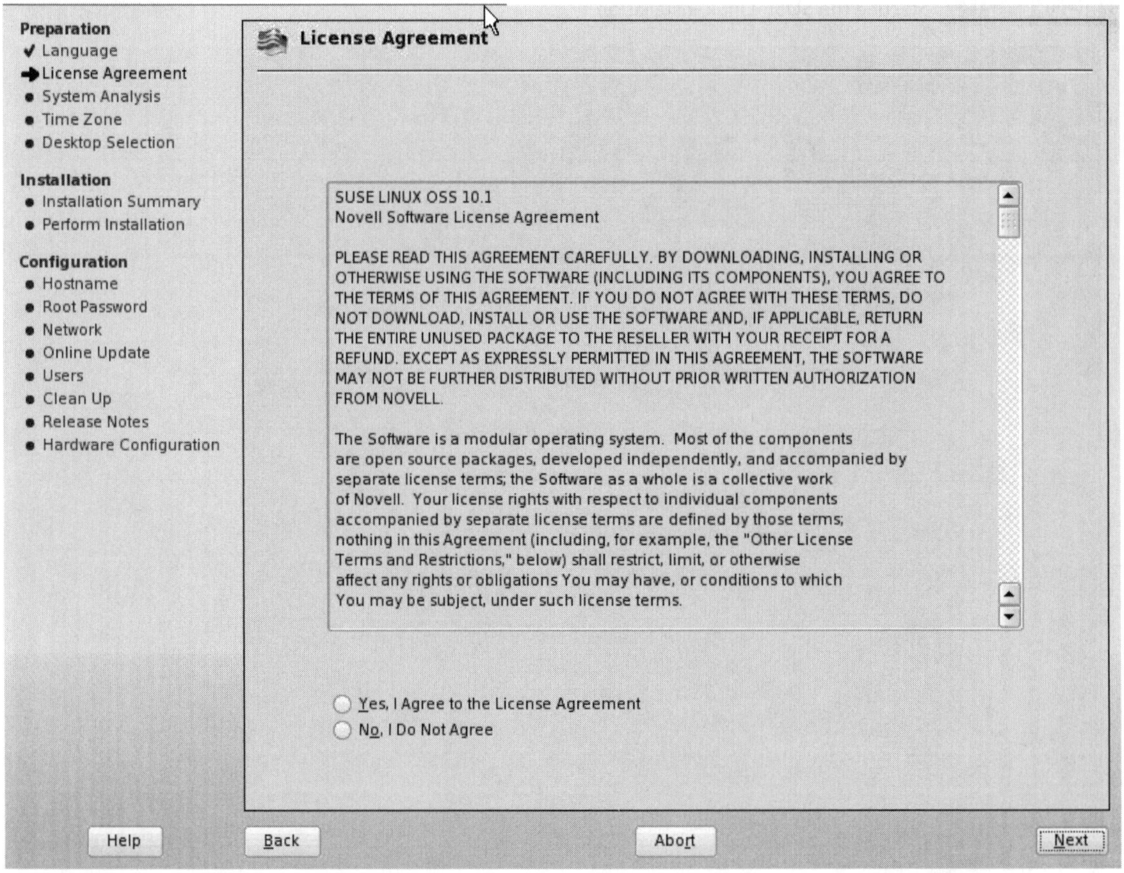

FIGURE 3-23   Selecting the Installation Mode

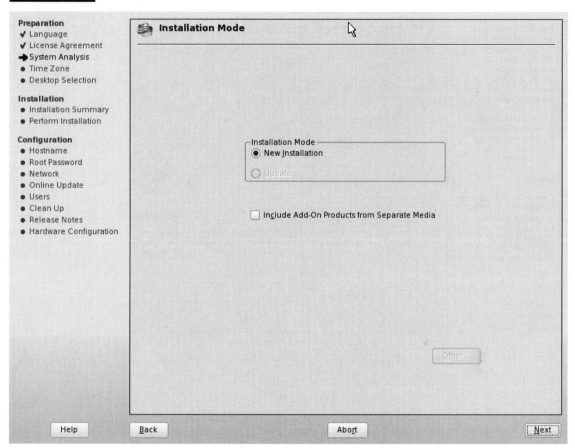

14. If the current date and time displayed in the lower-right corner of the screen are not correct, select Change and make the necessary adjustments; then select Apply.

15. Select Next. The Desktop Selection screen is displayed, as shown in Figure 3-24.

16. In the Desktop Selection screen, select KDE. If you don't like using KDE, you can also choose from the following desktop options:

   ■ **GNOME**   GNOME is a graphical desktop environment.

   ■ **Other**   This option allows you to configure either a minimal graphical system or a text-only system.

FIGURE 3-24 Selecting your desktop

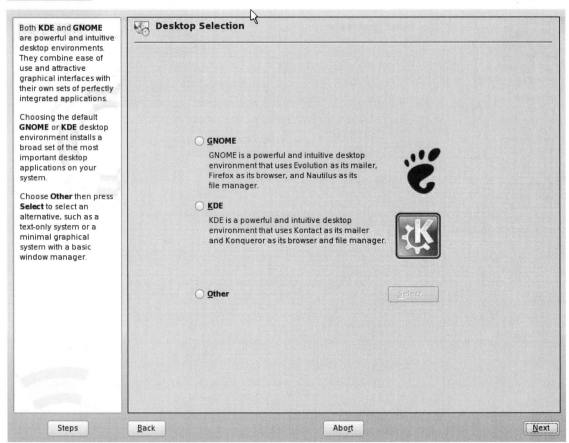

17. Select Next.

18. Select the Expert tab. The installation creates an installation proposal that you can either accept or modify, as shown in Figure 3-25.

19. Customize your disk partitioning by completing the following:

   a. Select Partitioning.

   b. Select Create Custom Partition Setup; then select Next.

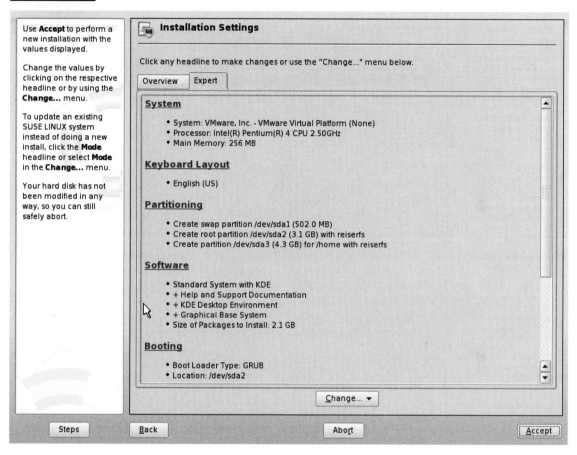

FIGURE 3-25 Viewing the default installation proposal

c. Select Custom Partitioning; then select Next. The Expert Partitioner screen is displayed, as shown in Figure 3-26.

d. Select your hard disk drive in the device list. Notice that Linux refers to the first SCSI hard drive in your system as /dev/sda. If you had two SCSI hard disks, the second one would be labeled /dev/sdb. If you have IDE hard drives in the system, they will be labeled /dev/hda, /dev/hdb, etc.

e. Select Create.

FIGURE 3-26 Customizing the partitioning proposal

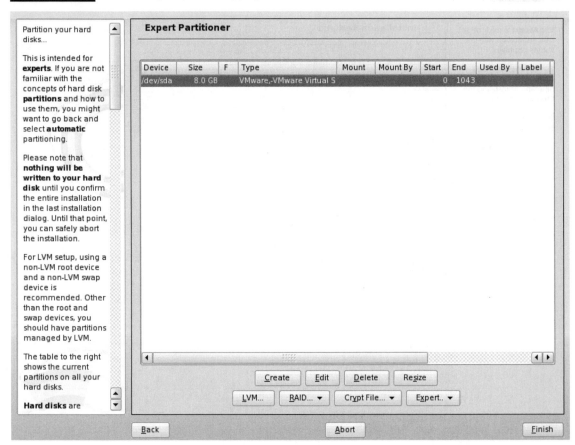

f. Select Primary Partition; then select OK. The screen in Figure 3-27 is displayed.

g. Verify that 0 is displayed in the Start Cylinder field.

h. In the End field, enter **+200M.**

i. In the Mount Point drop-down list, select /boot.

j. Verify that Format is selected and that the File System drop-down list is set to Reiser; then select OK. The new partition should be displayed. If you're using a SCSI hard disk drive, the new partition should be labeled /dev/sda1, indicating that it is the first partition on the first SCSI drive.

FIGURE 3-27   Creating a new partition

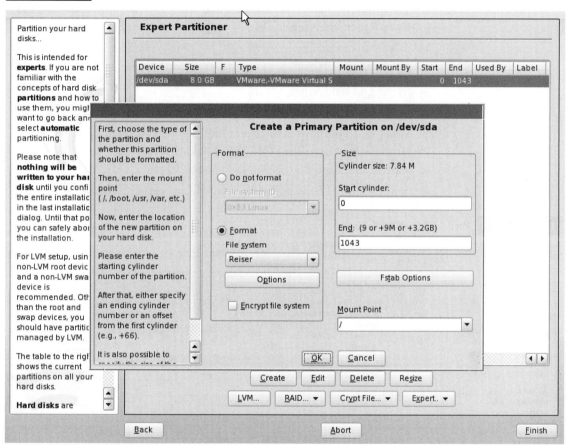

k. Select Create.

l. Select Primary Partition; then select OK.

m. In the End field, enter a *value* that is equal to twice the amount of RAM installed in your system. For example, if you have 256MB of RAM installed, you would enter **+512M.**

n. In the File System drop-down list, select Swap.

o. Select OK.

p. Select Create.

q. Select Primary Partition; then select OK.

r. In the End field, enter **+6GB**.

s. In the Mount Point drop-down list, select /.

t. Verify that Format is selected and that the File System drop-down list is set to Reiser; then select OK.

u. Select Create.

v. Select Primary Partition; then select OK.

w. In the End field, enter **+2GB**.

x. In the Mount Point drop-down list, select /var.

y. Verify that Format is marked and that the File System drop-down list is set to Reiser; then select OK. You should have a list of partitions that appears similar to that shown in Figure 3-28.

z. Select Finish. The Installation Settings screen is displayed.

FIGURE 3-28   Partitioning the hard drive

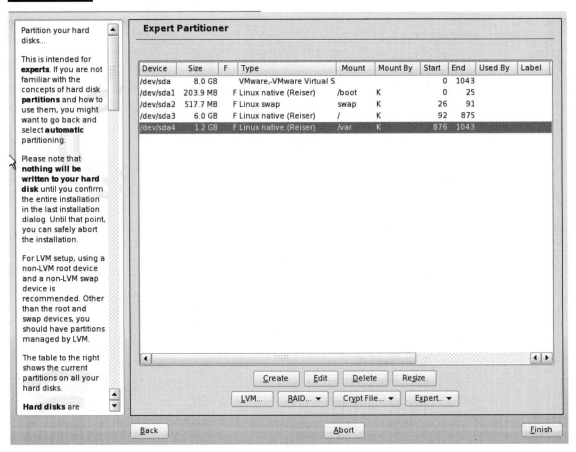

20. Customize the software packages that will be installed by completing the following:

   a. Select Software.

   b. Select Details. The screen in Figure 3-29 is displayed.

   c. In the left column, highlight Games.

   d. In the right column, select csmash.

   e. Select Accept.

21. In the Installation Settings screen, select Accept.

FIGURE 3-29 Configuring software

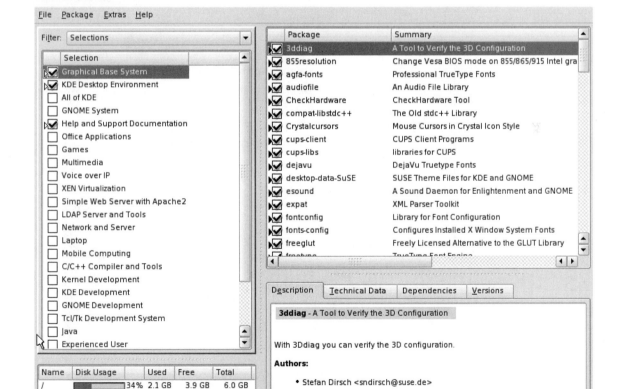

22. When prompted to confirm the installation, select Install. At this point, you can take a break and relax while Linux is installed. The Installation Wizard displays a progress meter that allows you to track the progress of the installation process, as shown in Figure 3-30.

23. After the packages have been copied, the system will reboot and the Hostname and Domain Name screen is displayed, as shown in Figure 3-31.

24. In the Hostname field, enter a hostname of **linux1**.

25. In the Domain Name field, enter your organization's *domain name*; then select Next.

FIGURE 3-30   Monitoring the progress of the installation

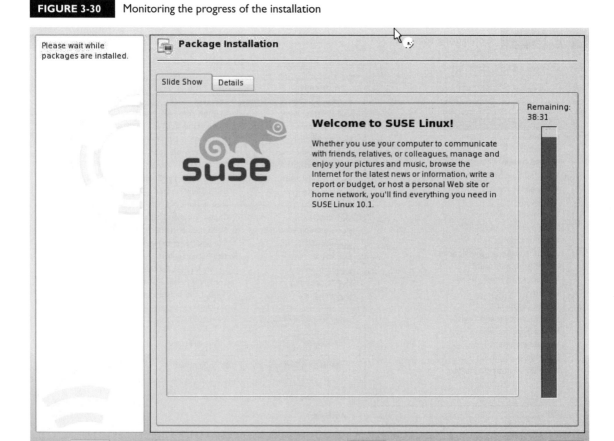

FIGURE 3-31   Viewing the default host and domain names

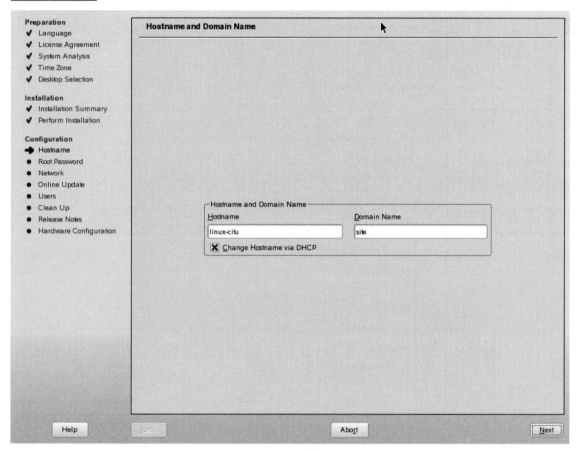

26. In the Password for the System Administrator "root" screen, enter a password of **tuxPenguin1** in the password fields; then select Next. The Network Configuration screen is displayed, as shown in Figure 3-32.

27. Review the information displayed in the Network Configuration screen; then select Next. We'll spend more time working with the network configuration in a later chapter.

28. When prompted to test your connection to the Internet, select Yes if your system is connected to the Internet through a LAN or modem; otherwise, select No.

29. Select Next.

FIGURE 3-32   Viewing the network configuration

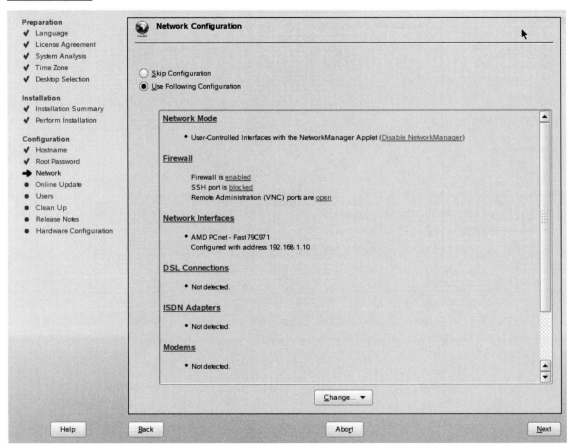

30. When prompted with the results of the test, select Next.

31. In the Online Update Configuration screen, select Configure Later; then select Next. We'll discuss how to configure updates in a later chapter. The User Authentication Method screen is displayed, as shown in Figure 3-33.

32. As you can see in Figure 3-33, you can choose several different methods for authenticating users to the system. This topic is fairly complex and we will address it in depth later in this book. For now, select Local; then select Next. The New Local User screen is displayed, as shown in Figure 3-34.

FIGURE 3-33 Configuring user authentication methods

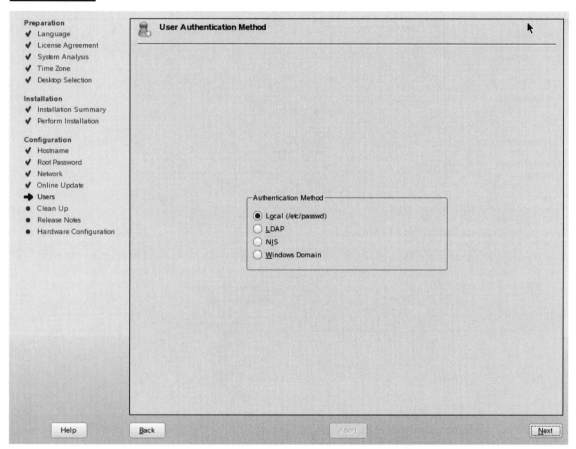

33. Remember that you should not use the root user account for day-to-day work. Instead, you should create a standard user account for this purpose. In the New Local User screen, enter the following:

- User's Full Name: **Tux Penguin**
- Username: **tux**
- Password: **M3linux273**

FIGURE 3-34   Configuring a new local user

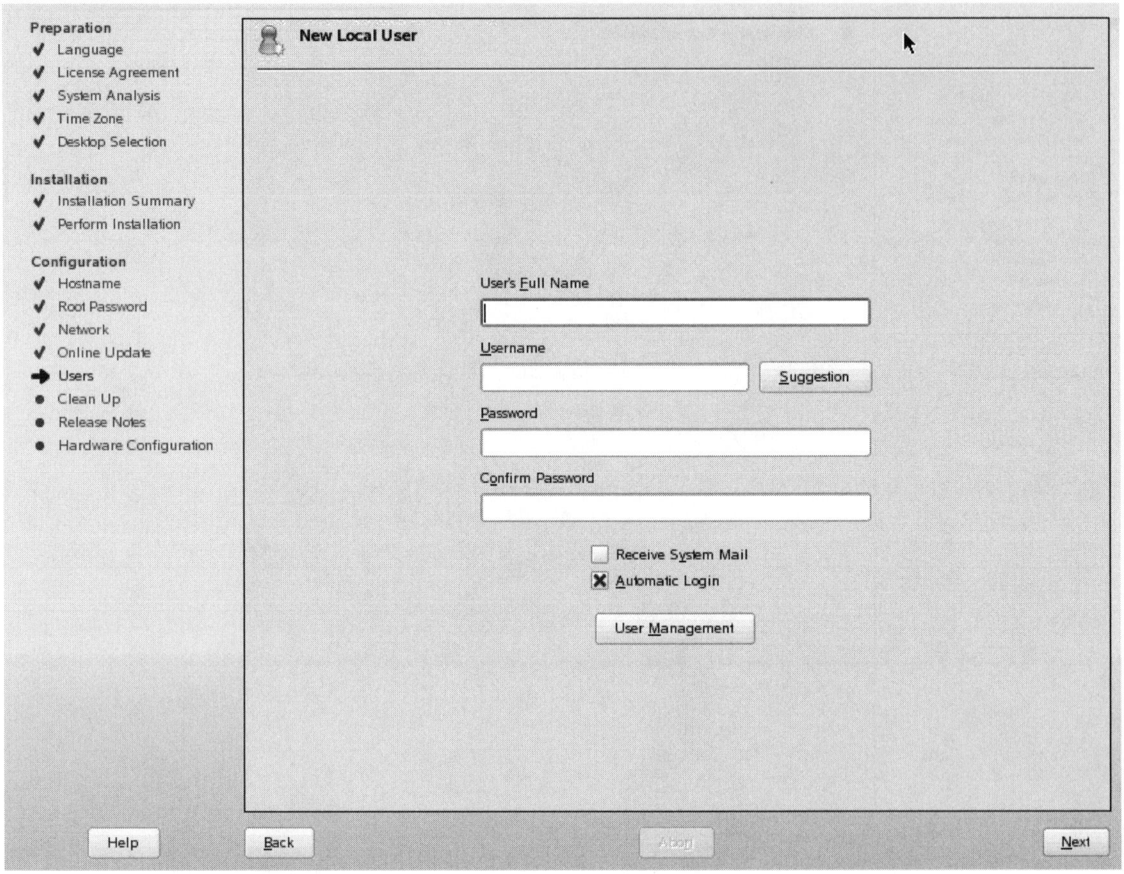

34. Deselect Automatic Login; then select Next. Wait while the system is updated.

35. In the Release Notes screen, read the information displayed; then select Next. The hardware configuration screen is displayed, as shown in Figure 3-35.

36. We'll discuss configuring your system hardware later in this book. For now, just select Next. Wait while the system is configured.

37. In the Installation Completed screen, select Finish. The system will reboot.

38. When the system has finished rebooting, you will see a login screen similar to that shown in Figure 3-36. Login as **tux** with a password of **M3linux273**.

FIGURE 3-35   Viewing the hardware configuration

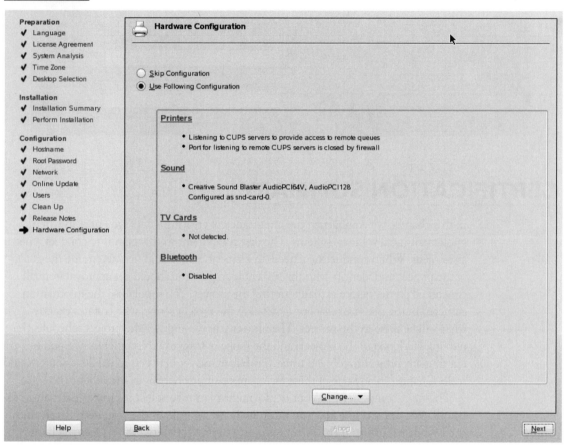

If you chose to use VMware to install your Linux system, you need to install a service called VMware Tools. This service optimizes your video, keyboard, and mouse to work with the virtual machine. Open a Web browser and navigate to http://www.vmware.com/support to view the latest instructions on how to do this. You can also use the Help menu in VMware to view instructions.

Congratulations! You now have a running Linux system. As we go through the rest of this book, you will learn how to configure and manage this system.

FIGURE 3-36	Logging in for the first time

CERTIFICATION SUMMARY

In this chapter, we emphasized the importance of creating a deployment plan when implementing new Linux systems. The first component in this plan is to conduct a needs assessment. When conducting a needs assessment, you should first determine the goals of the project and identify who the stakeholders are. You should get approval from all concerned parties before actually starting the project. You should use the information gathered in the needs assessment to develop the project scope, which states exactly what will be done in the project. The project scope comprises the project schedule, the resources assigned to the project, and the range of tasks to be completed. We pointed out that any project involves a three-way balancing act between schedule, resources, and scale. Changes in any one of these factors necessitate changes in the other two.

The next component in your deployment plan is to select a Linux distribution to install. We emphasized that you must evaluate the role of the system to determine the best distribution. If the system is going to provide network services to client systems, then a Linux distribution optimized to function as a server would be the best choice. If the system is going to be used as a desktop system, then a distribution optimized to function as a workstation would be the best choice. We also emphasized the importance of technical support. An unsupported distribution may be a fine choice for an experimental lab system, but a supported distribution is a better choice for systems that will be used in a production environment.

The next component in your deployment plan is to verify that your hardware is compatible with your chosen Linux distribution. We pointed out that most distributions included some type of hardware compatibility list. You should check your hardware against this list. You should also verify that your hardware meets your distribution's minimum system requirements. We emphasized that you must download the correct version of the distribution for your CPU's architecture.

After verifying your hardware, you should next plan your file system. We emphasized that the Linux file system requires more forethought and planning than the file system in other operating systems. We pointed out that you could choose from the ext2, ext3, or Reiser file systems when implementing a Linux system. We discussed the advantages and disadvantages of each file system. We also pointed out that the hard disk in a Linux system should have multiple partitions. We emphasized that your swap partition should be at least twice the size of your system RAM. We also emphasized that you should consider creating separate partitions for the /, /boot, /home, /opt, /tmp, /usr, and /var directories.

Next, you need to specify the software that will be installed on your Linux system. We emphasized that there are many packages that you can choose from when implementing a Linux system. However, you should only install the software that will be needed on the system. We also pointed out that most packages have dependencies that must be taken into account when installing your Linux system.

After specifying your software, your deployment plan should next specify which user accounts need to be created on the system. We pointed out that all Linux systems have the superuser account, root. We emphasized that root should only be used for administrative tasks. You should create an additional standard user account for completing day-to-day tasks. Any other users who will use the system will also need user accounts.

Next, you need to gather networking information for your system. You first need to specify whether the system will use static or dynamic IP addressing. If the system will use static addressing, then you need to gather the appropriate IP address, subnet mask, router address, and DNS server address for your network. You also need to define the hostname that will be used by the system as well as the DNS domain that the system will reside in. We also pointed out that most distributions include a host-based firewall that is used to prevent other systems on the network from connecting to your system. If the system will function as a server, you need to identify which IP ports will need to be opened in the host firewall to allow network clients to connect to the system.

Next, you need to identify your installation source in your deployment plan. We pointed out that most system administrators install Linux using CDs or a DVD. We discussed how you could download ISO images from your Linux vendor's Web site and burn them to optical discs. We also pointed out that the installation files can be copied to a network server, allowing you to complete an installation over the wire using the SMB, NFS, HTTP, or FTP protocol. This strategy also allows you to install a Linux system directly from an installation repository on the Internet. We also pointed out that you can use VNC to remotely install Linux from a Web browser running on a different computer.

With this information gathered, your deployment plan is complete. We emphasized that keeping this documentation on hand can be extremely valuable when the system needs maintenance later on. With the deployment plan in hand, you're ready to install a Linux system. We pointed out that the Linux+ exam expects you to be able to install one of the following Linux distributions:

- SUSE Linux
- Mandrake
- Red Hat Fedora
- TurboLinux

You can choose one of these four distributions. In this chapter, we elected to install SUSE Linux.

✓ TWO-MINUTE DRILL

Plan a Linux Installation

❑ Installing Linux requires more planning than other operating systems.

❑ System administrators don't like to plan or document their work.

❑ Properly planning and documenting a Linux deployment will save time and money in the long run.

❑ The first component in a Linux deployment plan is a needs assessment.

❑ You should ask the following questions in your needs assessment:

   ❑ What are the goals of the project?

   ❑ Who are the stakeholders?

   ❑ What is the scope of the project?

❑ The project scope is composed of three factors that must remain in balance:

   ❑ Schedule

   ❑ Resources

   ❑ Scale

❑ Using project management software can help you plan and manage your deployment.

❑ Your deployment plan should specify which distribution you are going to use.

❑ You should determine the role of the system before selecting a distribution.

❑ Systems used in a production environment should provide technical support.

❑ You should verify that your software will run on your selected distribution before deploying it.

❑ You should check your distribution's HCL to determine if your hardware is compatible.

❑ You should verify that your hardware meets your distribution's minimum system requirements.

❑ You need to determine your CPU's architecture before downloading a distribution.

❑ You need to plan your file system in your deployment plan.

- ❑ You should select one of the following file systems:
    - ❑ ext2
    - ❑ ext3
    - ❑ Reiser
- ❑ You should create separate partitions for different directories in your file system to ensure system stability.
- ❑ Your swap partition should be twice the size of your system RAM.
- ❑ Your implementation plan should specify the software packages you intend to install on your system.
- ❑ You should install only the packages needed.
- ❑ You need to keep package dependencies in mind when installing software.
- ❑ Your deployment plan should specify which user accounts will be created on the system.
- ❑ The root user account is the superuser.
- ❑ You should only use root for administrative tasks.
- ❑ You should create a standard user account for day-to-day tasks.
- ❑ Your deployment plan should include networking parameters.
- ❑ Systems can have the IP addressing information dynamically or statically assigned.
- ❑ You need to determine how the host-based firewall will be configured in your deployment plan.
- ❑ Your deployment plan should specify what installation source will be used to install Linux.
- ❑ You can download ISO images from your Linux vendor's Web site and burn them to a CD or DVD.
- ❑ You can copy the Linux installation files to a server on your network and install across the wire using the SMB, NFS, HTTP, or FTP protocols.
- ❑ You can install directly from the Internet using the HTTP or FTP protocols.
- ❑ You can configure VNC to complete an installation from a remote workstation using a Web browser.

Install Linux

❑ To practice installing Linux, you should purchase a lab system or use VMware.

❑ If you choose to use VMware, you will need to use VNC to complete the installation through a Web browser.

❑ Back up any important data from the hard drive before installing; otherwise, it will be erased when the disk is partitioned.

❑ You only need to know how to install one Linux distribution for your Linux+ exam.

❑ If you're using VMware to install Linux, you need to install VMware Tools after the installation is complete.

SELF TEST

Plan a Linux Installation

1. When conducting a needs assessment, what questions should you ask? (Choose two.)

   A. What problem will this installation fix?

   B. Which distribution should I use?

   C. Where can I get the best price on a new server?

   D. Who is requesting the new systems?

2. Which of the following is a properly stated goal in a needs assessment?

   A. Mike's boss wants a new server, so we're gong to install it.

   B. We're going to install Linux.

   C. We need a new Linux system.

   D. The new Linux system will provide a network database to increase the documentation team's productivity by an anticipated 20 percent.

3. Suppose Karen from Customer Service approaches you and asks for a new Linux server for her team. Who else should you talk to as a part of your needs assessment? (Choose two.)

   A. Karen's boss

   B. Karen's co-workers

   C. The Technical Support supervisor

   D. Your hardware vendor

4. Which of the following are components of your project scope? (Choose two.)

   A. Customer demands

   B. Management decision-making

   C. Schedule

   D. Scale

5. You're responsible for implementing five new Linux servers in your organization's Technical Support department. The Technical Support supervisor has asked that four additional servers be added to the project. Due to time constraints, he won't allow you to adjust the original schedule to accommodate the additional servers. Which of the following is the most appropriate response?

   A. Ignore the request.

   B. Inform the supervisor that additional resources will have to be added to the project.

   C. Resign in protest.

   D. Cheerfully agree to the request and then miss the deadline.

6. You're installing new Linux systems that will be used by software engineers to develop advanced computer-aided design applications. Which distributions would be the best choice for this deployment? (Choose two.)

   A. Red Hat Enterprise Linux ES

   B. Red Hat Enterprise Linux AS

   C. Red Hat Desktop

   D. Red Hat Enterprise Linux WS

   E. SUSE Linux Enterprise Server

   F. SUSE Linux Enterprise Desktop

7. You're installing a new Linux system that will be used by an administrative assistant to type documents, create presentations, and manage e-mail. Which distribution would be the best choice for this deployment?

   A. Red Hat Enterprise Linux ES

   B. Red Hat Enterprise Linux AS

   C. Red Hat Desktop

   D. Red Hat Enterprise Linux WS

   E. SUSE Linux Enterprise Server

   F. SUSE Linux Enterprise Desktop

8. You're installing a new Linux server that will be used to host mission-critical database applications. This server will be heavily utilized by a large number of users every day. Which distributions would be the best choice for this deployment? (Choose two.)

   A. Red Hat Enterprise Linux ES

   B. Red Hat Enterprise Linux AS

   C. Red Hat Desktop

   D. Red Hat Enterprise Linux WS

   E. SUSE Linux Enterprise Server

   F. SUSE Linux Enterprise Desktop

9. You're planning to install Linux on a system that you've built out of spare parts. Several components in the system aren't listed on your distribution's HCL. This system will be used by your team's administrative assistant to manage employee schedules, send and receive e-mail, and track employee hours. What should you do?

    A. Install the distribution anyway and hope for the best.

    B. Install the distribution and then install the latest product updates.

    C. Replace the incompatible parts with supported hardware.

    D. Spend three days scouring the Internet looking for drivers.

10. You're planning to install Fedora on a system that uses a Pentium IV Celeron CPU. Which distribution architecture should you download?

    A. IA-64

    B. x86-Celeron

    C. x86-64

    D. x86

    E. PPC

11. You're planning to install Fedora on a system that uses a 64-bit AMD CPU. Which distribution architecture should you download?

    A. IA-64

    B. x86-AMD

    C. x86-64

    D. x86

    E. PPC

12. You're installing a new Linux system. This system will be used by a civil engineer to model the behavior of buildings and bridges during an earthquake. This system must run as fast as possible. It must protect the integrity of the data if the system goes down unexpectedly. If it does go down, the system needs to be back up and running as quickly as possible. Which file system would be the best choice?

    A. VFAT

    B. FAT32

    C. Reiser

    D. ext3

    E. ext2

13. Which partition is used for virtual memory by a Linux system?

    A. pagefile

    B. swap

    C. /swap

    D. /boot

    E. /tmp

14. If your system has 1GB of RAM installed, how big should your swap partition be?

    A. 256MB

    B. 1GB

    C. 512GB

    D. 2GB

15. Which of the following directories should have their own partition? (Choose three.)

    A. /bin

    B. /boot

    C. /etc

    D. /usr

    E. /home

    F. /root

    G. /dev

16. You're installing a new Linux server. This system will function as an e-mail server for your organization. What ports should you open on its host firewall? (Choose three.)

    A. 110

    B. 80

    C. 25

    D. 143

    E. 443

Install Linux

17. You need to install Linux on a workstation. The hard drive has been wiped and is ready for the new operating system. You insert your first Linux installation CD in the CD drive and boot the system. Instead of starting the installation routine, the screen displays an error message indicating that an operating system couldn't be found. What's the most likely cause of the problem?

    A. Your Linux CD is damaged.

    B. The hard drive is failing and needs to be replaced.

    C. The CD drive is malfunctioning.

    D. The boot device order is set incorrectly in the BIOS.

18. Your Linux system uses two SCSI hard disk drives. The first drive is assigned SCSI ID 0; the second drive is assigned SCSI ID 1. Which of the following refers to the second SCSI drive in the system?

    A. /dev/sda

    B. /dev/sdc

    C. /dev/sdb

    D. /dev/sdd

19. Your Linux system uses a single IDE hard disk drive. Which of the following refers to the first partition on the IDE drive?

    A. /dev/hda1

    B. /dev/hdb1

    C. /dev/hda2

    D. /dev/hdb2

20. Your Linux system uses a single IDE hard disk drive. Which of the following refers to the second partition on the IDE drive?

    A. /dev/hda1

    B. /dev/hdb1

    C. /dev/hda2

    D. /dev/hdb2

21. Your Linux system uses two SCSI hard disk drives. The first drive is assigned SCSI ID 0; the second drive is assigned SCSI ID 1. Which of the following refers to the first partition on the second SCSI drive in the system?

    A. /dev/sda1

    B. /dev/sdc1

    C. /dev/sdb1

    D. /dev/sdd1

LAB QUESTION

You're responsible for managing the Linux systems in your organization. An engineer named Mike has sent you an e-mail asking you to upgrade the hardware and software he and his fellow engineers use to design the products sold by your company. Currently, they use Pentium IV 2.0 GHz systems running Red Hat 7.3. He would like to upgrade to newer systems that use 64-bit CPUs, 2GB of RAM, and RAID 5 disk arrays. He would also like to upgrade to a newer Linux distribution as well. Outline the process you will follow to complete this task.

SELF TEST ANSWERS

Plan a Linux Installation

1. ☑ **A and D.** You should determine why the new systems are needed and who will be using them.
   ☒ **B and C** are incorrect. Software and hardware are irrelevant at this stage of the assessment.

2. ☑ **D.** This response clearly states the goal of the project and it is measurable.
   ☒ **A, B,** and **C** are incorrect. These responses don't clearly define the goal of the project nor are they measurable.

3. ☑ **A and B.** Karen's boss and her co-workers are key stakeholders in the project.
   ☒ **C** and **D** are incorrect. These individuals are not stakeholders in the project.

4. ☑ **C and D.** The project scope is composed of schedule, scale, and resources.
   ☒ **A and B** are incorrect. Customer demands and management decisions can influence the project scope, but they shouldn't dictate the scope.

5. ☑ **B.** The best response to this situation is to have a frank discussion with the stakeholder and point out the consequences of the decision. Either the scale will have to be reduced or more resources must be added to the project to complete it in the same timeframe.
   ☒ **A, C,** and **D** are incorrect. Rather than confront the issue, these responses skirt about the problem. Ignoring the request will make the stakeholder unhappy. Agreeing to the request and then failing to come through will likewise make the stakeholder unhappy and will reflect poorly on you. Resigning doesn't help anyone involved.

6. ☑ **D and F.** Technically, any Linux distribution could be used in this role. However, options D and F are specifically optimized for these kinds of tasks.
   ☒ **A, B, C,** and **E** are incorrect. **A, B,** and **E** are wrong because these distributions are designed specifically for providing network services. **C** is incorrect because Red Hat Desktop is optimized for basic workstation tasks such as word processing.

7. ☑ **C.** Red Hat Desktop is optimized for basic workstation tasks such as word processing.
   ☒ **A, B, D, E,** and **F** are incorrect. **A, B,** and **E** are wrong because these distributions are designed specifically for providing network services. **D** and **F** could conceivably be used for this task. However, they are designed for high-end computing tasks commonly associated with engineering, software design, and graphics work.

8. ☑ **B and E.** These distributions are designed for high-demand network servers.
   ☒ **A, C, D,** and **F** are incorrect. **A** is designed for moderate-demand servers. **C, D,** and **F** are designed for workstation use.

9. ☑ **C.** The best approach is to use supported hardware.
    ☒ **A, B,** and **D** are incorrect. **A** is incorrect because hoping for the best is a sure recipe for disaster. **B** and **D** could potentially work; however, it may be some time before a driver is available for the unsupported hardware.

10. ☑ **D.** The Pentium IV Celeron CPU uses the Intel x86 architecture.
    ☒ **A, B, C,** and **E** are incorrect. **A** is used by Itanium CPUs. **B** is a distracter. **C** is incorrect because the Celeron CPU uses a 32-bit architecture. **E** is used by Apple systems.

11. ☑ **C.** The 64-bit AMD CPU uses a 64-bit x86 architecture.
    ☒ **A, B, D,** and **E** are incorrect. **A** is used by Itanium CPUs. **B** is a distracter. **D** is incorrect because the CPU in question uses a 64-bit architecture. **E** is used by Apple systems.

12. ☑ **C.** The Reiser file system is the fastest and it uses journaling to speed crash recovery.
    ☒ **A, B, D,** and **E** are incorrect. **A** and **B** are older FAT file systems used in older versions of Windows. **D** could conceivably work in the scenario listed in the question and could be considered a correct answer. However, Reiser is usually faster than ext3 in most situations. **E** is incorrect because ext 2 takes a long time to check the file system after a crash.

13. ☑ **B.** Linux systems use a dedicated swap partition for virtual memory.
    ☒ **A, C, D,** and **E** are incorrect. **A** and **C** are a distracters. **D** and **E** are system directories.

14. ☑ **D.** The swap partition should be at least twice the size of the installed RAM.
    ☒ **A, B,** and **C** are incorrect because the swap partition would be too small for a system with this much RAM.

15. ☑ **B, D,** and **E.** You should consider creating separate partitions for /boot, /usr, and /home.
    ☒ **A, C, F,** and **G** are incorrect. While you can create separate partitions for these directories, this won't influence the stability of the system.

16. ☑ **A, C,** and **D.** Port 110 is used by the POP3 e-mail protocol. Port 25 is used by the SMTP e-mail protocol. Port 143 is used by the IMAP e-mail protocol.
    ☒ **B** and **E** are incorrect. Web servers use these ports.

Install Linux

17. ☑ **D.** The most likely cause of this problem is that the system is set to boot off the hard drive first. When it can't find the operating system on the hard drive, the error message is displayed.
    ☒ **A, B,** and **C** are most likely incorrect. While these options are remotely possible, the most likely cause is simply a misconfigured boot order in the BIOS.

18. ☑ **C.** /dev/sdb points to the second SCSI drive installed in a system.
    ☒ **A, B,** and **D** are incorrect. These options point to the first, third, and fourth SCSI drives in the system.

19. ☑ **A.** /dev/hda1 points to the first partition on the first IDE hard drive in the system.
☒ **B, C,** and **D** are incorrect. **B** points to the first partition on the second IDE drive. **C** points to the second partition on the first IDE drive. **D** points to the second partition on the second IDE drive.

20. ☑ **C.** /dev/hda2 points to the second partition on the first IDE hard drive in the system.
☒ **A, B,** and **D** are incorrect. **A** points to the first partition on the first IDE drive. **B** points to the first partition on the second IDE drive. **D** points to the second partition on the second IDE drive.

21. ☑ **C.** /dev/sdb1 points to the first partition on the second SCSI drive in the system.
☒ **A, B,** and **D** are incorrect. **A** points to the first partition on the first SCSI drive. **B** points to the first partition on the third SCSI drive. **D** points to the first partition on the fourth SCSI drive.

LAB ANSWER

To address Mike's request, you should follow the process outlined in this chapter. Do the following to create your deployment plan:

- **Complete a needs assessment.** Spend some time discussing the request with Mike. Isolate the problem Mike is trying to solve with the upgrade. Does Mike really need the new system, or does he just want new hardware? How will the new equipment enhance the productivity of Mike's team? How soon are the new systems needed? You should also spend some time interviewing Mike's co-workers gathering the same information from them.

  You need to then identify other stakeholders affected by the request and get their buy-in as well. You should discuss the proposal with Mike's supervisor and make sure funding is available for the project. You should also meet with your own supervisor and make sure he will allocate your time to the project. You should identify members of management who must approve the project and get their approval as well.

  With this information in hand, you should document the project scope in your deployment plan. Identify the schedule, resources, and scale of the project. Get all the stakeholders to agree on the scope before proceeding.

- **Select a distribution.** Use the information from the needs assessment to determine which distribution you will use. Record this decision and the rationale behind it in your deployment plan. Because Mike needs high-end workstations for his team, you may want to consider distributions such as Red Hat Enterprise Linux WS or SUSE Linux Enterprise Desktop. Because the systems will be used by the engineers to complete tasks that are critical to the mission of your company, you should plan to purchase an appropriate level of support with the distribution you choose.

Because Mike wants to use 64-bit hardware, you need to make sure a 64-bit version of the distribution you choose is available. You should also check the distribution's hardware compatibility list and system requirements to obtain the specifications needed for the new hardware you'll purchase.

You should also check the software Mike's team uses to do their work and make sure it is compatible with the distribution you want to use.

- **Plan the file system.** The next part of your deployment plan should specify the file system type and partitions you will use on the systems' hard drives. Given the requirements, you will probably want to use the ext3 or Reiser file systems. You should be sure to create separate partitions for the directories discussed in this chapter. Remember that the swap partition should be twice the size of the system RAM. Many administrators forget to account for the size of the swap partition when planning the file system.

- **Specify your software.** The next part of your plan should specify the software packages that will need to be installed. Use your interviews with Mike and his co-workers to identify exactly which packages must be installed.

- **Define user accounts.** Next, identify who will need user accounts on each machine. Will Mike's team need access to each other's systems, or will each system only provide access to its owner?

- **Gather networking information.** Your deployment plan should also specify how the network boards in Mike's new systems would be configured. Because these systems are desktop workstations, you should probably use your organization's DHCP server to dynamically assign IP address information each time the system boots. You also need to define hostnames for each system in your plan along with your organization's domain name. You should also specify how the host firewall on each system will be configured. Because these are workstation systems, you will probably define few, if any, exceptions in the firewall rules.

- **Define an installation source.** The easiest way to install these systems will be to download a DVD ISO image from your chosen distribution's Web site and burn it to disc.

With this information in hand, you're ready to start the project. You can then order the new hardware and download the distribution. Set your new systems up in a lab and install the operating system and software. Verify that they are working correctly before transferring them to Mike's team.

Finally, file your deployment plan for future reference. You never know when that information will be needed again.

4

Getting Help

One of the great things about Linux is that documentation and help information are abundantly available for your use. Pick any Linux operating system task or utility and you can probably find documentation that will teach you how to accomplish what you need to do. In this chapter, we're going to teach you how to use four excellent resources for getting help when using Linux.

However, before doing so, there are a few key things about Linux documentation materials that you need to understand. First of all, the vendor who provided your Linux distribution probably provides some kind of general system documentation for you to use. However, this system documentation is probably quite minimal. (For some distributions, it may be non-existent.)

This is because each service or application you install on a Linux distribution (hopefully) includes documentation for that particular service. If you think about all the different packages that are available for Linux, you can see that it would be an extremely daunting task for a Linux vendor to try to develop their own documentation describing how to use all of these packages. Instead, they rely on others in the open source community to document all of the various applications and services that can be used on Linux.

This brings us to the second point you need to keep in mind when working with Linux documentation: The programmer who wrote a particular service or utility is probably the person who wrote the associated documentation. Very little Linux software documentation is actually written by professional technical writers. This means there are wide variations in the quality of the documentation from one piece of software to another. Some programmers are actually quite good at writing documentation. They write well and they understand how to structure information from easy concepts to more difficult ones.

Unfortunately, other programmers aren't very good at writing documentation. In fact, they can be absolutely terrible at documenting their software. The key mistake they make is that they assume the reader has the same knowledge level as they do. (This presents a contradiction of sorts. If the reader has the same knowledge level as the author, then he or she doesn't need the documentation.) When you encounter this kind of documentation, you'll quickly notice that the instructions are incomplete and generally unhelpful.

on the **Ū** o b *If you encounter this situation and have some extra time to spare, most programmers would love to have someone volunteer to help write documentation for their products. As we'll see later in this chapter, most Linux help sources include a contact e-mail address that you can use to contact the author.*

The third point you need to keep in mind is that most Linux documentation sources are not print-based. Back in the early days of Linux, many distributions did include a thick printed manual. The first Linux distribution I installed back in 1995, Caldera's OpenLinux version 1.0, included a manual such as this. Today, however, printed manuals are a rarity. As you can imagine, printing manuals of this size is very expensive and it isn't the best thing for the environment. Therefore, nearly all documentation sources for your Linux distribution are made available in an electronic format.

on the job *Some people I've worked with over the years get nervous when a printed manual isn't available. However, I happen to think it's a good thing. Not only does the electronic approach save trees, it also increases the searchability of the information. I love being able to pull up exactly what I need when I need it. I hate thumbing through page after page of documentation trying to find the information.*

In fact, other operating system vendors are following suit. Microsoft Windows used to include a thick printed manual when you purchased a box copy. Over the years, the thickness of the manual got thinner and thinner. Today, most of the Windows documentation is available online in the Help and Support utility. Novell has done the same thing with their NetWare operating system.

INSIDE THE EXAM

Getting Help in Linux

Knowing how to get help when working with Linux is a critical part of a Linux administrator's job role. When a problem happens, you need to be able to find an answer fast.

Therefore, on the Linux+ exam, you need to be able to demonstrate that you know how to use the various tools available for finding help. You need to be very familiar with the following resources:

- man
- info

- README files
- Web-based resources

When using man and info, you need to know how to launch the utility, navigate through the information displayed, and exit. When using README files, you need to know where the files are located and how to view them on screen. You also need to be familiar with the more popular Web-based information resources such as The Linux Documentation Project.

In this chapter, we'll introduce you to the various sources for getting help when working with Linux. The following topics will be covered:

- Using man pages
- Using info
- Using other documentation and troubleshooting resources

Let's begin by discussing how to use man to get help with your Linux system.

CERTIFICATION OBJECTIVE 4.01

Use man Pages

One of the primary means used by the Linux operating system to maintain system documentation is through the use of manual (man) pages. These manual pages contain documentation about the operating system itself as well as any applications installed on the system. These man pages are viewed using a utility called *man*.

The man utility was original developed and used by the UNIX operating system. It has been ported to Linux and provides the same functionality as on a UNIX system. It can be used to display a manual page for a particular Linux command, utility, or file.

The man utility is an extremely useful tool when managing a Linux system. Let's face it, there are a lot of commands and utilities even on a basic Linux system. Some of the commands and utilities are used frequently; others are used very rarely. It's very difficult for the average Linux administrator to remember the syntax and options used by every possible command and utility, especially for those you don't use frequently.

The man utility is a real lifesaver. If you ever find yourself at a loss when working with a particular command or utility, you can use man to display the corresponding man page and remind yourself of how it's used. We love man!

In addition to system commands and utilities, man pages are also maintained for most of the packages on your system. Whenever you install a package on Linux, the man pages containing the documentation for the software are installed. This allows you to use man to view documentation for these packages as well.

In this part of this chapter, we'll review the following man topics:

- The man directory structure
- Manual sections
- Using man to view documentation

The man Directory Structure

The actual pages displayed by man are maintained in several directories beneath the directory specified in the MANPATH environment variable. On a SUSE Linux 10.1 system, the MANPATH variable is set to the /usr/local/man, /usr/share/man, /usr/X11R6/man, and /opt/gnome/share/man directories.

You can check the value of the MANPATH variable on your system by entering **env | more** at a shell prompt. When you do, a list of environment variables is displayed. Look for a variable named MANPATH, as shown in Figure 4-1.

| **FIGURE 4-1** | Viewing the MANPATH environment variable |

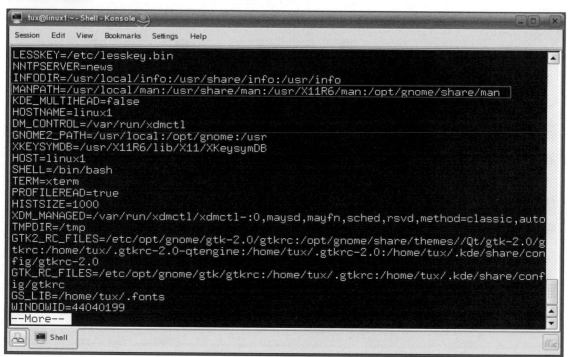

In Figure 4-1, the MANPATH variable lists the four directories mentioned above, each separated by a colon.

Before going much further, it's important to note that the man utility can be implemented in different ways on different Linux distributions. For example, the Fedora distribution doesn't use the MANPATH environment variable, by default. Instead, it uses the MANPATH directive in the /etc/man.config file to specify the directories where man pages are stored.

Beneath the directories specified in the MANPATH variable or in the MANPATH directive in the man.config file are a series of directories denoted by man1, man2, man 3, etc., as shown in Figure 4-2.

FIGURE 4-2   Viewing man directories

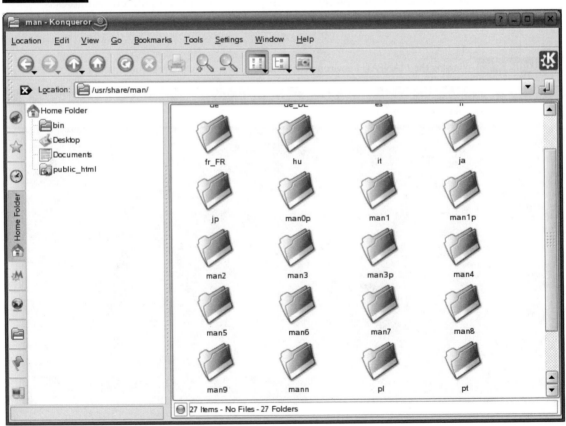

on the **Job**   *Some of the directories shown in Figure 4-2 aren't used for manual sections. Directories such as hu, it, and jp are used for man pages that have been localized into a language other than English.*

Manual Sections

All of the man pages contained in the man directories together comprise the *manual*. Each of the directories shown in Figure 4-2 represents a *section* of the manual. The standards used by man page authors divide the manual into the sections shown in Table 4-1.

Manual pages are categorized and stored in the appropriate directory, depending upon the type of software they are associated with. Many of the man pages you will use in this course will be stored in Section 1: Shell Commands and Section 8: Administrative Utilities.

Using man to View Documentation

Using man to look up information is really easy. All you have to do is enter **man** followed by the name of the utility you need information about. For example, the ls command is a very useful shell command that you can use to display a list of files in a directory, as shown in Figure 4-3.

TABLE 4-1	Sections used in man pages

Section	Content
1	Programs and shell commands that can be used by any user
2	System functions provided by the Linux kernel
3	Library functions
4	Special files found in /dev
5	File format descriptions and conventions
6	Games
7	Miscellaneous conventions
8	Administrative utilities used by the root user
9	Kernel routine documentation

FIGURE 4-3 Viewing files with the ls utility

In Figure 4-3, the contents of the /home/tux directory have been displayed using the ls command. In a Linux system, the ~ character represents the current user's home directory The **tux@linux1** text in the shell prompt tells you who is currently logged in to the shell. As you can see, the /home/tux directory contains four directories:

- bin
- Desktop
- Documents
- public_html

Don't worry about what these directories are used for right now. We'll cover the Linux file system in a later chapter. For now, just understand that you can use ls to view the contents of a directory. Notice in Figure 4-3 that we simply entered the command **ls**. The ls command is actually quite powerful. It can be used with a variety of options that customize how it works and how the data it returns is displayed. How do you know what these options are and how to use them? You use the man utility to display the manual page for the ls command. To do this, simply enter **man ls** at a shell prompt. When you do, the screen shown in Figure 4-4 is displayed.

SCENARIO & SOLUTION

You're managing a Linux system and need to use the useradd utility to add a new user. You can't remember the syntax for using this utility. What command can you use to do this?	You can use man to display the manual page for useradd. Simply enter **man useradd** at the shell prompt.

FIGURE 4-4   Viewing the man page for the ls utility

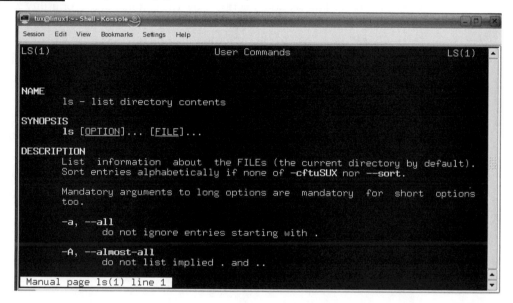

A given man page consists of several elements, as shown in Figure 4-4. Some man pages will include many sections; others will only include a few. Most man pages will include the following:

- **Title**   The title section is the first line of the man page. It lists the name of the utility, command, or file discussed in the man page followed by the section number. In Figure 4-4, notice that the first line reads LS(1). This indicates the man page describes the ls utility and is located in Section 1 of the manual. Remember from Table 4-1 that Section 1 of the manual contains manual pages for commands and utilities that all users on the Linux system can use.

- **NAME**   The NAME section simply displays the name of the command, file, or utility and a short abstract about what it does. In Figure 4-4, the NAME section indicates that the ls utility is used to list directory contents.

- **SYNOPSIS**   The SYNOPSIS section provides a brief description of the syntax for using a particular command or utility. If the manual page documents a configuration file, such as smb.conf, the SYNOPSIS section provides a brief overview of what the file is used for. In Figure 4-4, the SYNOPSIS section of the man page for the ls utility displays the syntax for using the command from the shell prompt. It tells you that you can enter **ls** followed by a list of possible options and file names.

- **DESCRIPTION** The DESCRIPTION section provides the meat of the manual page. This section describes how the command, file, or utility works in detail. It also provides a list of options that can be used. For example, in Figure 4-4, the man page specifies that you can use the –a or -all option with the ls utility to display hidden directories and files in the file system. (The names of hidden directories and files begin with a period). Using this option with ls is shown in Figure 4-5.

    Notice that the output from ls is considerably longer in Figure 4-5 than in Figure 4-4. That's because the –a option causes hidden directories and files to be displayed along with normal files and directories. Without a man page, you probably would have never known that you could use the –a option with ls!

- **AUTHOR** The AUTHOR section displays the name of the programmer who wrote the command, utility, or service referenced in the man page. This is shown for the ls utility in Figure 4-6.

- **REPORTING BUGS** The REPORTING BUGS section provides an e-mail address you can use to any report bugs you discover in the utility or the documentation, as shown in Figure 4-6.

FIGURE 4-5   Using the –a option with the ls utility

FIGURE 4-6	Viewing additional man page sections for the ls utility

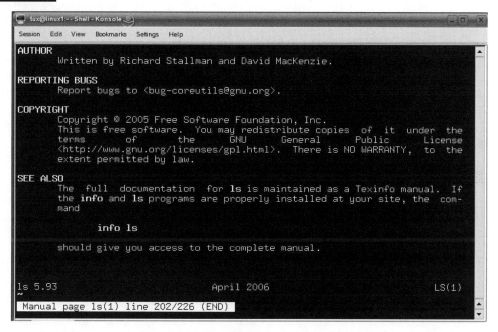

- **COPYRIGHT** The COPYRIGHT section provides you with details about who owns the copyright to the command, utility, or service referenced in the man page. It also provides you with redistribution information, as shown in Figure 4-6.

- **SEE ALSO** The SEE ALSO section provides you with a list of man pages or other resources that are related to the current man page. For example, in Figure 4-6, the SEE ALSO section directs the user to use the **info ls** command to view the complete manual for the ls command.

- **Version Number and Revision Date** As you can see in Figure 4-6, the very last line of the man page displays the version number of the program and the revision date.

on the Job *All sections other than NAME are optional. Authors are free to add new sections not shown the list above if their particular program requires them. You may see man pages for other utilities or services that contain sections such as OPTIONS, FILES, ENVIRONMENT, or DIAGNOSTICS.*

As you use man to display a manual page, a status indicator is shown at the very bottom of the display. This status indicator tells you what manual page is being displayed, the current line displayed, and how far into the document you are. This status indicator is shown in Figure 4-7.

In Figure 4-7, the status indicator shows that the ls(1) manual page is displayed. It also indicates that line 29 is the top line currently displayed and that the current text displayed resides about 20 percent of the way through the entire document.

on the **Job**

The version of man included with Fedora doesn't include a status display.

With a man page displayed, you can use the following keystrokes to navigate around within the page:

DOWN ARROW	Scrolls down one line in the page.
UP ARROW	Scrolls up one line in the page.
PAGE DOWN	Scrolls down 14 lines in the page.
PAGE UP	Scrolls up 14 lines in the page.
SPACEBAR	Scrolls down 26 lines in the page.
HOME	Moves you to the beginning of the page.
END	Moves you to the end of the page.
Q	Unloads the current man page and exits the man utility.

Let's next discuss how you can search for information in a man page.

Searching Within a man Page

Some man pages are short and concise; others are quite long and extensive. When working with a man page, it's very likely that you will need to search for a specific term within the page itself.

For example, if you're using the ls command, you may need to view extended information about files and directories in your file system. Notice in Figure 4-3

FIGURE 4-7   Viewing the man status indicator

```
Manual page ls(1) line 29/226 20%
```

that ls, by default, only displays the names of the files or directories within the current directory. What if you need to view extended information, such as permissions, ownership, file size, or modification dates? This is called the long listing format. Which ls option can format the output in this manner?

You can search for specific information within a man page by entering a forward-slash (/) followed by the search term you want to search for. For example, to find out how to obtain a long listing format from ls, load the man page for ls by entering **man ls**. Then, enter **/long** to search for the text string "long" in the man page. This is shown in Figure 4-8.

When you press ENTER, the first instance of "long" is located in the man page, as shown in Figure 4-9.

Obviously, this instance of "long" isn't the one we wanted. To find the next instance, simply press N. After pressing N several times, the instance we wanted to find is located, as shown in Figure 4-10.

As you can see in Figure 4-10, using the –l option with the ls utility will display its output in long format, which shows permissions, ownership, size, and modification dates for files and directories. This is shown in Figure 4-11.

| **FIGURE 4-8** | Searching for the text string "long" in a man page |

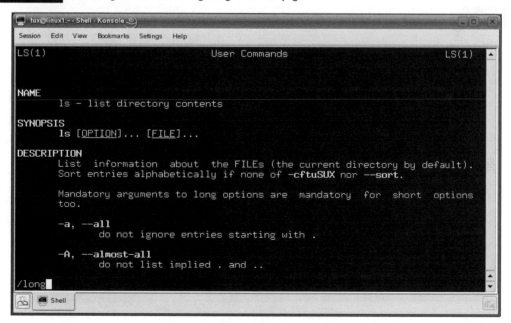

FIGURE 4-9   Locating the text string "long" in a man page

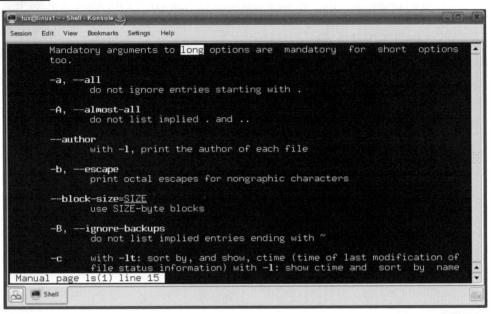

FIGURE 4-10   Finding the right instance of "long" in a man page

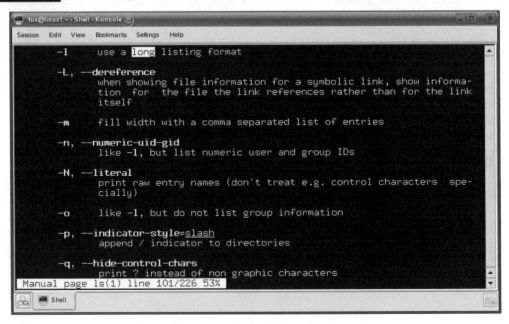

FIGURE 4-11   Using the ls utility to display long format listings

```
tux@linux1:~ - Shell - Konsole
Session  Edit  View  Bookmarks  Settings  Help

tux@linux1:~> ls -l
total 0
drwxr-xr-x 2 tux users   48 2006-10-10 14:47 bin
drwx------ 2 tux users  320 2006-10-10 14:52 Desktop
drwx------ 2 tux users   80 2006-10-10 14:47 Documents
drwxr-xr-x 2 tux users   80 2006-10-10 14:47 public_html
tux@linux1:~>

        Shell
```

In addition to searching within a man page, you can also search across man pages. Let's discuss how this is done next.

Searching Across man Pages

Many times, you will need to search for information in a man page for a utility, but you can't quite remember exactly how the command is spelled. Remember that man requires you to know the name of the command, utility, or file to view its associated manual page. If, for some reason, you can't remember, you can use two different tools to search across man pages:

■ **man –k**   Using the –k option with man allows you to search across all manual page names and descriptions to find a specific keyword. For example, suppose you wanted to remove a directory from your file system, but you can't remember which utility is used to do it. You can enter **man –k remove** at the shell prompt to view a list of man pages that include the term "remove." When you do, the screen in Figure 4-12 is displayed.

SCENARIO & SOLUTION

You need to use useradd to add a new user to your Linux system. You want to create a home directory for the user when you create the account. You've opened the man page for useradd. What can you type to search for home directory information in the man page?	You can type **/home** and press ENTER. This will help you find all instances of "home" in the man page. You can press N until you arrive at the instance you need.

FIGURE 4-12   Using man –k to search for text in man pages

In Figure 4-12, you can see that the rmdir command can be used to remove a directory. Now that you know the name of the command, you can enter **man rmdir** to learn how to use it.

■ **apropos**   The apropos utility does basically the same thing as the man –k command. You can use this utility to search across man page names and descriptions to search for a text string. For example, to search for man pages that have the string "remove" in their text, you would enter **apropos remove**.

With this in mind, let's practice using man in the following exercise.

SCENARIO & SOLUTION

You need to change the password for a user on your Linux system. You know there is a utility that will do this, but you can't remember what it's called. What command can you enter from a shell prompt to search for man pages that talk about changing passwords?	You can enter one of two commands: • man –k password • apropos password Either of these commands will search man page names and descriptions to find all references to "password."

EXERCISE 4-1

Using man Pages

In this exercise, you will practice using the man utility to view manual pages for Linux utilities. Complete the following:

1. Boot your Linux system and log in.
2. Start a terminal session. If you're using SUSE Linux, you can do this by selecting the Terminal icon in the kicker panel, shown in the next illustration.

   If you're using Fedora, you can select Applications | Accessories | Terminal.
3. At the shell prompt, enter **man cp**.
4. Answer the following questions:
   - What does the cp utility do?
   - What does the –r option do when used with cp?
   - Who wrote the cp utility?
   - To what e-mail address can you send any bugs you discover?
   - In what man section does the cp page reside?
   - If you wanted the cp utility to prompt you before overwriting an existing file, what option would you use?
5. Close man by pressing Q.

CERTIFICATION OBJECTIVE 4.02

Use info

In addition to man, you can also use the info utility to view documentation for commands, utilities, services, and files on your Linux system. You might be asking, "Why do I need info if I've already got man?" The two utilities do serve a similar purpose; however, they do it in a different way.

The man utility is a "down-and-dirty" reference utility. Man pages are packed with information, but they aren't really instructional in nature. Essentially, man says, "Here's the utility and its syntax. You go figure out how to use it."

The info utility, on the other hand, is more of a learning utility. Most info nodes contain the same information as a man page. However, info nodes are usually more verbose and can actually teach you how to use a particular Linux tool.

on the

Job *Instead of calling them pages, we refer to units of information displayed by the info utility as nodes. You'll see why they are called nodes later in this chapter.*

Let's discuss how to use info to view system documentation.

Using info to View System Documentation

Launching info is done in much the same manner as man. You simply enter **info** followed by the name of the command, utility, service, or file you need to learn about. For example, earlier in this chapter, you used man to view information about the ls utility. To use info to learn about the ls utility, you simply enter **info ls**. When you do, the image in Figure 4-13 is displayed:

FIGURE 4-13 Using info to view information about the ls utility

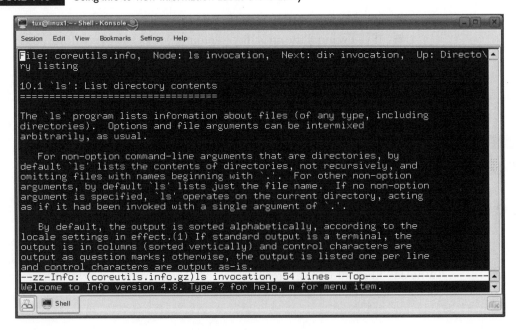

Right away, you'll notice several differences between man and info. The information available in the ls man page is fairly minimal. Conversely, the information available in info is much more verbose. The info node explains what the ls utility does and what you can expect when you use it.

Notice in Figure 4-13 that the top line of the info display shows information about the page currently displayed. The file that contains the information is named coreutils.info. Within the coreutils.info file, the *ls invocation* node is currently being displayed. The next node in the file is named *dir invocation*.

To navigate within the info interface, you can use the following keystrokes:

DOWN ARROW	Scrolls down one line at a time.
UP ARROW	Scrolls up one line at a time.
PAGE DOWN	Scrolls down one page at a time.
PAGE UP	Scrolls up one page at a time.
SPACEBAR	Scrolls down one page at a time.
DEL or BACKSPACE	Scrolls up one page at a time.
HOME	Moves you to the beginning of the node.
END	Moves you to the end of the node.
N	Takes you to the next node.
P	Takes you to the previous node.
Q	Unloads the current man page and exits the man utility.

One of the key differences between info and man is the fact that info divides the information up into nodes where man displays all information related to the particular utility or command in a single page. If you scroll down in the ls info node, you'll see a menu containing links to other related nodes. This is shown in Figure 4-14.

To jump to one of these nodes, arrow down to the desired menu item and then press ENTER. For example, if you wanted to learn how to sort output from the ls command, you would arrow down to the Sorting the Output menu item shown in Figure 4-14 and then press ENTER. When you do, a new node is opened, as shown in Figure 4-15.

To return back to the original node, just press L.

Let's next discuss how to search within an info node.

SCENARIO & SOLUTION	
You've viewed the man page for rmdir. However, it didn't provide enough information for you to use it correctly. You need more information. What command can you use from the shell prompt to do this?	You can enter **info rmdir** to view detailed information about how to use the rmdir utility.

Searching for Information in info

Just as you can search for information using the man utility, you can also search for information using info. If you want to search for information within the node displayed, press CTRL-S. When you do, the I-search prompt is displayed, as shown in Figure 4-16.

At the I-search prompt, enter the ***text*** you want to search for and press ENTER. The first instance of the text you entered after your current cursor location is displayed, as shown in Figure 4-17.

Pressing CTRL-S again will jump to the next instance of the string you entered.

Let's practice using info in the following exercise.

FIGURE 4-14   Using info menus

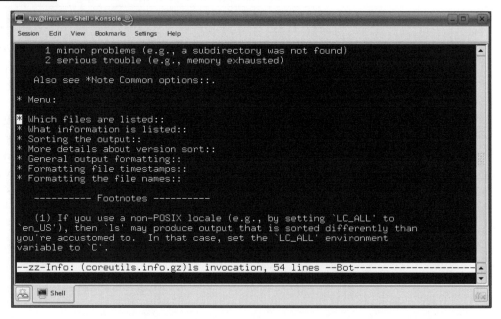

FIGURE 4-15   Viewing a new node in info

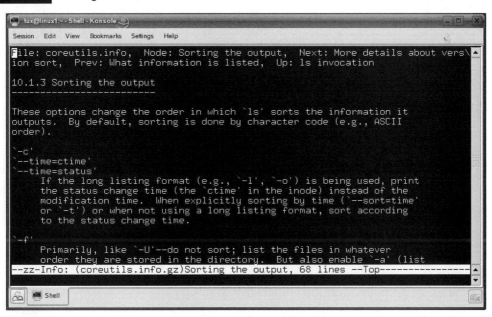

FIGURE 4-16   Searching for information in an info node

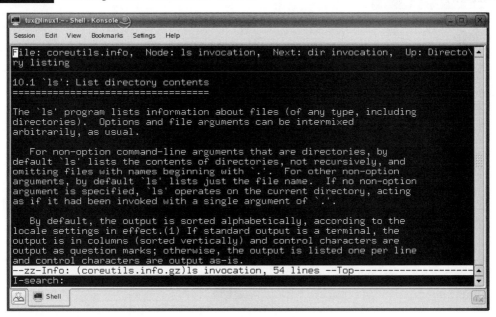

FIGURE 4-17 Viewing search results in info

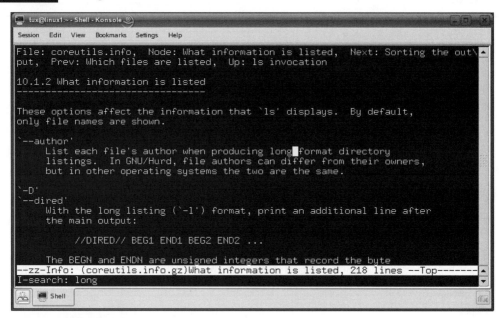

EXERCISE 4-2

Using info

In this exercise, you will practice using the info utility to view documentation for your Linux system. Complete the following:

1. If not already done, boot your Linux system and log in.
2. Start a terminal session.
3. At the shell prompt, enter **info rm**.
4. Answer the following questions:
   - What does the rm utility do?
   - What does the –v option do when used with rm?
   - In which node does the rm documentation reside?
   - What node comes before the current node?
   - What node comes after the current node?

- If you wanted the rm utility to prompt you before deleting each file, which option would you use?
- If you wanted to be sure a deleted file could not be recovered, would rm be the right utility to use?

5. Close info by pressing Q.

In addition to man pages and info nodes, you can also view information about the software installed on your system using other resources. Let's discuss these next.

CERTIFICATION OBJECTIVE 4.03

Use Other Documentation and Troubleshooting Resources

As you work in the industry, you'll probably notice that most Linux administrators use man and info as their primary documentation resource. However, you should be aware that there are many other sources of information available to you in addition to man and info. In this section, we're going to explore these other resources. We'll cover:

- Using README files
- Using Web-based resources

Let's begin by discussing the README file.

Using README Files

Whenever you install a software package on your Linux system, including those installed during the system installation process, a README file is usually copied to your file system. README files are one of the most valuable yet underutilized information resources on your Linux system. They usually contain fantastic information, but very few users or system administrators actually read them. You should break this pattern and become familiar with the README files on your system.

Let's begin this section of this chapter by discussing information that README files usually contain.

What's in a README File?

Unlike man pages or info nodes, the structure of a README file is somewhat less rigid in the industry. Essentially, the README file is a catchall for important information about its associated software package. A sample README file is shown in Figure 4-18.

Information contained in a typical README file could include the following:

- **Program Version Number**   This is the version number of the package installed on your system.

- **Program Description**   This part of the README file provides an overview of the package.

- **Changes**   Many README files will provide a list of changes in the current version of the software.

- **Installation and Configuration Information**   Some README files provide instructions to help you install and configure the package.

FIGURE 4-18   A sample README file

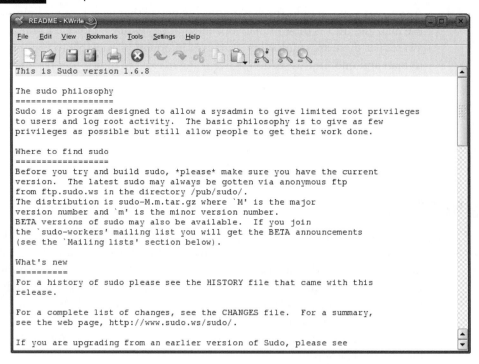

- **Known Issues**   One of the most valuable components included in many README files is a list of known issues. I can't tell you how many times I've tried to troubleshoot a problem with a particular piece of software only to find out that the issue was already listed in the README file. Frequently, the README file will even include instructions on how to address the issue.

- **Bug Reporting**   Most README files will include contact information that you can use to report any bugs you discover while using the software.

- **Copyright Information**   Nearly all README files include copyright information about the software package.

After installing a software package, one of the first things you should do is read the README file. You'll be amazed at the wealth of information these files contain.

With this information in mind, let's next discuss where these README files are located on your Linux system.

Locating README Files

One of the reasons most users and system administrators fail to read the README files associated with their software is the fact that they can be somewhat difficult to find. Some packages will display their README files during the installation process; others won't. The funny thing is, even if the README file is displayed during installation, most users still don't read them! This is a mistake. I promise that you will save yourself hours of troubleshooting time if you will take five minutes and read the README.

If the README file isn't displayed during the installation process, then you will need to locate it manually to read it. Most README files are stored in /usr/share/doc/packages, as shown in Figure 4-19.

Notice that within /usr/share/doc/packages, each package has its own directory created. The README file for the package is stored in this directory.

Some software packages include other documentation resources in this directory along with the README file. Again, the information in this directory is a treasure trove of information that is usually overlooked.

Also, be aware that the package directories that contain the README files on a Fedora system are located in /usr/share/doc instead of /usr/share/doc/packages.

FIGURE 4-19	README files stored in /usr/share/doc/packages

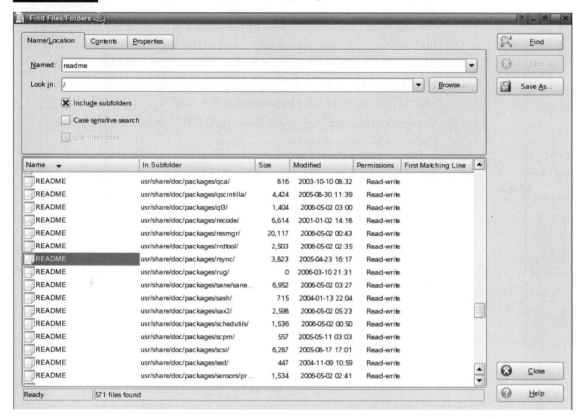

By convention, README files are always text files that can be read with a variety of text editors such as vi, gedit, or Kwrite. We'll discuss how to use text editors in more detail in the next chapter. You can also use the cat utility to simply display the contents of the README file on screen. For example, if you wanted to view the README file for the zip software package, you could enter **cat /usr/share/doc/ packages/zip/README | more**. The README file would then be displayed on the screen a page at a time, as shown in Figure 4-20.

Using |more after the cat command causes the text to be displayed one page at a time. If you omit this, the text will scroll down the screen so fast that you won't be able to read it. We'll discuss the more and less options later in this book.

FIGURE 4-20   Using cat to view a README file

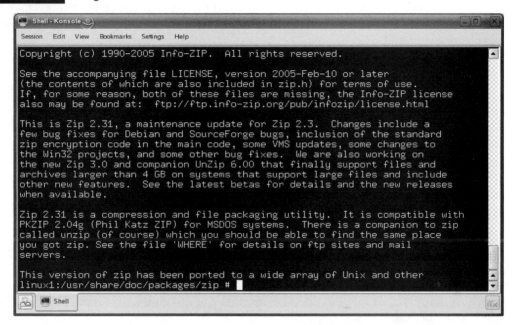

In addition to documentation and help files on your local system, you can also access a wealth of Linux information on the Internet. Let's discuss this next.

Using Web-Based Resources

When administering a Linux system, one of the best resources you have for viewing documentation and getting help is the Internet. There is a staggering amount of information available, most of it free, that will help you learn about Linux and troubleshoot problems you may encounter.

SCENARIO & SOLUTION

You've just installed the RealPlayer package on your SUSE Linux system and want to read its README file. In what directory in the file system would you find this file?	On a SUSE Linux system, README files are stored in /usr/share/doc/packages. To find the RealPlayer README file, you would navigate to the /user/share/doc/packages/RealPlayer directory.

The sheer volume of information available and the frequency with which it changes precludes an exhaustive listing in this part of the chapter. However, we do need to cover the following Web-based Linux resources in this part of this chapter:

- Using The Linux Documentation Project Web site
- Using Linux vendor Web sites
- Using search engines

Let's begin by discussing one of my favorite Internet resources: The Linux Documentation Project.

Using the Linux Documentation Project Web Site

The Linux Documentation Project (TLDP) is a fantastic resource for configuration and setup information for your Linux system. The TLDP Web site, shown in Figure 4-21, can be accessed at http://tldp.org.

FIGURE 4-21   The Linux Documentation Project Web site

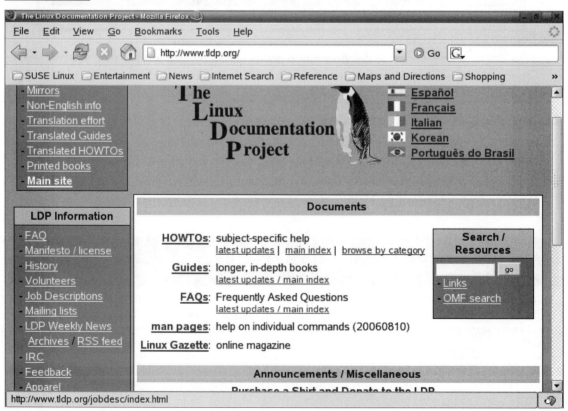

TLDP is a group of volunteers who contribute their time to write documentation for Linux. I, for one, sincerely appreciate their efforts! The TLDP Web site contains a wealth of information in the form of:

- **HOWTO documents** The TLDP Web site contains hundreds of HOWTO documents that describe how to set up or configure various aspects of a Linux system. A sample HOWTO that discusses how to configure the FTP service on a Linux system is shown in Figure 4-22.

   I can't tell you how many times I have found an answer to my deepest darkest Linux questions in a HOWTO on the TLDP Web site. I strongly recommend that you peruse the HOWTOs on this site to get a feel for what is available.

- **Linux Guides** The TLDP Web site even provides full-length online books that you can read. These guides cover topics from Linux basics to kernel programming. The best part is that they are free!

FIGURE 4-22 Using a HOWTO to set up an FTP server

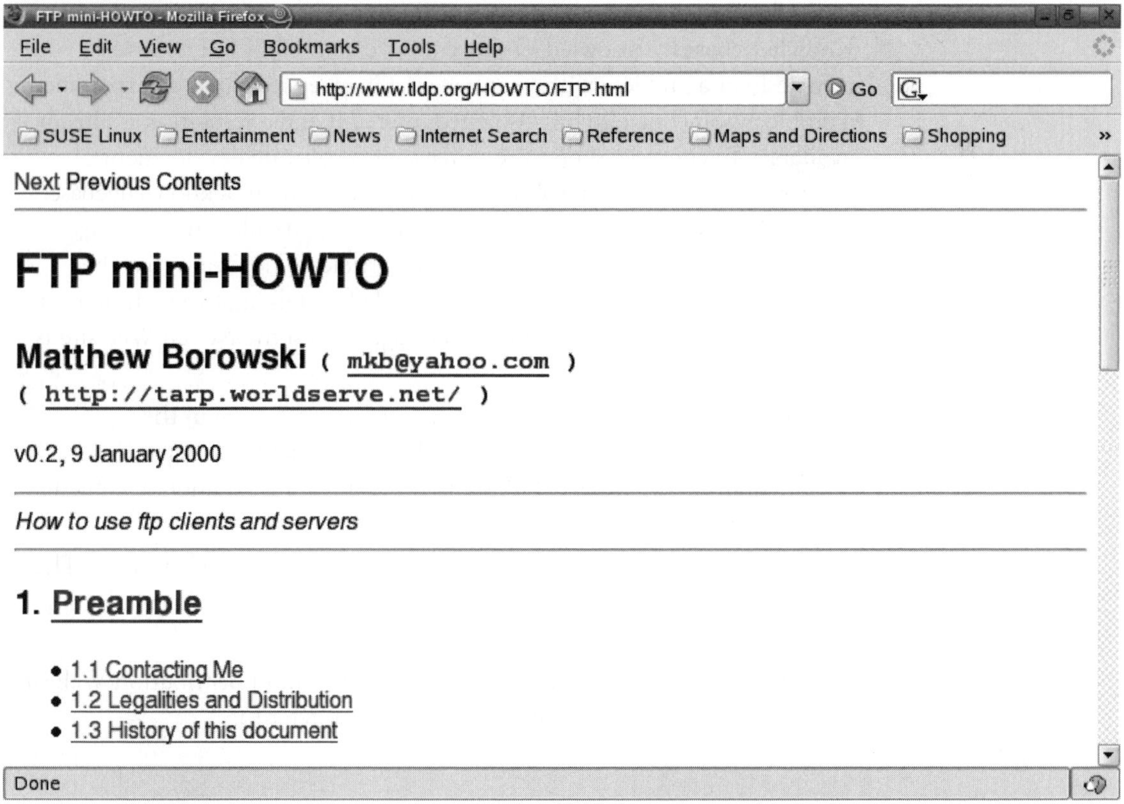

FTP mini-HOWTO - Mozilla Firefox

File   Edit   View   Go   Bookmarks   Tools   Help

http://www.tldp.org/HOWTO/FTP.html   Go

SUSE Linux   Entertainment   News   Internet Search   Reference   Maps and Directions   Shopping

Next Previous Contents

FTP mini-HOWTO

Matthew Borowski (mkb@yahoo.com)
(http://tarp.worldserve.net/)

v0.2, 9 January 2000

How to use ftp clients and servers

1. Preamble

- 1.1 Contacting Me
- 1.2 Legalities and Distribution
- 1.3 History of this document

Done

■ **FAQs** The TLDP Web site also provides a limited number of FAQs on a range of topics. These can be handy resources when you need to troubleshoot problems on your Linux systems.

■ **The Linux Gazette** The TLDP provides free access to an online Linux magazine called the Linux Gazette. New issues are posted in each month's issue that cover a variety of Linux topics and issues.

In addition to the TLDP Web site, you should also become very intimate with your Linux vendor's Web site. Let's discuss this next.

Using Linux Vendor Web Sites

The TLDP Web site is an excellent resource for learning how to configure your Linux system. However, it doesn't include much in the way of troubleshooting information. If you're working with a Linux system and encounter a problem, you'll need to use other Web-based resources to locate an answer. One of the best is your Linux vendor's Web site. Most Linux vendors provide a wealth of invaluable information on their Web sites that you can leverage, including:

■ **Knowledgebases** Knowledgebases can save your life if you need to troubleshoot a problem with your system. Chances are, if you're experiencing a problem, someone else has also encountered it and a resolution is already available. To conserve support resources, most software development organizations post these resolutions on their Web site in a knowledgebase. These knowledgebases allow you to search for a particular error message or symptom and display a list of matching articles. The idea is that they want you to check the knowledgebase first before talking to a tech support representative. The SUSE Linux knowledgebase on the Novell Web site is shown in Figure 4-23.

As you can see in Figure 4-23, you can enter a search term in the Search field. You can also specify that the search include articles, tips, documentation, the SUSE SDB, support technical information documents (TIDs), WIKIs, and blogs.

Unfortunately, not all distributions have an extensive knowledgebase. The availability of this type of information should actually play an important part in your choice of distributions.

■ **Documentation** In addition to knowledgebases, most distribution Web sites also include online documentation that you can refer to.

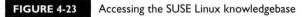

FIGURE 4-23   Accessing the SUSE Linux knowledgebase

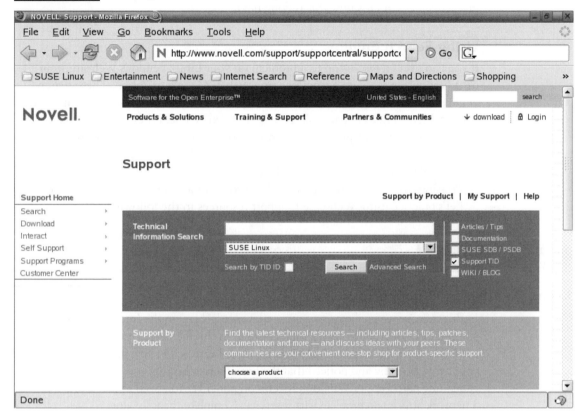

- **Support Forums**   Some distributions also include support forums that you can use to resolve problems. Some vendors actually monitor their support forums and assign a support technician to answer questions. Other vendors rely on forum participants to resolve each other's problems. Either way, these forums are a fantastic resource when you need to fix an error in a Linux system.

on the
job   *Forum participants expect you to do your homework before posting a question. Be sure you have already consulted readily available sources of information such as man pages and info nodes before you post a question on the forum. If you don't, other forum participants may give you an RTFM response!*

In addition to vendor Web sites, you can also use search engines to resolve problems. Let's discuss how this is done next.

Using Search Engines

If you can't find a resolution to a problem on your Linux vendor's Web site, your next best option is to use a search engine such as Google or Yahoo. These search engines can locate and link you to a variety of Web sites that contain a solution to your problem. They are particularly helpful if you've encountered a particular error message. You can copy and paste the text of the error message in the search field and then start the search. Again, chances are someone else has already experienced the same problem and has already posted a resolution.

Pressing CTRL-S again will jump to the next instance of the string you entered.

Let's practice using Web-based support resources in the following exercise.

EXERCISE 4-3

ON THE CD

Using Web-Based Support Resources

In this exercise, you will practice using a knowledgebase on the Internet to locate a resolution to a problem with a Linux system. In this scenario, you are a network administrator responsible for your organization's Linux server systems. You've monitored your network traffic and noticed that the Linux server hosting your Samba service is generating port scans of Windows systems on port 137. You need to determine if this is a network attack or a problem with a service. Complete the following:

1. If not already done, boot your Linux system and log in.
2. Start a Web browser such as Firefox or Konqueror.
3. Navigate to http://support.novell.com.
4. In the Choose a Product drop-down list, select SUSE Linux.
5. In the Search field, enter **port scan 137**.
6. Select Search.
7. Review the list of results. Do you see an article that describes your problem?

   You should see an article with a title of *10094458: Linux system doing port scans from port 137*, as shown in Figure 4-24.

8. Review the article. What's the resolution to the problem?

FIGURE 4-24   Knowledgebase search results

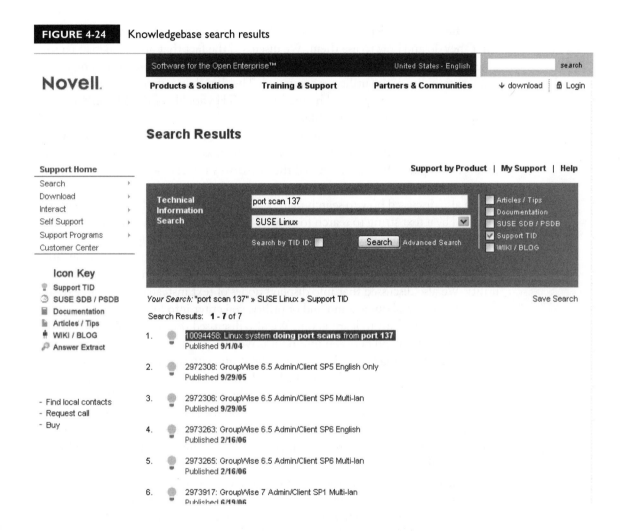

That's it for this chapter! You now know how to use a host of documentation and troubleshooting information for your Linux system. You know what they say: Knowledge is power!

CERTIFICATION SUMMARY

In this chapter, you learned about the various sources of information you can use to learn about your Linux system. We first reviewed how to use the man utility to view manual pages. We related that most commands and utilities on your Linux system have a man page associated with them that contains information about what they do and how to use them. We discussed the fact that all of the man pages together comprise the manual. The manual is divided into sections according to the functionality of the utility or command. The files that comprise the manual are stored in the directory specified by the MANPATH variable or the MANPATH directive in the /etc/man.config file.

To use man, you simply enter **man** and the name of the command, utility, file, or service that you need to learn more about. We reviewed the different sections used in most man pages. We also reviewed the keystrokes you can use to navigate within a man page.

We also discussed how to search man pages. We pointed out that you can enter / followed by a text string to search for a word within a single man page. You can also use man –k or the apropos utility to search for text across man pages.

After discussing the man utility, we then turned our attention to the info utility. We pointed out that info displays more extensive documentation than the man utility. We also discussed that info displays nodes of text instead of pages of text. To view information about a command or utility, you enter **info** followed by the name of the utility you want to learn about. We also discussed the keystrokes you can use to navigate within and between info nodes. We also pointed out that you can search info nodes for a string of text by pressing CTRL-S and entering a string of text.

After discussing info, we then looked at alternative sources of documentation and troubleshooting help. The first source we discussed is the README files included with most software packages installed on the system. We pointed out that these files are located in /usr/share/doc/packages or /usr/share/doc, depending on which distribution you're using. We discussed the contents typically included in a README file.

We then looked at a variety of Web-based resources on the Internet you can use to find information about your Linux system. We first pointed out that The Linux Documentation Project Web site provides extensive configuration information in the form of HOWTOs and guides. We also pointed out that you can use the documentation, knowledgebases, and FAQs on your Linux vendor's Web site to learn more about your system and troubleshoot specific problems. We ended the chapter discussing how you can use search engines such as Google or Yahoo to search for resolutions to errors you may encounter on your Linux system.

TWO-MINUTE DRILL

Use man Pages

- ❑ Manual (man) pages are one of the primary means for maintaining documentation on a Linux system.
- ❑ Manual pages are viewed using the man utility.
- ❑ Manual pages are maintained for most commands, utilities, services, and configuration files on your system.
- ❑ The location of the man pages in your file system is stored in the MANPATH environment variable or in the MANPATH directive in the /etc/man.config file.
- ❑ All of the man pages together comprise the manual.
- ❑ The manual is divided into the following sections:
  - ❑ Section 1: User programs and shell commands
  - ❑ Section 2: Kernel functions
  - ❑ Section 3: Library functions
  - ❑ Section 4: Special files found in /dev
  - ❑ Section 5: File format descriptions and conventions
  - ❑ Section 6: Games
  - ❑ Section 7: Miscellaneous conventions
  - ❑ Section 8: Utilities used by root
  - ❑ Section 9: Kernel routines
- ❑ Man pages are categorized into the various manual sections.
- ❑ To view a man page, enter **man** followed by the name of the utility or command that you need information about.
- ❑ Man pages are divided into sections.
- ❑ Some of the more commonly used man page sections include the following:
  - ❑ NAME
  - ❑ SYNOPSIS
  - ❑ DESCRIPTION
  - ❑ AUTHOR

- ❏ REPORTING BUGS
- ❏ COPYRIGHT
- ❏ SEE ALSO
- ❏ To search for text within a man page, you enter / followed by the text you want to search for.
- ❏ To search for text across man pages, you can use one of the following:
  - ❏ man –k
  - ❏ apropos

Use info

- ❏ In addition to man, you can also use the info utility to view system documentation.
- ❏ The info utility displays more in-depth information than the man utility.
- ❏ The information displayed by the info utility is called a node.
- ❏ To use info, enter **info** at the shell prompt followed by the name of the command, utility, or configuration file you need to learn about.
- ❏ To search for information in info, press CTRL-S and enter the term you want to search for.

Use Other Documentation Sources

- ❏ Most packages installed on a Linux system include a README file.
- ❏ README files often contain valuable information, but are underutilized by most system administrators and users.
- ❏ README files usually contain the following types of information:
  - ❏ Version numbers
  - ❏ Program descriptions
  - ❏ Change logs
  - ❏ Installation and configuration information
  - ❏ Known issues
  - ❏ Bug reporting information
  - ❏ Copyright information

❑ README files are usually located in /usr/share/doc/packages or /usr/share/doc in most distributions.

❑ You can view README files using any text editor or the cat utility.

❑ You can also view tremendous amounts of information about your Linux system on the Internet.

❑ One of the best resources on the Web for Linux is The Linux Documentation Project Web site at http://www.tldp.org.

❑ The TLDP Web site is best when you need setup and configuration information.

❑ The TLDP Web site contains the following information:

    ❑ HOWTOs

    ❑ Guides

    ❑ FAQs

    ❑ Online magazines

❑ Your Linux vendors' Web site is also an invaluable source for information.

❑ Linux vendors' Web sites are best when you need troubleshooting information.

❑ Most Linux vendors' Web sites include the following types of information:

    ❑ Knowledgebases

    ❑ Documentation

    ❑ Support forums

❑ Less well-known vendors may not have much information available on their Web site.

❑ Search engines such as Google or Yahoo can also be invaluable tools when trying to troubleshoot a problem with a Linux system.

❑ You can use search engines to search on the text of an error message displayed by the operating system.

SELF TEST

Use man Pages

1. Which utility is used to view manual pages?
   A. man
   B. manual
   C. viewman
   D. Kwrite

2. Which environment variable contains the directory where man page files are located?
   A. MANUAL
   B. MANUALPATH
   C. MANPAGEPATH
   D. MANPATH

3. Which file can be used to configure the path to the man page files?
   A. /etc/man.config
   B. /etc/man.conf
   C. /etc/man.txt
   D. /etc/manual.conf

4. Which of the following manual sections contains man pages for administrative utilities used by the root user?
   A. 1
   B. 3
   C. 8
   D. 9

5. Which of the following manual sections contains man pages for utilities and commands that can be used by any user?
   A. 9
   B. 1
   C. 3
   D. 7

6. You need to learn about the options available for the mkdir utility. Which command will display its manual page?

   A. cat mkdir | more

   B. cat mkdir | man

   C. manual mkdir

   D. man mkdir

7. You need to learn about the options available for the chmod utility. Which command will display its manual page?

   A. cat chmod | man

   B. manual chmod

   C. man chmod

   D. display chmod man page

8. Which section in a man page provides a brief review of the syntax used for a particular command or utility?

   A. REVIEW

   B. SYNOPSIS

   C. DESCRIPTION

   D. SYNTAX

9. Which section in a man page provides a list of man pages or other resources related to the particular command or utility?

   A. DESCRIPTION

   B. VERSION

   C. SEE ALSO

   D. REFERENCES

10. You're using man to view the man page for the chown utility. Which keystroke will unload the current man page and exit man?

   A. CTRL-U

   B. X

   C. CTRL-X

   D. Q

11. You're using man to view the man page for the Samba service. Which keystrokes can you use to search for the term "password" in the man page?

    A. /"password"

    B. CTRL-S

    C. /password

    D. search "password"

12. After searching for a term within a man page, you need to jump to the next instance of the term in the page. Which keystroke will do this?

    A. Q

    B. P

    C. N

    D. S

13. You need to search for man pages that relate to the Samba service. Which command will do this?

    A. man –s samba

    B. man –k samba

    C. search samba | man

    D. which samba

14. You need to search for man pages that relate to the PAM service. Which command will do this?

    A. which pam

    B. man –s pam

    C. search pam | man

    D. apropos pam

Use info

15. You need to use info to view information about using the smbpasswd utility. Which command will do this?

    A. info /smbpasswd

    B. info "smbpasswd"

    C. show info smbpasswd

    D. info smbpasswd

16. While viewing an info node, which keystroke can be used to navigate to the next node?

  A. /next

  B. P

  C. N

  D. L

17. While viewing an info node, which keystroke can be used to navigate to the previous node?

  A. P

  B. /prev

  C. N

  D. /up

18. While viewing an info node, which keystroke can be used to navigate to the beginning of the node?

  A. B

  B. /top

  C. HOME

  D. T

Use Other Documentation Sources

19. Where are the README files for the packages installed on a Fedora system located?

  A. /bin/packages/README

  B. /usr/share/README

  C. /usr/share/doc

  D. /bin/share/doc

20. What is the URL for The Linux Documentation Project Web site?

  A. http://www.linuxdoc.com

  B. http://www.linuxdocumentationproject.org

  C. http://www.tldp.org

  D. http://www.linuxdocs.org

21. You need to troubleshoot an error encountered with the httpd service on a Linux server. Which resource would be the best place to search for a resolution?

  A. The httpd info node

  B. The Linux Documentation Project

    C. The knowledgebase on your vendor's Web site

    D. The httpd man page

22. You need to learn how to set up and configure the Samba service on a Linux server. Which resource would be the best place to search for instructions?

    A. The samba info node

    B. The Linux Documentation Project

    C. The knowledgebase on your vendor's Web site

    D. The samba man page

23. You need to look up an error code displayed when your Linux workstation booted. Which resource would be the best place to search for a resolution?

    A. info

    B. The Linux Documentation Project

    C. A search engine such as Google or Yahoo

    D. man

LAB QUESTION

You're responsible for managing the Linux systems in your organization. You have been assigned by your supervisor to implement a Linux server as an HTTP application-level gateway between your organization's network and the Internet. You've never done this before. Describe the process you would follow to learn how to complete this task.

SELF TEST ANSWERS

Use man Pages

1. ☑ **A.** The man utility is used to view man pages. If an info node isn't available for a particular command or utility, then info may actually display a man page as well.
☒ **B, C,** and **D** are incorrect. **B** and **C** are distracters. **D** can't be used because manual pages are stored in gzip archives.

2. ☑ **D.** The MANPATH environment variable stores the path to the man pages on most Linux distributions.
☒ **A, B,** and **C** are incorrect. These responses are distracters.

3. ☑ **A.** You can use the /etc/man.config file to specify the path to the man files on many Linux distributions.
☒ **B, C,** and **D** are incorrect. These responses are distracters.

4. ☑ **C.** Section 8 of the manual contains man pages for utilities and commands used by root.
☒ **A, B,** and **D** are incorrect. Section 1 contains pages for commands that can be used by any user. Section 3 contains pages for library functions. Section 9 contains kernel routine documentation.

5. ☑ **B.** Section 1 of the manual contains man pages for commands that can be used by any user.
☒ **A, C,** and **D** are incorrect. Section 9 contains kernel routine documentation. Section 3 contains pages for library functions. Section 7 contains man pages for miscellaneous conventions.

6. ☑ **D.** The man mkdir command will display the man page for mkdir.
☒ **A, B,** and **C** are incorrect. These responses are distracters.

7. ☑ **C.** The man chmod command will display the man page for chmod.
☒ **A, B,** and **D** are incorrect. These responses are distracters.

8. ☑ **B.** The SYNOPSIS section of a man page provides a review of the syntax used for a command or utility.
☒ **A, C,** and **D** are incorrect. **A** is a distracter. **C** provides in-depth instructions for using the command or utility. **D** is a distracter.

9. ☑ **C.** The SEE ALSO section of a man page provides a list of related resources.
☒ **A, B,** and **D** are incorrect. **A** provides in-depth instructions for using the command or utility. **B** and **D** are distracters.

10. ☑ **D.** Pressing Q will exit man.
    ☒ **A, B,** and **C** are incorrect. Each of these responses is a distracter.

11. ☑ **C.** To search for the text "password" in a man page, you enter **/password**.
    ☒ **A, B,** and **D** are incorrect. Each of these responses is a distracter.

12. ☑ **C.** After entering a search term, pressing N will take you to the next instance of that term in a man page.
    ☒ **A, B,** and **D** are incorrect. **A** causes man to exit. **B** and **D** are distracters.

13. ☑ **B.** Entering **man –k samba** will search across man pages for the term "samba."
    ☒ **A, C,** and **D** are incorrect. These responses are distracters.

14. ☑ **D.** Entering apropos pam will search across man pages for the term "pam."
    ☒ **A, B,** and **C** are incorrect. These responses are distracters.

Use info

15. ☑ **D.** Entering **info smbpasswd** will cause info to display information about the smbpasswd utility.
    ☒ **A, B,** and **C** are incorrect. These options are distracters.

16. ☑ **C.** Pressing N will jump to the next node.
    ☒ **A, B,** and **D** are incorrect. **A** and **B** are distracters. **D** will cause info to jump up a level.

17. ☑ **A.** Pressing P will jump to the previous node.
    ☒ **B, C,** and **D** are incorrect. **B** and **D** are distracters. **C** will cause info to jump to the next node.

18. ☑ **C.** Pressing the HOME key will take you to the first line in an info node.
    ☒ **A, B,** and **D** are incorrect. These responses are distracters.

Use Other Documentation Sources

19. ☑ **C.** The README files on a Fedora system are located in /usr/share/doc.
    ☒ **A, B,** and **D** are incorrect. These responses are distracters.

20. ☑ **C.** The URL to The Linux Documentation Project Web site is http://www.tldp.org.
    ☒ **A, B,** and **D** are incorrect. These URLS don't exist.

21. ☑ **C.** Of the options presented, the knowledgebase on your Linux vendor's Web site would be the best place to search for a resolution to a problem on your system. You could also look in the appropriate README files or use a search engine to research the error.

☒ **A, B,** and **D** are not the best choices. **A** and **D** may provide some help, but their focus is on documenting how utilities and commands work. Usually, info nodes and man pages don't provide extensive troubleshooting information. **B** may provide some help, but it doesn't usually provide extensive troubleshooting information either.

22. ☑ **B.** Of the options presented, The Linux Documentation Project Web site provides extensive information about how to set up and configure services such as Samba.
☒ **A, C,** and **D** are not the best choices. **A** and **D** may provide some setup and configuration guidance, but the information provided isn't as extensive as that available on the TLDP Web site. Usually, info nodes and man pages don't provide extensive setup instructions. **B** may provide some help, but it doesn't usually provide extensive troubleshooting information either.

23. ☑ **C.** Of the options presented, a search engine would be the best option for researching a solution to an error code. Your Linux vendor's knowledgebase would also be a good choice.
☒ **A, B,** and **D** are not the best choices. **A** and **D** probably won't provide information on error codes. **B** may provide some help, but it doesn't usually provide error code information either.

LAB ANSWER

There are many ways to attack this problem. A good approach would be to begin by learning all you can about HTTP application-level gateways on Linux. This information is available in the guides posted on The Linux Documentation Project Web site (http://www.tldp.org). There you will learn how an application-level gateway works as well as the various packages available for Linux that provide this functionality. You could also spend some time using a search engine such as Google or Yahoo to research Linux application-level gateways.

One of the key results of this research is a decision on which package to use. Once you make this decision, you could then use the TLDP Web site to download a HOWTO document that describes how to set up an application-level gateway. For example, you could use the *Firewall and Proxy Server HOWTO* to learn how to set up a variety of different firewall and application-level gateway solutions. You could also refer to the appropriate info and man pages to learn how to customize your services to accomplish the needs of your organization.

With this information in hand, you would then be ready to create a deployment plan for the new system, as discussed in the previous chapter.

5

Using Linux
Text Editors

O ne of the key skills you will need when working with any Linux system (and for your Linux+ exam) is the ability to use a text editor effectively. Why? Because most of the system configuration tasks you need to complete in Linux, whether you're configuring the operating system itself or a service running on the system, are completed using a text editor and a text file.

This represents a significant difference between Linux and other operating systems, such as Windows. Under Windows, most of your configuration settings are stored in a database called the *Registry*. This information is stored in logical sections called *keys*, shown in Figure 5-1.

These keys are stored in a hierarchy; a given key can contain a number of subkeys. These keys contain values that store the system's configuration information. For example, in Figure 5-2, the Wallpaper value is set to the Wallpaper1.bmp file. This value sets the image used for the background of the Windows desktop.

The Registry is a good concept, but one of the key problems with it is that it isn't designed with the end user in mind. While a Registry editor named Regedit.exe is supplied with Windows, you are strongly discouraged from manually editing values in the Registry. Instead, you're supposed to let the operating system along with applications installed on the system make any and all changes to the Registry.

on the
() o b

One of the reasons for this is the fact that the Registry stores data in many different formats. Some values accept regular text strings; other values require data to be entered in binary format. Unless you're really good at your binary math, you could really mess up your Windows system by entering the wrong binary value.

Linux, on the other hand, doesn't use a central repository of all system configuration information like the Windows Registry. Instead, all of your configuration information is stored in a variety of text files. Most of these file are stored in the /etc directory in your Linux file system. For example, the text file used to configure the NTP service on your

FIGURE 5-1

Windows
Registry keys

Viewing Registry
values in Regedit

system (which is used to synchronize the system time with other network computers) is
the /etc/ntp.conf file, shown in Figure 5-3.

Instead of forbidding you from manually editing these configuration files, as
Windows does with the Registry, Linux *expects* you to know how to edit these files
to customize the way your system runs. Therefore, you must know how to use Linux
text editors to manage your system.

At this point, you may be thinking, "I know how to use text editors on other
operating systems. I can use Notepad on Windows. Why are we devoting an entire
chapter to text editors in this book?" There are two reasons:

■ Knowing how to use a text editor is absolutely critical to being able to
   manage a Linux system. If you can't use a text editor, you will struggle with
   the topics presented throughout the rest of this book.

■ Linux editors, frankly, are difficult for most new users to learn how to use,
   especially if you're coming from a Windows background.

Viewing the /etc/
ntp.conf file

```
# --- GENERAL CONFIGURATION ---
#
# Undisciplined Local Clock. This is a fake driver intended for backup
# and when no outside source of synchronized time is available. The
# default stratum is usually 3, but in this case we elect to use stratum
# 0. Since the server line does not have the prefer keyword, this driver
# is never used for synchronization, unless no other other
# synchronization source is available. In case the local host is
# controlled by some external source, such as an external oscillator or
# another protocol, the prefer keyword would cause the local host to
# disregard all other synchronization sources, unless the kernel
# modifications are in use and declare an unsynchronized condition.
#
server 127.127.1.0
fudge   127.127.1.0 stratum 10

#
# Drift file.  Put this in a directory which the daemon can write to.
# No symbolic links allowed, either, since the daemon updates the file
# by creating a temporary in the same directory and then rename()'ing
# it to the file.
#
driftfile /var/lib/ntp/drift
:
```

INSIDE THE EXAM

Using Linux Text Editors

For your Linux+ exam, you only need to be familiar with the vi text editor. In this chapter, however, we're going to present other text editors that you may find easier to use than vi. Just be aware that you probably won't see any questions on the exam covering these tools.

Therefore, you should pay special attention to vi. You need to be very familiar with how to open a file in vi, edit it, and save your changes.

Therefore, in this chapter, we're going to spend a significant amount of time learning how to use a variety of Linux text-editing tools. The following topics will be covered:

- Using non-graphical Linux text editors
- Using graphical Linux text editors

Let's begin this chapter by discussing how to use text editors to configure your Linux system.

CERTIFICATION OBJECTIVE 5.01

Use Non-Graphical Linux Text Editors

As we've discussed above, knowing how to use a text editor is a key skill necessary for managing a Linux system. Most configuration changes are made by making changes to a text file. Therefore, you must know how to use Linux text editors.

Be aware, however, that a growing number of front-ends are becoming available that allow you to make changes to your configuration files without directly editing a configuration file with a text editor. One of the best front-ends currently available, in my opinion, is YaST (Yet another Setup Tool), which is installed with SUSE Linux. A typical YaST front-end is shown in Figure 5-4.

FIGURE 5-4 Making configuration changes with YaST

Using YaST, you can install software, manage hardware settings, partition hard drives, configure bootloaders, configure network boards, configure users and groups, and configure settings for the services running on your system.

Many other distributions also use configuration front-ends. For example, Fedora provides several different utilities that can be used to configure system settings, network settings, services, and users. These are shown in Figure 5-5.

Admittedly, I like using these graphical front-ends. In the early days of Linux, however, these tools didn't exist. Every configuration change made had to be done with a text editor. As these tools have matured and become more pervasive, more and more Linux administrators are starting to use them as an alternative to manually editing configuration files.

FIGURE 5-5	Fedora configuration tools

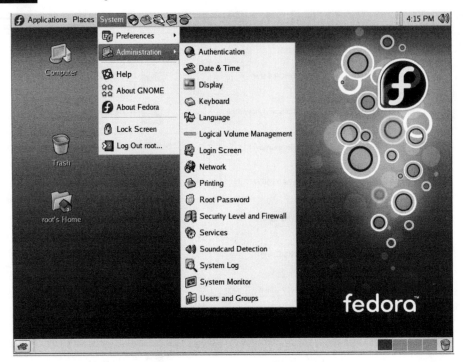

Why, then, are we spending an entire chapter discussing text manipulation tools? The reason is twofold:

- The Linux+ exam doesn't cover these graphical configuration utilities. If you want to pass the exam, you've got to be familiar with the text-based configuration files and the text editors used to manage them.

- Good Linux administrators use graphical front-ends only for convenience. They don't rely on them. In other words, a good Linux admin should be intimately familiar with the configuration text files behind the graphical interface, not just with the interface itself.

With this in mind, let's dig in and start learning about text editors. We're first going to look at editors that don't use a graphical user interface. We'll cover the following in this part of the chapter:

- Using the vi editor
- Using the Emacs editor

We'll start by reviewing how to use the vi editor.

Using the vi Editor

The vi editor is a very basic program that can be used to edit text files on a Linux system. The vi editor has been around for quite some time and I dare say that it is one of the more widely used text editors used by Linux administrators.

Be aware that the choice of which text editor to use on a Linux system can incite the same type of holy war among Linux aficionados as the debate over which distribution is the "best." With text editors, some swear by vi; others by Emacs. We're going to review both in this chapter and then let you decide which you prefer.

However, even if you decide that you prefer Emacs, you should still make sure you are very familiar with vi. Not only is vi the editor tested on the Linux+ exam, it's also a much smaller program than Emacs. In fact, it's small enough to fit on a floppy. If you ever need to boot a Linux system from an emergency floppy diskette, vi is one of the few editors small enough to fit on a disk.

There are actually two versions of vi. The older version is called simply vi. The newer version is called vim (Vi IMproved). On older systems, you may be actually using vi when you enter **vi** at a shell prompt. However, on most newer Linux distributions, you are probably actually using the newer vim version of vi.

The executable for the vi program is a file on your system's hard drive called vim. On most distributions, the vim executable is located in the /bin directory. A symbolic link file named vi is placed in your /usr/bin directory that points to the /bin/vim executable. This is shown in Figure 5-6.

Notice in Figure 5-6 that the vi file actually points to the vim file in the same directory. However, the vim file in /usr/bin itself is only a symbolic link that points to the /bin/vim executable file.

FIGURE 5-6

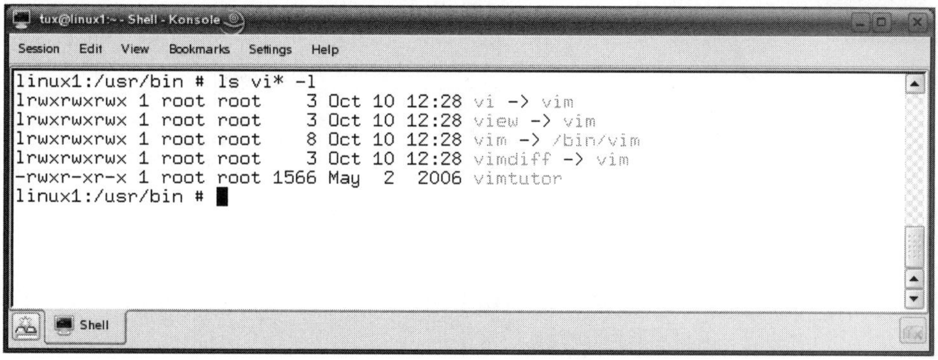

tux@linux1:~ - Shell - Konsole
Session Edit View Bookmarks Settings Help
linux1:/usr/bin # ls vi* -l
lrwxrwxrwx 1 root root 3 Oct 10 12:28 vi -> vim
lrwxrwxrwx 1 root root 3 Oct 10 12:28 view -> vim
lrwxrwxrwx 1 root root 8 Oct 10 12:28 vim -> /bin/vim
lrwxrwxrwx 1 root root 3 Oct 10 12:28 vimdiff -> vim
-rwxr-xr-x 1 root root 1566 May 2 2006 vimtutor
linux1:/usr/bin #
Shell

vi links to /bin/vim

on the

J o b *A symbolic link is simply a file that points to another file elsewhere in the file system. We'll discuss symbolic links in depth in Chapter 6.*

The result is that no matter what command you type at the shell prompt (**vi** or **vim**), the vim editor is loaded. For example, in Figure 5-7, the vi command has been entered at a shell prompt of a Fedora system. Notice, however, that the vim editor has been loaded, as shown in the welcome screen.

With this in mind, let's discuss how to open text files in vi.

Opening Files in vi

To open a file from the shell prompt to manipulate in vi, simply enter **vi *file name***. For example, in Figure 5-8, notice that there is a file named myfile.txt in the tux user's home directory.

Because the file resides in the current directory, you can simply enter **vi myfile.txt** at the shell prompt to load this file into the vi editor. This is shown in Figure 5-9.

If the file resides in a directory other than the current directory, you then need to include the full path to the file. For example, suppose your current directory is /tmp and you need to open the /var/log/messages file in vi. To do this, you would enter **vi /var/log/messages** at the shell prompt.

It's also possible to create a new text file using vi. To do this, simply enter **vi** followed by the name of the file you wish to create at the shell prompt. If you don't include a path with the file name, then the file will be created in the current directory. If you specify a path, then the file will be created in that directory.

For example, in Figure 5-10, the current directory is /home/tux and the command **vi yourfile.txt** has been entered at the shell prompt. Notice that a blank file has been opened in the vi editor interface, as indicated by the [New File] text at the

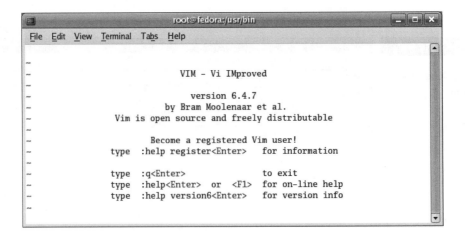

FIGURE 5-7

Using vim

FIGURE 5-8   Contents of the /home/tux directory

FIGURE 5-9   Opening a text file in the vi editor

FIGURE 5-10   Creating a new file with vi

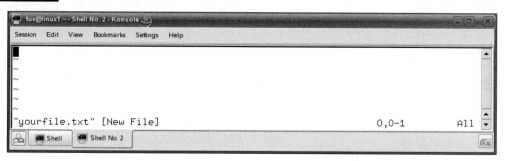

bottom of the screen. It's important to note that, when creating a new file with vi, the file isn't actually created on disk until you write the file (also known as *saving*). Until you do, all the lines of text you enter in the vi interface are saved only in a memory buffer. If you don't save the file, you will lose it!

on the
Job

Remember that Linux directory and file names are case-sensitive. A file named Yourfile.txt is not the same file as one named yourfile.txt. We'll discuss case-sensitivity in more detail in the next chapter.

Now, let's discuss vi modes.

vi Modes

So far, so good, right? Most of the students I teach vi to can handle opening a file in vi or creating a new file. However, once the file is opened, things start to get a little confusing. That's because vi uses four different operating modes:

- Normal mode
- Command mode
- Insert mode
- Replace mode

By default, vi opens or creates a file in normal mode. You'll notice in the preceding figures that the vi interface doesn't include any pull-down menus that you can use to complete operations on the current file, such as writing, searching, or closing. Instead, you must use commands in command and normal modes to accomplish these tasks.

SCENARIO & SOLUTION

You need to edit a file named /etc/smb.conf. What command would you enter at the shell prompt to do this with the vi editor?	You would enter **vi /etc/smb.conf**.
You need to create a new file in the /tmp directory named notes.txt. What command would you enter to do this with the vi editor?	You would enter **vi /tmp/notes.txt**.
Your current directory at the shell prompt is /home/mhuffman. In this directory is a file named contacts. What command would you enter at the shell prompt to open this file with vi?	You could use two different commands. You could, of course, use the full path to the file by entering **vi /home/mhuffman/contacts**. However, because the file exists in the current directory, you could also enter simply **vi contacts**.

The confusing part for most of my students is the fact that, while in command or normal mode, you can't actually edit the file! Unless you happen to hit the right key, nothing happens on the screen if you try to change the text of the file. To do this, you must first enter insert mode. To enter insert mode, you can press any one of the following keys on the keyboard:

- I
- INSERT
- S

After pressing one of these keys, you can then actually edit the text of the file. You can tell you're in insert mode by the --INSERT-- text displayed at the bottom of the vi interface. This is shown in Figure 5-11.

Pressing INSERT a second time will cause vi to switch to replace mode. Insert mode is analogous to using a word processor in insert mode. Any text you type is inserted wherever the cursor is located in the file. All text that may already exist after the cursor is moved down a space for each character typed.

Replace mode, on the other hand, is analogous to overtype mode. When you type in new characters, the new characters overwrite any existing characters. You can toggle back to insert mode by pressing INSERT again.

While in insert mode, you can add text, change text, or delete text from the file. However, you can't perform any file operations. For example, if you make changes to a file and want to save them, you can't do so while in insert mode. To do this, you must first switch back to normal mode. This is done by pressing ESC. In Figure 5-12, we've switched from insert mode back into command mode by pressing ESC.

In normal mode, you can enter a variety of different commands to delete lines of text or search the file for particular words. You can also enter command mode where you can save the current file or exit the editor. We'll review these commands later in this section. To switch back to insert mode, just press I, INSERT, or S.

FIGURE 5-11   The vi editor in insert mode

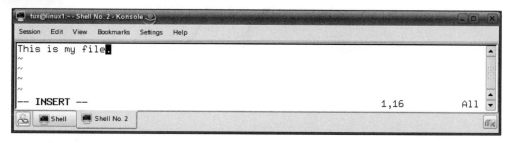

FIGURE 5-12 Switching back to normal mode in vi

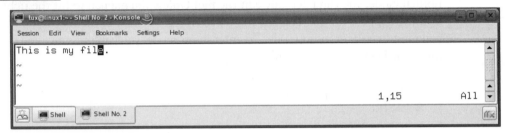

Now that you know how to open a file in vi and how to switch between modes, let's discuss how you edit text in insert mode.

Working in Insert Mode

Once you have opened a file in vi and entered insert mode, you can edit the text as you would with any other text editor. Note that, on the left side of the screen, you see several lines of tildes (~). These characters aren't actually in the file. These characters simply indicate that these lines don't exist in the file. After adding lines to the file, you'll see that the tildes disappear one at a time.

You can navigate around to different insertion points in the file by pressing the arrow keys as well as the PAGE UP, PAGE DOWN, HOME, and END keys. You can add text by simply typing characters on the keyboard. You can remove text by pressing DELETE. However, be warned that you can't use the BACKSPACE key!

SCENARIO & SOLUTION

You're using the vi editor in normal mode. How can you switch to insert mode?	You can use one of three different keystrokes: • I • INSERT • S
You're using the vi editor in insert mode. How can you switch to replace mode?	You can press the INSERT key.
You're using the vi editor in replace mode. How can you switch to normal mode?	You can press the ESC key.

This is another point of confusion with new vi users. From years of using word processors, we've become used to using the BACKSPACE key to backspace over mistakes in a file. This simply can't be done in vi. If you need to delete characters, you'll have to get used to using the DELETE key. To add a new line, simply press ENTER.

Once you're done editing the text, you can then switch back to normal mode by pressing ESC. From normal mode, you can also enter command mode. Let's discuss what you can do in command mode next.

Using Command Mode Commands in vi

As we've discussed earlier, the vi editor doesn't provide menus to accomplish common file tasks. Instead, you have to enter commands in command mode. In this topic, we're going to review some of the commands you can use and what they do.

To enter command mode in vi, you must first enter normal mode (if you were previously in insert mode) and then enter a colon (:). When you do, a command prompt is displayed at the bottom of the screen, as shown in Figure 5-13.

You can then enter commands at this prompt to accomplish file-related tasks. Obviously, one of the most important tasks you'll need to complete in command mode is to write the file to disk. This is done by entering **w** at the command prompt. Be sure to press ENTER after entering the command. After entering **w** at the command prompt, a message is displayed at the bottom of the screen indicating that the file has been written to disk. This is shown in Figure 5-14.

Entering **w** *file_name* at the command prompt will write the file to a different file name. You can also enter the following other commands at the command prompt:

- **exit** Writes the current file and then closes vi.
- **wq** Also writes the current file to disk and closes vi.
- **q** Closes vi without saving the current file. This can only be used if the file hasn't been changed. If the file has been changed, then you must enter **q!**.

FIGURE 5-13   The vi command mode command prompt

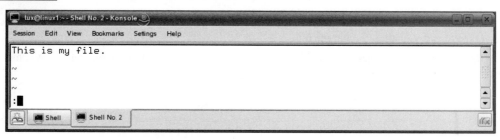

FIGURE 5-14 Writing file changes to disk

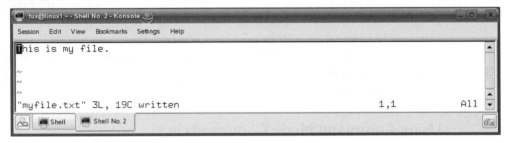

In addition to commands that are entered at the command prompt, you can also enter commands in normal mode. Let's discuss these commands next.

Entering Commands in vi Normal Mode

Normal mode commands aren't entered at the command prompt, as the preceding commands were. Instead, these commands are entered *without* entering a **:** first. If you are in insert mode, press ESC to return to normal mode. Then you can enter the following commands:

- **dw**   Deletes the word that comes immediately after the cursor, including the space following the word. The text is saved in a memory buffer.
- **de**   Deletes the word that comes immediately after the cursor, not including the space. The text is saved in a memory buffer.

SCENARIO & SOLUTION

You're entering changes to a text file in vi. How do you save your file?	You would type **:w**.
You've made significant changes to a text file using vi. You realize that you've made so many mistakes that it would be best to start over. What command can you type to exit vi without saving the file?	You would type **:q!**.
You've finished entering changes to a text file in vi. How do you save your file and exit the editor?	You could use either of the following two commands to do this: • **:exit** • **:wq**

FIGURE 5-15   Displaying the vi status line

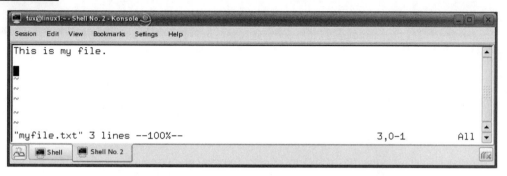

- **d$**   Deletes from the insertion point to the end of the line. The text is saved in a memory buffer.
- **dd**   Deletes the entire current line. The text is saved in a memory buffer.
- **p**   Inserts the text deleted in the last deletion operation after the current cursor location.
- **u**   Undoes the last action.
- CTRL-G   Displays a status line at the bottom of the interface. This displays the name of the file, the total number of lines in the file, and the current cursor location. This is shown in Figure 5-15.
- **/search_term**   Searches for the next instance of the term specified. For example, entering **/init** searches for the next instance of the text "init" after the cursor. Pressing N after executing a search will search for the next instance of the search term. In Figure 5-16, the **/file** command has been entered while in normal mode. The first instance of *file* has been highlighted as a result.

FIGURE 5-16   Searching for text in vi

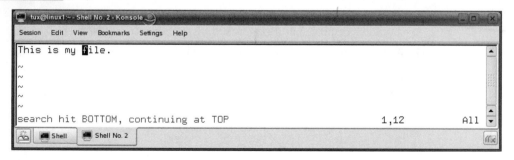

SCENARIO & SOLUTION

You need to search for the term "init" in a text file opened in vi. What command would you enter to do this?	You would enter **/init**.
You've placed your vi cursor before a word that you need to delete from a text file. Which command could you enter to do this?	If you want to delete the word and the space that follows it, you would enter **dw**. If you wanted to only delete the word and not the following space, you would enter **de**.
You're entering changes in a text file in vi. You just deleted a word that you didn't want to delete. How can you reverse the change?	You can enter **u** to undo your last change.

As you can see, vi is a simple, yet fairly powerful text editor. The only complaint I have about vi is that its user interface can be difficult to learn. However, once you've used vi for a while, it will become second nature to you. Therefore, let's spend some time practicing with vi in the following exercise.

EXERCISE 5-1

Using the vi Editor

In this exercise, you will practice using the vi editor to create and manipulate text files. Complete the following:

1. If not already done, boot your Linux system and log in using your standard (non-root) user account.

2. Open a terminal session. The session should open with your user's home directory as the current directory. You can check this by entering **pwd** at the shell prompt. If your user account is named tux, then the current directory should be displayed as /home/tux. This is shown in Figure 5-17.

3. At the shell prompt enter **vi test.txt**. The vi editor should run with test.txt open as a new file.

4. Press the INSERT key on your keyboard. You should now be in insert mode.

FIGURE 5-17   Checking the current directory with the pwd command

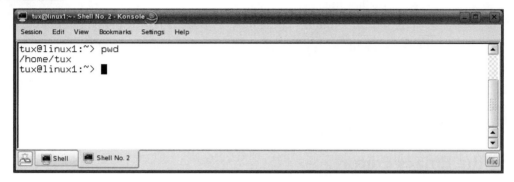

5. Enter the following text in the file:

Usu agam legere delicata ut, per democritum scriptorem an. Nec te zzril possim tincidunt, at qui probo mucius gubergren. Ea mei paulo cetero oportere, at pertinax liberavisse pri.

6. Save your file by completing the following:

   a. Press ESC to return to normal mode.

   b. Enter **:w**. You should see a message indicating that the file was written.

7. Exit vi by entering **:exit**.

8. Reload test.txt in vi by entering **vi test.txt** at the shell prompt.

9. Display the status line by pressing CTRL-G while in normal mode.

10. Use the arrow keys to move the cursor to the beginning of the first word in the first line of the file.

11. Search for all occurrences of the text "at" by completing the following:

    a. While in normal mode, enter **/at**. The first instance should be highlighted.

    b. Find the next instance by pressing the N key.

    c. Find the remaining instance by pressing N until you reach the end of the file.

12. Practice deleting text by doing the following:

    a. While in normal mode, use the arrow keys to place the cursor on the first letter of the word *legere*.

    b. Delete the word *legere* and the space that follows it by pressing **dw**.

    c. Use the arrow keys to move the cursor to the period at the end of the last line.

    d. Put the contents of the memory buffer after the period by entering **p**.

13. Exit the file without saving your changes by entering **:q!**.

You now have sufficient skills to use vi to manage a typical Linux system! Let's next look at using another Linux text editor: Emacs.

Using the Emacs Editor

Emacs is a slightly more advanced editor than vi. Like, vi, Emacs has been around a long time and has many devotees. It even comes in three different variations: two text-based versions and a graphical version. In this part of the chapter, we're going to cover the following:

- Using Emacs
- Using Quick Emacs

Let's begin by looking at the basic Emacs editor.

Using Emacs

Admittedly, vi is a very basic editor. If you're craving a more powerful editor, then Emacs may be the text editor for you. One of the key advantages of Emacs is the fact that it provides a menu-driven interface as well as keyboard shortcuts, much like the old DOS EDIT.COM program. It also allows you to use the mouse to move the cursor around the screen and click on menu items.

Many Linux administrators I've associated with prefer Emacs to vi for editing text files. Admittedly, its interface is more intuitive than vi. My problem, personally, is that I learned Linux using vi and I have a hard time switching over. Folks who learned Linux with Emacs probably feel the same way about vi, of course.

Knowing how to use Emacs isn't a requirement for the Linux+ exam. However, we're going to spend a few pages covering this editor to give you a feel for how it works. Like my associates, you may find that you prefer it to vi.

To use Emacs, you may need to install the Emacs package on your Linux system. Some distributions include it in the base install, many don't. Almost all distributions include the vi editor in the base installation, however. We'll discuss the process for installing software packages on your system later in the book.

To use Emacs, open a terminal session and enter **emacs** at the shell prompt. When you do, the interface shown in Figure 5-18 is displayed.

As you can see, Emacs uses a graphical, menu-driven interface that you can manipulate using either the keyboard or the mouse. If you click on a menu item with your mouse, a menu is displayed just as you would expect with any graphical application. The File menu is shown in Figure 5-19.

Notice that many Emacs menu options also have a keyboard shortcut associated with them. For example, to open a new file, you could select File | Open File or you could press CTRL-X followed by CTRL-F on the keyboard. When you do either of these options, the screen in Figure 5-20 is displayed.

Notice in Figure 5-20 that the text "Find file: ~/" is displayed at the bottom of the screen. The tilde indicates that you are in your home directory (in this case, /home/tux). At this prompt, you can enter the name of the file you want to open. If you want to create a new file, you can enter the name for the new file.

With Emacs running and a file loaded, you can perform many of the text manipulations that you are probably already familiar with if you're familiar with using a word processor. For example, you can select Edit | Copy to copy text and Edit | Paste to paste text. You can select File | Save (current buffer) to save a file. You can also select File | Exit Emacs to exit the program.

FIGURE 5-18

Using Emacs

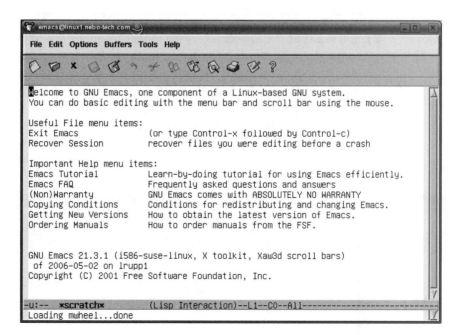

FIGURE 5-19

The Emacs File
menu

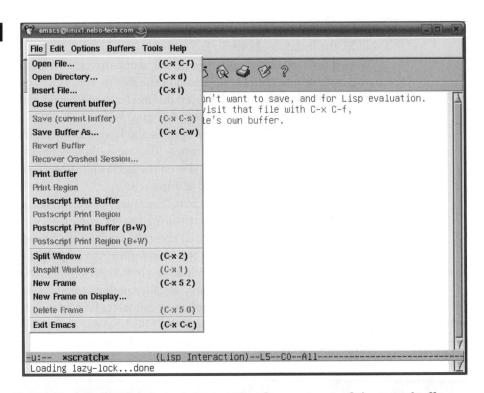

FIGURE 5-20

Opening a file in
Emacs

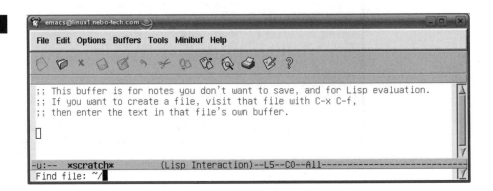

on the

Job *You'll see that the Emacs interface makes frequent use of the term* **buffers.** *As with vi, Emacs loads a file into a buffer in RAM when you open or create it. Any changes you make with the editor are saved in the buffer. When you select Save, the contents of the buffer are written out to disk.*

The one thing that will trip you up when working with Emacs is the fact that the keyboard shortcuts for these typical operations are very different than the standard shortcuts used by most other applications. For example, if you look at the Edit menu

FIGURE 5-21

The Emacs Edit
menu

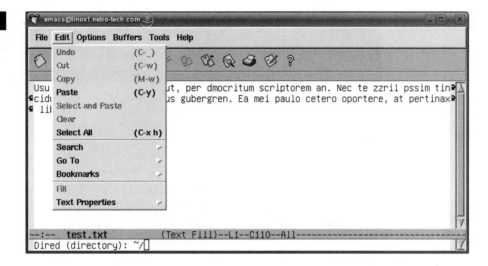

FIGURE 5-21

The Emacs Edit
menu

in Figure 5-21, you'll see that the Copy keyboard shortcut is ALT-W, not the CTRL-C
shortcut you are probably familiar with.

Likewise, the Paste keyboard shortcut is CTRL-Y, not CTRL-V. The Save shortcut is
CTRL-X CTRL-W, not CTRL-S.

Another key difference between vi and Emacs is the fact that Emacs can have
multiple buffers open at once. With vi, you can open and work on one file at time.
Emacs can open multiple files. You can toggle between the open buffers using the
Buffers menu, shown in Figure 5-22.

As you can see, using Emacs is very similar to using standard word processing
applications such as Microsoft Word or OpenOffice.org. It's really not much of a
stretch to move from one of these programs to Emacs. Moving to vi, on the other
hand, takes a lot more work. That's why, I suspect, many Linux administrators prefer
Emacs to vi.

In addition to the standard version of Emacs, there's also a more minimal version of
Emacs available that you can use called Quick Emacs. Let's look at this version next.

FIGURE 5-22

The Emacs
Buffers menu

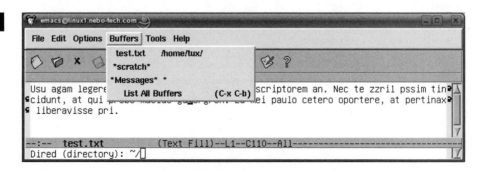

Using Quick Emacs

Quick Emacs is a sized-down version of the standard Emacs editor. One of the problems with the standard version of Emacs is its size. As we discussed earlier, if you have a major system meltdown and need to boot Linux from a floppy diskette, it's very likely that you will need a text editor to fix problems. The standard version of Emacs won't fit on a floppy. However, Quick Emacs will! If you like Emacs, you'll love Quick Emacs. There's not much Emacs can do that Quick Emacs can't.

To use Quick Emacs, you'll need to install the qemacs package on your Linux system. Once installed, you can start the program by simply entering **qemacs** at a shell prompt. When you do, the qemacs interface is displayed, as shown in Figure 5-23.

As you can see in Figure 5-23, Quick Emacs doesn't provide a menu-driven interface as Emacs does. Therefore, you'll need to know your Emacs keyboard shortcuts to use Quick Emacs. Other than that, Quick Emacs works in exactly the same way as the standard version Emacs.

Let's practice working with Emacs in the following exercise.

SCENARIO & SOLUTION

What keyboard shortcut can you use to open a file in Emacs?	You would press CTRL-X CTRL-F on the keyboard.
What keyboard shortcut can you use to save a file in Emacs?	You would press CTRL-X CTRL-S on the keyboard.
You want to use Quick Emacs on your system. However, when you enter **qemacs** at the shell prompt, an error occurs indicating the command can't be found. What's causing this problem?	You need to install the qemacs package on your system.

EXERCISE 5-2

Using the Emacs Editor

In this exercise, you will practice using the Emacs editor to create and manipulate text files. To complete this exercise, you will need to install Emacs on your Linux system. Since we haven't covered installing packages yet, I'm going to show you how to do this the "easy way" using YaST. If you're not using SUSE Linux, then you'll need to refer to Chapter 8 to learn how to use the rpm utility to install software packages.

Complete the following:

1. If not already done, boot your Linux system and log in using your standard (non-root) user account.

2. Install Emacs by doing the following:

   a. With your mouse, select K Menu | System | YaST (Control Center).

   b. When prompted for a password, enter your root user's *password*. If you used the installation exercise presented earlier in this book to set up your Linux system, your root user's password is **tuxPenguin1**.

   c. Select OK.

   d. Select Software | Software Management.

   e. In the Search field, enter **emacs**, then select Search.

   f. Select the following packages:

      ■ emacs

      ■ emacs-info

      ■ emacs-x11

      This is shown in Figure 5-24.

   g. Click Accept.

   h. If prompted, insert the requested CDs or DVDs in your optical drive. Wait while the packages are installed.

   i. When prompted to install more packages, select No.

   j. Close your YaST window.

3. Open a terminal session. The session should open with your user's home directory as the current directory. You can check this by entering **pwd** at the shell prompt. If your user account is named tux, then the current directory should be displayed as /home/tux.

FIGURE 5-24 Installing Emacs

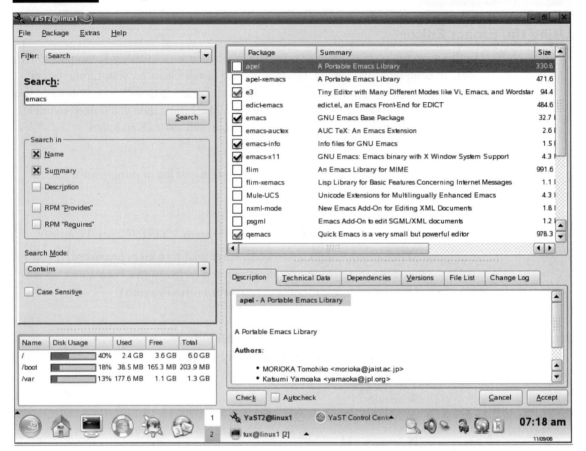

4. At the shell prompt, display a listing of files in the current directory by entering **ls**.

5. Verify that the test.txt file you created in the previous exercise is in your home directory.

6. At the shell prompt enter **emacs**.

7. Select File | Open File.

8. At the Find File prompt, enter **test.txt**. The test.txt file should be opened in the editor window, as shown in Figure 5-25.

9. Switch to the scratch buffer by selecting Buffers | Scratch. Read the message about the purpose of the scratch buffer.

FIGURE 5-25

Loading a file in Emacs

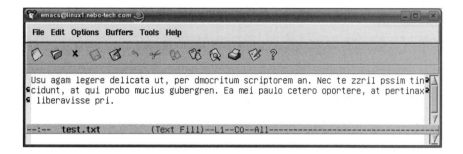

10. Create a new file by selecting File | Open File.

11. At the Find File prompt, enter **test2.txt**. A blank Emacs screen should be displayed.

12. Enter the following text in the test2.txt buffer:

```
Et reque everti atomorum vel, eos sale partiendo id, quaeque
salutandi vis at. At vis cibo partem, mazim mandamus at pro.
```

13. Select File | Save (Current Buffer). You should see a message at the bottom of the screen indicating that the test2.txt file has been written, as shown in Figure 5-26.

14. Switch to the test.txt buffer by selecting Buffers | test.txt.

15. Use your mouse to highlight the first sentence in test.txt.

16. Select Edit | Copy.

17. Switch to the test2.txt buffer.

18. Place the cursor at the end of the last line after the period.

19. Paste the copied text by pressing CTRL-Y.

20. Save your changes to the file by pressing CTRL-X CTRL-S. You should see a message indicating that the file was written to disk.

FIGURE 5-26

Saving a file in Emacs

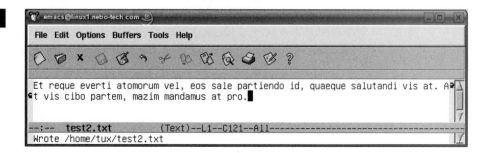

FIGURE 5-27 Viewing files created with Emacs

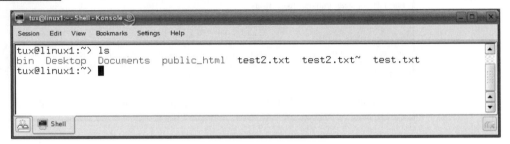

21. Exit Emacs by pressing CTRL-X CTRL-C.

22. At the shell prompt, enter **ls**. You should now see the test2.txt file listed in your home directory, as shown in Figure 5-27.

    Notice that there is also a file named test2.txt~. This is a backup file created by Emacs when you modified the original test2.txt file. This can be a real lifesaver. If you ever make a serious error in a file that you're working with, you can revert to the prior version using this backup file.

23. View the contents of test2.txt by entering **cat ./test2.txt** at the shell prompt.

Before we finish with this chapter, we need to discuss the graphical text editors that are available on a typical Linux system.

CERTIFICATION OBJECTIVE 5.02

Use Graphical Text Editors

In addition to the text-based editors we've discussed to this point, you can also use a variety of graphical text editors if you've installed a graphical Linux system that uses the KDE or GNOME desktops. These graphical editors aren't covered on the Linux+ exam. However, they are much easier to use than the text-based editors discussed earlier. In fact, many Linux administrators prefer to use these editors instead of vi or Emacs.

However, you need to remember that these editors can only be used if the following conditions are true:

- The system is working properly.
- The system has X Windows, a window manager, and a desktop installed.
- Your X Window System has been configured properly to work with your hardware.

If any of these conditions aren't met, you must use a text-based editor. Basically, graphical editors work fine for day-to-day tasks. However, in an emergency, you probably won't be able to use them.

There are many different graphical editors available. For our purposes here, we're going to discuss three of my favorites:

- Kate
- XEmacs
- gedit

Let's begin by looking at the Kate editor

Using Kate

Kate is perhaps my favorite graphical Linux text editor. Kate is usually installed by default if you install a standard KDE system. It can be started by entering **kate** at a shell prompt or by selecting K Menu | Utilities | Editor | Kate in the KDE desktop interface, as shown in Figure 5-28.

When you do, the Kate editor is opened, as shown in Figure 5-29.

You use Kate just as you would any standard word processor. In fact, you'll notice that most of the menu names, menu items, and keyboard shortcuts are pretty much the same as those used by standard word processing programs.

For example, you can select File | Open to open an existing text file. You can also select File | New to create a new file. You can save a file by selecting File | Save or pressing CTRL-S, just as you would in most word processors. You can use the following to cut, copy, and paste text:

- Cut (File | Cut): CTRL-X
- Copy (File | Copy): CTRL-C
- Paste (File | Paste): CTRL-V

Kate even includes a spelling checker. You can't do that with vi!

In addition to Kate, you can also use a version of Emacs designed specifically to work in the X Windows environment. Let's look at this editor next.

Launching the Kate text editor

Using Kate

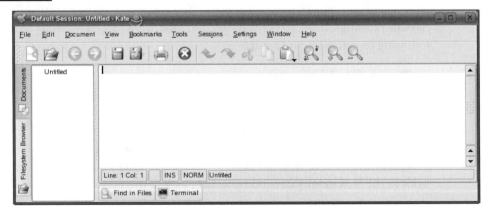

Using XEmacs

If you install the xemacs package on your Linux system, you can then use a version of Emacs designed to work within the KDE or GNOME graphical desktop environments. This version is executed by running the xemacs command from a shell prompt or from the Utilities | Editors | XEmacs desktop menu item. The XEmacs interface is shown in Figure 5-30.

The interface for XEmacs is very similar to that used by the standard version of Emacs, so we won't spend a lot of time discussing it here. Just be aware that if you really like Emacs, a graphical version is also available.

Finally, let's look at gedit.

Using gedit

If you're working on a Linux system that uses the GNOME desktop, then your default graphical text editor is a package called gedit. The gedit text editor is very

FIGURE 5-30

Running XEmacs

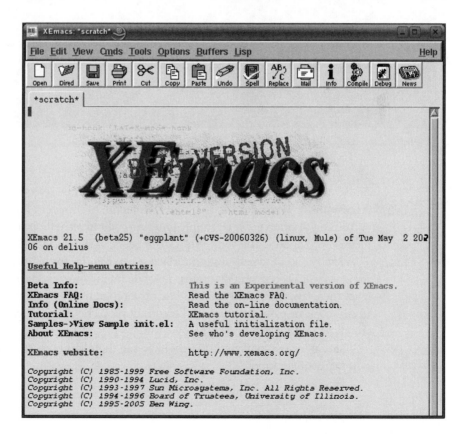

FIGURE 5-31   Running gedit

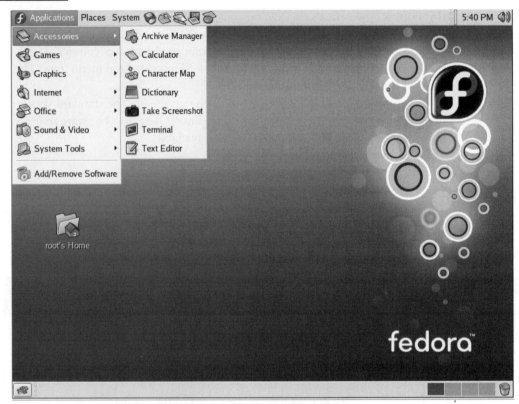

similar to the Kate editor we discussed earlier. It is run by selecting Applications |
Accessories | Text Editor in the GNOME menu, as shown in Figure 5-31.

You can also run gedit by simply entering **gedit** at a shell prompt. Whichever
method you choose, the gedit interface appears, as shown in Figure 5-32.

As with Kate, the gedit user interface is very similar to the interfaces used by
standard word processing programs. The File menu allows you to create new files,
open files, save files, print files, and exit the program. The Edit menu allows you
to cut, copy, or paste text within the current file. The Search menu allows you to
search for and replace text within the file.

That's it for text editors. You now have the tools you need to manage your Linux
systems' configuration.

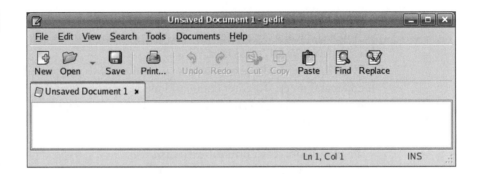

FIGURE 5-32

The gedit user
interface

CERTIFICATION SUMMARY

In this chapter, you learned how to use a variety of Linux text editors. We first emphasized the important role text editors play in Linux system management tasks. Unlike other operating systems that use a database to store system and application settings, Linux stores this information in a variety of text files. To configure a Linux system, you need to know how to edit these files.

Normally we wouldn't spend much time learning how to use text editors. However, because Linux text editors are a little harder to use than text editors on other operating systems, we spent a considerable amount of time learning how to operate them. We pointed out that there are a variety of graphical front-ends now available to make system configuration tasks easier. However, we pointed out that a good system administrator needs to understand the underlying configuration files being manipulated by these utilities. To do that, you must know how to use a text editor.

We began by learning how to use text-based text editors. The most commonly used editor (and the one you will be tested on in the Linux+ exam) is the vi editor. Although vi is a relatively simple editor, it is small, it doesn't require a graphical environment, and it can fit on a floppy diskette. This makes it ideal for use in emergency repair situations when you need to boot a malfunctioning system from a floppy.

To run vi, simply enter **vi** at a shell prompt. To run vi and load a file, enter **vi *file name*** at a shell prompt. If the file name you specify doesn't exist, vi will create a new file for you.

We then discussed the four different modes that vi can operate in. In normal mode, you can't directly edit the text of the file. To do this, you need to switch to insert mode or replace mode by pressing the INSERT key, the s key, or the I key. To return to normal mode, you just press the ESC key.

Once in insert mode or replace mode, you can edit the text file just as you would with most typical word processors. The key difference is the fact that you can't use the BACKSPACE key to erase text.

We then discussed the commands you can enter to perform file-related operations in command mode. To enter command mode, you first switch to normal mode and then enter a full colon (:). This causes a command prompt to be displayed that you can use to enter vi commands, including the following:

- **w**   Writes the current file to disk.
- **exit**   Writes the current file and then closes vi.
- **wq**   Also writes the current file to disk and closes vi.
- **q**   Closes vi without saving the current file.
- **q!**   Closes vi without saving the current file even if the file has been modified.

We then discussed the text manipulation commands that you can enter in normal mode. These commands are entered without entering a colon (:). You can enter the following:

- **dw**   Deletes the word that comes immediately after the cursor, including the space following the word.
- **de**   Deletes the word that comes immediately after the cursor, but not the following space.
- **d$**   Deletes from the insertion point to the end of the line.
- **dd**   Deletes the entire current line.
- **p**   Inserts deleted text after the current cursor location.
- **u**   Undoes the last action.
- **/term**   Searches for the specified term in the file.

We then shifted gears and looked at the Emacs editor. Emacs is a more powerful text-based editor that many administrators prefer over vi. It can use either keyboard commands or a menu-driven interface that can be manipulated with your mouse. You will need to install the Emacs package on your Linux system before you can use the program.

To run Emacs, you simply enter **emacs** at a shell prompt. Emacs saves files being worked on in memory buffers and uses the term *buffers* to refer to files being edited.

Within Emacs, you can do the following:

- Open a file (File | Open File): CTRL-X CTRL-F
- Copy text (Edit | Copy): ALT-W
- Cut text (Edit | Cut): CTRL-W
- Paste text (Edit | Paste): CTRL-Y
- Exit the program (File | Exit Emacs): CTRL-X CTRL-C

In addition to Emacs, you can also use a scaled-down version of Emacs called Quick Emacs. Quick Emacs can do just about everything that Emacs can do, but is considerably smaller. To use Quick Emacs, you must first install the qemacs package on your system. Then you can start the program by entering **qemacs** at the shell prompt.

We next reviewed some of the graphical editors that you can use on a Linux system. We pointed out that these editors are very similar to standard word processors, using most of the standard keyboard shortcuts and menu items. While these editors may be appropriate for day-to-day work, they usually can't be used in an emergency situation because they require X Windows to be running.

We first looked at the Kate editor. Kate is a standard graphical text editor provided with the KDE desktop. We also looked at the XEmacs editor, which is a graphical version of Emacs designed to work within X Windows. Finally, we looked the gedit text editor, which is the default editor used within the GNOME environment.

✓ ## TWO-MINUTE DRILL

Use Non-Graphical Linux Text Editors

❑ You must be able to use a text editor to manage a Linux system.

❑ Linux uses text files to store operating system and application configuration settings.

❑ Most of your configuration files reside in /etc.

❑ Many graphical configuration utilities are now available for most Linux distributions; however, you still need to be familiar with manually editing configuration files with a text editor.

❑ The vi editor is one of the most commonly used Linux text editors.

❑ The older version of vi was called *vi*; the newest version is called *vim* (Vi IMproved).

❑ You can open a file with vi by entering **vi *file name***. If the file doesn't exist, a new file will be created.

❑ Linux directory and file names are case-sensitive.

❑ The vi editor opens in normal mode by default.

❑ You can't directly edit files in vi when you are in normal mode.

❑ To switch to insert mode, press I, S, or the INSERT key.

❑ In insert mode, you can directly edit the text of a file.

❑ You can't use the BACKSPACE key to delete text in insert mode.

❑ Pressing INSERT while in insert mode will cause vi to switch to replace mode.

❑ To switch back to normal mode, press ESC.

❑ From within normal mode, you can enter a full colon (:) to switch to command mode.

❑ In command mode, you can enter file-related commands.

❑ Entering **:w** will write the current file to disk.

❑ Entering **:exit** will write the current file to disk and exit vi.

❑ Entering **:q** will exit vi.

❑ Entering **:q!** will exit vi without saving changes to a modified file.

❑ You can enter text manipulation commands from within normal mode in vi.

❑ Entering **dw** deletes the word that comes immediately after the cursor, including the space following the word.

❑ Entering **de** deletes the word that comes immediately after the cursor, not including the space.

❑ Entering **d$** deletes from the insertion point to the end of the line.

❑ Entering **dd** deletes the entire current line.

❑ Entering **p** inserts the text deleted in the last deletion operation after the cursor.

❑ Entering **u** undoes the last action.

❑ Pressing CTRL-G displays a status line at the bottom of the interface.

❑ Entering **/search_term** searches for the term specified.

❑ In addition to the vi editor, you can also use Emacs.

❑ Emacs is a more powerful text-based editor.

❑ Emacs provides a menu-driven interface that can be used with a mouse.

❑ You can run Emacs by entering **emacs** from the shell prompt.

❑ You will have to install the Emacs package on your system before you can run it.

❑ To open a file in Emacs, select File | Open File or press CTRL-X CTRL-F.

❑ To copy text in Emacs, select Edit | Copy or press ALT-W.

❑ To cut text in Emacs, select Edit | Cut or press CTRL-W.

❑ To paste text in Emacs, select Edit | Paste or press CTRL-Y.

❑ To exit Emacs, select File | Exit Emacs or press CTRL-X CTRL-C.

❑ Whenever you modify a file, Emacs saves a backup copy named with a tilde (~).

❑ A scaled-down version of Emacs is available called Quick Emacs.

❑ Quick Emacs is much smaller than Emacs and can fit on a floppy diskette.

Use Graphical Text Editors

❑ In addition to vi and Emacs, you can also use a variety of graphical text editors from within X Windows to edit configuration text files.

❑ To use these editors, you need to have X Windows, a window manager, and a desktop environment installed on your Linux system.

- ❑ Graphical text editors are appropriate for day-to-day tasks, but they usually can't be used in an emergency situation where you're trying to rescue a failing system.
- ❑ Kate is the standard graphical text editor installed with the KDE desktop.
- ❑ Kate works much like a standard word processor such as Microsoft Word or OpenOffice.org.
- ❑ You run Kate by selecting its icon from the KDE menu or by entering **kate** at a shell prompt.
- ❑ The menu items and keyboard shortcuts used by Kate are very similar to those used by standard word processing software.
- ❑ A graphical version of Emacs is available called XEmacs.
- ❑ XEmacs is a special version of Emacs designed to work within X Windows.
- ❑ The default editor used in the GNOME desktop environment is gedit.
- ❑ You run gedit by selecting its icon from the GNOME menu or by entering **gedit** from the shell prompt.
- ❑ Like Kate, gedit functions much like a standard word processor.
- ❑ The menu items and keyboard shortcuts used by gedit are very similar to those used by standard word processing software.

SELF TEST

Use Non-Graphical Linux Text Editors

1. Where are operating system and application configuration parameters stored on a Linux system?

A. In text files

B. In the Registry

C. In .ini files

D. In the system database

2. Where are most configuration files stored in the Linux file system?

A. /boot

B. /var

C. /usr

D. /etc

3. Where can you find the vi symbolic link file on most Linux distributions?

A. /usr/bin

B. /boot

C. /etc

D. /var/vi

4. Which of the following is an advantage of the vi editor?

A. It provides a syntax checker.

B. It provides a menu-driven user interface.

C. It is small enough to fit on a floppy.

D. It can be used to edit Microsoft Word files.

5. You have a terminal window open and the current directory is /tmp. You need to use vi to open a file named vnc in the /etc/xinetd.d directory on your system. Which of the following commands will do this?

A. vi vnc

B. vi /tmp/vnc

C. vi /etc/xinetd.d/vnc

D. vi /etc/xinetd.d

6. You have a terminal window open and the current directory is your user's home directory. You need to create a new file in your home directory named resources.txt using vi. Which of the following commands will do this?

   A. vi resources.txt –new

   B. vi resources

   C. vi ~/resources

   D. vi resources.txt

7. Which mode does vi open in by default?

   A. Command mode

   B. Insert mode

   C. Normal mode

   D. Replace mode

8. You've opened a text file named list.txt in vi. You move the cursor using the arrow keys to the point in the file where you need to make several changes. You try to type, but nothing happens. Why is this happening?

   A. The vi editor is in insert mode. You need to switch to normal mode.

   B. The vi editor is in normal mode. You need to switch to insert mode.

   C. The vi editor is in insert mode. You need to switch to replace mode.

   D. The text file is corrupt.

9. Which keystroke will switch vi from normal mode to insert mode?

   A. DELETE

   B. ESC

   C. INSERT

   D. F1

10. You're using vi to edit a text file in insert mode. Because of the nature of the changes you're making to the file, you need to switch to replace mode. Which keystroke will do this?

    A. ESC

    B. CTRL-X CTRL-R

    C. :

    D. INSERT

11. You're using vi to edit a file in insert mode. You need to switch back to normal mode. Which keystroke will do this?

    A. INSERT

    B. :

C. ESC

D. BACKSPACE

12. You're using vi to edit a file in insert mode. You try to use the BACKSPACE key to delete a word, but nothing happens. What's wrong with the system?

A. You need to switch to normal mode.

B. You need to switch to replace mode.

C. Nothing is wrong. BACKSPACE doesn't work in vi.

D. You need to switch to command mode.

13. You've created a new file using vi and now need to save the file. Which command will do this?

A. :s

B. :w

C. :save

D. :writeln

14. You've created a new file using vi and need to save the file to disk and exit the program. Which command will do this? (Choose two.)

A. :w

B. :se

C. :wq

D. :exit

E. :q

15. You've made several changes to a configuration file using vi. You realize that you've made a myriad of mistakes and want to quit without saving the changes so you can start over. Which command will do this?

A. :q!

B. :exit

C. :q

D. :exit!

16. You're working with a file in vi in normal mode. You locate a word in the file that needs to be deleted and place your cursor at the beginning of that word. Which command will delete this word without deleting the space that follows the word?

A. dw

B. de

C. d$

D. dd

17. You're viewing a configuration file in vi in normal mode. You need to locate a directive named *server* in the file. However, the file is very long and you don't want to scan through it line by line. What command can you use to search for this term?

A. /server

B. search=server

C. /"server"

D. find "server"

18. Which keystroke will open a file in the Emacs text editor?

A. CTRL-X CTRL-F

B. CTRL-O

C. CTRL-X CTRL-O

D. CTRL-G

19. Which keystroke will save a file in the Emacs text editor?

A. CTRL-X CTRL-F

B. CTRL-W

C. CTRL-X CTRL-S

D. CTRL-S

20. Which command will start Quick Emacs from the shell prompt?

A. Emacs

B. quickemacs

C. QuickEmacs

D. qemacs

Use Graphical Text Editors

21. Which of the following is an advantage of using a graphical text editor in Linux?

A. It can be used in an emergency repair situation.

B. It is small enough to fit on an emergency boot diskette.

C. It can be used to work on Microsoft Word files.

D. It is generally easier to use than a text-based editor.

22. Which desktop environment uses Kate as the default graphical text editor?

A. GNOME

B. Sawfish

    C. KDE

    D. ICE

23. Which command can be used from the shell prompt to run the graphical version of Emacs?

    A. **xemacs**

    B. **gemacs**

    C. **emacs -gui**

    D. **emacs -x**

24. Which desktop environment uses gedit as the default graphical text editor?

    A. GNOME

    B. Sawfish

    C. KDE

    D. ICE

LAB QUESTION

You're responsible for managing the Linux systems in your organization. You need to change the configuration of the xntpd daemon running on one of your servers to use a different time provider. To do this, you need to open the /etc/ntpd.conf file and change the server=192.168.1.2 line in the file to server=192.168.1.254. Outline the steps you would follow to accomplish this task with vi.

SELF TEST ANSWERS

Use Non-Graphical Linux Text Editors

1. ☑ **A.** Linux uses text files to store configuration parameters for both the operating system and for applications or services running on the system
   ☒ **B, C,** and **D** are incorrect. **B** is incorrect because Linux doesn't use a Registry like Windows does. **C** is incorrect. While .ini files are text files, they are primarily used on older Windows systems to store configuration information. **D** is incorrect because Linux doesn't use a system database.

2. ☑ **D.** Most Linux configuration files are stored in the /etc directory or in a subdirectory of /etc.
   ☒ **A, B,** and **C** are incorrect. **A** is incorrect because the basic boot-up files are stored in /boot. **B** is incorrect because the /var directory is used to store mainly log files. However, there are instances when configuration files can be stored in /var. We'll discuss when this happens when we discuss setting up a DNS server later in this book. **C** is incorrect because system utilities are stored in /usr.

3. ☑ **A.** Depending upon your distribution, either the vi program itself or a symbolic link to the vim program will be stored in /usr/bin.
   ☒ **B, C,** and **D** are incorrect. **B** is incorrect because the basic boot-up files are stored in /boot. **C** is incorrect because configuration files are stored in /etc. **D** is a distracter.

4. ☑ **C.** One of the advantages of vi is that it can fit on a floppy diskette, allowing you to use it as an emergency boot disk.
   ☒ **A, B,** and **D** are incorrect. **A** is incorrect because vi doesn't provide a syntax checker. **B** is incorrect because vi doesn't provide a menu-driven interface. **D** is incorrect because vi can only be used to edit text files, not word processing files.

5. ☑ **C.** Because the file to be loaded doesn't reside in the current directory, you have to provide the full path to the file along with its file name when starting vi.
   ☒ **A, B,** and **D** are incorrect. **A** will only work if the file is in the current directory. **B** will only work if the file resides in /tmp. **D** doesn't include the file name.

6. ☑ **D.** Because you haven't specified a path, the file will be created in the current directory, which is what you want.
   ☒ **A, B,** and **C** are incorrect. **A** uses invalid syntax. **B** fails to include the correct file name. It's missing the file extension. **C** also uses invalid syntax for vi.

7. ☑ **C.** By default, vi opens in normal mode.
   ☒ **A, B,** and **D** are incorrect. **A** is incorrect because you must enter **:** to switch to command mode. **B** is incorrect because you must press INSERT to switch to insert mode. **D** is incorrect because you must press INSERT twice to switch to replace mode.

8. ☑ **B.** The vi editor opens by default in normal mode. You must press INSERT to switch to insert mode to start editing the file.

   ☒ **A, C,** and **D** are incorrect. **A** is incorrect. You can't edit in normal mode. **C** is incorrect because the editor is in normal mode. **D** is a distracter.

9. ☑ **C.** Pressing INSERT switches vi from normal mode to insert mode.

   ☒ **A, B,** and **D** are incorrect. **A** deletes text in vi. **B** switches from insert mode back to normal mode. **D** is a distracter.

10. ☑ **D.** Pressing INSERT while in insert mode will switch vi to replace mode.

    ☒ **A, B,** and **C** are incorrect. **A** will switch vi back to normal mode. **B** is a distracter. **C** switches vi into command mode.

11. ☑ **C.** Pressing ESC while in insert mode switches vi to normal mode.

    ☒ **A, B,** and **D** are incorrect. **A** would switch vi to replace mode. **B** would switch vi to command mode. **D** is a distracter.

12. ☑ **C.** The BACKSPACE key doesn't work in vi.

    ☒ **A, B,** and **D** are incorrect. **A** is incorrect because BACKSPACE only moves the cursor backwards in normal mode. **B** is incorrect because BACKSPACE doesn't work in replace mode either. **D** is incorrect because the focus moves from the text to the command prompt in command mode.

13. ☑ **B.** Entering **:w** will save the current file in vi without exiting the program.

    ☒ **A, C,** and **D** are incorrect. These responses are distracters.

14. ☑ **C** and **D.** Entering **:exit** will cause vi to save the current file and exit the program as will entering **:wq**.

    ☒ **A, B,** and **E** are incorrect. **A** will only save the file. **B** is a distracter. **E** exits vi without saving and will only work if the file hasn't been modified.

15. ☑ **A.** Entering **:q!** will exit vi without saving changes to the current file.

    ☒ **B, C,** and **D** are incorrect. **B** will save the file and exit. **C** won't work because the file has been modified. **D** is a distracter.

16. ☑ **B.** Entering **de** in normal mode will cause vi to delete the word without deleting the space that follows the word.

    ☒ **A, C,** and **D** are incorrect. **A** is incorrect because it will delete the space following the word. **C** is incorrect because it will delete the entire rest of the line. **D** is incorrect because it will delete the entire line.

17. ☑ **A.** Entering **/server** will search for the term "server" in the file.

    ☒ **B, C,** and **D** are incorrect. They are all distracters.

18. ☑ **A.** Pressing CTRL-X CTRL-F will open a file in Emacs.
    ☒ **B, C,** and **D** are incorrect. They are distracters.

19. ☑ **C.** Pressing CTRL-X CTRL-S will save a file in Emacs.
    ☒ **A, B,** and **D** are incorrect. **A** is incorrect because it is used to open a new file. **B** and **D** are distracters.

20. ☑ **D.** If the package is installed, entering **qemacs** will start Quick Emacs on your Linux system.
    ☒ **A, B,** and **C** are incorrect. These responses are distracters.

Use Graphical Text Editors

21. ☑ **D.** If you're used to working with word processors, you will probably find graphical Linux text editors much easier to use than text-based editors.
    ☒ **A, B,** and **C** are incorrect. **A** is incorrect because you usually can't use graphical editors in an emergency repair situation. **B** is incorrect. Because most graphical editors require a variety of dependent packages, they probably won't fit on a floppy diskette. **C** is incorrect. Graphical text editors can only work on text files, not word processing files.

22. ☑ **C.** KDE uses Kate as the default text editor.
    ☒ **A, B,** and **D** are incorrect. **A** is incorrect because GNOME uses gedit for the default editor. **B** and **D** are window managers, not desktops.

23. ☑ **A.** If the appropriate packages are installed, entering **xemacs** at the shell prompt will cause XEmacs to run on your system.
    ☒ **B, C,** and **D** are incorrect. These responses are distracters.

24. ☑ **A.** GNOME uses gedit as the default graphical editor.
    ☒ **B, C,** and **D** are incorrect. **B** and **D** are window managers, not desktops. **C** uses Kate for the default graphical editor.

LAB ANSWER

To accomplish this task, you should first open a terminal session. Then, you would enter **vi /etc/ntpd.conf** at the shell prompt to open the file in vi. The next task is to locate the appropriate directive. To do this, while in normal mode, enter **/server**. Press N repeatedly until you reach the right instance of "server" in the file.

With the right line located, you could move the cursor over to the beginning of the IP address after the = sign. Then enter **d$** to delete the rest of the line. Now you could insert the new IP address after the = sign by pressing INSERT to switch to insert mode and entering the appropriate text. Once done, press ESC to return to normal mode, and then save the file and exit vi by entering **:exit**.

6

Managing the
Linux File System

I t's time to dig in and really start working with Linux! All of the chapters preceding this chapter have been designed to build a foundation of knowledge and skills that you will use throughout the rest of this book. In this chapter, we're going to take what you've learned thus far and apply it to learn how to manage partitions, directories, and files on a Linux system.

If you're coming to Linux from a Windows background, this chapter may be challenging for you. The Linux file system is similar to the DOS or Windows file systems in many ways, but it is radically different in many others. My experience with students new to Linux is that there are just enough similarities to give them a false sense of security when they initially start learning about the file system. Then, as we dig deeper and start working with more advanced tasks, they start to get very frustrated.

Hopefully, we can make things as easy to understand as possible as we work through this chapter. If I can emphasize one thing that will make your life easier as you learn about the Linux file system here, it would be to encourage you to

INSIDE THE EXAM

Managing the Linux File System

Be prepared to be tested very heavily on this chapter in your Linux+ exam. We're going to be covering five separate Linux+ certification objectives in this chapter. Depending on which exam form you receive when you take your test, you may see 15–20 percent of your exam questions coming from this chapter alone.

Much of the content of the preceding chapters is somewhat conceptual in nature, meaning they emphasize *knowing* something instead of *doing* something. This chapter will be completely different. Most of the topics we're going to cover here will require you to actually perform certain tasks on a Linux system. If you haven't set up a lab system to

practice on yet, I strongly recommend that you do so before proceeding. Refer back to the lab exercise in Chapter 3 for instructions on how to do this.

Once your lab system is up and running, you should practice completing the examples and exercises presented in this chapter over and over until you feel thoroughly comfortable with the tasks and utilities involved. When you take your Linux+ exam, you may be asked questions such as "Which command is used to delete a directory?" You need to be familiar enough with the contents of this chapter to instantly know exactly how to respond. That can be best accomplished through repeated practice.

remember that Linux file and directory names are case-sensitive! Windows and DOS users and administrators tend to really struggle with this aspect of the Linux file system. When you see a command or file name in an example or exercise in this book, remember that you must use the correct case shown; otherwise, you won't get the same results on your system!

With this in mind, let's review what we're going to talk about in this chapter. The following topics will be covered:

- An introduction to the Linux file system
- Completing common file system tasks
- Managing disk partitions
- Working with removable media
- Backing up data

Let's begin this chapter by introducing you to the Linux file system.

CERTIFICATION OBJECTIVE 6.01

Describe the Linux File System

"An introduction to file systems?" you ask. "Didn't we already talk about ext2, ext3, and Reiser back in Chapter 3?" Yes, we did. However, these are more properly termed *disk* file systems. They are used to define how data is stored on your Linux system's hard disk drive. A disk file system is a specific implementation of a *file system* in general. There are other implementations of file systems in addition to disk file systems, including database file systems and network file systems, such as the Network File System (NFS) or the Server Message Block (SMB) file system.

Instead of discussing a specific type of file system in this part of the chapter, we're instead going to discuss the Linux file system in general. Specifically, we're going to review the following:

- The role of the file system
- The hierarchical structure of the Linux file system
- Linux file types

Let's begin by discussing the role of the file system.

The Role of the Linux File System

So what exactly is the role of the file system in general on a Linux system (or any other operating system, for that matter)? We're talking about a system that stores information on a storage device in such a manner that:

- The data is organized and can be easily located.
- The data can be easily retrieved at any later point in time.
- The integrity of the data is preserved.

In other words, if you save a file to a storage device, you should be able to find it later on and retrieve it, assured that its contents will be exactly the same as when it was saved. It doesn't matter whether you're saving data to a floppy diskette, a hard drive, or a USB thumb drive; you must use some type of file system to accomplish these three goals.

Let's review how the Linux file system organizes the data to make it easily locatable and retrievable.

The Hierarchical Structure of the Linux File System

The file system used by Linux uses a hierarchical structure to organize and store data. This is shown in Figure 6-1.

Notice that the topmost directory in the structure is the **/** directory, also called the *root* directory. This has nothing to do with your root user account. It simply specifies that this directory is the root of your hierarchical file system tree.

Beneath the root directory are a series of subdirectories. Specifications for how these directories are to be named are contained in the Filesystem Hierarchy Standard (FHS). The FHS provides Linux software developers and system administrators with a standard directory structure for the file system, ensuring consistency between systems and distributions. You can view more information about the FHS at http://www.pathname.com/fhs/. The FHS defines the directories that should appear under the root directory (/) as well as the directories that should appear under the /usr and /var directories. These include the following:

- **/bin** This directory contains executable files necessary to manage and run the Linux system, including shells (such as bash) and file system management utilities such as cp and rm.

FIGURE 6-1   The hierarchical structure of the Linux file system

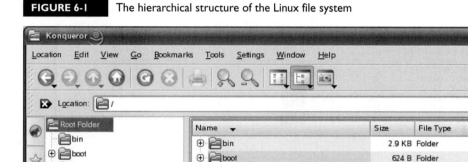

- **/boot**   This directory contains your bootloader files, which are required to boot your system.
- **/dev**   This directory contains special files that are used to represent the various hardware devices installed in the system. Remember when we installed Linux? We said that the first SCSI hard disk drive in your system was called sda and the first IDE hard drive in your system was called hda. The files that represent these devices are stored in /dev, as shown in Figure 6-2.

   Other hardware devices are also represented by files in /dev. A sampling is shown in Table 6-1.

FIGURE 6-2   Files in /dev

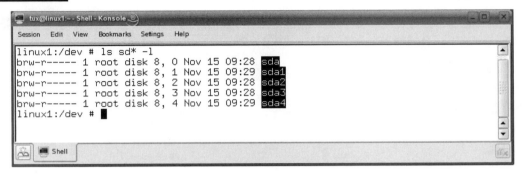

- **/etc**   This directory contains text-based configuration files used by the system as well as services running on the system. You can edit these files with a text editor to customize how Linux behaves. Some of the more important files in this directory include those shown in Table 6-2.

- **/home**   This directory contains subdirectories that serve as home directories for each user account on your Linux system.

- **/lib**   This directory contains code libraries used by programs in /bin and /sbin. Your kernel modules are also stored in the modules subdirectory of /lib.

- **/media**   This directory is used by some Linux distributions (such as SUSE Linux) to mount external devices, including CD drives, DVD drives, and floppy drives. This is done using a series of subdirectories, shown in Figure 6-3.

- **/mnt**   This directory is used by some Linux distributions (such as Fedora or Red Hat) to mount external devices, including CD drives, DVD drives, and floppy drives. As with the /media directory on a SUSE system, a series of subdirectories are used to do this, as shown in Figure 6-4.

TABLE 6-1   Hardware Represented by Files in /dev

Device	Device File in /dev
Floppy Drive	/dev/fd0
SCSI CD-ROM Drive	/dev/scd0
IDE CD-ROM Drive	/dev/hdc (if the drive is the master IDE device on the secondary IDE channel in the system)
Serial Port	/dev/ttyS0
Parallel Port	/dev/lp0

TABLE 6-2	Some of the Configuration Files in /etc

File	Function
/etc/fstab	Lists the partitions and file systems that will be automatically mounted when the system boots.
/etc/group	Contains local group definitions.
/etc/grub.conf	Contains configuration parameters for the GRUB bootloader (assuming it's being used on the system).
/etc/hosts	Contains a list of hostname-to-IP address mappings the system can use to resolve hostnames.
/etc/inittab	Contains configuration parameters for the init process.
/etc/init.d/	A subdirectory that contains startup scripts for services installed on the system. On a Fedora or Red Hat system, these are located in /etc/rc.d/init.d.
/etc/modules.conf	Contains configuration parameters for your kernel modules.
/etc/passwd	Contains your system user accounts.
/etc/shadow	Contains encrypted passwords for your user accounts.
/etc/X11/	Contains configuration files for X Windows.

FIGURE 6-3

Subdirectories of /media

FIGURE 6-4

Subdirectories of /mnt

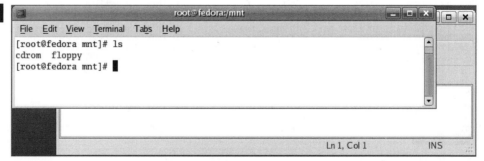

- **/opt** This directory contains files for some programs you install on the system.
- **/proc** This directory is a little different from the other directories in this list. /proc doesn't actually exist in the file system. Instead, it's a pseudo file system that is dynamically created whenever it is accessed. It's used to access process information from the Linux kernel.

Within /proc are a number of different subdirectories, as shown in Figure 6-5.

Notice that each of these subdirectories is identified with a number, not a name. These numbers correspond to the process ID (PID) number of the associated process running on the system. In Figure 6-6, top is being run to display the running processes on the system.

The PID column, on the far-left side of the display, lists the PID number of each process. The actual name of the command used to create the process is displayed in the far-right column of the display. For example, the process associated with the top program itself has a PID of 14235. If you look in the /proc/14235 directory, you can view information about the top process running on the system, as shown in Figure 6-7.

FIGURE 6-5   Subdirectories of /proc

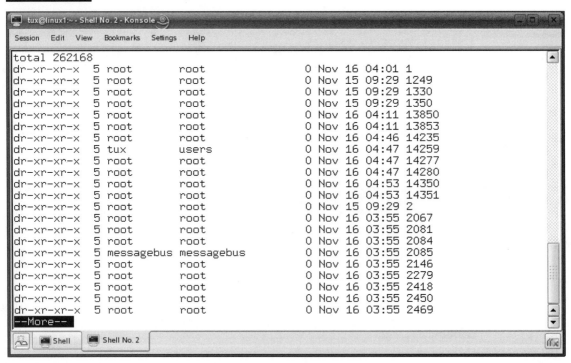

FIGURE 6-6   Using top to display running processes

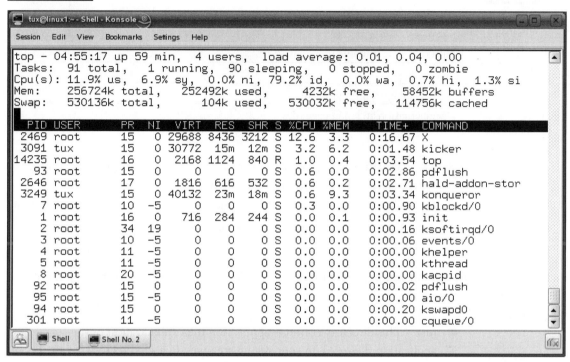

- **/root**   This directory is the root user's home directory. Notice that it is located separately from the home directories for other users in /home.
- **/sbin**   This directory contains important system management and administration files, such as fdisk, fsck, ifconfig, init, mkfs, shutdown, and halt.

FIGURE 6-7   Viewing information about the top process in /proc

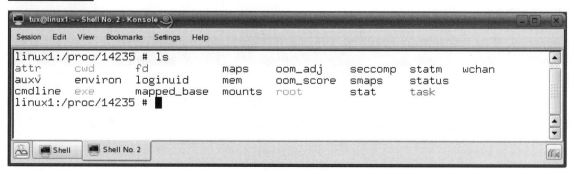

TABLE 6-3   Subdirectories of /usr

Subdirectory	Contents
bin	Most of your executable programs
lib	Library files
sbin	System administration programs
share	Documentation and man page files

- **/srv**   This directory contains subdirectories where services running on the system (such as httpd and ftpd) save their files.
- **/sys**   This directory contains information about the hardware in your system.
- **/tmp**   This directory contains temporary files created by you or by the system.

on the
Ĵob

The system will periodically delete old files out of the /tmp directory. Don't save anything in /tmp that you want to keep!

- **/usr**   This directory contains application files. In fact, most of the application files used on your system are saved in a subdirectory of /usr. These subdirectories include those shown in Table 6-3.
- **/var**   This directory contains a variety of variable data, including your system log files. Some of the typical subdirectories contained in /var are shown in Table 6-4.

With this structure in mind, let's next discuss the types of files used by the Linux file system.

TABLE 6-4   Subdirectories of /var

Subdirectory	Contents
lib	Library files created by various services and applications running on the system
log	Log files from your system and from services running on the system
spool	Print queues

SCENARIO & SOLUTION

Which device file points to the floppy disk in a Linux system?	The /dev/fd0 file points to the first floppy diskette in the system.
Which device file points to an IDE CD-ROM drive connected as the slave drive on the primary IDE channel?	The /dev/hdb file points to the slave device on the primary IDE channel.
Which directory contains your Linux system's configuration files?	Your system's configuration files are saved in /etc.

Types of Files Used by Linux

When working with Linux, you need to be aware of the fact that there are a number of different file types used by the file system. This is another area where the Linux file system differs significantly from the Windows file system. With a Windows file system you basically have two entry types in the file system:

- Directories
- Files

Granted, you can have normal files, hidden files, shortcut files, word processing files, executable files, and so on. However, these are all simple variations of the basic file when working with Windows.

With Linux, however, there are a variety of different file types used by the file system. These include the file types shown in Table 6-5.

TABLE 6-5   Linux File Types

File Type	Description
Regular files	These files are similar to those used by the file systems of other operating systems—for example, executable files, OpenOffice.org files, images, text configuration files, etc.
Links	These files are pointers that point to other files in the file system.
FIFOs	FIFO stands for First In First Out. These are special files used to move data from one running process on the system to another. A FIFO file is basically a queue where the first chunk of data added to the queue is the first chunk of data removed from the queue. Data can only move in one direction through a FIFO.
Sockets	Sockets are similar to FIFOs in that they are used to transfer information between sockets. With a socket, however, data can move bi-directionally.

With this introduction to the Linux file system in mind, you're ready to start learning how to complete common file system tasks. Let's do that next.

CERTIFICATION OBJECTIVE 6.02

Complete Common File System Tasks

Just as with any other operating system, you need to be able to create, copy, and move files and directories in the Linux file system. In this part of this chapter, we're going to spend some time reviewing how this is done.

If you have any experience working with the command line in other operating systems, such as DOS or Windows, you may be thinking that these tasks are trivial in nature. Believe it or not, these tasks are actually quite difficult for many of my students when they first learn how to use Linux. I frequently see students trying to using old DOS commands when working with the file system at the Linux shell prompt.

on the
Job

I even catch myself doing this on occasion. I was presenting a demo for students just last week and needed to copy some files on a Linux system. Without thinking, I entered copy instead of cp at the shell prompt and, of course, it didn't work. I was red-faced!

When working with the Linux file system, remember that the following commands don't work:

copy
del

As with Windows, you can perform file system manipulation tasks from either the shell prompt or from within the Linux GUI. Many who are coming to Linux from a Windows background are tempted to perform these tasks solely using the GUI utilities provided with most distributions.

While these graphical utilities are handy and easy to use, you should also learn how to do these tasks from the shell prompt. I realize that this goes against standard practice with Windows systems. I've worked with many Windows users who don't know the command prompt even exists on their systems. With Linux, however, you should become proficient with the shell commands first and then use the GUI utilities for convenience. I say this for the following reasons:

- Most employers and co-workers won't take you seriously as a Linux administrator if you can't use the shell prompt. It just goes with the territory.
- Many Linux systems, especially those deployed as servers, don't run X Windows. Supporting a GUI environment requires a lot of CPU overhead. Many server admins prefer to devote those CPU cycles to system services instead of moving the mouse cursor on the screen. In this situation, you need to know how to do things from the shell prompt.
- You need to know how to complete these tasks from the shell prompt to pass your Linux+ exam.

For your Linux+ exam, there are a large number of file system manipulation commands that you must be proficient with. In this chapter, we're going to group these commands together into the following tasks:

- Navigating the file system
- Managing files and directories
- Running executable files
- Searching the file system

As we cover each of these groups of tasks, you'll be presented with an exercise that will help you learn how to use the associated commands. I strongly recommend that you practice working with these commands until they become second nature to you. You'll be glad you did when you take your exam!

Let's begin by learning how to get around in the file system using shell prompt commands.

Navigating the File System

As you work with the Linux file system, one of the most common tasks you will need to complete is to move around between the different directories on your hard disks. Your Linux system provides the following commands that you can use from the shell prompt to do this:

- pwd
- cd
- ls

Let's start by learning how to use the pwd command.

Using the pwd Command

The pwd command is a relatively simple utility. It simply displays the current directory on the screen. (*pwd* stands for Present Working Directory.) This utility can be exceptionally useful if your shell profile hasn't been configured to display the current directory as a part of the shell prompt. To use pwd, simply enter **pwd** at the shell prompt. This is shown in Figure 6-8.

In Figure 6-8, you can see that the current directory is set to /home/tux.

on the
job

The ~ character in the shell prompt is shorthand that refers to the current user's home directory. Because we're logged in as the tux user in Figure 6-8, the ~ points to /home/tux.

At this point, you know how to identify what directory you're in. More than likely, you're going to need to change to a different directory in the file system at some point. Let's discuss how to do this next.

Using the cd Command

The cd command is used from the Linux shell prompt to change directories in the file system. To use this command, simply enter **cd** followed by the name of the directory you want to switch to. There are two ways you can do this. If you enter **cd** and then the name of a directory *without* specifying the full path to the directory, cd will assume that the directory is a subdirectory of the current directory. For example, in Figure 6-9 the **cd Documents** command has been issued.

Because the command was issued from /home/tux, cd changed directories to /home/tux/Documents. This is called using a *relative path*. The path specified with the command is relative to some other point in the file system, in this case, the /home/tux directory.

FIGURE 6-8   Using pwd to display the current directory

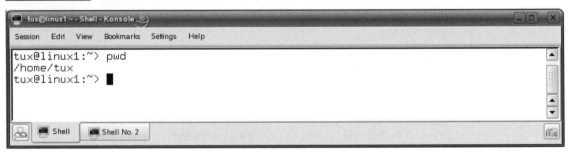

| FIGURE 6-9 | Using the cd command with relative paths |

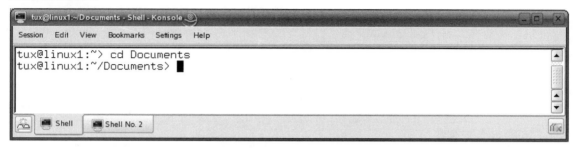

You can also use *absolute paths* with the cd command. When you use an absolute path, you specify the full path, starting from /, to the directory you want to change to. For example, in Figure 6-10, the **cd /var/log** command has been issued.

Because we specified an absolute path, the cd command knew that the var/log directory didn't exist in the current directory. Instead, the path was determined from the root directory (/) and the current directory was changed to it.

on the
job
If you enter cd at the shell prompt without specifying a path, it will automatically change directories to the home directory of the currently logged-in user.

You can also use the cd command to move up the file system hierarchy. You can do this by entering **cd ..**. This will change the current directory to the next directory higher in the hierarchy. In Figure 6-11, the **cd ..** command has been issued, changing the directory from /var/log to /var.

Let's next look at the ls command.

| FIGURE 6-10 | Using the cd command with absolute paths |

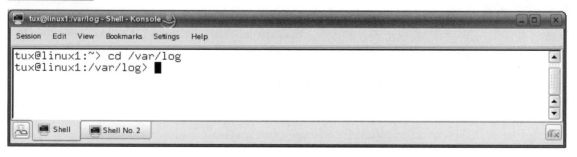

| FIGURE 6-11 | Using cd to move up in the file system hierarchy |

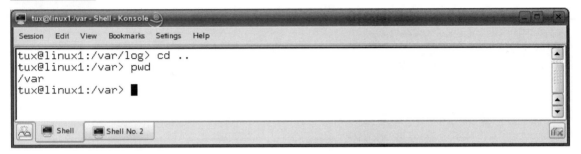

Using the ls Command

To this point, you've learned how to view the current directory and change to other directories in the file system. Now you need to learn how to list the files and subdirectories that may exist within a directory. This is done using the ls command. If you enter **ls** at the shell prompt, the contents of the current directory are listed on the screen, as shown in Figure 6-12.

As with the cd command, you can also provide an absolute path when using ls. This will cause ls to display the contents of the directory you specify. Consider the example shown in Figure 6-13.

In Figure 6-13, the ls /var/log command has been issued, causing the contents of /var/log to be displayed. When working with ls, you can use a variety of options to customize how it works. Some of these options include the following:

- –a   Displays all files, including hidden files.
- –l   Displays a long listing of the directory contents. This is a very useful option. You can use it to see the file names, ownership, permissions, modification date, and size. A sample is shown in Figure 6-14.

| FIGURE 6-12 | Using ls to view the contents of the current directory |

FIGURE 6-13 Using absolute paths with the ls command

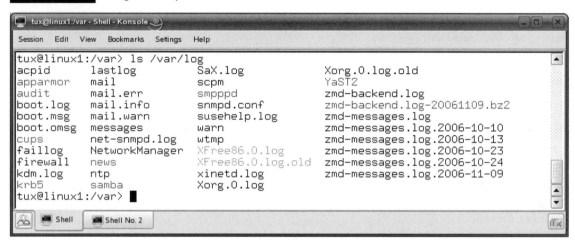

■ **–R** Displays directory contents recursively; that is, it displays the contents of the current directory as well as the contents of all subdirectories. Depending on the number of entries in the directory, you may want to append | more after using this option. This will cause the more utility to pause the display one page at a time. An example is shown in Figure 6-15 where the ls –R | more command has been issued from the /var/log directory.

FIGURE 6-14 Using the –l option with the ls command

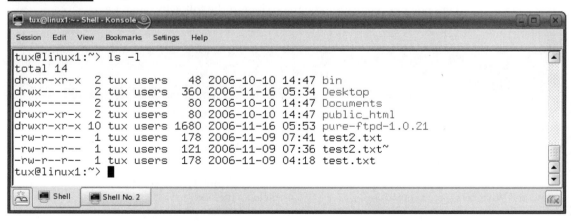

FIGURE 6-15   Using the –R option with the ls command

This list is only a sampling of the different options you can use with ls. You can
view the ls man page or info node to learn more.

Let's practice navigating the file system in the following exercise.

SCENARIO & SOLUTION

What command would you enter at the shell prompt to determine the current directory?	You would enter **pwd**.
What command would you enter if you wanted to change to your home directory?	You could enter **cd** or **cd ~**.
You need to see how large a file is in the current directory. What command can you use?	You could enter **ls –l** to generate a long listing that includes file sizes.

EXERCISE 6-1

Navigating the File System

In this exercise, you will practice using shell commands to navigate the Linux file system. Complete the following:

1. Boot your Linux system and log in as a standard user. If you used the lab exercise in Chapter 3 to install your system, you can log in as tux with a password of M3linux273.

2. Open a terminal session.

3. Determine your current working directory by entering **pwd** at the shell prompt. What's the current directory?

4. Change directories to /etc by entering **cd /etc** at the shell prompt.

5. Generate a listing of the current directory by entering **ls**.

6. Generate a long listing of the current directory by entering **ls –l**.

7. Generate a long list and pause the output a page at a time by entering **ls –l | more**. Page your way through the listing.

8. Switch back to your home directory by entering **cd ~**.

Let's now shift gears and discuss shell commands that you can use to manage files and directories.

Managing Files and Directories

In addition to navigating among the directories in the file system, there will be many occasions when you need to manage those directories and the files they contain. In this part of the chapter, you will learn how to complete the following tasks:

- Creating files and directories
- Viewing file contents
- Deleting files and directories
- Copying and moving files and directories
- Creating links

Let's start with the process you should follow to create new files and directories in your file system.

Creating Files and Directories

From time to time, you will need to create new files and directories in your Linux file system. Creating a new file can be accomplished using the touch command from the shell prompt. To use touch, enter **touch** followed by the name of the file you want to create. In Figure 6-16, the command touch myfile.txt was issued from within the home directory of the tux user.

After entering touch, the ls –l command was entered. You can see in Figure 6-16 that a 0-byte file was created named myfile.txt in /home/tux. If you wanted to create the file elsewhere in the file system, you could use an absolute path with the file name.

You can also use shell commands to create new directories. This is done using the mkdir command. As with touch, you can enter **mkdir** from the shell prompt followed by the name of the directory you want to create. For example, in Figure 6-17, the mkdir MyFiles command has been issued from the home directory of the tux user.

Notice in the output from the ls –l command that a new directory named MyFiles was created in /home/tux. Of course, you could use an absolute path with the directory name if you wanted to create it somewhere other than the current directory.

FIGURE 6-16 Using touch to create a new file

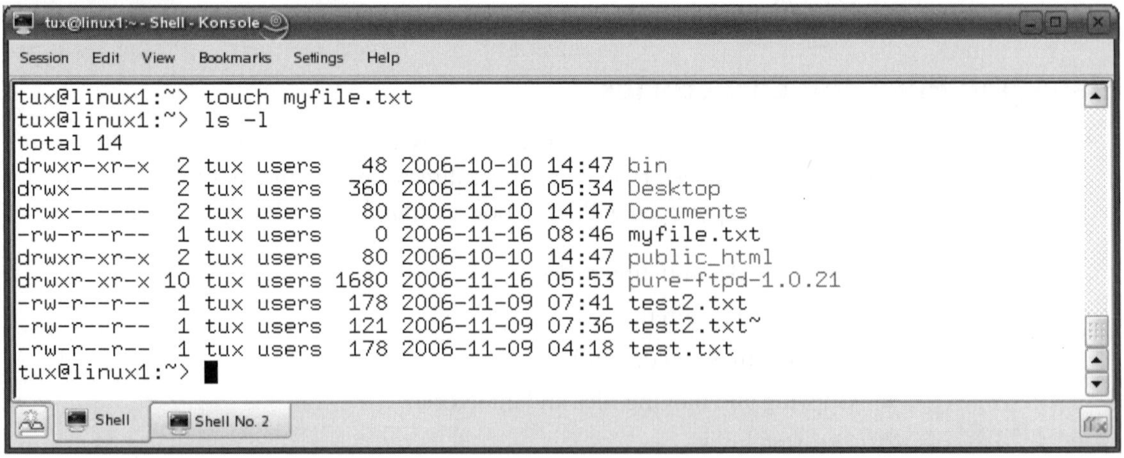
tux@linux1:~ - Shell - Konsole
Session Edit View Bookmarks Settings Help
tux@linux1:~> touch myfile.txt
tux@linux1:~> ls -l
total 14
drwxr-xr-x 2 tux users   48 2006-10-10 14:47 bin
drwx------ 2 tux users 360 2006-11-16 05:34 Desktop
drwx------ 2 tux users   80 2006-10-10 14:47 Documents
-rw-r--r-- 1 tux users   0 2006-11-16 08:46 myfile.txt
drwxr-xr-x 2 tux users   80 2006-10-10 14:47 public_html
drwxr-xr-x 10 tux users 1680 2006-11-16 05:53 pure-ftpd-1.0.21
-rw-r--r-- 1 tux users 178 2006-11-09 07:41 test2.txt
-rw-r--r-- 1 tux users 121 2006-11-09 07:36 test2.txt~
-rw-r--r-- 1 tux users 178 2006-11-09 04:18 test.txt
tux@linux1:~>
Shell
Shell No. 2

SCENARIO & SOLUTION

You are working on a Linux system and need to create a new file named params in /tmp. What command would you use?	You would enter **touch /tmp/params**.
What command would you enter if you wanted to create a new directory named backup in the /tmp directory?	You could enter **mkdir /tmp/backup**.

Let's next discuss how to view the contents of a text file.

Viewing Text File Contents

As we discussed in the previous chapter, your Linux system and the services that run on it are configured using simple text files stored in (usually) the /etc directory in the file system. Because Linux uses text files to configure just about everything, you will frequently need to view the contents of files.

In the previous chapter, you learned how to use text editors to open a file for viewing and editing. This works very well. However, there will be many occasions when you simply want to quickly view a text file on screen and don't want to have

FIGURE 6-17   Using mkdir to create a new directory

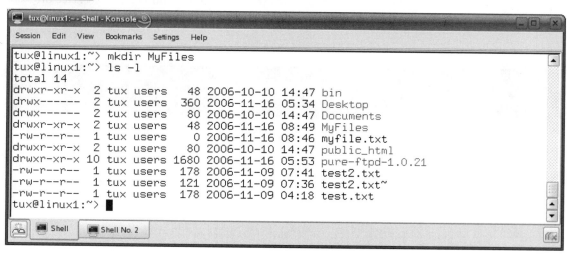

to load up a text editor. Linux provides you with a variety of command-line tools that you can use to do this. These include the following:

- **cat** The cat *filename* command will display the specified text file on screen. This command doesn't pause the output, so if you use it to view a long file, you may need to append | more to the command to pause the output a page a time.

- **less** The less *filename* command can also be used to display the specified text file on screen, much like cat. However, the less command automatically pauses a long text file one page at time. You can use the SPACEBAR, PAGE UP, PAGE DOWN, and ARROW keys to navigate around in the file.

- **head** The head *filename* command is used to display the first couple of lines of a text file on the screen.

- **tail** The tail *filename* command is used to display the last couple of lines of a text file on screen. The tail command is particularly useful when displaying a log file on screen. When viewing a log file, you probably only want to see the end of the file. You probably don't care about log entries made several days ago. You can use tail to see just the last log entries added to the end of the file.

   The tail command also includes the –f option, which is very useful. You can use this to monitor the file specified in the command. If new content is added to the end of the file (such as a log file) the addition will be displayed on screen. In Figure 6-18, the tail –f /var/log/messages command has been issued to monitor the file for new entries.

   This can be very helpful when troubleshooting a misbehaving service or configuration problem on the system.

SCENARIO & SOLUTION

You are working on a Linux system and need to view the /etc/xinetd.conf file. What command would you use?	You could enter **cat /etc/xinetd.conf**.
You need to view the last few lines of the /var/log/messages file. What command can you use to do this?	You could enter **tail /var/log/messages**.

FIGURE 6-18   Using tail with the –f option to monitor a log file

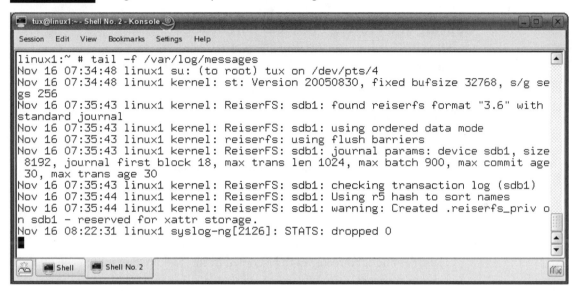

In addition to creating and viewing files, you will also need to know how to delete existing files and directories. Let's discuss how this is done next.

Deleting Files and Directories

As with any operating system, there will be times when you will need to delete an existing file or directory from the Linux file system. Deleting files and directories can be accomplished using two shell commands:

- **rmdir**   This utility can be used to delete an existing directory. To use it, simply enter **rmdir** *directory_name*—for example, **rmdir MyFiles**. Be aware, however, that rmdir requires that the directory be empty before it will delete it.

- **rm**   The rm utility is a more powerful deletion utility that can be used to delete either a file or a populated directory. To delete a file, simply enter **rm** *filename*. To delete a directory, enter **rm –r** *directory_name*.

on the
()ob   *Be careful with rm! By default, it won't prompt you to confirm a deletion operation. It assumes that you really meant to delete the file or directory. If you want rm to prompt you before deleting a file or directory, include the –i option.*

Let's next review how you can copy and move files.

Copying and Moving Files and Directories

In addition to creating and deleting files and directories in the Linux file system, you can also copy or move them. You use the following utilities to accomplish these tasks:

- **cp** This utility is used to copy files or entire directory structures from one location in the file system to another. For example, to copy a file named /tmp/schedule.txt to your home directory, you could enter **cp /tmp/schedule.txt ~**. Because cp copies the file, the original file is left intact.

  To copy an entire directory structure, you need to include the –R option, which specifies that the directory contents be recursively copied. For example, in Figure 6-19, the cp –R ~/MyFiles ~/backup command was issued in the tux user's home directory. This caused the MyFiles directory and all of its files and subdirectories to be copied to the backup directory in the user's home directory.

- **mv** The mv command is used much like cp. However, it will copy the specified file to the new location in the file system and then delete the original. For example, to move a file named mylog.txt from /tmp to /var/log, you would enter **mv /tmp/mylog.txt /var/log**.

*The mv command is also used to rename files. Simply enter **mv** followed by the file to be renamed and then the new file name. For example, to rename schedule.txt to schedule.old, you would enter **mv schedule.txt schedule.old**.*

FIGURE 6-19   Using the cp command to copy a directory structure

SCENARIO & SOLUTION

You are working on a Linux system and need to delete a file named /tmp/config.txt. What command would you use?	You could enter **rm /tmp/config.txt**.
You need to copy /tmp/mystuff.txt to your home directory. What command can you use to do this?	You could enter **cp /tmp/mystuff.txt ~**.
You need to rename a file in your home directory from myfile.txt to yourfile.txt. What command would you use to do this?	You could enter **mv ~/myfile.txt ~/yourfile.txt**.

Before we end this topic, let's spend some time discussing link files.

Creating Links

As we discussed earlier in this chapter, the Linux file system supports a file type called a link file. Link files are pointers that redirect you to a different file in the file system. On Linux you can create two different types of link files:

- **Hard**   A hard link is a file that points directly to the inode of another file. An inode stores basic information about a file in the Linux file system, including its size, device, owner, and permissions. Because the two files use the same inode, you can't tell which file is the pointer and which is the pointee after the hard link is created.

- **Symbolic**   A symbolic link file also points to another file in the file system. However, a file that is a symbolic link has its own inode. Because the pointer file has its own inode, the pointer and the pointee in the file system can be easily identified. For example, in the previous chapter, you saw that the vi file is symbolic-linked to the vim file.

To create a link file, you use the ln command. The syntax is ln *pointee_file pointer_file*. Using ln without any options creates a hard link. If you want to create a symbolic link, you use the –s option. For example, in Figure 6-20, the ln command has been used to create a symbolic link between a file named schedule.txt and a file named sched.

Using the ls command, you can see that schedule.txt actually points to the sched file.

Let's practice managing files in the following exercise.

FIGURE 6-20   Using ln to create a symbolic link

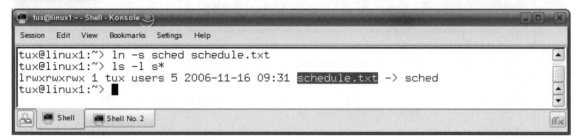

```
tux@linux1:~> ln -s sched schedule.txt
tux@linux1:~> ls -l s*
lrwxrwxrwx 1 tux users 5 2006-11-16 09:31 schedule.txt -> sched
tux@linux1:~>
```

EXERCISE 6-2

Managing Files and Directories

In this exercise, you practice managing files and directories using shell commands. Complete the following:

1. With your Linux system running and authenticated as a regular user, switch to your home directory by entering **cd** at the shell prompt.

2. Create a new directory in your home directory by entering **mkdir MyFiles**.

3. Enter **ls** and verify that the new directory exists.

4. Create a new file in the MyFiles directory called myfile.txt by entering **touch ~/MyFiles/myfile.txt**.

5. Enter **ls ~/MyFiles** and verify that the file exists.

6. Change to your root user account by entering **su –** and entering your root password. If you used the exercises in Chapter 3 of this book to set up your system, your root user password is **tuxPenguin1**.

7. View your system log file by entering **cat /var/log/messages |more**.

8. Page through a few pages of the file, then press CTRL-C to break out to the shell prompt.

9. View the last few entries in the log file by entering **tail /var/log/messages**.

10. Switch back to your regular user account by entering **exit**.

11. Delete the MyFiles directory in your home directory by entering **rm –r ~/MyFiles**.

12. Enter **ls** and verify that the directory and its contents are gone.

13. Make a copy of your home directory files and subdirectories in /tmp by entering **cp –R ~ /tmp**.

14. View the contents of /tmp by entering **ls /tmp**. Verify that your home directory was copied.

15. Create a symbolic link from a file named docs in your home directory to the /usr/share/doc directory by entering **ln –s /usr/share/doc/ ~/docs**.

16. Enter **ls –l**. Verify that the docs file points to /usr/share/doc/.

17. Enter **cd docs**.

18. Enter **pwd**. What directory are you in?

19. Enter **ls**. You should see the contents of the /usr/share/doc/ directory even though you are still in ~/doc.

Now that you know how to manage files in the Linux file system, we need to change our focus a little bit and discuss how to run an executable file from the shell prompt.

Running Executables

Running executables is the one task that I've observed to frustrate new Linux users over the years. Therefore, we're going to spend a page or two discussing how you go about running an executable file from the shell prompt on a Linux system.

As you have progressed through this book, you've already run a number of programs from the shell prompt. For example, you've used the man, vi, and cp programs to accomplish various tasks on your system. These programs are executable files that exist in the Linux file system and are loaded into memory when you call them from the shell prompt. No problem so far, right?

Notice, however, that you didn't have to provide the path to these files when you ran them from the shell prompt. However, these commands do have an absolute path associated with them. You can determine what this absolute path is using the which command. For example, in Figure 6-21, the which command has been used to determine where the vi utility resides in the file system.

FIGURE 6-21   Using the which command

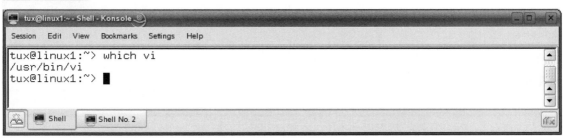

Notice that the vi file resides in /usr/bin. However, when you've run vi in previous chapters, you haven't entered **/usr/bin/vi** to run the program. Instead, you've simply run the vi command. This is because the /usr/bin directory is contained in your system's PATH environment variable. All of the directories contained in this variable are shown in Figure 6-22.

on the
Ö o b

You can view all of your environment variables by entering env |more *or echo* **$PATH** *at the shell prompt.*

Notice that there are many directories other than just /usr/bin in the PATH variable. Any time you enter a command at the shell prompt, the Linux operating system searches through the directories listed in your PATH environment variable for the executable you specified. Assuming the file is found, the program is then run. This is a very useful feature of Linux (and most other operating systems as well). It allows you to run frequently used programs without having to memorize their paths from any directory in the file system.

FIGURE 6-22   Viewing the PATH environment variable

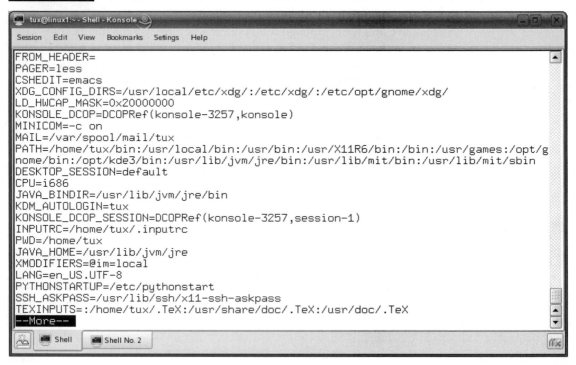

Now comes the more difficult part. What do you do if the program you want to run isn't listed in your PATH environment variable? You have two options. First, you can prepend the absolute path to the executable you want to run to the command. For example, suppose you wanted to run a program named install.pl located in /home/tux. To do this, you would enter **/home/tux/install.pl** at the shell prompt.

The second option is to add the path to the executable to your PATH environment variable. You would do this only if the executable you want to run will be run many times and will stay in the same location. In the example above, you wouldn't want to do this because you would probably only run the install.pl executable once to install an application.

However, if the executable will be used many times, adding its path to the PATH variable can be very handy. To do this, enter **PATH=$PATH:*new_path***. For example, if you wanted to add a directory named apps in your tux user's home directory to the PATH variable, you would enter **PATH=$PATH:/home/tux/apps**. Be sure to include $PATH. This preserves the existing entries in the PATH variable. If you don't, the directory you specify will overwrite all of the existing directory entries in your PATH variable! After adding the path, you must then export the new variable by entering **export PATH** at the shell prompt. You can then check your PATH variable by entering **echo $PATH** at the shell prompt. This is shown in Figure 6-23.

At this point, I need to make you aware of a mistake commonly made by new Linux users and administrators. Consider the runme executable shown in Figure 6-24.

Notice that the executable resides in the current directory. If you're coming to Linux from Windows or DOS, you may assume that, because the file resides in the current directory, you should be able to enter the name of the executable at the shell prompt. Notice what happens in Figure 6-25 when I do.

As you can see, the operating system can't find the file. This is an important point to keep in mind when working with Linux. The operating system looks *only* in the PATH environment variable when searching for an executable called at the

FIGURE 6-23   Adding a directory to the PATH environment variable

FIGURE 6-24   Viewing an executable file in the current directory

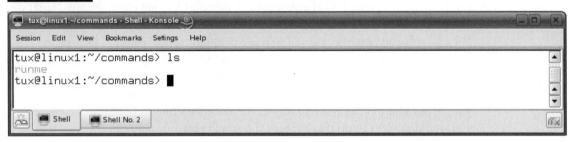

shell prompt. It does *not* look in the current directory. Other operating systems, such as Windows, look in both.

So what can you do? As mentioned above, you could add the directory to your PATH variable or you could enter the full path to the file. However, because the file resides in the current directory, you can simply prepend ./ before the file name. This indicates to the operating system that the file resides in the current directory. In the example shown in Figure 6-25, you could simply enter **./runme** at the shell prompt.

Let's now move on and talk about searching for files in the file system.

Searching the File System

One of my great weaknesses in life is the fact that I have a terrible memory. You can call me on the phone and relate some bit of information and I am pretty much guaranteed to forget what you told me by the time I hang up. This problem can be very embarrassing when I run into someone I've known and worked with for years and find myself unable to recall their name.

FIGURE 6-25   Trying to run an executable from the current directory

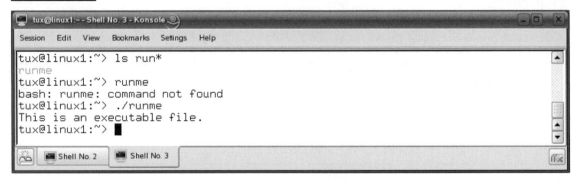

SCENARIO & SOLUTION

You are working on a Linux system and need to determine where the ls command resides in the file system. What command would you use?	You could enter **which ls**.
You need to see the directories contained in the PATH environment variable. What command could you enter to do this?	You could enter **echo $PATH**.
You need to run an executable file in your home directory named config.pl. Assuming your current directory is your home directory, what command would you enter?	You could enter **./config.pl** or **~/config.pl**.

This fallibility, unfortunately, carries over into my work life. I can't tell you how many times I've created a file, saved it, and then promptly forgot where I saved it. To help people like me, Linux includes utilities that you can use to search for files in the file system. It also includes utilities that you can use to search for specific content within a file. In this part of this chapter, you'll learn the following:

- Using find
- Using locate
- Using grep

Let's begin by learning how to use the find utility.

Using find

The find utility is fantastic tool that you can use to search the Linux file system. To use find, enter **find *path* –name *"filename"*** at the shell prompt. Replace *path* with the place in the file system where you want to start looking. Replace *filename* with the name of the file you want to search for. (Don't forget to use quotation marks!) You can use wildcard characters such as * to broaden your search results.

For example, suppose you wanted to find all of the log files stored in your file system that have a .log extension. You could enter **find / –name *"*.log"***. The find utility would then locate all files with an extension of .log starting in the root directory of the file system and searching all subdirectories. This is shown in Figure 6-26.

The find utility is flexible. You can also use the **–user *"username"*** option to search for files owned by a specific user, or use the **–size *"size"*** option to search for files of a specified size. You can use a + sign before the size value to search for

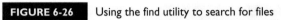

FIGURE 6-26   Using the find utility to search for files

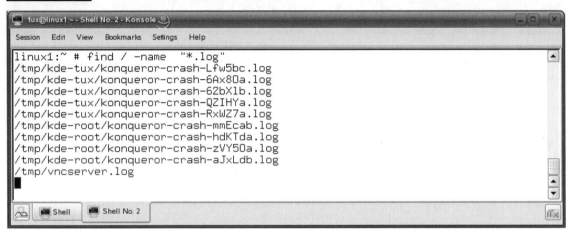

files larger than the specified size, or a – sign before the size value to search for files smaller than the specified size. The find utility has many other options. You can use the man page for find to see everything it has to offer.

In addition to find, you can also use locate to search for files in the file system.

Using locate

The locate utility functions in much the same manner as find. However, it has one distinct advantage over find. Whenever you execute a search with find, it manually walks through each directory in the path you name in the command looking for the specified files. This process can take some time.

Alternatively, the locate utility builds an index of the files in the file system. Then, when you execute a search, locate simply runs a query of the index. It doesn't actually search the file system directly. The result is that locate runs much faster than find in most situations.

To use locate, you must first install the findutils-locate package on your system. This process is shown on a SUSE Linux system using the YaST utility in Figure 6-27. (We'll discuss installing packages in more detail in Chapter 8.)

With the package installed, the index of files in the file system (named locatedb) will be create in /var/log. This index will be updated each day with the latest changes to the file system. However, you can also manually update the index using the updatedb command from the shell prompt. Because updatedb does all the dirty work for the locate utility, it can take some time to complete and will use up a lot of system resources in the process.

FIGURE 6-27   Using YaST to install the findutils-locate package

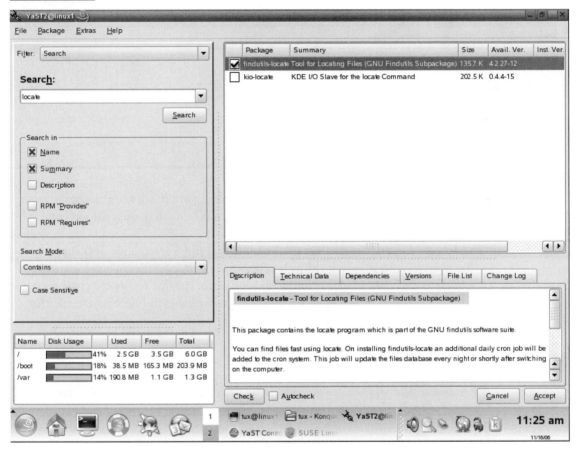

With the index updated, you can search for files by simply entering **locate**
filename at the shell prompt. For example, if you wanted to search for a file named
snmpd.conf, you could enter **locate snmpd.conf**. This is shown in Figure 6-28.

Notice that locate found several files in Figure 6-28 that had the text snmpd.conf
somewhere in the file name.

With this in mind, let's next discuss how to use grep.

Using grep

Thus far, we've discussed utilities that search for files in the file system. However,
Linux also provides a utility called grep that you can use to search for content within
a file. The grep utility is extremely useful. Using grep, you can search through a file

FIGURE 6-28   Using locate to search for files

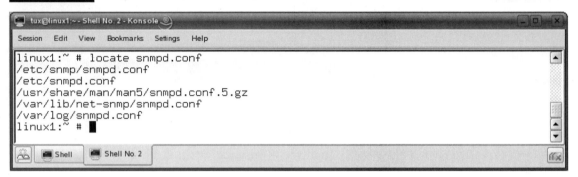

for a particular text string. This can come in handy when you want to search a very large log file for a specific message. You can also use grep to search through multiple files to locate a particular text string.

To use grep, you would enter **grep *search_text file***. For example, let's suppose you want to want to search through your /var/log/messages file for any log entries related to the VNC service running on your Linux system. You would enter **grep vnc /var/log/messages**. The grep utility would then display each line from the file that contained your search term, as shown in Figure 6-29.

FIGURE 6-29   Searching for content with grep

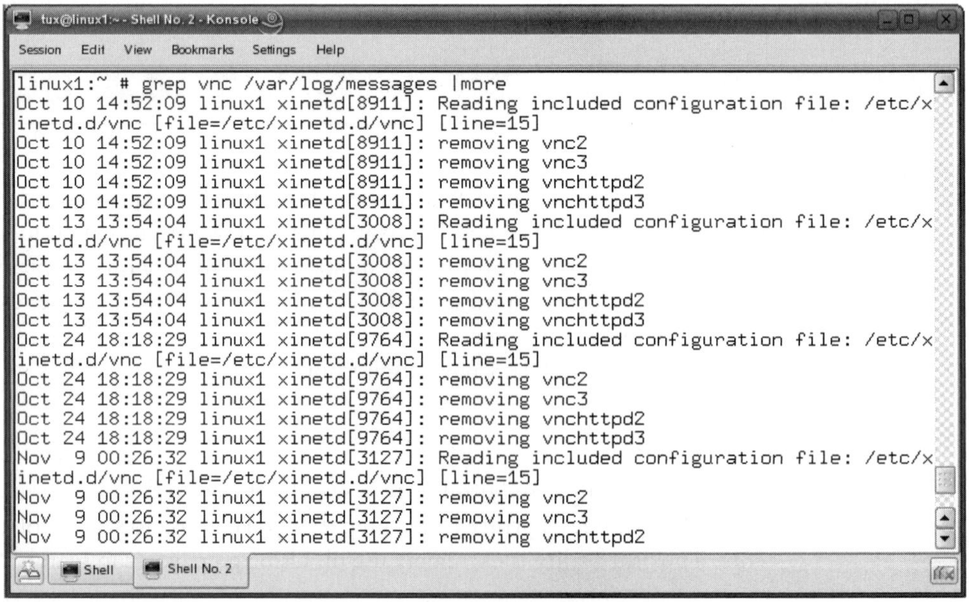

SCENARIO & SOLUTION

You are working on a Linux system and need to determine where the crontab resides in the file system. What command would you use?	You could enter **find / −name "crontab"**. Or, if the findutils-locate package is installed, you could enter **locate crontab**.
You need to find a line that contains the directive "server" in your /etc/ntp.conf file. What command could you use to do this?	You could enter **grep server /etc/ntp.conf**.

When working with grep, you can use the following options:

- ■ **−i** Ignores case when searching for the search text.
- ■ **−l** Doesn't display the actual matching line of text. Only displays the names of the files that contain the matching text.
- ■ **−r** Searches recursively through subdirectories of the path specified.

Let's practice using Linux search tools in the following exercise.

EXERCISE 6-3

ON THE CD

Using Linux Search Tools

In this exercise, you will practice using Linux search tools. Complete the following:

1. Verify that you are logged in to your Linux system.
2. Change to your root user account by entering **su −** and entering your root password. If you used the exercises in Chapter 3 of this book to set up your system, your root user password is **tuxPenguin1**.
3. Search for a file named xinetd.conf by entering **find / −name "xinetd.conf"** at the shell prompt. Where is this file located?
4. At the shell prompt, enter **locate / −name "xinetd.conf"**.
5. Locate references to the xinetd.conf file in your system log file by entering **grep xinetd.conf /var/log messages**. What can you learn about this file from the output of grep?

Now it's time to work with disk partitions.

Manage Disk Partitions

When you initially installed your Linux system, you defined a series of partitions on your hard disk drives to host your file system. Depending on which distribution you installed, you probably used some kind of graphical or menu-driven partitioning utility to accomplish this.

After the system has been in use for a while, it's likely that you will need to add more storage space at some point. If you install a new hard disk in the system, you will need to partition it and create a file system on it. To do this, most distributions provide you with some type of graphical partitioning utility. For example, on a SUSE Linux system, you can use the YaST Partitioner module to manage the partitions on your system. This utility is shown in Figure 6-30.

These utilities work great; however, for your Linux+ certification exam, you have to know how to manage your partitions from the command line. In this part of the chapter, you will learn the following:

- Using fdisk to create disk partitions
- Building a file system with mkfs
- Mounting a partition with mount
- Checking the file system with fsck

Let's begin by learning how to use fdisk.

Using fdisk to Create Disk Partitions

The fdisk utility is used from the command line to create or delete partitions at the shell prompt. To use fdisk to create a new partition, first open a terminal session. Then, at the shell prompt, change to your root account by entering **su –** followed by your root user's password.

At the shell prompt, enter **fdisk** *device*. For example, if you wanted to create a partition on the third SCSI hard disk in your system, you would enter **fdisk /dev/sdc**. In Figure 6-31, a new hard disk has been installed in the system and fdisk is being used to create a partition.

Notice in Figure 6-31 that, because this is a new disk in the system, it has to be initialized with a disk label. The fdisk utility takes care of this for you when you load the program. However, the change won't be applied until you write the disk.

FIGURE 6-30   Using YaST to manage disk partitions

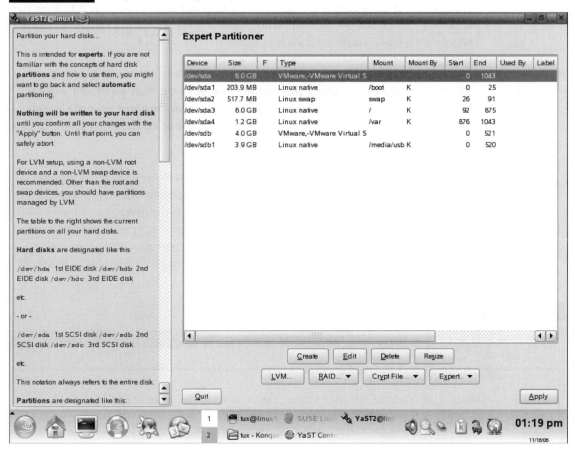

FIGURE 6-31   Running fdisk

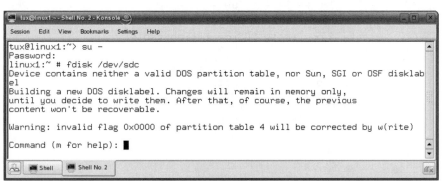

With fdisk running, you have a Command: prompt that you can use to enter fdisk commands. At this point, one of the best things you can do is to press M to view the fdisk help. When you do, a list of commands is displayed that you can use to perform actions with fdisk. These are shown in Figure 6-32.

on the Job

Notice in Figure 6-32 that you can press D to delete an existing partition. Be very careful about using this action. Any data on that partition will be lost! Once the changes are committed to disk, they are not reversible. You can back off from changes made with fdisk without committing them to disk by pressing Q. With fdisk, Q is your friend!

Before creating a partition, you should press P to view any existing partitions on the disk. This will help you determine if there is sufficient space and, if there is, what number must be assigned to a new partition created on the disk.

To create a new partition, you press N. You can then specify whether you want to create a primary disk partition or an extended disk partition. Any hard disk in your system can have up to four partitions defined in its partition table. These can

---

FIGURE 6-32 fdisk commands

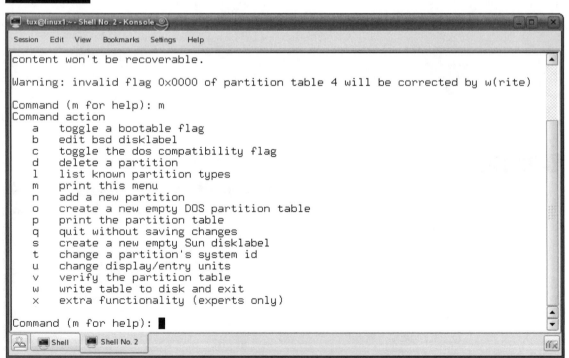

```
tux@linux1:~ - Shell No. 2 - Konsole

Session   Edit   View   Bookmarks   Settings   Help

content won't be recoverable.

Warning: invalid flag 0x0000 of partition table 4 will be corrected by w(rite)

Command (m for help): m
Command action
   a   toggle a bootable flag
   b   edit bsd disklabel
   c   toggle the dos compatibility flag
   d   delete a partition
   l   list known partition types
   m   print this menu
   n   add a new partition
   o   create a new empty DOS partition table
   p   print the partition table
   q   quit without saving changes
   s   create a new empty Sun disklabel
   t   change a partition's system id
   u   change display/entry units
   v   verify the partition table
   w   write table to disk and exit
   x   extra functionality (experts only)

Command (m for help):

  Shell    Shell No. 2
```

be either primary or extended partitions. Generally speaking, you can simply use primary partitions.

However, if you want to create more than four partitions on the disk, you should create at least one extended partition. Extended partitions are great. Within one extended partition, you can create many logical partitions. This allows you to get around the four-partition limitation. The general rule of thumb is to create your primary partitions first, then create your extended partition and create your logical partitions within it.

To create a primary partition, press P when prompted. To create an extended partition, press E. You are then prompted to specify a partition number, as shown in Figure 6-33.

You need to specify the next available partition number for the partition being created. In other words, if your disk already has two partitions on it, you would enter 3. If you try to enter a partition number that's already being used by an existing partition, the fdisk utility will complain!

At this point, you must specify the size of the partition. This is done by specifying the beginning and ending cylinders. You first specify the cylinder that you want to

FIGURE 6-33   Specifying the partition number

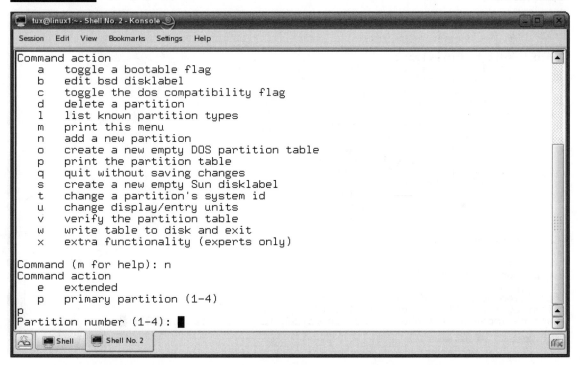

begin the partition on. By default, fdisk displays the next available cylinder. If you don't have any partitions on the disk, this will be cylinder 1. If you already have partitions on the disk, the next unused cylinder will be listed. After specifying your start cylinder, you have several options for specifying the overall size of the partition, as shown in Figure 6-34.

You can:

- Enter the last cylinder to be used in the partition.
- Enter the size of the partition in megabytes by entering *size*M. For example, you could create an 800MB partition by entering **800M**.

After specifying the size, you should verify your new partition by pressing P. This will display all partitions for the disk, as shown in Figure 6-35.

It's important to note that, at this point, the partition hasn't been written to disk. All changes are saved in memory before being committed to disk. This allows you to experiment, make mistakes, and so on with your partitions before actually making changes.

FIGURE 6-34 Specifying the size of the new partition

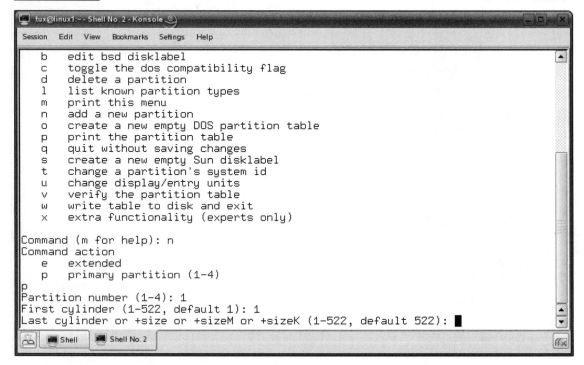

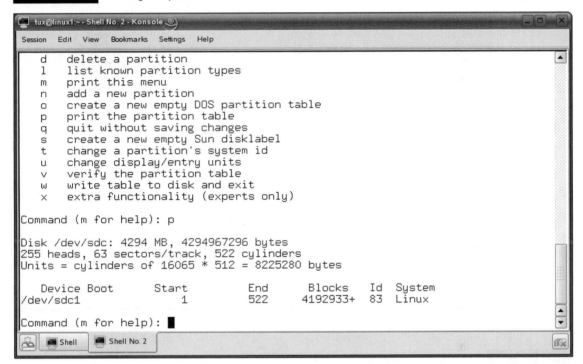

FIGURE 6-35   Viewing disk partitions with fdisk

```
      d    delete a partition
      l    list known partition types
      m    print this menu
      n    add a new partition
      o    create a new empty DOS partition table
      p    print the partition table
      q    quit without saving changes
      s    create a new empty Sun disklabel
      t    change a partition's system id
      u    change display/entry units
      v    verify the partition table
      w    write table to disk and exit
      x    extra functionality (experts only)

Command (m for help): p

Disk /dev/sdc: 4294 MB, 4294967296 bytes
255 heads, 63 sectors/track, 522 cylinders
Units = cylinders of 16065 * 512 = 8225280 bytes

   Device Boot      Start         End      Blocks   Id  System
/dev/sdc1               1         522     4192933+   83  Linux

Command (m for help): ▮
```

Before committing the partition to disk, however, you may need to change the partition type. Notice in Figure 6-35 that, by default, the partition being created is a standard Linux partition. Usually, this is sufficient. However, suppose you were creating a swap partition. You would need to use a different type of partition. This is done by pressing T and then entering the ID of the partition type you want to change to. You can press L to list all of the valid partition types and their associated ID numbers, as shown in Figure 6-36.

For example, notice in Figure 6-36 that the ID for a Linux swap partition is 82. You could press T and specify a partition ID of **82** if you wanted to change the partition to a swap partition.

At this point, you're ready to commit your partition to disk. If you're unhappy with the partitioning proposal, you can always press Q to quit without applying the new partitions. If you are happy, however, you can apply your changes by pressing W. This will commit the partition to disk and exit fdisk, as shown in Figure 6-37.

FIGURE 6-36   Linux partition types

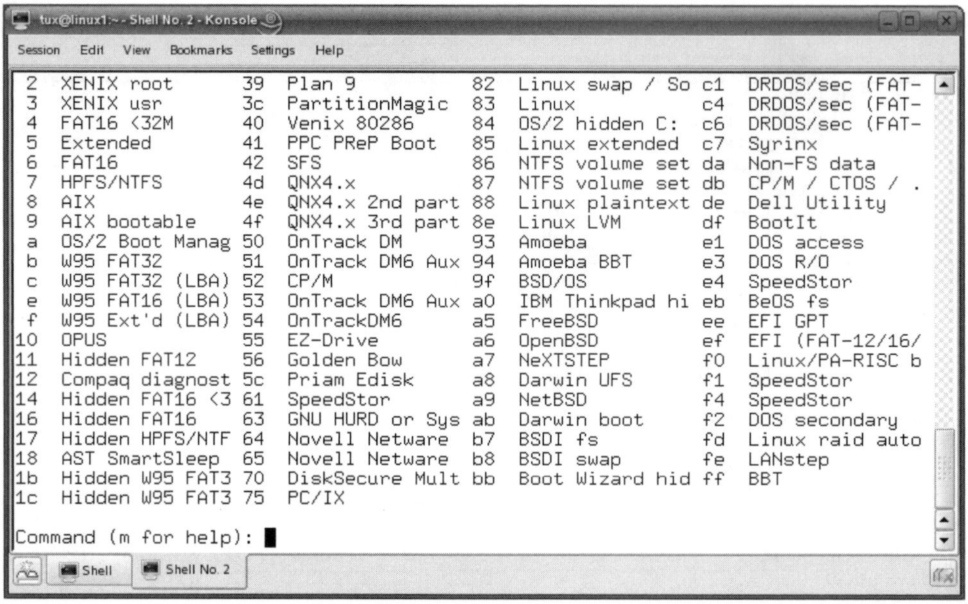

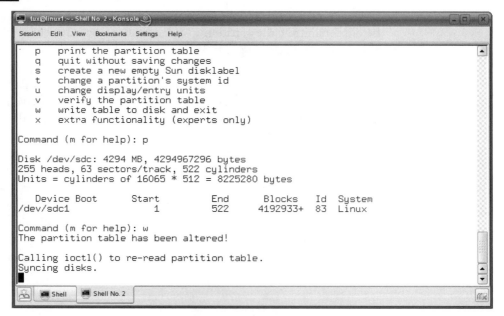

FIGURE 6-37   Committing a new partition to disk

Now that you know how to create a partition with fdisk, let's next learn how to make a file system using mkfs.

Building a File System with mkfs

Even though we've created a partition with fdisk, we can't use it yet. That's because it hasn't been formatted with a file system yet. This is accomplished using one of the following commands:

■ **mkfs** This utility is used to make an ext2 or ext3 file system on a partition. You can even use it to create a FAT file system on the partition (which is used by Windows and DOS). You specify which file system you want to use by entering the –t option and the type of file system. For example, if you wanted to create an ext3 file system on the first partition on your third SCSI hard disk drive in your system, you would enter **mkfs –t ext3 /dev/sdc1**.

■ **mkreiserfs** This utility is used to make a Reiser file system on a partition. For example, if you wanted to create a Reiser file system on the first partition on your third SCSI hard drive in your system, you would enter **mkreiserfs /dev/sdc1**. When you do, a screen is displayed and a proposal is presented.

Many of these parameters can be customized using mkreiserfs options. See the utility's man page for more information. Usually, however, the default parameters work just great. When prompted to continue, press Y to format the partition.

SCENARIO & SOLUTION	
You've just added a second SCSI hard disk to your Linux system. What command would you use to create a partition on it?	You would enter **fdisk /dev/sdb**.
You've just created a new partition on your Linux system and need to change it to a swap partition. How would you do this at the fdisk command prompt?	You could press T and then enter **82**.

Logical Volume Management (LVM) is an option you can use when partitioning Linux hard disk drives. It provides an alternative to the traditional process of creating disk partitions. Instead, you create volume groups from storage devices in your system. From the volume group, you allocate space to specific storage volumes, which are managed by the logical volume manager. Instead of mounting partitions, you mount storage volumes at mount points in your file system. This provides you with a great deal of flexibility when allocating space on the system. For example, if you mount a volume at /usr and a volume on /home and the /home directory begins to run out of space, you can reallocate space from the volume mounted at /usr to the volume mounted at /home. You can't do that with traditional disk partitions!

Once the partition has been formatted, you can then mount and use it. Let's review how you mount a partition next.

Mounting a Partition with mount

One of the key differences between Linux and other operating systems (such as Windows) is the fact that you need to mount a file system before you can use it. This is another one of those "gotchas" that trip up new Linux administrators. You even have to mount CDs, DVDs, and floppies before you can use them! We'll talk about mounting removable media later in this chapter.

The good news is that the process of mounting a partition is relatively easy. This is done using the mount command. The mount utility mounts the partition into an existing directory in your file system. When you switch to that directory, you are actually switching to the partition.

SCENARIO & SOLUTION

You've just added a second partition to the first SCSI hard disk in your Linux system. What command would you use to format it with the ext3 file system?	You would enter **mkfs −t ext3 /dev/sda2**.
You've just created the first partition on the second SCSI hard disk in your Linux system. What command would you use to format it with the Reiser file system?	You would enter **mkreiserfs /dev/sdb1**.

This is another one of those "gotchas" that new Linux admins sometimes struggle with. Other operating systems, such as Windows, reference partitions on the disk using a drive letter, such as C: or D:. For example, if you had a hard disk in a Windows system that had two partitions on it, the first one would be accessed using drive letter C:. The second partition would be accessed using drive letter D:. Each drive letter has its own separate hierarchy of directories and files.

Not so with Linux! Linux instead uses a virtual file system (VFS) that creates a single hierarchy that encompasses all partitions on all storage devices in the system. Switching to the directory where the partition is mounted switches you to that partition.

on the **Job**   *Newer versions of Windows also permit you to mount a partition in a directory as well. In my opinion, however, it isn't nearly as elegant as the way it's done under Linux.*

To use mount to mount a partition, first switch to your root account using su. Then enter **mount –t** *file_system_type device mount_point* at the shell prompt. I know this looks complicated, but it really isn't. For example, in the preceding topics we've worked through scenarios where we've created and formatted a partition on the third SCSI drive in a Linux system. Suppose you wanted to mount it in a directory named /mnt/extraspace; to do this, you would enter **mount –t reiserfs /dev/sdc1 /mnt/extraspace** at the shell prompt. Then, whenever you switched to /mnt/extraspace, you would be switching to the new partition you just created. If you don't know what type of file system is used by the partition, you can use the –a option with mount instead of –t. This will cause mount to try to mount the partition using all supported file system types until one is successful.

on the **Job**   *On most distributions, the /mnt directory is the default directory for mounting local and remote file systems. You don't have to use it, of course. You could mount a partition into any directory you want. However, by convention, /mnt is used for this purpose. On some distributions (such as Red Hat or Fedora), it's also the default location for mounting removable devices as well. Other distributions, such as SUSE, use /media as the default location for mounting removable media.*

You can also use the –o option with the mount command to include a variety of mounting options with the command. For example, you could use –o ro to mount the partition as read-only. See the man page for mount for a complete listing of all the available options.

FIGURE 6-38   Viewing mounted file systems with mount

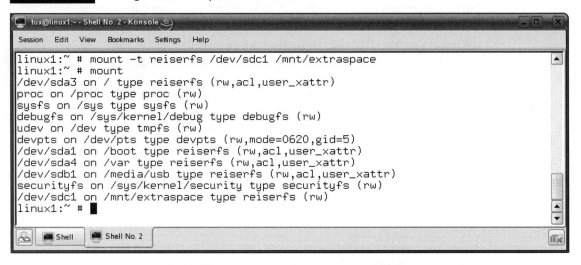

```
linux1:~ # mount -t reiserfs /dev/sdc1 /mnt/extraspace
linux1:~ # mount
/dev/sda3 on / type reiserfs (rw,acl,user_xattr)
proc on /proc type proc (rw)
sysfs on /sys type sysfs (rw)
debugfs on /sys/kernel/debug type debugfs (rw)
udev on /dev type tmpfs (rw)
devpts on /dev/pts type devpts (rw,mode=0620,gid=5)
/dev/sda1 on /boot type reiserfs (rw,acl,user_xattr)
/dev/sda4 on /var type reiserfs (rw,acl,user_xattr)
/dev/sdb1 on /media/usb type reiserfs (rw,acl,user_xattr)
securityfs on /sys/kernel/security type securityfs (rw)
/dev/sdc1 on /mnt/extraspace type reiserfs (rw)
linux1:~ # 
```

After mounting the partition, you can use the mount command with no switches to view all mounted file systems, as shown in Figure 6-38.

If you look at the last line of the output from mount, you'll see that /dev/sdc1 is mounted on /mnt/extraspace and uses the Reiser file system. In addition, whenever you mount or unmount a partition, the /etc/mtab file is updated with a list of mounted file systems. You can view this file as well to see a list of mounted file systems.

on the
job
You can also view /proc/mounts to see a list of mounted file systems. Another useful utility for viewing mounted partitions is df. This utility displays your partitions, where they're mounted, how much space has been used, and how much free space is still available.

If, for some reason, you wanted to unmount a partition, you can use the umount command. To umount a partition, simply enter **umount** followed by the device or the mount directory for the partition. For example, to umount the partition shown in Figure 6-38, you would enter **umount /dev/sdc1** or **umount /mnt/extraspace**.

on the
job
Notice that the command is "umount," not "unmount." This is yet another Linux gotcha!

This brings up yet another issue when working with Linux. Just because you mount a file system with mount does not mean it will stay mounted if you reboot the system.

FIGURE 6-39   Viewing the /etc/fstab file

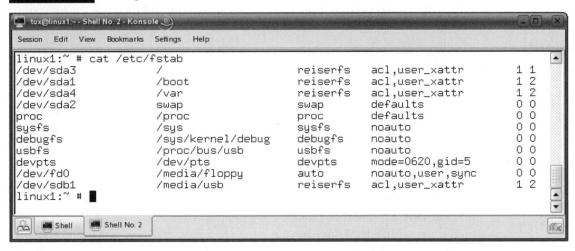

As long as the system stays running, the partition will stay mounted. However, if you reboot, the partition won't be remounted when the system starts back up.

You can remedy this using the /etc/fstab file. This file contains a list of file systems that the operating system mounts whenever it boots. A typical /etc/fstab file is shown in Figure 6-39.

I know this file looks a little confusing at first, but it actually isn't. Each line in the /etc/fstab file specifies a separate file system to be mounted on boot. Each line is composed of six fields, listed in Table 6-6.

TABLE 6-6   Fields in the /etc/fstab file

Field	Function
1	Specifies the device and partition to be mounted—for example, /dev/sda3.
2	The directory (mount point) where the partition is to be mounted.
3	The file system type of the partition.
4	Various mount options. See the man page for mount for a complete description of each one.
5	Specifies whether or not the file system should be dumped. 0 means don't dump. 1 means dump.
6	Specifies the order in which fsck should check the file system at reboot. The root partition should be set to a value of 1. Other partitions should have a value of 2.

Let's suppose we want to add the partition we created in the examples presented earlier. We could open /etc/fstab in an editor, such as vi, and then add the following line:

```
/dev/sdc1     /mnt/extraspace     reiserfs     acl,user_xattr     1     2
```

This specifies that the /dev/sdc1 partition be mounted in /mnt/extraspace using the Reiser file system. It also specifies that access control lists be enabled for the file system (a very good thing to do!) and that extended user attributes be enabled for the file system as well. Now, whenever you reboot the system, the partition will be automatically mounted.

You can also use command-line utilities to create and mount swap partitions on your Linux system. You can create swap partitions using the mkswap command. First, create the partition that will be used as a swap partition using fdisk. Then enter **mkswap *device*** at the shell prompt. For example, to covert the second partition on the second IDE hard drive in your system to a swap partition, you would enter **mkswap /dev/hdb2** at the shell prompt. After converting the partition to a swap partition, you need to enable it using the /sbin/swapon command.

Before we finish with partitions, let's talk about fsck.

Checking the File System with fsck

As with any other operating system, your Linux partitions can sometimes encounter problems. These problems can be caused by a variety of conditions; however, my experience has been that the number one source of partition corruption issues is a power outage that results in an unclean shutdown of the system. If your system goes

SCENARIO & SOLUTION

You've just formatted the second partition on the first SCSI hard disk with the ext3 file system. What command would you enter to mount it in /mnt/scsi1?	You would enter **mount −t ext3 /dev/sda2 /mnt/scsi1**.
You've just formatted the first partition on the second SCSI hard disk in your Linux system with the Reiser file system. What command would you enter to mount it in /mnt/scsi2?	You would enter **mount −t reiserfs /dev/sdb1 /mnt/scsi2**.

down without properly unmounting a mounted partition, it's very likely that data corruption will occur.

on the **Job**   *This a good argument for implementing an uninterruptible power supply (UPS) on your systems. Linux doesn't like going down unexpectedly!*

If something like this happens, you need to check your file systems for errors and make repairs, if necessary. This is done using the fsck utility (fsck stands for File System ChecK). To use this utility, you must first umount the file system you want to check. Then enter **fsck** *device* at the shell prompt. For example if you wanted to check the file system on the first partition of the third SCSI hard drive in your system, you would enter **fsck /dev/sdc1**. The utility will then check the file system and report any errors encountered (or the lack thereof). Sample output from fsck is shown in Figure 6-40.

Notice in Figure 6-40 that reiser-fsck was run. If you run fsck without any options, it will query your /etc/fstab file to determine the file system type of the partition you

---

FIGURE 6-40   Using fsck to check a file system

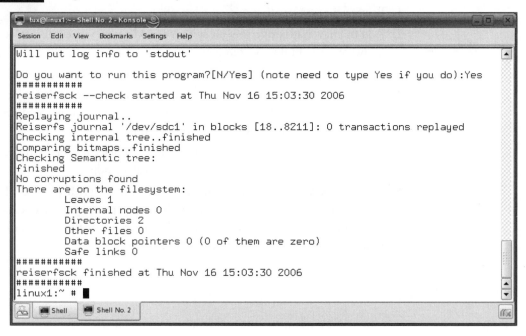

want to check and then load the appropriate module for the file system. Versions of fsck exist for Reiser, ext2, and ext3 file systems. After the check is complete, you can remount the partition using the mount command.

Now that you know how to manage partitions on a Linux system, let's practice in the following exercise.

EXERCISE 6-4

Managing Linux Partitions

In this exercise, you will practice working with Linux partitions. If you're using standard hardware, you'll need to add a second hard disk drive to your system to complete this exercise. Be sure there isn't anything on it you want to save because it's going to get erased!

If you're using VMware, you can simply add a new virtual disk to your system by powering the off the virtual machine and then selecting Edit Virtual Machine Settings | Add | Hard Disk.

Complete the following:

1. Power your system off.
2. Add the new hard drive to your system or add a new virtual disk to your VMware virtual Linux system.
3. Power your system on and log in as your regular Linux user.
4. Change to your root user account by entering **su –** and entering your root password. If you used the exercises in Chapter 3 of this book to set up your system, your root user password is **tuxPenguin1**.
5. At the shell prompt, enter **fdisk /dev/device**. Replace *device* with the appropriate device for your system, such as **sdb** or **hdb**.
6. View the existing partitions on the device by pressing P. If you don't have any free space to create a partition on this drive, press D to delete existing partitions. Be sure you don't have any data on the disk that you want to save! Deleting the partition will erase all data!

7. Create a new partition by pressing N.

8. Specify a primary partition by pressing P.

9. Create the first partition on the disk by entering **1**.

10. Specify a first cylinder of **1**.

11. Use the default for the last cylinder by pressing ENTER.

12. Verify your new partition by pressing P.

13. Write the partition to disk by pressing W.

14. Format the new partition using the ext3 file system by entering **mkfs –t ext3 /dev/*device***. Replace ***device*** with the appropriate partition for your system— for example, **sdb1** or **hdb1.**

15. Wait while the file system is applied.

16. Create a new directory in /mnt named newdisk by entering **mkdir /mnt/newdisk**.

17. Mount the new file system in this directory by entering **mount –t auto /dev/ *device* /mnt/newdisk**.

18. Verify that the disk was mounted by entering **mount**.

19. Configure the file system to be automatically mounted every time the system boots by entering **vi /etc/fstab** at the shell prompt.

20. Add the following line to the file:

```
/dev/device /mnt/newdisk ext3 acl,user_xattr 1 2
```

21. Save your changes and exit vi.

22. Check your new file system by first unmounting it. Enter **umount /mnt/ newdisk** at the shell prompt.

23. Enter **fsck /dev/*device*** at the shell prompt. The fsck utility should report that the file system was clean.

24. Remount the device.

25. Return to your regular user account by entering **exit**.

Let's change our focus and talk about how to use removable media on a Linux system.

CERTIFICATION OBJECTIVE 6.04

Use Removable Media

One of the more difficult aspects of working with a Linux system for those coming to Linux from Windows tends to be the subject of how to use removable media, including floppies, CDs, and DVDs. Using these types of storage on a Windows system is trivial. You just insert the disc and everything just works.

Using removable media with a Linux system, on the other hand, takes a little more effort. However, with a little bit of practice, it will become second nature to you. In this part of this chapter, you'll learn how to make it all work. Specifically, we're going to discuss the following tasks:

- Working with floppies
- Working with optical devices
- Working with USB and FireWire devices

Let's begin by discussing how to work with good ol' floppy disk drives.

Working with Floppies

I'll never forget the first time I tried to use a floppy disk with a Linux system many years ago in the mid-1990s. I inserted the diskette into the drive and ... nothing happened! I spent the better part of a day trying to figure out what I was doing wrong.

The issue? I didn't know you had to mount a floppy on a Linux system before you could use it. Linux doesn't use drive letters to refer to removable devices such as floppies. Instead, these devices are mounted in a directory in the file system, just like partitions on a hard drive. As we've already discussed previously, the mount command is used to mount file systems on Linux. It's also use to mount file systems on floppies.

To mount a floppy from the shell prompt, you must first change to your root account using the su command. Then enter **mount –t vfat** *device mount_point*. For example, if you wanted to mount the floppy diskette in your A: drive in /media/floppy, you would enter **mount –t vfat /dev/fd0 /media/floppy**. This is shown in Figure 6-41.

Notice in Figure 6-41 that the last line in the output from mount shows that /dev/fd0 is mounted on /media/floppy with a file system type of vfat. When you switch to the /media/floppy directory in your file system, you are accessing the file system on the floppy diskette.

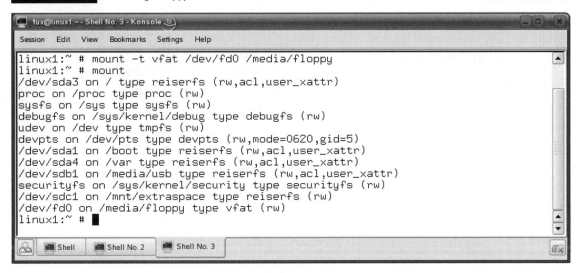

FIGURE 6-41   Mounting a floppy diskette

On other distributions, such as Red Hat or Fedora, the default mount point for floppy diskettes is /mnt/floppy.

There is an easier way, however, to mount floppies. Take a look at the /etc/fstab file in Figure 6-42.

Notice that there is a line that reads:

```
/dev/fd0    /media/floppy    auto    noauto,user,sync    0    0
```

This line specifies that the floppy diskette be mounted by default into /media/floppy. The auto parameter specifies that the system detect the file system of the media automatically. Therefore, you can simply enter **mount /dev/fd0** at the shell prompt and the floppy will be automatically mounted using these parameters.

You can also implement a service called autofs on your system to help you with mounting removable media. When configured and running, it will automatically detect when a diskette or other removable media has been inserted and mount it for you. Configuring this service goes beyond the scope of this course and isn't required for your Linux+ exam, so we're not going to cover it here.

FIGURE 6-42   Viewing the /etc/fstab file

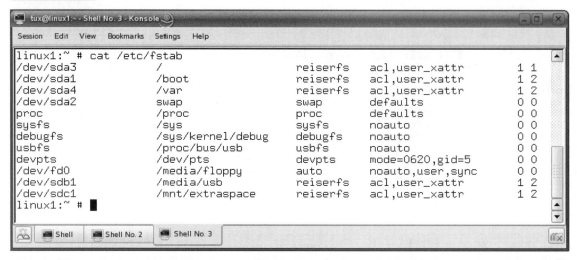

Before you remove a mounted floppy diskette from a drive, you must also unmount it. Just as with partitions, this is done using the umount command. To unmount a floppy, you enter **umount** *device* or **umount** *mount_point*. For example, to unmount your A: drive, you would enter **umount /dev/fd0**.

Let's next discuss mounting optical drives.

Working with Optical Devices

Just like partitions or floppy diskettes, you must also mount optical drives, such as CDs or DVDs, before you can use them. The only real difference is the mount point used and the file system type. For CDs and DVDs, you can use the file system type of iso9660 with the mount command. On distributions such as SUSE Linux, you mount CDs in one of the three following directories:

- /media/cdrom
- /media/cdrecorder
- /media/dvd

On distributions such as Red Hat or Fedora, your directories for mounting optical devices are located in /mnt.

FIGURE 6-43   Mounting a CD

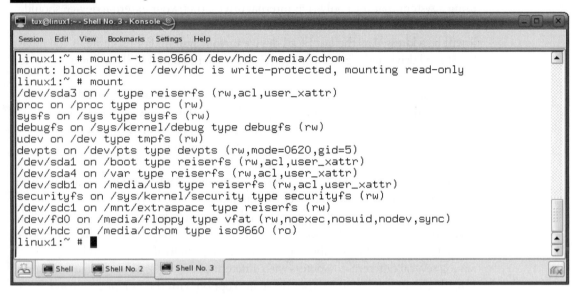

To mount a CD on a Linux system, insert it in your CD drive. Change to your root account and then enter **mount –t iso9660** *device mount_point*. For example, if your CD drive is /dev/hdc and you want to mount the disc into /media/cdrom, you would enter **mount –t iso9660 /dev/hdc /media/cdrom**. This is shown in Figure 6-43.

As with floppies, you can make the mounting process for optical devices easier by adding an entry to your /etc/fstab file. Consider the following:

```
/dev/hdc      /media/cdrom     iso9660     noauto,user,sync     0     0
```

Adding this line makes it such that you only need to enter **mount /dev/hdc** to mount an optical device. As with any mounted file system, you should use umount to unmount a CD or DVD before ejecting it.

Let's next discuss mounting external storage devices.

Working with USB and FireWire Devices

Most Linux distributions are compatible with external storage devices using a USB or FireWire interface. Because Linux is plug-n-play–compatible, it should automatically detect a new device when you connect an external storage device (such as a flash drive or an external hard drive).

Most Linux distributions will address these devices as a SCSI device. If you're using a system that uses only IDE internal drives, then your external device should be addressed through /dev/sda. If you already have SCSI devices in your system, then it will be addressed as the last SCSI device in your system. For example, if you have a SCSI hard drive and a SCSI DVD drive, then your external USB or FireWire device will be /dev/sdc.

To verify this, you can check your /var/log/messages file after connecting the device. You should see a kernel message indicating that a new SCSI disk was attached. In Figure 6-44, a USB flash drive has been connected to the system at /dev/sdd, indicating that it is the fourth SCSI device in the system.

If necessary, you can then use the same procedure discussed previously to create a partition on the device and then create a file system. If a file system has already been created on the device, you only need to mount it.

You mount USB or FireWire devices in the same way that you mount a typical hard disk partition. One issue that comes up here is that you may not be entirely sure what file system is being used on the external device, especially if the drive is being used among several different computers with different operating systems. Because of this, I highly recommend that you use the –t auto option with the mount command. This will cause mount to try to detect for you what file system has been used on the device.

Other than that, mounting a USB or FireWire device is relatively easy. Simply enter **mount –t auto** *device mount_point*. For example, if I wanted to mount an external flash drive that is the fourth SCSI device in the system in the /media/THUMBDRIVE directory, I would enter **mount –t auto /dev/sdd /media/THUMBDRIVE**. This is shown in Figure 6-45.

FIGURE 6-44   Checking /var/log/messages for detection of an external USB storage device

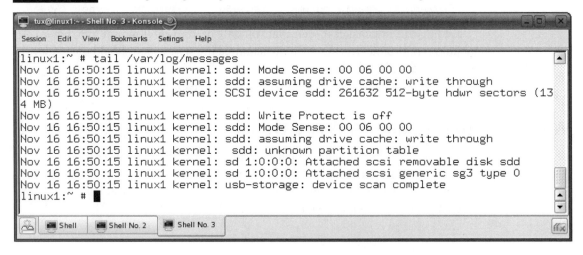

FIGURE 6-45   Mounting a USB flash drive

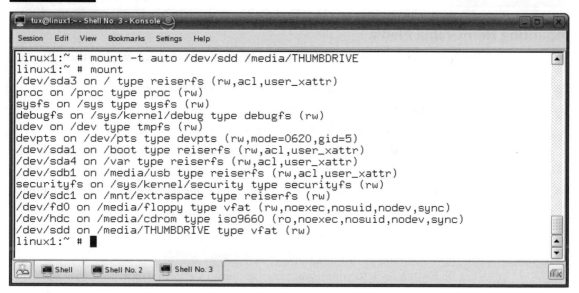

```
linux1:~ # mount -t auto /dev/sdd /media/THUMBDRIVE
linux1:~ # mount
/dev/sda3 on / type reiserfs (rw,acl,user_xattr)
proc on /proc type proc (rw)
sysfs on /sys type sysfs (rw)
debugfs on /sys/kernel/debug type debugfs (rw)
udev on /dev type tmpfs (rw)
devpts on /dev/pts type devpts (rw,mode=0620,gid=5)
/dev/sda1 on /boot type reiserfs (rw,acl,user_xattr)
/dev/sda4 on /var type reiserfs (rw,acl,user_xattr)
/dev/sdb1 on /media/usb type reiserfs (rw,acl,user_xattr)
securityfs on /sys/kernel/security type securityfs (rw)
/dev/sdc1 on /mnt/extraspace type reiserfs (rw)
/dev/fd0 on /media/floppy type vfat (rw,noexec,nosuid,nodev,sync)
/dev/hdc on /media/cdrom type iso9660 (ro,noexec,nosuid,nodev,sync)
/dev/sdd on /media/THUMBDRIVE type vfat (rw)
linux1:~ #
```

As with any other device, you can add an entry to your /etc/fstab file to make the process easier. In addition, you must unmount the device before you remove it from the system using the umount command.

Let's practice mounting devices in the following exercise.

SCENARIO & SOLUTION

You need to mount a CD that you've inserted in your system's CD drive. Assuming your CD-ROM drive is the master drive on the secondary IDE channel, what command would you enter to mount it in /mnt/cdrom?	You would enter **mount –t iso9660 /dev/hdc /mnt/cdrom**.
How does Linux view USB or FireWire removable devices?	It sees them as additional SCSI devices.

EXERCISE 6-5

Mounting Removable Media

In this exercise, you will practice mounting removable media. Complete the following:

1. With your system up and running, open a terminal session.
2. Change to your root user account.
3. Insert a formatted floppy diskette into your system's floppy drive.
4. At the shell prompt, enter **mount –t vfat /dev/fd0 /media/floppy** (SUSE) or **mount –t vfat /dev/fd0 /mnt/floppy** (Fedora).
5. Change to your floppy disk by entering **cd /media/floppy** or **cd /mnt/floppy**.
6. Get a listing of the files on the disk by entering **ls**.
7. Change to your home directory by entering **cd**.
8. Unmount the floppy by entering **umount /dev/fd0**.
9. Switch back to your regular user account by entering **exit**.

Now that you know how the Linux file system works and how to complete common file system tasks, let's talk about how you go about backing up the file system.

CERTIFICATION OBJECTIVE 6.05

Back Up Data

One of the key roles that you must perform as a Linux system administrator is to ensure that the data on the systems you are responsible for is protected. One of the best ways that you can do this is to back up the data. Having a backup creates a redundant copy of the data so that if a disaster occurs, the data can be restored.

It's important that you remember that data is stored, for the most part, on mechanical devices in your Linux system. Hard drives have motors and other moving parts that slowly wear out over time. In fact, hard drives usually have a mean time between failures (MTBF) value assigned to them by the manufacturer. This MTBF basically gives you an estimate of how long a drive will last before it fails. Basically, it's not a matter of *if* a hard drive will fail, it's a matter of *when*.

I relate this because I want you to take backing up seriously. Many system administrators, frankly, get very lazy about running backups. It's an easy task to blow off, thinking "I'll run a backup tomorrow…." Before you know it, it's been weeks since the last time you ran a backup.

If you're employed by an organization to maintain their systems and you fail to run backups, I can just about guarantee that you will lose your job if a disaster happens. Several years ago, I participated on a support call with a system administrator whose system had completely died. He had called us in a last-ditch effort hoping that we would have some kind of magic solution that would get his system back. When we told him that we couldn't and that he would have to reinstall and restore from his backups, there was silence on the other end of the phone for a long time. He got a little choked up and whispered "I don't have any backups. I'm going to lose my job over this." Take my advice, develop a backup plan and stick to it religiously.

There are several components to a backup plan. In this part of this chapter, we're going to discuss the following:

- Selecting a backup medium
- Selecting a backup strategy
- Using Linux backup utilities

Let's begin by discussing how to select a backup medium.

Selecting a Backup Medium

Back in the "old days," we really only had two choices for backing up data: floppies or a tape drive. Floppies didn't hold much and were notoriously unreliable, so most system admins opted for tape drives.

Today, many admins still use tape drives to back up their data. Tape drives use magnetic tape, much like the tape used in an 8mm video camera, to store data. Tape drives store a lot of data and are relatively inexpensive. They are a great choice for backing up data on your Linux system.

However, tape drives have several limitations. First of all, they wear out. Tape drives have a lot of mechanical parts that wear out over time. The tape itself is run over the top of a read/write head in the tape drive, so it wears out over time as well due to friction. Second, tapes are relatively slow. Backing up large quantities of data can take hours.

As a result, many admins are exploring other media for backing up system data. For a while, read/write CDs and DVDs were in vogue for backups. As long as hard drives didn't get much larger than 4–8GB, they worked just fine. However, in the last five years, hard drives have dramatically increased in size. Backing up a 200GB hard drive with DVDs today is similar to backing up a 100MB hard drive with floppy diskettes 15 years ago. Yes, it can be done, but it's a painful, time-consuming process. Unless the amount of data you're backing up is relatively small, I don't recommend this option.

Another option that many system administrators are exploring (and one that I really like personally) is the use of removable USB or FireWire hard drives. Back in the old days, we used tape drives to back up our hard drives because hard disks were extremely expensive. The general rule of thumb back in the early 1990s was "$1 per megabyte" when buying a hard disk. It was just too expensive to use hard drives for backups. In addition, we didn't have a good, hot-swappable, fast external interface for hard drives. Therefore, tape was one of the few viable options.

Today, however, the price of hard drives has dropped dramatically. You can buy a removable USB or FireWire hard drive for less than a penny per megabyte. Using external hard drives for backups has two distinct advantages. First, they are much, much faster than tapes. Backups that took hours on a tape drive take minutes on a hard disk. Second, hard drives tend to be more reliable than tape drives.

Of course, using hard drives for backups isn't a perfect solution. One of the key disadvantages is the fact that the disk partition must be mounted on the removable drive to run a backup. If something bad were to happen to the system that destroyed data on the main hard drive while the removable drive was connected, it could potentially destroy data on the removable drive as well.

As with any backup medium, you have to weigh the benefits and drawbacks when deciding to use external hard drives for backups.

At any rate, you first need to select the backup medium you will use, purchase the appropriate equipment, and connect it to your system. Once that's in place, you next need to select a backup strategy.

Selecting a Backup Strategy

When creating a backup plan, you have several different options for how you will conduct your backups. You need to consider the following:

- Selecting a backup type
- Selecting a backup schedule
- Determining what to back up

Let's start by choosing a backup type.

Selecting a Backup Type

Depending upon the backup utility you choose to use, you will usually have at least three different types of backups that you can use (sometimes more). These include the following:

- **Full** In a full backup, all specified files are backed up, regardless of whether or not they've been modified since the last backup. After being backed up, each file is flagged as having been backed up.
- **Incremental** During an incremental backup, only the files that have been modified since the last backup (full or incremental) are backed up. After being backed up, each file is flagged as having been backed up.
- **Differential** During a differential backup, only the files that have been modified since the last full backup are backed up. Even though they have been backed up during a differential backup, the files involved are *not* flagged as having been backed up.

To determine your backup strategy, you need to select from the above backup types. For example, you could run a full backup every time. This strategy is thorough and exhaustive. It's also the fastest strategy when you need to restore data from a backup.

However, full backups can take a very long time to complete. This is because every single file is backed up regardless of whether or not it's changed since the last backup. Therefore, many administrators mix full backups with incremental or differential backups.

If you use a full/incremental strategy, you run a full backup once a week, usually when the system load is lightest, such as Friday night. Then you run incremental backups each of the other six days in the week. Using this strategy, you should end up with one full backup and six incremental backups for each week. The advantage of this strategy is primarily speed. Because incrementals only back up files that have changed since the last full *or* incremental backup, they usually run very fast. The drawback to this strategy is that you must restore six backups in exactly the correct order. The full backup is restored first followed by the first incremental, then the second incremental, and so on. This can be a slow process.

Alternatively, you can also use full with differentials. In this strategy, you run a full backup on Friday night, usually. Then you run a differential each of the other nights of the week. Remember that a differential backup only backs up files that have changed since the last full backup, *not* since the last differential. Therefore, each day's backup gets progressively bigger. The main advantage to this strategy is that restores are really fast. Instead of seven backups to restore, you only have to restore two—the last full backup first, followed by the last differential backup (and no others!). The disadvantage to this method is that the differential backups start out very fast, but can become almost as long as a full backup by the time you reach the last day in the cycle.

on the Job *Whatever you do, don't mix incremental and differential backups together! Your backups will lose data.*

Whichever strategy you choose, you should be sure to keep a rotation of backups. Many administrators will rotate their backup media such that they have three to four weeks worth of past backups on hand. You never know when a file that was deleted two weeks ago will suddenly be needed again!

In addition, you should be sure to verify your backups. Most backup utilities provide you with the option of checking your backup after it's complete against the original files. If you don't, you may have errors in your backup.

Now that you've selected a backup type, you next need to set a backup schedule.

Selecting a Backup Schedule

You can use whatever backup schedule works best for you. However, most admins work on a weekly rotation, as discussed previously. Pick one day for your full backup and then the remaining days of the week for your incremental or differential backups.

You should also schedule your backups to occur when the load on the system is at its lightest. Late in the evening or in the early morning are usually best, depending on your organization's schedule.

Finally, you need to specify what will be backed up. Let's discuss this next.

Determining What to Back Up

Most Linux systems you're going to be working with will probably consume a fairly large amount of disk space, depending on the packages you've installed. You need to decide how much of this consumed disk space is going to be backed up.

One option is to back up the entire system. This is a safe, thorough option. However, it's also somewhat slow due to the sheer amount of data involved. Many administrators choose not to do this. Instead, they only back up critical data on the system, such as user data and configuration information. The theory behind this strategy is that you could, in the event of a disaster, simply re-install a new system and then restore the critical data to it. If you choose this strategy, then you should consider backing up the following directories in your Linux file system:

- /etc
- /home
- /opt

- /root
- /var
- /srv

Notice that this strategy doesn't back up your Linux system or its utilities. Instead, it only backs up your configuration files, your user data, your log files, and your web/ftp files.

Once you've determined what to back up, the next part of your plan is to determine what you'll back it up with.

Using Linux Backup Utilities

When working with Linux, you have a host of different utilities at your disposal to conduct a backup. Many come with the operating system; others can be obtained from third parties. For your Linux+ exam, you need to be familiar with the tools that are common to most distributions and are run from the shell prompt. In this part of the chapter, we're going to look at the following:

■ Using tar
■ Using cpio

Let's begin by looking at the venerable tar utility.

Using tar

The tar utility has been around for a very long time and is a very commonly used Linux backup tool. The acronym "tar" stands for tape archive. The tar utility takes a list of specified files and copies them into a single archive file (.tar). The .tar file can then be compressed with the gzip utility on your Linux system, resulting in a file with a .tar.gz extension.

The tar utility can be used to send backup jobs to a variety of backup media, including tape drives and removable hard disk drives. The syntax for using tar to create backups is tar –cvf *filename directory*. The –c option tells tar to create a new archive. The –v option tells tar to work in verbose mode, displaying each file being backed up on screen. The –f option specifies the name of the tar archive to be created.

For example, if you wanted to create a backup of the /home directory named backup.tar on an external USB hard drive mounted in /media/usb, you would enter **tar –cvf /media/usb/backup.tar /home**. This is shown in Figure 6-46.

As you can see in Figure 6-47, a tar archive named backup.tar was created in the /media/usb directory. When opened with the Ark graphical utility, you can see that the home directory was backed up into a single archive file.

If you wanted to back up to a tape drive, you could do this by replacing the file name parameter in the tar command to the device name for your tape drive. On most distributions, the first SCSI tape drive in the system is referenced through

FIGURE 6-46   Using tar to create a backup

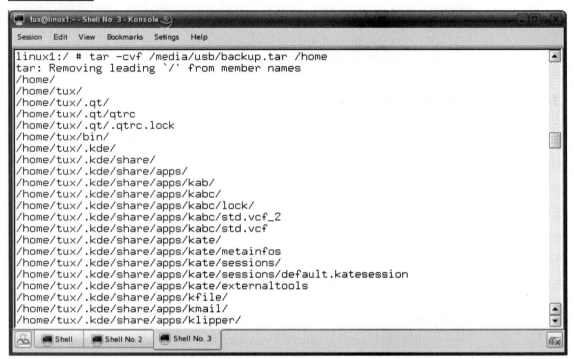

```
linux1:/ # tar -cvf /media/usb/backup.tar /home
tar: Removing leading `/' from member names
/home/
/home/tux/
/home/tux/.qt/
/home/tux/.qt/qtrc
/home/tux/.qt/.qtrc.lock
/home/tux/bin/
/home/tux/.kde/
/home/tux/.kde/share/
/home/tux/.kde/share/apps/
/home/tux/.kde/share/apps/kab/
/home/tux/.kde/share/apps/kabc/
/home/tux/.kde/share/apps/kabc/lock/
/home/tux/.kde/share/apps/kabc/std.vcf_2
/home/tux/.kde/share/apps/kabc/std.vcf
/home/tux/.kde/share/apps/kate/
/home/tux/.kde/share/apps/kate/metainfos
/home/tux/.kde/share/apps/kate/sessions/
/home/tux/.kde/share/apps/kate/sessions/default.katesession
/home/tux/.kde/share/apps/kate/externaltools
/home/tux/.kde/share/apps/kfile/
/home/tux/.kde/share/apps/kmail/
/home/tux/.kde/share/apps/klipper/
```

/dev/st0. Therefore, you could enter **tar –cvf /dev/st0 /home** if you wanted to run the same backup as in the previous example, but send it to a SCSI tape drive instead.

To restore a tar archive, simply enter **tar –xvf** *filename*. For example, to extract the archive we just created, you would enter **tar –xvf /media/usb/backup.tar**. This will extract the archive into the current working directory. If the archive has been zipped, you can also use the –z option to unzip the archive before extracting it.

In addition to tar, you can also use cpio to create backups. Let's discuss how it is used next.

Using cpio

The cpio utility can also be used to make archive files just like tar. A key difference between tar and cpio is the fact that you must provide cpio with a list of files and directories to back up from the standard input. This can be done using cat to display the contents of a text file or by generating a listing using find or ls.

For example, let's suppose you wanted to back up the contents of the /home directory on your Linux system. To use cpio to do this, you must somehow generate

FIGURE 6-47   Viewing the contents of a tar archive file

a listing of files and directories and send it to cpio. Then you must redirect the output from cpio to a file. This can be done using the find utility, discussed earlier. You could switch to /home and then enter **find . –print –depth | cpio –ov > /media/usb/backup.cpio**. The find utility will generate a listing of all files in the current directory. Because the –print option was used, find will print the full name of each file to the screen (the standard output). Because the –depth option was also used, find checks the contents of each directory before processing the directory itself.

The key here is the fact that we've used the | command to pipe the standard output from find to the standard input of cpio. (We'll talk more about piping later in this book.) The cpio utility uses this as a list of files and directories to archive. The –o option tells cpio to create a new archive. The –v option simply tells cpio to run verbosely, displaying the name of each file and directory as it's processed. Finally, we have to redirect the standard output from cpio (the archive) to a file in the file system. This is done by entering **>** followed by the name of the archive file. The resulting archive is shown in Figure 6-48.

To restore files from a cpio archive, you run cpio from the shell prompt using the –i option and specifying the name of the archive to process. When you do, the archive files will be extracted into the current working directory. For example, we could extract the archive we just created by entering **cpio –iv < /media/usb/backup.cpio**.

FIGURE 6-48   Viewing a cpio archive file

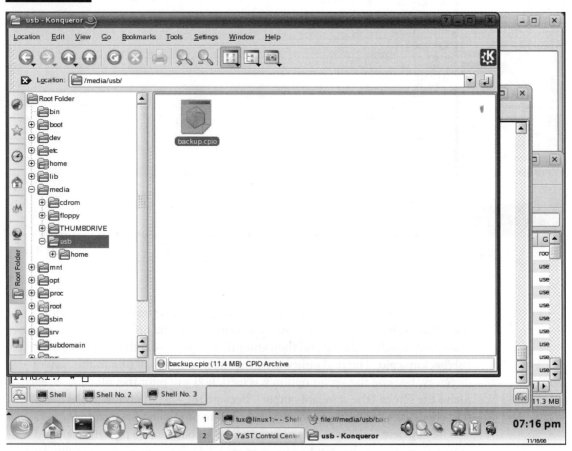

SCENARIO & SOLUTION

You've decided to implement full backups once a week with daily incremental backups. Is this a valid strategy?	Yes, this is a valid strategy that is used by many organizations around the world. It makes the backup process very fast, but can slow down restores.
You need to create a backup of the /home directory on a SCSI tape drive connected to your Linux system. What tar command could you enter at the shell prompt to do this?	You could enter **tar –cfv /dev/st0 /home**.
You want to use cpio to create a backup of the /home directory named backup.cpio on a FireWire removable hard drive mounted at /mnt/Firewire. What command would you use to do this?	You could enter **find /home –print –depth	cpio –ov > /mnt/Firewire/backup.cpio**.

Let's practice backing up in the following exercise.

EXERCISE 6-6

Backing Up Data

In this exercise, you will practice backing up data. This exercise assumes that you have completed exercise 6-5. If you haven't, then you will have to select an alternative path to save the backup file. Complete the following:

1. With your system up and running, open a terminal session.
2. Change to your root user account.
3. At the shell prompt, enter **tar –cvf /mnt/newdisk/backup.tar /home**.
4. Enter **ls /mnt/newdisk**. Verify that the backup file exists.
5. Switch back to your regular user account by entering **exit**.

You are becoming quite the Linux expert. It won't be long before you are ready to tackle your Linux+ exam!

CERTIFICATION SUMMARY

In this chapter, we reviewed a variety of topics related to managing the Linux file system. We began this chapter by introducing you to the Linux file system. We first differentiated between a general file system and a specific disk file system such as Reiser or ext3. We then pointed out that the role of the Linux file system is to organize data such that it can be easily located and retrieved as well as reliably preserved.

We then related that Linux uses a hierarchical file system. The topmost directory of this hierarchy is the root directory (/). We then discussed the role of the various standard directories used in a typical Linux system as specified in the Filesystem Hierarchy Standard (FHS). These include:

- /bin
- /boot
- /dev
- /etc
- /home
- /lib
- /media
- /mnt
- /opt

- /proc
- /root
- /sbin
- /srv
- /sys
- /tmp
- /usr
- /var

We then discussed the four different types of files used on a Linux system: regular files, links, FIFOs, and sockets.

With this background information in hand, we turned our attention to common Linux file system tasks. We emphasized that, while most of these tasks can be performed using graphical utilities, the Linux+ exam expects you to know how to complete them from the shell prompt.

We first learned how to navigate through the Linux file system using the pwd, cd, and ls commands. We then discussed how to manage files and directories. We pointed out that you could create new files using the touch command. You can also create new directories using the mkdir command.

We then discussed utilities you can use to view the contents of text files on screen. We pointed out that you can use cat, less, head, or tail to do this. We also pointed out that you can use the –f option with tail to monitor changes to a text file, such as a log file, as they are made.

We also reviewed the utilities you can use to delete files and directories, including rmdir and rm. To copy and move files and directories, you can use the cp and mv utilities. We pointed out that mv can also be used to rename files or directories. We also discussed link files. We pointed out that link files point to other files or directories in the file system. We related that you can create either hard links or symbolic links using the ln command.

At this point, we changed gears and talked about running executables in Linux. We pointed out that you can use the which command to find out where the executables for system utilities, such as ls, cp, man, etc., reside in the file system. We also discussed the PATH environment variable, which allows you to type system commands without having to know the full path to the executable file. We pointed out that if an executable resides in a directory that isn't included in the PATH variable, you have to either specify the full path to the file at the command line to run it or add the path to the PATH variable. We also emphasized that the Linux operating system doesn't check the current working directory when you enter a command at the shell prompt.

We then discussed utilities that you can use to search for files or directories in the Linux file system. We reviewed how to use the find and locate commands to find specific files or directories. We pointed out that find manually walks the file system hierarchy to conduct its searches, which can be somewhat slow. As an alternative, the locate utility creates a database of files in the file system. When you search with locate, it queries its database instead of walking the file system hierarchy, which is much faster. We also reviewed how to use grep to find content within text files.

The next topic we discussed was how to manage disk partitions. We first pointed out that you must partition a disk before you can use it in a Linux system. This is done using the fdisk utility. We reviewed the steps for creating a new partition using this command. We emphasize that you must actually commit your changes to disk before fdisk actually writes the new partitions you create.

We then discussed how to format a partition with a file system. This is done using the mkfs utility. We related that you use mkfs to create ext2 or ext3 file systems. The mkreiserfs utility is used to create Reiser file systems.

After a partition has been formatted, you can then mount it using the mount command. We pointed out that Linux mounts all partitions in directories within the same file system. It doesn't use drive letters as Windows and DOS do. Switching to a directory in the file system where a partition is mounted switches you to that device. We discussed the syntax for mounting a partition with mount. We pointed out that mount can also be used to display mounted partitions. To unmount a partition, you use the umount command.

We discussed the role of the /etc/fstab file. We pointed out that a mounted file system won't stay mounted after the system is rebooted if it doesn't have an entry in the /etc/fstab file. We reviewed the six fields used for each fstab entry. We also discussed how you can add a new entry to ensure a file system is mounted at system boot.

We then related that partitions can, occasionally, become damaged. If this happens, you can use the fsck utility to check and repair the partition.

We then reviewed how mount can also be used to mount removable media in the file system. Just as partitions are mounted in a directory, removable devices are also mounted in a directory in the file system. You access these devices through the directory where they are mounted (called a mount point). We reviewed the procedure for mounting floppy diskettes, optical discs, USB, and FireWire devices. We pointed out that, if you don't know what kind of file system is used by a removable device, you can use the –t auto option to allow the mount utility to automatically determine the correct parameter to use.

We ended this chapter by discussing how to back up your Linux file system. We emphasized the importance of conducting backups on a regular schedule. We then discussed the elements required to create a backup plan for your systems. The first step is to select a backup medium. We discussed the advantages and disadvantages of tape drives, recordable optical drives, and removable hard drives.

The next step is to select a backup strategy. We discussed how full, incremental, and differential backups work and how to combine them to design your own backup strategy. We also emphasized the importance of rotating your backup media as well as verifying your backup.

The next step is to determine your backup schedule and then to decide what to back up. We reviewed the directories in the file system that are commonly backed up, including /etc, /home, /opt, /root, /var, and /srv.

We ended the chapter by reviewing some of the Linux backup utilities that you can use to back up your system. We first reviewed the syntax for using tar, both with hard disks and with tape drives. We then reviewed the syntax for using cpio.

✓ TWO-MINUTE DRILL

Describe the Linux File System

❑ The role of the file system is to store and organize data such that it can be easily located and retrieved.

❑ The file system must also preserve data intact.

❑ Linux uses a hierarchical file system.

❑ The Linux file system hierarchy is based on the Filesystem Hierarchy Standard (FHS).

❑ The topmost directory is /.

❑ Other standard directories are created beneath / and serve functions defined in the FHS.

❑ The Linux file system uses regular files, links, FIFOs, and sockets.

Complete Common File System Tasks

❑ Most file system management tasks can be completed using either graphical or command-line tools.

❑ The pwd command is used to display the current directory.

❑ The cd command is used to change directories.

❑ The ls command is used to display directory contents.

❑ Using ls with the –l option displays additional details about files and directories.

❑ Using ls with the –R option displays directory contents recursively.

❑ The touch command is used to create new files.

❑ The mkdir command is used to create new directories.

❑ You can use cat to view a text file on screen.

❑ You can also use less to view a text file on screen.

❑ The less command pauses the display one line at a time.

❑ The head command can be used to display the first few lines of a text file.

❑ The tail command can be used to display the last few lines of a text file.

❑ The tail command used with the –f option can monitor a text file for changes.

❑ You can use rmdir to delete an empty directory.

❑ You can use rm to delete populated directories or files.

❑ The cp command is used to copy files.

❑ The mv command is used to move files.

❑ The Linux file system allows you to create link files that point to other files or directories in the file system.

❑ Hard links point directly to the inode of another file.

❑ Symbolic links have their own inode.

❑ Links are created using the ln command.

❑ The which command is used to display the location of files in the file system.

❑ The PATH environment variable makes it such that you don't have to include the full path when running Linux commands.

❑ If an executable's path isn't included in PATH, you must either enter the full path with the command or add the path to PATH.

❑ The Linux operating system doesn't check the current directory when you enter a command at the shell prompt.

❑ You can use the find utility to locate files or directories in the file system.

❑ The find utility manually walks the file system hierarchy to search for files.

❑ You can use locate to search for files or directories.

❑ The locate utility maintains a database of all files in the file system.

❑ When locate conducts a search, it searches the database instead of the file system.

❑ You can use grep to search for text within a file.

Manage Disk Partitions

❑ You must partition and format a disk before you can mount it in the Linux file system.

❑ The fdisk utility is used to partition disks.

❑ You have to set the partition type when partitioning disks.

❑ Partition changes are only saved in memory until you commit them to disk.

❑ After partitioning a disk, you need to format it with mkfs or mkreiserfs.

❑ After formatting a disk you can mount it using the mount command.

❑ The /etc/mtab file can be used to view mounted file systems.

❑ You can also use /proc/mounts to view mounted file systems.

❑ You can unmount a mounted file system using the umount command.

❑ All file systems must be unmounted before shutting Linux down.

❑ Mounted file systems won't be remounted on reboot unless they have an entry in the /etc/fstab file.

❑ The /etc/fstab file specifies mount points and other options for specific devices.

❑ The fsck utility is used to check and repair file systems.

Use Removable Media

❑ Removable devices must be mounted in the Linux file system before they can be accessed.

❑ The mount command can be used to mount floppy diskettes.

❑ Floppies usually use the vfat file system type.

❑ The first floppy diskette in your system is /dev/fd0.

❑ The /media/floppy and /mnt/floppy directories are used for mounting floppies.

❑ You can use /etc/fstab to automate the process of mounting a floppy.

❑ You must use umount to unmount a floppy before you can remove it from the system.

❑ CDs and DVDs must be mounted in the file system before they can be accessed.

❑ CDs and DVDs are mounted using the iso9660 file system type.

❑ CDs and DVDs are usually mounted in /media/cdrom, /media/cdrecorder, /media/dvd, or /mnt/cdrom.

❑ Linux sees USB and FireWire devices as additional SCSI devices.

❑ USB and FireWire devices are mounted using mount.

❑ If you don't know what type of file system is used on a USB or FireWire device, you can use –t auto to let mount try to determine the correct file system type.

Back Up Data

❑ It is absolutely critical that you regularly back up your system.

❑ Tape drives are commonly used to back up data.

❑ Tape drives hold a large amount of data and are relatively inexpensive.

❑ Tape drives are also slow and tend to wear out.

❑ Rewritable CDs and DVDs are an option for backups, but they usually don't hold enough information.

❑ Removable hard drives are becoming a popular solution for running backups.

❑ Removable hard drives are very fast and hold a lot of data; however, they are also susceptible to the same corruption issues as the hard disk being backed up.

❑ Full backups back up everything and flag the files as having been backed up.

❑ Incremental backups back up everything that has been modified since the last full or incremental backup and flag the files as having been backed up.

❑ Differential backups back up everything that has been backed up since the last full backup. It doesn't flag the files as having been backed up.

❑ You can mix full backups with incremental or differential backups, but you can't mix incremental and differential backups.

❑ You should keep a three- to four-week rotation of backups.

❑ You should verify your backups.

❑ You should set a schedule for your backups.

❑ You should carefully determine which directories to back up.

❑ You should consider backing up /etc, /home, /opt, /root, /var, and /srv.

❑ You can use tar to create backup files.

❑ The tar utility works with most backup media.

❑ You can also use cpio to archive data.

SELF TEST

Describe the Linux File System

1. Which of the following are roles of the Linux file system? (Choose two.)
   - A. Create automatic backups of system data.
   - B. Make data easily locatable.
   - C. Preserve data integrity.
   - D. Provide the user with a command-line interface.
   - E. Provide the user with a graphical user interface.

2. Which directory contains file system management utilities such as cp or rm?
   - A. /bin
   - B. /dev
   - C. /var
   - D. /usr

3. Which directory is a pseudo file system that is dynamically created when it is accessed?
   - A. /var
   - B. /opt
   - C. /proc
   - D. /sys

Complete Common File System Tasks

4. Which directory does the ~ character represent when used with file system commands?
   - A. /var
   - B. The current directory
   - C. The current user's home directory
   - D. The root user's home directory

5. You need to generate a listing of files and directories within the /var directory, including files in subdirectories. Which command will do this?
   - A. ls /var
   - B. ls –l /var
   - C. ls –f /var
   - D. ls –R /var

6. You need to view the last few lines of your /var/xinetd.log file. Which is the best command to do this?

    A. tail /var/xinetd.log

    B. cat /var/xinetd.log |more

    C. head /var/xinetd.log

    D. less /var/xinetd.log

7. You need to delete the Temp directory within your user's home directory. Given that Temp has files in it, which is the best command to do this?

    A. rmdir Temp

    B. rmdir ~/Temp

    C. rm Temp

    D. rm ~/Temp

8. You need to copy the Documents directory within your user's home directory to the /tmp directory. Given that Documents has files and subdirectories within it, which is the correct command to do this?

    A. cp ~/Documents /tmp

    B. cp –R ~/Documents /tmp

    C. cp ~/Documents ~/tmp

    D. cp –R ~/Documents ~/tmp

9. You want to create a symbolic link in your home directory that will link the manual file to the /usr/share/doc/manual directory. Which is the correct command to do this?

    A. ln –s /usr/share/doc/manual ~/manual

    B. ln /usr/share/doc/manual ~/manual

    C. ln –s ~/manual /usr/share/doc/manual

    D. ln ~/manual /usr/share/doc/manual

10. You need to run an executable file named install located in the current directory. Which is the best command to do this?

    A. install

    B. ./install

    C. ~/install

    D. $PATH:install

11. You need to find a file named myfile.txt somewhere in your Linux file system. Which is the correct command to do this?

    A. find / -name "myfile.txt"

    B. find "myfile.txt"

    C. find / –name myfile.txt

    D. find –name "myfile.txt"

12. You need to find all entries in your /var/log/messages file that contain the term "scsi." Which is the correct command to do this?

    A. grep /var/log/messages "scsi"

    B. grep "scsi" /var/log/messages

    C. grep /var/log/messages scsi

    D. grep scsi /var/log/messages

Manage Disk Partitions

13. You need use fdisk to format the slave drive on the secondary IDE channel. Which is the correct command to do this?

    A. fdisk /dev/hdd

    B. fdisk /dev/sdd

    C. fdisk /dev/hda4

    D. fdisk /dev/hdb2

14. You need to format the first partition on the slave drive on the secondary IDE channel using the ext3 file system. Which is the correct command to do this?

    A. mkext3fs /dev/hdd1

    B. mkfs –t ext3 /dev/hdd1

    C. mkfs –t ext3 /dev/hda4

    D. mkreiserfs –t ext3 /dev/hdd1

15. Which file is used to automatically mount file systems when the system initially boots?

    A. /etc/mtab

    B. /proc/mounts

    C. /etc/inittab

    D. /etc/fstab

Use Removable Media

16. You need to mount a CD disc on /media/cdrecorder. Given that the CD drive is the slave drive on the secondary IDE channel, which is the best command to do this?

    A. mount –t iso9660 /dev/hdd /media/cdrecorder

    B. mount –t cdrom /dev/hdd /media/cdrecorder

    C. mount –t iso9660 /dev/hdc /media/cdrecorder

    D. mount –t iso9660 /dev/hda ~/cdrecorder

17. You need to mount a USB flash drive on your Linux system. Given that your Linux system doesn't currently have any SCSI adapters or devices installed, which file represents the flash drive when it is inserted?

    A. /dev/hda

    B. /dev/usb

    C. /dev/sda

    D. You must install a SCSI adapter for the USB device to be recognized.

Back Up Data

18. Which type of backup backs up all files modified since the last full backup and does not flag the files as having been backed up?

    A. Full

    B. Incremental

    C. Differential

    D. Partial

19. You need to create a backup of /etc to a removable hard disk drive mounted at /mnt/USB. Which tar command will do this?

    A. tar –cfv /mnt/USB/backup.tar /etc

    B. tar –xfv ~/backup.tar /etc

    C. tar –xzf /mnt/USB/backup.tar /etc

    D. tar –cfv /mnt/USB/backup.tar ~/etc

LAB QUESTION

You've just installed a new hard disk drive to increase the storage space in your Linux system. The drive is an IDE hard disk drive and is the master drive on the secondary IDE channel. Outline the steps you would need to complete to be able to access the new disk.

SELF TEST ANSWERS

Describe the Linux File System

1. ☑ **B and C.** The role of the file system is to make data easily locatable and to preserve its integrity.
☒ **A, D,** and **E** are incorrect. **A** is provided by file system utilities. **D** is provided by the shell. **E** is provided by X Windows.

2. ☑ **A.** File system utilities are located in /bin.
☒ **B, C,** and **D** are incorrect. **B** contains your device files. **C** contains variable data. **D** contains application files.

3. ☑ **C.** The /proc file system is a pseudo file system.
☒ **A, B,** and **D** are incorrect. **A** contains variable data. **B** contains application files. **D** contains hardware information.

Complete Common File System Tasks

4. ☑ **C.** The ~ character represents the home directory of the current user.
☒ **A, B,** and **D** are incorrect. **A** contains variable system data. **B** is a distracter. **D** is only true if the current user is root.

5. ☑ **D.** The ls –R /var command will generate a listing of /var and its subdirectories.
☒ **A, B,** and **C** are incorrect. **A** only displays a listing of /var. **B** displays a long listing of /var only. **C** is a distracter.

6. ☑ **A.** The tail utility will display the last few lines of the file.
☒ **B, C,** and **D** are incorrect. **B** will eventually display the last lines, but it will take a while to get to them. **C** displays the beginning of the file. **D** will, likewise, eventually display the last lines, but it will take a while to get to them.

7. ☑ **D.** The rm command will delete the Temp directory and its subdirectories.
☒ **A, B,** and **C** are incorrect. **A** won't work because Temp has files in it. **B** won't work because Temp has files in it. **C** will only work if the current directory is ~.

8. ☑ **B.** The –R switch copies data recursively.
☒ **A, C,** and **D** are incorrect. **A** won't copy subdirectories. **C** won't copy subdirectories and uses incorrect syntax to refer to /tmp. **D** also uses incorrect syntax to refer to /tmp.

9. ☑ **A.** The –s option creates a symbolic link with the ln command.
☒ **B, C,** and **D** are incorrect. **B** creates a hard link. **C** uses the wrong order of files and directories. **D** also uses the wrong order of files and directories and creates a hard link.

10. ☑ **B.** You must use ./ to run a file in the current directory if that directory isn't included in the PATH environment variable.

    ☒ **A, C,** and **D** are incorrect. **A** will only work if the current directory is in PATH. **C** will only work if the current directory is your home directory. **D** is a distracter.

11. ☑ **A.** The find / –name "myfile.txt" command uses the correct syntax.

    ☒ **B, C,** and **D** are incorrect. **B** omits the –name parameter and search directory. **C** omits the quotes around the search term. **D** omits the search directory.

12. ☑ **D.** The grep scsi /var/log/messages command uses the correct syntax.

    ☒ **A, B,** and **C** are incorrect. **A** uses the wrong order of options and uses quotes. **B** uses quotes. **C** uses the wrong order of options.

Manage Disk Partitions

13. ☑ **A.** The fdisk /dev/hdd command uses the correct syntax.

    ☒ **B, C,** and **D** are incorrect. **B** references the fourth SCSI device. **C** references the fourth partition on the first IDE hard disk on the primary channel. **D** references the second partition on the second IDE hard disk on the primary channel.

14. ☑ **B.** The mkfs –t ext3 /dev/hdd1 command uses the correct syntax.

    ☒ **A, C,** and **D** are incorrect. **A** uses an invalid command. **C** references the wrong device. **D** can't be used to make an ext3 partition.

15. ☑ **D.** The /etc/fstab file is used to automatically mount file systems at boot.

    ☒ **A, B,** and **C** are incorrect. **A** only displays a list of currently mounted file systems. **B** also only displays a list of currently mounted file systems. **C** contains information for the init process.

Use Removable Media

16. ☑ **A.** The mount –t iso9660 /dev/hdd /media/cdrecorder command uses the correct syntax.

    ☒ **B, C,** and **D** are incorrect. **B** uses an invalid file system type. **C** references the wrong device. **D** references the wrong device and mount point.

17. ☑ **C.** The device will be referenced by /dev/sda because there are no other SCSI devices in the system.

    ☒ **A, B,** and **D** are incorrect. **A** references the first IDE disk in the system. **B** is a distracter. **D** is incorrect. You don't need a SCSI adapter in the system to use USB external storage.

Back Up Data

18. ☑ **C.** A differential backup backs up all files modified since the last full backup and does not flag the files as having been backed up.

☒ **A, B,** and **D** are incorrect. **A** is incorrect because a full backup flags files as having been backed up and backs up all files regardless of when they were last backed up. **B** is incorrect because incrementals flag files as having been backed up. **D** is a distracter.

19. ☑ **A.** The tar –cfv /mnt/USB/backup.tar /etc command uses the correct syntax.

☒ **B, C,** and **D** are incorrect. **B** extracts an archive instead of creating one. **C** also extracts an archive instead of creating one. **D** references the wrong directory for backing up.

LAB ANSWER

To accomplish this, you must first use fdisk to create a primary partition on /dev/hdc. This partition should be of type 83 Linux Native. Once written to disk, you should then use either mkfs or mkreiserfs to format /dev/hdc1 with a file system. Then you need to create a directory in /mnt to serve as a mount point. Once done, you can then mount the /dev/hdc1 file system in the mount point directory you created. To ensure the partition is remounted when the system reboots, you should add the appropriate entry in /etc/fstab.

7

Working with Linux Users and Groups

O ne of the great things about Linux is the fact that it is a true multi-user operating system. A single Linux system can be configured with one, two, five, ten, or more user accounts. Each user on the system is provided with his or her own computing environment that is unique to the user. For example, in Figure 7-1, the current user is named **ksanders**.

Notice that ksanders has her own directory in /home named **ksanders**. Within her home directory, she has a variety of subdirectories, including the following:

■ **Desktop**   Contains the files and icons displayed on ksanders' desktop.

■ **Documents**   Contains ksanders' documents.

■ **public_html**   Contains ksanders' personal Web pages.

FIGURE 7-1   The ksanders user's system environment

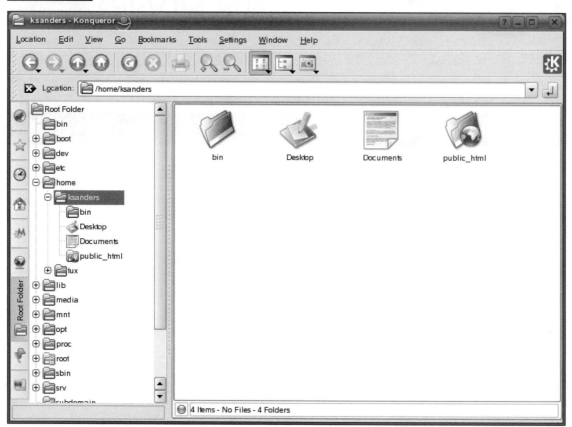

When ksanders logs in to the system, her own desktop preferences are displayed and she has access to her files stored in /home/ksanders. If a different user logs in, his or her desktop preferences are displayed and access is provided to that user's home directory.

If the system has been configured to work on a computer network, then users can even log in to the system remotely and access their desktop and home directory as if they were sitting in front of the computer. In this scenario, multiple users can be logged in and using the same computer at the same time.

Because Linux is a multi-user operating system, we need some way to control who has access to what in the system. For example, suppose you have a Linux system with five user accounts:

- ksanders
- jelison
- hsaez
- ebuchannan
- aebbert

You need some way to make sure each of these users can access what they need in the file system and nothing more. For example, you need to ensure that hsaez can access her files but can't access jelison's files and directories. Imagine what a nightmare it would be if one user on the system could access and tinker with files owned by a different user.

I had an experience early in my career where this actually happened. My first job out of college was with a microchip manufacturer. This particular employer ran several shifts each day. To save money, the cubicles and computers used by day shift workers were shared with night shift workers. In the Navy, they call this "hot-bunking."

Because of this, I shared my chair and computer system with a night shift employee. I started my shift at 8:00 A.M. and he ended his shift at 7:00 A.M. The computer system we shared was a blazing fast 486 DX2 66 system running Windows 3.1.

Now, early versions of Windows, such as Windows 3.x, as well as the entire Windows 9x family, including Windows 95, 98, and Me, were not true multi-user operating systems. In fact, with Windows 3.1, you didn't even have to log in. That meant whoever used the computer had full access to the entire file system. In my hot-bunking employment situation, my night shift compatriot had full and unfettered access to my files and I likewise had access to his files during the daytime.

At first, we managed to stay out of each other's way reasonably well. However, as time passed, this got to be a real problem. The problem was that, at this point in time, a 500MB hard drive was considered "cutting edge" and the first 1GB hard disk drives were just starting to come onto the market (although they were far too expensive for most of us to actually buy).

Because we were limited to a 500MB hard drive, we were constantly running out of disk space. You can probably guess what started to happen. During the day, I'd need more disk space on our shared system and I'd poke around the file system looking for files that could be deleted. My compatriot did the same thing at night. It didn't take long for us to start deleting each other's important files. As the wise philosopher George Carlin has noted, "Have you ever noticed that your junk is stuff and other people's stuff is junk?" My night shift compatriot would delete my "junk" so he could save his "stuff." I would do the same thing during the day.

The moral of this story is that you must implement some kind of file system access controls that prevent users from accessing "stuff" they shouldn't. Linux does just this using users, groups, ownership, and permissions. In this chapter, we're going to discuss the following topics:

- Working with users and groups
- Managing ownership, permissions, and quotas

Let's begin this chapter by introducing you to Linux users and groups.

INSIDE THE EXAM

Working with Linux Users and Groups

To pass your Linux+ exam, you must know Linux users, groups, ownership, and permissions inside and out! These concepts are central to the management of a Linux system. If you don't understand them, you are very likely to fail the exam.

To be properly prepared, you should understand how users are implemented on Linux, the difference between system and regular users, and how to manage accounts from the command line. You should also know how groups are used on Linux and how to manage them from the command line as well.

You should also understand the three Linux permissions and how they affect user access to files in the file system. You should know how to use command-line utilities to modify permissions assigned to a file or directory. You should also know how to use command-line utilities to manage file ownership.

CERTIFICATION OBJECTIVE 7.01

Manage Users and Groups

To control access to a Linux system and the data it contains, we need to do two things:

- We need to require users to supply a set of credentials before they will be granted access to the system.
- We need access controls that specify what individual users can do with files and directories in the file system after they have logged in.

We're going to address the first condition in this part of the chapter. To control overall access to the system itself, we need to implement users and groups. In this part of this chapter, we're going to discuss how to do this. Specifically, we're going to cover the following:

- Linux user accounts
- Linux groups

Let's begin by discussing how Linux user accounts work.

Linux User Accounts

One of the key problems in the employment situation I described at the beginning of this chapter is the fact that my Windows 3.1 system didn't use any user accounts. Whoever sat down in front of the computer and turned it on had full access to all of the data on the hard drive. It didn't matter if it was myself, my co-worker, the custodian, or (of more concern) a corporate spy from a competitor. This was a great weakness of this particular operating system.

To remedy this problem, I needed a workstation operating system that used true user accounts. Fortunately, the days of the "userless" operating system are all but gone. Most modern operating systems include some type of user authentication system based on user accounts. Linux in particular performs this function very well. In this part of this chapter, we're going to discuss the following:

- How Linux user accounts work
- Where Linux user accounts are stored
- Creating and managing user accounts from the command line

Let's begin by discussing how Linux user accounts work.

How Linux User Accounts Work

You've probably noticed as we've worked through the various exercises in this course that you must log in before you can use your Linux system. This is called *authentication*. To authenticate, you must supply the following credentials:

■ Username

■ Password

There are a variety of other authentication methods available for Linux systems. Instead of manually entering usernames and passwords, you can configure Linux to use smart cards, proximity cards, or biometric readers.

After logging in, your user's unique system environment is created. In Figure 7-2, the ksanders user has logged in to the local system. Her customized desktop preferences have been loaded and access has been granted to her home directory in /home/ksanders.

FIGURE 7-2	The ksanders system environment

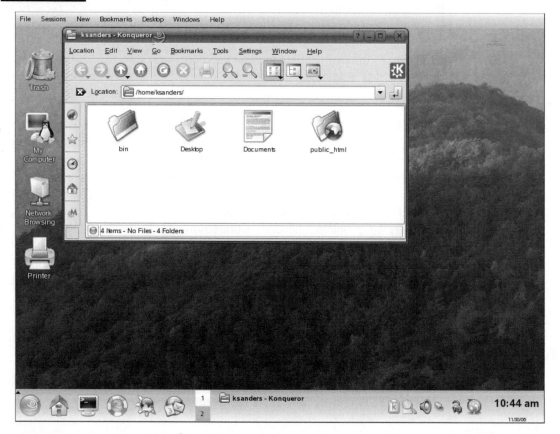

If another user were to log in to the same system, his or her preferences would be loaded instead of ksanders' preferences. They would also be provided with access to their home directory. An important point to remember is that files saved in a given user's home directory are protected from all other users on the system. For example, if ksanders were to save files in /home/ksanders, the tux user on this system would not be able to access them.

By default, all user home directories are created and maintained in the /home directory. For example, in Figure 7-3 two user accounts have been created on the Linux system, tux and ksanders.

Both users have home directories created for them in /home. There is one exception to this rule, however. Remember that all Linux systems use a superuser account named root. Notice in Figure 7-3 that there is no home directory in /home for the root user account. Is root homeless? Actually, no. The root user account is

FIGURE 7-3   User accounts in /home

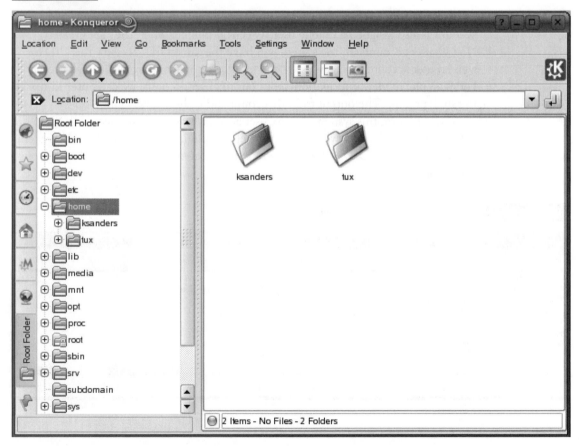

given a home directory too. However, it isn't maintained in /home. Instead, the root user's home directory is /root. If you look carefully in Figure 7-3, you'll see a directory named root at the root of the file system. This is root's home directory and, of course, only root can access this directory.

You can view information about any user account on your system using the finger *username* command from the shell prompt. For example, if I wanted to view information about the ksanders account on my Linux system, I would enter **finger ksanders**. When I do, useful information about the ksanders account is displayed, as shown in Figure 7-4.

Notice that finger displays the following information about the ksanders account:

- **Login** This is the username that is used to authenticate to the system.
- **Name** This is the user's full name.
- **Directory** This is the user's home directory.
- **Shell** This is the default shell that will be provided to the user.
- **Last Login** This displays the last time the user logged in and where from.

In addition to having a home directory and default shell assigned, each user account is also assigned a unique user ID (UID) number when they are created. No two user accounts on the system will have the same UID. To view the UID for a given user account, you can use the id *username* command from the shell prompt. For example, to view information about our tux user account, we can enter **id tux** at the shell prompt. The output from this command is shown in Figure 7-5.

Notice that on this system, the tux user account has been assigned a UID of 1000. On a SUSE Linux system, the first regular user account created on the system is always assigned a UID of 1000. The next user account will be assigned a UID of 1001, and so on.

FIGURE 7-4   Using finger to view user account information

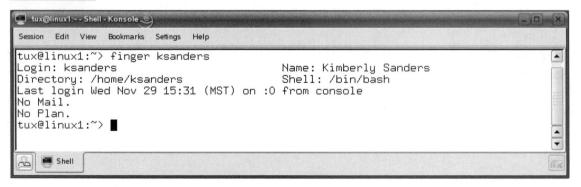

FIGURE 7-5   Using the id command to view the UID for a user account

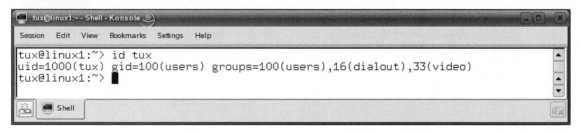

Other distributions may use a different numbering scheme for the UID, however. For example, UIDs on a Fedora system start at 500 instead of 1000. In Figure 7-6, you can see that the tux user on this Fedora system has a UID of 500 because it was the first standard user account created.

Notice that the preceding paragraphs refer to UIDs assigned to standard user accounts. What about the root user? The root user account is always assigned a UID of 0 on most Linux distributions. This is shown in Figure 7-7.

It's this UID that the operating system actually uses to control access to files and directories in the file system. We'll discuss this in more detail later in the chapter. For now, however, we need to discuss where Linux user accounts are saved in the system. Let's do that next.

Where Linux User Accounts Are Stored

Linux is a very flexible operating system. One of its flexible features is the location of user accounts on the system. When you originally installed the system, your distribution may have given you several options for where you wanted to store your user accounts. For example, the User Authentication Method selection screen from the SUSE Linux installer is shown in Figure 7-8.

FIGURE 7-6   Viewing the UID of a user on a Fedora system

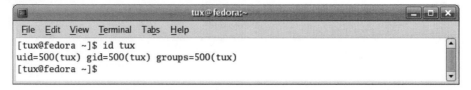

FIGURE 7-7   Viewing the UID of the root user account

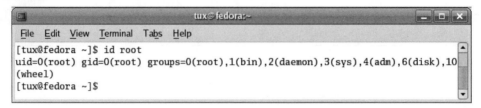

```
[tux@fedora ~]$ id root
uid=0(root) gid=0(root) groups=0(root),1(bin),2(daemon),3(sys),4(adm),6(disk),10
(wheel)
[tux@fedora ~]$
```

Notice that this screen allows you to choose from the following authentication methods:

■ **Local**   This option stores user accounts in the /etc/passwd file. This has been the default configuration used by Linux systems for many years.

■ **LDAP**   This is a newer option that many Linux administrators are starting to adopt. Instead of storing user accounts in a file in the file system, user accounts are stored in a directory service provided by OpenLDAP. Unlike local authentication, which is a flat file, the directory service is hierarchical

FIGURE 7-8   Selecting a user authentication method

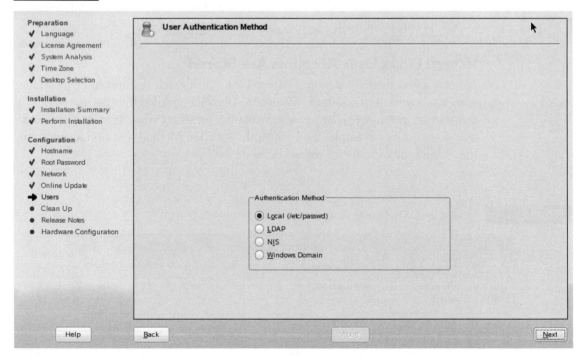

in nature, allowing you to sort and organize your user accounts by location, function, or department. The database that hosts the directory can also be replicated among several different Linux systems. This allows you to maintain one single set of user accounts that can be used by several different systems.

on the
Job *Essentially, the LDAP option moves Linux in the direction of other server operating systems that use directory services, such as Novell's eDirectory or Microsoft's Active Directory.*

- **NIS** This option stands for *Network Information Service*. NIS is also designed to provide centralized user account management when you have multiple systems that all need the same user accounts. To do this, NIS configures systems to all use a common passwd and shadow file.
- **Windows Domain** If you have a Windows domain controller in your network (or another Linux server running the Samba service), you can configure your Linux system to use the user accounts in the domain to authenticate to the local system.

exam

Watch *For your Linux+ exam, you primarily need to be concerned with the Local option. All Linux distributions can use the /etc/passwd and /etc/shadow files for authentication.*

Which of these options is best? It depends on what you need your system to do. If the system is a standalone workstation, the Local option is usually sufficient. You could also optionally use the LDAP option as well.

If your system is going to participate on a network where lots of different users will need access to your system, then you may want to consider using LDAP, NIS, or Windows Domain authentication.

For our purposes here, we're going to focus on the Local option. This option stores user and group information in the following files in the file system:

- **/etc/passwd** This file contains the user account information for your system.
- **/etc/shadow** This file contains passwords for your user accounts.
- **/etc/group** This file contains your system's groups. (We'll discuss groups later in this chapter.)

Let's look at the /etc/passwd file first.

The /etc/passwd File   If configured to use local authentication, your /etc/ passwd file contains your system's user accounts. Each user account on your system is represented by a single line in the file, as shown in Figure 7-9.

Each account record is composed of several different fields in the line, separated by a colon (:). These are organized as follows:

```
Username:Password:UID:GID:Full_Name:Home_Directory:Default_Shell
```

For example:

```
ksanders:x:1001:100:Kimberly Sanders:/home/ksanders:/bin/bash
```

Here's what these fields contain:

- **Username**   The Username field simply identifies the username the user will supply when logging in to the system. In this example, it is ksanders.
- **Password**   This is a legacy field. At one time, the user's password was stored in encrypted form in this field in the passwd file. However, for security reasons, the password has been moved from /etc/passwd to /etc/shadow. (We'll look at this file in more detail later.) Therefore, only the character x is shown in this field.
- **UID**   This is the user ID for the user account. We discussed the UID earlier in this chapter. In this example, the UID for the ksanders account is 1001.
- **GID**   This field references the group ID number of the user's default group. In this example, the GID for the ksanders account is 100. As we'll see later in this chapter, this references the users group.
- **Full_Name**   This field contains the user's full name. In this example, it's Kimberly Sanders.
- **Home_Directory**   This field contains the path to the user's home directory. In this case, the home directory is /home/ksanders.
- **Default_Shell**   This field specifies the shell that will be used by default. For ksanders, this is /bin/bash (the Bourne-Again SHell).

You probably noticed in Figure 7-9 that there are a lot of user accounts listed in the /etc/passwd file on my system. Your first instinct may be that I've created a lot of users on my system. Actually, this isn't the case. I've only created two standard users: tux and ksanders. All of the other user accounts are *system* user accounts. They aren't used for login. Instead, they are used by services running on the system. When one of these services needs to do something in the Linux file system, it does so as its associated user account from /etc/passwd.

For example, suppose I've logged into the ftp service on my Linux system as an anonymous user and uploaded a file. This file needs to be written to the ftp service's

FIGURE 7-9   Viewing the /etc/passwd file

default directory in the file system. When it writes, it does so as the ftp user. By doing this, we can use permissions (discussed later in the chapter) to control what a given service can or can't do.

Let's next look at the /etc/shadow file.

The /etc/shadow File   With most Linux distributions that use local authentication, your users' passwords will be stored in encrypted format in the /etc/shadow file. This file is linked to the /etc/passwd file we discussed previously. Each of the user accounts listed in /etc/passwd has a corresponding entry in /etc/shadow, as shown in Figure 7-10.

As with /etc/passwd, each user account is represented by a single line in the /etc/shadow file. Each record is composed of the following fields, each separated by a colon:

```
Username:Password:Last_Modified:Min_Days:Max_Days:Days_Warn:Disabled_Days:Expire
```

For example, the record for ksanders is as follows:

```
ksanders:$2a%05$fHzL5vsuk3ilLIuispxqKuCFEPg50ZhF8KshQyIZH7SDERJooEJTC:13481:0:99999:7:-1::
```

FIGURE 7-10 Viewing the /etc/shadow file

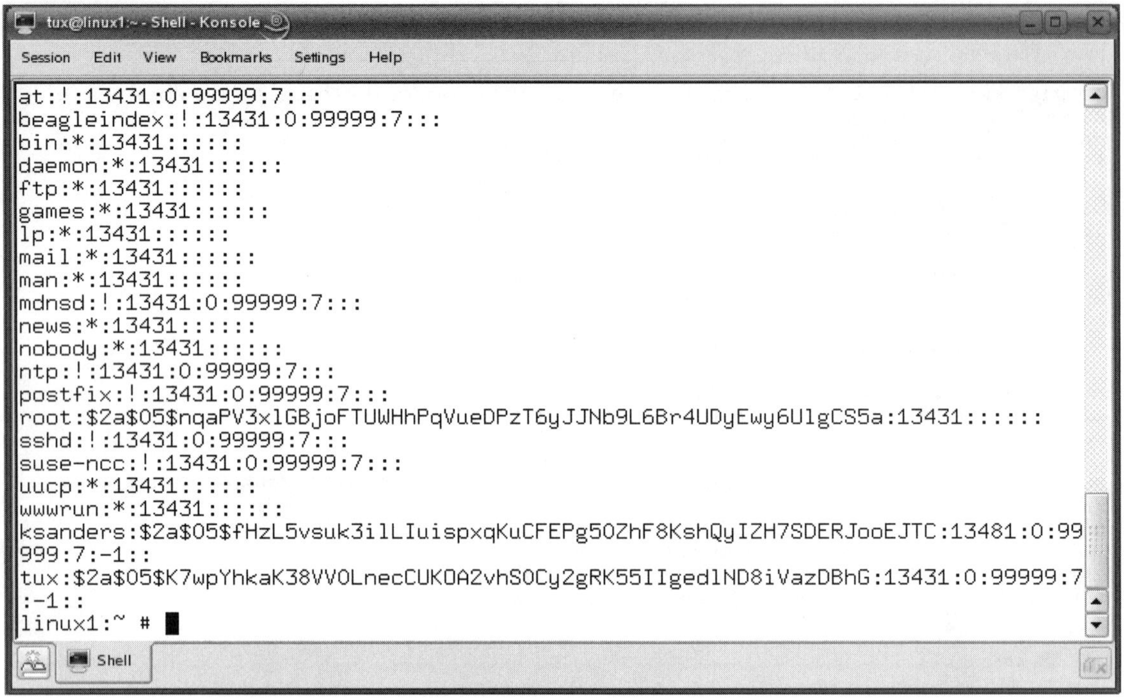

Here's what each of these fields contain:

- **Username** This is the user's login name from /etc/passwd.
- **Password** This is the user's password in encrypted format. In the preceding example, the password for ksanders is Sanders1. However, to prevent someone from copying the /etc/shadow file and grabbing your user passwords from it, they are stored in encrypted format. You may notice that several of the system user accounts have a simple asterisk in this field (*). This indicates that these accounts aren't allowed to log in to the system. For example, if I tried to log in to my system as ftp, I would be denied access even though the ftp user account exists.
- **Last_Modified** This field displays the number of days since January 1, 1970 that the password was last changed. In this example, it's been 13481 days.
- **Min_Days** This field displays the minimum number of days required before a password can be changed. In this example, it is set to 0 days.

- **Max_Days**   This field displays the maximum number of days before a password must be changed. In this example, it is set to 99999 days. Effectively, this means a password isn't required.
- **Days_Warn**   This field displays the number of days prior to password expiration that the user will be warned of the pending expiration. In this case, it's set to 7 days.
- **Disabled_Days**   This field displays the number of days to wait after a password has expired to disable the account. In this example, it is set to –1. This value disables this functionality.
- **Expire**   This field displays the number of days since January 1, 1970 after which the account will be disabled. In this example, it is set to a null value, indicating the account never expires.

As you can see, it is very important that these two files stay synchronized with each other. If they get out of whack, then it's possible that a user may not be able to log in or a service may not be able to access the file system correctly.

The good news is that these files usually stay in sync as they are supposed to without any intervention on the part of the administrator. The only times I've seen these two files become unsynchronized is when the administrator decides to manually edit these files with a text editor. I strongly discourage this practice. Your Linux system includes a wide variety of utilities that are used to manage user accounts and passwords on your system. (We'll discuss how to use these utilities later in this chapter.) You should always use these utilities instead of a text editor to manage user accounts. Doing so will ensure that both files are edited appropriately and stay synchronized with each other.

To verify your /etc/passwd and /etc/shadow files, you can use the pwck command at the shell prompt. This utility will verify each line in the two files and make sure they are valid. Any errors are reported on the screen. This is shown in Figure 7-11.

FIGURE 7-11   Using pwck to verify your /etc/passwd and /etc/shadow files

As you can see in Figure 7-11, pwck found that the home directory specified for the suse-ncc system user account didn't exist. Everything else checked out. If, for some reason, the /etc/passwd and the /etc/shadow files were out of synchronization, you could use the pwconv command at the shell prompt to fix the files. This utility will add any missing user accounts from /etc/passwd to /etc/shadow.

Next we discuss how you manage user accounts.

Creating and Managing User Accounts from the Command Line

As we've encountered with many of the other tasks discussed in this book, you can manage user accounts on your Linux system with either graphical utilities or from the command line. For example, SUSE Linux includes the YaST Users module, shown in Figure 7-12, to manage user accounts.

Likewise, Fedora includes the User Manager utility, which can also be used to manage user accounts graphically. This utility is shown in Figure 7-13.

As with everything else, these graphical utilities are just fine to use. I'll admit that I use them the majority of the time. However, you must know how to use the command-line user management utilities, both to be a truly effective Linux admin and to pass your Linux+ exam. Therefore, we're going to focus on command-line tools in this chapter. Once you're comfortable with them, feel free to experiment with their graphical equivalents.

In this chapter, we're going to cover the following tools:

- Using useradd
- Using passwd
- Using usermod
- Using userdel

Let's begin by learning how to use useradd.

SCENARIO & SOLUTION

You open /etc/passwd in a text editor and notice that the password for a particular user account is set to x. Why is this?	That's because the password is actually saved in encrypted format in /etc/shadow.
Your Linux system has a large number of user accounts. You need to check them to verify that they are configured properly. What command could you use to do this?	You would enter **pwck** at the shell prompt.

FIGURE 7-12   Using YaST to manage user accounts

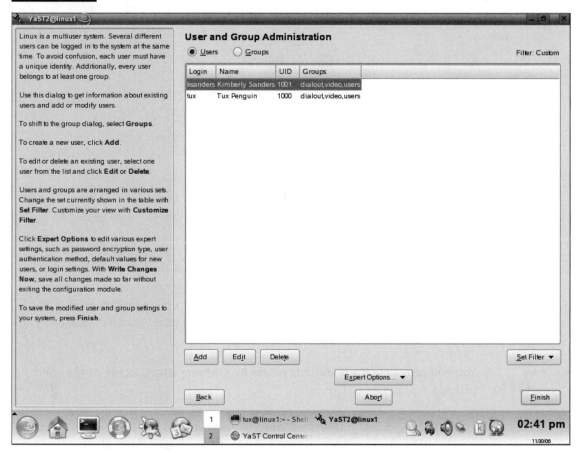

Using useradd   As its name implies, the useradd utility is used to add users to the Linux system. The syntax for useradd is useradd *options username*. For example, suppose I wanted to create a user account named lmorgan using default parameters. I would enter **useradd lmorgan** at the shell prompt, as shown in Figure 7-14.

When I do, the lmorgan account is created using the default parameters contained in the following configuration files:

■ **/etc/default/useradd**   This file contains defaults used by the useradd utility. A sample is shown in Figure 7-15.

Notice that this file specifies that the default group for new users is the group with a GID of 100 (that's the users group). It also specifies that a home directory

FIGURE 7-13   Using User Manager to manage user accounts

for the user be created in /home. The inactive account parameter is set to –1 and the account is set to never expire. The default shell is set to /bin/bash. In addition, the user is also made a member of the video and dialout groups in addition to the default groups. As with any Linux configuration file, if you don't like these values, you can simply edit the useradd file with a text editor to customize it the way you like.

on the

job

You can also view these default values by entering useradd –D *at the shell prompt.*

■ **/etc/login.defs**   This file contains values that can be used for the GID and UID parameters when creating an account with useradd. It also contains defaults for creating passwords in /etc/shadow. A sample of this file is shown in Figure 7-16.

FIGURE 7-14   Adding a user using default values with useradd

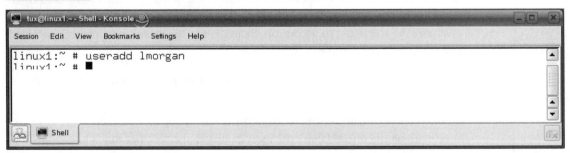

FIGURE 7-15 Default values in /etc/default/useradd

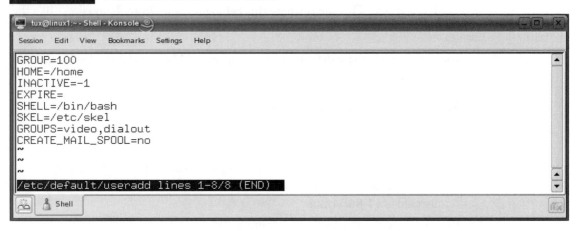

Notice that this file specifies default values for the fields we reviewed earlier in /etc/shadow for each user account. It also specifies defaults used when useradd is assigning a UID to a new account. Remember that, earlier in this

FIGURE 7-16 Default values in /etc/login.defs

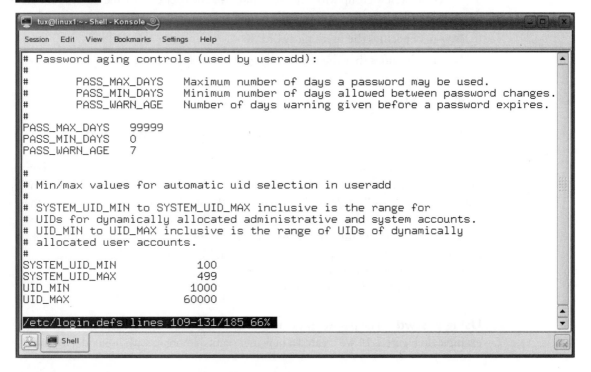

chapter, we noted that SUSE Linux starts UIDs at 1000 while Fedora starts UIDs at 500. This file is where this behavior comes from. If you don't like the defaults, you can always edit this file to match your preferences.

You can override these defaults when using useradd by specifying a list of options in the command line. You can use the following:

- **–c** Includes the user's full name.
- **–e** Specifies the date when the user account will be disabled. Format the date as *yyyy-mm-dd*.
- **–f** Specifies the number of days after password expiration before the account is disabled. Use a value of –1 to disable this functionality, e.g., useradd –f –1 jmcarthur.
- **–g** Specifies the user's default group.
- **–G** Specifies additional groups that the user is to be made a member of.
- **–M** Specifies that the user account be created without a home directory.
- **–m** Specifies the user's home directory.
- **–n** Used only on Red Hat or Fedora systems. By default, these systems create a new group with the same name as the user every time an account is created. Using this option will turn *off* this functionality.
- **–p** Specifies the user's password.
- **–r** Specifies that the user being created is a system user.
- **–s** Specifies the default shell for the user.
- **–u** Manually specifies a UID for the user.

For example, suppose I wanted to create a new user account for a user named Jackie McArthur on a Linux system. Further suppose that I want to specify a user name of jmcarthur, a full name of Jackie McArthur, a password of tux123, and that a home directory be created. To do this, I would enter **useradd –c "Jackie McArthur" –m –p "tux123" –s "/bin/bash" jmcarthur** at the shell prompt. After doing so, the account will be created in /etc/passwd, as shown in Figure 7-17.

Notice that useradd used the parameters we specified in the command line. For parameters we didn't specify, such as the GID and UID, the defaults from /etc/default/useradd were used instead.

Let's next look at the passwd utility.

Using passwd   The passwd utility is used to change an existing user's password. For example, in Figure 7-14 we created a new user named lmorgan with useradd. However,

FIGURE 7-17 Viewing a new user created with useradd

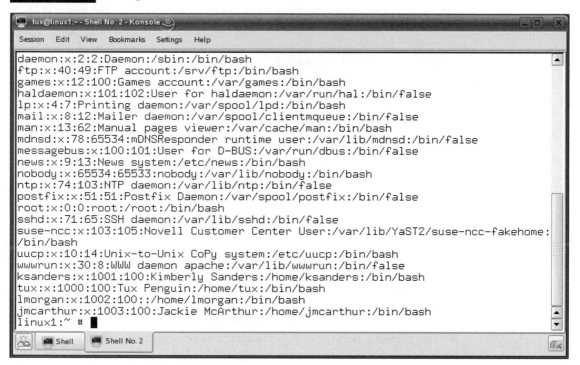

because we didn't use the –p option in the command line, the lmorgan account doesn't have a password and is locked. You can find out this information using the –S option with passwd. For example, we could enter **passwd –S lmorgan** at the shell prompt. This is shown in Figure 7-18.

Notice that LK is displayed in the output. This indicates that the account is locked. The remaining parameters are various other password parameters, such as the date of the last password change, the minimum number of days required before

FIGURE 7-18 Viewing password status with passwd

a password can be changed, the maximum number of days before a password must be changed, the number of days prior to password expiration when the user will be warned of the pending expiration, and the number of days to wait after a password has expired to disable the account.

In short, this account is unusable. To enable this account, we need to add a password. We can do this using passwd. The syntax is passwd *username*. In this case, you would enter **passwd lmorgan**. When you do, you are prompted to enter a password for the specified user, as shown in Figure 7-19.

Enter the password you want to use at the prompts. After doing so, you can enter **passwd –S lmorgan** again to view the account status, as shown in Figure 7-20.

Notice that the account status is set to PS, indicating that the password has been set and is valid. When working with passwd, you can also use the following options:

- **–l** Locks the user's account. This option invalidates the user's password.
- **–u** Unlocks a user's account.
- **–d** Removes a user's password.
- **–n** Sets the minimum number of days required before a password can be changed.
- **–x** Sets the maximum number of days before a password must be changed.
- **–w** Sets the number of days prior to password expiration when the user will be warned of the pending expiration.
- **–i** Sets the number of days to wait after a password has expired to disable the account.

Now that you know how to create a new user and how to set a user's password, let's next review how you go about modifying an existing user account.

FIGURE 7-19   Setting a user's password with passwd

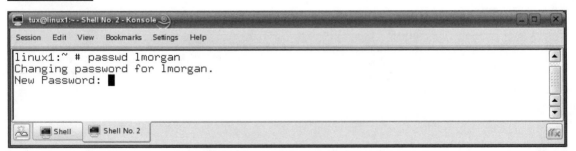

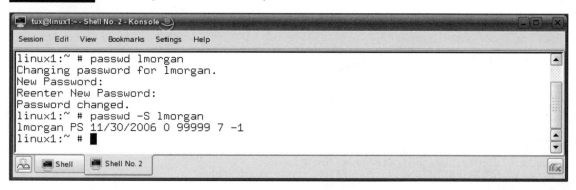

FIGURE 7-20   Rechecking the user's status with passwd

Using usermod   From time to time, you will need to modify an existing user account. This can be done from the command line using the usermod utility. The syntax for usermod is very similar to that used by useradd. You enter **usermod** *options username* at the shell prompt. The options for usermod are likewise similar to those used by useradd. They include the following:

- **–c**   Edits the user's full name.
- **–e**   Sets the date when the user account will be disabled. Format the date as *yyyy-mm-dd*.
- **–f**   Sets the number of days after password expiration before the account is disabled. Use a value of –1 to disable this functionality.
- **–g**   Sets the user's default group.
- **–G**   Specifies additional groups that the user is to be made a member of.
- **–l**   Changes the username.
- **–L**   Locks the user's account. This option invalidates the user's password.
- **–m**   Sets the user's home directory.
- **–p**   Sets the user's password.
- **–s**   Specifies the default shell for the user.
- **–u**   Sets the UID for the user.
- **–U**   Unlocks a user's account that has been locked.

For example, suppose my jmcarthur user has recently married and changed her last name to Sanders. I could update her user account to reflect this change by entering **usermod –l jsanders –c "Jackie Sanders" jmcarthur** at the shell prompt. When I do, the user's account information is updated in /etc/passwd, as shown in Figure 7-21.

FIGURE 7-21   Viewing a modified user account

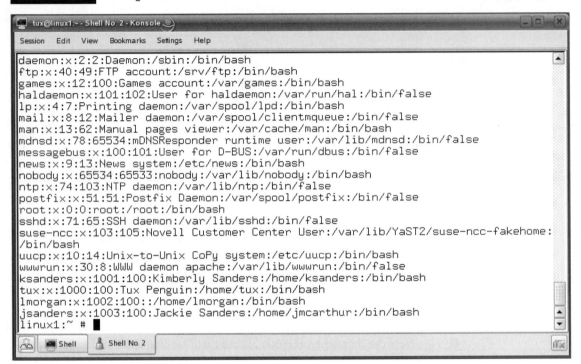

```
daemon:x:2:2:Daemon:/sbin:/bin/bash
ftp:x:40:49:FTP account:/srv/ftp:/bin/bash
games:x:12:100:Games account:/var/games:/bin/bash
haldaemon:x:101:102:User for haldaemon:/var/run/hal:/bin/false
lp:x:4:7:Printing daemon:/var/spool/lpd:/bin/bash
mail:x:8:12:Mailer daemon:/var/spool/clientmqueue:/bin/false
man:x:13:62:Manual pages viewer:/var/cache/man:/bin/bash
mdnsd:x:78:65534:mDNSResponder runtime user:/var/lib/mdnsd:/bin/false
messagebus:x:100:101:User for D-BUS:/var/run/dbus:/bin/false
news:x:9:13:News system:/etc/news:/bin/bash
nobody:x:65534:65533:nobody:/var/lib/nobody:/bin/bash
ntp:x:74:103:NTP daemon:/var/lib/ntp:/bin/false
postfix:x:51:51:Postfix Daemon:/var/spool/postfix:/bin/false
root:x:0:0:root:/root:/bin/bash
sshd:x:71:65:SSH daemon:/var/lib/sshd:/bin/false
suse-ncc:x:103:105:Novell Customer Center User:/var/lib/YaST2/suse-ncc-fakehome:
/bin/bash
uucp:x:10:14:Unix-to-Unix CoPy system:/etc/uucp:/bin/bash
wwwrun:x:30:8:WWW daemon apache:/var/lib/wwwrun:/bin/false
ksanders:x:1001:100:Kimberly Sanders:/home/ksanders:/bin/bash
tux:x:1000:100:Tux Penguin:/home/tux:/bin/bash
lmorgan:x:1002:100::/home/lmorgan:/bin/bash
jsanders:x:1003:100:Jackie Sanders:/home/jmcarthur:/bin/bash
linux1:~ # ▮
```

on the
Ⓙⓞb   *If there's a space in the name, then you will need to enclose it in quotes when using the usermod command. For example, we used the jsanders –c "Jackie Sanders" jmcarthur command to set the full name of the user.*

The last user-related topic we need to cover here is that of deleting user accounts. Let's discuss how to do this next.

Using userdel   From time to time, you will also need to remove a user account from your Linux system. This can be done from the shell prompt using the userdel utility. To delete a user, simply enter **userdel** *username*. For example, if we wanted to delete the lmorgan account we created earlier, we would enter **userdel lmorgan** at the shell prompt.

It's important to note that, by default, userdel will *not* remove the user's home directory from the file system. If you do want to remove the home directory when you delete the user, you need to use the –r option in the command line. For example, entering **userdel –r lmorgan** will remove the account and delete her home directory.

SCENARIO & SOLUTION

You want to create a user account for Viola Hammer named vhammer. What command would you enter at the shell prompt to create the account, specifying her full name, creating a home directory, setting her password to jkl123, and specifying a default shell of bash?	You would enter **useradd –c "Viola Hammer" –m –p "jkl123" –s "/bin/bash" vhammer**.
You need to check the password status of the vhammer account. What command would you enter?	You would enter **passwd –S vhammer** at the shell prompt.
What command would you use to delete the vhammer account without removing her home directory?	You would enter **userdel vhammer**.

Let's practice managing users in the following exercise

Managing User Accounts from the Command Line

In this exercise, you will practice creating and modifying user accounts from the shell prompt of your Linux system. Complete the following:

Boot your Linux system and log in as a standard user. If you used the lab exercise in Chapter 3 to install your system, you can log in as **tux** with a password of **M3linux273**.

Open a terminal session and change to your root user account by entering **su –** at the shell prompt and entering your root user's password. If you installed your system according to the instructions in Chapter 3, root's password is **tuxPenguin1**.

Create a user account for yourself by doing the following:

Determine a *username* and *password* for yourself. A common convention is to use your first initial with your last name.

At the shell prompt, enter **useradd –c "*your_full_name*" –m –p "*your_password*" –s "/bin/bash" *your_username***.

At the shell prompt, enter **tail /etc/passwd**. Verify that your new user account was created.

Create a user account using your system's default settings by entering **useradd dtracy** at the shell prompt.

At the shell prompt, enter **tail /etc/passwd**. Verify that your new user account was created. Notice that the new user is missing many parameters. Add these parameters by doing the following:

Enter a full name for the dtracy user account by entering **usermod –c "Richard Tracy" dtracy** at the shell prompt.

At the shell prompt, enter **tail /etc/passwd**. Verify that the full name was added to the dtracy account.

Give dtracy a password by entering **passwd dtracy** at the shell prompt.

When prompted, enter a new *password* for dtracy.

Now that you know how to manage users, we need to discuss how to manage groups. Let's do that next.

Linux Groups

Like other operating systems, Linux uses groups to make managing the system easier. In this part of this chapter, we're going to discuss the following:

- How Linux groups work
- Managing groups from the command line

Let's begin by discussing how Linux groups work.

How Linux Groups Work

Groups make our lives as system administrators easier! To understand why, let's take a look at a scenario. Suppose you have seven users on a Linux system. Of these users, five of them need almost the same level of access to files in the file system. Without groups, you would need to assign the necessary permissions separately to each of the five user accounts. That means you would be doing the same exact task five times over. That may not sound so bad, but just suppose you had 100 users that all needed the same level of access. What a waste of time!

Instead, you can implement groups on your Linux system. With groups, you assign permissions to the group and then make all the users that need that level of access members of the group. That's much easier! You only need to make one set of assignments. If something changes in the level of access needed, you only need to make the change once to the group. All of the group members then automatically receive the change. Once again, this is much easier than the alternative!

If your Linux system has been configured to use local authentication, your groups are defined in the /etc/group file. A sample of this file is shown in Figure 7-22.

FIGURE 7-22 Viewing entries in the /etc/group file

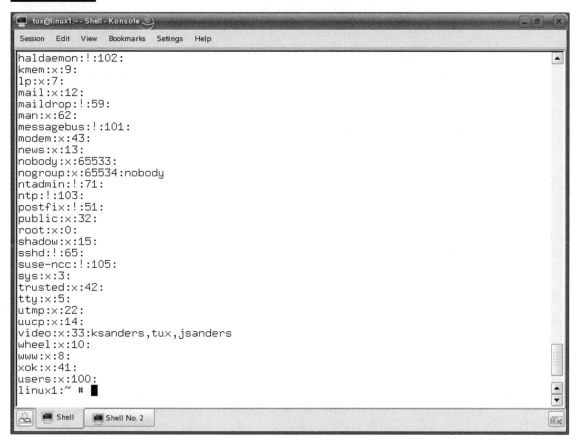

As with the /etc/passwd and the /etc/shadow files, each line in /etc/group is a single record that represents one group. Each record is composed of the following four fields:

```
Group:Password:GID:Users
```

For example, in Figure 7-22, the record for the video group reads as follows:

```
video:x:33:ksanders,tux,jsanders
```

- ■ **Group** Specifies the name of the group. In the example above, the name of the group is video.
- ■ **Password** Specifies the group password.

- **GID** Specifies the group ID (GID) number of the group. In this example, the GID of the video group is 33.
- **Users** Lists the members of the group. In this case, the ksanders, tux, and jsanders users are members of the video group.

Some distributions, such as Fedora, use an additional group file to store group passwords. Just as /etc/shadow is used to store encrypted passwords for users defined in /etc/passwd, the /etc/gshadow file is sometimes used to define group passwords for groups defined in /etc/group.

A sample /etc/gshadow file is shown in Figure 7-23.

As with /etc/shadow, each line in /etc/gshadow represents a record for a single group. Each record is composed of the following fields:

```
Group_Name:Password:Group_Admins:Group_Members
```

With this in mind, let's review how you can manage your groups with command-line tools.

Managing Groups from the Command Line

As with users, you can also manage groups with either command-line or graphical tools. For example, both YaST and User Manager can be used to create, modify, or delete groups on your Linux system as well as user accounts.

FIGURE 7-23

Viewing the /etc/ gshadow file

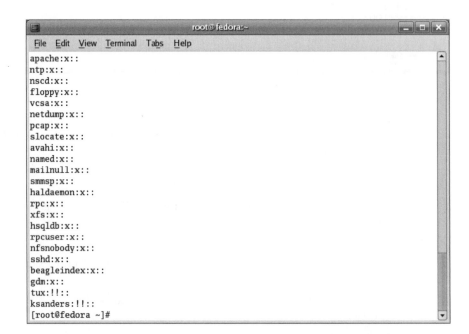

However, for the reasons specified earlier, we're going to focus on managing groups from the shell prompt in this chapter. We will review the following tools:

- Using groupadd
- Using groupmod
- Using groupdel

Let's begin by looking at groupadd.

Using groupadd   As you can probably guess from its name, the groupadd utility is used to add groups to your Linux system. The syntax for using groupadd at the shell prompt is relatively simple. Just enter **groupadd *options groupname***. For example, if I wanted to add a group named dbusers, I would enter **groupadd dbusers** at the shell prompt. When I do, a group is added to /etc/group using default parameters specified in /etc/login.defs.

When using groupadd, you can override the defaults in /etc/login.defs and customize the way the group is created using the following options:

- **–g**   Specifies a GID for the new group.
- **–p**   Specifies a password for the group.
- **–r**   Specifies that the group being created is a system group.

Let's next look at groupmod.

Using groupmod   You may have noticed that the groupadd command didn't add one key component to the new group: Users! What good is a group if you don't have any users occupying it?

To modify a group, including adding users to the group membership, you use the groupmod utility. The syntax for using groupmod is similar to that used by usermod. Enter **groupmod *options group*** at the shell prompt. You can use the following options with the command:

- **–g**   Changes the group's GID number.
- **–p**   Changes the group's password.
- **–A**   Adds a user account to the group.
- **–R**   Removes a user account from the group.

In the preceding topic, we added a group named dbusers to the system. If we wanted to add ksanders to the group, we would enter **groupmod –A "ksanders" dbusers** at the shell prompt.

SCENARIO & SOLUTION

You want to create a new group on a Linux system for marketing employees. This group should be named mkt. What command would you enter to do this, assuming you want to use system defaults for creating the group?	You would enter **groupadd mkt**.
You want to add the user vhammer as a member of the mkt group. What command would you use to do this?	You would enter groupmod –A **"vhammer" mkt** at the shell prompt.

Finally, let's look at deleting groups.

Using groupdel If, for some reason, you need to delete an existing group from the system, you can do so using the groupdel command at the shell prompt. For example, to delete the dbusers group, you would enter **groupdel dbusers**.

Let's practice managing groups in the following exercise.

EXERCISE 7-2

ON THE CD

Managing Groups from the Command Line

In this exercise, you will practice creating and modifying groups from the shell prompt of your Linux system.

Suppose your company is putting together a new research and development team that will be using your Linux system. You need to create a new group for users who will be members of this team. Complete the following:

1. Verify that you are logged in to your system.
2. If necessary, switch to your root user account with the **su – command**.
3. Create a new group named research by doing the following:
   a. At the shell prompt, enter **groupadd research**.
   b. Add your user account and the dtracy user account (created in the previous exercise) to the research group by entering **groupmod –A "dtracy,*your_username*" research** at the shell prompt.
   c. Verify the users were added to the group by entering **tail /etc/group** at the shell prompt.

Now that you know how to create, delete, and modify Linux users and groups, we need to add additional components to our security equation: ownership, permissions, and quotas.

CERTIFICATION OBJECTIVE 7.02

Manage Ownership, Permissions, and Quotas

Recall that earlier in this chapter we identified two tasks we need to accomplish when working with Linux:

- Control who can access the system.
- Define what users can do after they have logged in to the system.

We addressed the first point in the preceding topics. We control who accesses the system by implementing users and groups. In this part of this chapter, we're going to address the second point. We need to define what users can do after they have logged in to the system. We're going to do this by discussing the following topics:

- Managing ownership
- Managing permissions
- Implementing disk quotas

Let's begin by discussing file and directory ownership.

Managing Ownership

To effectively control who can do what in the file system, you need to first consider who "owns" files and directories. We're going to discuss the following in this regard:

- How ownership works
- Managing ownership from the command line

Let's start by discussing how ownership works.

How Ownership Works

Anytime a user creates a new file or directory, his or her user account is assigned as that file or directory's "owner." For example, suppose the ksanders user logs in to her Linux system and creates a file named contacts.odt using OpenOffice.org in her home directory. Because she created this file, ksanders is automatically assigned ownership of contacts.odt. By right-clicking on this file in the system's graphical user interface and selecting Properties | Permissions, you can view who owns the file. This is shown in Figure 7-24.

Notice in Figure 7-24 that there are two owners for contacts.odt. The first is the name of the user who owns the file. In this case, it's ksanders. In addition, the group

FIGURE 7-24   Viewing file ownership in the Linux GUI

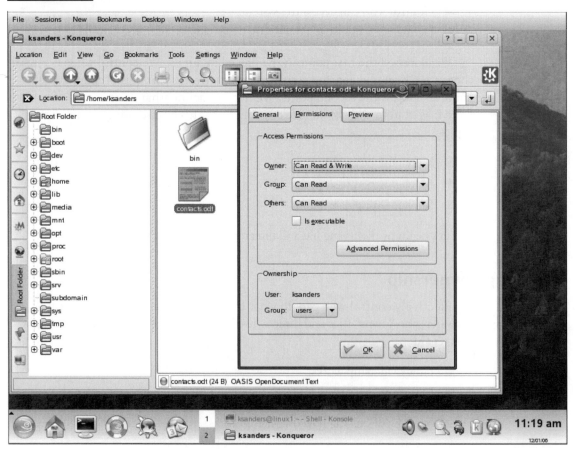

FIGURE 7-25   Viewing file ownership from the command line

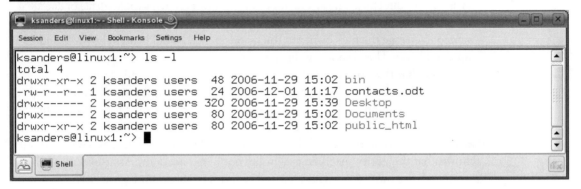

users owns the file as well. That's because the primary group that ksanders belongs to is users.

You can also view file ownership from the command line using the ls –l command. This has been done in ksanders' home directory in Figure 7-25.

Notice in Figure 7-25 that the third column in the output displays the name of the file or directory's owner (ksanders) while the fourth column displays the name of the group that owns it (users).

While file and directory ownership is automatically assigned at creation, it can be modified. Let's discuss how this is done next.

Managing Ownership from the Command Line

File and directory ownership isn't a fixed entity. Even though ownership is automatically assigned at creation, it can be modified. You can specify a different user and/or group as the owner of a given file or directory. To change the user who owns a file, you must be logged in as root. To change the group that owns a file, you must be logged in as root or as the user who currently owns the file.

This can be done with either graphical or command-line tools. Staying true to the form of this chapter, we're going to focus on command-line utilities, including the following:

- Using chown
- Using chgrp

Let's begin by learning how to use chown.

Using chown   The chown utility can be used to change the user or group that owns a file or directory. The syntax for using chown is chown *user.group file* or *directory*. For example, suppose I have a file named myfile.txt in /tmp that is owned by root. If I wanted to change the file's owner to the ksanders user, I would enter **chown ksanders /tmp/myfile.txt**. This is shown in Figure 7-26.

Notice that this command changed the user who owns the file to ksanders. However, also notice that the group that owns the file is still root. This was assigned when the file was created because root's primary group is named root. If I wanted to change this to the users group, of which ksanders is a member, I would enter **chown .users /tmp/myfile.txt**. Notice that I used a period (.) before the group name to tell chown that the entity specified is a group, not a user account. After executing this command, the owning group is changed to users, as shown in Figure 7-27.

I could have actually changed both the user and the group that owns the file all at once with a single chown command. In the example above, I could have entered **chown ksanders.users /tmp/myfile.txt**. This tells chown that the user to change ownership to is ksanders and the group to change ownership to is users.

on the **j**ob *You can use the –R option with chown to change ownership on many files at once recursively.*

Let's also look at the chgrp utility.

Using chgrp   In addition to chown, you can also use chgrp to change the group that owns a file or directory. Simply enter **chgrp *group file*** or ***directory***. For example, to change the group ownership of the /tmp/myfile.txt file discussed in the previous examples from root to users, you could enter **chgrp users /tmp/myfile.txt**.

FIGURE 7-26   Changing file ownership with chown

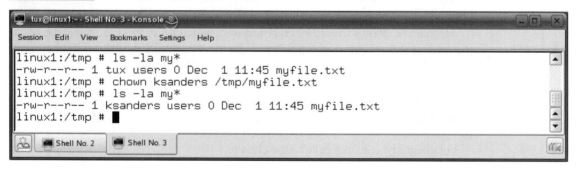

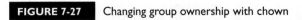

FIGURE 7-27   Changing group ownership with chown

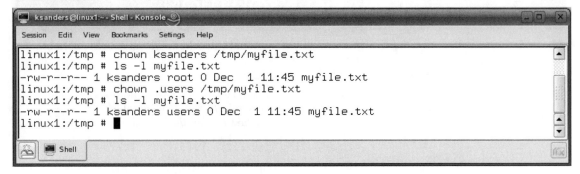

```
linux1:/tmp # chown ksanders /tmp/myfile.txt
linux1:/tmp # ls -l myfile.txt
-rw-r--r-- 1 ksanders root 0 Dec  1 11:45 myfile.txt
linux1:/tmp # chown .users /tmp/myfile.txt
linux1:/tmp # ls -l myfile.txt
-rw-r--r-- 1 ksanders users 0 Dec  1 11:45 myfile.txt
linux1:/tmp # █
```

Let's practice managing ownership in the following exercise.

EXERCISE 7-3

ON THE CD

Managing Ownership

In this exercise, you will practice modifying file and directory ownership from the shell prompt of your Linux system. Complete the following:

1. Verify that you are logged in to your system.

2. If necessary, switch to your root user account with the su – command.

3. Change to the /var/opt directory by entering **cd /var/opt** at the shell prompt.

4. Create a new directory named RandD by entering **mkdir RandD** at the shell prompt.

5. At the shell prompt, enter **ls –l**. Notice that the root user account and the root group are the owners of the new directory.

6. Change ownership of the directory to your user account and the research group by entering **chown *your_username*.research RandD** at the shell prompt.

7. Enter **ls –l** again at the shell prompt. Verify that ownership of the RandD directory has changed to your user account and the research group.

SCENARIO & SOLUTION

You want to change the ownership of a directory named /var/mkt to the vhammer user account and the mkt group. What command would you enter?	You would enter **chown vhammer.mkt /var/mkt**.
You want to set the mkt group as the owner of the /var/mkt/collateral.odt file. What command would you use to do this?	You could use either of the following commands: **chown .mkt /var/mkt/collateral.odt** **chgrp mkt /var/mkt/collateral.odt**

Now that you understand users, groups, and owners, you are finally ready to work with Linux file system permissions. Let's discuss how this is done next.

Managing Permissions

Managing ownership represents only a part of what needs to be done to control access to files and directories in the Linux file system. Ownership only specifies who owns what. It doesn't say what you can or can't do with files and directories. To do this, you need to set up and manage *permissions*. You need to understand the following:

- How permissions work
- Managing permissions from the command line
- Working with default permissions
- Working with special permissions

Let's start by explaining how permissions work.

How Permissions Work

Unlike ownership, permissions are used to specify exactly what a particular user may do with files and directories in the file system. These permissions may allow a user to view a file, but not modify it. They may allow a user to open and modify a file. They may allow a user to even run an executable file. Permissions may be configured to prevent a user from even seeing a file within a directory.

Each file or directory in your Linux file system stores the specific permissions assigned to it. These permissions together constitute the *mode* of the file. Any file or directory can have the permissions shown in Table 7-1 in its mode.

TABLE 7-1		Linux Permissions	
Permission	**Symbol**	**Effect on Files**	**Effect on Directories**
Read	r	Allows a user to open and view a file. Does not allow a file to be modified or saved.	Allows a user to list the contents of a directory.
Write	w	Allows a user to open, modify, and save a file.	Allows a user to add or delete files from the directory.
Execute	x	Allows a user to run an executable file.	Allows a user to enter a directory.

These permissions are assigned to each of three different entities for each file and directory in the file system:

■ **Owner** This is the user account that has been assigned to be the file or directory's owner. Permissions assigned to the owner apply only to that user account.

■ **Group** This is the group that has been assigned ownership of the file or directory. Permissions assigned to the group apply to all user accounts that are members of that group.

■ **Others** This entity refers to all other users who have successfully authenticated to the system. Permissions assigned to this entity apply to these user accounts.

on the **Job**

Be aware that permissions are additive. That means it is possible for one user account to receive permissions assigned to more than one entity. For example, suppose I assign the read and write permissions to a file to Owner and the execute permission to Group. If ksanders is the file Owner, users is the Group, and ksanders is a member of users, then ksanders receives both the permissions assigned to Owner and Group. Her effective permissions would be rwx!

Also, be very careful about what permissions you assign to Others. Basically, every user on the system belongs to Others; therefore, any permission you grant to Others gets assigned to everyone. In some cases, this can be very useful. However, in others, it can get you in a lot of trouble! Just ask yourself before assigning permissions, "Do I really want everyone to have this kind of access to the file or directory?"

You can use the ls –l command to view the permissions assigned to each of these entities for any file or directory in the file system. Consider the example shown in Figure 7-28.

The first column displayed is the mode for each file and directory. The first character is either a "d" or a "–". This simply indicates whether or not the associated entry is a directory or a file. As you can see, contacts.odt is a file while Desktop is a directory.

The next three characters are the permissions assigned to the entry's owner. For example, contacts.odt has rw– assigned to its owner (which is the ksanders user). This means ksanders has read and write permissions to the file, but not execute. Because the file isn't an executable, that permission isn't needed anyway. If the file were an executable and the execute permission were assigned, an x would have replaced the – in this part of the mode. Because the owner has read and write permissions to the file, ksanders can open the file, edit it, and save the changes.

The next three characters are the permissions assigned to the owning group. In this case, it is the users group. Any user on the system who is a member of the users group is granted r–– access to the contacts.odt file. This means they have the read right, allowing them to open a file and view its contents, but they aren't allowed to save any changes to the file.

The last three characters in the mode are the permissions assigned to others, meaning any legitimately authenticated user on the system who isn't the owner and

FIGURE 7-28   Viewing the file mode with ls –l

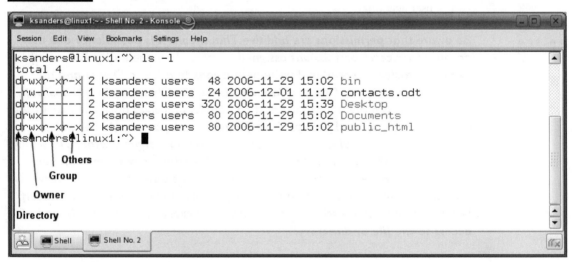

isn't a member of the owning group. In this example, these users are also assigned r–– rights to the contacts.odt file, again, granting them read access.

Before we progress any farther, you should know that permissions for each entity can also be represented numerically. This is done by assigning a value to each permission, as shown in Table 7-2.

Using these values, you can represent the permissions assigned to the Owner, Group, or Others with a single number. Simply add up the value of each permission. For example, suppose Owner is assigned read and write permissions to a file. To determine the numeric value of this assignment, simply add the values of read and write together (4+2=6). You will many times see a file or directory's mode represented by three numbers. Consider the example shown in Figure 7-29.

In this example, the associated file owner has read and write permissions (6), the owning group has the read permission (4), and others also have the read permission (4). Using the ls –l command, this mode would be represented as –rw–r–r––.

So what do you do if these permissions aren't correct? You use the chmod utility to modify them! Let's discuss how this is done next.

Managing Permissions from the Command Line with chmod

I realize that I'm sounding like a broken record, but, just as with most of the other tasks in this chapter, you can modify permissions either graphically or from the command line. For example, using the Konqueror file browser in the KDE Desktop environment, you can right-click any file or directory and then select Properties | Permissions. The screen in Figure 7-30 is displayed.

You then can use drop-down lists for Owner, Group, and Others to specify what each entity can do with the file or directory. When you select OK, the file or directory's mode is changed to match what you specified.

However, for your Linux+ exam, you must be able to accomplish this same task using command-line tools. The one you use to modify permissions is chmod. To use chmod to modify a file's permissions, you must either own the file or you must be logged in as root. Any other users will not be allowed to do this.

There are several different syntaxes that can be used with chmod. The first is to enter **chmod *entity=permissions filename*** at the shell prompt. You substitute u for

TABLE 7-2		
	Permission	**Value**
Numeric Values	Read	4
Assigned to	Write	2
Permissions	Execute	1

FIGURE 7-29

Representing
permissions
numerically

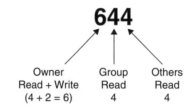

Owner, g for Group, and o for Others in the entity portion of the command. You
substitute r, w, and/or x for the permissions portion of the command. For example,
suppose I wanted to change the mode of contacts.odt to –rw–rw–r–– (giving the

FIGURE 7-30   Setting permissions in Konqueror

Owner and Group read and write permissions while giving Others only read access). I would enter **chmod u=rw,g=rw,o=r contacts.odt** at the shell prompt (assuming the file resides in the current directory). After doing so, the mode is adjusted with the permissions assigned by chmod, as shown in Figure 7-31.

You can also use chmod to toggle a particular permission on or off using the **+** or **–** signs. For example, suppose I want to turn off the write permission I just gave to Group for the contacts.odt file. I could enter **chmod g–w contacts.odt** at the shell prompt. When I do, the specified permission is turned off, as shown in Figure 7-32.

If I wanted to turn the permission back on, I would enter **chmod g+w contacts .odt**. You can substitute u or o to modify permission to the file or directory for Owner and Others as well.

Finally, you can also use numeric permissions with chmod. This is the option I use most often. You can modify all three entities at once with only three characters. To do this, enter **chmod *numeric_permission filename***.

Going back to our earlier example, suppose I wanted to grant read and write permissions to Owner and Group, but remove all permissions to Others. That would mean Owner and Group's permissions would be represented numerically as 6. Because Others gets no permissions, its permissions would be represented by 0. I could implement this by entering **chmod 660 contacts.odt** at the shell prompt. When I do, the appropriate changes are made, as shown in Figure 7-33.

FIGURE 7-31	Changing the mode with chmod

```
ksanders@linux1:~ - Shell No. 2 - Konsole
Session  Edit  View  Bookmarks  Settings  Help

ksanders@linux1:~> ls -l
total 4
drwxr-xr-x  2 ksanders users   48 2006-11-29 15:02 bin
-rw-r--r--  1 ksanders users   24 2006-12-01 11:17 contacts.odt
drwx------  2 ksanders users  320 2006-11-29 15:39 Desktop
drwx------  2 ksanders users   80 2006-11-29 15:02 Documents
drwxr-xr-x  2 ksanders users   80 2006-11-29 15:02 public_html
ksanders@linux1:~> chmod u=rw,g=rw,o=r contacts.odt
ksanders@linux1:~> ls -l
total 4
drwxr-xr-x  2 ksanders users   48 2006-11-29 15:02 bin
-rw-rw-r--  1 ksanders users   24 2006-12-01 11:17 contacts.odt
drwx------  2 ksanders users  320 2006-11-29 15:39 Desktop
drwx------  2 ksanders users   80 2006-11-29 15:02 Documents
drwxr-xr-x  2 ksanders users   80 2006-11-29 15:02 public_html
ksanders@linux1:~>

  Shell    Shell No. 2
```

FIGURE 7-32 Removing a permission with chmod

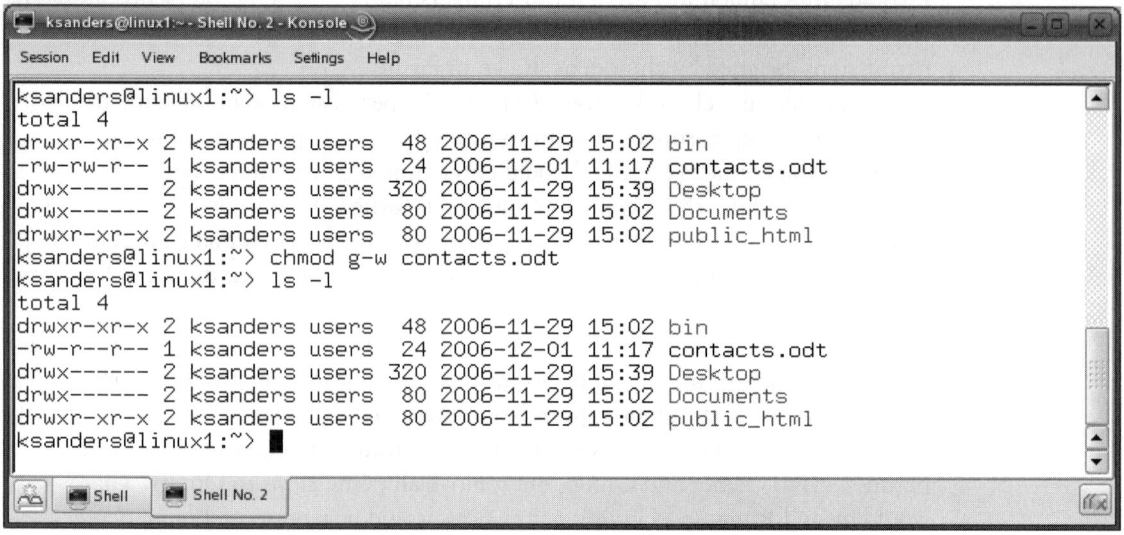

```
ksanders@linux1:~ - Shell No. 2 - Konsole
Session  Edit  View  Bookmarks  Settings  Help
ksanders@linux1:~> ls -l
total 4
drwxr-xr-x 2 ksanders users  48 2006-11-29 15:02 bin
-rw-rw-r-- 1 ksanders users  24 2006-12-01 11:17 contacts.odt
drwx------ 2 ksanders users 320 2006-11-29 15:39 Desktop
drwx------ 2 ksanders users  80 2006-11-29 15:02 Documents
drwxr-xr-x 2 ksanders users  80 2006-11-29 15:02 public_html
ksanders@linux1:~> chmod g-w contacts.odt
ksanders@linux1:~> ls -l
total 4
drwxr-xr-x 2 ksanders users  48 2006-11-29 15:02 bin
-rw-r--r-- 1 ksanders users  24 2006-12-01 11:17 contacts.odt
drwx------ 2 ksanders users 320 2006-11-29 15:39 Desktop
drwx------ 2 ksanders users  80 2006-11-29 15:02 Documents
drwxr-xr-x 2 ksanders users  80 2006-11-29 15:02 public_html
ksanders@linux1:~> █

   Shell      Shell No. 2
```

on the
job
You can use the –R option with chmod to change permissions on many files at once recursively.

FIGURE 7-33 Using numeric permissions with chmod

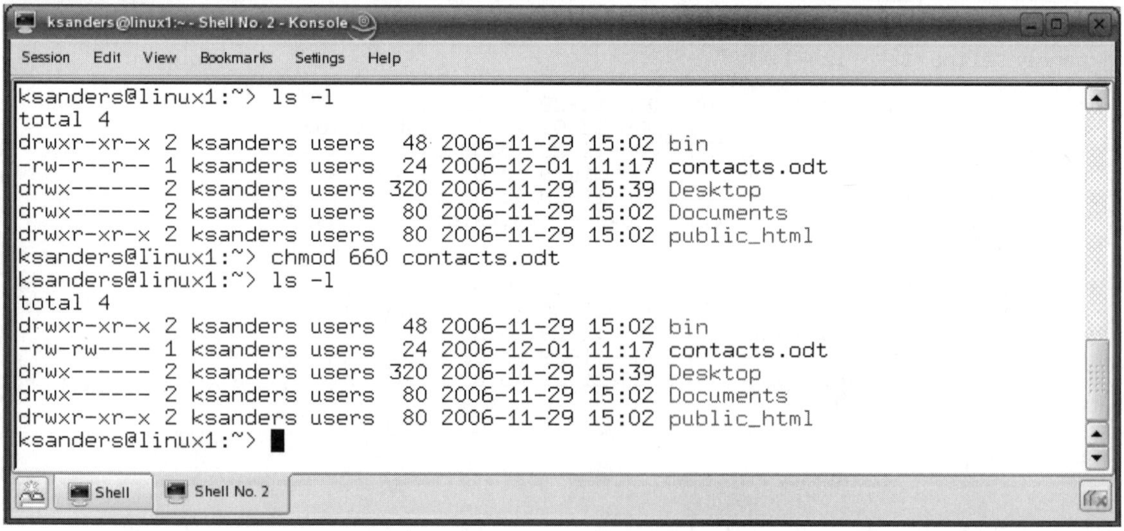

```
ksanders@linux1:~ - Shell No. 2 - Konsole
Session  Edit  View  Bookmarks  Settings  Help
ksanders@linux1:~> ls -l
total 4
drwxr-xr-x 2 ksanders users  48 2006-11-29 15:02 bin
-rw-r--r-- 1 ksanders users  24 2006-12-01 11:17 contacts.odt
drwx------ 2 ksanders users 320 2006-11-29 15:39 Desktop
drwx------ 2 ksanders users  80 2006-11-29 15:02 Documents
drwxr-xr-x 2 ksanders users  80 2006-11-29 15:02 public_html
ksanders@linux1:~> chmod 660 contacts.odt
ksanders@linux1:~> ls -l
total 4
drwxr-xr-x 2 ksanders users  48 2006-11-29 15:02 bin
-rw-rw---- 1 ksanders users  24 2006-12-01 11:17 contacts.odt
drwx------ 2 ksanders users 320 2006-11-29 15:39 Desktop
drwx------ 2 ksanders users  80 2006-11-29 15:02 Documents
drwxr-xr-x 2 ksanders users  80 2006-11-29 15:02 public_html
ksanders@linux1:~> █

   Shell      Shell No. 2
```

SCENARIO & SOLUTION

You want to change the permissions of a directory named /var/mkt to the following: Owner: Read, Write, Execute Group: Read Others: No Permissions How could you do this with a single command?	You would enter **chmod 740 /var/mkt**.
Currently, the permissions assigned to the /var/mkt/ product_prd.odt file are: Owner: Read, Write Group: Read, Write Others: No Permissions What command would you enter to remove the write permission from Group?	You could enter either of the following commands: **chmod g–w /var/mkt/product_prd.odt** **chmod 640 /var/mkt/product_prd.odt**

Let's practice managing permissions in the following exercise.

EXERCISE 7-4

Managing Permissions

In this exercise, you will practice modifying permissions from the shell prompt of your Linux system. You will create a design document for your hypothetical Research and Design team and modify its permissions to control access.

Complete the following:

1. Verify that you are logged in to your system.

2. If necessary, switch to your root user account with the su – command.

3. Change to the /var/opt/RandD directory by entering **cd /var/opt/RandD** at the shell prompt.

4. Create a design document for your team and restrict access to it by doing the following:

   a. Create a new file named design_doc.odt by entering **touch design_doc.odt** at the shell prompt.

   b. At the shell prompt, enter **ls –l**. Notice that the root user account and the root group are the owners of the new file.

    c. Change ownership of the directory to your user account and the research group using the chown command.

    d. Enter **ls –l** again at the shell prompt. Verify that ownership of the RandD directory has changed to your user account and the research group. Also, notice that Owner has rw– permissions to the file, but Group only has r––permission.

    e. Grant Owner rw– permissions by entering **chmod g+w** at the shell prompt.

    f. Enter **ls –l** again at the shell prompt. Notice that Owner and Group now both have read/write access to the file.

    g. Notice that Others have read access to the file. You need to keep this document confidential, so remove this access by entering **chmod 660 design_doc.odt** at the shell prompt.

    h. Enter **ls –l** again. Verify that Others have no permissions to this file.

5. Next, you need to control access to the research directory itself using permissions. Do the following:

    a. At the shell prompt, enter **cd /var/opt**.

    b. At the shell prompt, enter **ls –l**. Notice that Owner has full access to the RandD directory, but Group is missing the write permission to the directory. Also notice that Others can read the directory contents (r) and can enter the directory (x).

    c. Grant Group full access to the directory and remove Others access to the directory completely by entering **chmod 770 RandD** at the shell prompt.

    d. Enter **ls –l** at the shell prompt. Verify that Owner and Group have full access while Others has no access.

Let's next discuss how to work with default permissions.

Working with Default Permissions

You may have noticed as we've worked through exercises and examples in this course that whenever you create a new file or directory in the file system, a default set of permissions is automatically assigned without any intervention on your part.

By default, Linux assigns rw–rw–rw– (666) permissions to every file whenever it is created in the file system. It also assigns rwxrwxrwx permissions to every directory created in the file system. However, these aren't the permissions the files or directories actually end up with. Let's take a look at an example.

Suppose ksanders was to create a new directory named revenue in her home directory and a file named projections.odt in the revenue directory. Based on what we just discussed, the revenue directory should have a mode of rwxrwxrwx and the projections.odt file should have a mode of rw–rw–rw–. However, this isn't the case, as shown in Figure 7-34.

Notice that the revenue directory has a mode of rwxr–xr–x (755). This means the directory owner has read, write, and execute permissions to the directory. Group and Others have read and execute permissions to the directory. Likewise, notice that the projections.odt file has a mode of rw–r––r–– (644). The file owner has read and write permissions while Group and Other have only the read permission.

These aren't the default permissions Linux is supposed to assign! Why did this happen? It's because the default permissions are too liberal. Think about it. The default directory mode would allow anyone on the system to enter any directory and delete any files they wanted to! Likewise, the default file mode would allow any user on the system to modify a file you created. What a nightmare!

To increase the overall security of the system, Linux uses a variable called *umask* to automatically remove permissions from the default mode whenever a file or directory is created in the file system. The value of umask is a three-digit number, as shown in Figure 7-35 (ignoring the first 0).

For most Linux distributions, the default value of umask is 022. Each digit represents a numeric permission value to be removed. The first digit references—you guessed it—Owner, the second references Group, the last references Other.

FIGURE 7-34   Viewing default permissions assigned to new files and directories

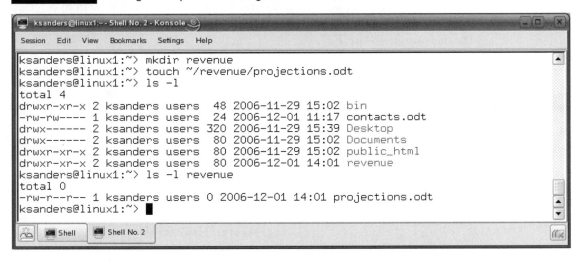

FIGURE 7-35   Viewing the value of umask

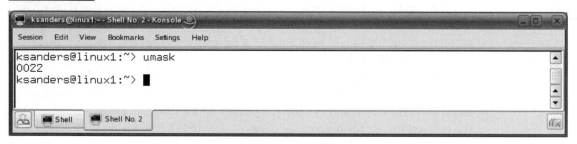

Because a 0 is listed for Owner, no permissions are removed from the default mode for a file or directory owner. However, because a 2 is listed for Group and Other, the write permission is removed from the default mode whenever a file or directory is created in the file system. The function of umask is shown in Figure 7-36.

The default value of umask works for most Linux admins. However, there may be situations where you need to tighten up or loosen the permissions assigned when a file or directory is created in the file system. To do this, you need to change the value assigned to umask.

This can be done in two ways. First, if you only need to make a temporary change to umask, you can enter **umask *value*** at the shell prompt. For example, if you wanted to remove the execute permission that is automatically assigned to Others whenever a new directory is created, you could enter **umask 023**. This would cause the write permission (2) to be removed from Group upon creation as well as write (2) and execute (1) from Others. This will effectively disallow anyone from entering the new directory except for the directory owner or members of the owning group. This is shown in Figure 7-37.

FIGURE 7-36

How umask
works

```
                                            Files
                    Default Mode : rw-rw-rw-
              Subtracted by umask : ----w--w-
                                    ──────────
                          Result:  rw-r-r--

                                          Directories
                    Default Mode:  rwxrwxrwx
              Subtracted by umask:  ----w--w-
                                    ──────────
                          Result:  rwxr-xr-x
```

FIGURE 7-37   Modifying umask from the command line

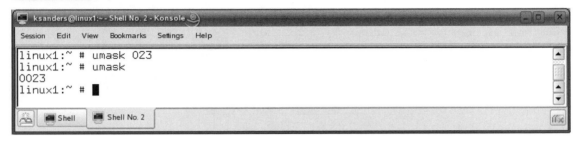

Notice that, because the value of umask was changed, the execute permission (x) was removed from Others in the mode when the temp directory was created.

This method for modifying umask works great; however, it isn't persistent. If you were to restart the system, umask would revert back to its original value. That's because the value of umask is automatically set each time the system boots using the umask parameter in the /etc/profile file, shown in Figure 7-38.

If you want to make your change to umask permanent, simply edit /etc/profile in a text editor and set the value of umask to your desired value.

Let's next look at special permissions.

SCENARIO & SOLUTION

Your umask variable is currently set to 022. What does this do?	A umask variable of 022 specifies the following permissions removed when a file or directory is created in the file system: Owner: No permissions removed (0) Group: The Write permission is removed (2) Others: The Write permission is removed (2)
Suppose you want to alter your umask variable such that the following permissions are assigned by default when a file or directory is created: Owner: Read, Write, Execute Group: Read, Write Others: Read What command would you enter to do this?	You would enter **umask 013**.

FIGURE 7-38   Setting umask in /etc/profile

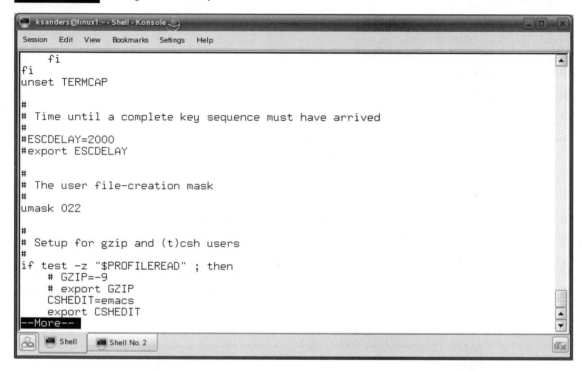

Working with Special Permissions

Most of the tasks you will complete with permissions will be with the read, write, and execute permissions. However, there are several other special permissions that you can assign to files and directories in your file system. These are shown in Table 7-3.

These special permissions are referenced as an extra digit added to the beginning of the file or directory's mode. As with regular permissions, each of these special permissions has a numerical value assigned to it as shown here:

- SUID: 4
- SGID: 2
- Sticky Bit: 1

You can assign these special permissions to files or directories using chmod. Just add an extra number to the beginning of the mode that references the special permissions you want to associate with the file or directory.

TABLE 7-3	Special Permissions		
Permission	**Description**	**Effect on Files**	**Effect on Directories**
SUID	Set User ID Can only be applied to binary executable files (not shell scripts).	When an executable file with the SUID set is run, the user who ran the file temporarily becomes the file's owner.	None.
SGID	Set Group ID Can be applied to binary executable files (not shell scripts).	When a user runs an executable file with SGID set, the user temporarily becomes a member of the file's owning group.	When a user creates a file in a directory that has SGID set, the file's owner is set to the user's account (as per normal). However, the owning group assigned to the new file is set to the owning group of the parent directory.
Sticky Bit		None.	When the Sticky Bit is assigned to a directory, users can only delete files within the directory for which they are the owner of the file or the directory itself. This negates the effect of having the write permission to a directory, which could allow a user to delete files in a directory that he or she doesn't own.

For example, suppose you wanted to apply the SUID and SGID permissions to a file named runme that should be readable and executable by Owner and Group. You would enter **chmod 6554 runme** at the shell prompt. This specifies that the file have SUID (4) and SGID (2) permissions assigned (for a total of 6 in the first digit). It also specifies that Owner and Group have read (4) and execute permissions (1) assigned (for a total of 5 in the second and third digits). It also specifies that Others be allowed to read (4) the file, but not be able to modify or run it (for a total of 4 in the last digit).

Let's practice managing default and special permissions in the following exercise.

EXERCISE 7-5

ON THE CD

Managing Default and Special Permissions

In this exercise, you will practice modifying default permissions with umask and creating files. You will also practice adding special permissions to directories. Complete the following:

1. Verify that you are logged in to your system.

2. If necessary, switch to your root user account with the su – command.

3. Change to the /var/opt/RandD directory by entering **cd /var/opt/RandD** at the shell prompt.

4. You need to create several Research and Development documents in the RandD directory. However, you need to make sure these documents are secure from prying eyes. Recall from the previous exercise that Others are automatically granted read access to files when you create them. You don't want this to happen. You need Others to have no access at all to any documents created. Do the following:

   a. Change the default permissions by entering **umask 027** at the shell prompt.

   b. Verify the value of umask by entering **umask** at the shell prompt. It should display 0027.

   c. Create a new file named schedule.odt by entering **touch schedule.odt** at the shell prompt.

   d. Enter **ls –l** at the shell prompt. Verify that Owner has rw–, Group has r––, and Others has ––– permissions.

5. In a previous exercise we granted Owner and Group rwx permissions to the RandD directory. However, having the write permission to the directory allows anyone in the research group to delete any file in the directory. We want to configure the directory such that users in the research group can only delete files they actually own. Do the following:

   a. At the shell prompt, enter **cd /var/opt**.

   b. At the shell prompt, add the Sticky Bit permission to the RandD directory by entering **chmod 1770 RandD**.

   c. At the shell prompt, enter **ls –l**. Notice that a "T" has been added to the last digit of the Others portion of the mode of the RandD directory. This indicates that the sticky bit has been set.

6. Experiment with the new permissions you just added by logging in as different users in the system and testing what the permissions will and won't allow you to do.

7. In a previous exercise, we created a user named dtracy. However, because we didn't use the –m option when we created him, he doesn't have a home directory. Using what you've learned, do the following:

   a. Create the appropriate home directory for dtracy in /home.

   b. Look at the other home directories and determine the ownership and permissions that should be assigned.

   c. Use command-line utilities to set the ownership and permissions for dtracy's home directory.

   d. Run pwck when you're done to verify that the account is configured correctly.

Let's end this chapter by discussing disk quotas.

Implementing Disk Quotas

Disk quotas are a valuable management tool when you're administering a Linux system. The problem here is that, because Linux is a multi-user system, it's possible for one or two users to completely monopolize all the disk space available in the file system. This is especially a problem in today's networked world where users are downloading large music files and even larger movie files from the Internet. How do you keep these users from consuming more than their fair share of disk space? You use disk quotas.

Put simply, disk quotas establish space limitations for users on the system. You can specify that users are each allowed only a certain amount of disk space (a quota). Users are not allowed to exceed this quota.

To implement quotas on your Linux file system, you first need to install the quota package on your system. Some distributions, especially server distributions, install this package as part of the base installation. Most distributions, however, will require you to install it separately after the system has been set up.

on the
ⓘ o b

*See the next chapter to learn how to install packages on a Linux system. If you want to check and see if quota is already installed on your system, enter **rpm –qi quota** at the shell prompt.*

To establish quotas, complete the following:

1. Verify that the quota package has been installed on your system.

2. Open a terminal session and change to your root user account with su.

3. Configure your mounted file systems to use quotas by doing the following:

   a. Open your /etc/fstab file in a text editor.

   b. Add the usrquota and grpquota parameters to the mount options for the file system you want to establish quotas on. For example, in Figure 7-39, quotas have been established for the / file system.

   c. Save your changes to the file and exit the editor.

   d. Restart your system so the changes can take effect.

FIGURE 7-39   Establishing quotas on the / file system

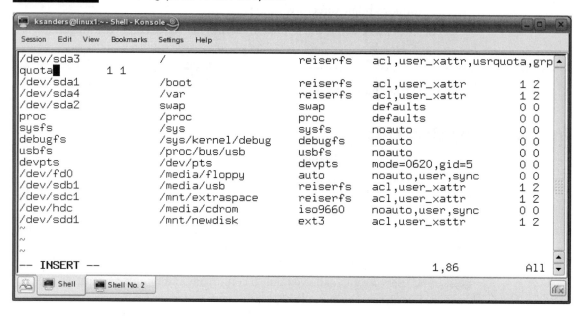

4. After the system has rebooted, create your quota files by doing the following:

   a. Open a terminal session and switch to your root user account with su.

   b. At the shell prompt, enter **quotacheck –amvug**.

   The quotacheck utility is used to scan the file system for disk usages as well as create quota files. The options used with quotacheck above do the following:

   ■ **–a**: Checks all mounted file systems.

   ■ **–m**: Forces check on mounted file systems.

   ■ **–u**: Checks users.

   ■ **–g**: Checks groups.

   ■ **–v**: Operates in verbose mode.

   As the system is checked, you should see several messages appear on screen, as shown in Figure 7-40.

   You can disregard the messages about old quota files. When quotacheck is complete, two files named aquota.user and aquota.groups should have been created in the mount point of your mounted file system, as shown in Figure 7-41.

FIGURE 7-40 Viewing output from quotacheck

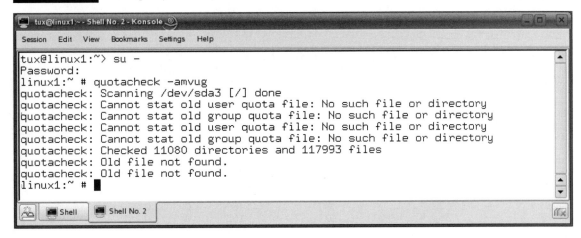

5. Enable quotas on your file system by entering **quotaon –av** at the shell prompt.

on the **job** *You will need to use chkconfig or insserv to configure the quota service to automatically start each time the system boots. We'll talk about how to do this later in this book.*

6. View current disk space used by your users by entering **repquota –av** at the shell prompt. A report is displayed on the screen showing how much space each user is consuming, as shown in Figure 7-42.

Notice in Figure 7-42 that no limits have been configured for any users.

FIGURE 7-41 Viewing newly created quota files

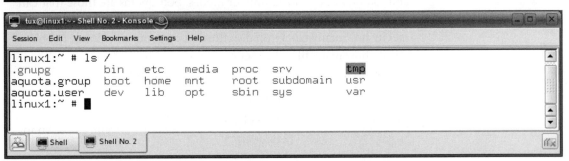

FIGURE 7-42   Generating the quota report

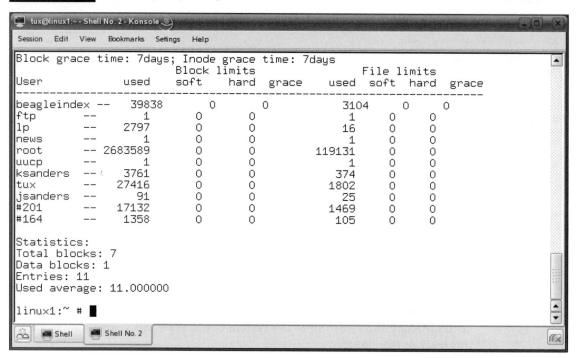

7. Create disk quotas for your users by doing the following:

   a. At the shell prompt, enter **edquota –u *username***. A screen similar to that shown in Figure 7-43 is displayed.

     In this example, quotas are being set for ksanders. Notice that the quota file has been opened in the vi editor. Also notice that you can set hard and soft quotas for blocks and for inodes. Soft quotas are those that can be temporarily exceeded. Hard quotas cannot be exceeded. Block quotas specify how many blocks on disk the user can consume. Inode quotas specify how many files the user can own.

   b. Use the vi editor to set block and/or inode soft and hard quotas.

   c. Save your changes and exit the editor.

   d. Repeat this process for each of your users.

FIGURE 7-43   Setting user quotas

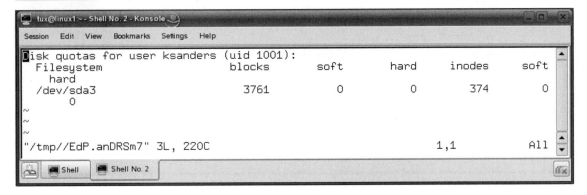

on the   *You can enter edquota –p source_user destination_user to copy quotas from*

Job   *one user to another.*

8. Create disk quotas for your groups by doing the following:

   a. At the shell prompt, enter **edquota –g** *groupname*.

   b. Use the vi editor to set block and/or inode soft and hard quotas.

   c. Save your changes and exit the editor.

9. In the preceding steps, you created soft quotas for blocks and/or inodes. The default value is to allow users to exceed their soft quotas for a maximum of seven days. This is the *grace period*. You can change this by doing the following:

   a. At the shell prompt, enter **edquota –t**. The screen in Figure 7-44 is displayed.

   b. Edit your grace period settings.

   c. Save your changes and exit vi.

10. Check your new quotas by entering **repquota –av** at the shell prompt. You should now see quotas established for your users. In Figure 7-45 quotas have been established for the ksanders user.

Your system is now protected from disk space hogs! Let's practice establishing disk quotas in the following exercise.

FIGURE 7-44 Setting the soft quota grace period

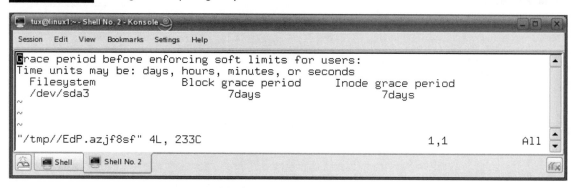

FIGURE 7-45 Viewing newly established disk quotas

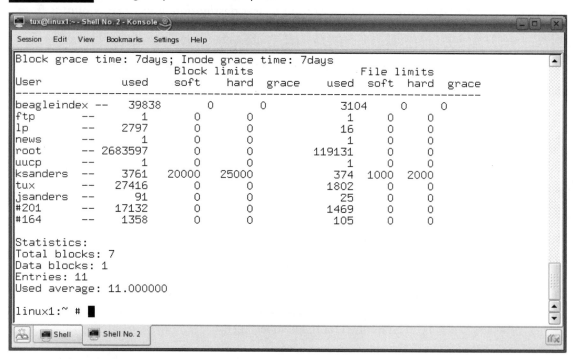

EXERCISE 7-6

Establishing Disk Quotas

In this exercise, you will practice implementing disk quotas on your Linux system. Complete the following:

1. Verify that you are logged in to your system.
2. If necessary, switch to your root user account with the su – command.
3. Configure your mounted file systems to use quotas by doing the following:
   a. Open your /etc/fstab file in a text editor.
   b. Add the usrquota and grpquota parameters to the mount options for the / file.
   c. Save your changes to the file and exit the editor.
   d. Restart your system so the changes can take effect.
4. After the system has rebooted, create your quota files by doing the following:
   a. Open a terminal session and switch to your root user account with su.
   b. At the shell prompt, enter **quotacheck –amvug**.

   You can disregard the messages about old quota files. When quotacheck is complete, two files named aquota.user and aquota.groups should have been created in /.
5. Enable quotas on your file system by entering **quotaon –av** at the shell prompt.
6. View current disk space used by your users by entering **repquota –av** at the shell prompt. A report is displayed on the screen showing how much space each user is consuming. Notice that no limits have been configured for any users.
7. Create disk quotas for your users by doing the following:
   a. At the shell prompt, enter **edquota –u** *your_username*.
   b. Use the vi editor to set the following:
      - Block Hard Quota: **15000**
      - Block Soft Quota: **10000**
      - Inode Hard Quota: **1000**
      - Inode Soft Quota: **800**
   c. Save your changes and exit the editor.
   d. Repeat this process for the rest of your users.
8. Check your new quotas by entering **repquota –av** at the shell prompt. You should now see quotas established for your users.

You are now an expert at working with Linux users, groups, and permissions!

CERTIFICATION SUMMARY

We started this chapter discussing the need for a basic level of file system security on a Linux system. We reviewed a scenario where multiple users on the same system were able to access each other's files and the problems that were encountered as a result. The way to prevent these problems is to first control who can access the system and then control what they can access once they are in.

The first part is accomplished by using Linux user accounts. With user accounts, users must supply a valid username and password (called credentials) before they are allowed to access the system. This is called "logging in." We pointed out that the Linux operating system will customize the system environment based on the username of the user who logged on. Users will have access to their own home directory and a customized desktop environment. We pointed out that, by default, user home directories are located in /home, except for the root user, whose home directory is located in /root. You can view specific information about a particular user using the finger *username* command at the shell prompt.

We also pointed out that each Linux user account has a unique ID number called the UID. No two users on the system have the same UID. SUSE Linux, by default, starts UIDs for standard users at 1000. Other distributions, such as Fedora, start UIDs at 500. No matter what distribution you're using, the root user's UID is always set to 0. You can view a user's UID (as well as group membership) using the id *username* command.

We then discussed the various locations where user accounts can be saved on a Linux system. Using local authentication, user accounts are saved in /etc/passwd and /etc/shadow. Using LDAP authentication, user accounts are saved in an LDAP-compliant directory service. Using NIS authentication, user account files are distributed among several systems using the NIS service. Using Windows Domain authentication, user accounts are stored in a central database on a Windows (or Linux Samba) domain controller.

We pointed out that, for the Linux+ exam, you only need to be familiar with the local authentication method. In this configuration, the /etc/passwd file contains your user account information while the /shadow file contains your users' encrypted passwords. The /etc/passwd file stores user accounts in the following format:

```
Username:Password:UID:GID:Full_Name:Home_Directory:Default_Shell
```

We also pointed out that the /etc/passwd file contains both standard and system user accounts. Standard user accounts are used for login. System user accounts can't be used for login. Instead, they are used by system services when they need to access the file system.

The /etc/shadow file stores user password information in the following format:

```
Username:Password:Last_Modified:Min_Days:Max_Days:Days_Warn:Disabled_Days:Expire
```

The /etc/passwd and /etc/shadow files must stay synchronized. To do this, you should avoid editing these files directly with a text editor. Instead you should use the various user and password management tools on your system. To check your files, you can use the pwck command. If you suspect the files are out of sync, you can use the pwconv command to add accounts from /etc/passwd to /etc/shadow.

We then discussed the different utilities you can use from the shell prompt to manage user accounts on your Linux system. To add a user, you use the useradd utility. If you don't supply any options when creating a user with useradd, the defaults contained in the /etc/default/useradd and /etc/login.defs files are used.

To set a user's password, you can use the passwd utility at the shell prompt. To view the status of a user's account, you can use the –S option with passwd. To modify an existing user account, you use the usermod utility. To remove a user account, you use the userdel utility. By default, userdel will not remove a user's home directory when deleting an account. If you want to remove the user's home directory, you can use the –r option with userdel.

We then shifted gears and discussed the role of Linux groups. Groups ease system administration by allowing you to group together users who need a common level of access to files and directories in the file system. Linux groups are stored in /etc/group. Group records in /etc/group are represented using the following syntax:

```
Group:Password:GID:Users
```

Some distributions store group passwords (if implemented) in /etc/group. Other distributions store them in a separate file (in encrypted format) in /etc/gshadow, much in the same manner as user accounts are stored in /etc/passwd and /etc/shadow. You create groups in your Linux system using the groupadd command. If you don't specify any options with the groupadd command, the group is created using default parameters found in /etc/login.defs.

To add users to a group, you must use the –A option with the groupmod command at the shell prompt. You can also remove groups using the groupdel command.

We then turned to a discussion of ownership, permissions, and quotas. We pointed out that users and groups only control who can access the system. They don't control what the user can do with files or directories in the file system. To do this, we need to implement ownership and permissions.

We pointed out that, whenever a user creates a file or directory, that user is automatically assigned to be its owner. In addition, the group the user belongs to becomes the file or directory's group owner. These defaults can be changed; however, you must be logged in as root to change a file or directory's owner or be logged in as its owner to change its group.

To modify ownership, you use the chown command. This command can change both the user and/or the group that owns a file or directory. If you only want to change the group, you can also use the chgrp command.

We then pointed out that ownership alone can't control user access to files and directories. To fully control access, we need Linux file system permissions. Permissions define what a user can and cannot do with a given file or directory. Linux uses the following permissions:

- Read
- Write
- Execute

Linux assigns permissions to the following entities:

- Owner
- Group
- Others

The permissions assigned to Owner, Group, and Others together constitute a file or directory's mode. We also emphasized that Linux permissions are additive. If a given user is both an owner and member of the owning group, then he or she receives permissions assigned for a file or directory to Owner and Group.

We then pointed out that permissions can be represented numerically for Owner, Group, and Others using the following values:

- Read: 4
- Write: 2
- Execute: 1

By adding up each permission assigned to a given entity, you can represent all of the permissions assigned with a single number. For example, a value of 7 indicates that all permissions have been assigned. A value of 5 indicates read and execute permissions have been assigned.

We then discussed the chmod tool that is used to manage permissions from the shell prompt. The chmod utility can use any of the following syntaxes to assign permissions to Owner, Group, and/or Others:

- chmod u=rw,g=rw,o=r *file_or_directory*
- chmod u+rw,g+rw,o+r *file_or_directory*
- chmod 664 *file_or_directory*

At this point, we began a discussion of default Linux permissions. We pointed out that, by default, Linux automatically assigns new files with rw–rw–rw– permissions and new directories with rwxrwxrwx permissions upon creation. However, to increase security, the umask variable is used to automatically remove some permission. The default umask value is 022, which removes the write permission from Group and Others when a file or directory is created. We pointed out that you can change the value of umask by entering **umask** *value* at the shell prompt.

We also briefly discussed the special permissions that you can assign, including:

- SUID: 4
- SGID: 2
- Sticky Bit: 1

We pointed out that you assign these permissions with chmod by adding an extra digit before the Owner digit in the command using the values shown above.

We ended the chapter by discussing how to implement disk quotas. We pointed out that disk quotas are used to prevent users from using up too much disk space. To implement quotas, you must first install the quota package on your Linux system. We then reviewed the procedure for setting up quotas for mounted file systems. We pointed out that you can set quotas for the number of blocks a user is allowed to consume (disk space) and the number of inodes a user may consume (number of files). For both of these parameters, you can set hard and soft limits. A user may temporarily exceed soft limits for a time you define as the *grace period*. A user may not exceed a hard limit. You can enter the **repquota –av** command at the shell prompt to view a report displaying hard and soft limits as well as current user space usage.

✓ # TWO-MINUTE DRILL

Manage Users and Groups

❑ You need to control who can access a Linux system and what they can do with files and directories in the file system after they are in.

❑ To authenticate to a system, a user must supply a username and password (called credentials).

❑ Linux restores user-specific information when a user logs in, such as a home directory and desktop environment.

❑ User home directories are created in /home by default.

❑ The root user's home directory is in /root.

❑ You can use the finger command to view information about a user account.

❑ Every Linux user account has a unique user ID (UID) number assigned to it.

❑ The root user's UID is 0.

❑ The starting UID for standard users is 1000 on some distributions and 500 on others.

❑ You can use the id command to view a user's UID.

❑ You can use many different authentication methods with a Linux system.

❑ For your Linux+ exam, you need to know how to use local authentication.

❑ Using local authentication, user accounts are stored in /etc/passwd and /etc/shadow.

❑ The /etc/passwd file stores user account information.

❑ The /etc/shadow file stores encrypted user passwords.

❑ You can use the pwck utility to verify that /etc/passwd and /etc/shadow are synchronized.

❑ You can use the pwconv utility to copy missing users from /etc/passwd to /etc/shadow.

❑ You can use the useradd utility to add users to a Linux system.

❑ When used without any options, useradd uses the system defaults contained in /etc/default/useradd and /etc/login.defs to create user accounts.

❑ You can use the passwd utility to set a user's password.

❑ The passwd utility can also be used to check the status of a user account.

❑ You can use the usermod utility to modify an existing user account.

❑ You can use the userdel utility to delete an existing user account.

❑ By default, userdel will not remove a user's home directory unless you specify the –r option with the command.

❑ Linux groups can be used to ease administration by grouping like user accounts together.

❑ User accounts are stored in /etc/group.

❑ Some distributions store group passwords in /etc/gshadow.

❑ You use the groupadd utility to add a new group to your system.

❑ You use the groupmod utility to add or remove users to an existing group.

❑ You use the groupdel utility to delete an existing group.

Manage Ownership, Permissions, and Quotas

❑ Ownership defines which user and group owns a particular file or directory in the file system.

❑ You can use the ls –l command to view ownership.

❑ You can use the chown utility to configure user and group ownership of a file or directory.

❑ You can use the chgrp utility to change group ownership.

❑ You must be logged in as root to change user ownership.

❑ You must be logged in as root or as the file/directory owner to change group ownership.

❑ Permissions are used to define what users may or may not do with files or directories in the file system.

❑ Linux uses the read, write, and execute permissions for files and directories.

❑ Linux permissions are assigned to Owner, Group, and Others.

❑ Linux permissions are additive.

❑ The permissions assigned to Owner, Group, and Others constitute the file or directory's mode.

❑ Permissions can be represented numerically: read=4, write=2, and execute=1.

❑ Summing all permissions assigned to an entity, such as Owner, allows you to represent all assigned permissions with a single number.

- ❏ You use the chmod utility to modify permissions.
- ❏ Linux assigns rw–rw–rw– permissions by default to new files and rwxrwxrwx permissions to new directories.
- ❏ These permissions are too relaxed for most situations, so the umask variable is used to subtract specific permissions from the defaults.
- ❏ The default value of umask is 022, which subtracts the write permission (2) from Group and Others.
- ❏ You can modify the value of umask to change the default permissions assigned upon creation.
- ❏ Linux also includes three default special permissions: Sticky Bit, SUID, and SGID.
- ❏ You assign special permissions with chmod by adding an additional digit before the Owner digit in the command.
- ❏ You can use the quota package to implement disk quotas in the file system.
- ❏ Quotas prevent users from consuming too much disk space.
- ❏ You can set quotas for the number of blocks a user is allowed to consume (disk space) and the number of inodes a user may consume (number of files).
- ❏ You can set hard and soft limits.
- ❏ A user may temporarily exceed soft limits for a time you define as the grace period.
- ❏ A user may not exceed a hard limit.
- ❏ You can enter the **repquota –av** command at the shell prompt to view a report displaying hard and soft limits as well as current user space usage.

SELF TEST

Manage Users and Groups

1. Which of the following commands will display the UID of a user named dcoughanour when entered at the shell prompt?

    A. id dcoughanour

    B. finger dcoughanour

    C. UID dcoughanhour

    D. info dcoughanour

2. Which of the following files is used to store user accounts on a Linux system that has been configured to use local authentication?

    A. /etc/shadow

    B. /etc/users

    C. /etc/passwd

    D. /etc/local/accounts

3. Which of the following files is used to store user passwords on a Linux system that has been configured to use local authentication?

    A. /etc/shadow

    B. /etc/users

    C. /etc/passwd

    D. /etc/local/accounts

4. Consider the following entry in /etc/passwd:

```
ksanders:x:1001:100:Kimberly Sanders:/home/ksanders:/bin/bash
```

What is the primary group for this user?

    A. ksanders

    B. home

    C. 1001

    D. 100

5. Consider the following entry in /etc/shadow:

```
ksanders:$2a%05$fHzL5vsuk3ilLIuispxqKuCFEPg50ZhF8KshQyIZH7SDERJooEJTC:13481:30:60:7:-1::
```

How often must this user change her password?

A. Every 30 days.

B. Every 60 days.

C. Every 7 days.

D. This feature is disabled. The user isn't required to change her password.

6. You need to create a new user account on a Linux system for Mike Huffman named mhuffman. Mike's password should be set to "Panguitch" and he needs a home directory created in /home/mhuffman. Which of the following commands will do this?

A. useradd –c "Mike Huffman" –m –p "Panguitch" mhuffman

B. usermod "Mike Huffman" –p "Panguitch" mhuffman

C. useradd mhuffman

D. useradd mhuffman –c "Mike Huffman" –m –p Panguitch

7. A user named Diana Grow has recently married and changed her last name to Nelson. You need to change her username on her Linux system. Which command will do this?

A. usermod –l "dgrow" –c "Diana Nelson" dnelson

B. usermod –l "dnelson" –c "Diana Nelson" dgrow

C. useradd dnelson

D. usermod –c "dgrow" –l "dnelson" Diana Grow

8. You need to delete a user account named jcarr from your Linux system and remove his home directory contents. Which of the following commands will do this?

A. userdel jcarr

B. usermod --delete --rmhome jcarr

C. userdel –r jcarr

D. userdel --rmhome jcarr

9. Which file is used to store group information on a Linux system that has been configured to use local authentication?

A. /etc/groups

B. /etc/local/group

C. /etc/groupinfo

D. /etc/group

10. Which of the following commands can be used to add the users mhuffman, dnelson, and jcarr to a group named editors on a Linux system?

A. groupadd –A "mhuffman,dnelson,jcarr" editors

B. groupmod –A "mhuffman,dnelson,jcarr" editors

C. groupmod editors –A "mhuffman,dnelson,jcarr"

D. groupmod –R "mhuffman,dnelson,jcarr" editors

11. Which of the following commands will remove a user named dnelson from a group named editors?

A. groupadd –R "dnelson" editors

B. groupmod –A "dnelson" editors

C. groupmod editors –R "dnelson"

D. groupmod –R "dnelson" editors

Manage Ownership, Permissions, and Quotas

12. You need to change the owner of a file named /var/opt/runme from mireland, who is a member of the users group, to dnelson, who is a member of the editors group. Assuming you want to change both user and group owners, which command will do this?

A. chown mireland dnelson /var/opt/runme

B. chown –u "dnelson" –g "editors" /var/opt/runme

C. chown dnelson /var/opt/runme

D. chown dnelson.editors /var/opt/runme

13. Which permission, when applied to a directory in the file system, will allow a user to enter the directory?

A. Read

B. Write

C. Execute

D. Access Control

14. A user needs to open a file, edit it, and then save the changes. What permissions does he need to do this? (Choose two.)

A. Read

B. Write

C. Execute

D. Modify

15. A file named employees.odt has a mode of rw–r––r––. If mhuffman is not the file's owner but is a member of the group that owns this file, what can he do with it?

A. He can open the file and view its contents, but he can't save any changes.

B. He can open the file, make changes, and save the file.

    C. He can change ownership of the file.

    D. He can run the file if it's an executable.

16. A file named myapp has a mode of 755. If dnelson doesn't own this file and isn't a member of the group that owns the file, what can she do with it?

    A. She can change the group that owns the file.

    B. She can open the file, make changes, and save the file.

    C. She can change ownership of the file.

    D. She can run the file.

17. You need to change the permissions of a file named schedule.odt such that the file owner can edit the file, users who are members of the group that owns the file can edit it, and users who are not owners and don't belong to the owning group can view it but not modify it. Which command will do this?

    A. chmod 664 schedule.odt

    B. chmod 555 schedule.odt

    C. chmod 777 schedule.odt

    D. chmod 644 schedule.odt

18. Your Linux system's umask variable is currently set to a value of 077. A user named jcarr (who is a member of the users group) creates a file named mythoughts.odt. What can users who are members of the users group do with this file?

    A. They can view the file, but they can't modify or save it.

    B. They can open, modify, and save the file.

    C. They can open, modify, and save the file. They can also execute the file if it is an executable.

    D. They have no access to the file at all.

19. An executable file has the SUID permission set. If this file is run on the system, who owns the file?

    A. The user who created the file remains the owner.

    B. The user who ran the file becomes the file's permanent owner.

    C. The user who ran the file becomes the file's temporary owner.

    D. The root user becomes the file's owner.

20. Which mount options need to be included in /etc/fstab to enable quotas when a file system is mounted? (Choose two.)

    A. groupquotas=on

    B. usrquota

    C. grpquota

    D. userquotas=on

    E. fsquota

21. With the quota package installed on your Linux system, what parameters can you set quotas for in the file system? (Choose two.)

    A. Blocks

    B. Permissions

    C. Inodes

    D. Ownership

    E. Number of Users

    F. Number of Groups

LAB QUESTION

The users on your Linux system have been consuming excessive amounts of disk space. You've just added a new 300GB hard drive to the system and mounted it at /home in the file system and copied your users' old data to the new disk. After instructing the users to delete unnecessary files, you decide to implement quotas on this disk to prevent this from happening again. Outline the steps you would follow to do this.

SELF TEST ANSWERS

Manage Users and Groups

1. ☑ **A**. Entering **id dcoughanour** will display the UID of that user account.
   ☒ **B, C,** and **D** are incorrect. **B** will display user information about dcoughanour, but it won't display his UID. **C** and **D** are distracters.

2. ☑ **C**. The /etc/passwd file stores user account information.
   ☒ **A, B,** and **D** are incorrect. **A** stores user passwords, not user account information. **B** and **D** are distracters.

3. ☑ **A**. The /etc/shadow file stores user passwords on most Linux distributions.
   ☒ **B, C,** and **D** are incorrect. **B** is a distracter. **C** used to be used to store passwords on Linux systems a long time ago. However, most systems use shadow passwords now. **D** is a distracter.

4. ☑ **D**. The GID of ksander's primary group is 100. On most distributions, this is the users group.
   ☒ **A, B,** and **C** are incorrect. **A** is the user's username. **B** lists the directory where home directories are stored. **C** is the UID of the ksanders user.

5. ☑ **B**. The user must change her password every 60 days. The value of 60 in the record shown specifies that the maximum age of a password is 60 days. After that, the user must change to a new password.
   ☒ **A, C,** and **D** are incorrect. **A** refers to the number of days the user must use the same password before being allowed to change it. **C** specifies the number of days prior to password expiration that a warning message will be displayed to the user. **D** is a distracter.

6. ☑ **A**. Entering **useradd -c "Mike Huffman" –m –p "Panguitch" mhuffman** will create the user mhuffmann, set its full name to Mike Huffman, create a home directory (–m), and set the user's password to Panguitch.
   ☒ **B, C,** and **D** are incorrect. **B** uses usermod instead of useradd. The usermod utility can only be used to modify an existing account. **C** will actually work to create the user account. However, it won't create a home directory nor will it set the user's password. **D** uses incorrect syntax for using useradd.

7. ☑ **B**. Entering **usermod –l "dnelson" –c "Diana Nelson" dgrow** at the shell prompt will rename the dgrow user account to dnelson.
   ☒ **A, C,** and **D** are incorrect. **A** changes dnelson to dgrow instead of dgrow to dnelson. **C** creates a new user account named dnelson, but it doesn't remove the old account. **D** uses incorrect syntax for the usermod command.

8. ☑ C. Entering **userdel –r jcarr** will delete jcarr's account and remove his home directory.
☒ A, B, and D are incorrect. A will delete the jcarr account, but his home directory will remain in the file system. B is a distracter. D is incorrect. The userdel command doesn't have a --rmhome option. However, you could use --remove-home with userdel and it would remove the home directory.

9. ☑ D. The /etc/group file stores group information.
☒ A, B, and C are incorrect. A, B, and C are distracters.

10. ☑ B. Entering **groupmod –A "mhuffman,dnelson,jcarr" editors** at the shell prompt will add the mhuffman, dnelson, and jcarr user accounts to the editors group.
☒ A, C, and D are incorrect. A is incorrect because you can't use the –A option with the groupadd command. C creates a new user account named dnelson, but it doesn't remove the old account. D uses incorrect syntax for the usermod command.

11. ☑ D. Entering **groupmod –R "dnelson" editors** will remove the dnelson user account from the editors group.
☒ A, B, and C are incorrect. A is incorrect because it uses groupadd instead of groupmod. You can't add or remove users from a group with groupadd. B adds dnelson to editors; it doesn't remove the account. C uses incorrect syntax for groupmod.

Manage Ownership, Permissions, and Quotas

12. ☑ D. Entering **chown dnelson.editors /var/opt/runme** will change the user and group owners of the runme file to dnelson and editors.
☒ A, B, and C are incorrect. A uses incorrect syntax. B uses incorrect syntax. C changes the user assigned to the runme file, but it doesn't change the group owner.

13. ☑ C. The execute permission allows a user to enter a directory in the file system.
☒ A, B, and D are incorrect. A allows the user to list the directory contents, but it doesn't allow the user to enter the directory. B allows the user to delete or create files in a directory, but it doesn't allow access to the directory itself. D doesn't exist in Linux. It's a NetWare file system right.

14. ☑ A and B. The user must have read and write permissions to open and modify a file.
☒ C and D are incorrect. C is used to run an executable file. D doesn't exist in Linux. It's a NetWare file system right.

15. ☑ A. In the mode shown, Group is given the read permission only. Because mhuffman is a member of the group, he can only open and view file contents. He can't modify and save the file.
☒ B, C, and D are incorrect. B is incorrect because Group doesn't have the write permission. C is incorrect. Only root can change a file's owner. D is incorrect because Group doesn't have the execute permission.

16. ☑ **D.** Because dnelson isn't the owner and isn't a member of the owning group, she is granted the rights assigned to Others, which are read (4) and execute (1). This allows her to run the file.
☒ **A, B,** and **C** are incorrect. **A** is incorrect. Only root or the file's owner can change group ownership. **B** is incorrect. The write permission must be assigned to Others to modify and save the file. **C** is incorrect. Only root can change a file's ownership.

17. ☑ **A.** Entering **chmod 664 schedule.odt** will grant Owner and Group read (4) and write (2) permissions. It will also grant Others read (4) permission.
☒ **B, C,** and **D** are incorrect. **B** is incorrect because it grants Owner, Group, and Others read (4) and execute (1) permissions. **C** is incorrect because it grants Owner, Group, and Others read (4), write (2), and execute (1) permissions. **D** is incorrect because Group isn't granted the write (2) permission.

18. ☑ **D.** Because umask is set to 077, all permissions (read=4, write=2, execute=1) are removed from Group and Others. Therefore, members of the owning group have no access to the file.
☒ **A, B,** and **C** are incorrect. **A** is incorrect. The read permission is required to view the file. **B** is incorrect. The read and write permissions must be assigned to open, modify, and save the file. **C** is incorrect. The read, write, and execute permissions must be assigned to open, modify, save, or run the file.

19. ☑ **C.** The SUID permission causes the user who runs the file to temporarily become the file's owner.
☒ **A, B,** and **D** are incorrect. **A** is incorrect. The user who runs the file temporarily becomes its owner. **B** is incorrect. The user running the file is only temporarily assigned to be the file's owner. **D** is only correct if the user running the file is root. Even in this case, root would only be the owner temporarily.

20. ☑ **B** and **C.** You need to add the usrquota and grpquota options to the mount options for the file system.
☒ **A, D,** and **E** are incorrect. These responses are distracters.

21. ☑ **A** and **C.** The quota package can set quotas on blocks and inodes in the file system.
☒ **B, D, E,** and **F** are incorrect. **B** is incorrect. Quotas don't apply to permissions. **D** is incorrect. Quotas don't apply to ownership. **E** is incorrect. Quotas don't apply to the number of users. **F** is incorrect. Quotas don't apply to the number of groups.

LAB ANSWER

To enable quotas on the file system mounted on /home, you would first install the quota package on your system. This package can be downloaded from http://www.sourceforge.net or installed from your distribution's installation CD.

Then, open a terminal session and change to your root user account. Open /etc/fstab in a text editor and add usrquota and grpquota to the list of mount options for the file system mounted at /home. Restart the system so the mount options can take effect.

Next, after the system has rebooted, you would open a terminal session again, change to root, and enter **quotacheck –amvug** at the shell prompt. This will scan the file system for usage and create your quota files. In this case, aquota.user and aquota.groups will be created in /home.

Once this is done, you would next enable quotas on the file system by entering **quotaon –av** at the shell prompt. You would then enter **edquota –u** *username* to set hard and soft limits for blocks and inodes in the file system. You would repeat this process for each user. You could also, optionally, enter **edquota –g** *groupname* to set quotas for your groups. If desired, you could also enter **edquota –t** to set the grace period for your soft limits.

At this point, quotas have been established on the file system mounted at /home. You can now enter **repquota –av** to view the quotas you just set as well as view how much space your users are consuming.

8

Installing and Managing Software on Linux

As a Linux system administrator, you need to know how to install and manage software on a Linux system. "Ha!" you're thinking. "How hard can it be to install software? I've been installing software on my Windows system for years." Actually, installing software on Linux can be somewhat challenging to those new to this operating system. It's not that installing software on Linux is more difficult than on other operating systems, such as Windows. It's just that it is very different.

If you have experience installing Windows or DOS applications, you need to momentarily shelve what you already know about installing software and be prepared to approach the process from a new perspective. My past experience has been that if students new to Linux hang on too tightly to their "Windows-way" of doing things, they really struggle when working with Linux software. There just aren't enough similarities. If, on the other hand, you will let Windows go and learn how to do things in a new way, you're going to be just fine.

With this in mind, let's review what we're going to talk about in this chapter. The following topics will be covered:

■ Installing software on Linux
■ Managing installed software

Let's begin this chapter by introducing you to the process required to install software on your Linux system.

INSIDE THE EXAM

Installing and Managing Linux Software

Be prepared to answer a moderate number of installation-related items when you take your Linux+ exam. Be sure you know the shell commands that are used to manage Linux RPM packages, including how to install packages, uninstall packages, and query the RPM database for information about installed packages.

You also need to be familiar with the process used to build software from a source package. Be sure you know what the configure, make, and make install commands do. Also be sure you are comfortable with the role, function, and syntax of the Makefile file.

CERTIFICATION OBJECTIVE 8.01

Install Software on Linux

As with many of the other tasks we've discussed in this book, you can use a variety of tools to install and manage software on a Linux system. Some of these tools are run from the shell prompt; others are graphical utilities that can be used from within the KDE or GNOME desktop environment. For example, the SUSE Linux distribution includes the Software Management module within the YaST configuration utility. This is shown in Figure 8-1.

FIGURE 8-1   Using the YaST Software Management module

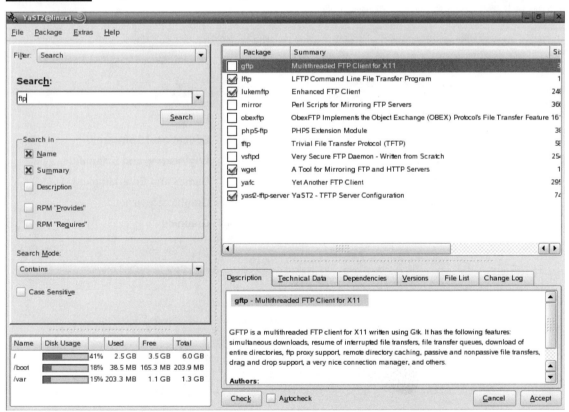

The Software Management module allows you to perform a variety of software administrative tasks, such as installing, updating, or removing packages. Other distributions provide similar graphical utilities. For example, on Fedora, you can select Applications | Add/Remove Software from the GNOME desktop to launch the Package Manager graphical utility, shown in Figure 8-2.

These graphical utilities have many advantages. In addition to the easy-to-use interface, most will also automatically detect and resolve package dependencies for you. We'll discuss how dependencies work later in this chapter.

However, we're not going to spend much time with these utilities in this chapter. This is done for a variety of reasons. First of all, as with most of the other tasks we've discussed in this chapter, a good Linux admin needs to know how to manage software from the command line. You really need to understand what's going on "under the hood" of the graphical utility.

| **FIGURE 8-2** | Using the Package Manager utility |

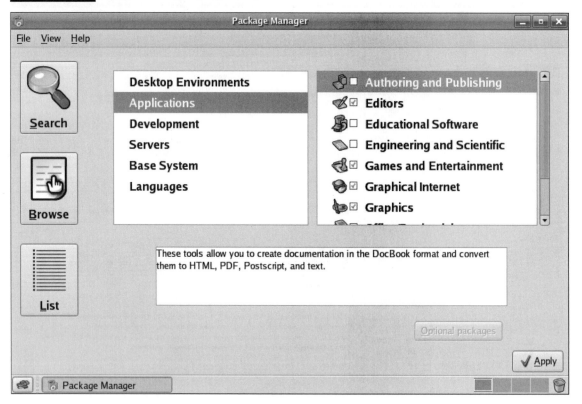

In addition, most graphical management utilities can only manage software *packages*. Many of the programs you will install on a Linux system will be installed from a source package. These types of programs must be untarred and compiled from source code. The only way to do this is from the shell prompt. Finally, the Linux+ exam requires you to know how to manage software from the shell prompt. Therefore, you must know how to complete these tasks using command-line utilities.

In accordance, we're going to review the following topics in this part of the chapter:

- Obtaining Linux software
- Installing software from source packages
- Installing software packages

Let's begin by reviewing where you can get Linux software for your system.

Obtaining Linux Software

One of the things that I love most about Linux is the fact that there is a wealth of software available for your system from a variety of sources, most at little or no cost. Back in the early days of Linux, this wasn't the case. In fact, one of the great impediments that prevented the widespread adoption of Linux in the early days was the lack of applications, particularly office productivity applications.

Today, however, that has all changed. You name a particular task you need to complete with a Linux system and you can probably find an application or service somewhere that can handle the job.

on the *The availability of the OpenOffice.org productivity suite, in my opinion, has*
Job *played a very important role in the acceptance and adoption of Linux on the desktop. Linux has always held an edge in the server room. Its reliability, scalability, and flexibility made it a natural fit in the server role. However, the uptake of Linux on the desktop has been much slower. One of the key issues was that less computer-savvy users needed a desktop environment similar to Windows as well as a productivity suite similar to those provided by Microsoft Office. With the KDE and GNOME desktops, the first condition has been addressed. With the OpenOffice.org suite, the second condition has been addressed as well. It's not there yet, but I predict that within the next five to ten years, you'll see a dramatic influx of Linux systems at users' desks.*

So where can you get Linux software? As we discussed earlier in this book, the Linux development model violates most of the accepted norms. With other operating systems, you obtain software by visiting your local computer store and purchasing a box copy of your desired application. A few "edgy" vendors may actually allow you to purchase your application online and download a copy.

With Linux, however, this usually isn't the case. As I was writing this, I visited the Web site of a well-known big-box computer store to see how many boxed applications they offer for Linux. Guess how many? Only three! In fact, two of the three were actually Linux distributions, not applications. The point is, most of your Linux software is obtained from alternative sources. Let's take a look at a few here.

Sources for Linux Software

You can obtain software for your Linux system from a variety of sources other than the computer store. The first source you should be aware of (and a source that many administrators overlook) is your distribution CDs or DVD. Many distributions include a cornucopia of applications and services that you can install. For example, the SUSE Linux 10.1 DVD includes hundreds of application and service RPMs in the subdirectories of the suse directory, as shown in Figure 8-3.

In addition to your distribution disc, you can also download software for your Linux system from a host of Web sites on the Internet. Most open source applications have their own Web sites where you can learn about the software and download the latest version. For example, you can visit http://www.pureftpd.org to learn about and download the pure-ftpd service, which is used to configure an FTP service on your Linux system. This Web site is shown in Figure 8-4.

In addition to individual project Web sites, you can also use several other Web sites that provide you with links to many different programs from a single location. One of my favorites is http://www.rpmfind.net/linux/RPM. This Web site provides an RMP repository that you can search to locate and download an RPM package for your Linux system. This Web site is shown in Figure 8-5.

Another great source for Linux software is SourceForge (http://sourceforge.net). The SourceForge Web site is a central repository for open source software. As of the date this was written, there were over 100,000 different programs available on this site. As with the rpmfind Web site, you can search SourceForge to locate and download a particular package. For example, in Figure 8-6, I've conducted a search for the pure-ftpd package discussed above. The results are displayed with links that will allow you to download the appropriate programs.

FIGURE 8-3   Applications and services on the distribution DVD

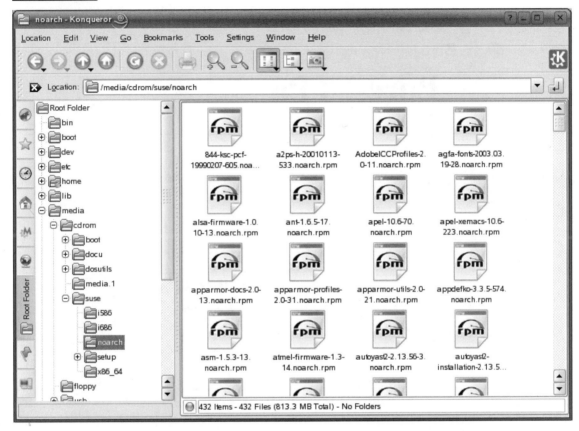

As you can see, you can download just about anything you need from these Web sites. In addition, you can also use the following Web sites to download software for your Linux system:

- **Tucows**   http://linux.tucows.com
- **Freshmeat**   http://www.freshmeat.net
- **Linux Online**   http://www.linux.org/apps

The point is that software is readily available for you to use on your system. Spend some time reviewing what's available on these sites. You'll be glad you did!

FIGURE 8-4   Obtaining software from an open source project Web site

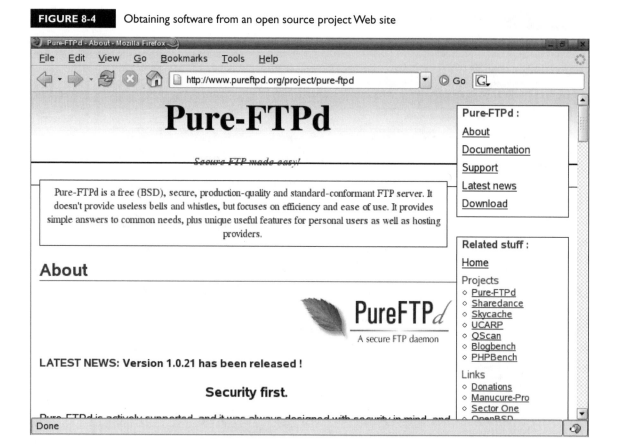

When you download a program from one of these sites, you should check your download and verify that it didn't get corrupted along the way. Let's talk about how this is done next.

Verifying Your Downloads

For the most part, files downloaded from the Internet arrive at your local system intact. However, it is possible for corruption to occur. There are few things more frustrating than downloading a file, especially a distribution ISO image, only to find that the file got corrupted somewhere along the way.

The good news is that you can check your files after they are downloaded to verify that the copy on your local system is the same as the copy on the server you downloaded from. This can be done by creating and comparing the file's *checksum value* against the source file. A checksum is a value generated by calculating the

FIGURE 8-5   Using the RPM repository on rpmfind.net

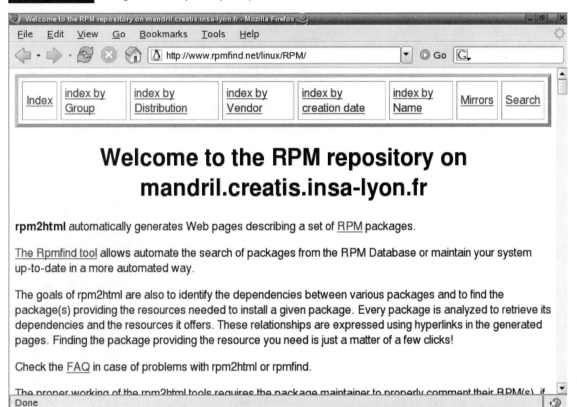

contents of a file using a Message Digest 5 (MD5) algorithm. For example, if you were downloading a DVD ISO image from http://www.suse.org, you could view the checksum for the file using the link provided in the download page. This would display the checksum values for the source file, as shown in Figure 8-7.

After downloading the file, you could then use the sum command from the shell prompt to calculate a checksum for the local copy of the file. To do this, you simply enter **sum** *path/filename*. For example, if you downloaded the SUSE-Linux-10.1-GM-DVD-i386.iso file to the /root directory, you would enter **sum /root/SUSE-Linux-10.1-GM-DVD-i386.iso**. The sum utility reads the file and generates a checksum value for the file and displays it onscreen. You can then compare the checksum for the original file on the Web site against the checksum for the local file. If the checksums are the same, you're in good shape. That means the files are identical. No corruption occurred during transit.

FIGURE 8-6 Searching for software on the SourceForge Web site

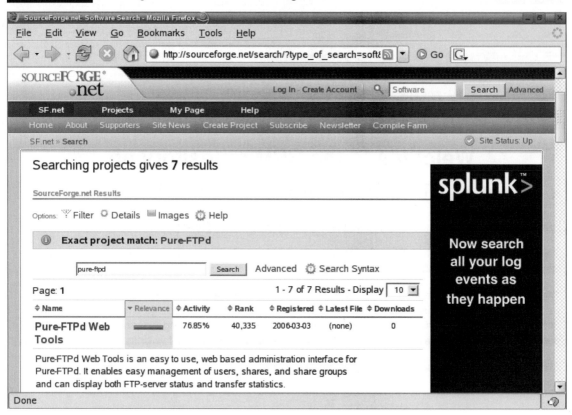

FIGURE 8-7 Viewing source file checksum values

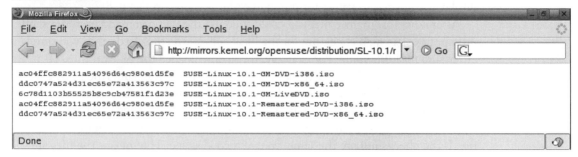

SCENARIO & SOLUTION

You need to install an RPM package named barcode on your Linux system. Where could you look to find this software?	You could look on your distribution's installation CD. For a more updated version, you could visit http://www.rpmfind.net or http://sourceforge.net.
You've just downloaded a file named SUSE-Linux-10.1-Remastered-i386-CD2.iso. What command would you use to generate a checksum value on the file?	You would change to the directory where the file resides and then enter **sum SUSE-Linux-10.1-Remastered-i386-CD2.iso**.

However, if the checksums are different, that indicates that somehow the two copies of the file are different in some way. More than likely, something happened during the download process that corrupted the local copy. In this situation, don't try to salvage the local copy. Delete it and download a new copy and verify the checksum values again.

Let's practice using Web resources to obtain Linux software in the following exercise.

EXERCISE 8-1

Using Web Resources to Obtain Linux Software

In this exercise, you will practice using Web resources to download Linux software. The following steps were accurate as of the time this book was written. Because of the ever-changing nature of the Web, you may need to modify these steps as new versions of software are released and Web sites are updated.

With this in mind, complete the following:

1. Boot your Linux system and log in as a standard user. If you used the lab exercise in Chapter 3 to install your system, you can log in as **tux** with a password of **M3linux273**.

2. Open a Web browser and navigate to http://wwwsourceforge.net.

3. In the Search field on the SourceForge home page, enter **pure-ftpd**, then select Search.

4. Locate the Pure-FTPd Download link in the list of search results and select it.

5. In the list of latest file releases, select the Download link for the latest version of Pure-FTPd in tar.gz format.

6. Save the file to your home directory (~). (Your browser may prompt you to open the file with a graphical archive utility. Don't select this option.)

7. In your browser, navigate to http://www.rpmfind.net/linux/RPM.

8. Scroll down to the Search field and enter **gftp**, then select Search.

9. In the list of search results identify the appropriate RPM package for your distribution and architecture.

10. Select the appropriate link to download the correct RPM for your system and save the file to your home directory.

11. Close your browser window.

Now you're ready to start installing files. Let's review how this is done next.

Installing Software from Source Code

Many of the applications and services you will install on a Linux system will be delivered as source code, not as a binary executable. When you install the software on your local system, you actually compile the source code from the installation files into a binary executable that can be run.

For example, let's suppose you wanted to install and configure an FTP service on your local Linux system. You've done some research and determined that the pure-ftpd service is the one you want to use to set up your FTP server. When you download and extract the installation files, you notice that a directory named src is created. Within this directory are a number of text files that contain the source code for the pure-ftpd service. An example of one of the source code files for this service is shown in Figure 8-8.

Distributing software in this manner has many advantages. Key among these is the fact that you don't have to create a separate executable and installation package for each delivery architecture and platform. You can have the installation process detect the type of system the software is being installed on and compile the software appropriately. The key disadvantage to this approach is the fact that it makes the installation process somewhat complex. Users must have a compiler installed on

FIGURE 8-8   Viewing a program's source code

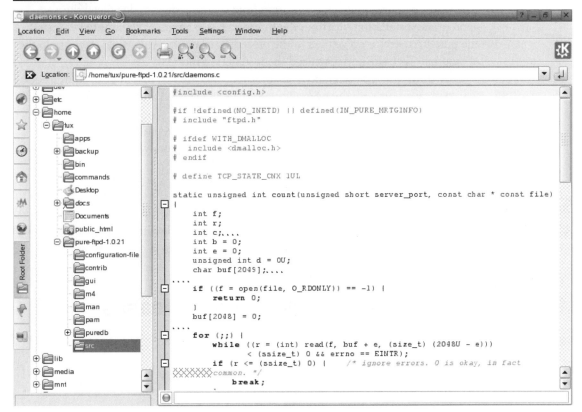

their system; otherwise, they won't be able to compile the source code into a binary executable. In addition, the user must know the proper procedure for compiling the source code and installing the resulting executable.

Fortunately, a standard process for completing this task has been adopted by most developers. This process is composed of the following elements:

- Preparing the installation files
- Compiling the executable
- Installing the executable

Let's begin by discussing how to prepare the installation files.

Preparing the Installation Files

The first step in installing an application from source code is to download the appropriate installation files from the Internet. For example, if you wanted to install the pure-ftpd service we've used in the preceding examples, you would navigate to the appropriate Web site and download the installation files.

One thing you'll notice about installation files used to install from source code is that they are usually distributed as a tarball file (tarred and gzipped). This is shown in Figure 8-9.

Because these applications are distributed as tarballs, you must first unzip and untar them after downloading them from the Internet before you can do anything else.

FIGURE 8-9   Downloading tarball files

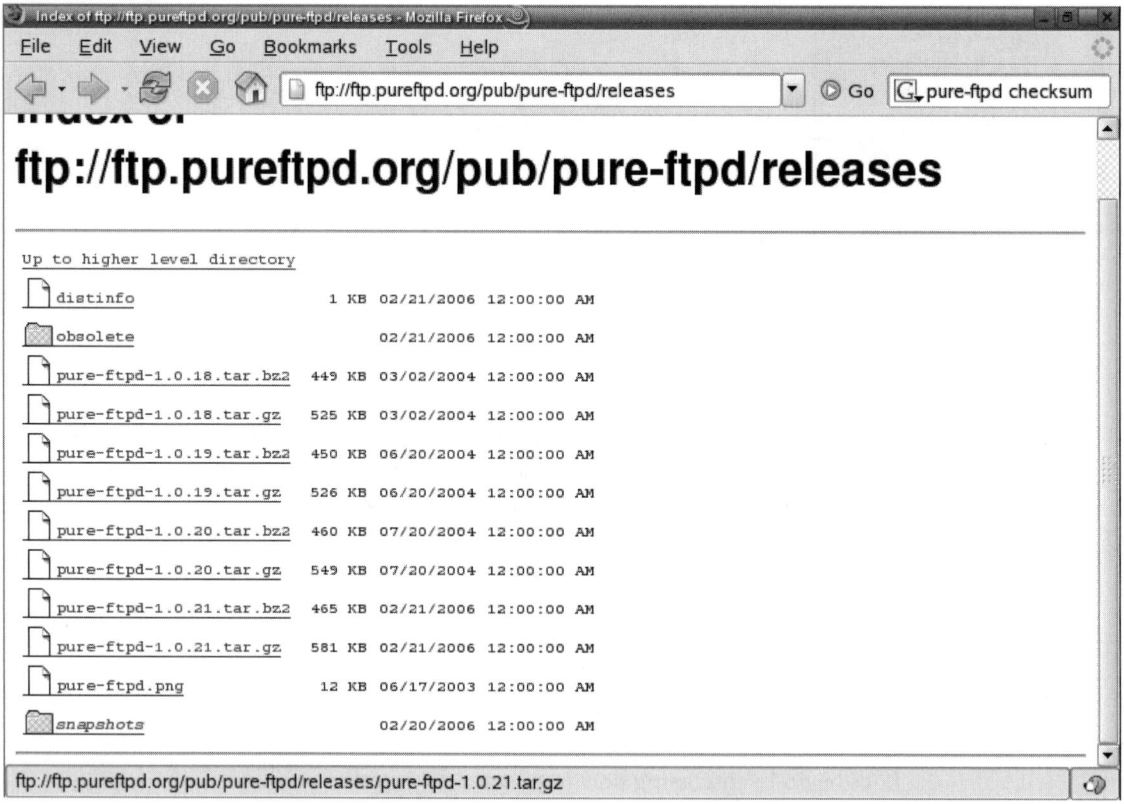

This is done using the tar command. Recall from Chapter 6 that the tar command is used to create archive files. It can also be used to extract files from archives such as tarballs.

To do this on your system, switch to the directory where you downloaded the tarball using the cd command from the shell prompt. Then enter **tar –zxvf ./*filename***. The –z option tells tar to use gzip to decompress the tarball first. The –x option tells tar to extract the files from the decompressed archive file. The –v option tells tar to operate verbosely, displaying each file onscreen as it is processed. The –f option tells tar the name of the file to extract.

For example, suppose you downloaded the pure-ftpd-1.0.21.tar.gz file shown in Figure 8-9. To extract this file, you would enter **tar –zxvf ./pure-ftpd-1.0.21.tar.gz** at the shell prompt. This is shown in Figure 8-10.

FIGURE 8-10 Extracting a tarball file

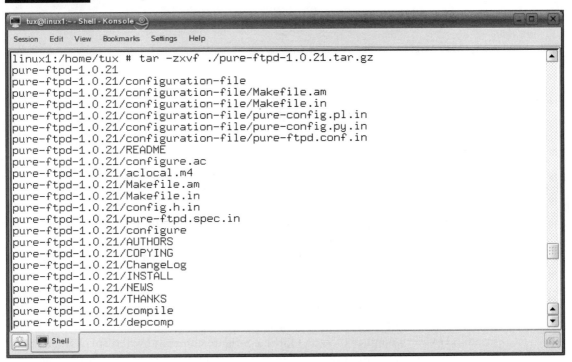

FIGURE 8-11 Application installation files

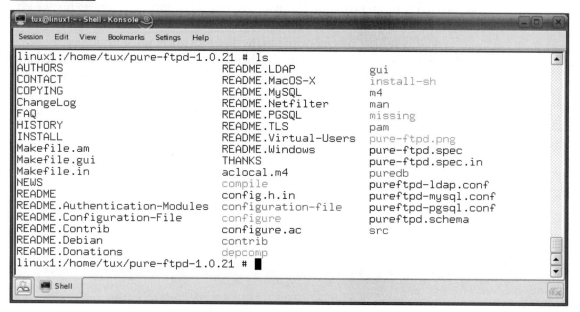

Notice in Figure 8-10 that the files are extracted to a directory named pure-ftpd-1.0.21 in the current directory. This directory contains the source code files that will be used to create the executable program. It also contains a variety of utilities needed to help create the executable. These are shown in Figure 8-11.

With the files extracted, we next need to prepare the installation files to be compiled. This is done using the configure command shown in Figure 8-12. To run this command, verify that you're in the directory created when the tarball was extracted. Then enter **./configure** at the shell prompt. This is shown in Figure 8-12.

The configure file is a script that does two things when it is run. First, it checks your system to make sure all the necessary components required to compile the program are available. One of the most important things it checks for is the existence of a compiler compatible with the C programming language. If you don't have a C compiler, such as the GNU C Compiler (gcc) or the GNU C++ Compiler (gcc-c++), the configure command will display an error on the screen instructing you to install a compiler and then run configure again.

FIGURE 8-12 Running configure

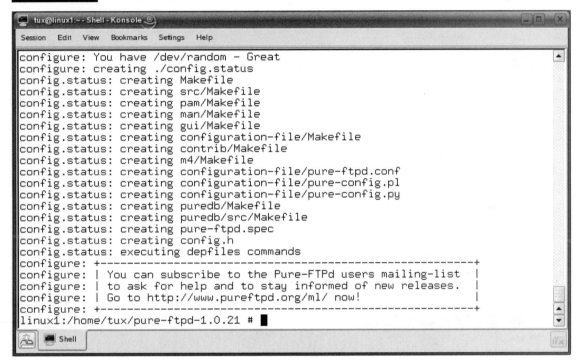

It also verifies that your overall system environment is compatible with the program you're going to install.

Second, it also creates a very important file called Makefile. Because most source code applications are designed to be deployed on a variety of distributions and architectures, the installation program needs to know how to customize the source code files such that the resulting executable will run on your particular system. Notice in Figure 8-12 that one of the last things the configure script did was to create a series of Makefile files. The Makefile file contains specific instructions for how the executable should be compiled to run on your platform, as shown in Figure 8-13.

While not required, it's usually a good idea to check the Makefile file after running configure to verify that the program is going to be installed in the manner you want. If you see something you want to change, you can use a text editor to make the appropriate changes and save the file.

FIGURE 8-13 Viewing Makefile

Once configure has been run and the Makefile file is ready, the next step in the process is to actually compile the executable. Let's discuss how this is done next.

Compiling the Executable

At this point in the process, the program you want to install still only exists as source code in your file system. Before you can run it, you must convert the text-based source code into a binary executable file. This is done using the make command. The make command calls your system's C compiler (such as gcc) and directs it to read the source code files, using the specifications and options listed in the Makefile file, and generate a compiled executable file.

FIGURE 8-14 Using the make command to compile source code

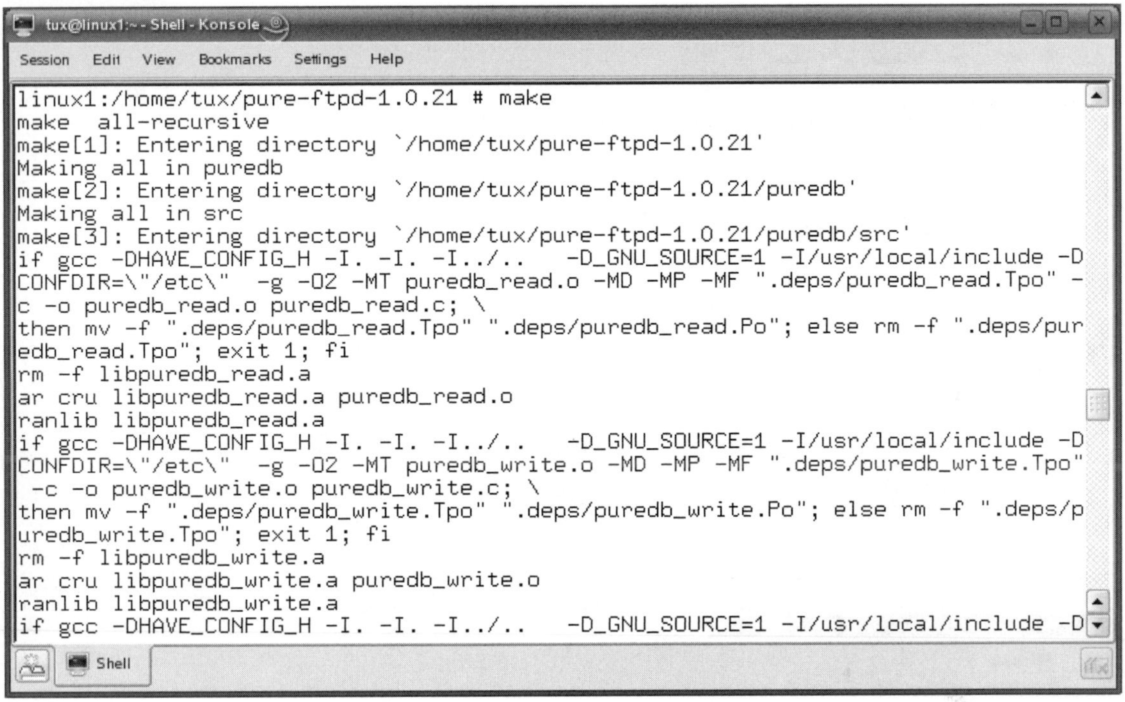
tux@linux1:~ - Shell - Konsole
Session Edit View Bookmarks Settings Help
linux1:/home/tux/pure-ftpd-1.0.21 # make
make all-recursive
make[1]: Entering directory `/home/tux/pure-ftpd-1.0.21'
Making all in puredb
make[2]: Entering directory `/home/tux/pure-ftpd-1.0.21/puredb'
Making all in src
make[3]: Entering directory `/home/tux/pure-ftpd-1.0.21/puredb/src'
if gcc -DHAVE_CONFIG_H -I. -I. -I../..   -D_GNU_SOURCE=1 -I/usr/local/include -D
CONFDIR=\"/etc\" -g -O2 -MT puredb_read.o -MD -MP -MF ".deps/puredb_read.Tpo" -
c -o puredb_read.o puredb_read.c; \
then mv -f ".deps/puredb_read.Tpo" ".deps/puredb_read.Po"; else rm -f ".deps/pur
edb_read.Tpo"; exit 1; fi
rm -f libpuredb_read.a
ar cru libpuredb_read.a puredb_read.o
ranlib libpuredb_read.a
if gcc -DHAVE_CONFIG_H -I. -I. -I../..   -D_GNU_SOURCE=1 -I/usr/local/include -D
CONFDIR=\"/etc\" -g -O2 -MT puredb_write.o -MD -MP -MF ".deps/puredb_write.Tpo"
 -c -o puredb_write.o puredb_write.c; \
then mv -f ".deps/puredb_write.Tpo" ".deps/puredb_write.Po"; else rm -f ".deps/p
uredb_write.Tpo"; exit 1; fi
rm -f libpuredb_write.a
ar cru libpuredb_write.a puredb_write.o
ranlib libpuredb_write.a
if gcc -DHAVE_CONFIG_H -I. -I. -I../..   -D_GNU_SOURCE=1 -I/usr/local/include -D
Shell

This is done by entering **make** at the shell prompt without any options while you are still in the directory created when you untarred the tarball file. This is shown in Figure 8-14.

Be aware, however, that make only creates the executable. Before you can use it, it needs to be actually installed on the system; doing this will copy the executable, startup scripts, and documentation files to the appropriate directories in your file system. Let's discuss how this is done next.

Installing the Executable

To actually install the program on your system, you use the make command a second time. However, this time you specify a target with make named INSTALL.

FIGURE 8-15   The INSTALL target in the Makefile file

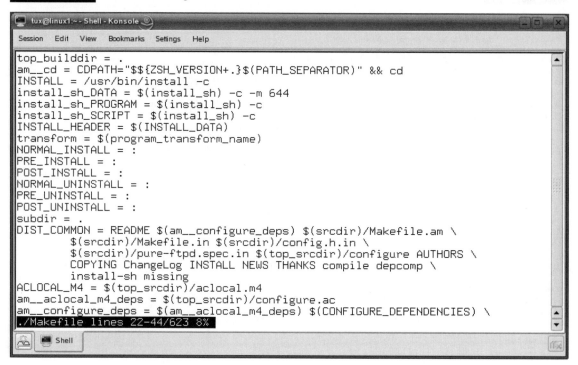

This tells make to install the program using the information specified in the INSTALL portion of the Makefile file, shown in Figure 8-15.

To do this, make sure you're still in the directory created when you untarred the tarball file. Then enter **make install** at the shell prompt. The make utility will then follow the instructions in the Makefile file to install the application, as shown in Figure 8-16.

At this point, the application or service is ready to run. Simply enter the appropriate commands at the shell prompt.

FIGURE 8-16   Installing the program with make install

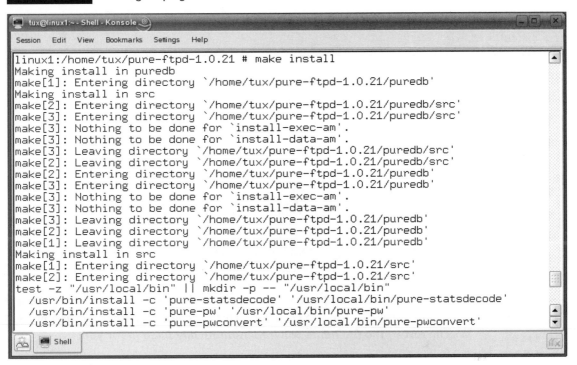

SCENARIO & SOLUTION

You've just downloaded a file named newapp-2.10.tar.gz. What command would you use to extract it?	You would switch to the directory where the file resides and then enter **tar –zxvf ./newapp-2.10.tar.gz**.
You've downloaded and extracted an application from a tarball. You've run configure and make. What command should you run next?	You need to run **make install** to actually install the compiled executable.

Let's practice installing software from source code in the following exercise.

EXERCISE 8-2

Building Software from Source Code

In this exercise, you will practice installing the Pure-FTPd software from the tarball you downloaded in the previous exercise. Complete the following:

1. With your system running, open a terminal session.

2. Change to your root user account by entering **su –** followed by your root user's *password*.

3. Use the cd command to change to the directory where you saved the Pure-FTPd tarball file.

4. At the shell prompt, enter **tar –zxvf ./pure-ftpd-*version*.tar.gz**. Replace *version* with the current version number of the tarball you downloaded.

on the

Job

You can use the tab complete feature of Linux to make the entering of these commands easier. To use tab complete, enter tar –zxvf ./pure- and then press TAB. The rest of the file name will be automatically filled in for you!

5. Use the cd command to change to the directory created by tar. This should be pure-ftpd-*version*.

6. Enter **ls** to view the files extracted from the tarball.

7. At the shell prompt, enter **./configure**.

The configure script will check your system and verify that the software can be installed. You must have a C compiler installed on your system. If you followed the steps presented in the Chapter 3 installation exercise, you should have this compiler already installed. If configure reports that you're missing a compiler, locate the gcc RPM package on your distribution CD and install it entering **rpm –i** at the shell prompt. See the next section of this chapter for details on how to use rpm.

8. When the configure script is done, compile the executable by entering **make** at the shell prompt.

9. When the compilation is complete, install the executable by entering **make install** at the shell prompt.

10. Start the service by entering **/usr/local/sbin/pure-ftpd &** at the shell prompt.

11. Test the system by entering **ftp localhost** at the shell prompt.

12. When prompted, enter a username of **anonymous**. You should be logged in to the FTP server at this point.

13. Close the connection by entering **quit**.

At this point, you have a functioning FTP server running on your Linux system! However, it won't be accessible by other workstations yet because your system's host firewall is probably blocking traffic on the IP ports used by the FTP protocol. We'll address how to open up ports in Chapter 15.

In addition to installing software from source code, you can also install programs using preconfigured packages. Let's discuss how this is done next.

Installing Software Packages

In addition to installing software from source code, you can also install precompiled, preconfigured applications and services on your Linux system using *packaged software*. With packaged software, the source code is prebuilt and configured for a particular system architecture and, in some cases, a specific Linux distribution.

In this part of this chapter, we're going to discuss the following:

- The role and function of a package manager
- Installing RPM packages

Let's start by discussing the package manager.

The Role and Function of a Package Manager

To use software packages, you must have some type of software package manager installed. On distributions such as SUSE, Red Hat, and Fedora (as well as many others), you use the Red Hat Package Manager (RPM) to manage RPM packages on your Linux system. Other distributions may use a different package manager. For example, the Debian distribution has its own package management system that is similar to the RPM system.

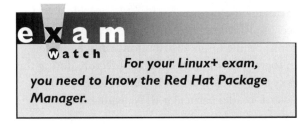

For your Linux+ exam, you need to know the Red Hat Package Manager.

Regardless of which one you use, the role of a package manager is to do the following:

- Install new packages
- Update existing packages
- Verify package files
- Query installed packages
- Uninstall packages

To make this happen, the RPM Package Manager has its own database, stored in /var/lib/rpm, that it uses to keep track of what packages are installed in the system. Whenever you install, uninstall, or update a package, the appropriate changes are made to this database.

on the
Job
On rare occasions, the rpm database can get corrupted. This can cause numerous headaches with the packages installed on the system. You can use the rpm --rebuilddb command from the shell prompt to try to restore the database to a functioning state.

Let's next discuss how you use the RPM Package Manager to install package files.

Installing RPM Packages

The great thing about RPM is the fact that it makes it much easier to install and manage software than the source code option we discussed earlier in this chapter, especially for new or novice Linux users. Frankly, you have to know your stuff with Linux to install and compile source code. You're likely to find that the skills and knowledge required is way beyond that of most of your end users.

RPM packages, on the other hand, are quite easy to install. Instead of having to download and extract a tarball file, most RPM packages are downloaded in a single file that you process directly. You don't have to untar, configure, make, and make install the file the way you do with source code installs.

Instead, you simply use the rpm utility to install a package file. Before I show you how to do this, we first need to discuss the naming conventions used by RPM packages. This is very important because RPM packages are built for a specific CPU architecture and sometimes even for a specific Linux distribution. Unlike source code installs, which customize the program for the particular architecture during the installation process, RPM packages come precompiled for a specific architecture. That means there may be multiple versions of a particular RPM available to accommodate different platforms.

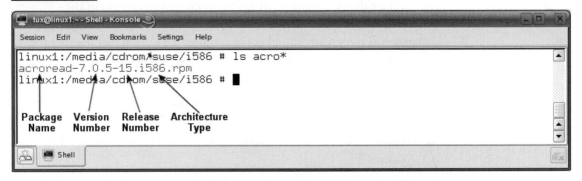

FIGURE 8-17   A sample RPM

The important point is to make sure you're downloading and installing the correct version of a given RPM for your particular system. You can check this by looking at the name of the RPM package. Consider the example shown in Figure 8-17.

This RPM is used to install the Acrobat Reader application from Adobe Systems. Different parts of the file name are used to indicate different information about the package, including the following:

- **Package Name**   This part of the file name simply identifies the name of the package. In this example, the name of the package is acroread.
- **Version Number**   This part of the file name specifies the version of the software in the package. In this case, the software version is 7.0.5.
- **Release Number**   This part of the file name indicates the current release of the software version. On occasion, errors are encountered in the process of creating an RPM package. When a new package release is made available for the same version of the software that fixes an error, the release number is incremented. In the example in Figure 8-17, the release number is 15.

    This field may also include an optional distribution designator that indicates that the package has been compiled for a specific Linux distribution. The designators include:
    - **fc*x***   Specifies that the package is intended for Fedora Core version *x*. For example, fc4 indicates the package is for Fedora Core 4.
    - **rhl*x***   Specifies that the package is intended for Red Hat Linux version *x*.
    - **suse*xxx***   Specifies that the package is intended for SUSE Linux version *xxx*. For example, suse101 indicates that the package is intended for SUSE Linux 10.1.

- **Architecture Type** This part of the file name specifies the CPU architecture that the software inside the package will run on. In the preceding example, the architecture is specified as i586. That means the software will run on any Intel Pentium or later CPU. You may also see the following architectures specified in a package's file name:

    - **i386** Specifies that the software will run on an Intel 80386 or later CPU.
    - **i686** Specifies that the software will run on an Intel Pentium II or later CPU.
    - **athlon** Specifies that the software is intended to run on an AMD Athlon CPU.
    - **ppc** Specifies that the software is intended to run on the PowerPC CPU.
    - **noarch** Specifies that the package is not architecture-dependent.

As with source code software installation files, RPM packages can be located on your distribution installation CD or DVD as well as from a variety of locations on the Internet. After downloading an RPM package, you should use the sum command to generate a checksum and compare it to the checksum of the original file, as we discussed earlier.

In addition, you can also use the rpm command to check the authenticity of the package. Doing so lets you know whether the package you downloaded came directly from the organization responsible for maintaining the software or whether it has been altered in some way by a third party. This is done by entering **rpm --checksig** *package_ filename*. This command will query the package for its digital signing key. If anyone altered the package at some point, the key will become invalid.

For example, in Figure 8-18, the armagetron package has been downloaded from the Internet. To verify the integrity of the package, you first switch to the directory where the package file is stored. Then you can enter **rpm --checksig armagetron-0.2.7.1-38.i586.rpm** to check the digital signature applied. This is shown in Figure 8-18.

FIGURE 8-18   Checking the digital signature on an RPM file

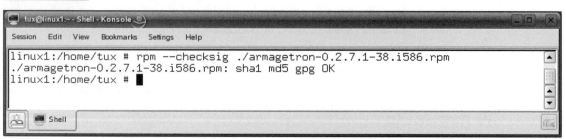

FIGURE 8-19   Installing a package file using rpm

Notice in Figure 8-18 that the output of the command says that the signature is OK, indicating that the package hasn't been altered by anyone since it was created.

Once you're confident that the package has arrived to your local system intact, you can install it using the rpm command again. This is done by entering **rpm –i** *package_filename*. The –i option tells the rpm utility to install the package specified. For example, you could install the package downloaded in Figure 8-18 by first switching to the directory where the package file is located. Then enter **rpm –i armagetron-0.2.7.1-38.i586.rpm**. This is shown in Figure 8-19.

The software is now installed on the system and ready for you to use. That was easy!

on the
()ob

If you know the full URL to the package you want to install, you can install it directly from the Internet. Just enter rpm –i url/filename.rpm.

You'll notice in Figure 8-19 that the rpm utility didn't provide much in the way of feedback as it was installing the package. Some Linux administrators prefer it this way; others prefer to see some visual queues that indicate the progress of the installation. This can be done using the –ihv option with rpm, as shown in Figure 8-20.

FIGURE 8-20   Installing a package file using the –ihv option

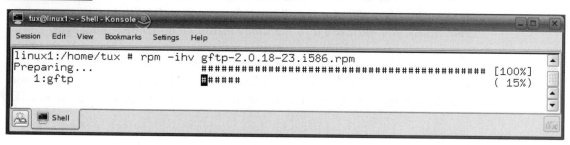

The –h option tells rpm to print hash marks on the screen as a progress indicator. The –v option tells rpm to operate verbosely, printing output to the screen.

on the Job

Personally, I prefer the –ihv option when I use rpm. It's not much of an issue when installing small packages. However, installing a large RPM package can take several minutes. If you don't use the –ihv option, the session will just sit there while the installation process runs. This makes me uneasy because I don't know if everything is processing correctly or not. If it takes too long, I start to wonder if something caused rpm to hang. I much prefer seeing a visual progress indicator, even if it is only a bunch of hash marks, to let me know that everything is progressing normally.
If you're the type of person who is obsessed with details, you can get even more information about the installation by using the –vv option with the rpm utility.

One of the fantastic features of the rpm utility is that it automatically calculates dependencies for you. You need to understand that a given Linux software package may be dependent upon another package being installed on the system before it can work properly. If this is the case, the dependent package is called a *dependency*. When you run the rpm utility, it queries the package you want to install and automatically checks to see if you have the dependent packages installed. If not, it will generate an error and prompt you to install the necessary packages required for the software to work.

If you want to check for dependencies without actually installing the software, you can use the –test option with the rpm utility. If there are any failed dependency tests, they will be printed on the screen, allowing you to install the necessary software. You can skip the dependency tests completely and install the package even if dependent software isn't present (not a good idea, by the way) by using the –nodeps option with rpm.

on the Job

One of the things that I love about the graphical software management utilities, such as YaST, is the fact that they not only calculate dependencies for you, but they will also install them for you as well. With the command-line rpm utility, you must use it to manually install all dependent packages.

After running rpm, you can then use the installed software. Some packages will create a menu item or icon in your KDE or GNOME desktop environment that you can use to launch the application. For example, the armagetron package we installed

FIGURE 8-21   Running an installed package using the K menu

earlier is started by selecting K Menu | Games | Arcade | Armagetron. This is
shown in Figure 8-21.

Other packages, particularly those that installed system services, will have to be
started from the shell prompt using a startup script or by running the executable file
name. For example, in Figure 8-22, the gftp FTP client we installed previously has
been run by entering **gftp** at the shell prompt.

FIGURE 8-22   Running an installed package from the shell prompt

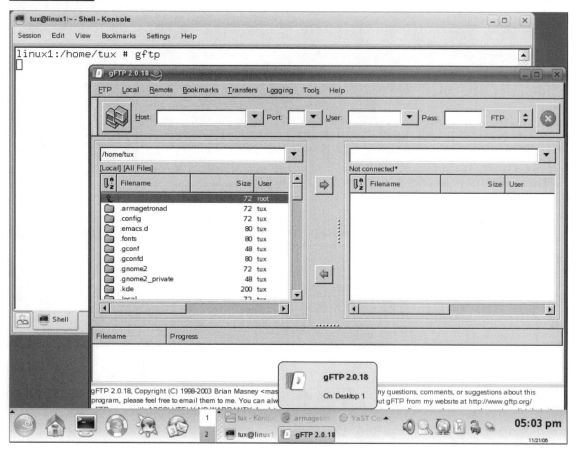

SCENARIO & SOLUTION	
You've just downloaded a file named BitTorrent-4.0.3-17.i586.rpm. Will this package run on a Pentium III 800 MHz CPU?	Yes. Because the file name specifies i586 as the architecture, it will run on any Intel Pentium or later CPU.
You've just downloaded a file named BitTorrent-4.0.3-17.i586.rpm. What command would you use to install it and display a progress indicator on the screen?	You would switch to the directory where the RPM package resides and enter **rpm –ihv BitTorrent-4.0.3-17.i586.rpm** at the shell prompt.

Let's practice installing software from an RPM package in the following exercise.

EXERCISE 8-3

Installing RPM Packages

In this exercise, you will practice installing the gftp client you downloaded in the first exercise in this chapter. Complete the following:

1. With your system running, open a terminal session.

2. If necessary, change to your root user account by entering **su –** followed by your root user's *password*.

3. Use the cd command to change to the directory where you saved the gftp RPM file.

4. At the shell prompt, enter **rpm –ihv ./gftp-version.i586.rpm**. Replace *version* with the current version number of the RPM package you downloaded.

5. Run the gftp client by entering **gftp &** at the shell prompt.

6. Test the client by entering **localhost** in the Host field and entering **anonymous** in the User field. You should be logged in to your local ftp server.

7. Close your gftp window.

Now that you know how to install software both from source code and from an RPM package, let's shift gears and discuss how you manage installed software on your system.

CERTIFICATION OBJECTIVE 8.02

Manage Installed Software

If you've worked with computers at all, you know that over a period of time you occasionally need to repair or even uninstall software from a system. The same holds true with Linux. In this part of this chapter, we're going to spend a few pages learning how to manage software that is currently installed on the system. We're going to discuss the following:

- Uninstalling software
- Updating software
- Querying packages
- Verifying packages

Let's begin by discussing how you uninstall software on Linux.

Uninstalling Software

Believe it or not, you will probably need to uninstall a lot of software as a Linux system administrator. It's not because there's anything wrong with the software itself; it's because most Linux distributions install a host of packages on a given system as a part of the base installation proposal. Unless you take the time during the install process to manually specify exactly which software is to be installed, it's very likely that many software packages will be installed on your systems that aren't needed. At best, these unnecessary packages use up disk space; at worst, they could potentially open up security holes in the system.

After installing any Linux system, I strongly recommend that you spend a few minutes reviewing the software that was included in the installation. If you've got unnecessary software on the system, uninstall it!

The good news is that it is relatively easy to uninstall software from a Linux system. In this part of the chapter, we're going to discuss how to uninstall software in the following scenarios:

- Uninstalling software compiled from source code
- Uninstalling RPM packages

Let's first look at how you go about uninstalling software that was installed from source code.

Uninstalling Software Compiled from Source Code

In the first part of this chapter, we spent some time discussing how to compile and install software from a source code package. The process for uninstalling software of this variety is very similar to the installation process.

on the
(i) o b

For most applications or services that are installed using the standard build process we discussed earlier, you must (in most cases) have access to your installation files to uninstall the associated software. The issue here is that many Linux administrators delete the installation source files once the installation process is complete to save disk space. If you do this, you've just deleted the files you'll need if you ever decide to uninstall the software. I recommend that you create a protected directory in your file system somewhere that only root can access and keep your source installation files in it. Yes, it does take up a little bit of disk space, but you'll have the files you need if uninstalling ever becomes necessary.

The uninstall process can vary slightly from product to product. Some applications or services may include an uninstall script in the files you extract from the tarball. If this is the case, you can execute this script to uninstall the application from your system.

Other products may include an UNINSTALL target in their Makefile file. If this is the case, you must first run configure from the directory created when you originally extracted the downloaded tarball file, just as you did when you first installed the software. Then, instead of running make install, you run make uninstall. This will cause the make utility to follow the instructions in the uninstall portion of the Makefile file to remove the software from your system. In Figure 8-23, we've used the make uninstall command to remove the pure-ftpd service from the system.

How do you know what method to use? The tarball you downloaded should include a README file of some sort that documents both the install and the uninstall process for the particular software you are working with. Check this file first. If the information isn't available, then check the FAQ or knowledgebase on the Web site of the organization that produced the software. One of these resources should provide you with the steps you need to follow to uninstall the software.

Let's next discuss how you uninstall an RPM package.

Uninstalling RPM Packages

As with installing RPM packages, the process for uninstalling them is relatively easy and straightforward. To do this, enter **rpm –e** *package_name* at the shell prompt. The –e option tells the rpm utility to erase the specified package. For example, in Figure 8-19 we installed the armegetron-0.2.7.1-38.i586.rpm package using rpm. We could uninstall this same package by entering **rpm –e armagetron** at the shell prompt.

FIGURE 8-23   Uninstalling software using the make uninstall command

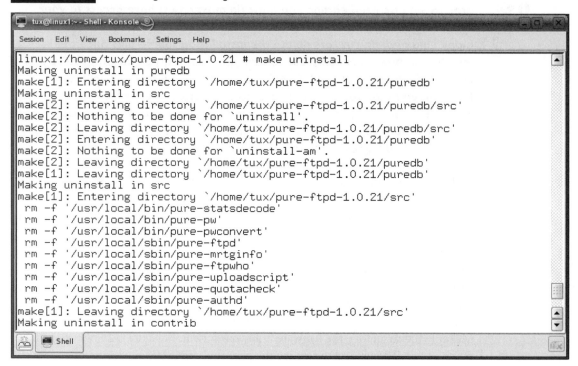

Be warned that the rpm utility checks dependencies during uninstall as well as install operations. If other software is installed on the system that is dependent on the package you are trying to uninstall, an error message will be displayed listing the dependent packages. You must first uninstall those packages before you can continue.

SCENARIO & SOLUTION

You need to uninstall an application that was originally installed from source code on your system. You've run ./configure in the installation directory. What command do you need to run next?	You need to run **make uninstall** from the installation directory.
You need to uninstall a package named BitTorrent from your system. What command would you use to do this?	You would enter **rpm –e BitTorrent** at the shell prompt.

Let's practice uninstalling an RPM package in the following exercise.

EXERCISE 8-4

Uninstalling RPM Packages

In this exercise, you will practice uninstalling the gftp client you installed in the previous exercise. Complete the following:

1. With your system running, open a terminal session.

2. If necessary, change to your root user account by entering **su –** followed by your root user's *password*.

3. At the shell prompt, enter **rpm –e gftp**. You should see a message indicating that gftp has been erased.

Let's next discuss how you can update RPM packages.

Updating Software

The ability of the rpm utility to manage dependencies is a real time-saver. However, it brings up the issue of updates. What if you have a package installed that needs to be updated, but it has many other packages that are dependent on it? Do you have to uninstall all of them before you can update the package? That would be a real pain!

Fortunately, this isn't the case. The rpm utility can be used to update an existing package without having to uninstall all of its dependent packages. This is done using the –U option with rpm. Using this option, the rpm utility will remove any existing older packages and then install a newer version of the package. For example, suppose you had an older version of gftp installed on your system and wanted to upgrade to version 2.0.18. To do this, you would enter **rpm –U gftp-2.0.18-23.i586.rpm** at the shell prompt.

Let's now discuss how you can query packages installed on your system.

Querying Packages

In addition to installing and upgrading packages on your system, the rpm command can also be used to query packages for information. This can be done using the –q (for *query*) option with rpm. Using the –q option, you can list all the packages installed on the system, view the version and release number of a specific package installed on the system, or view details about a package.

The –q option requires that you specify exactly what you want to query. For example, if you want to generate a list of all packages installed on the system, you would enter **rpm –qa**. A list of installed packages will then be displayed on the screen. This is shown in Figure 8-24.

Be warned that the list will probably be very long! If you need information about a specific package, you can use the following options with –q:

■ **–i** This option displays summary information about a specific package. For example, in Figure 8-25, the rpm –qi postfix command has been issued at the shell prompt to display information about the postfix package installed on the system.

■ **--whatrequires** This option displays a list of packages that require the specified packages. For example, entering **rpm –q --whatrequires postfix** will display a list of packages that require the postfix package.

FIGURE 8-24   Using rpm to list all installed packages

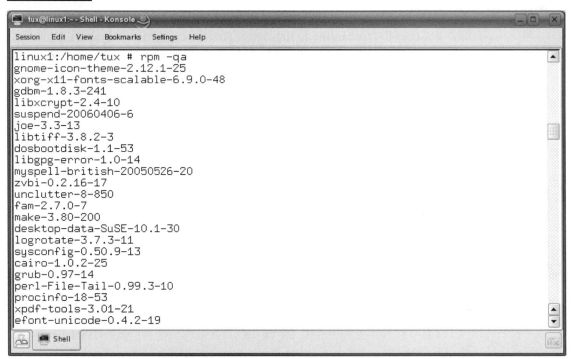

FIGURE 8-25   Viewing information about the postfix package using rpm

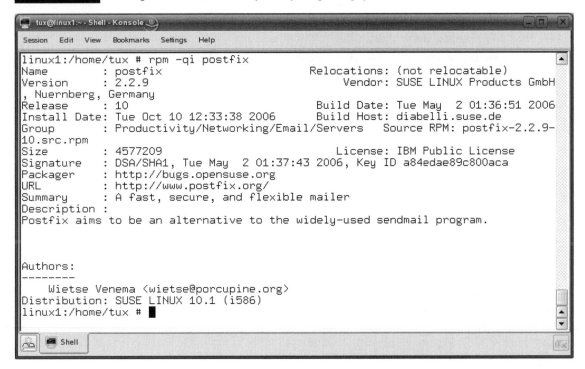

- **–l**   This option displays a list of files that are included in an RPM package.
- **--provides**   This option displays the functionality the specified package supplies.
- **--requires**   This useful option displays the functionality required by the specified package. For example, in Figure 8-26, the rpm –q --requires postfix command has been entered at the shell prompt.

Notice that a list of system requirements is displayed on the screen. Some of the information displayed refers to specific packages, such as netcfg. Other lines refer to specific utilities or executables, such as /sbin/ip. If you want to find out what packages provide the ip executable specified, you can enter **rpm –q --whatprovides ip** at the shell prompt. The rpm utility will then determine the name of the package that provides this program. In Figure 8-27, you can see that the iproute2-2.6.15-14 package provides the ip executable.

Before ending this chapter, let's discuss how you can use the rpm utility to verify packages.

FIGURE 8-26 Using the –q --requires option with rpm

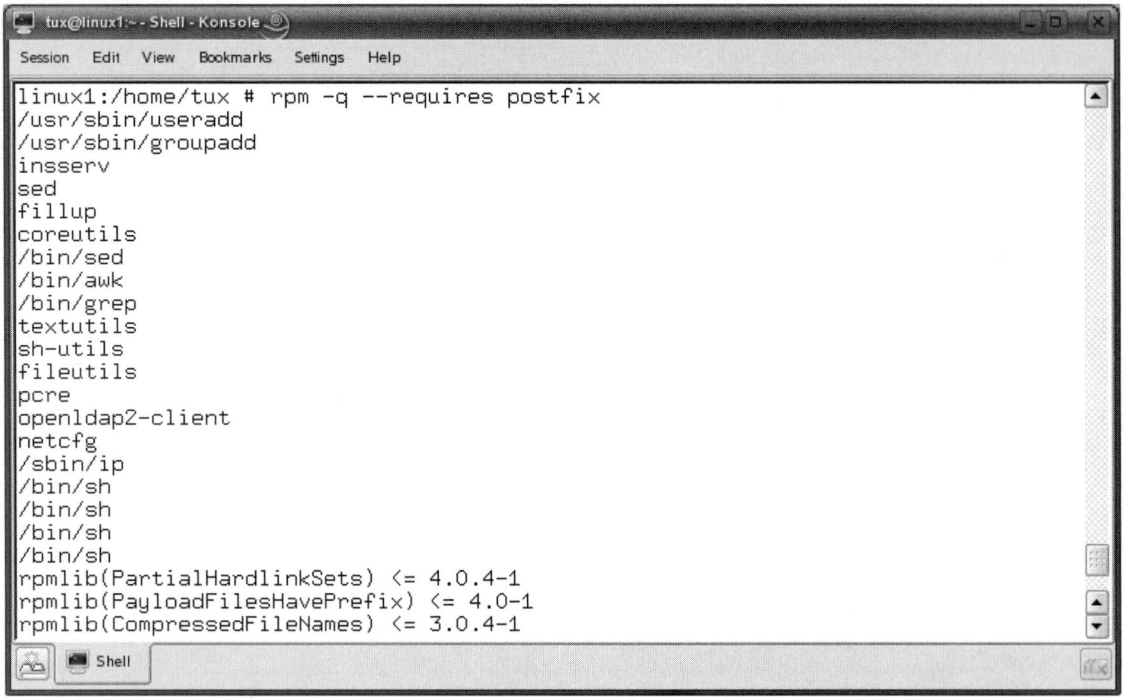

tux@linux1:~ - Shell - Konsole
Session Edit View Bookmarks Settings Help
linux1:/home/tux # rpm -q --requires postfix
/usr/sbin/useradd
/usr/sbin/groupadd
insserv
sed
fillup
coreutils
/bin/sed
/bin/awk
/bin/grep
textutils
sh-utils
fileutils
pcre
openldap2-client
netcfg
/sbin/ip
/bin/sh
/bin/sh
/bin/sh
/bin/sh
rpmlib(PartialHardlinkSets) <= 4.0.4-1
rpmlib(PayloadFilesHavePrefix) <= 4.0-1
rpmlib(CompressedFileNames) <= 3.0.4-1
Shell

Verifying Packages

In addition to querying packages, the rpm utility can also be used to verify packages on your system. As you are probably (painfully) aware, software can get corrupted, deleted, or otherwise messed up on any given computer system, regardless of the operating system. You can use the rpm utility to verify your installed packages and make sure everything is working the way it is supposed to. This is done using the –V option.

FIGURE 8-27 Using the –q --whatprovides option with rpm

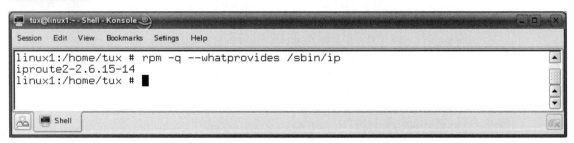

tux@linux1:~ - Shell - Konsole
Session Edit View Bookmarks Settings Help
linux1:/home/tux # rpm -q --whatprovides /sbin/ip
iproute2-2.6.15-14
linux1:/home/tux #
Shell

FIGURE 8-28   No errors detected by rpm

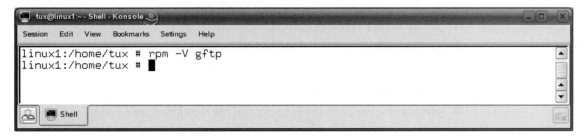

You can use –V to verify a single package by specifying its package name, such as
rpm –V gftp. You can also verify all packages on the system by entering **rpm –Va**.
Regardless of which option you choose, rpm will return no output if no errors are
found. For example, in Figure 8-28, the rpm –V gftp command was issued at the
command prompt. Because the package had no errors, nothing was written to the
screen and the rpm utility exited.

If an error does occur, rpm prints out the error message and the associated file
name, as shown in Figure 8-29.

The error messages generated during the verification process follow the
syntax of:

```
SM5DLUGT c file_name
```

The parameters in the error message stand for the following:

- **S**   Indicates a problem in the size of a file.
- **M**   Indicates a problem with a file's mode.
- **5**   Indicates a problem with the MD5 checksum of a file.

FIGURE 8-29   Errors detected by rpm

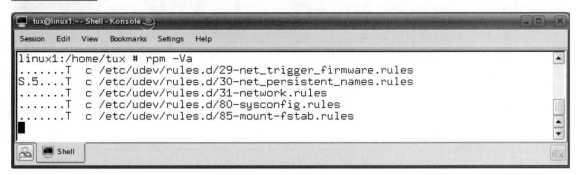

- **D**   Indicates a problem with a file's revision numbers.
- **L**   Indicates a problem with a file's symbolic link.
- **U**   Indicates a problem with a file's ownership.
- **G**   Indicates a problem with a file's group.
- **T**   Indicates a problem with the modification time of a file.
- **c**   Indicates the specified file is a configuration file.
- ***file_name***   Specifies the name of the file that failed verification.

For example, refer back to Figure 8-29. Any time one of the preceding letters is represented by a **.** in the output, it indicates that no problem was found with this parameter for the specified file. A letter displayed indicates a problem was found for this particular parameter for the specified file. For example, in Figure 8-29, the /etc/udev/rules.d/30-net_persistent_names.rules file had errors S, 5, and T, indicating there was a problem with the size, checksum, and modification time of the file. We also know that it is a configuration file because there's a c on the line as well.

In Figure 8-29, notice that all of the errors encountered by rpm were associated with configuration files. This actually isn't a problem. Configuration files, naturally, get modified all the time and, hence, fail to verify.

If other files, such as executables, fail to verify, then you should be more concerned. Based on the output from rpm –V, you may determine that you need to repair an installed package. You can use rpm to do this as well, using the –U --replacepkgs option. For example, if we determined that we needed to reinstall the gftp package, we could enter **rpm –U --replacepkgs gftp-2.0.18-23.i586.rpm** at the shell prompt to force rpm to install the gftp package from the original rpm even though it is already installed.

SCENARIO & SOLUTION

You currently have bind-9.1.0-12.i586.rpm installed on your system and want to upgrade to bind-9.3.2-17.i586. rpm. What command would you use to do this?	You need to enter **rpm –U bind-9.3.2-17.i586.rpm**.
You need to view summary information about the bind package installed on your system. What command would you use to do this?	You would enter **rpm –qi bind** at the shell prompt.

Let's practice managing RPM packages in the following exercise.

EXERCISE 8-5

Managing RPM Packages

In this exercise, you will practice managing RPM packages installed on your system. Complete the following:

1. With your system running, open a terminal session.

2. If necessary, change to your root user account by entering **su –** followed by your root user's *password*.

3. List all of the RPM packages installed on your system by entering **rpm –qa** at the shell prompt.

4. View information about the rpm utility itself by entering **rpm –qi rpm | more**.

5. Identify packages that require the rpm package by entering **rpm –q --whatrequires rpm**. What packages require rpm?

6. Identify components required by the rpm utility by entering **rpm –q --requires rmp**. What is required by rpm?

7. One of the components required by rpm is libz.so.1. Determine what package provides this component by entering **rpm –q --whatprovides libz.so.1**. What package provides this component?

That's it for this chapter! The terms *tarball* and *rpm* should no longer frighten you because you know how to effectively manage software on a Linux system!

CERTIFICATION SUMMARY

In this chapter, we discussed how you go about managing software on a Linux system. We first pointed out that you can use either graphical or command-line tools to manage software on a Linux system. We emphasized that a good Linux admin shouldn't be dependent on the graphical tools to manage software. He or she should also know how to use command-line software management tools. We also pointed out that not all software can be managed using graphical utilities. In addition, the Linux+ exam focuses on command-line utilities.

We then spent time reviewing the various resources available to you for obtaining Linux software. These include the following:

- Your installation CD or DVD
- Open source project Web sites
- http://www.rpmfind.net
- http://www.sourceforge.net
- http://linux.tucows.com
- http://www.freshmeat.net
- http://www.linux.org

We also pointed out that you should verify your downloads using checksums whenever possible. You should generate a checksum using the sum command on the file you downloaded and compare it to the checksum provided on the Web site where you obtained it.

We then discussed the process you need to follow to install software from source code. We pointed out that most software installed in this manner is distributed in tarball format. After downloading the file, you need to use the tar –zxvf command to extract the files from the tarball file. Once extracted, you switch to the new directory created when the tarball was extracted and run **./configure**. This script checks your system and creates the Makefile file.

You then run the make command to create the binary executable file from the source code text files using the instructions provided in the Makefile file. Once done, you use the make install command to install the executable on the system.

We then shifted gears and reviewed the process for installing software using RPM files. We pointed out that you have to use a package manager to manage packaged software, such as the Red Hat Package Manager (RPM). RPM packages are precompiled software packages that the package manager can install on your system. Because they are precompiled, you need to verify that a given package is compatible with your system before installing it. To do this, you need to review the package file name. The package file name includes the following information:

- Package name
- Version number
- Release number
- Compatible distribution (optional)
- Architecture type

You can enter **rpm --checksig** to verify the digital signature of an RPM package before you install it. You can then enter **rpm –i** to actually install the package file on your system. We pointed out that many RPM packages are dependent on other packages being installed on the system for them to work properly. If these packages aren't present, the software won't run. The rpm utility automatically checks to see if dependent software is installed before it installs a new package. You can also run **rpm –test** to check for dependencies before installing.

We then discussed the process you need to follow to uninstall software from your Linux system. We pointed out that the process required depends on how the software was installed in the first place. Software installed from source code will use either an uninstall script in the original installation files or an UNINSTALL target in the Makefile file that is called using the configure and the make uninstall commands. To uninstall an RPM package, you enter **rpm –e**.

We also pointed out that you can use the rpm command to update an existing package to a newer version. This is done using the rpm –U command. The rpm command can also be used to query and verify RPM packages. To query a package, you use the –q option with rpm. To verify a package, you use the –V option. If you determine that a package has been damaged, you can re-install an existing package by entering **rpm –U --replacepkgs**.

✓ # TWO-MINUTE DRILL

Install Software on Linux

❑ You can use either graphical or command-line tools to manage Linux software.

❑ A good Linux administrator can use either type of utility.

❑ A great deal of software is freely available for Linux systems.

❑ Your distribution CDs or DVD is a great resource for Linux software.

❑ A variety of Web sites are available for downloading Linux software.

❑ If possible, you should verify your downloads by comparing a checksum value you create with the sum command against the checksum value specified on the Web site where you obtained the file.

❑ To install from source code, you first download and extract a tarball file.

❑ In the installation directory, you run configure, make, and make install.

❑ The configure command checks your system to verify compatibility and creates the Makefile file.

❑ The make command compiles a binary executable from the source code text using the specifications in the Makefile file.

❑ The make install command installs the compiled executable.

❑ RPM packages are installed using the Red Hat Package Manager (RPM).

❑ RPM packages are compiled for a specific architecture and sometimes a specific Linux distribution.

❑ You can tell what architecture a package file is intended for by looking at the file name, which contains the following information:

  ❑ Package name
  ❑ Version number
  ❑ Release number
  ❑ Compatible distribution (optional)
  ❑ Architecture type

❑ You can enter **rpm --checksig** to verify the digital signature of an RPM package before you install it.

❑ You can enter **rpm –i** to install a package file on your system.

Manage Installed Software

❑ The process required to uninstall software from a Linux system depends on how the software was installed in the first place.

❑ Software installed from source code will use one of the following:

    ❑ An uninstall script in the original installation files

    ❑ An UNINSTALL target in the Makefile file that is called using the configure and the make uninstall commands.

❑ To uninstall an RPM package, you use the rpm –e command.

❑ You can update an existing package to a newer version using the rpm –U command.

❑ The rpm command can be used to query and verify RPM packages.

❑ To query a package, you use the –q option with rpm.

❑ To verify a package, you use the –V option with rpm.

❑ If you determine that a package has been damaged, you can re-install an existing package by entering **rpm –U --replacepkgs**.

SELF TEST

Install Software on Linux

1. What type of software can be managed with a graphical software utility such as YaST?

   A. RPM packages

   B. Text-based script files

   C. Software compiled from downloaded source code

   D. Programs compiled from source code written by the end user

2. You've just downloaded a file named FC-6-i386-DVD.iso to the /home/tux directory on your Linux system. What command would you use to generate a checksum value?

   A. checksum /home/tux/ FC-6-i386-DVD.iso

   B. sum /home/tux/ FC-6-i386-DVD.iso

   C. verify /home/tux/ FC-6-i386-DVD.iso

   D. rpm –V /home/tux/ FC-6-i386-DVD.iso

3. You've just downloaded a file named FC-6-i386-DVD.iso and have generated a checksum value. The value generated is slightly different from that shown on the download Web site. What does this imply?

   A. The downloaded copy is different than the original; but the download is still usable as long as the differences are minor.

   B. The version number is incremented by 1 when the file was downloaded.

   C. The downloaded copy is different than the original copy and shouldn't be used.

   D. The downloaded copy is exactly the same as the original copy.

4. You've just downloaded a file named BitTorrent-5.0.1.tar.gz to your home directory. Assuming the current directory is ~, what command would you enter at the shell prompt to extract all of the files from this archive?

   A. gzip –d ./ BitTorrent-5.0.1.tar.gz

   B. tar –axvf ./ BitTorrent-5.0.1.tar.gz

   C. tar –xvf ./ BitTorrent-5.0.1.tar.gz

   D. tar –zxvf ./ BitTorrent-5.0.1.tar.gz

5. What does the configure script do in an application's installation directory? (Choose two.)

   A. It compiles the source code into a binary executable.

   B. It checks the local system to verify that the necessary components are available.

    C. It copies the binary executable and other files, such as documentation, to the appropriate directories in the file system.

    D. It creates the Makefile file.

    E. It verifies that the installation files haven't been corrupted or tampered with.

6. What does the make command do when installing an application from source code?

    A. It compiles the source code into a binary executable.

    B. It checks the local system to verify that the necessary components are available.

    C. It copies the binary executable and other files, such as documentation, to the appropriate directories in the file system.

    D. It creates the Makefile file.

    E. It verifies that the installation files haven't been corrupted or tampered with.

7. What does the make install command do when installing an application from source code?

    A. It compiles the source code into a binary executable.

    B. It checks the local system to verify that the necessary components are available.

    C. It copies the binary executable and other files, such as documentation, to the appropriate directories in the file system.

    D. It creates the Makefile file.

    E. It verifies that the installation files haven't been corrupted or tampered with.

8. Where does the RPM Package Manager store its database of installed packages?

    A. /var/lib/rpm

    B. /etc/rpm

    C. /var/rpmdb

    D. /tmp/rpm

9. You've just downloaded an RPM package file named evolution-2.6.0-41.i586.rpm to your home directory. Assuming the current directory is ~, what command could you use to check the digital signature of the downloaded file to verify that it hasn't been tampered with?

    A. rpm –checksig ./evolution-2.6.0-41.i586.rpm

    B. rpm –verify ./evolution-2.6.0-41.i586.rpm

    C. rpm –tamperproof ./evolution-2.6.0-41.i586.rpm

    D. rpm –signature ./evolution-2.6.0-41.i586.rpm

10. You've just downloaded an RPM package file named evolution-2.6.0-41.i586.rpm to your home directory. Assuming the current directory is ~, what command could you use to install the package on your system, displaying a progress indicator as the installation is completed?

- **A.** rpm –i ./evolution-2.6.0-41.i586.rpm
- **B.** rpm –ihv ./evolution-2.6.0-41.i586.rpm
- **C.** rpm –install ./evolution-2.6.0-41.i586.rpm
- **D.** rpm –install --progress ./evolution-2.6.0-41.i586.rpm

11. You've just downloaded an RPM package file named evolution-2.6.0-41.i586.rpm to your home directory. Assuming the current directory is ~, what command could you use to check the package for dependencies? (Choose two.)

- **A.** rpm –i ./evolution-2.6.0-41.i586.rpm
- **B.** rpm –test ./evolution-2.6.0-41.i586.rpm
- **C.** rpm –V ./evolution-2.6.0-41.i586.rpm
- **D.** rpm –deps ./evolution-2.6.0-41.i586.rpm
- **E.** rpm –checkdeps ./evolution-2.6.0-41.i586.rpm

Manage Installed Software

12. You need to uninstall the Pure-FTPd service from your Linux system. You've switched to the directory where the original installation files are located. What's the first command you need to enter to uninstall this package?

- **A.** ./configure
- **B.** make
- **C.** make remove
- **D.** make uninstall

13. You've installed an RPM package file named evolution-2.6.0-41.i586.rpm on your Linux system. What command would you use to uninstall this package?

- **A.** rpm –U evolution
- **B.** rpm –U --remove evolution
- **C.** rpm –i --remove evolution
- **D.** rpm –e evolution

14. You currently have an RPM package file named evolution-2.2.0-2.i586.rpm installed on your Linux system. You've recently downloaded the evolution-2.6.0-41.i586.rpm package from http://www.sourceforge.net. What command would you use to install the newer version of this package?

    A. rpm –U evolution-2.6.0-41.i586.rpm

    B. rpm –i evolution-2.6.0-41.i586.rpm

    C. rpm –i --upgrade evolution-2.6.0-41.i586.rpm

    D. rpm –e evolution-2.2.0-2.i586.rpm

15. You currently have an RPM package file named evolution-2.6.0-41.i586.rpm installed on your Linux system. What command would you enter to display summary information about the package?

    A. rpm –s evolution-2.6.0-41.i586.rpm

    B. rpm –qs evolution-2.6.0-41.i586.rpm

    C. rpm –qi evolution-2.6.0-41.i586.rpm

    D. rpm –V --summary evolution-2.6.0-41.i586.rpm

16. You've used the rpm command with the –q --requires option to determine the components required by the rpm package. One of the required components is /usr/bin/perl. What command would you enter to find out which RPM package provides this component?

    A. rpm –q --whatprovides /usr/bin/perl

    B. rpm –qs --requires /usr/bin/perl

    C. rpm –qi --requires /usr/bin/perl

    D. rpm –q --provides perl

17. You've used the rpm command with the –V option to verify an rpm package installed on your system. The output from the command listed the following error code:

```
S.5....T c /opt/kde3/share/config/kdm/kdmrc
```

    What does this error code indicate? (Choose two.)

    A. There's a problem with the size of the file.

    B. There's a problem with the mode of the file.

    C. There's a problem with the timestamp of the file.

    D. There's a problem with a file's revision numbers.

    E. There's a problem with a file's ownership.

LAB QUESTION

You've just downloaded a tarball file from http://www.sourceforge.net named rdesktop-1.5.0.tar.gz. The file is currently saved in the /root directory. Outline the steps you would follow to install this software on your Linux system.

SELF TEST ANSWERS

Install Software on Linux

1. ☑ **A.** Most graphical software management utilities can only manage RPM package files.
   ☒ **B, C,** and **D** are incorrect. **B** is incorrect because script files can't be managed by graphical software management utilities. **C** is incorrect because programs compiled from source code usually can't be managed by graphical software management utilities. **D** is incorrect for the same reason.

2. ☑ **B.** The sum /home/tux/ FC-6-i386-DVD.iso command will generate a checksum value for the file specified.
   ☒ **A, C,** and **D** are incorrect. **A** is a distracter. There's no such utility as checksum. **C** is a distracter. There's no such utility as verify. **D** can be used to verify an RPM package, but it won't work with an ISO image; nor will it generate a checksum value.

3. ☑ **C.** A variance in the checksum values indicates the two copies of the file are different in some way. You shouldn't use the file in this situation because it probably is corrupt.
   ☒ **A, B,** and **D** are incorrect. **A** is correct in that the two files are different. However, you shouldn't use the file. **B** is a distracter. The version number isn't incremented when a file is copied. **D** is incorrect. A variance in the checksum values indicates the two copies of the file are different in some way.

4. ☑ **D.** To extract the file, you would enter **tar –zxvf ./ BitTorrent-5.0.1.tar.gz**.
   ☒ **A, B,** and **C** are incorrect. **A** will decompress the file, but it won't extract the files from the tar archive. **B** uses an incorrect option (–a). **C** omits the –z option required to first decompress the file before extracting files from the archive.

5. ☑ **B and D.** The configure script is used to check the local system to make sure it has the components required to install and run the software. It also creates the Makefile file.
   ☒ **A, C,** and **E** are incorrect. **A** is performed by the make command. **C** is performed by the make install command. **E** is performed by the sum command.

6. ☑ **A.** The make command compiles the text-based source code into a binary executable that can be run on the system.
   ☒ **B, C, D,** and **E** are incorrect. **B** is performed by the configure command. **C** is performed by the make install command. **D** is also performed by the configure command. **E** is performed by the sum command.

7. ☑ **C.** The make install command actually installs the program and its associated support files (such as documentation and configuration files) into the appropriate directories in the file system.

☒ **A, B, D,** and **E** are incorrect. **A** is performed by the make command. **B** is performed by the configure command. **D** is also performed by the configure command. **E** is performed by the sum command.

8. ☑ **A.** The RPM database is stored in /var/lib/rpm.

☒ **B, C,** and **D** are incorrect. Each of these options is a distracter.

9. ☑ **A.** The rpm –checksig ./evolution-2.6.0-41.i586.rpm command would be used to check the file's digital signature.

☒ **B, C,** and **D** are incorrect. **B** is incorrect because the –verify option isn't valid. To run a verify, you would use –V. However, this option requires that the package be installed first and won't check the package's digital signature. **C** and **D** also use invalid rpm command options.

10. ☑ **B.** The rpm –ihv ./evolution-2.6.0-41.i586.rpm command will install the file and display a progress indicator composed of hash marks on the screen as the installation progresses.

☒ **A, C,** and **D** are incorrect. **A** will install the file correctly. However it won't display a progress indicator on the screen. **C** and **D** are distracters that use invalid rpm command options.

11. ☑ **A** and **B.** The rpm –i ./evolution-2.6.0-41.i586.rpm and the rpm –test ./evolution-2.6.0-41.i586.rpm commands will both automatically check the package for required dependencies and prompt you if any are missing.

☒ **C, D,** and **E** are incorrect. **C** would verify the package if it were already installed. However, it can't be used to test for dependencies before installing a package. **D** and **E** are distracters that use invalid rpm command options.

Manage Installed Software

12. ☑ **A.** The ./configure command would be used first to generate the Makefile file. This file contains the UNINSTALL target that can then be used with the make utility to uninstall the software.

☒ **B, C,** and **D** are incorrect. **B** is used to compile the executable from the source code text using the parameters in the Makefile file. **C** is a distracter. **D** would be the next command used *after* running the configure script to actually uninstall the service's files from the file system.

13. ☑ **D.** To erase the rpm from the system, you would enter **rpm –e evolution**.

☒ **A, B,** and **C** are incorrect. **A** could be used to upgrade the rpm if you had a newer version and specified its full name on the command line. **B** uses invalid syntax. **C** also uses invalid syntax for the rpm command.

14. ☑ **A.** The rpm –U evolution-2.6.0-41.i586.rpm command will upgrade the existing rpm to the newer version.

    ☒ **B, C,** and **D** are incorrect. **B** could be used to install the rpm if it didn't already exist in the system. However, because a prior version is already installed, the –i option will generate an error when run. **C** is a distracter that uses invalid rpm command syntax. **D** could conceivably be part of a correct response. This command will uninstall the old version from the system. However, you would then have to use the command in response **B** to install the new version. Using the –U option accomplishes both steps at the same time.

15. ☑ **C.** The rpm –qi evolution-2.6.0-41.i586.rpm command will query the package and display summary information on the screen.

    ☒ **A, B,** and **D** are incorrect. Each of these responses is a distracter that uses incorrect rpm command syntax.

16. ☑ **A.** The rpm –q --whatprovides /usr/bin/perl command will display the name of the package that provides this component. You could also just enter **rpm –q --whatprovides perl** to get the same information.

    ☒ **B, C,** and **D** are incorrect. **B** and **C** are distracters that use invalid rpm command syntax. **D** is incorrect because it will display the components provided by the perl package.

17. ☑ **A and C.** The S, 5, and T in the error code indicate that there is a problem with the file's size, MD5 checksum, and timestamp. The c indicates that the file is a configuration file, so these errors may or may not be significant.

    ☒ **B, D,** and **E** are incorrect. **B** would be indicated by an M in the error code. **D** would be indicated by a D in the error code. **E** would be indicated by a U in the error code.

LAB ANSWER

To install this package, you would first open a terminal session on the system and switch to your root user account using the su – command (if necessary). You would then switch to the /root directory by entering **cd /root**.

If a checksum is available on the Web site where the tarball archive was downloaded, you would enter **sum ./rdesktop-1.5.0.tar.gz** and compare the resulting checksum value against the original checksum. If they are the same, you're in good shape! If not, then you know that the copy of the file on your local hard drive is somehow different from the original file on the Web site. This is not a good thing. You should download a new copy and run the sum command against it again to verify that it arrived intact.

At this point, you need to decompress and extract the installation files from the archive. This can be done by entering **tar –zxvf ./rdesktop-1.5.0.tar.gz** at the shell prompt. Doing this creates a new directory in /root named rdesktop-1.5.0. The files from the archive are extracted to this directory.

With the files extracted from the tarball, you can now start the installation process. To do this, first switch to the installation directory by entering **cd rdesktop-1.5.0** at the shell prompt. You should probably enter **ls** and verify that files needed to run the installation are present in the directory.

To start the install, you first enter **./configure** at the shell prompt. This script will check the system and verify its architecture and Linux distribution. It will also verify that you have all the necessary components installed, such as a C compiler. It will also create the Makefile file that contains the parameters necessary for the software to be installed on your particular system. If desired, you could use cat or less to view the Makefile file and verify that it is configured the way you want.

After the configure script is done, you then compile the binary executable from the source code by entering **make** at the shell prompt. When it's done, you would then enter **make install** to install the executable and its associated support files in the appropriate location in the file system.

With the software installed, you could then run the **rdesktop** executable from the shell prompt and verify that the program is functioning correctly.

9
Using the Linux Shell

I t's time to become better acquainted with the Linux shell! As we've progressed through this book, we've spent a lot of time working from the command line on our Linux system. The command-line interface we've been using is provided by the Linux *shell*. That's why we frequently refer to the *shell prompt*. You've learned how to use shell commands to manage the file system, manage users and groups, edit text files, and install applications. The shell prompt works great for executing commands such as these.

However, it also works very well for a variety of other tasks as well. The shell is actually a very powerful tool in and of itself for managing the Linux operating system. In this chapter, we're going to explore how to do this. We're going to discuss the following topics:

- ■ Introducing the Bourne Again Shell
- ■ Working with Linux environment variables
- ■ Managing shell command inputs and outputs
- ■ Creating shell scripts

INSIDE THE EXAM

Using the Linux Shell

As you've probably ascertained as you've progressed through this book, the Linux+ certification program has a heavy emphasis on using the command line to do just about everything. You're not going to be tested on graphical configuration utilities such as linuxconf or YaST. Therefore, you need to become very proficient with the Linux shell to pass your Linux+ exam. You should be particularly familiar with the bash shell.

You should become very comfortable working with environment variables as well as redirecting inputs and outputs from the command line. On your Linux+ exam, be prepared to see questions that expect you to know how to set the values of environment variables and make them persistent at shell startup. Also be prepared for questions that require you to know how to redirect output from a command into another program for processing.

In addition, you will be expected to know how to create basic shell scripts. You should be familiar with the basic structure of a shell script, how to make it executable, and how to read user input and assign the data to a variable.

Let's begin this chapter by introducing you to the Bourne Again Shell.

Use the Bourne Again Shell

Earlier in this book, we reviewed several of the shells available for you to use on your Linux system when we introduced you to the command-line environment. Depending upon your needs and preferences, you can select from the Bourne shell (sh), the Korn shell (ksh), the C shell (csh), and so on.

However, the default shell used on most Linux systems is the Bourne Again Shell (bash). (It's also the shell you need to know for your Linux+ exam!). The bash shell has been around for a very long time. It originated on the UNIX operating system back in the 1970s and was ported to the earliest Linux distributions in the early 1990s. Today, bash has become one of the most widely used shells on Linux as well as other operating systems, including Apple's OS X and even (optionally) Novell's NetWare.

Therefore, we're going to focus our discussion here on the bash shell. The bash shell does some cool things that make it the shell of choice for many Linux users and administrators. In this part of this chapter, we're going to review the following:

- Reviewing the bash configuration files
- Using command history
- Using command completion

Let's begin by reviewing the files used to configure the bash shell.

Reviewing the bash Configuration Files

You can customize your shell environment within bash using several configuration files. The files actually used depend on whether you are using a *login shell* or a *non-login shell*. A login shell is in use if your Linux system boots to a text-based login screen and you use it to log in to the system. In other words, a login shell is what you are using if your system boots to runlevel 3. This is shown in Figure 9-1.

FIGURE 9-1	
	Fedora Core release 5 (Bordeaux)
	Kernel 2.6.15-1.2054_FC5 on an i686
Using a login shell	
	fedora login: _

Even if your system is configured to boot into a graphical environment (runlevel 5), you're still running a login shell. It's hiding behind your desktop. If you open a terminal session within your desktop environment, however, you are not using a login shell. Instead, you are running a non-login shell. This is shown in Figure 9-2.

Why do we care? Because the type of shell you're using dictates what configuration files are read to customize your shell environment. These files are listed in Table 9-1.

If you're using a non-login shell, things are pretty straightforward. The bash shell simply reads ~/.bashrc from the user's home directory.

If you're using a login shell, bash first reads /etc/profile and runs the configurations specified in that file. After that, however, things get a little more complex. As you may

FIGURE 9-2   Using a non-login shell

TABLE 9-1   bash Shell Configuration Files

bash Configuration File	Type of Shell	Function
~/.bashrc	Non-login shells (Although login shells on most distributions read this file as well. It is usually called from one of the configuration files listed below)	Stores individual users' shell preferences
/etc/profile	Login shells	Contains configuration parameters that are applied system-wide
~/.bash_profile	Login shells	Stores individual users' shell preferences
~/.bash_login	Login shells	Stores individual users' shell preferences
~/.profile	Login shells	Stores individual users' shell preferences
~/.bash_logout	Login shells	Specifies actions to be performed when a user logs out from the shell

have noticed in Table 9-1, several of the files listed sound like they do exactly the same thing. You're right, they do. The issue here is that not all distributions use *all* of these files. For example, a Fedora system uses ~/.bashrc, ~bash_profile, and ~bash_logout. This is shown in Figure 9-3.

Alternatively, on a SUSE Linux system, the ~/.bashrc and ~/.profile files are used instead. This is shown in Figure 9-4.

When a login shell is run, the bash shell program searches for configuration files in the following order:

1. ~/.bash_profile
2. ~/.bash_login
3. ~/.profile

FIGURE 9-3   bash configuration files on Fedora

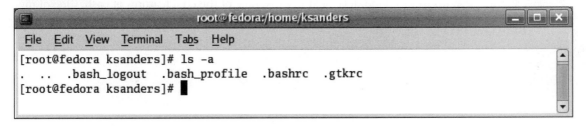

```
root@fedora:/home/ksanders
File  Edit  View  Terminal  Tabs  Help
[root@fedora ksanders]# ls -a
.  ..  .bash_logout  .bash_profile  .bashrc  .gtkrc
[root@fedora ksanders]#
```

FIGURE 9-4   bash configuration files on SUSE

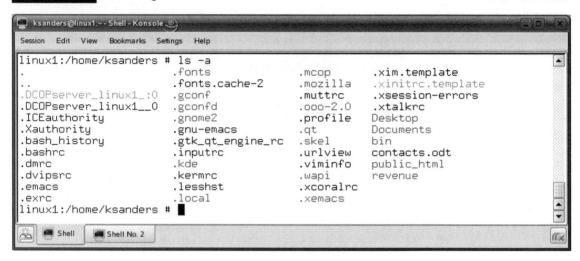

It uses the first file it finds and ignores all of the rest. As you can see in Figures 9-3 and 9-4, this isn't much of an issue on SUSE and Fedora. Remember that .bashrc is not read by bash when loading a login shell (although it is usually called by .bash_profile or .profile, so it actually is used for a login shell in reality). Therefore, bash, after reading /etc/profile, reads .bash_profile on a Fedora system. On a SUSE system, bash reads .profile after reading /etc/profile.

The .bash_logout file is only used when you log out of a login shell.

on the
Job
You can run multiple terminal sessions at the same time on your Linux system. In the graphical environment, you can simply run multiple terminal programs or open multiple tabs within a single terminal program.
In a text environment, you can press ALT-F1 to switch to the first session, ALT-F2 to switch to the second session, and so on up to ALT-F6.

With this in mind, let's next discuss some of the cool features of bash. One of my favorites is command history. Let's look at it next.

SCENARIO & SOLUTION

Which configuration file is used when a user opens a non-login bash shell?	The ~/.bashrc file is used.
You want to make a change that will be applied to all users on your Linux system whenever they open a bash shell. Which configuration file would you use to do this?	The best way to do this would be to add the change to /etc/profile. Alternatively, you could also make the change to the appropriate hidden bash configuration file in each user's home directory.

Using Command History

The bash shell supports command history. Every time you enter a command at the shell prompt, that command is saved in the ~/.bash_history file in your home directory, as shown in Figure 9-5.

FIGURE 9-5   Storing shell commands in .bash_history

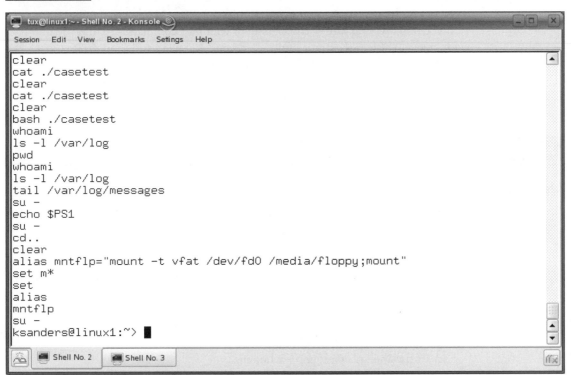

FIGURE 9-6	Searching your command history

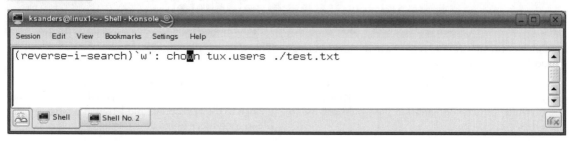

If you use cat to view this file, you'll see that it is just a simple (hidden) text file that contains all of your previously entered shell commands, one on each line. This file is continually updated each time you enter a shell command.

If you press the UP ARROW key at the shell prompt, bash will read this file and display the last command you entered. If you press the UP ARROW key repeatedly, you can scroll through a list of your last used commands. When you arrive at the one you want, simply press ENTER to execute the command. I love this feature, especially if I need to retype a very long, complex command. Just hit the UP ARROW key and press ENTER!

If you don't want to arrow through all of your past commands to find the one you want, you can also enter a part of the command you need and then press CTRL-R. The bash shell will search through your command history and display the most recent matching command. The result is shown in Figure 9-6.

Let's practice using command history in the following exercise.

EXERCISE 9-1

Using Command History

In this exercise, you will practice using command history in the bash shell. Complete the following:

1. Boot your Linux system and log in as a standard user. If you used the lab exercise in Chapter 3 to install your system, you can log in as **tux** with a password of **M3linux273**.

2. At the shell prompt, enter **ls –l /var/log**.

3. At the shell prompt, enter **pwd**.

4. At the shell prompt, enter **whoami**.

5. Run the ls command in step 2 again by pressing the UP ARROW key three times and then pressing ENTER.

6. Use the UP ARROW key to run the pwd command again.

7. Use the UP ARROW key to run the whoami command again.

In addition to command history, the bash shell also offers command completion. Let's talk about this feature next.

Using Command Completion

I also love the command completion feature offered by the bash shell. This feature is extremely helpful when you need to enter a very long file name in a command line. The command completion feature allows you to simply press the TAB key while entering a command at the shell prompt. When you do, the bash shell "guesses" what it is you want to type and then automatically completes the command for you.

For example, in Figure 9-7, a file named vmware-linux-tools.tar.gz exists in root's home directory. I need to extract this tarball archive so I can install the application it contains. If I wanted to, I could type out the full command **tar –zxvf ./vmware-linux-tools.tar.gz** at the shell prompt and tar would take care of this for me.

However, if you're like me, your fingers don't always do what you tell them to do. I tend to make a lot of typos when I'm typing commands, especially when dealing with long file names as in this example. Therefore, I could also opt to use command completion to take care of the typing for me. I could enter **tar –zxvf ./vmw** at the shell prompt, as shown in Figure 9-7.

Then I can press the TAB key. When I do, the bash shell looks at the files in the current directory that begin with vmw and determines that I probably am referring to the vmware-linux-tools.tar.gz file. It then tacks this file on to the end of my command, as shown in Figure 9-8.

All I then have to do is press ENTER. Command completion is great!

FIGURE 9-7   Entering part of a command at the shell prompt

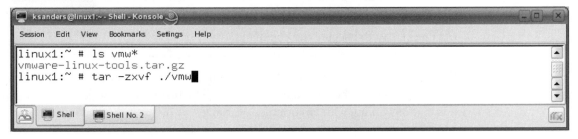

| FIGURE 9-8 | Using command completion |

Let's practice using command completion in the following exercise.

EXERCISE 9-2

Using Command Completion

In this exercise, you will practice using command completion in the bash shell. Complete the following:

1. If necessary, boot your Linux system and log in as a standard user. If you used the lab exercise in Chapter 3 to install your system, you can log in as **tux** with a password of **M3linux273**.
2. Change to your root user account by entering **su –** followed by your root password.
3. At the shell prompt, type **tail /var/log/m**, but don't press ENTER yet.
4. Press the TAB key twice. A list of all files in /var/log/ that start with "m" should be displayed.
5. Add an **e** to the command, but don't press ENTER yet. Your command prompt should display tail /var/log/me.
6. Press the TAB key. The command should automatically display tail /var/log/ messages.
7. Press ENTER to execute the command.

Now that you know how to use the bash shell, let's talk about some of the tasks that you need to know how to complete with it. The first topic we're going to deal with is that of working with environment variables.

CERTIFICATION OBJECTIVE 9.02

Manage Linux Environment Variables

Whenever you start a bash shell, several different variables are used to define critical parameters the shell needs to run properly. Because these variables define the shell environment, they are called *environment variables*. In this part of this chapter, we're going to spend some time learning about environment variables. Specifically, we're going to cover the following topics:

- What environment variables are
- Managing environment variables
- Creating user-defined variables
- Creating aliases

Let's begin by reviewing what environment variables are.

What Are Environment Variables?

Before you can understand what an environment variable is, you must first understand what a variable itself is. The best way to describe variables is to envision a bucket in which a variety of substances can be stored. This bucket has a name, such as "MyStuff," and you can fill it with sand, rocks, water, soil, and so on. If the bucket is already full of a particular substance, such as sand, you must empty it before you can fill it with another substance, such as rocks.

That's essentially how a variable in a Linux system works. It's an area in your system's RAM that's reserved to store whatever values you want to put in it. Essentially, it's a like a "bucket" in memory. Just as you must empty out a real bucket before you can pour a new substance in, you must also empty out a variable before you can assign a new value to it.

On your Linux system, you can define and use two different types of variables:

- User-defined
- Environment

User-defined variables are just that. They are "buckets" in memory that you create yourself. You can assign user-defined variables with a name of your choice. You can also assign whatever contents you want to them. User-defined variables can be very useful when working with shell scripts, discussed later in this chapter.

FIGURE 9-9 Changing to the home directory with the cd command

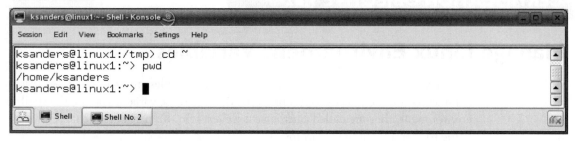

Environment variables, on the other hand, are initially created, named, and populated by the operating system itself. As the name implies, environment variables are used to configure the system's computing environment. Environment variables are frequently accessed and used by programs you run from the shell prompt. Using the information stored in these variables makes these programs much more flexible and robust.

For example, suppose we were to enter the **cd ~** command at the shell prompt, as shown in Figure 9-9.

You know from prior chapters in this book that this command will switch the current directory in the shell to the user's home directory, no matter what user is currently logged in. Notice in Figure 9-9 that, because ksanders is currently logged in, the cd ~ command changed the current directory to /home/ksanders. Also notice that nowhere in the command did we specify /home/ksanders. The cd command somehow knew that ~ pointed to /home/ksanders. If I were logged in as jmcarthur, however, the cd ~ command would have changed the current directory to /home/jmcarthur.

The question is, how does the cd command know what directory in the file system to switch to? The cd command checked the value of an environment variable named HOME. As you can see in Figure 9-10, the value of the HOME environment variable is set to the home directory path of the current user.

FIGURE 9-10 Viewing the value of the HOME environment variable

FIGURE 9-11   Viewing the value of the HOME environment variable for the tux user

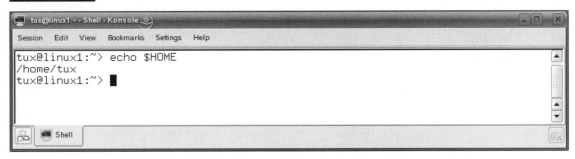

Because ksanders is currently logged in, the value of HOME is set to /home/ksanders. If, however, I were to log in as a user named tux, the value of the HOME environment variable is changed by the system to /home/tux. This is shown in Figure 9-11.

Your Linux system defines a number of environment variables like the HOME variable we just looked at. Some of the more pertinent environment variables commonly used on most Linux distributions are listed in Table 9-2.

Now that you know what environment variables are and the names of variables commonly used on a Linux system, let's next discuss how you go about managing your environment variables.

SCENARIO & SOLUTION

Which environment variable specifies the name of the bash configuration file used to configure the shell environment?	The ENV variable.
Which environment variable contains the path to the prior current directory?	The OLDPWD variable.
Which environment variable configures your shell prompt?	The PS1 variable.

TABLE 9-2   Commonly Used Environment Variables

Environment Variable	Stores	Default Value
BASH and SHELL	The full path to the shell executable	/bin/bash
CPU	The type of CPU installed in the system	Depends on your system. An Intel Pentium IV computer would have a value of i686
DISPLAY	The location where your X Windows display should be sent	0.0 (the local video card and monitor)
ENV	The name of the file bash read to configure its environment	~/.bashrc
EUID	The user ID (UID) of the current user	The UID number of the current user
HISTFILE	The path to the bash command history file	~/.bash_history
HISTSIZE	The number of commands saved in the command history file	1000
HOME	The path to the current user's home directory.	The current user's home directory
HOST and HOSTNAME	The hostname of the system	The hostname you assigned when you installed the system
INFODIR	The path to your system's info program	/usr/local/info:/usr/share/info:/usr/info
LOGNAME	The username of the current user	The username of the current user
MAIL	The path to the current user's mailbox file	/var/spool/mail/*username*
MANPATH	The path to your system's man program	/usr/local/man:usr/share/man:/usr/X11R6/man:/opt/gnome/share/man
OLDPWD	The path to the prior current directory	Depends on what your prior current directory was
OSTYPE	The type of operating system currently being run	Linux
PATH	A list of directories to be searched when running a command from the shell prompt	Depends on your distribution
PS1	The characters used to create the shell prompt	Depends on your distribution
PWD	The path to the current working directory	Depends on what your current directory is

Managing Environment Variables

For the most part, the values assigned to your environment variables by the system are usually sufficient for most tasks. However, there are occasions when you will need to manipulate the values assigned to your environment variables. To do this, you need to know how to manage them. In this part of this chapter, we'll discuss how to do just that. The following topics will be addressed:

- Viewing variables and their values
- Setting the value of a variable
- Making variables persistent

Let's begin by discussing how to view the value of a variable.

Viewing Variables and Their Values

If you need to see the value assigned to a variable on your system, you can use a variety of different commands from the shell prompt. If you need to see the value of a single variable, you can use the echo command. The syntax is echo $*variable*. For example, if I wanted to view the value of the PATH variable, I would enter **echo $PATH** at the shell prompt. This is shown in Figure 9-12.

As you can see in Figure 9-12, the contents of the PATH variable are displayed on the screen. Notice that when we use the echo command we must place a $ before the name of the variable. This is very important. The $ character tells the echo command that the text that follows is not a literal string, but is instead the name of a variable and that echo should retrieve the value of the variable and display it on the screen. If you omit the $ character, the echo command will display your variable name on the screen. For example, in Figure 9-13, the echo PATH command has been issued.

FIGURE 9-12   Using the echo command to view the value of a variable

FIGURE 9-13 Omitting the $ when entering the echo command

Notice that echo simply displayed "PATH" on the screen. That's because it didn't know that "PATH" was the name of a variable. The echo command thought you wanted the text string "PATH" displayed. Don't forget the $ character when using echo with variables!

As you saw above, the echo command works great for displaying the contents of a variable on the screen. However, it can only display the variables you specify. That means you have to know the name of the variables you want to view. What if you don't know the exact name of the variable? What if you want to view all of your variables at once?

In these situations you can use other shell commands to view your variables and their associated values. One of these is the set command. If you enter **set** at the shell prompt, all of your variables, including environment and user-defined variables, are displayed on the screen. Because the output of set can be very long, you should use | **more** with set to pause the output displayed one page at a time. (We'll discuss redirection later in this chapter.) For example, in Figure 9-14, the set | more command has been issued at the shell prompt.

As you can see, each variable is displayed along with its associated value. In addition to the set command, you can also use the env command to view your system's environment variables. As with set, the output of env can be very long, so you should append | **more** to the command to pause the display one page at a time. For example, in Figure 9-15, the env | more command has been issued.

As with set, the env command displays each variable and its current value. However, notice that env doesn't sort the variables. The set command actually sorts the variables alphabetically, which I really like!

These commands—echo, set, and env—all can be used to show you variables and their values. However, what if you need to change the value assigned to a variable? Let's talk about how this is done next.

FIGURE 9-14 Using the set command to view variables and their values

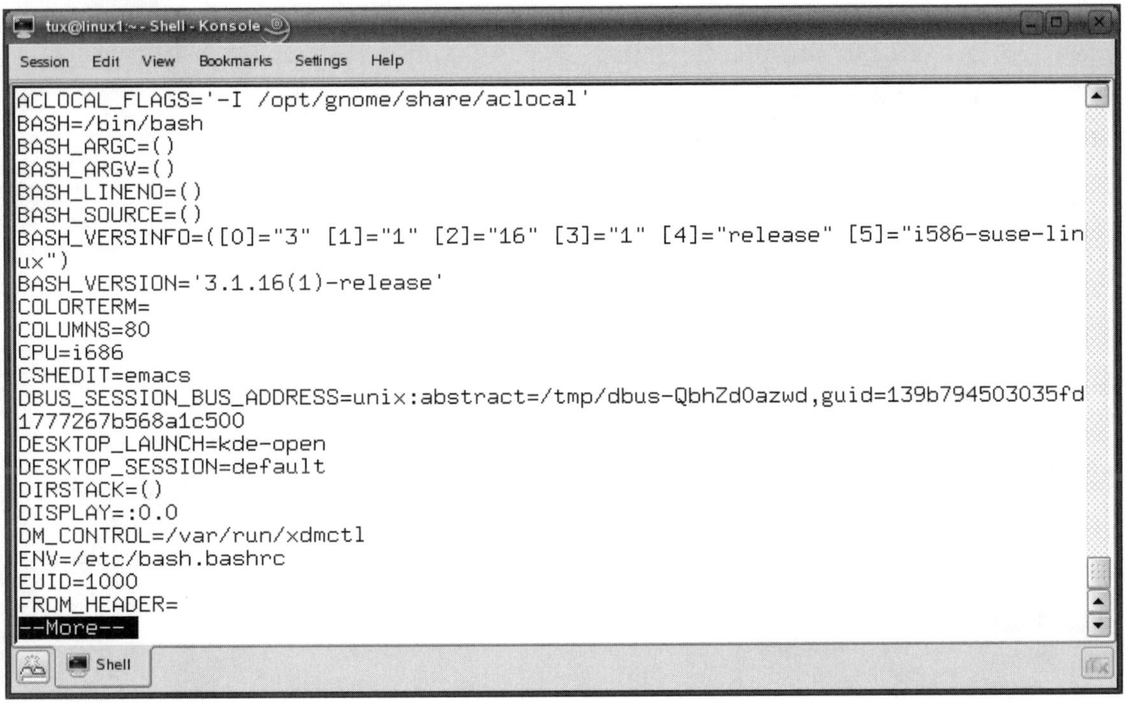
tux@linux1:~ - Shell - Konsole
Session Edit View Bookmarks Settings Help
ACLOCAL_FLAGS='-I /opt/gnome/share/aclocal'
BASH=/bin/bash
BASH_ARGC=()
BASH_ARGV=()
BASH_LINENO=()
BASH_SOURCE=()
BASH_VERSINFO=([0]="3" [1]="1" [2]="16" [3]="1" [4]="release" [5]="i586-suse-lin
ux")
BASH_VERSION='3.1.16(1)-release'
COLORTERM=
COLUMNS=80
CPU=i686
CSHEDIT=emacs
DBUS_SESSION_BUS_ADDRESS=unix:abstract=/tmp/dbus-QbhZd0azwd,guid=139b794503035fd
1777267b568a1c500
DESKTOP_LAUNCH=kde-open
DESKTOP_SESSION=default
DIRSTACK=()
DISPLAY=:0.0
DM_CONTROL=/var/run/xdmctl
ENV=/etc/bash.bashrc
EUID=1000
FROM_HEADER=
--More--
Shell

Setting the Value of a Variable

As we discussed earlier, most of the environment variables used on a Linux system work great using the values assigned to them by the system.

on the job

In fact, there are many environment variables that you should not change! For example, changing the value of the HOSTNAME variable could cause problems with many services running on your system.

However, there are times when you will need to change the value assigned to an environment variable. For example, you may need to add an additional directory to the end of the PATH variable. This can be a handy way to make life easier for your users (and for you as well). In addition, you may need to edit the DISPLAY variable to configure your X Windows System to send its display to a remote computer. Likewise, you may want to alter the shell prompt to display different information.

To do these tasks, you need to change the value of an environment variable. This is relatively easy to do. Simply enter ***variable=value*** at the shell prompt. For example, suppose you installed an application in /var/opt/mydb named myapp.

FIGURE 9-15   Using the env command to view variables and their values

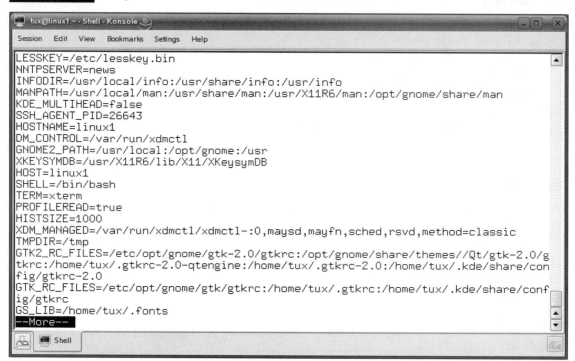

This path doesn't currently exist in your PATH variable and you want to add it so you won't have to use the full path when you want to run the program. To do this, you can enter **PATH=$PATH:/var/opt/mydb** at the shell prompt, as shown in Figure 9-16.

An important point to notice here is that I specified **$PATH** in the variable assignment command. This includes the current value of the PATH variable in

FIGURE 9-16   Setting the value of the PATH environment variable

the new value assignment. I then concatenated **:/var/opt/mydb** to the existing list of paths. If you don't include $PATH in your reassignment, then the current directories in your PATH variable will be *erased* and replaced by the new path you specify in the command! When this happens, your system will start to experience a host of problems!

on the

Job *Remember that setting the value of an environment variable will erase its current contents. If you want to preserve the current contents, use the technique just shown. If you do actually want to erase the contents of the variable and replace it with a new value, then you can simply enter* variable=value *at the shell prompt.*

However, we've still one more task to complete. We've assigned the value of PATH to include an additional directory. However, the new value of the PATH variable applies only to the current shell. If I were to open up another terminal session, the change that I made to PATH will not be applied. This is shown in Figure 9-17.

As you can see in Figure 9-17, the value of PATH doesn't include /var/opt/mydb even though I'm still logged in as the same user. To make the assignment apply to all shells, I need to export the new value of the variable. To do this, I enter **export** *variable* at the shell prompt. In this example, I need to enter **export PATH** at the shell prompt, as shown in Figure 9-18.

After doing so, the new value assigned to PATH is made available to all other shells, including any subshells created by the current shell.

Making Variables Persistent

One problem you will encounter in this process, however, is the fact that any new value you add to an environment variable will be lost after the system reboots. If the

| **FIGURE 9-17** | New variable value not exported |

```
tux@linux1:~ - Shell No. 2 - Konsole
Session   Edit   View   Bookmarks   Settings   Help

tux@linux1:~> echo $PATH
/home/tux/bin:/usr/local/bin:/usr/bin:/usr/X11R6/bin:/bin:/usr/games:/opt/gnome/
bin:/opt/kde3/bin:/usr/lib/jvm/jre/bin:/usr/lib/mit/bin:/usr/lib/mit/sbin
tux@linux1:~> █
```

| **FIGURE 9-18** | Exporting the new value of a variable |

change you made needs to be persistent across system restarts, then you need to edit one of your bash configuration files, discussed at the beginning of the chapter, and add the variable assignment to the file.

In the preceding example, I probably want my new PATH variable value assignment to be automatically made each time the system restarts. I don't want to have to manually set the value of PATH and export it each time the system reboots.

To do this, I can use the command to set the value of PATH to include /var/opt/mydb as well as the command to export the PATH variable to one of the following bash configuration files:

- ~/.bashrc
- ~/.bash_login
- /etc/profile
- ~/.profile
- ~/.bash_profile

on the **Job** *Adding the commands to /etc/profile will cause the change to be applied to all users. If you want to apply the change to only a single user, then you should use the configuration files found in that user's home directory.*

You need to determine which files your particular distribution uses. For example, in Figure 9-19, I've added the following commands to the ~/.profile file in the tux user's home directory:

```
PATH=$PATH:/var/opt/mydb
export PATH
```

Now, whenever the system boots and tux logs in, the /var/opt/mydb path is automatically added to his PATH environment variable. Because I added the command to the ~/.profile file in the tux user's home directory, it will not be added to any other user's PATH variable.

FIGURE 9-19   Making variable value assignments persistent

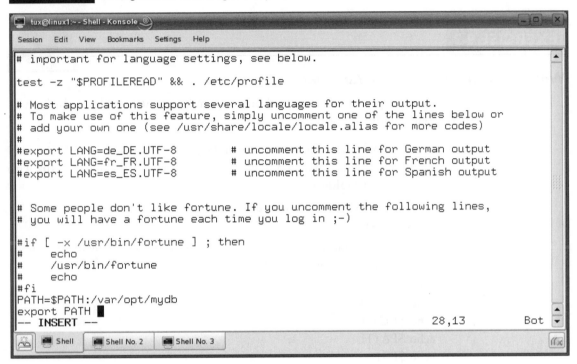

SCENARIO & SOLUTION

You need to view the value of the HOME variable. What command could you enter at the shell prompt to do this?	To view just the value of HOME, you could enter **echo $HOME**. You could also use **set** or **env**.
You want to add the ~/temp directory to the end of the list of directories in your PATH variable. What command would you enter at the shell prompt to do this?	You need to preserve your existing directories, so you would need to enter **PATH=$PATH:~/temp**. You would also need to enter **export PATH**.
You've added a directory to the PATH environment variable. However, when you reboot your system, the directory is missing. Why is this?	The changes aren't persistent. To make them persistent, you need to edit a bash configuration file and add the changes to it.

Let's practice working with environment variables in the following exercise.

EXERCISE 9-3

Working with Environment Variables

In this exercise, you will practice working with environment variables in the bash shell. Complete the following:

1. If necessary, boot your Linux system and log in as a standard user. If you used the lab exercise in Chapter 3 to install your system, you can log in as **tux** with a password of **M3linux273**.

2. Change to your root user account by entering **su –** followed by your root password.

3. At the shell prompt, view the value of the following environment variables by entering the following commands:

   echo $PWD
   echo $HOME
   echo $EUID
   echo $PATH
   echo $PS1

4. Change your shell prompt to display the currently logged-in user, the name of the Linux host, the current time, the full path to the current working directory, and a colon by doing the following:

   a. At the shell prompt enter **PS1="[\u@\h \t \w]:"**. The prompt should immediately change.

   b. At the shell prompt, enter **export PS1**.

   c. At your shell prompt, enter **ls –a**. Which file would you edit on your particular distribution if you wanted to make the changes to your PS1 environment variable persistent?

With this in mind, let's now talk about creating user-defined variables.

Creating a User-Defined Variable

In the preceding topics, we've focused on working with environment variables. These variables are automatically defined for you each time the system boots.

FIGURE 9-20   Creating a user-defined variable

However, you can actually create your own, customized variables as well. It sounds hard, but it really isn't. In fact, this is done in exactly the same way as when working with environment variables. Simply enter *variable=value* at the shell prompt.

For example, suppose I wanted to create a variable named ME and set it to a value of "Robb Tracy". I can do this by entering **ME="Robb Tracy"** at the shell prompt. Once done, a variable named ME is added to my list of variables and is set to a value of Robb Tracy. You can use the echo command to view the value of the ME variable, as shown in Figure 9-20.

As with environment variables, a user-defined variable is only available to the current instance of the shell. To make it available to other shells, including subshells created by the current shell, you need to export it with the export command. In this instance, I would enter **export ME** at the shell prompt.

In addition to echo, you can also use set or env to view user-defined variables just as you did with environment variables. An example of using set to view the ME variable I just created is shown in Figure 9-21.

As with environment variables, you can make a user-defined variable persistent by adding the appropriate commands to one of the bash configuration files discussed previously. When creating user-defined variables, keep the following rules in mind:

- Variable names can contain letters or numbers, but may not begin with a number.
- Variable names may contain "-" or "_" characters.
- While not required, you should try to use all uppercase characters when naming your variables. Notice when you enter set or env that all of your system's environment variables use uppercase names. You should do the same.

The last variable-related topic we need to address here is that of aliases. Let's discuss how aliases work next.

FIGURE 9-21   Using the set command to view the value of a user-defined variable

Creating Aliases

Aliases are really cool. Aliases are similar to variables in many ways, but have a very different function. An alias is basically a shortcut to a different file or command on your Linux system. When your system boots, a series of aliases are automatically created for you. You can view these by entering **alias** at the shell prompt. This is shown in Figure 9-22.

Notice in Figure 9-22 that a series of commands are listed that aren't really commands at all. Instead, they are aliases that point to real commands. For example, if you type **dir** at the shell prompt, the output from alias tells us that the ls –l command is actually run. Likewise, typing **..** will actually execute the cd .. command.

You can create your own aliases too. To do this, just enter **alias** *name=“command”* at the shell prompt. For example, suppose you want to be able to enter **longlist** at the

FIGURE 9-22 Viewing system-generated aliases

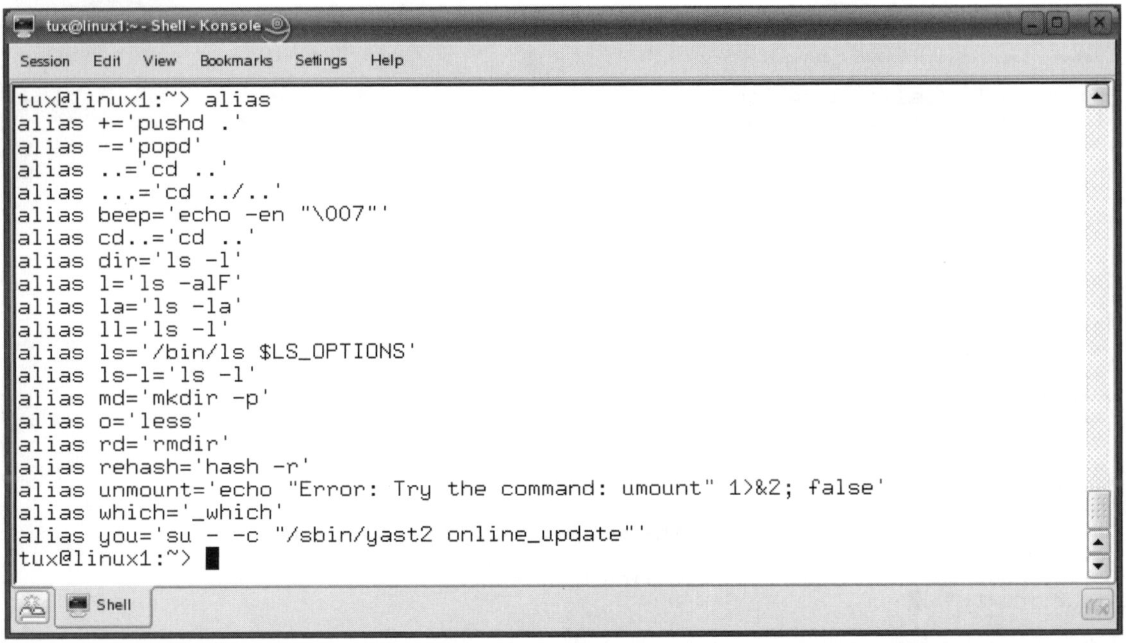
tux@linux1:~ - Shell - Konsole
Session Edit View Bookmarks Settings Help
tux@linux1:~> alias
alias +='pushd .'
alias -='popd'
alias ..='cd ..'
alias ...='cd ../..'
alias beep='echo -en "\007"'
alias cd..='cd ..'
alias dir='ls -l'
alias l='ls -alF'
alias la='ls -la'
alias ll='ls -l'
alias ls='/bin/ls $LS_OPTIONS'
alias ls-l='ls -l'
alias md='mkdir -p'
alias o='less'
alias rd='rmdir'
alias rehash='hash -r'
alias unmount='echo "Error: Try the command: umount" 1>&2; false'
alias which='_which'
alias you='su - -c "/sbin/yast2 online_update"'
tux@linux1:~>
Shell

shell prompt to view a long listing of a directory. You could enter **alias longlist="ls –l"** at the shell prompt. This is shown in Figure 9-23.

Now, if I enter **longlist** at the shell prompt, the ls –l command is executed and its output is displayed on screen. This is shown in Figure 9-24.

You can even include multiple commands within a single alias. To do this, separate the commands in the alias command line with a semi-colon (;). For example, if you wanted to create an alias that would mount a CD inserted in your CD drive and then generate a long listing of the files it contains, you could enter the following at the shell prompt:

```
alias mntcd="mount -t iso9660 /dev/cdrom /media/cdrom;ls -l /media/cdrom"
```

After doing so, you can enter **mntcd** at the shell prompt to mount the CD and generate a listing of its files.

As with variables, any aliases you define with the alias command are not persistent. If you reboot the system, they will be gone when the system comes back up. As with variables, you can make your aliases persistent by adding them to one of the bash

FIGURE 9-23	Creating a new alias using the alias command

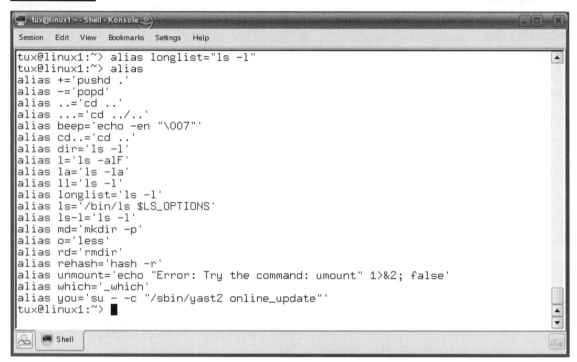

configuration files. You can add them to /etc/profile if you want to make the aliases available to all users on the system. You can also add them to one of the hidden bash configuration files in a particular user's home directory if you want them to be available only to that particular user.

SCENARIO & SOLUTION

You need to view all of the aliases on your system. What command could you enter at the shell prompt to do this?	To view all of the aliases, you enter **alias** at the shell prompt.
You want to add an alias named logs to your system that will display the last few lines of your /var/log/messages file. What command would you enter to do this?	You would enter **alias logs="tail /var/log/messages"** at the shell prompt.

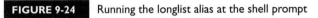

FIGURE 9-24 Running the longlist alias at the shell prompt

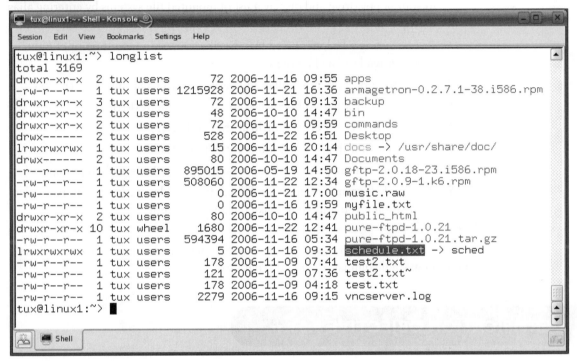

Let's practice working with aliases in the following exercise.

EXERCISE 9-4

Working with Aliases

In this exercise, you will practice creating aliases in the bash shell. To complete this exercise, you will need a DOS-formatted floppy diskette that is compatible with your computer's hardware. Once you have it ready, do the following:

1. If necessary, boot your Linux system and log in as a standard user. If you used the lab exercise in Chapter 3 to install your system, you can log in as **tux** with a password of **M3linux273**.

2. Change to your root user account by entering **su –** followed by your root password.

3. Create an alias named mntflp that will automatically mount a floppy diskette in your floppy drive and display a list of mounted file systems by entering **alias mntflp="mount –t vfat /dev/fd0 /media/floppy;mount"** at the shell prompt.

   If you're using a Fedora or Red Hat distribution, use a mount point of /mnt/floppy instead of /media/floppy.

4. At the shell prompt, enter **alias** and verify that the alias has been created.

5. Insert a DOS-formatted floppy diskette in your floppy drive.

6. Test your alias by entering **mntflp** at the shell prompt.

7. Verify that your floppy is mounted in the mount table.

8. Dismount your floppy by entering **umount /dev/fd0** at the shell prompt.

9. At your shell prompt, enter **ls –a**. Which file would you edit on your particular distribution if you wanted to make the alias persistent?

Now that you know how to manage variables, it's time to discuss how to redirect output from shell commands. Let's do that next.

CERTIFICATION OBJECTIVE 9.03

Manage Shell Command Inputs and Outputs

The bash shell (as well as most other Linux shells) is extremely powerful and flexible. One of the features that make it this way is its ability to manipulate command input and output. In this part of this chapter, we're going to explore how to do this. Specifically, we're going to cover the following:

- Standard bash file descriptors
- Redirecting output and input for shell commands
- Piping information

Let's begin by reviewing bash shell file descriptors.

Standard bash File Descriptors

Before you can learn how to redirect or pipe outputs from a bash command, you must first understand bash shell *file descriptors*. There are three file descriptors

FIGURE 9-25

bash shell file
descriptors

that are available for every command you enter at a shell prompt. These are
shown in Figure 9-25.

These three file descriptors include the following:

- **stdin** This file descriptor stands for *standard input*. Standard input is the
  input provided to a particular command to process. The stdin for a command
  is represented by the number 0.
- **stdout** This file descriptor stands for *standard output*. Standard output is
  simply the output from a particular command. For example, the directory
  listing generated by the ls command is its stdout. The stdout for a command
  is represented by the number 1.
- **stderr** This file descriptor stands for *standard error*. Standard error is the
  error code generated, if any, by a command. The stderr for a command is
  represented by the number 2.

Not all commands will use all three of these descriptors, but many do. Let's take a
look at some examples. Suppose I display the contents of a file in the home directory
of the tux user by entering **cat ./test2.txt**, as shown in Figure 9-26.

The cat command displayed the contents of the file on the screen. This is the
stdout of the cat command. Now suppose I enter the same command, but specify a
file that doesn't exist, as shown in Figure 9-27.

Because the file doesn't exist, the cat command generates an error. This is the
stderr of the cat command. Knowing these descriptors, you can redirect where each
one goes when the command is executed. Let's discuss how this is done next.

FIGURE 9-26   Viewing the stdout of the cat command

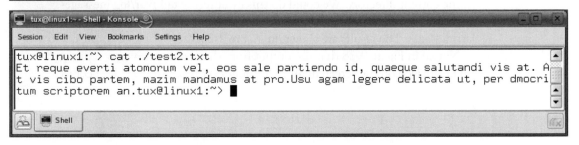

FIGURE 9-27   Viewing the stderr of the cat command

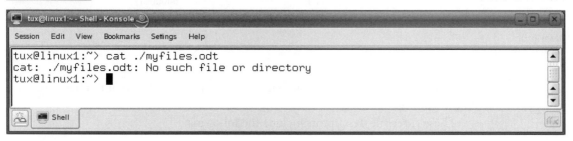

Redirecting Output and Input for Shell Commands

Using the three descriptors you can manipulate where a command gets its input from and where it sends its outputs. In this part of this chapter, we're going to review how you can do this from the command line. We'll discuss the following:

- Redirecting output
- Redirecting input

Let's begin by discussing how to redirect outputs.

Redirecting Output

The bash shell allows you to manipulate where the output from a command goes after it is generated. By default, it is displayed on the screen. However, you can specify that it be sent elsewhere. For example, it is very common to redirect output from a command from the screen to a text file in the file system, especially if the output from the command is very long.

Redirection is accomplished using the **>** character in the command line. The syntax for redirecting output is *command output>filename_or_device*. For example, suppose we want to use the tail command to view the last few lines of our system log file /var/log/messages and we want to save the output to a file named lastmessages in the current directory. We could do this by entering **tail /var/log/messages 1> lastmessages**. This tells the shell to redirect the stdout (1) to a file named lastmessages. The results are shown in Figure 9-28.

Notice in Figure 9-28 that the output from the command is truly redirected. It isn't displayed on the screen at all. All stdout text is sent to the file specified.

FIGURE 9-28   Redirecting stdout to a text file

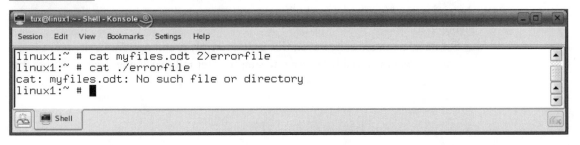

```
tux@linux1:~ - Shell - Konsole

Session   Edit   View   Bookmarks   Settings   Help

linux1:~ # tail /var/log/messages 1>lastmessages
linux1:~ # cat ./lastmessages
Dec  8 12:53:19 linux1 SuSEfirewall2: Setting up rules from /etc/sysconfig/SuSEf
irewall2 ...
Dec  8 12:53:21 linux1 SuSEfirewall2: Firewall rules successfully set
Dec  8 12:53:23 linux1 SuSEfirewall2: batch committing...
Dec  8 12:53:23 linux1 SuSEfirewall2: Error: iptables-batch failed, re-running u
sing iptables
Dec  8 12:53:25 linux1 SuSEfirewall2: Firewall rules successfully set
Dec  8 12:53:25 linux1 kernel: bootsplash: status on console 0 changed to on
Dec  8 13:03:03 linux1 zmd: ShutdownManager (WARN): Preparing to sleep...
Dec  8 13:03:04 linux1 zmd: ShutdownManager (WARN): Going to sleep, waking up at
 12/09/2006 12:43:03
Dec  8 13:52:57 linux1 syslog-ng[2231]: STATS: dropped 0
Dec  8 14:03:15 linux1 su: (to root) tux on /dev/pts/3
linux1:~ #

  Shell
```

on the
Job   *If you don't enter a file descriptor number in the command, the shell will assume that you want to only redirect the stdout output from the command. In the example in Figure 9-28, therefore, you could enter* tail /var/log/messages >lastmessages *and get the same result.*

You can use the same technique to redirect stderr from the screen to a file. For example, if I were to use the cat command to try to display a file that doesn't exist, I can redirect any error messages generated to a file by entering **cat *filename* 2>*errfilename***—for example, **cat myfiles.odt 2>errorfile**. Because the file doesn't exist, the cat command generates an error message (stderr) instead of regular output (stdout). This is shown in Figure 9-29.

FIGURE 9-29   Redirecting stderr to a text file

```
tux@linux1:~ - Shell - Konsole

Session   Edit   View   Bookmarks   Settings   Help

linux1:~ # cat myfiles.odt 2>errorfile
linux1:~ # cat ./errorfile
cat: myfiles.odt: No such file or directory
linux1:~ #

  Shell
```

This command specifies that the stderr (2) from the cat command be redirected to a file named errorfile in the current directory. Because it's redirected, the stderr output is not displayed on the screen. It's only written to the specified file.

on the Job

When you redirect output to a file that doesn't exist, the shell will automatically create it for you. This is what happened in the preceding examples. However, if the file already exists, be warned that the shell will, by default, erase the existing file and replace it with the new output. If you want to append the new output to an existing file without erasing its contents, then you should use >> instead of >.

You can even redirect both stderr and stdout to text files at the same time. To do this, you add two redirection instructions to the command, one for the stdout and one for the stderr. The syntax for doing this is *command 1>stdout_filename 2>stderr_filename*. This will send stdout to one file and stderr to a different file. You can also send both outputs to the same file. To do this, use the syntax of *command 1>filename 2>&1*. This syntax causes the stdout to first be sent to the specified file, and then stderr (2) output is redirected to the stdout output (&1).

If you're going to use this option, it's very important to remember to use the & symbol before the 1. This tells the shell that the character that follows is a file descriptor and not a file name. If you omit this character, then the shell will write stderr output to a separate file named 1.

Now that you know how to redirect output from a command, we next need to discuss how to redirect command inputs. Let's do that next.

Redirecting Input

Just as you can specify where output from a command is sent, you can also specify where a command's inputs (stdin) come from as well. To do this, you simply reverse the character that we used previously for redirecting output. The syntax you use is *command <input_text_or_file*.

For example, I could enter **tail </var/log/messages** at the shell prompt. This sends the text string "/var/log/messages" to the tail command as an input, as shown in Figure 9-30.

For most commands, however, this isn't a terribly useful option. In the preceding example, it would probably be easier to simply enter **tail /var/log/messages**. Where this

FIGURE 9-30   Redirecting stdin

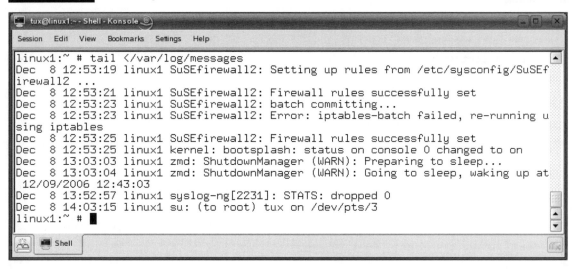

option really shines is when you need to send a lot of text to a command that is expecting it.

For example, you can send a list of words from a text file to the sort command and have it sort them for you. In Figure 9-31, I've used the vi editor to create a text file named words that contains text.

FIGURE 9-31   Creating an input file in the vi editor

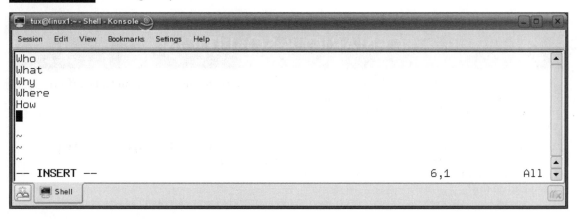

FIGURE 9-32   Redirecting input at the command line

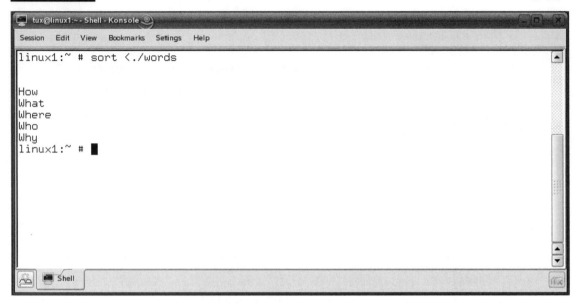

With this file created, I can specify that it be used as an input with the sort command. I would do this by entering **sort <./words** at the shell prompt. The output is then displayed on the screen as shown in Figure 9-32.

SCENARIO & SOLUTION

You want to write the stdout from the mount command to a file named mountedfs and the stderr to a file named fserr. What command would you use to do this?	You would enter **mount 1>mountedfs 2>fserr**.
You want to write the stdout from the top command to a file named myprocesses without overwriting the existing contents of the file. What command would you use to do this?	You would enter **top 1>>myprocesses or top >myprocesses**.

Let's practice working with redirection in the following exercise.

EXERCISE 9-5

ON THE CD

Redirecting Input and Output

In this exercise, you will practice redirecting input and output. Complete the following:

1. If necessary, boot your Linux system and log in as a standard user. If you used the lab exercise in Chapter 3 to install your system, you can log in as **tux** with a password of **M3linux273**.

2. Change to your root user account by entering **su –** followed by your root password.

3. Use tail to view the last lines of your /var/log/messages file and redirect the standard output to a text file in your home directory by entering **tail /var/log/ messages 1>lastlines**.

4. Enter **ls l*** and verify that the lastlines file was created.

5. Use the **cat** command to view the lastlines file.

6. Append the last lines of the content of your /var/log/firewall log file to lastlines by entering **tail /var/log/firewall 1>>lastlines** at the shell prompt.

7. Send standard error to a log file by entering **tail /var/log/mylog 2>errorout** at the shell prompt.

8. View the errorout file with cat. Why was an error generated by the preceding command?

9. Using the vi editor, create a new file named mywords in your home directory. Add the following words to the file, each on a separate line:

Linux	Greatest
Is	Operating
The	System!

10. Save the file and exit vi.

11. Send the mywords file to the stdin of the sort command by entering **sort <./mywords** at the shell prompt.

12. The sort command should send the words from the file to the stdout (the screen) in alphabetical order.

In addition to redirecting input or output from a command, you can also pipe outputs. Let's discuss how this is done next.

Piping Information

Redirection is great, but it has one weakness. It only allows us to redirect to or from a file in the file system or a system device. What if we needed to redirect the output from one command to the input of another command? Can this be done? You bet it can! This is done using pipes.

As we've gone through the various exercises and examples presented thus far in this book, we've many times used piping to send output from one command to another. In this part of the chapter, we're going to explain how this is done. We'll cover the following:

- Using pipes to move information between commands
- Using awk and sed to manipulate text

Let's begin by learning how to use pipes to move information between shell commands.

Using Pipes to Move Information Between Commands

Pipes are extremely useful when you're working at the shell prompt. As I mentioned, we've actually used pipes many times so far in this course. Now you're going to learn exactly why we did what we did.

For example, many times we've used | more with the cat or ls commands. The pipe character (|) used in the command tells the shell to take the output of the first command and send it on to the second program specified.

For example, if I enter **cat /var/log/messages | more** at the shell prompt, the cat command reads the contents of the /var/log/messages file and sends it to the stdout. Normally, this would be displayed on the screen. However, because we are using a pipe, the shell knows that it should not display the stdout from cat on the screen. Instead, it takes the stdout from cat and sends it as the stdin for the next command listed—in this case, the more command. The more command then takes the output from cat and performs its manipulations on it, which is to display the text on the screen one line at a time.

Pipes can be used with any command that produces output of some sort and accepts input of some sort. A great example is the grep command. You can use grep alone from the command line, of course. However, it's very handy when used in a pipe in conjunction with another command. The syntax of the command is *command* | grep *expression*. Doing this pipes the output of the first command to the input of grep, which then searches the information for the specified expression.

FIGURE 9-33	Piping output to grep

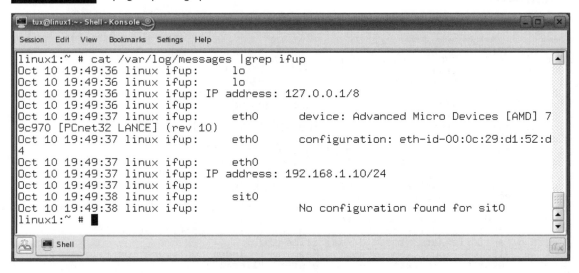

For example, suppose you are using the cat command to display the contents of the /var/log/messages file on the screen. You're only interested in displaying log file entries created when the network interfaces in the system were brought up. You could filter out the output of cat by piping it to grep and searching for the expression "ifup" in the output of cat. To do this, you would enter **cat /var/log/messages | grep ifup**, as shown in Figure 9-33.

Notice that only the entries in the output of cat that match the expression "ifup" are displayed on the screen by grep.

on the *Job* **Remember that when you are piping information, only the last command in the pipe actually displays output on the screen. The output from all of the other commands is redirected to the input of the next command in the pipe and is not displayed on the screen.**

Let's look at another example. Suppose I wanted to use cat again to display the contents of /var/log/messages and I want to use grep to filter out only those lines that have to do with the xinetd service. I enter **cat /var/log/messages | grep xinetd** at the shell prompt. The result is shown in Figure 9-34.

Notice that there are too many entries to fit on a single screen in the terminal window. What can we do? We can actually include multiple commands within a pipe.

FIGURE 9-34 Too much output from grep

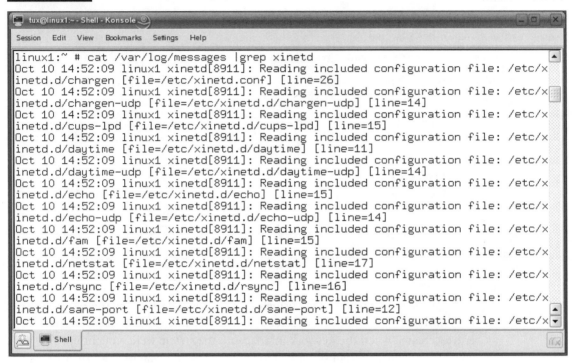

In this situation we need to use cat to generate the initial output, then filter it through grep to find only those entries that have "xinetd" in them, and then send the output of grep to the more command so that the display is paused one screen at a time. To do this, you would enter **cat /var/log/messages | grep xinetd | more** at the shell prompt. The result is shown in Figure 9-35.

SCENARIO & SOLUTION

You want to use the mount command to find out where the /dev/sda2 device is mounted in the file system. What command could you enter to filter the display from the mount command to show only this line?	You would enter **mount	grep sda2**.

FIGURE 9-35   Using multiple commands within a single pipe

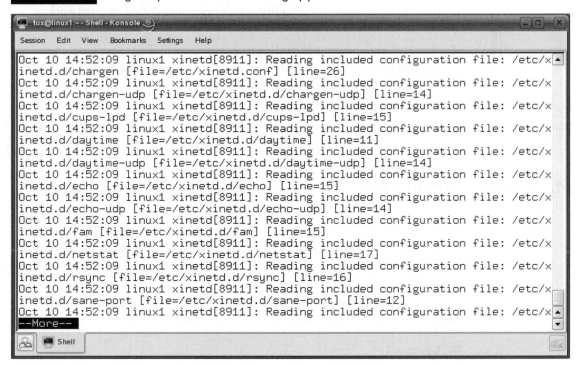

```
tux@linux1:~ - Shell - Konsole

Session   Edit   View   Bookmarks   Settings   Help

Oct 10 14:52:09 linux1 xinetd[8911]: Reading included configuration file: /etc/x
inetd.d/chargen [file=/etc/xinetd.conf] [line=26]
Oct 10 14:52:09 linux1 xinetd[8911]: Reading included configuration file: /etc/x
inetd.d/chargen-udp [file=/etc/xinetd.d/chargen-udp] [line=14]
Oct 10 14:52:09 linux1 xinetd[8911]: Reading included configuration file: /etc/x
inetd.d/cups-lpd [file=/etc/xinetd.d/cups-lpd] [line=15]
Oct 10 14:52:09 linux1 xinetd[8911]: Reading included configuration file: /etc/x
inetd.d/daytime [file=/etc/xinetd.d/daytime] [line=11]
Oct 10 14:52:09 linux1 xinetd[8911]: Reading included configuration file: /etc/x
inetd.d/daytime-udp [file=/etc/xinetd.d/daytime-udp] [line=14]
Oct 10 14:52:09 linux1 xinetd[8911]: Reading included configuration file: /etc/x
inetd.d/echo [file=/etc/xinetd.d/echo] [line=15]
Oct 10 14:52:09 linux1 xinetd[8911]: Reading included configuration file: /etc/x
inetd.d/echo-udp [file=/etc/xinetd.d/echo-udp] [line=14]
Oct 10 14:52:09 linux1 xinetd[8911]: Reading included configuration file: /etc/x
inetd.d/fam [file=/etc/xinetd.d/fam] [line=15]
Oct 10 14:52:09 linux1 xinetd[8911]: Reading included configuration file: /etc/x
inetd.d/netstat [file=/etc/xinetd.d/netstat] [line=17]
Oct 10 14:52:09 linux1 xinetd[8911]: Reading included configuration file: /etc/x
inetd.d/rsync [file=/etc/xinetd.d/rsync] [line=16]
Oct 10 14:52:09 linux1 xinetd[8911]: Reading included configuration file: /etc/x
inetd.d/sane-port [file=/etc/xinetd.d/sane-port] [line=12]
Oct 10 14:52:09 linux1 xinetd[8911]: Reading included configuration file: /etc/x
--More--

    Shell
```

Let's practice working with pipes in the following exercise.

EXERCISE 9-6

ON THE CD

Using Pipes

In this exercise, you will practice using pipes to send stdout from one command to the stdin of another. Complete the following:

1. If necessary, boot your Linux system and log in as a standard user. If you used the lab exercise in Chapter 3 to install your system, you can log in as **tux** with a password of **M3linux273**.

2. Change to your root user account by entering **su –** followed by your root password.

3. View all entries in your system log that contain the word "network" by piping the output from cat to grep. Enter **cat /var/log/messages | grep network** at the shell prompt to do this.

4. Notice that the output from the preceding command was very long. Pipe the output from cat to grep to more by entering **cat /var/log/messages | grep network | more** at the shell prompt.

Before we end this topic, we need to talk about one more thing: using the awk and sed commands to manipulate output. Let's do that next.

Manipulating stdout Text

When you redirect or pipe output, there may be occasions when you want to filter the output such that only certain portions are actually passed along. We actually did this to an extent by piping output to grep in the previous examples. Using grep, we filtered the output such that only lines containing matching text made it through.

In addition to grep, we can also use two other tools on a Linux system to match and modify text in the output from a command. In this part of this chapter, we're going to learn how to do this using the following commands:

- Using sed
- Using awk

Let's begin by looking at sed.

Using sed

The sed command is a *stream* text editor. Unlike the interactive text editors that you've already learned how to use in this book, such as vi, a stream editor takes a stream of text as its stdin and then performs operations on it that you specify. Then, sed sends the results to stdout, which is to the screen by default. You can use the following commands with sed:

- **s**   Replaces instances of a specified text string with another text string. The syntax for using the s command is sed s/*term1*/*term2*/. For example, in Figure 9-36, I've used the cat command to display a file in the tux user's home directory named test2.txt. I then use cat to read test2.txt and then

FIGURE 9-36   Using sed to replace text

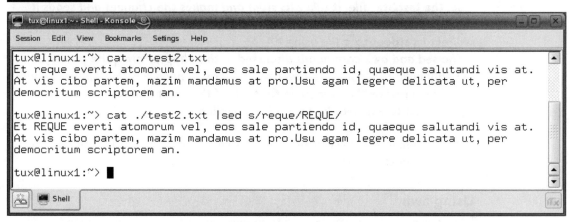

pipe the stdout to the stdin of the sed command and specify that the term "reque" be replaced with "REQUE."

■ **d**   Deletes the specified text. For example, to delete every line of text from the stdin that contains the term "eos," you would enter **sed /eos/d**. This is shown in Figure 9-37.

FIGURE 9-37   Using sed to delete lines of text

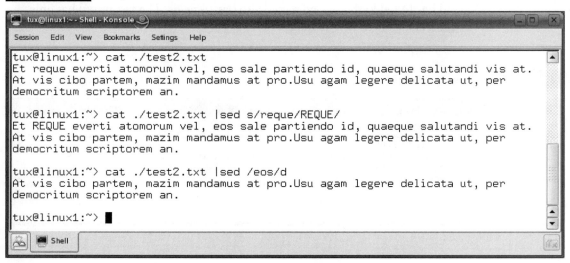

on the **Job**

Remember, sed doesn't actually modify the source of the information—in this case, the test2.txt file. It takes its stdin and makes the changes and sends it to the stdout. If you want to save the changes made by sed, then you need to redirect its stdout to a file using >.

The sed and awk commands discussed in this chapter are quite powerful. We only have space here to cover the basics you need for your Linux+ exam. You should review the man page for both of these commands and use this information to explore the possibilities available.

In addition to sed, you can also use awk to manipulate output. Let's discuss how this is done next.

Using awk

Like grep and sed, awk can be used to receive output from another command as its stdin and manipulate it in a manner you specify. However, the way awk does this is a little bit different. The awk command treats each line of text it receives as a record. Each word in the line, separated by a space or tab character is treated as a separate field within the record.

For example, consider the text file displayed by the cat command shown in Figure 9-38.

According to awk, this file has three records because it has three separate lines of text. Each line of text has a carriage return/linefeed character at the end that creates a new line. This is the character awk uses to define the end of a record. The first record has 14 fields; the second record also has 14 fields. The last record has only 3 fields. These are shown in Table 9-3.

FIGURE 9-38   Viewing the test2.txt file

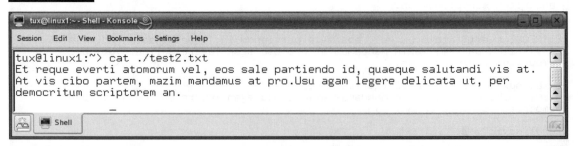

TABLE 9-3	Viewing a Text File as a Database												
Record	Field1	Field2	Field3	Field4	Field5	Field6	Field7	Field8	Field9	Field10	Field11	Field12	Field13
1	Et	reque	everti	atomorum	vel,	eos	sale	partiendo	id,	quaeque	salutandi	vis	at.
2	At	vis	cibo	partem,	mazim	mandamus	at	pro.Usu	agam	legere	delicata	ut,	per
3	democritum	scriptorem	an.										

Notice that white space, not punctuation, delimits the fields. Each field is referenced as $field\_number$. For example, the first field of any record is referenced as $1, the second as $2, and so on.

Using awk, we can specify a field in a specific record and manipulate it in some manner. The syntax for using awk is awk '*pattern {manipulation}*'. For example, we could enter **cat ./test2.txt | awk '{print $1,$2,$3}'** to print out the first three words ("fields") of each line ("records"). Because we didn't specify a pattern to match on, awk simply prints out the first three words of every line. This is shown in Figure 9-39.

You can also include a pattern to specify exactly which records to search on. For example, suppose we only wanted to display the first three fields of any record that includes the text "em" somewhere in the line. To do this, you add a pattern of /em/ to the command. This is shown in Figure 9-40.

FIGURE 9-39	Using awk to print the first three fields of each record

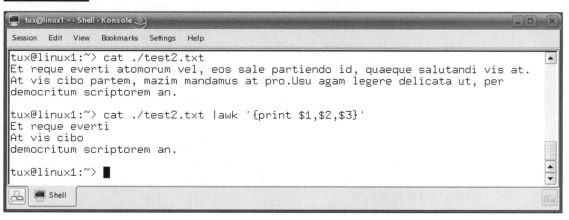

FIGURE 9-40 Using search patterns in an awk command

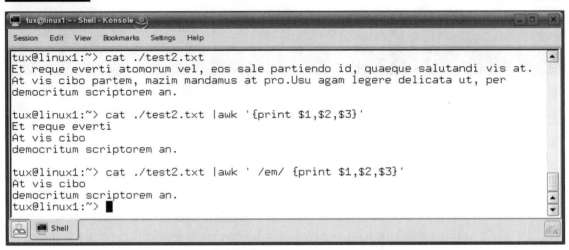

Notice that awk only displayed the second and third records because they contain the term "em" somewhere in the line whereas the first line does not (and, hence, isn't included in the output).

You can also add your own text to the output. Just add it to the manipulation part of the command within quotes. In fact, you can also add control characters to output as well. You can use the following:

- **\t** Inserts a tab character.
- **\n** Adds a new line character.
- **\f** Adds a formfeed character.
- **\r** Adds a carriage return character.

For example, in Figure 9-41, I've entered:

```
cat ./test2.txt |awk '/em/ {print "Field 1: "$1"\t", "Field 2:
"$2"\t", "Field 3: "$3"\t"}'
```

This causes each field to be labeled Field 1, Field 2, and Field 3. It also inserts a tab character between each field. As with sed, awk doesn't modify the original file. It sends its output to stdout (the screen). If you want to send it to a file, then you can redirect it using >.

FIGURE 9-41   Adding text to the output of awk

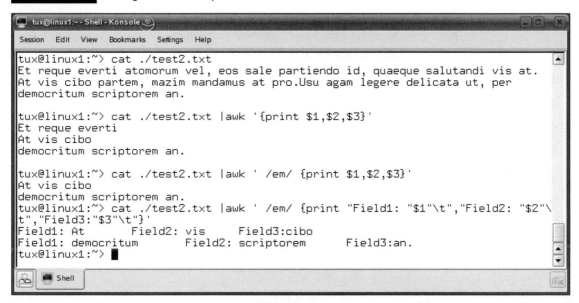

```
tux@linux1:~> cat ./test2.txt
Et reque everti atomorum vel, eos sale partiendo id, quaeque salutandi vis at.
At vis cibo partem, mazim mandamus at pro.Usu agam legere delicata ut, per
democritum scriptorem an.

tux@linux1:~> cat ./test2.txt |awk '{print $1,$2,$3}'
Et reque everti
At vis cibo
democritum scriptorem an.

tux@linux1:~> cat ./test2.txt |awk ' /em/ {print $1,$2,$3}'
At vis cibo
democritum scriptorem an.
tux@linux1:~> cat ./test2.txt |awk ' /em/ {print "Field1: "$1"\t","Field2: "$2"\
t","Field3:"$3"\t"}'
Field1: At      Field2: vis     Field3:cibo
Field1: democritum      Field2: scriptorem      Field3:an.
tux@linux1:~> █
```

Let's practice working with awk and sed in the following exercise.

EXERCISE 9-7

Using awk and sed

In this exercise, you will practice using pipes to send stdout from one command to the stdin of another. Complete the following:

1. If necessary, boot your Linux system and log in as a standard user. If you used the lab exercise in Chapter 3 to install your system, you can log in as **tux** with a password of **M3linux273**.

2. At the shell prompt, use the ls command to verify that the test.txt file we created in an earlier chapter's exercises still exists in your home directory.

   If it doesn't exist, use vi to create the file and enter the following as its contents:

   ```
   Usu agam legere delicata ut, per democritum scriptorem an. Nec
   te zzril possim tincidunt, at qui probo mucius gubergren. Ea mei
   paulo cetero oportere, at pertinax liberavisse pri.
   ```

3. Open test.txt in the vi editor.

4. Add a carriage return, if it doesn't already exist, to the end of each line of text.

5. Save your changes and exit vi.

6. Use sed to replace the word "oportere" with the word "democritum" and send the output to a new file named testsed.txt by completing the following:

   a. At the shell prompt, enter **cat ~/test.txt |sed s/oportere/democritum/ 1>testsed.txt**.

   b. Use the cat command to verify that the word was replaced in the testsed.txt file.

7. Use awk to print the second word in each line of the test.txt file that has the characters "us" in it. Enter **cat ~/test.txt |awk '/us/ {print $2}'** at the shell prompt.

8. Which line matched and which word was subsequently printed on the screen?

Let's end this chapter by reviewing how to create shell scripts.

CERTIFICATION OBJECTIVE 9.04

Create Shell Scripts

One of the cool things about Linux is the fact that it allows you to create your own powerful *shell scripts* that you can run right from your shell prompt. A shell script is a text file that contains a series of commands that are executed by the shell. Shell scripts can be used to run multiple commands at once. They can also be used to read input from the end user or from shell commands, and make decisions based on the input.

In this part of the chapter, we're going to show you how to create basic shell scripts. To do this, you need to know the following:

e x a m

ⓦatch *Shell scripts range from very simple to extremely complex. For your Linux+ exam, you only need to know how to create a basic script. If you master the topics we're covering here, you should be in good shape for your exam.*

- How shell scripts work
- Creating a basic script
- Using control structures

Let's begin by discussing how shell scripts work.

How Shell Scripts Work

To understand how shell scripts work, you need to know the following:

- The components of a shell script
- How shell scripts are executed

Let's begin by discussing the components that comprise a shell script.

The Components of a Shell Script

As we mentioned, a shell script is a simple text file that contains a series of commands that are executed from top to bottom. A sample shell script named runme is shown in Figure 9-42.

Notice that this script contains several parts:

- **#!/bin/bash** The first line of any shell script must specify which shell the script is written to run under. In this case, the /bin/bash shell is specified. When a script is run, a subshell will be created using the shell specified here and the script contents will be processed in it.

- **#A sample script that….** This part of the script is a comment that describes what the script does. Notice that this part of the script begins with a **#** character to indicate that the text that comes after it is a comment. Because it is a comment, this part of the script is not displayed on the screen when it is run. Comments are optional. The script will run just fine without them.

FIGURE 9-42   A sample shell script

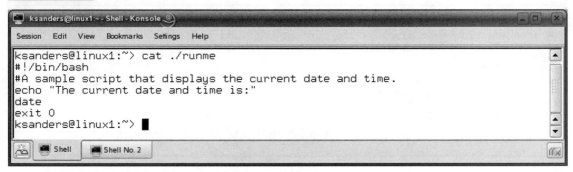

```
ksanders@linux1:~> cat ./runme
#!/bin/bash
#A sample script that displays the current date and time.
echo "The current date and time is:"
date
exit 0
ksanders@linux1:~>
```

However, it's considered good form to include a comment at the beginning of your scripts right after the shell declaration that describes what the script does and, optionally, who wrote it.

- **echo, date** These elements in the script are simple commands that are typically used at the shell prompt. The echo command is used to display text on the screen. The date command is used to display the current date and time on the screen.

- **exit 0** This part of the script is its end. It tells the shell what to do after it is done running the commands in the script. In this case, it tells the shell to exit the script.

When we run this script, the output shown in Figure 9-43 is displayed on the screen. Notice that this script first displayed the text specified by the echo command. Then the next command was processed, which directed the shell to run the date command. When the script was done, the shell exited the script and returned you to the command prompt.

How Shell Scripts Are Executed

Notice in Figure 9-43 that, to run the script I created, I had to call the shell (/bin/bash) and then tell it what script to execute (./runme). This is one option for running a script.

However, there's a second option (and a better one in my opinion) for running shell scripts. Remember in an earlier chapter when we talked about permissions? Recall that one of the file permissions you could assign to a file is named *execute*.

FIGURE 9-43	Running the sample shell script

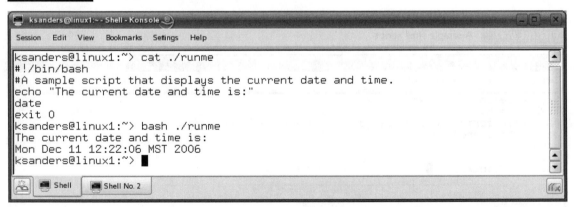

| FIGURE 9-44 | Changing the execute permission on a script file |

With the execute permission assigned, any file, including a text file, can be allowed to execute from the shell prompt. This is a great option for making scripts easy for end users to run.

To do this, simply enable the execute attribute for Owner, Group, and/or Others. As you learned earlier, this is done using the chmod command. In the example we're working with here, I can configure the runme file to be executed by the file Owner by entering **chmod u+x ./runme** at the shell prompt. Then I can run the runme script by simply entering its name at the shell prompt, just as I would with any other system command. This is shown in Figure 9-44.

If desired, I could have also given the execute permission to Group and/or Others as well.

There is one other issue you need to be aware of when working with scripts and that is the issue of paths. Notice in Figure 9-44 that I had to enter **./runme** at the shell prompt. Even though the file resided in the current directory, the current directory (in this case, /home/ksanders) is not in my PATH environment variable.

If you're creating scripts for yourself, then this probably doesn't pose a problem. By now, you should be familiar enough with Linux to understand why you have to specify the path to the file at the shell prompt and know how to do it. However, if you're creating a script for your end users to run, this may present a problem. To save yourself frustration, you should consider putting the script in a directory that is part of the PATH or adding the directory to your existing PATH.

One option you can use is the ~/bin directory in each user's home directory. Most Linux distributions automatically create a directory named /bin for each user. Then, one of the bash configuration files, discussed at the beginning of this chapter, is used to automatically add ~/bin to the PATH environment variable when a shell is started. This is shown in Figure 9-45.

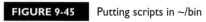
FIGURE 9-45   Putting scripts in ~/bin

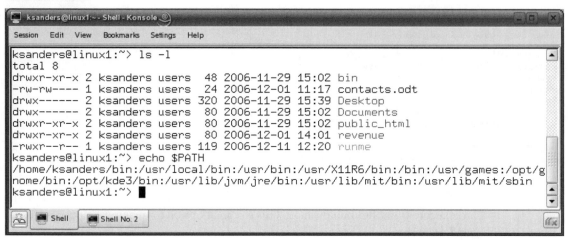

Because it's in the PATH, any files you put in ~/bin can be run from the shell prompt without specifying the full path to the file. You could also, of course, create your own directory and manually edit your bash configuration files to add it to your user's PATH environment variable as well.

With this background in mind, let's spend some time discussing how to create a basic shell script.

Creating a Basic Script

As we mentioned earlier, shell scripts can be extremely basic or extremely complex. The example we reviewed earlier was a very simple script. It echoed text on the screen and ran one command. For your Linux+ exam, you need to be able to create scripts that are more complex than this one. Therefore, in this part of the chapter, we're going to cover the following topics:

- Displaying text on the screen
- Adding commands to a script
- Reading input from the user

Let's begin by discussing how to display text on the screen in a shell script.

Displaying Text on the Screen

This task is pretty easy. As you saw in the earlier examples we reviewed, you can display text on the screen in a shell script using the echo command. The syntax for using echo is to simply enter **echo "*text_to_be_displayed*"** in the script file.

For example, in Figure 9-42, we entered **echo "The current date and time is:"** to display the associated text on the screen. Because the shell script simply calls and runs the echo command, you can use all of the options you would use if you were to run echo at the shell prompt. Check out the man page for echo to see what's available.

In addition to displaying text on the screen, you can also run commands from the script. Let's review how this is done next.

Adding Commands to a Script

To run a shell command from within a script, simply enter the appropriate command in the script with all of the options you want to include with it. In Figure 9-42, we used the date command to display the current date and time. You can include just about any command you want in your shell scripts. Just remember to put each command on a separate line unless you are using pipes to move data between commands.

Let's make things a little more interesting by discussing how to gather input from the user in a script.

Reading Input from the User

Up to this point, our scripts have been very simple and non-interactive, meaning that the user simply types the command at the shell prompt and the script does whatever it's been written to do.

However, you can make your scripts more flexible by making them interactive, meaning that you can have your scripts ask the user a question and then capture their input for processing. This is done using the echo command discussed previously in conjunction with the read *variable* command. The echo command is used to present the user with a question. The read *variable* command is used to pause the script, present a prompt on the screen, and read the information the user supplies into a variable you define. Consider the example shown in Figure 9-46.

In this script, the user is prompted for the name of the directory he or she wants to add to the PATH environment variable. The read command provides the user with a prompt to enter the directory name. When the user presses the ENTER key, the value he or she typed is assigned to the variable named MYNEWPATH.

FIGURE 9-46   Querying the user for input in a shell script

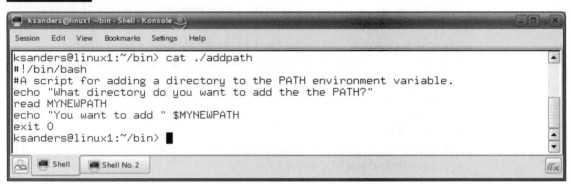

```
ksanders@linux1:~/bin> cat ./addpath
#!/bin/bash
#A script for adding a directory to the PATH environment variable.
echo "What directory do you want to add the the PATH?"
read MYNEWPATH
echo "You want to add " $MYNEWPATH
exit 0
ksanders@linux1:~/bin>
```

Once the variable was stored in memory, the echo command was used a second
time to display the value of MYNEWPATH on the screen. Now, we didn't actually
modify the PATH variable yet. To do this, we need to add some more commands to
the shell script. The best way to approach this is to ask yourself: "If I were doing this
from the shell prompt, what commands would I need?" Then enter the commands in
the script and try it out.

In this example, we need to add the directory specified by the user to PATH and
then export PATH. This could be done using the command shown in Figure 9-47.

If you've done any programming, you probably noticed that we didn't have to
declare the MYNEWPATH variable anywhere in the script. With many scripting
and programming languages, you have to first declare a variable, set its size, and
specify what type of information (text string, real number, integer, Boolean value,

FIGURE 9-47   Adding commands to the shell script

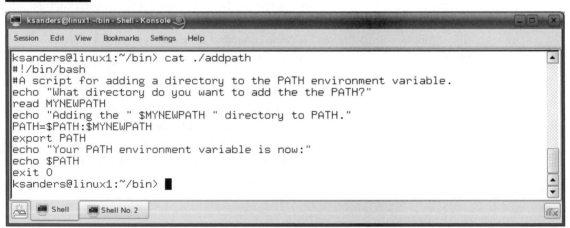

```
ksanders@linux1:~/bin> cat ./addpath
#!/bin/bash
#A script for adding a directory to the PATH environment variable.
echo "What directory do you want to add the the PATH?"
read MYNEWPATH
echo "Adding the " $MYNEWPATH " directory to PATH."
PATH=$PATH:$MYNEWPATH
export PATH
echo "Your PATH environment variable is now:"
echo $PATH
exit 0
ksanders@linux1:~/bin>
```

FIGURE 9-48   Adding non-declared variables together

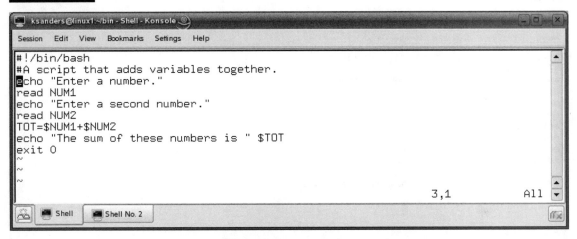

and so on) it will contain. The bash shell is a little more forgiving. The bash shell will create the variable in memory dynamically for you from the read command and assign the user's input as its value.

Of course, bash does let you declare and type the variable if you want to. This is done using the declare command in the script. This can be useful if you want to have the user enter numbers in a read command. The issue here is that the bash shell interprets anything entered at the read command as text, even if the user enters a number. Consider the script shown in Figure 9-48.

When run, this script asks the user for two numbers, adds them together and assigns the result to a variable named TOT, and echoes the value of TOT on the screen. Notice what happens when the script is run in Figure 9-49.

Because we didn't declare the NUM1, NUM2, or TOT variables, bash treated them all as simple text. No arithmetic took place. However, if we declare these

FIGURE 9-49   The results of not declaring variables

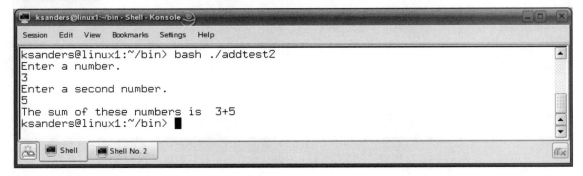

FIGURE 9-50   Declaring and typing variables in a script

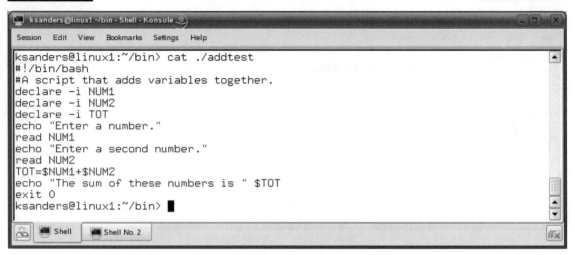

variables and type them as integers, something very different will happen. Consider a revised version of this script, shown in Figure 9-50.

Notice that NUM1, NUM2, and TOT are declared at the beginning of the script using the –i (integer) option. Now the bash shell will interpret the user's input as a whole number, not as text. When we use the + operator on the variables in the script, they are actually added, not just concatenated, as shown in Figure 9-51.

You're doing great! We've gone from relatively simple scripts to ones that are a little more complex. Let's ratchet things up a notch and add some control structures to our scripts.

FIGURE 9-51   Adding declared variables in a script

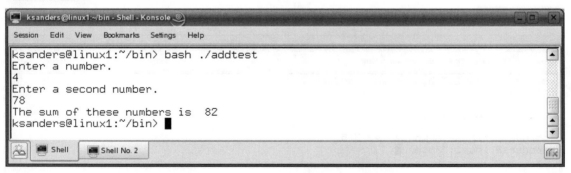

SCENARIO & SOLUTION

You need to write a script that will mount a CD in your CD-ROM drive and then display the contents of the CD on screen. How would you do this?	You could use the following script: ``` #!/bin/bash #A script for mounting a CD. mount -t iso9660 /dev/cdrom /media/cdrom ls -l /media/cdrom exit 0 ```
You've saved the script above as mntmycd. What command would you enter to make it executable by the file owner?	You would enter **chmod u+x mntmycd**.

Using Control Structures in Scripts

In addition to interactivity, it can also be very beneficial to add control structures to your shell scripts. Our scripts, to this point, have executed straight through from beginning to end. This works fine, but what if we need the script to make some decisions? Based on user input or output from a command, you may want the script to determine a course of action. This is done by implementing control structures in the script. We're going to discuss the following about this type of script element:

- Using if/then/else structures
- Using case structures

Let's begin by reviewing if/then statements.

Using if/then Structures

Using an if/then/else structure within your shell script gives your script the ability to execute different commands based on whether or not a particular condition is true or false. The structure appears as follows:

```
if condition then
    commands
else
    commands
fi
```

The if part of the structure tells the shell to determine if the specified condition is true or false. If it is true, then the commands under the then part of the structure are run.

If the condition evaluates to false, then the commands under the else part of the structure are run.

For example, in the script we've been working with so far in this part of the chapter, we've asked the user to enter the name of a directory they want to add to the PATH environment variable. When we add the directory to PATH, the shell doesn't check to see if the directory the user entered actually exists. It would be beneficial to run a quick test and verify that the specified directory exists. If it does, we should go ahead and add it to the PATH variable. If not, we should post an error message on the screen telling the user what happened. The script shown in Figure 9-52 does this very thing.

In this example, the [–e "$MYNEWPATH"] condition calls a utility called test and directs it to check and see if the directory contained in the MYNEWPATH variable exists (as specified by the –e option). If test returns a value of TRUE, then the steps immediately under the if statement are executed.

However, if the test program returns a value of FALSE, then the statements under the else portion of the structure are executed. In this case, an error message will be displayed indicating that the directory doesn't exist. When we run this script and supply a valid directory, the output in Figure 9-53 is displayed.

You can also use a related structure in your scripts called case. Let's discuss how to use it next.

FIGURE 9-52   Using an if/then/else structure in a shell script

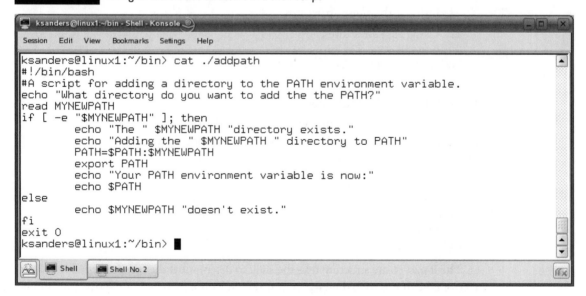

```
ksanders@linux1:~/bin> cat ./addpath
#!/bin/bash
#A script for adding a directory to the PATH environment variable.
echo "What directory do you want to add the the PATH?"
read MYNEWPATH
if [ -e "$MYNEWPATH" ]; then
        echo "The " $MYNEWPATH "directory exists."
        echo "Adding the " $MYNEWPATH " directory to PATH"
        PATH=$PATH:$MYNEWPATH
        export PATH
        echo "Your PATH environment variable is now:"
        echo $PATH
else
        echo $MYNEWPATH "doesn't exist."
fi
exit 0
ksanders@linux1:~/bin>
```

| FIGURE 9-53 | Running our script using an if/then/else structure |

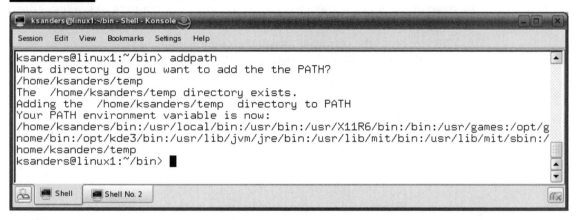

```
ksanders@linux1:~/bin> addpath
What directory do you want to add the the PATH?
/home/ksanders/temp
The  /home/ksanders/temp directory exists.
Adding the  /home/ksanders/temp  directory to PATH
Your PATH environment variable is now:
/home/ksanders/bin:/usr/local/bin:/usr/bin:/usr/X11R6/bin:/bin:/usr/games:/opt/g
nome/bin:/opt/kde3/bin:/usr/lib/jvm/jre/bin:/usr/lib/mit/bin:/usr/lib/mit/sbin:/
home/ksanders/temp
ksanders@linux1:~/bin> ▮
```

Using case Structures

The case statement is really just a glorified if/then statement. The if/then statement works fantastic if we have a condition that can be evaluated in one of two ways. In the preceding example, the condition could be evaluated as true or false. However, what do you do if you have a condition that could be evaluated in many different ways, but you still want your script to take certain actions based on how it evaluates? You use the case statement instead.

on the
ⓘob

You could also use a whole series of if/then statements instead of a case statement. However, it can get really messy and is considered poor form. If you have a condition that can be evaluated to return more than two responses, you should probably use a case statement.

The syntax for using a case structure is as follows:

```
case variable in
     response_1 ) commands
                  ;;
     response_2 ) commands
                  ;;
     response_3 ) commands
                  ;;
esac
```

Essentially, the case statement compares the value of the variable listed to the list of responses within the case statement. If a match is found, then the commands associated with that response are run. Commands for all other list items are ignored.

For example, we could write a script that asks the user what month they were born in. Based on the response they give, you could cause the script to provide a customized response using a case statement. A sample script that does this is shown in Figure 9-54.

This script asks the user what month they were born in and then determines the season of their birth using a case structure. Five options are provided:

- December, January, or February
- March, April, or May
- June, July, or August
- September, October, or November
- *

Notice in Figure 9-54 that the different terms on the same line are separated with a pipe character (|). This means "or." If the user's response matches one of the terms, then the command associated with its line is executed. In Figure 9-55, the script has been run and the user has responded with a birth month of June.

Because the value of the MYMONTH variable matched the line in the case statement for June, the echo command for June, July, or August response was run.

FIGURE 9-54   Using a case statement

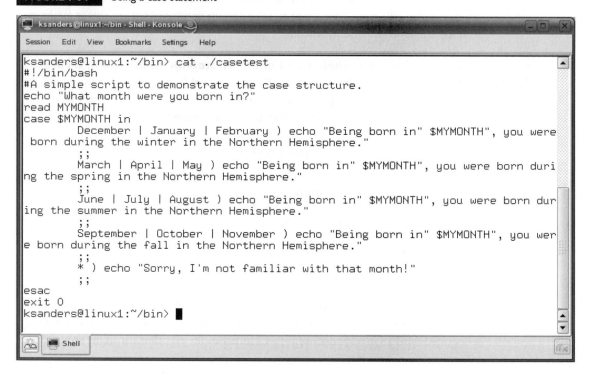

```
ksanders@linux1:~/bin> cat ./casetest
#!/bin/bash
#A simple script to demonstrate the case structure.
echo "What month were you born in?"
read MYMONTH
case $MYMONTH in
        December | January | February ) echo "Being born in" $MYMONTH", you were
 born during the winter in the Northern Hemisphere."
        ;;
        March | April | May ) echo "Being born in" $MYMONTH", you were born duri
ng the spring in the Northern Hemisphere."
        ;;
        June | July | August ) echo "Being born in" $MYMONTH", you were born dur
ing the summer in the Northern Hemisphere."
        ;;
        September | October | November ) echo "Being born in" $MYMONTH", you wer
e born during the fall in the Northern Hemisphere."
        ;;
        * ) echo "Sorry, I'm not familiar with that month!"
        ;;
esac
exit 0
ksanders@linux1:~/bin> 
```

FIGURE 9-55   Running a script that uses a case statement

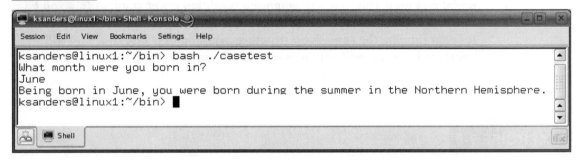

```
ksanders@linux1:~/bin> bash ./casetest
What month were you born in?
June
Being born in June, you were born during the summer in the Northern Hemisphere.
ksanders@linux1:~/bin> ▊
```

Notice that we added one extra response at the end of the case statement using an asterisk *. This option allows us to provide the user with feedback in the event that the response they supply doesn't match any of the other items listed in the case statement.

on the *Job*

The if/then/else and case structures are called branching structures. *Based on how a condition evaluates, the script branches in one direction or another. You can also use* looping *control structures within a shell script. Looping structures are a little more complex and you aren't likely to encounter any questions related to them on the Linux+ exam, so we're not going to cover them here.*

Looping structures come in two varieties, the while *loop and the* until *loop. A while loop executes over and over until a specified condition is no longer true. The structure of a while loop is:*

```
while condition
do
      script commands
done
```

A while loop will keep processing over and over and over until the condition evaluates to false.

In addition to a while loop, you can also use an until loop in your script. It works in the opposite manner. An until loop, on the other hand, runs over and over as long as the condition is false. As soon as the condition is true, it stops. The structure for an until loop is as follows:

```
until condition
do
      script commands
done
```

The biggest danger with looping structures is that it is possible to get stuck in an infinite loop. This happens when the condition never changes to a value that will break the loop. In this situation, the script gets "hung" because it keeps running the same loop structure over and over and over and will continue to do so until you manually break out of it using the CTRL-C key.

Let's practice working with basic shell scripts in the following exercise.

EXERCISE 9-8

Creating a Basic Shell Script

In this exercise, you will practice creating a basic shell script. This script will ask the user for a series of three numbers. It will then ask the user if he or she wants to sum the three numbers or average them. You will also add the execute permission to the file to allow the file owner to run it.

Complete the following:

1. If necessary, boot your Linux system and log in as a standard user. If you used the lab exercise in Chapter 3 to install your system, you can log in as **tux** with a password of **M3linux273**.

2. Change to the ~/bin directory.

3. At the shell prompt enter **vi ~/domath**.

4. Enter the following script:

```
#!/bin/bash
#A script to do some simple math.
clear
declare -i A
declare -i B
declare -i C
declare -i ANSWER
echo "Enter the first number:"
read A
echo "Enter the second number:"
read B
echo "Enter the third number:"
read C
echo "What would you like to do with these numbers?"
echo "P: Add them up!"
echo "V: Average them!"
```

```
echo "Enter your choice:"
read CHOICE
case $CHOICE in
        p | P )  ANSWER=A+B+C
        ;;
        v | V )  ANSWER=A+B+C
                    ANSWER=$ANSWER/3
        ;;
esac
echo "Your answer is" $ANSWER "."
exit 0
```

5. Save your changes to the script and exit vi.

6. Make the script executable by the file owner by entering **chmod u+x ./domath** at the shell prompt.

7. Test the script by entering **domath** at the shell prompt.

8. Test the script and verify that it works.

You are now an experienced bash shell user! Let's review what you learned in this chapter.

CERTIFICATION SUMMARY

In this chapter, you learned about working with the bash shell on your Linux system. Because the Linux+ exam has a heavy emphasis on command-line utilities, you need to be very familiar with the bash shell.

We began by discussing bash configuration files. We pointed out that there are two types of shells on a Linux system:

■ Login shells

■ Non-login shells

When running a login shell, /etc/profile is read first to initially configure the shell environment. The shell then searches for the following files in the user's home directory in the following order:

■ .bash_profile

■ .bash_login

■ .profile

The shell will read the first of these files found and use it to configure the shell environment for the current user. Different distributions will use different bash configuration files.

We then discussed the command history function of the bash shell. Using command history, you can press the UP ARROW key to scroll through a list of previously entered commands. These commands are saved in the .bash_history file in each user's home directory.

The bash shell also offers command completion. Using command completion, you can enter part of a command and then press the TAB key to automatically finish the command for you.

At this point in the chapter, we then turned to a discussion of environment variables. Environment variables are used to configure the shell environment. These variables are automatically populated when the bash shell is started, but you can modify many of them if needed. You can view the value of an environment variable using the following utilities:

- echo
- set
- env

To set the value of a variable, you can enter **_variable_name=value_**. For example, to add the /var/opt directory to the value of the PATH environment variable, you can enter **PATH=$PATH:/var/opt** at the shell prompt. This assigns the current value of the PATH variable ($PATH) concatenated with :/var/opt to PATH. After assigning a new value to an environment variable, you need to enter **export variable_name** at the shell prompt to make the new value available to other shells, including subshells launched by the current shell.

It's important to remember that any change you make to an environment variable is not persistent. To make it persistent, you need to edit one of the bash configuration files discussed in this chapter to make the value assignment to the variable each time a shell is started.

We also pointed out that you can create your own variables from the shell prompt. This is done using the same technique as described for environment variables. Like environment variables, user-defined variables have to be exported in order for them to be available to other shells.

We then turned our discussion to a special type of variable called an alias. An alias is a shortcut to commands on your Linux system. Many aliases are usually defined automatically when a shell is started by most distributions. You can view these using the alias command. You can also define your own aliases by entering **alias _alias_name="commands"_** at the shell prompt. Like variables, alias definitions aren't persistent. To make them persistent, you need to add the appropriate commands to one of your bash configuration files.

We then shifted gears and addressed the issue of managing the inputs and outputs of shell commands. Most shell commands have three file descriptors:

- stdin (0)
- stdout (1)
- stderr (2)

You can redirect stdout and stderr output from a command to a file by adding 1>*filename* or 2>*filename* to any command. If the specified file doesn't exist, the shell will create it. If it does exist, its contents will be overwritten. If you want to preserve the existing contents of the file, use >> instead of >. You can also send input from a file to a command's stdin using the < character.

In addition to redirecting to a file, you can also use a pipe to redirect stdout from one command to the stdin of another. This is done by entering **command | command** at the shell prompt. In fact, you can use many different commands in the same pipe.

We then discussed using pipes to manipulate and modify text coming from a command's stdout with the awk and sed tools. The sed utility is a stream editor. Like a regular interactive text editor, the sed stream editor can be used to edit text coming from another command's stdout. You can use command-line options to search and replace or delete text and display them on screen or write them to a file.

The awk command can also be used to manipulate a stream of text. The awk utility views each line arriving at its stdin as a record. Each word in the line is treated as a field. Using this metaphor, you can use awk to reference a specific field (word) in a specific record (line).

We ended this chapter by discussing how to create shell scripts. A shell script is a text file that is interpreted and run by the bash shell. A shell script can contain a series of commands that automate tasks and process information for you. A shell script is composed of the following parts:

- #!/bin/bash
- #Comments
- *shell commands*
- exit 0

Shell scripts can be edited with any text editor. They can be executed in one of two ways:

- Entering **/bin/bash** *script_file_name*.
- Adding the execute permission to the script file using the chmod utility and entering the file name of the script at the shell prompt.

In addition, you can also add the path to the script file to your PATH environment variable so users won't have to remember the full path to the file to use it. Alternatively, you can also move the script file to a directory that is already in the users' PATH environment variable, such as ~/bin.

In addition to running commands from a script, you can also read input from the user and assign it to a variable using the read *variable_name* command in a script. Script variables don't need to be declared if you are going to read text into them. However, if you want to read numbers into them that will be actually treated as numbers (so you can perform arithmetic functions, for example), then you need to declare them first using the declare –i *variable_name* command in the script.

You can also use control structures in your scripts. Control structures allow you to configure your scripts such that they branch or loop based on conditions that you supply. To make a script that branches in two directions, you can use an if/then/else structure in your script. If the condition you specify in the structure is true, then one set of commands (under then) is executed. If the condition is false, then the commands under the else portion of the structure are executed. The syntax for using if/then/else structures in a script is as follows:

```
if condition then
      commands
else
      commands
fi
```

If you want more than two branches in your script, then you can use the case structure. The case structure is an advanced if/then/else statement. With a case structure, you can evaluate multiple conditions and execute a series of commands that are executed according to which condition is true. The case structure is a handy way to replace multiple if/then/else statements in a script. The syntax for using the case structure is as follows:

```
case variable in
      condition_1 ) commands
      ;;
      condition_2 ) commands
      ;;
      condition_3 ) commands
      ;;
esac
```

✓ TWO-MINUTE DRILL

Use the Bourne Again Shell

❏ The default shell for most Linux distributions is the bash shell.

❏ Shells used to log in to the system are login shells.

❏ Shells opened after the user has logged in are non-login shells.

❏ The .bashrc file is used to configure non-login shells.

❏ The /etc/profile file is the first file read when creating a login shell.

❏ After the /etc/profile file is read, the bash shell looks for one of the following configuration files in the user's home directory:

   ❏ .bash_profile

   ❏ .bash_login

   ❏ .profile

❏ The first of these files found is the one used to configure the user's shell environment.

❏ The bash shell saves your command history in .bash_history.

❏ Pressing the UP ARROW key displays the last commands entered at the shell prompt.

❏ The bash shell offers command completion using the TAB key.

Manage Linux Environment Variables

❏ Environment variables are used to define the shell environment.

❏ You can view the values of your environment variables using the echo, set, or env shell commands.

❏ You must use a $ when referencing an environment variable to specify that the text is a variable name, not a string.

❏ You can set the value of an environment variable by entering *variable_name=value* at the shell prompt.

❏ After setting the value of a variable, you must export it using the export command.

❏ The value you assign to an environment variable is not persistent.

❑ To make a variable assignment persistent, you need to add the appropriate commands to one of your bash configuration files.

❑ You can also create user-defined variables in the same manner as environment variables.

❑ User-defined variables need to be exported in order for them to be used by other shells.

❑ You can create aliases on your system to create shortcuts to commands.

❑ You can view existing aliases using the alias command.

❑ You can define a new alias by entering **alias *alias_name=command***.

❑ Aliases are not persistent. You must add the appropriate commands to one of your bash configuration files to make them persistent.

Manage Shell Command Inputs and Outputs

❑ Most Linux shell commands have three standard file descriptors:

  ❑ stdin (0)

  ❑ stdout (1)

  ❑ stderr (2)

❑ You can redirect output (stdout and stderr) from the screen to a file using the > character after the command.

❑ Using 1>*filename* redirects stdout to the specified file.

❑ Using 2>*filename* redirects stderr to the specified file.

❑ Using > causes the specified file to be created if it doesn't exist. If it does exist, the file's contents will be overwritten.

❑ Using >> will cause the specified file's existing contents to be preserved and the new output appended to the end.

❑ You can use < to specify a file to be used as the stdin for a command.

❑ Using pipes allows you to move the stdout from one command to the stdin of another command.

❑ The syntax for using pipes is *command1 | command2*.

❑ You can use multiple commands within a single pipe.

❑ You can use awk and sed to manipulate the output from a command by including them in a pipe.

❑ The sed command can be used to replace or delete text from a command's stdout.

❑ The awk command treats command output like a database.

❑ Lines of text are seen as records.

❑ Words within a line of text are seen as fields.

❑ Using awk you can reference a specific field (word) within a specific record (line).

Create Shell Scripts

❑ Shell scripts are text files that contain a variety of commands that can be used to automate tasks and process information.

❑ All shell scripts begin with #!/bin/bash to specify that the bash shell should be used to run the script.

❑ You should include a comment at the beginning of each script that describes what it does.

❑ Your shell scripts should end with exit 0 to tell the script to exit.

❑ You can run shell scripts by running **/bin/bash** *script_file_name* or by adding the execute permission to the script file.

❑ You can read user input in a script using read *variable_name* in a script.

❑ To make your scripts more powerful, you can add branching structures in a script.

❑ Control structures allow you to configure your scripts such that they branch or loop based on conditions that you supply.

❑ To make a script that branches in two directions, you can use an if/then/else structure in your script.

❑ If the condition you specify in the structure is true, then one set of commands (under then) is executed.

❑ If the condition is false, then the commands under the else portion of the structure are executed.

❑ If you want more than two branches in your script, then you can use the case structure.

❑ With a case structure, you can evaluate multiple conditions and execute a series of commands that are executed according to which condition is true.

SELF TEST

Use the Bourne Again Shell

1. Which shell is the default shell used on most Linux distributions?
   A. ksh
   B. csh
   C. sh
   D. bash

2. Which configuration file is read when a non-login bash shell is run?
   A. .bashrc
   B. .bash_profile
   C. .bash_login
   D. .profile

3. Which configuration file is the first file read when a login bash shell is run?
   A. ~/.bashrc
   B. ~/.bash_profile
   C. ~/.bash_login
   D. ~/.profile
   E. /etc/profile

4. Which file contains a list of your most recently entered shell commands?
   A. ~/.history
   B. ~/.bash_history
   C. /etc/bash_history
   D. ~/.bash_commands

5. Which keystroke is used for the command completion feature of bash?
   A. ENTER
   B. F1
   C. TAB
   D. UP ARROW

Manage Linux Environment Variables

6. You want to configure your X Windows System to display your graphical desktop on a remote Linux system. Which environment variable would you need to modify to do this?

   A. ENV

   B. XWIN

   C. DISPLAY

   D. DESKTOP

7. You want to add the ~/temp directory to your system's PATH environment variable. You want to be sure you don't overwrite the existing directories in your path, so you enter **PATH=PATH:~/temp** at your shell prompt. Did you do this correctly?

   A. Yes, this command will work correctly.

   B. No, you must first export the variable before you set it.

   C. No, you must use a $ before each PATH variable name in the command.

   D. No, you must use a $ before the second PATH variable name in the command.

8. Which commands can you use to view the values currently assigned to your environment variables? (Choose two.)

   A. set

   B. display

   C. var

   D. show

   E. env

9. You want to view a list of the aliases currently defined on your Linux system. What command can you issue at the shell prompt to do this?

   A. alias

   B. alias –l

   C. display alias

   D. env alias

10. You want to create a new alias named mntflp that will mount a floppy diskette in your floppy drive, display the entry from the mount command that shows the floppy mounted, and display a long listing of files on the floppy diskette. Which command will do this?

   A. mntflp="mount –t vfat /dev/fd0 /media/floppy;mount | grep fd0;ls –l /media/floppy"

   B. alias mntflp="mount –t vfat /dev/fd0 /media/floppy;mount | grep fd0;ls –l /media/floppy"

    C. alias mntflp="mount –t vfat /dev/fd0 /media/floppy,mount | grep fd0,ls –l /media/floppy"

    D. alias mntflp=mount –t vfat /dev/fd0 /media/floppy;mount | grep fd0;ls –l /media/floppy

Manage Shell Command Inputs and Outputs

11. Which file descriptor refers to the text a command displays on the screen after the command has finished processing? (Choose two.)

    A. stdin

    B. stdout

    C. stdscreen

    D. stdoutput

    E. stderr

12. You want to send the standard output and the standard error from the tail /var/log/firewall command to a file named lastevents in the current directory. Which command will do this?

    A. /tail/var/log/firewall 1>lastevents 2>lastevents

    B. /tail/var/log/firewall >lastevents

    C. /tail/var/log/firewall 1>lastevents 2>&1

    D. /tail/var/log/firewall 1&2>lastevents

13. You want to send the contents of the logfile.txt file in the current directory to the sort command to sort them alphabetically and display them on the screen. Which command will do this?

    A. sort <./logfile.txt

    B. sort –i ./logfile.txt

    C. sort <./logfile.txt –d "screen"

    D. sort <./logfile.txt >screen

14. You want to send the contents of the logfile.txt file in the current directory to the sort command to sort them alphabetically and display them on the screen. Which command will do this?

    A. cat ./logfile.txt --sort

    B. cat ./logfile.txt | sort <./logfile.txt

    C. sort < | cat ./logfile.txt

    D. cat ./logfile.txt | sort

15. You want to display on screen the sixth, seventh, and eighth words in any line of /var/log/
    messages that has the term "syslog" in it. Which of the following commands will do this?
    A. cat /var/log/messages | awk '/syslog/ {print $6,$7,$8}'
    B. cat /var/log/messages | awk '/syslog/ {print 6,7,8}'
    C. cat /var/log/messages | awk /syslog/ {print $6,$7,$8}
    D. cat /var/log/messages | awk 'syslog {print 6,7,8}'

Create Shell Scripts

16. Which of the following elements must be included at the beginning of every shell script?
    A. #Comment
    B. #!/bin/bash
    C. exit 0
    D. #begin script

17. You've created a shell script in your home directory named myscript. How can you execute it?
    (Choose two.)
    A. Enter **/bin/bash ~/myscript** at the shell prompt.
    B. Enter **myscript** at the shell prompt.
    C. Select Start > Run at the shell prompt, then enter **~/myscript** and select Run.
    D. Enter **run ~/myscript** at the shell prompt.
    E. Enter **chmod u+x ~/myscript**, then enter **myscript** at the shell prompt.

18. Which command will create a new variable named TOTAL and set its type to be "integer"?
    A. variable –i TOTAL
    B. declare –i TOTAL
    C. declare TOTAL –t integer
    D. TOTAL=integer

LAB QUESTION

You need to create a script that can be used by the root user to mount removable media. The script
should display a prompt on the screen asking the user if he or she wants to mount a CD or a floppy.
After mounting the appropriate device, the corresponding entry from the mount command should be
displayed on the screen along with a listing of files on the device. Your script should also account for
user error. Outline the process you will follow to create and implement this script.

SELF TEST ANSWERS

Use the Bourne Again Shell

1. ☑ **D.** The bash shell is the default shell on most Linux distributions.
   ☒ **A, B,** and **C** are incorrect. While these shells are available on most distributions, the Bourne Again SHell (bash) is usually the default shell used.

2. ☑ **A.** A non-login shell reads the ~/.bashrc file to define the user's shell environment.
   ☒ **B, C,** and **D** are incorrect. **B** is used by login bash shells to set the user environment. **C** is also used by login bash shells to set the user environment. **D** is incorrect for the same reason.

3. ☑ **E.** The /etc/profile file is read when a bash login shell is first opened.
   ☒ **A, B, C,** and **D** are incorrect. **A** is read by non-login shells (although it may be read by login shells as well through one of the other configuration files). **B** is read, if it exists, but only after /etc/profile has been read. The same is true of **C** and **D**.

4. ☑ **B.** The ~/.bash_history file contains a list of your most recent shell commands.
   ☒ **A, C,** and **D** are incorrect. **A, C,** and **D** are distracters. There are no such files.

5. ☑ **C.** The TAB key is used with command completion.
   ☒ **A, B,** and **D** are incorrect. **A** is used to enter a command in the shell. It can't be used with command completion. **B** is a distracter. **D** is incorrect. It is used with command history, not command completion.

Manage Linux Environment Variables

6. ☑ **C.** The DISPLAY environment variable is used to configure where the X Windows desktop is displayed.
   ☒ **A, B,** and **D** are incorrect. **A** contains the name of the bash configuration file read when the shell was started. **B** is a distracter. There's no environment variable named XWIN. **D** is incorrect for the same reason.

7. ☑ **D.** You must reference the PATH variable using $PATH after the = sign. Otherwise, PATH will be interpreted as a literal string of text.
   ☒ **A, B,** and **C** are incorrect. **A** is incorrect because the $ has been omitted on the second instance of PATH in the command. **B** is incorrect. You export a variable after it has been created or modified. **C** is incorrect. The $ is only required on the second instance of PATH in the command.

8. ☑ **A and E.** You can use the set or the env command to view your variables.

☒ **B, C, and D** are incorrect. B, C, and D are distracters that use invalid commands.

9. ☑ **A.** The alias command is used to view your system's aliases.

☒ **B, C, and D** are incorrect. Each of these responses is a distracter and invalid.

10. ☑ **B.** The alias mntflp="mount –t vfat /dev/fd0 /media/floppy;mount | grep fd0;ls –l /media/floppy" command will create the mntflp alias.

☒ **A, C, and D** are incorrect. A omits the alias command. C is incorrect because it separates commands in the alias with commas instead of semi-colons. D is incorrect because it omits the quotes around the command in the alias.

Manage Shell Command Inputs and Outputs

11. ☑ **B and E.** The stdout and stderr file descriptors represent output displayed on screen (by default) by most commands.

☒ **A, C, and D** are incorrect. A refers to the standard input descriptor. C and D are distracters.

12. ☑ **C.** The /tail/var/log/firewall 1>lastevents 2>&1 command will send both stdout and stderr to the same file.

☒ **A, B, and D** are incorrect. A will cause the stdout to be overwritten by the stderr. B will only write the stdout to the file. D is a distracter that uses incorrect syntax.

13. ☑ **A.** The sort <./logfile.txt command will send the file to the stdin of the sort command.

☒ **B, C, and D** are incorrect. B is a distracter that uses incorrect syntax, as do C and D.

14. ☑ **D.** The cat ./logfile.txt | sort command will send the output of cat (containing the contents of the file) to the stdin of the sort command.

☒ **A, B, and C** are incorrect. A is a distracter that uses incorrect syntax, as do B and C.

15. ☑ **A.** The cat /var/log/messages | awk '/syslog/ {print $6,$7,$8}' command will find instances of "syslog" in the stdout of cat and print the sixth, seventh, and eighth words in each matching line.

☒ **B, C, and D** are incorrect. B is incorrect because it omits the $ characters needed to reference the fields in each record. C is incorrect because it omits the quotes need to enclose the awk options. D is incorrect because it omits the $ characters and also fails to enclose the search term in slashes "/ /".

Create Shell Scripts

16. ☑ **B.** The #!/bin/bash element must be included at the beginning of every bash shell script.

☒ **A, C, and D** are incorrect. A is expected, but not required. C should also be included in every script, but it comes at the end of the file. D is a distracter.

17. ☑ **A and E.** You can enter **/bin/bash ~/myscript** or **chmod u+x ~/myscript** to make the script execute.

    ☒ **B, C,** and **D** are incorrect. **B** won't work because the script text file, by default, isn't executable unless you change its permissions. **C** and **D** are distracters.

18. ☑ **B.** The declare –i TOTAL command will create the TOTAL variable and type it as integer.

    ☒ **A, C,** and **D** are incorrect. Each of these responses is a distracter that uses incorrect syntax.

LAB ANSWER

You should begin this task by outlining exactly what the script should do and in what order. A flowchart or sticky-notes on the wall work well for this task. Once done, you should create a new file using a text editor. The file should have a descriptive name such as mntdev. Then enter the following lines in the file:

```
#!/bin/bash
#A script to mount removable media.
echo "Which device do you want to mount?"
echo "A Floppy Diskette"
echo "E CD Disc"
read MYCHOICE
case $MYCHOICE in
     a | A )      mount -t vfat /dev/fd0 /media/floppy
             mount |grep fd0
             ls /media/floppy
             ;;
     e | E )      mount -t iso9660 /dev/cdrom /media/cdrom
             mount |grep cdrom
             ls /media/cdrom
             ;;
     * )     echo "Sorry, that's not a valid device."
             ;;
esac
exit 0
```

At this point, you could enter **/bin/bash ./mntdev** at the shell prompt to verify that it works correctly. Once you've fixed all the bugs, you can then make the file executable by entering **chmod u+x ./mntdev** at the shell prompt.

At this point, you need to decide whether or not you want to be able to run the file without specifying its full path at the shell prompt. If you don't want to use the full path, then you can move the script to a directory already contained in your PATH environment variable. Alternatively, you could also add the current directory to your PATH environment variable and export it.

10

Managing Linux Processes and Services

Y ou've learned a great deal about Linux so far in this book. We started off easy, learning about the historical origins of Linux and the different roles it can play in your organization. As we've progressed through each chapter, you've been introduced to increasingly more challenging Linux concepts and skills. In the last chapter, we really ratcheted things up when we talked about creating shell scripts. In this chapter, we're going to build on the previous chapter by talking about how the Linux operating system handles executable programs and scripts when they are run. Then we'll spend some time learning how to manage executables while they are running on the system. We'll discuss the following topics:

- How Linux handles processes
- Managing running processes
- Scheduling processes

INSIDE THE EXAM

Managing Linux Processes and Services

For your Linux+ exam, you need to be very familiar with how Linux handles running processes. You need to understand the heredity of Linux processes as well as the difference between user processes and system processes (daemons).

You should know how to use shell commands to view processes running on the system.

You need to know how to run a process in the foreground and in the background. You should also know how to kill a process from the command line. Finally, you need to know how to use at and cron to configure a service to run automatically in the future.

Let's begin this chapter by discussing how Linux handles processes.

CERTIFICATION OBJECTIVE 10.01

Describe How Linux Handles Processes

The key to being able to effectively manage Linux processes is to first understand how processes function within the operating system. In this part of this chapter, we're going to discuss the following:

- What exactly is a process?
- The heredity of Linux processes

Let's begin by discussing what a process is.

What Exactly Is a Process?

So, what exactly is a "process"? This term tends to be used in a variety of different ways in the computing industry, so it can be difficult sometimes to nail down exactly what it means. In this part of this chapter we'll help you understand what a process is by discussing the following:

- Processes defined
- Types of processes

Processes Defined

For our purposes here, a *process* is a program that has been loaded from a long-term storage device, usually a hard disk drive, into system RAM and is currently being processed by the CPU on the motherboard.

Many different types of programs can be executed to create a process. On your Linux system, the types of programs listed in Table 10-1 can be loaded into RAM and executed by the CPU.

Remember that the Linux operating system can run many processes "concurrently" on a single CPU. Depending on how your Linux system is being used, it may have only a few processes running at a given point in time or it may have hundreds of processes running concurrently.

| TABLE 10-1 | Linux Programs |

Type of Program	Description
Binary executables	These are programs that were originally created as a text file using a programming language, such as C or C++. The text file was then run through a compiler to create a binary file that can be processed by the CPU. Remember when you learned how to install applications from source code in a previous chapter? You were using a compiler (gcc) to compile the text file you downloaded into a binary executable.
Internal shell commands	Some of the commands you enter at the shell prompt are actual binary files in the file system that are loaded and run by the CPU. For example, when you enter **rpm** at the shell prompt, you load the rpm binary file into memory. Other commands, however, are not binary executables. Instead, they are commands that are rolled into the shell program itself. For example, if you enter **exit** at a shell prompt, you are actually running an internal shell command. There is no executable file in the file system named "exit." Instead, the computer code associated with the exit function is stored within the shell program code itself.
Shell scripts	These are text files that are executed through the shell itself. You can include commands to run binary executables within the text of any shell script. You created shell scripts in the previous chapter.

In the preceding paragraph, I put the term *concurrently* in quotes because most CPUs can't truly run multiple processes at the same time. Instead, the Linux operating system quickly switches between the various processes running on the CPU, making it appear as if the CPU is working on multiple processes concurrently. However, the CPU actually only executes a single process at a time. All other currently "running" processes wait in the background for their turn. The operating system maintains a schedule that determines when each process is allowed access to the CPU. This is called *multitasking*. Because the switching between processes happens so fast, it appears, to you and me at least, that the CPU is executing multiple processes at the same time.

on the
Üob
Newer, dual-core CPUs can actually execute more than one process at a time. Because there are two cores within the CPU, one core can execute one process while the other core works on another.

The Linux operating system uses several types of processes. Let's review those next.

Types of Processes

Not all processes on your Linux system are the same. Some processes are created by the end user when he or she executes a command from the shell prompt or though the X Windows graphical interface. These processes are called *user processes*. User processes are usually associated with some kind of end-user program running on the system.

For example, if you were to run the OpenOffice.org suite (oofromtemplate) from the shell prompt to create a spreadsheet, two user processes for the OpenOffice.org program would be created. This is shown in Figure 10-1.

The key point to remember about user processes is that they are called from within a shell and are associated with it.

However, not all processes running on your system are user processes. In fact, most processes executing on a given Linux system will probably be of a different type called *system processes* or *daemons*. Unlike a user process, a system process (usually) does not provide an application for an end user to use. Instead, they are used to provide system services, such as a Web server, an FTP server, a file service such as Samba, a print service such as CUPS, a logging service, and so on. These processes run in the background and usually don't provide any kind of user interface.

For example, consider the processes shown in Figure 10-2.

Notice that the system has many system processes running, including cupsd, hald, resmgrd, mdsnd, auditd, cron, qmgr, sshd, powersaved, and xinetd.

on the **Job** *System processes are usually (but not always) noted with a "d" at the end of the name, which stands for* daemon.

FIGURE 10-1 User processes created by OpenOffice.org

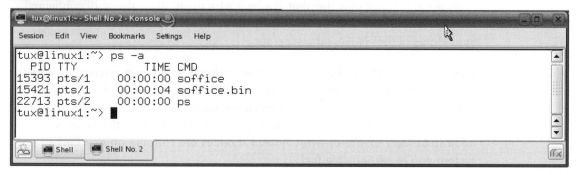

FIGURE 10-2   System processes

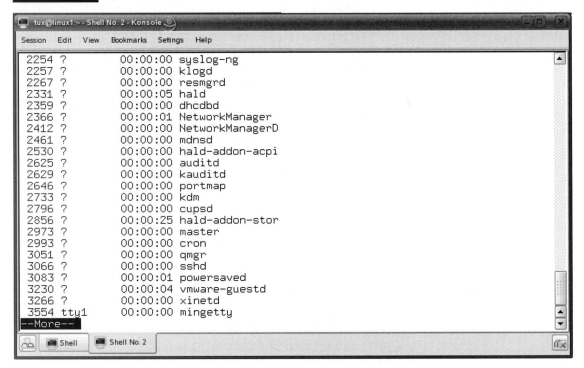

System processes are usually (but not always) loaded by the system itself when it is booted up. Therefore, they are not associated with a particular shell instance. This is another key difference between user processes and system processes. User processes are tied to the particular shell instance they were called from. System processes, on the other hand, are not.

By default, most Linux distributions boot with many, many daemons configured to automatically start at boot. Some of these daemons are critical to the overall functioning of the system; others are not.

on the *Job*

One of the first things I do after implementing a new Linux system, whether as a server or as a workstation, is to turn off all the daemons that aren't needed. Running unnecessary daemons consumes memory and CPU time. More seriously, it can also open up gaping security holes in the system. You need to be very aware of what system services are running on any Linux system you're responsible for!

SCENARIO & SOLUTION

You enter the **ls –l /tmp** command at the shell prompt. What kind of program did you load to create the ls process?	You loaded a binary executable named /bin/ls from the file system into your system RAM where it could be executed by the CPU.
When you enter **ls –l /tmp** at the shell prompt, what type of process did you create?	Because the command was issued by a user from within a shell and the command is associated with the shell, you created a user process.
You need to use the at daemon to schedule future jobs. You start the daemon by entering **rcatd start** at the shell prompt. What type of process did you create?	Because the atd process was started using an init script, it isn't associated with the terminal even though it was started from a shell prompt. Therefore, it is a system process.

To understand what daemons are critical to the overall function of the system and which aren't, you need to understand the heredity of Linux processes. Let's discuss this next.

The Heredity of Linux Processes

Right now, you're probably asking yourself: "What on earth is the 'heredity' of Linux processes? What is this guy talking about?" It sounds complicated, but it actually isn't. In this part of the chapter, we're going to review the following:

- The parent/child relationship between processes
- The heredity of processes

Let's first look at the parent/child relationship that exists between all processes.

The Parent/Child Relationship Between Processes

Understand that any process running on a Linux system can launch additional processes. The process that launched the new process is called the *parent process*. The new process itself is called the *child process*.

This parent/child relationship constitutes the *heredity* of Linux processes. Because any process, including child processes, can launch additional processes, it is possible to have many generations of processes running on a system. This is shown in Figure 10-3.

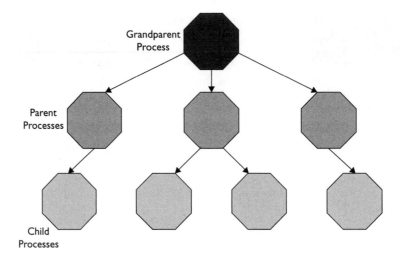

In Figure 10-3, the first parent process spawned three child processes. Each of these three child processes spawned child processes of their own, making the first parent process a grandparent! Do you see now why we call it a "heredity" of processes?

For any process on a Linux system, then, we need to be able to uniquely identify it as well as its heredity. Whenever a process is created on a Linux system, it is assigned two resources:

- **Process ID (PID) Number** This is a number assigned to each process that uniquely identifies it on the system.
- **Parent Process ID (PPID) Number** This is the PID of the process' parent process.

By assigning these two numbers to each process, we can track the heredity of any process through the system. With this in mind, let's next discuss the structure of the process heredity on Linux.

The Heredity of Processes

Notice in Figure 10-3 that I've depicted a "grandparent" process that spawned all of the other processes. This figure is drawn from a conceptual standpoint to illustrate the nature of the parent/child relationships between processes. However, it also can be used to describe the hierarchy of generations in a Linux system.

FIGURE 10-4

The init
process as the
grandparent of all
other processes

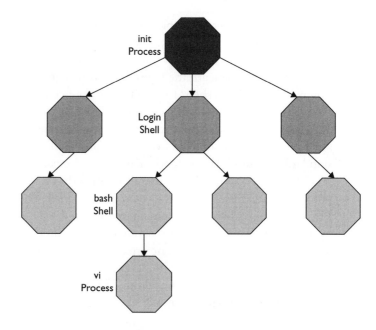

There really is a "grandparent" process that spawns all other processes. This is the init process. The kernel loads the init process automatically during bootup. The init process then launches child processes, such as a login shell, that in turn launch other processes, such as that used by the vi utility, as shown in Figure 10-4.

While other processes are assigned a PID randomly from the operating system's table of available PID numbers, the init process is always assigned a PID of 1. This brings up an interesting point. If the init process is the first process from which all other processes descend, what then is its PPID? Does it even have one? Actually, it does. Because the init process is launched directly by the Linux kernel (which always has a PID of 0), the PPID of the init process is always 0. This is shown in Figure 10-5.

FIGURE 10-5

The PPID of the
init process

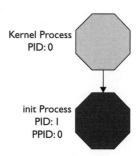

The init process is responsible for launching all system processes that are configured to automatically start on bootup. It also creates a login shell that is used for login.

This brings up an important point. Notice in Figure 10-4 that I've placed a second bash shell beneath the login shell. You might ask: "Couldn't you just run vi from within the login shell? Do you have to launch a second bash shell?"

Actually, in this figure, vi was, in fact, launched from the login shell. Why, then, does it show a second shell between the vi process and the login shell? It's because any time you run a command from within any shell (whether it's a login shell or a standard shell session), a second shell session is created, called a subshell, and the process for the command you entered is run within it. The subshell is a separate process in and of itself and has its own PID assigned. The PPID of the subshell is the PID of the shell where the command was entered.

The subshell process remains active for as long as the command that was entered at the shell prompt is in use. The process for the command runs within the subshell and is assigned its own PID. The PPID of the command's process is, of course, the PID of the subshell it's running within. When the command process is complete and has exited, the subshell is terminated and control is returned back to the original shell session.

on the **Ü** o b *This process of creating a new subshell and running the command process within it is called **forking**.*

For example, in Figure 10-6, the user has issued the vi command at the shell prompt of a bash shell. A new subshell is created and the vi process is run within it. When the user exits vi, the subshell is destroyed and control is returned to the original shell instance.

FIGURE 10-6

Running a process from the shell prompt

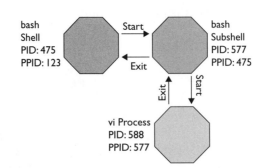

SCENARIO & SOLUTION

You have a process named su running on your Linux system. It has a PID of 3840. What is this number?	The PID is the process' ID number. It is used to uniquely identify the process on the system.
Your su process also has a PPID of 3709. What is this number?	The PPID is the PID of the process that created the su process (i.e., its parent process).
To what process can all processes running on your Linux system trace their heredity back to?	The init process (PID 1) is the grandparent of all Linux processes.

Now that you understand how Linux processes work, you're ready to start managing them. Let's do that next.

CERTIFICATION OBJECTIVE 10.02

Manage Running Processes

One of the key tasks you need to complete is to manage the processes running on the Linux systems you support. In this part of this chapter we're going to review how to do this. We're going to discuss the following topics:

- Starting system processes
- Viewing running processes
- Prioritizing processes
- Managing foreground and background processes
- Ending a running process

Let's begin by learning how to start processes.

Starting System Processes

There are two basic ways to start a process on a Linux system. For a user process, you simply enter the command or script name at the shell prompt. For example, to run the vi program, you simply enter **vi** at the shell prompt. When you do, the vi process is created, as shown in Figure 10-7.

FIGURE 10-7   Viewing the vi user process

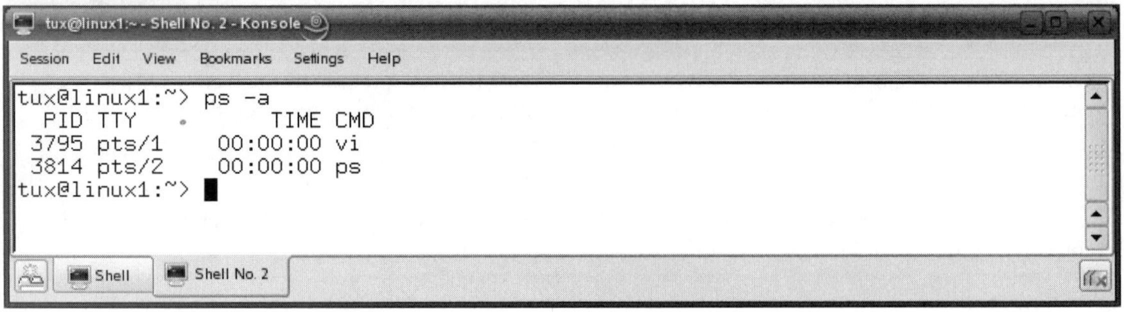

```
tux@linux1:~> ps -a
  PID TTY          TIME CMD
 3795 pts/1    00:00:00 vi
 3814 pts/2    00:00:00 ps
tux@linux1:~> █
```

For system processes, however, you use an *init script*. An init script is used by the init process to start processes on system boot. These scripts are stored in a specific directory on your Linux system. Which directory they are stored in depends on your Linux distribution. Most Linux distributions use one of two types of init scripts:

- **System V**   Linux distributions that use System V init scripts store them in the /etc/rc.d directory. Within /etc/rc.d are a series of subdirectories named rc0.d through rc6.d. Each of these directories is associated with a particular runlevel (which we'll discuss later in this book). Within each of these subdirectories are symbolic links that point to the init scripts for your system daemons, which reside in /etc/rc.d/init.d. Red Hat Linux and Fedora use System V–type init scripts.

- **BSD**   Other Linux distributions use BSD-style init scripts. These scripts reside in the /etc/init.d directory. Within /etc/init.d are a series of directories named rc0.d through rc6.d. As with System V init scripts, these directories are associated with specific runlevels. These directories contain links that point to the init scripts in /etc/init.d. SUSE Linux uses this type of init script.

In addition to using the init process to run these scripts, you can run these scripts from the command prompt. Simply enter **/etc/init.d/*script_name*** at the shell prompt (on a BSD-style system) or **/etc/rc.d/init.d/*script_name*** (on a System V–style system). If you're not sure of which script name you should use, you can use the ls command to generate a listing of scripts in the script directory. This is shown in Figure 10-8.

FIGURE 10-8   Init scripts in /etc/init.d

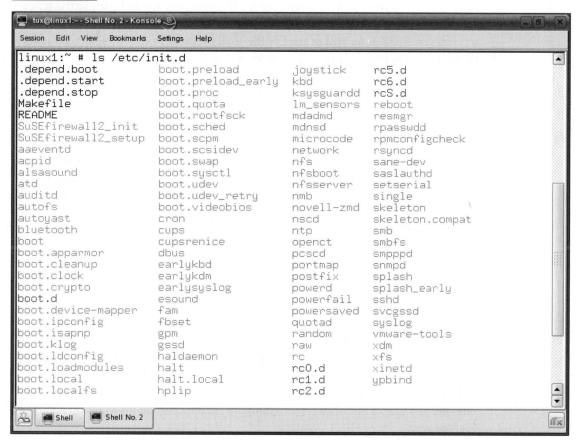

The actual scripts in your init directory depend on which services you've installed on your particular system. Whenever you use the rpm utility to install a service on your system, a corresponding init script is automatically installed in your init script directory. Once there, you can run any script by simply running it from the command prompt. The syntax is (on a BSD-style system):

```
/etc/init.d/script_name start | stop | restart
```

For example, to run the smb service, you would enter **/etc/init.d/smb start** at the shell prompt. To stop it, you would enter **/etc/init.d/smb stop**. To restart it, you would enter **/etc/init.d/smb restart**.

On some distributions, such as SUSE Linux, you can also use the rc script to start, stop, or restart a service process without having to specify the full path to the script file. The syntax is rc*script_name* start | stop | restart. For example, to start the smb service, you could enter **rcsbm start** at the shell prompt. To stop it, you could enter **rcsmb stop**. You could also use the restart option to restart it.

Now that you know how to start and stop system processes, let's discuss how you go about viewing your running processes.

Viewing Running Processes

As we've gone through this chapter, I've provided you with graphics that show the processes running on a Linux system. In this part of the chapter, we're going to discuss how to view running processes on your system. We'll cover the following tools:

- Using top
- Using ps

Let's begin by looking at the top utility.

Using top

Linux provides a wide variety of tools for viewing running processes on your system. One of my favorites is the venerable top utility. You run top by simply entering **top** at the shell prompt. When you do, the interface shown in Figure 10-9 is displayed.

In Figure 10-9, you can see that top displays some of your running processes, one on each line. The following columns are used to display information about each process:

- **PID**   The process ID of the process.
- **USER**   The name of the user that owns the process.
- **PR**   The priority assigned to the process. (We'll discuss process priorities later in this chapter.)
- **NI**   This is the nice value of the process. (We'll talk about what this means later in this chapter.)
- **VIRT**   The amount of virtual memory used by the process.
- **RES**   The amount of physical RAM the process is using (its resident size) in kilobytes.

- **SHR**   The amount of shared memory used by the process.
- **S**   The status of the process. Possible values include:
    - **D**   Uninterruptibly sleeping.
    - **R**   Running.
    - **S**   Sleeping.
    - **T**   Traced or stopped.
    - **Z**   Zombied.

FIGURE 10-9   Using top to view running processes

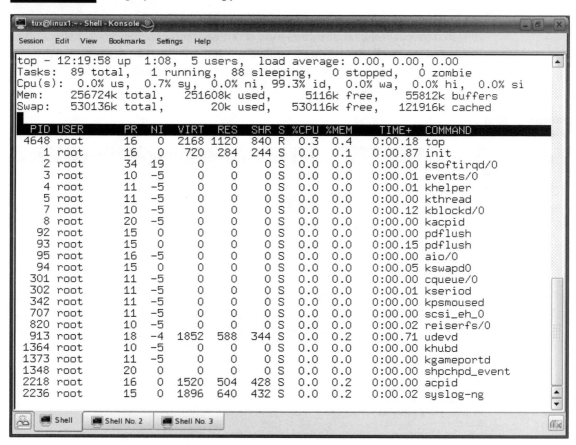

on the
Job *A zombied process is one where the process has finished executing and exited, but the process' parent didn't get notified that it was finished and hasn't released the child process' PID. A zombied process may eventually clear up on its own. If it doesn't, you may need to manually kill the parent process. We'll talk about how to do this later in the chapter.*

- **%CPU** The percentage of CPU time used by the process.
- **%MEM** The percentage of available physical RAM used by the process.
- **TIME+** The total amount of CPU time the process has consumed since being started.
- **COMMAND** The name of the command that was entered to start the process.

The key aspect I like about top is that it's dynamic. The screen is constantly updated to reflect the latest information about each process. You can sort the information as well. By pressing H while top is running, you can display the help screen, which provides you with the keystrokes required to sort by a particular category. This help screen is shown in Figure 10-10.

FIGURE 10-10 Viewing the top help screen

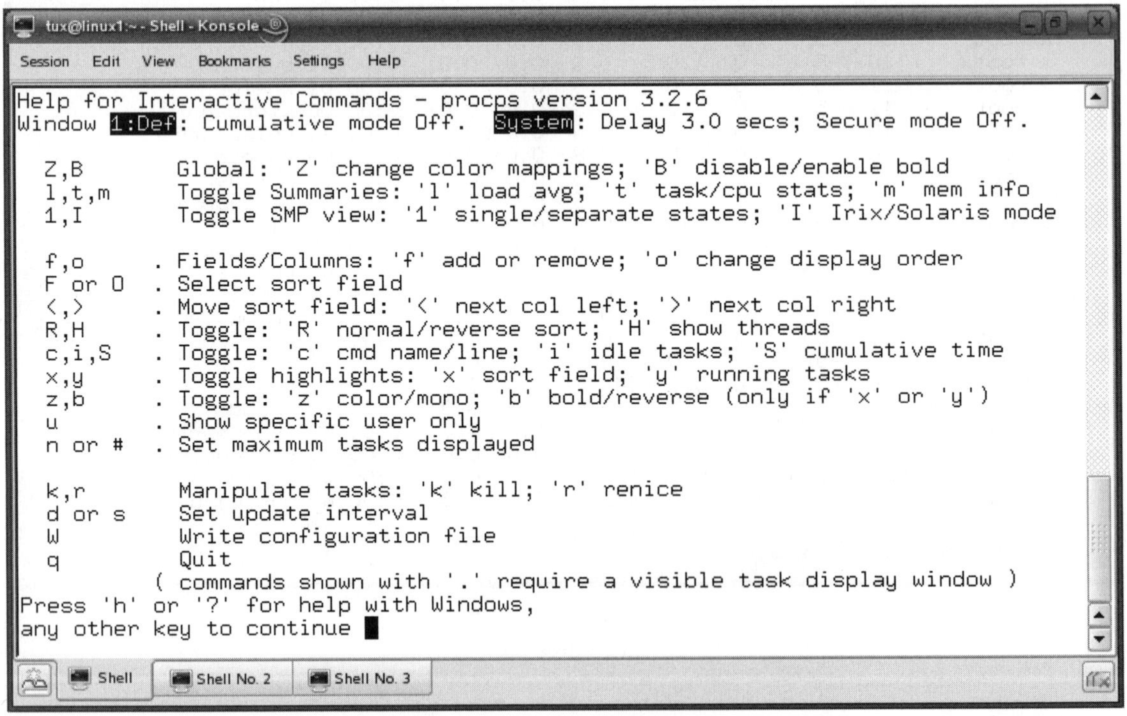

```
tux@linux1:~ - Shell - Konsole

Session   Edit   View   Bookmarks   Settings   Help

Help for Interactive Commands - procps version 3.2.6
Window 1:Def: Cumulative mode Off.  System: Delay 3.0 secs; Secure mode Off.

  Z,B       Global: 'Z' change color mappings; 'B' disable/enable bold
  l,t,m     Toggle Summaries: 'l' load avg; 't' task/cpu stats; 'm' mem info
  1,I       Toggle SMP view: '1' single/separate states; 'I' Irix/Solaris mode

  f,o     . Fields/Columns: 'f' add or remove; 'o' change display order
  F or O  . Select sort field
  <,>     . Move sort field: '<' next col left; '>' next col right
  R,H     . Toggle: 'R' normal/reverse sort; 'H' show threads
  c,i,S   . Toggle: 'c' cmd name/line; 'i' idle tasks; 'S' cumulative time
  x,y     . Toggle highlights: 'x' sort field; 'y' running tasks
  z,b     . Toggle: 'z' color/mono; 'b' bold/reverse (only if 'x' or 'y')
  u       . Show specific user only
  n or #  . Set maximum tasks displayed

  k,r       Manipulate tasks: 'k' kill; 'r' renice
  d or s    Set update interval
  W         Write configuration file
  q         Quit
            ( commands shown with '.' require a visible task display window )
Press 'h' or '?' for help with Windows,
any other key to continue █

  Shell    Shell No. 2    Shell No. 3
```

This screen also shows you how to use other options with top. For example, you can press F to display a list of columns that you can add to the display, as shown in Figure 10-11.

Fields that will be displayed are indicated with an asterisk (*). To add or remove a field, just press the appropriate letter. This will toggle the asterisk on or off to determine whether or not the field is displayed. You can also press U to specify that only the processes associated with a specific user be displayed.

I really like top. The only thing I don't like about it is that it only shows the top few processes on your system. There will be times when you need to see everything running on your system. In this situation, top just doesn't cut it. You need to use the ps utility.

FIGURE 10-11   Adding columns to the top display

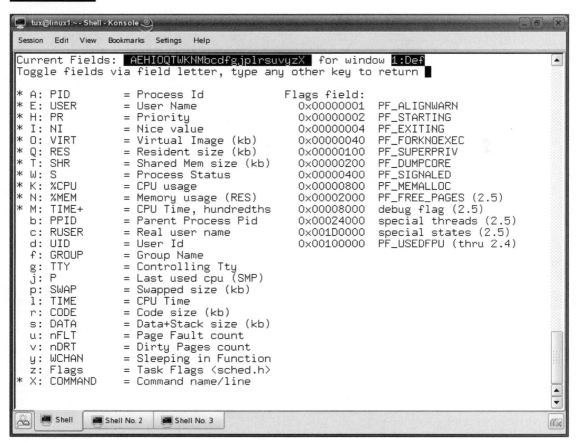

Using ps

The ps utility can be used to display running processes on your system. Unlike top, which displays processes dynamically, ps displays a snapshot of the current processes running.

exam

ⓦatch

As good a utility as it is, you probably won't see many, if any, questions on the Linux+ exam covering top. You will, *however, be expected to know how to use the ps utility.*

By simply entering ps, the processes associated with the *current* shell are displayed, as shown in Figure 10-12.

In Figure 10-12, the following processes are displayed by ps:

- **su** The su utility is in use inside this shell to switch to the root user account.
- **bash** The current bash shell session.
- **ps** Because ps was in use to list current processes, its process is also listed.

Notice that the following information is displayed by default:

- **PID** The process ID of the process.
- **TTY** The name of the terminal session (shell) that the process is running within.
- **TIME** The amount of CPU time used by the process.
- **CMD** The name of the command that was entered to create the process.

FIGURE 10-12 Using ps to display current shell processes

Notice in Figure 10-12 that only three processes were listed. On the system where ps was run in Figure 10-12, many different processes were running. I had top running in a separate shell. In addition, X Windows and the KDE desktop environment were running as well. Why didn't they show up in the list? It's because, by default, ps only shows processes associated with the current shell. Hence, only the shell, su, and ps processes are displayed.

To see all processes running on the system, you need to use the –e option with ps. An example is shown in Figure 10-13.

As you can see in Figure 10-13, the –e option results in many more processes being displayed by the ps command. Also notice that most of the processes shown in Figure 10-13 have a ? in the TTY column. This indicates a system process. Remember that system processes (daemons) are loaded by the init process at startup and, therefore, are not associated with any shell. Because of this, a ? is displayed in the TTY column in the output of ps.

FIGURE 10-13   Viewing all processes with ps –e

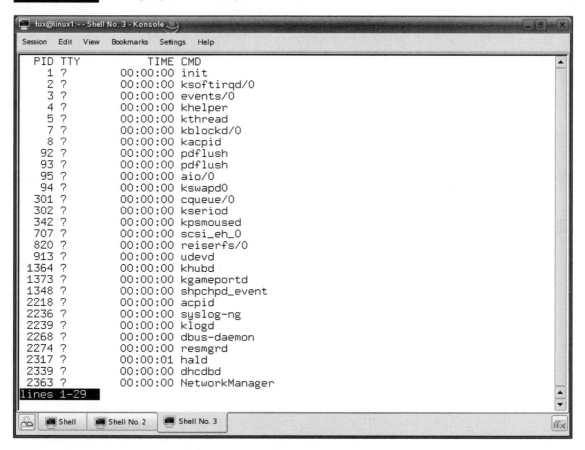

FIGURE 10-14 Viewing extended process information with ps –ef

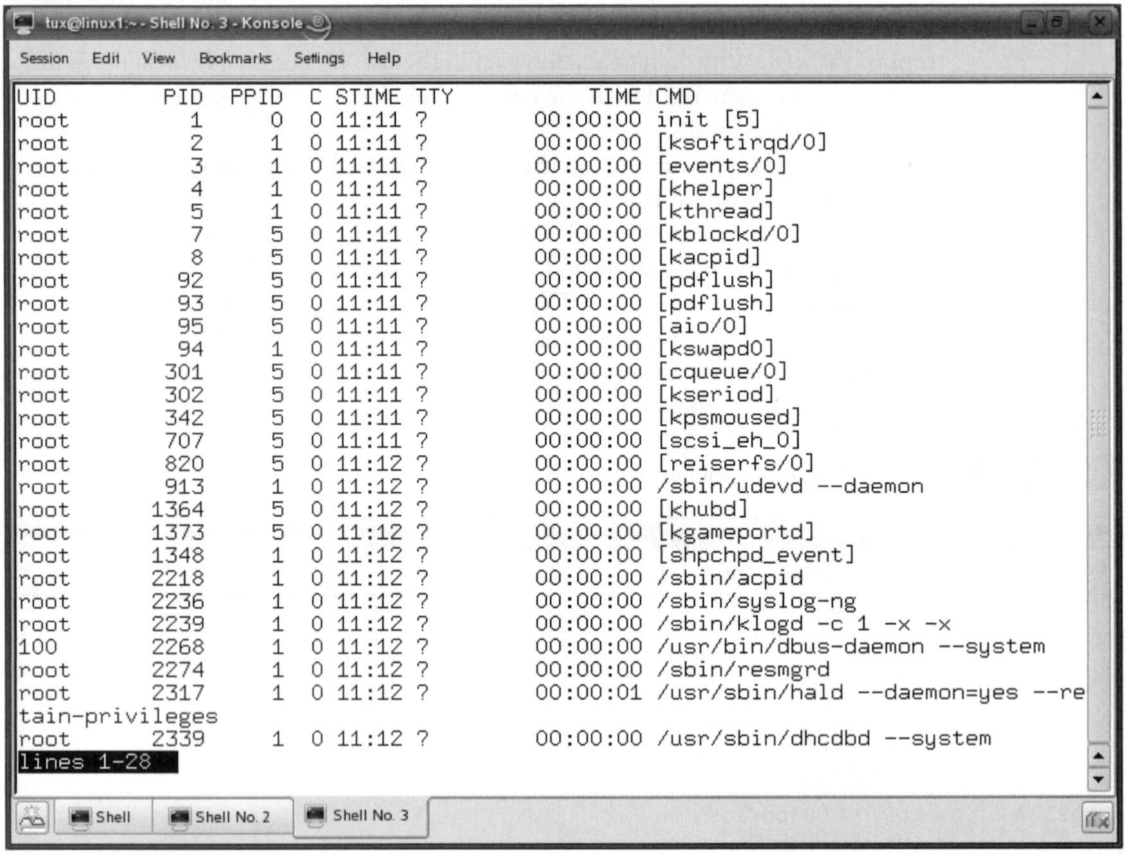

```
tux@linux1:~ - Shell No. 3 - Konsole

Session   Edit   View   Bookmarks   Settings   Help

UID         PID   PPID   C STIME TTY       TIME CMD
root          1      0   0 11:11 ?     00:00:00 init [5]
root          2      1   0 11:11 ?     00:00:00 [ksoftirqd/0]
root          3      1   0 11:11 ?     00:00:00 [events/0]
root          4      1   0 11:11 ?     00:00:00 [khelper]
root          5      1   0 11:11 ?     00:00:00 [kthread]
root          7      5   0 11:11 ?     00:00:00 [kblockd/0]
root          8      5   0 11:11 ?     00:00:00 [kacpid]
root         92      5   0 11:11 ?     00:00:00 [pdflush]
root         93      5   0 11:11 ?     00:00:00 [pdflush]
root         95      5   0 11:11 ?     00:00:00 [aio/0]
root         94      1   0 11:11 ?     00:00:00 [kswapd0]
root        301      5   0 11:11 ?     00:00:00 [cqueue/0]
root        302      5   0 11:11 ?     00:00:00 [kseriod]
root        342      5   0 11:11 ?     00:00:00 [kpsmoused]
root        707      5   0 11:11 ?     00:00:00 [scsi_eh_0]
root        820      5   0 11:12 ?     00:00:00 [reiserfs/0]
root        913      1   0 11:12 ?     00:00:00 /sbin/udevd --daemon
root       1364      5   0 11:12 ?     00:00:00 [khubd]
root       1373      5   0 11:12 ?     00:00:00 [kgameportd]
root       1348      1   0 11:12 ?     00:00:00 [shpchpd_event]
root       2218      1   0 11:12 ?     00:00:00 /sbin/acpid
root       2236      1   0 11:12 ?     00:00:00 /sbin/syslog-ng
root       2239      1   0 11:12 ?     00:00:00 /sbin/klogd -c 1 -x -x
100        2268      1   0 11:12 ?     00:00:00 /usr/bin/dbus-daemon --system
root       2274      1   0 11:12 ?     00:00:00 /sbin/resmgrd
root       2317      1   0 11:12 ?     00:00:01 /usr/sbin/hald --daemon=yes --re
tain-privileges
root       2339      1   0 11:12 ?     00:00:00 /usr/sbin/dhcdbd --system
lines 1-28

   Shell     Shell No. 2     Shell No. 3
```

Another thing you may notice in Figures 10-12 and 10-13 is that the amount of detail displayed by ps is rather limited as compared to top. You can use the –f option with ps to display more detail. In Figure 10-14, the –e and –f options have been used together in the ps command to display extended information about every process running on the system.

With the –f option, you can now view additional information, including the following:

■ **UID**   The user ID of the process' owner.
■ **PPID**   The PID of the process' parent process.

- **C** The amount of processor time utilized by the process.
- **STIME** The time that the process started.

If you really want to crank things up, you can also use the –l option with the ps command. The –l option displays the long format of the ps output. An example is shown in Figure 10-15.

With the –l option, you can view the following information about processes running on your system:

- **F** The flags associated with the process. This column uses the following codes:
  - **1** Forked, but didn't execute.
  - **4** Used root privileges.

FIGURE 10-15   Viewing long format output from ps –efl

```
tux@linux1:~ - Shell No. 3 - Konsole

Session   Edit   View   Bookmarks   Settings   Help

F S    UID    PID   PPID   C  PRI   NI ADDR  SZ WCHAN    TTY         TIME CMD
4 S      0      1      0   0   76    0 -    180 -        ?       00:00:00 init
1 S      0      2      1   0   94   19 -      0 ksofti   ?       00:00:00 ksoftirqd/0
1 S      0      3      1   0   70   -5 -      0 worker   ?       00:00:00 events/0
1 S      0      4      1   0   71   -5 -      0 worker   ?       00:00:00 khelper
1 S      0      5      1   0   71   -5 -      0 worker   ?       00:00:00 kthread
1 S      0      7      5   0   70   -5 -      0 worker   ?       00:00:00 kblockd/0
1 S      0      8      5   0   80   -5 -      0 worker   ?       00:00:00 kacpid
1 S      0     92      5   0   75    0 -      0 pdflus   ?       00:00:00 pdflush
1 S      0     93      5   0   75    0 -      0 pdflus   ?       00:00:00 pdflush
1 S      0     95      5   0   76   -5 -      0 worker   ?       00:00:00 aio/0
1 S      0     94      1   0   75    0 -      0 kswapd   ?       00:00:00 kswapd0
1 S      0    301      5   0   71   -5 -      0 worker   ?       00:00:00 cqueue/0
1 S      0    302      5   0   71   -5 -      0 serio_   ?       00:00:00 kseriod
1 S      0    342      5   0   71   -5 -      0 worker   ?       00:00:00 kpsmoused
1 S      0    707      5   0   71   -5 -      0 scsi_e   ?       00:00:00 scsi_eh_0
1 S      0    820      5   0   70   -5 -      0 worker   ?       00:00:00 reiserfs/0
5 S      0    913      1   0   78   -4 -    463 -        ?       00:00:00 udevd
1 S      0   1364      5   0   70   -5 -      0 hub_th   ?       00:00:00 khubd
1 S      0   1373      5   0   71   -5 -      0 gamepo   ?       00:00:00 kgameportd
1 S      0   1348      1   0   80    0 -      0 -        ?       00:00:00 shpchpd_event
5 S      0   2218      1   0   76    0 -    380 -        ?       00:00:00 acpid
5 S      0   2236      1   0   75    0 -    474 -        ?       00:00:00 syslog-ng
5 S      0   2239      1   0   76    0 -    413 syslog   ?       00:00:00 klogd
5 S    100   2268      1   0   77    0 -    888 -        ?       00:00:00 dbus-daemon
5 S      0   2274      1   0   77    0 -    450 -        ?       00:00:00 resmgrd
5 S      0   2317      1   0   76    0 -   1097 -        ?       00:00:01 hald
1 S      0   2339      1   0   75    0 -    464 -        ?       00:00:00 dhcdbd
5 S      0   2363      1   0   76    0 -   3013 stext    ?       00:00:00 NetworkManager
lines 1-29

     Shell       Shell No. 2      Shell No. 3
```

- **S** The state of the process. This column uses the following codes:
  - **D** Uninterruptible sleep.
  - **R** Running.
  - **S** Interruptible sleep.
  - **T** Stopped or traced.
  - **Z** Zombied.
- **PRI** The priority of the process.
- **NI** The nice value of the process. We'll talk about what this means in the next section.
- **SZ** The size of the process.
- **WCHAN** The name of the kernel function in which the process is sleeping. You will see a dash (–) in this column if the process is currently running.

Now that you know how to view running processes, we now need to discuss how to prioritize processes running on your system. Let's do that next.

Prioritizing Processes

Recall from the first part of this chapter that Linux is a multitasking operating system. It rotates CPU time between each of the processes running on the system, creating the illusion that all of the processes are running concurrently.

SCENARIO & SOLUTION	
You want to use the top utility to view processes running on your system. What command would you enter at the shell prompt?	You would simply enter **top** at the shell prompt.
You want to view a list of all processes associated with your current shell session. What command would you enter at the shell prompt?	You would enter **ps** at the shell prompt.
You need to see a list of system processes running on your system. What command would you enter at the shell prompt?	You would enter **ps –e** at the shell prompt.

Because Linux is a multitasking operating system, you can specify a priority level for each process. Doing so determines how much CPU time a given process gets in relation to other processes on the system.

By default, Linux tries to equalize the amount of CPU time given to all of the processes on the system. However, there may be times when you need to adjust the priority assigned to a process. Depending on how the system is deployed, you may want a particular process to have a higher priority than other processes. This can be done using several Linux utilities. In this part of the chapter, we'll review the following:

- Setting priorities with nice
- Setting priorities of running processes with renice

Let's begin by learning how to use the nice utility.

Setting Priorities with nice

The nice utility can be used on Linux to launch a program with a different priority level. Recall from our previous discussion of top and ps that each process running on your system has a PR and NI value associated with it. This is shown in Figure 10-16.

The PR value is the process' kernel priority. The higher the number, the higher the priority of the process. The lower the number, the lower the priority of the process. The NI value is the nice value of the process. The nice value is factored into the kernel calculations that determine the priority of the process. The nice value for any Linux process can range between –20 and +19. Again, the lower the number, the higher the priority of the process.

You can't directly manipulate the priority of a process, but you can manipulate the process' nice value. The easiest way to do this is to set the nice value when you initially run the command that launches the process. This is done using the nice command. The syntax for using nice is nice –n *nice_level command*.

For example, suppose I wanted to launch the vi program and increase its priority on the system by decreasing its nice level to a value of –5. Before doing so, vi runs on my system with a priority of 78. This is shown in Figure 10-17.

Notice in Figure 10-17 that the vi process has a default nice level of 0. The kernel uses this value to calculate the overall priority of the process, which comes out to a value of 78. I could adjust this priority level to a higher level by entering **nice –n –15 vi** at the shell prompt. After doing so, the priority and nice values of the vi process are decreased, increasing its priority level on the system. This is shown in Figure 10-18.

FIGURE 10-16 Viewing PR and NI values

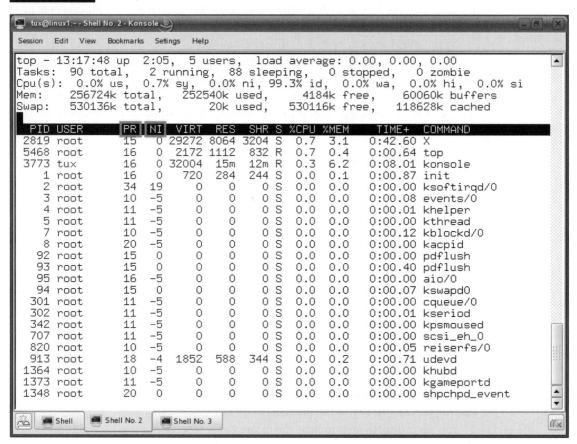

FIGURE 10-17 The default priority of vi

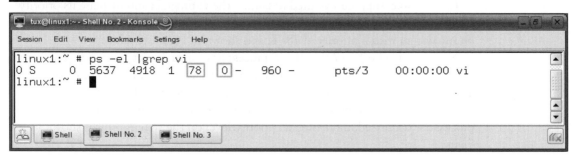

FIGURE 10-18   Changing the priority of vi with the nice command

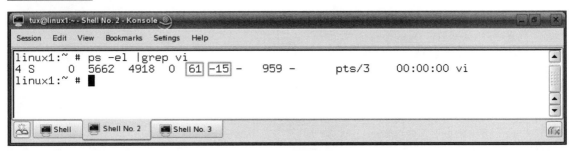

Notice in Figure 10-18 that the nice value was decreased to a value of –15. This caused the overall priority of the process to be reduced to a value of 61.

Be aware that Linux is hesitant to allow you to reduce the value of nice for processes running on the system. Because Linux is a true multi-user operating system, it's possible for multiple users on the same system to adjust the nice values of their own processes. Naturally, every user on the system thinks that his or her process is much more important than anyone else's and may be tempted to crank that nice value clear down to –20 for just about everything they run.

To keep this from happening, Linux won't let you adjust the nice value of a process below 0 unless you are logged in as root. Basically, if you aren't root, you won't be allowed to use a negative number with the nice command.

The nice command works great for modifying the nice value when running a command to start a process. But what can you do if the process you want to modify is already running? You can't use nice in this situation. You have to use the renice command instead. Let's discuss how renice works next.

Setting Priorities of Running Processes with renice

Instead of having to kill a process and restart it with nice to set its nice value, you can use the renice command to adjust the nice value of a process that is currently running on the system. The syntax for using this command is renice *nice_value PID*.

For example, in Figure 10-18, the PID of the vi process is 5662. If I wanted to adjust the priority of the vi process to a lower level without unloading the program, I could enter **renice 4 5662** at the shell prompt. This is shown in Figure 10-19.

FIGURE 10-19 Setting the priority of a running process with renice

As you can see in Figure 10-19, the nice value of the vi process was increased from –15 to 4. This caused the overall priority of the process to go from 61 to 84, decreasing the process' overall priority level. Just as with nice, you must be logged in as root to adjust the nice level of a running process to a negative number.

Now that you know how to prioritize running processes, here are some possible scenario questions and their answers.

SCENARIO & SOLUTION

One process on your Linux system has a nice value of 12, another has a nice value of 0. Which of these processes has a higher priority?	The process with a nice value of 0 has a higher priority.
You want to load a program named myapp from the shell prompt. This application will provide a key service on the system, so you want to assign it a nice value of –10. What command would you enter at the shell prompt?	You would first change to your root user account. Then you would enter **nice –n –10 myapp**.
With the myapp process running, you determine that it really doesn't need as high a priority as you gave it previously. The myapp process has a PID of 4560. What command can you enter to reduce the nice value to 0 without unloading the application?	You would enter **renice 0 4560** at the shell prompt.

Let's now shift gears and talk about foreground and background processes.

Managing Foreground and Background Processes

In this part of the chapter, we need to discuss running processes in the foreground and background. We'll address the following topics:

- Running processes in the background
- Switching processes between the background and the foreground

Running Processes in the Background

Recall from our earlier discussion of processes that, when you enter any command at the shell prompt, a subshell is created and the process is run within it. As soon as the process exits, the subshell is destroyed. During the time that the process is running, the shell prompt of the parent shell disappears. You can't do anything at the shell prompt unless you open a new terminal session.

This happens because the process runs in the *foreground*. This behavior is even more apparent when running a graphical application from the shell prompt. In Figure 10-20, the OpenOffice.org application has been launched from the shell prompt using the oofromtemplate command.

Notice in Figure 10-20 that the cursor in the shell is unavailable. It will remain so until OpenOffice is closed. Only then can additional commands be entered at this shell prompt.

This is the default behavior for all commands entered at the shell prompt, whether the program is a text-based shell program or a graphical X Windows program. However, it is possible to run the program in the *background*. If you do this, the program you launch will run normally. However, control will be returned immediately to the shell. You can then use the shell to launch other programs or perform other shell tasks.

Running a program in the background is very easy. All you have to do is append an ampersand (&) character to the command. This tells the shell to run the program in the background. In Figure 10-21, the OpenOffice application has been launched again. However, this time an ampersand was appended to the end of the command, causing it to run in the background.

Notice in Figure 10-21 that two values were displayed on the screen after the process was run in the background. The first value [1] is the background job ID that was assigned to the background job. The second value is the PID of the process.

Launching a graphical application in the foreground

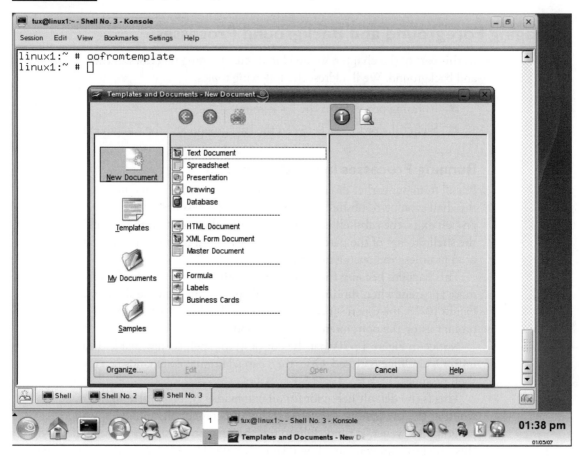

You can view all background jobs running on the system by entering **jobs** at the shell prompt. This is shown in Figure 10-22.

In Figure 10-22, the output of the jobs command displays the status of the job as well as the name of the command that was run to create the background job. Let's next discuss how to move jobs from the background to foreground and vice versa.

FIGURE 10-21   Running an application in the background

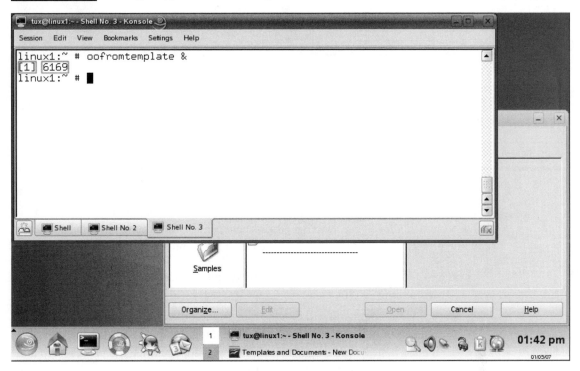

FIGURE 10-22   Viewing background jobs with the jobs command

FIGURE 10-23   Sending a foreground process to the background

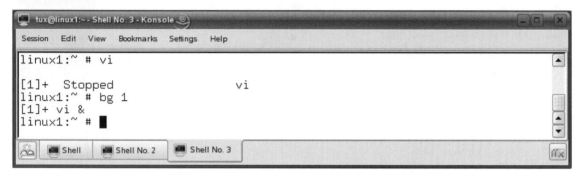

Switching Processes Between the Background and the Foreground

Just because a process was started in the background or the foreground doesn't mean it has to stay there. You can switch a process between the foreground and the background while it's running. This is done using the following commands:

- **fg** This command will move a background process to the foreground. The syntax is fg *job_ID*.
- **bg** This command will move a foreground process to the background. To use this utility, you must first assign the foreground job a background job ID. This is done by pressing CTRL-Z. When you do, you'll see the process stop and a background job ID assigned to the process. You can then enter **bg *job_ID*** to move the process to the background.

In Figure 10-23, the vi program was loaded as per normal into the foreground. It was then stopped using CTRL-Z, where it was assigned a job ID of 1. It was then sent to the background using the bg 1 command.

Now that you know how to switch processes between the foreground and the background, here are some possible scenario questions and their answers.

SCENARIO & SOLUTION

You want to load a program named myapp to run in the background. What command would you enter at the shell prompt?	You would enter **myapp &** at the shell prompt.
What command would you enter to move the myapp process from the background (job ID 2) to the foreground?	You would enter **fg 2** at the shell prompt.

Let's next discuss how to kill a running process.

Ending a Running Process

To this point in this chapter, we've done just about everything you can think of to processes on a Linux system. We've loaded them, viewed them, prioritized them, and moved them to the background. The one task we've yet to cover is to end a process that is running on the system.

Normally, you use the exit function that is coded into nearly all programs to end a running process. For example, you enter **:exit** in vi to exit the editor and end its process. Sometimes, however, they hang and no matter what you do, you can't get the process to close properly. In this situation, you may need to manually kill the hung process. This can be done in two ways:

- Using kill
- Using killall

Let's look at using the kill command first.

Using kill

The kill command is used to terminate a process. The syntax for using kill is kill *–signal PID*. The *PID* parameter is the PID of the process you want to kill. You can also send a specific kill signal to the process. This is one of the things about kill that I love. You actually have about 64 different types of kill signals that you can send to the process. The most useful of these include the following:

- **SIGHUP**   This is kill signal 1. This signal restarts the process. After a restart, the process will have exactly the same PID that it had before. This is a very useful option for restarting a service for which you've made changes in a configuration file.
- **SIGINT**   This is kill signal 2. This signal sends a CTRL-C key sequence to the process.
- **SIGKILL**   This is kill signal 9. This is a brute-force signal that kills the process. If the process was hung badly, this option will force it to stop. However, the process may not clean up after itself if this signal is used. The resources allocated to the process may remain allocated until the system is restarted.
- **SIGTERM**   This is kill signal 15. This signal tells the process to terminate immediately. This is the default signal sent by kill if you omit a signal in the command line. This signal allows the process to clean up after itself before exiting.

FIGURE 10-24   Killing a process with kill

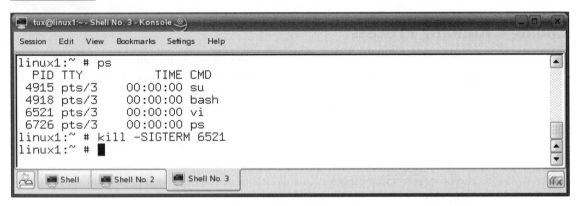

When using kill, you can use the text of the signal, such as SIGTERM, or you can use the signal's number, such as 15. You will need to use ps or top to first identify the PID of the process before you can use kill to stop it. For example, in Figure 10-24, the vi process is running with a PID of 6521.

In Figure 10-24, I've entered **kill –SIGTERM 6521** to kill the vi process. I could have also entered **kill –15 6521** and accomplished exactly the same task. Because the SIGTERM signal allows the process to return its resources before exiting, the vi process ends cleanly.

This brings up a mistake I've seen many new Linux admins make when working with kill. They frequently "go for the jugular" before trying less forceful signals first. Yes, using SIGKILL will work, but it's best if you try other, cleaner signals first. Only if these signals fail should you try a harsher signal.

If you experience a hung process that needs to be killed, I suggest you use the following sequence:

1. Send a SIGINT first. If it doesn't respond, then go on to step 2.

2. Send a SIGTERM. Usually, this will fix the problem and allow the process to exit cleanly. If it doesn't, then go on to step 3.

3. Send a SIGKILL.

In addition to kill, you can also use killall to kill processes. Let's review how this is done next.

Using killall

The killall command is very similar to the kill command. The syntax is almost the same. The key difference is that killall uses the command name of the process

SCENARIO & SOLUTION	
You need to kill a hung process (PID 3456) on your Linux system. You would like the process to clean up after itself after it is killed. What kill command would you use?	You would enter **kill –SIGTERM 3456** or **kill –15 3456** at the shell prompt.
You need to kill a hung process named myapp on your Linux system. You would like the process to clean up after itself after it is killed. What killall command would you use?	You would enter **killall –15 myapp** or **killall –SIGTERM myapp** at the shell prompt.

to be killed instead of its PID. For example, if I wanted to kill the vi process in Figure 10-24 with killall instead of kill, I would have entered **killall –15 vi**. This command sends the SIGTERM signal to the process named vi.

I strongly suggest that you spend some time reviewing the man page for killall. It's quite extensive and contains excellent information. For example, it will show you how to use the –u option with killall to end processes owned by a specific user.

Let's practice working with Linux processes in the following exercise.

EXERCISE 10-1

Working with Linux Processes

In this exercise, you will practice using shell commands to manage processes running on your system. Complete the following:

1. Boot your Linux system and log in as a standard user. If you used the lab exercise in Chapter 3 to install your system, you can log in as **tux** with a password of **M3linux273**.

2. Open a terminal session.

3. Switch to your root user account by entering **su –** followed by your root user's password.

4. Practice starting system processes by doing the following:

   a. At the shell prompt, enter **rcatd status**. What's the status of your at daemon? (For most distributions, the atd daemon is not configured to run by default.)

   b. Start the atd daemon by entering **rcatd start** at the shell prompt.

   c. Enter **rcatd status** again at the shell prompt. The atd service should now be shown as running.

5. Practice using top by doing the following:

   a. At the shell prompt, enter **top**.

   b. View your running processes.

   c. Press H to access the top help screen. Which keystroke will sort the display by CPU stats?

   d. Press T to sort the display by CPU stats. Which processes are using the most CPU time on your system?

   e. Press M to sort the display by memory usage. Which processes are using the most memory?

   f. Add columns by pressing F.

   g. Add the PPID column to the display by pressing B, then press SPACEBAR. You should now see the PPID of each process added to the display.

   h. Exit top by pressing Q.

6. Practice using the ps utility to view processes by doing the following:

   a. At the shell prompt, enter **ps**. What processes are associated with the current shell session?

   b. View all running processes on the system by entering **ps –ef | more** at the shell prompt.

   c. Press SPACEBAR until you find the atd service. What user name does atd run under? (On most distributions, it should run under the at user.)

   d. At the shell prompt, enter **ps –el | less**.

   e. Locate the Status (S) column.

   f. Press SPACEBAR until you find the atd service. What is the status of the service? (Because it isn't being used at the moment, it's probably sleeping.)

7. Practice managing process priorities by completing the following:

   a. At the shell prompt, enter **top**.

   b. What are the priority (PR) and nice (NI) values associated with the top processes? (For most distributions, these values should be 16 and 0.)

   c. Press Q to stop the top process.

   d. At the shell prompt, enter **nice –n –20 top**. Now what are the PR and NI values for the top process?

   e. Note the PID for the top process.

   f. Open a new terminal window and **su** to root.

   g. At the shell prompt, adjust the nice value of the top process while it's running by entering **renice 1 *top_PID***.

   h. Switch back to the first terminal session where top is running. What are its PR and NI values now?

   i. Press Q to exit top.

8. Practice switching processes between the foreground and the background by doing the following:

   a. Load top again by entering **top** at the shell prompt.

   b. In the terminal where top is running, press CTRL-Z.

   c. Note the background job ID number assigned to the process.

   d. At the shell prompt, enter **bg *background_job_ID***. The output from top disappears while the process runs in the background.

   e. Press CTRL-C.

   f. At the shell prompt, enter **fg *background_job_ID***. The output from top reappears as the process now runs in the foreground.

9. Practice killing processes by completing the following:

   a. Ensure that top is still running.

   b. Switch to your other terminal session where you're logged in as root.

   c. At the shell prompt, enter **ps –e |grep top**.

   d. Note the PID of the top process.

   e. At the shell prompt, enter **kill –SIGTERM *top_PID***.

   f. Switch back to the terminal session where top was running. Verify that top has exited.

   g. Load **top** again at the shell prompt.

   h. Switch back to your other terminal session where you're logged in as root.

   i. Kill the top process by entering **killall –15 top**.

   j. Switch back to your first terminal window and verify that top has exited.

It's time to make a quantum leap and change topics! We next need to discuss how to schedule processes on your Linux system.

Schedule Processes

So far in this chapter, you've learned how to execute and manage processes on a Linux system from the shell prompt. However, there will be many occasions when you will need a process to run automatically without any intervention on your part. Backups are a good example. One of the key problems with backups is not that system administrators perform them incorrectly; it's that they forget to perform them at all. One of the worst things you can do in your backup strategy is to rely on a human being to remember to run them.

Instead, you can configure your Linux system to run programs for you automatically. This removes the human element from the equation and ensures that the specified programs execute regularly and on time. There are two key utilities that can be used to schedule processes to run in the future. We'll discuss the following in this part of the chapter:

- Using the at daemon
- Using the cron daemon

Let's begin by learning how to use the at daemon.

Using the at Daemon

Using at is a great way to schedule a process to run once sometime in the future. The at service is a system daemon (called *atd*) that runs in the background on your system. Most Linux distributions install this service for you during the initial installation of the system. If not, you may need to install it manually from your installation CD using the rpm utility.

The startup script used to start the atd daemon is located in your init script directory, which should be either /etc/init.d or /etc/rc.d/init.d, depending on your particular distribution. The name of the script is atd, as shown in Figure 10-25.

Before attempting to use at, you need to make sure the atd daemon is running. You can do this by entering **rcatd start** at the shell prompt. You can also run the script file with its full path followed by **start** at the shell prompt to accomplish the same task.

FIGURE 10-25   The atd daemon startup script

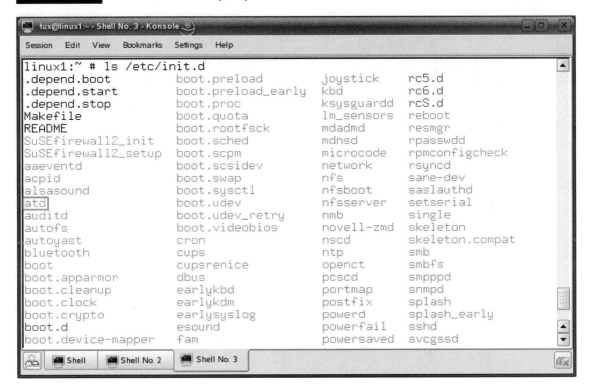

You also need to specify which users can and which users cannot create at jobs. This can be done by editing the following files:

- ■ **/etc/at.allow**   Users listed in this file are allowed to create at jobs.
- ■ **/etc/at.deny**   Users listed in this file are not allowed to create at jobs.

To use at to schedule a command to run at a future time, complete the following:

1. At the shell prompt enter **at** *time*. The at daemon is very flexible as to how you specify the *time* value in this command. Observe the syntax shown in Table 10-2.

    After entering the at command and a time value from Table 10-2, the at> prompt is displayed, as shown in Figure 10-26.

2. At the at> prompt, enter the command(s) that you want at to run for you. It's important to note that if your commands display output on the screen from the shell prompt, you won't see the output when the commands are run by at.

TABLE 10-2	at Command Time Syntax Options	

Type of Reference	Syntax	Description
Fixed	*HH:MM*	Specifies the exact hour and minute when the commands should be run. The at daemon assumes that the hour and minute specified is today unless that time is already past; then it assumes it is tomorrow. You can also add **am** or **pm** to the value to specify morning or afternoon.
	Noon	Specifies that a command be run at 12:00 P.M.
	Midnight	Specifies that a command be run at 12:00 A.M.
	Teatime	Specifies that a command be run at 4:00 P.M.
	MMDDYY or *MM/DD/YY* or *MM.DD.YY*	Specifies the exact month, date, and year when a command is to be run.
	HH:MM MMDDYY	Specifies the exact month, date, year, and time when a command is to be run.
Relative	now	Specifies that the command be run immediately.
	now + *value*	Specifies that the command be run at a certain time in the future. For example, you could enter any of the following: **now + 5 minutes** **now + 2 hours** **now + 3 days**
	today	Specifies that the command be run today. You can mix this value with a fixed value from above, such as **2 pm today**.
	tomorrow	Specifies that the command be run tomorrow. You can also mix this value with a fixed value, such as **2 pm tomorrow**.

FIGURE 10-26	The at> prompt

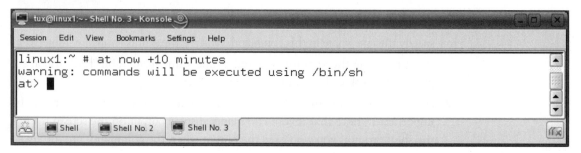

FIGURE 10-27   Viewing the at job number

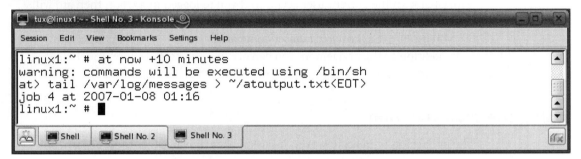

You have two different options for viewing the output. First of all, if you don't specify any alternative, at will e-mail the output to your local user account.

Alternatively, you can also redirect the output to a file. You learned how to do this earlier in this book. For example, if you wanted to run the tail /var/log messages command in the future with at, you could enter **tail /var/log/messages > ~/atoutput.txt** at the at> prompt to send the output from the command to a text file named atoutput.txt in your home directory.

3. Press ENTER if you want to add additional commands. You can run multiple commands within the same job. Each command should be on its own line.

4. When you're done entering commands, press CTRL-D. When you do, the at> prompt will disappear, the job will be scheduled, and a job number will be assigned. This is shown in Figure 10-27.

Once you've configured the job, you can use the atq command to view a list of pending at jobs. This is shown in Figure 10-28.

FIGURE 10-28   Viewing pending jobs

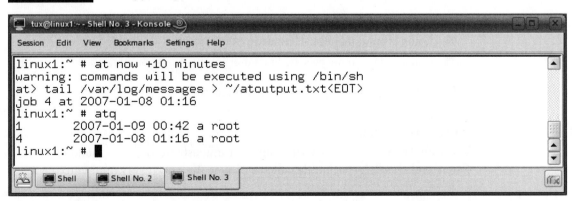

If you are logged in as a regular user, the atq command will display only the jobs associated with the current user account. If you're logged in as root, then atq will display all pending jobs for all users. If you need to remove a pending job from the list, you can use the atrm *job_number* command.

In addition to the at daemon, you can also use the cron daemon to schedule future jobs. Let's discuss how this is done next.

Using the cron Daemon

The at daemon is great; however, it has one key drawback. It can only schedule a job to run once in the future. That's not a problem if you only want the job to run once. However, there will be many times that you want a job to run in the future on a regular schedule. For example, you may need to run a process, such as a backup utility, every day at a certain time. In this situation, the at daemon doesn't cut it. We need a tool that can handle repetitious schedules.

The cron daemon can do just that. Unlike at, cron can run commands on a schedule you specify. It's a very powerful, very useful service.

on the
ⓘob

I use at occasionally. However, cron is a service that I use all of the time. In fact, I would have a hard time getting my work done without it.
Most of my clients' offices are many miles from my office. Making rounds just to run backups for all of my clients each day would take up all of my time. I don't dare trust my clients' administrative personnel to make sure backups occur each day.
Instead, I set up the cron daemon to run the backup process for me. That way, I know that backups are occurring on a regular schedule and that the correct command has been issued to create them.

In this part of the chapter, we'll discuss the following:

■ How cron works
■ Using cron to manage scheduled system jobs
■ Using cron to manage scheduled user jobs

Let's begin by learning how the cron service works.

How cron Works

The cron daemon is a service that runs continuously in the background on your system and checks a special file called a *crontab* file once every minute to see if

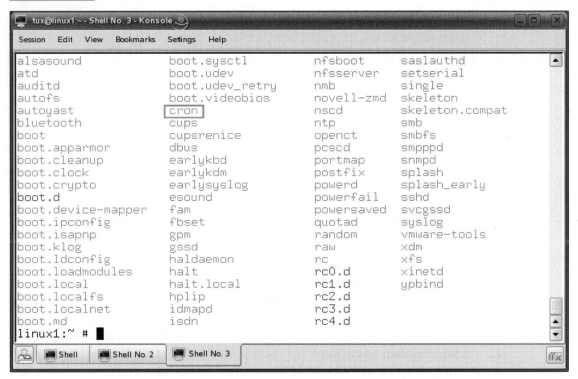

FIGURE 10-29 Viewing the cron init script

there's a scheduled job it should run. The cron daemon is managed using the cron init script in your init directory, as shown in Figure 10-29.

By default, the cron daemon is configured to run automatically every time the system boots on most Linux distributions. If not, you'll need to start it manually using the cron init script in your system's init directory.

You can configure cron to run system jobs or user-specific jobs. Let's talk about running system jobs first.

Using cron to Manage Scheduled System Jobs

Using cron to run scheduled system jobs is an extremely useful tool for a Linux system administrator. You can configure your systems to perform a wide variety of tasks on a regular schedule automatically, saving you a ton of time and effort. Remember when I mentioned the problems with running regular backups? Creating a system job in cron that runs a backup on a regular schedule saves me tons of time. If I don't have time to

FIGURE 10-30   The /etc/crontab file

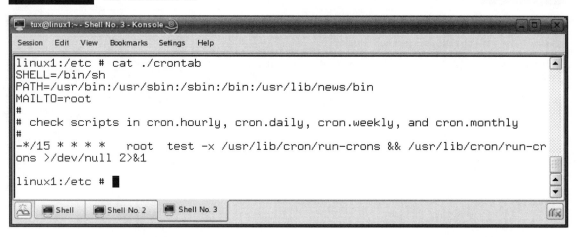

```
linux1:/etc # cat ./crontab
SHELL=/bin/sh
PATH=/usr/bin:/usr/sbin:/sbin:/bin:/usr/lib/news/bin
MAILTO=root
#
# check scripts in cron.hourly, cron.daily, cron.weekly, and cron.monthly
#
-*/15 * * * *    root   test -x /usr/lib/cron/run-crons && /usr/lib/cron/run-cr
ons >/dev/null 2>&1

linux1:/etc #
```

visit a client site on a particular day, I don't have to worry. I know that cron will run
a backup at the preconfigured time. All I have to do is drop by now and then to
verify that everything is still working properly and to perhaps rotate the backup media.
I love cron!

To run system jobs, the cron service uses the /etc/crontab file, shown in Figure 10-30,
to configure what jobs to run.

As you can see in Figure 10-30, the /etc/crontab file contains commands that are
used to run scripts found in four different directories:

- ■ **/etc/cron.hourly**   Contains cron scripts that are run every hour.
- ■ **/etc/cron.daily**   Contains cron scripts that are run every day.
- ■ **/etc/cron.weekly**   Contains cron scripts that are run once a week.
- ■ **/etc/cron.monthly**   Contains cron scripts that are run once a month.

All scripts found in any of these directories are automatically run by cron
according to the specified schedule. For example, the /etc/cron.daily directory
contains a variety of scripts that are used to clean up your system and rotate your
logs once each day. These scripts are shown in Figure 10-31.

If you have a system task that needs to be run on one of these four schedules, you
can simply create a script file, using the steps we covered earlier in this book, and
copy it into the appropriate cron directory in /etc.

FIGURE 10-31 /etc/cron.daily scripts

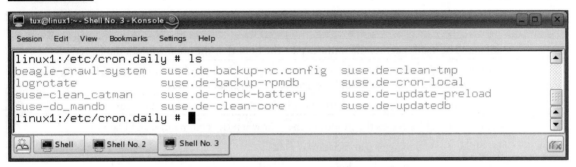

What do you do, however, if your system job needs to run on a schedule other than one of the four used by the cron directories? No problem. The cron daemon has got you covered. In addition to the four directories just presented, there's a fifth directory in /etc/ called cron.d, shown in Figure 10-32.

If you need a system job to run on a custom schedule, you can create a crontab file in this directory where it will be read and run by the cron daemon.

FIGURE 10-32 Viewing the cron.d directory

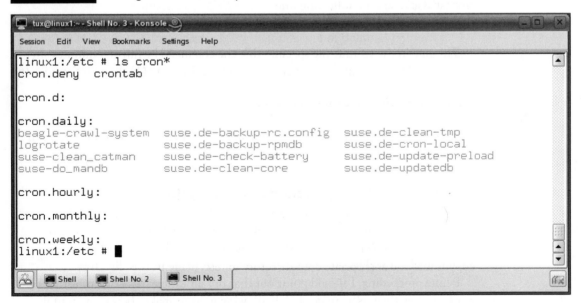

| TABLE 10-3 | crontab File Fields |

Field	Description
1	Minutes. This field specifies the minutes past the hour that the command should be run.
2	Hour. This field specifies the hour of the day when the command should be run. The cron daemon prefers military time, so you should use a value of 0 to 23 in this field.
3	Day. This field specifies the day of the month that the command should be run.
4	Month. This field specifies the month of the year when the command should be run.
5	Day of the week. Sunday is 0 and Saturday is 6.
6	The name of the command, including the full path, to be run.

How do you create a crontab file? It looks difficult but it really isn't. A crontab file is simply a text file that uses one line per job. Each line has six fields, separated by tabs, shown in Table 10-3.

Many times, you will see an asterisk (*) in one or more fields in a given cron tab file. This wild card means "match everything."

For example, suppose I wanted to run the tar command to back up the /home directory using the tar –cvf /media/usb/backup.tar /home command every day of every month, except Sundays, at 11:05 P.M. I could create a crontab file in /etc/ crontab.d and add the following line:

```
5    23    *    *    1-6    /bin/tar -cvf /media/usb/backup.tar /home
```

This line in the crontab file specifies that the command be run at 5 minutes after 11:00 P.M. (23) every day (*) of every month (*) on Monday (1) through Saturday (6).

System cron jobs run as the root user.

In addition to system cron jobs, individual users can also create their own cron jobs. Let's review how this is done next.

Using cron to Manage Scheduled User Jobs

Users on your system can create their own schedules using a crontab file that is associated with their user account. Unlike system crontab files, which are saved in /etc, user crontab files are stored in /var/spool/cron/tabs. If a user has created a crontab file, it will be saved under his or her username in this directory.

Before proceeding, I should point out that not all Linux system administrators want to allow their users to do this. If allowing users to make their own crontab

FIGURE 10-33   Using the crontab –e command

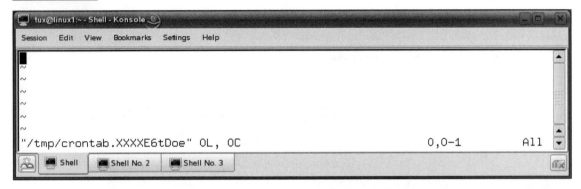

files and run programs on a schedule makes you nervous, you can lock the system to prevent them from doing so. To do this, you use an approach similar to that used when working with the at daemon.

The cron daemon will read the /etc/cron.allow and /etc/cron.deny files when it starts up to determine who can and who can't create crontab schedules. By default, only the /etc/cron.deny file is created automatically and it only contains a restriction for the guest user account. All other users are allowed to create crontab files to schedule jobs. If you create an /etc/cron.allow file, then *only* the users in that file will be allowed to create crontab files; all others will be denied.

With that out of the way, let's discuss how users can create their own crontab files. To do this, they can use the crontab –e command. After entering this command, the vi editor is opened with a new, blank crontab file loaded, as shown in Figure 10-33.

In this file, the user simply adds lines for each job they want to run using the syntax we reviewed previously. For example, in Figure 10-34, the tar command is run at 5:10 P.M. every day to back up the user's home directory to a file named ~/homebak.tar.

FIGURE 10-34   Creating a user crontab file

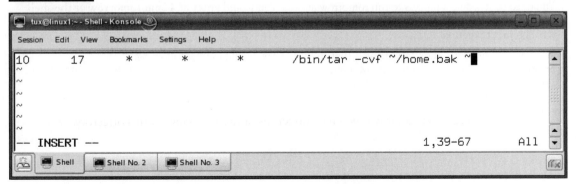

| **FIGURE 10-35** | Viewing the user's new crontab file |

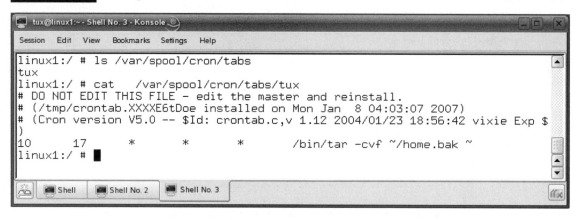

```
linux1:/ # ls /var/spool/cron/tabs
tux
linux1:/ # cat    /var/spool/cron/tabs/tux
# DO NOT EDIT THIS FILE - edit the master and reinstall.
# (/tmp/crontab.XXXXE6tDoe installed on Mon Jan  8 04:03:07 2007)
# (Cron version V5.0 -- $Id: crontab.c,v 1.12 2004/01/23 18:56:42 vixie Exp $
)
10       17      *       *       *       /bin/tar -cvf ~/home.bak ~
linux1:/ #
```

The file is edited using standard vi commands and keystrokes, which you learned early in this book. (I told you knowing how to use vi would come in handy!) When complete, exit vi and save the file. After doing so, a new crontab file for the user is created in /var/spool/cron/tabs, as shown in Figure 10-35. In addition, the cron service is reloaded so the new configuration can be applied.

In Figure 10-35, I used the cat command to view the tux user's crontab file. However, you can also use the crontab –l command to display your user's crontab file. You can also use the crontab –r command to remove your user's crontab file.

SCENARIO & SOLUTION

You need to schedule a process to run tomorrow at 12:00 P.M. What at command would you enter at the shell prompt to do this?	You would enter **at 12pm tomorrow** at the shell prompt.
You need to configure a crontab file such that the myappcleanup command is run every Monday through Friday at 11:05 P.M. How would the crontab line for this schedule be formatted?	You would use the following: 05 11 * * 1-5 myappcleanup

Let's practice working with Linux processes in the following exercise.

EXERCISE 10-2

ON THE CD

Scheduling with Linux Processes

In this exercise, you will practice using cron and at commands to schedule processes to run in the future on your system. Complete the following:

1. Boot your Linux system and log in as a standard user. If you used the lab exercise in Chapter 3 to install your system, you can log in as **tux** with a password of **M3linux273**.

2. Open a terminal session.

3. Switch to your root user account by entering **su –** followed by your root user's password.

4. Practice using the at daemon by doing the following:

   a. At the shell prompt, enter **rcatd status**.

   b. Verify that the at daemon is running. If it isn't, enter **rcatd start** at the shell prompt.

   c. At the shell prompt, enter **at now + 5 minutes**.

   d. At the at prompt, enter **ps –ef > ~/psoutput.txt**.

   e. Press ENTER.

   f. Press CTRL-D.

   g. Generate a listing of pending at jobs by entering **atq**. You should see the job you just created.

   h. Wait for the pending at job to complete.

   i. Check the ~/psoutput.txt file and verify that the output from the ps command was generated correctly.

   j. At the shell prompt, enter **at 2pm tomorrow**.

   k. At the at prompt, enter **ps –ef >> ~/psoutput.txt**.

   l. Press ENTER.

   m. Press CTRL-D.

   n. Generate a listing of pending at jobs by entering **atq**. You should see the job you just created. Note its job number.

   o. Remove the pending job by entering **atrm *job_number***.

   p. Enter **atq** again. The pending job should be gone.

5. Practice using cron by completing the following:

   a. Log out of your root user account by entering **exit**.

   b. At the shell prompt, enter **crontab –e**.

   c. Press INSERT.

   d. Configure your system to create a backup of your user's home directory every day at 5:05 P.M. by entering the following:

```
05    17    *    *    *    /bin/tar -cvf ~/mybackup.tar ~/
```

   (If you don't want to wait until 5:05 P.M., you could instead specify a time value that is only two or three minutes in the future.)

   e. Press ESC.

   f. Enter **:exit**. You should see a message on the screen indicating that a new crontab has been installed.

   g. Enter **crontab –l** and verify that the job was created correctly.

   h. Wait until the time you specified in the crontab file, then check your user's home directory and verify that the mybackup.tar file was created.

   i. Remove your user's crontab file by entering **crontab –r** at the shell prompt.

Well done! You now know how to manage Linux processes on your system! Not many can make that claim. Let's now review what you learned in this chapter.

CERTIFICATION SUMMARY

In this chapter, you learned how to manage Linux processes. We began this chapter by reviewing what a process is. We established that whenever you run a command from the shell prompt or when a daemon is run by init, a process is created on the system as the associated program's code is loaded into RAM and the code is executed by the CPU.

We pointed out that Linux is a multitasking operating system. Even though the CPU can only run one process at a time, Linux continually switches CPU time among many processes loaded into RAM, making it appear that the CPU is processing many processes concurrently.

We also pointed out that when the init process loads a daemon using an init script, a system process is created. When an end user enters a command at the shell prompt, a user process is created. User processes are associated with a shell session; system processes are not.

We then discussed the heredity of Linux processes. We pointed out that Linux processes can spawn other Linux processes. The process that spawned another process is called the parent. The new process that was created by the first process is called the child. Every Linux process has a parent process. All Linux processes can trace their heredity back to the init process, which is the first process loaded by the kernel on system boot.

Every Linux process is assigned a process ID (PID) that uniquely identifies the process on the system. Processes are also assigned a PPID, which is the PID of the process' parent process. Whenever you run a command from the shell prompt, a new shell (called a subshell) is created and the command is run within it. When the process is complete, the subshell is destroyed and control is returned to the original shell.

We then turned our attention to managing Linux processes. We first discussed how you go about creating processes. User processes are created by simply entering commands at the shell prompt. System processes are created by running a daemon startup script from your system's init directory. Some distributions use System V init scripts, which are stored in /etc/rc.d/init.d. Other distributions use BSD init scripts, which are stored in /etc/init.d.

We next discussed how to view running processes. The first utility we looked at was the top utility. You load top by entering **top** at the shell prompt. You can press the H key while top is running to view a help screen that will show you how to sort by a specific column or even add columns of data to the display.

You can also use the ps command to view running processes. By default, the ps command only displays running processes associated with the current shell session. To view all running processes, use the –e option with the ps command. You can also use the –f and –l options with ps to view extended process information.

Next, we discussed how to prioritize processes on your system. A process' overall priority is heavily influenced by its nice value. Nice values can range from –20 to +19. The lower the nice value, the higher the priority of the process. To adjust the nice value of a process when it's loaded, you can use the nice command. The syntax is nice –n *nice_value command*. You can't use a nice value lower than 0 unless you are logged in as root. You can also adjust the nice value of a running process without unloading it. This is done using the renice command. The syntax is renice *nice_value PID*.

Then we discussed how to run processes in the foreground and the background. By default, processes you launch from the shell prompt run in the foreground. In this situation, the shell prompt is locked until the process is complete. You can also run a process in the background. In this situation, the program runs, but it does so in the background and control is returned to the shell prompt, allowing you to run additional commands. This is done by simply appending the & character to the end of the command. When you do, the background process is assigned a job ID number.

You can move a process that is running in the background to the foreground by entering **fg *job_ID*** at the shell prompt. You can also move a foreground process into the background. To do this, first press CTRL-Z to stop the process. The process will then be assigned a job ID number. You can then enter **bg *job_ID*** to move the process to the background.

Finally, we discussed how to kill a running process from the shell prompt. You can use the kill or the killall commands to do this. Both of these commands use a variety of kill signals. Some of the most useful signals include:

- SIGHUP (1)
- SIGINT (2)
- SIGKILL (9)
- SIGTERM (15)

The syntax for kill is kill *–signal PID*. The syntax for killall is killall *–signal process_name*. When working with a hung process, you should try less aggressive kill signals, such as SIGINT and SIGTERM, before using more aggressive kill signals such as SIGKILL.

At this point in the chapter, we shifted gears and discussed how to schedule processes to run automatically in the future. If you only need the process to run once in the future, you can use the at daemon. Before you can use at, you need to make sure the atd daemon is running on your system. Then, you can enter **at *time*** at the shell prompt. The time value can be a fixed time, such as **10:00**, or a relative time, such as **tomorrow**. You will then be presented with an at> prompt where you can enter a list of commands to be run. Press CTRL-D when you're done. You can use the atq command to view a list of pending at jobs. You can also use the atrm command to remove a pending at job.

If you need to schedule a process to run on a recurring basis, then you need to use the cron daemon instead of at. The cron daemon can run system jobs or user jobs. System cron jobs are created by creating script files in one of the following directories:

- /etc/cron.hourly
- /etc/cron.daily
- /etc/cron.weekly
- /etc/cron.monthly

You can also create a crontab file and save it in the /etc/cron.d directory. A crontab file contains one line for each command that is to be run. Each line contains six fields:

- 1 Minutes
- 2 Hour
- 3 Day
- 4 Month
- 5 Day of the week
- 6 Command to be run

In addition to system jobs, you can also use cron to create user jobs. User cron jobs are stored in /var/spool/cron/tabs. A user can create a crontab file by entering **crontab –e** at the shell prompt. The user then creates one line for each scheduled command using the syntax just described. After creating the crontab file, you can use the crontab –l command to view your crontab file. You can also use the crontab –r command to remove your crontab file.

✓ # TWO-MINUTE DRILL

Describe How Linux Handles Processes

❑ Whenever you run a command from the shell prompt, a process is created on the system.

❑ When a process loads, the program's code is loaded into RAM and is executed by the CPU.

❑ Linux is a multitasking operating system.

❑ Most CPUs can only run one process at a time.

❑ Linux continually switches CPU time among the many processes loaded into RAM, making it appear that the CPU is processing many processes concurrently.

❑ When the init process loads a daemon from an init script, a system process is created.

❑ When an end user enters a command at the shell prompt, a user process is created.

❑ User processes are associated with a shell session; system processes are not.

❑ Linux processes can spawn other Linux processes.

❑ The process that spawned another process is called the parent.

❑ The new process that was created by the first process is called the child.

❑ Every Linux process has a parent process.

❑ All Linux processes can trace their heredity back to the init process, which is the first process loaded by the kernel on system boot.

❑ Every Linux process is assigned a process ID (PID) that uniquely identifies the process on the system.

❑ Processes are assigned a PPID value, which is the PID of the process' parent process.

❑ Whenever you run a command from the shell prompt, a subshell is created and the command is run within it.

❑ When the process is complete, the subshell is destroyed and control is returned to the original shell.

❑ User processes are created when you enter commands at the shell prompt.

❑ System processes are created when you run a daemon startup script from your system's init directory.

❑ Some distributions use System V init scripts, which are stored in /etc/rc.d/
    init.d.

❑ Some distributions use BSD init scripts, which are stored in /etc/init.d.

Manage Running Processes

❑ You can use the top utility to view system processes. You load top by entering
    top at the shell prompt.

❑ You can press the H key while top is running to view a help screen that will
    show you how to configure the data displayed by top.

❑ You can use the ps command to view running processes.

❑ By default, the ps command only displays running processes associated with
    the current shell session.

❑ You can use the –e option with the ps command to view all running processes.

❑ You can use the –f and –l options with ps to view extended process information.

❑ Linux allows you to prioritize processes running on your system.

❑ A process' overall priority is heavily influenced by its nice value.

❑ Nice values can range from –20 to +19.

❑ The lower the nice value, the higher the priority of the process.

❑ You can use the nice command to adjust the nice value of a process as it's loaded.

❑ To use nice, you enter **nice –n** *nice_value command*.

❑ You can't assign a nice value lower than 0 unless you are logged in as root.

❑ You can also adjust the nice value of a running process without unloading it
    using the renice command.

❑ The syntax for using renice is renice *nice_value PID*.

❑ By default, processes you launch from the shell prompt run in the foreground.

❑ Foreground processes lock the shell prompt until the process is complete.

❑ You can run Linux processes in the background.

❑ Background processes return control to the shell prompt.

❑ You can run a process in the background by appending a & character to the
    end of the command.

❑ When you load a process into the background, the process is assigned a job
    ID number.

❑ You can move a process that is running in the background to the foreground
    by entering **fg** *job_ID* at the shell prompt.

❑ You can move a foreground process into the background by pressing CTRL-Z to stop the process and then entering **bg *job_ID*** to move the process to the background.

❑ You can use the kill or the killall commands to kill a running process.

❑ There are many kill signals that can be sent using kill or killall; some of the most useful include:

  ❑ SIGHUP (1)

  ❑ SIGINT (2)

  ❑ SIGKILL (9)

  ❑ SIGTERM (15)

❑ To kill a process with kill, enter **kill *–signal PID*** at the shell prompt.

❑ To kill a process with killall, enter **killall *–signal process_name***.

❑ You should use less aggressive kill signals, such as SIGINT and SIGTERM, before attempting to use more forceful kill signals such as SIGKILL.

Schedule Processes

❑ If you only need the process to run once in the future, you should use the at daemon.

❑ You need to load the atd daemon before you can use at.

❑ You can load atd by entering **rcatd start** at the shell prompt.

❑ To schedule a command to run in the future with at, enter **at *time*** at the shell prompt.

❑ The at time value can be a fixed time, such as:

  ❑ HH:MM

  ❑ Noon

  ❑ Midnight

  ❑ Teatime

  ❑ MMDDYY, MM/DD/YY, or MM.DD.YY

❑ The at time value can also be a relative time, such as:

  ❑ now

  ❑ now +*x* minutes, hours, or days

  ❑ today

  ❑ tomorrow

❑ At the at> prompt, enter a list of commands to be run; press CTRL-D when you're done.

❑ If you don't redirect output from your commands to a file, the output will be e-mailed to your local user account.

❑ You can use the atq command to view a list of pending at jobs.

❑ You can use the atrm command to remove a pending at job.

❑ If you need to schedule a process to run on a recurring basis, you should use the cron daemon instead of at.

❑ The cron daemon can run system jobs or user jobs.

❑ System cron jobs are created by creating script files in the following directories:

   ❑ /etc/cron.hourly

   ❑ /etc/cron.daily

   ❑ /etc/cron.weekly

   ❑ /etc/cron.monthly

❑ You can also create system cron jobs by creating a crontab file in the /etc/cron.d directory.

❑ A crontab file contains one line for each command that is to be run; each line contains six fields:

   ❑ 1   Minutes

   ❑ 2   Hour

   ❑ 3   Day

   ❑ 4   Month

   ❑ 5   Day of the week

   ❑ 6   Command to be run

❑ You can use cron to create user jobs.

❑ User cron jobs are stored in /var/spool/cron/tabs.

❑ A user can create a crontab file by entering **crontab –e** at the shell prompt.

❑ After creating the crontab file, you can use the crontab –l command to view your crontab file contents.

❑ You can use the crontab –r command to remove your crontab file.

SELF TEST

Describe How Linux Handles Processes

1. Which of the following best describes a multitasking operating system?

    A. An operating system that can run multiple tasks concurrently on multiple CPUs.

    B. An operating system that can run a single task concurrently across multiple CPUs.

    C. An operating system that runs multiple tasks concurrently on a single CPU.

    D. An operating system that constantly switches CPU time between loaded processes.

2. You just entered **vi** at the shell prompt. What type of process was created on your Linux system?

    A. User

    B. System

    C. Daemon

    D. init

3. Your current shell session has a PID of 3456. You run the su command to change to the root user account. The su process has a PID of 3457. You then run vi from the shell prompt as root. The vi process has a PID of 3458. What is the PPID of the vi process?

    A. 3456

    B. 3457

    C. 3458

    D. 3459

4. Which process is the grandparent of all processes running on your Linux system?

    A. bash

    B. init

    C. sh

    D. ps

Manage Running Processes

5. You're running a Fedora Linux system that uses System V init scripts. Where are these scripts stored in your file system?

    A. /etc/init.d

    B. /etc/rc.d/init.d

C. /etc/sysv/init.d

D. /etc/init.d/rc.d

6. You want to use ps to display extended information about only the processes associated with your current terminal session. Which command will do this?

A. ps

B. ps –e

C. ps –f

D. ps –ef

7. What is a zombied process?

A. A process that has finished executing but whose parent process hasn't released the child process' PID.

B. A process that has stopped executing while waiting for user input.

C. A process that is being traced by another process.

D. A process that has gone to sleep and can't be interrupted.

8. Which ps option can be used to display all currently running processes?

A. –a

B. –e

C. –f

D. –l

9. The myapp process has a nice value of 1. Which of the following nice values would increase the priority of the myapp process? (Choose two.)

A. –15

B. 5

C. 19

D. 0

E. 2

10. Which of the following shell commands will load the myapp program with a nice value of –5?

A. myapp –n –5

B. nice –5 myapp

C. renice –5 myapp

D. nice –n –5 myapp

11. The myapp process (PID 2345) is currently running on your system. Which of the following commands will reset its nice value to –5 without unloading the process?

A. myapp –n –5 –p 2345

B. renice –n –5 2345

C. renice –5 2345

D. nice –n –5 2345

12. You want to load the myapp program from the shell prompt and run it in the background. Which command will do this?

A. myapp –b

B. myapp &

C. myapp –bg

D. load myapp into background

13. Which kill signal sends a CTRL-C key sequence to a running process?

A. SIGHUP

B. SIGINT

C. SIGKILL

D. SIGTERM

14. You need to kill a hung process. You know its process name, but you don't know its PID. Which utility can you use?

A. killall

B. kill

C. hangup

D. SIGKILL

Schedule Processes

15. It's currently 1:00 in the afternoon. You want to schedule the myapp program to run automatically tomorrow afternoon at 12:00. Which of the following at commands could you use? (Choose two.)

A. at 12pm tomorrow

B. at tomorrow –1 hour

C. at now + 1 day

D. at today +23 hours

E. at now +23 hours

16. Which of the following crontab lines will cause the /usr/bin/myappcleanup process to run at 4:15 A.M. on the first of every month?

A.	15	4	1	*	*	/usr/bin/myappcleanup
B.	15	4	*	1	*	/usr/bin/myappcleanup
C.	1	4	15	*	*	/usr/bin/myappcleanup
D.	4	1	*	*	15	/usr/bin/myappcleanup

LAB QUESTION

You need to configure your Linux system such that the /usr/bin/myappcleanup program is run once a week at 11:00 P.M. on Sundays. This program is extremely important and should be loaded with a nice value of –10. Describe the process you would follow to implement this configuration.

SELF TEST ANSWERS

Describe How Linux Handles Processes

1. ☑ **D.** A multitasking operating system constantly switches CPU time between loaded processes, creating the impression that the CPU is actually executing processes concurrently.
☒ **A, B,** and **C** are incorrect. **A** describes a multiprocessing operating system. **B** describes a distributed processing operating system. **C** is only possible if the CPU is a dual-core CPU. Even then, it can only execute two processes at a time.

2. ☑ **A.** Because the command was entered from the shell prompt, a user process was created.
☒ **B, C,** and **D** are incorrect. **B** and **C** would only be created if the process were a system process loaded through an init script. **D** is not a type of process and is incorrect.

3. ☑ **A.** Because the command was entered from the shell prompt, its parent process is the bash process, which has a PID of 3456.
☒ **B, C,** and **D** are incorrect. **B** is incorrect because the su process didn't create the vi process. **C** is incorrect because this PID is the PID of the vi process itself. **D** is incorrect because the PID isn't the PID of the parent process.

4. ☑ **B.** The init process is the grandparent of all other Linux processes on the system. All other processes can trace their heredity to init.
☒ **A, C,** and **D** are incorrect. **A** may be the parent of many processes, but it is still a descendant of the init process. The same is true of **C**. **D** is incorrect. It's the process name for the ps command.

Manage Running Processes

5. ☑ **B.** The init scripts for distributions that use System V init scripts are stored in /etc/rc.d/init.d.
☒ **A, C,** and **D** are incorrect. **A** is the correct directory for distributions that use BSD-style init scripts. Fedora uses System V init scripts, however. **C** is a distracter and is incorrect. **D** is incorrect. The init.d and rc.d directories are reversed.

6. ☑ **C.** The **ps –f** command will display extended information about processes associated with the current shell session.
☒ **A, B,** and **D** are incorrect. **A** will display processes associated with the current shell session, but only in summary format. **B** will display summary information about all processes running on the system. **D** will display extended information about all processes running on the system.

7. ☑ **A.** A zombied process is one where the process has finished executing, but the parent process wasn't notified and, therefore, hasn't released the child process' PID.
☒ **B, C,** and **D** are incorrect. **B** describes a sleeping process. **C** describes a traced or stopped process. **D** describes a process that is in uninterruptible sleep.

8. ☑ **B.** The ps –e command can be used to display a list of all running processes on the system.
☒ **A, C,** and **D** are incorrect. **A** will display all processes not associated with a terminal session. **C** will display extended process information, but only for processes associated with the current shell session unless used with the –e option. **D** will display process information in long format, but only for processes associated with the current shell session unless used with the –e option.

9. ☑ **A** and **D.** The lower the nice value, the higher the priority of the process. Therefore, nice values of 0 and –15 will increase the priority of the myapp process.
☒ **B, C,** and **E** are incorrect. Each of these nice values are higher than the original nice value of 0, which would only decrease the priority of the myapp process.

10. ☑ **D.** The nice –n –5 myapp command will load myapp with a nice value of –5.
☒ **A, B,** and **C** are incorrect. **A** is a distracter that uses incorrect syntax as does **B**. **C** is incorrect because the renice utility is used to reset the nice value of a process that is already running. It also uses the incorrect syntax for renice.

11. ☑ **C.** The renice –5 2345 command will reset the nice value of the myapp process while it's running.
☒ **A, B,** and **D** are incorrect. **A** and **B** use incorrect syntax. **D** is incorrect because the nice utility is used to set the nice value of a process as it is being loaded. It also uses the incorrect syntax for nice.

12. ☑ **B.** The myapp & command will cause myapp to run in the background.
☒ **A, C,** and **D** are incorrect. Each of these options uses incorrect syntax.

13. ☑ **B.** The SIGINT kill signal sends a CTRL-C key sequence to the specified process.
☒ **A, C,** and **D** are incorrect. **A** causes the process to unload and then reload with the same PID. **C** will use brute force to kill the process and may not allow the process to clean up after itself. **D** will kill the process but still allow it to clean up and release the resources it was assigned.

14. ☑ **A.** The killall utility uses the process name in the command line and can be used to kill the process in this scenario.
☒ **B, C,** and **D** are incorrect. **B** requires that you know the PID of the process to be killed. **C** and **D** are distracters and are incorrect.

Schedule Processes

15. ☑ **A** and **E.** You can enter **at 12pm tomorrow** or **at now +23 hours** to cause the atd daemon to run the specified command at 12:00 on the following day.
☒ **B, C,** and **D** are incorrect. **B** uses invalid at syntax. **C** will run the process the next day, but at 1:00 instead of 12:00. **D** uses invalid at syntax.

16. ☑ **A.** The 15 4 1 * * /usr/bin/myappcleanup crontab line will cause the myappcleanup process to be run at 4:15 on the first day of every month no matter what day of the week it is.
☒ **B, C,** and **D** are incorrect. **B** would cause the process to run at 4:15 A.M. every day in January only. **C** would cause the process to run at 4:01 A.M. on the 15th of every month. **D** uses an invalid number in the fifth column (day of the week) and also specifies the wrong time of day.

LAB ANSWER

The first thing you should do is open a shell session and su to your root user. We're assuming here that the myappcleanup program needs to run under the root user account. Once done, you should verify that cron is running by entering **rccron status** at the shell prompt. Most distributions configure cron to automatically run at runlevels 3 and 5 by default; however, it never hurts to check and make sure.

Once you've verified that cron is running, you should then enter **crontab –e** at the shell prompt. This will open the crontab file for the root user in the vi editor. Because the program needs to run on Sunday nights at 11:00 P.M., you need to configure your schedule in the crontab file as follows:

```
00    23    *    *    6
```

This tells cron to run the command at 23:00 (11:00 P.M.) on the sixth day of every day of the month (*) of every month (*).

Next, you need to add the command to load the /usr/bin/myappcleanup program with a nice value of –10 to the crontab file. This would be done adding the following to the line:

```
/user/bin/nice -n -10 /usr/bin/myappcleanup
```

When you're done, the crontab line should appear as follows:

```
00    23    *    *    6        /user/bin/nice -n -10 /usr/bin/myappcleanup
```

Then you would exit the vi editor and save the changes to the file. At this point, you should verify the crontab file by entering **crontab –l** at the shell prompt.

The cron service was automatically reloaded when you exited vi, so the daemon should have already read your new crontab file. All you have to do now is wait until Monday morning and verify that the process was executed. You could do this by viewing the last few lines of the /var/log/messages file.

11

Managing the Linux Boot Process

I n the previous chapter, you learned about Linux processes. We discussed the init process, which is the grandparent of all other processes. We also discussed how to use init scripts to start and stop services on the system. In this chapter, we're going to build upon this knowledge and go into depth about the Linux boot process. We'll discuss the following topics:

■ How the Linux boot process works

■ Configuring Linux bootloaders

■ Managing Linux runlevels

INSIDE THE EXAM

Managing the Linux Boot Process

For your Linux+ exam, you need to have a sound understanding of how the Linux boot process works. If you can draw a simple diagram of the process, you should be in good shape for the exam. In addition, you need to be very familiar with both the LILO and GRUB bootloaders. Given a particular Linux system, you need to be able to identify which bootloader it's using and know how to configure it. You also need to know how

to configure a bootloader to boot a system to either the Linux or Windows operating systems (i.e., a dual-boot system).

Finally, you need to know how to manage Linux runlevels. You need to know how to change runlevels from the shell prompt. You should know how to use the inittab file to specify the default runlevel for the system. You must also know how to specify which services run by default at each runlevel.

Let's begin this chapter by discussing how the Linux boot process works.

CERTIFICATION OBJECTIVE 11.01

Explain How the Linux Boot Process Works

A key concept for Linux administrators to understand is how the operating system boots. The Linux boot process is a little more complicated than the boot process used by many other operating systems that you may already be familiar with. Therefore, we're going to spend some time at the beginning of this chapter outlining how the process works. Understanding the boot process will be of great benefit to you when we discuss how to configure bootloaders and runlevels later in this chapter.

on the Job *Understand that the process we'll discuss in this chapter is generic in nature. Most Linux distributions will follow the same basic process, although the specific implementation of the process may vary between distributions. The process also varies between older and newer versions of the Linux kernel.*

The first time I booted a Linux system back in the 1990s, a string of unintelligible messages (at least to me) was displayed on the screen as the system started up. I had no idea what they were talking about. What's this vmlinuz thing anyway? Today, most of the Linux operating system's boot messages are hidden by splash screens on most popular distributions, as shown in Figure 11-1.

These splash screens make things pretty, but they also hide a lot of information that can be very useful to the system admin. Fortunately, with most distributions, you can still view these messages if you press the ESC key when the splash screen is displayed. A sample is shown in Figure 11-2.

on the Job *The messages often scroll by too quickly to be read. You can enter dmesg | more to review the messages displayed during the boot process.*

I highly recommend that you do this very thing after reading this part of this chapter. It will help solidify the boot process concepts we're going to be reviewing.

FIGURE 11-1 Linux splash screen

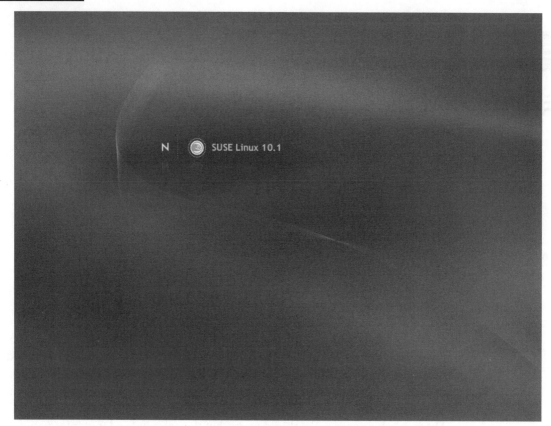

To make the Linux boot process more digestible, we're going to break it down into the following phases:

- The BIOS phase
- The bootloader phase
- The kernel phase

Let's start by discussing the BIOS phase.

FIGURE 11-2   Linux boot messages

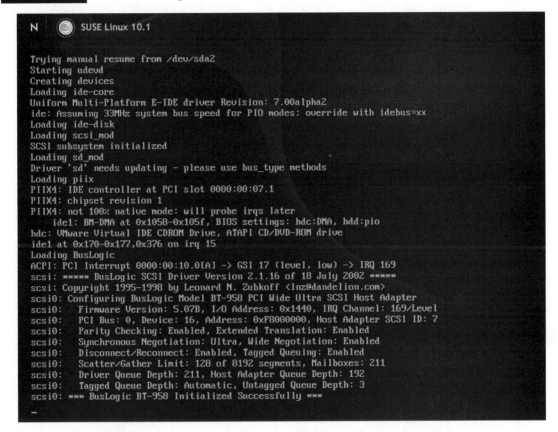

N   SUSE Linux 10.1

```
Trying manual resume from /dev/sda2
Starting udevd
Creating devices
Loading ide-core
Uniform Multi-Platform E-IDE driver Revision: 7.00alpha2
ide: Assuming 33MHz system bus speed for PIO modes; override with idebus=xx
Loading ide-disk
Loading scsi_mod
SCSI subsystem initialized
Loading sd_mod
Driver 'sd' needs updating - please use bus_type methods
Loading piix
PIIX4: IDE controller at PCI slot 0000:00:07.1
PIIX4: chipset revision 1
PIIX4: not 100% native mode: will probe irqs later
    ide1: BM-DMA at 0x1058-0x105f, BIOS settings: hdc:DMA, hdd:pio
hdc: VMware Virtual IDE CDROM Drive, ATAPI CD/DVD-ROM drive
ide1 at 0x170-0x177,0x376 on irq 15
Loading BusLogic
ACPI: PCI Interrupt 0000:00:10.0[A] -> GSI 17 (level, low) -> IRQ 169
scsi: ***** BusLogic SCSI Driver Version 2.1.16 of 18 July 2002 *****
scsi: Copyright 1995-1998 by Leonard N. Zubkoff <lnz@dandelion.com>
scsi0: Configuring BusLogic Model BT-958 PCI Wide Ultra SCSI Host Adapter
scsi0:    Firmware Version: 5.07B, I/O Address: 0x1440, IRQ Channel: 169/Level
scsi0:    PCI Bus: 0, Device: 16, Address: 0xF8000000, Host Adapter SCSI ID: 7
scsi0:    Parity Checking: Enabled, Extended Translation: Enabled
scsi0:    Synchronous Negotiation: Ultra, Wide Negotiation: Enabled
scsi0:    Disconnect/Reconnect: Enabled, Tagged Queuing: Enabled
scsi0:    Scatter/Gather Limit: 128 of 8192 segments, Mailboxes: 211
scsi0:    Driver Queue Depth: 211, Host Adapter Queue Depth: 192
scsi0:    Tagged Queue Depth: Automatic, Untagged Queue Depth: 3
scsi0: *** BusLogic BT-958 Initialized Successfully ***
_
```

The BIOS Phase

Regardless of what operating system you're using, when you first power on an x86 personal computer, the system BIOS is the first component to take charge of the boot process. The system BIOS is a ROM chip integrated in the motherboard that contains a series of very small programs and drivers that allow the CPU to communicate with basic system devices, such as the keyboard, I/O ports, the system speaker, system RAM, floppy disk drives, and hard drives.

on the
j o b   *Variable information about your system, such as the amount of RAM installed, the geometry of your hard drives, and the type of floppy disk installed, are stored in the CMOS chip. The BIOS uses the data in the CMOS chip to address these devices.*

The BIOS plays two key roles during the boot process. First, it tests the various system components and makes sure they are working properly. This is called the power on self test, otherwise affectionately known as POST. If the BIOS encounters any problems with system devices, it will either display a cryptic error message on the screen or it will sound a series of beeps in code. You can use your BIOS documentation—easily available on the Internet by searching on the motherboard model number or BIOS manufacturer, or sometimes included in the manual for your motherboard—to interpret these messages to determine what exactly is wrong with the system.

The second role played by the BIOS is that it selects a storage device to boot the operating system from. Most system setup programs (which are also small programs contained in the BIOS) allow you to configure the order in which the BIOS should look for bootable media. In Figure 11-3, the system has been configured to first look on the floppy disk drive, then on the local hard disk drive, then on the CD-ROM drive.

The BIOS will boot from the first bootable device it finds in the list. Recall back when we installed Linux early in this book. I told you that you need to be sure your BIOS is set to boot off the CD first, otherwise you probably won't be able to load the

FIGURE 11-3   BIOS boot media options

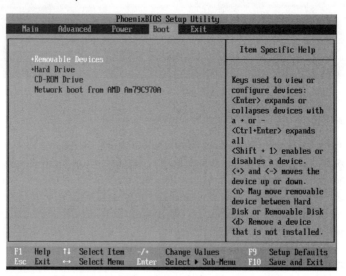

Linux installation program. This is why this happens. If the BIOS finds a bootable device higher up in the list, it won't get to the CD that you want to boot from.

So how does the BIOS know if a device is bootable or not? It looks in the first sector of the device, which is called the *boot sector*. On a hard disk drive, the boot sector contains the master boot record (MBR). Let's discuss the role of the MBR next in the bootloader phase.

The Bootloader Phase

After finishing the POST process, the BIOS really doesn't have much more to do. It has done its job and is ready to turn control of the system over to someone else. To do this, it needs to know where programming resides that can take over the system. To do this, it looks for the MBR on your system's hard drive.

The MBR resides in the boot sector of your system's hard disk drive. It plays a key role in the process of booting your Linux system. The MBR tells the system where a bootloader resides. The bootloader has a very important job. The issue here is that your computer needs an operating system of some type to access the hard disk drive and load data into RAM from it. At this point in the boot process, we need to load the operating system itself from the hard drive into memory. How do you load an operating system into memory from the hard drive if you need to have an operating system to load data from the hard drive?

This is the job of the bootloader. The *bootloader* is software that the BIOS can load from the MBR of the hard drive that will allow the CPU to access the disk and load the operating system into RAM. To do this, the bootloader is configured with the location of the operating system files on the hard disk drive.

The bootloader software itself may or may not actually be in the MBR. As we'll see later in this chapter, you can install some bootloaders within the MBR or you can install them within a partition somewhere else on the hard drive and place a pointer in the MBR. Other bootloaders actually reside in both places.

After loading the bootloader software into memory, the BIOS turns control of the system over to the bootloader. The bootloader may be configured to automatically load an operating system from the hard drive or it may be configured to provide end users with a menu that allows them to select which operating system to load.

With later Linux kernels, the bootloader may also create a temporary, virtual file system in your system RAM called a ramdisk. This file system is called *initrd image*.

on the
job

The term "initrd" stands for initial ramdisk.

This image contains a basic file system that can be used to complete a variety of startup tasks. The reason the initrd image is used is because Linux systems can use a wide variety of devices for the root (/) file system. Some devices may be created from a software RAID array (which we'll discuss later in this book); some devices may even reside on a different computer and are accessed through the NFS or Samba services. These types of file systems can't be mounted by the kernel until special software is loaded, which, of course, resides on those file systems. It can't be done!

To make the system boot correctly in these situations, the bootloader creates a small, virtual hard drive in memory called a ramdisk and transfers a temporary root file system from the initrd image to it. The Linux kernel can then use this temporary file system to load the software and complete the tasks required for it to mount the real file systems on these other types of devices.

The Kernel Phase

After selecting the operating system to run, the bootloader loads the operating system kernel into RAM from the hard drive. For our purposes, the bootloader loads the Linux kernel into RAM. The Linux kernel is located in the /boot directory in your file system, as shown in Figure 11-4.

Your kernel is the vmlinuz-*version*.gz file located in this directory. You may have noticed that the kernel is a .gz file. That's because the kernel resides as a compressed file on the hard drive. You may have noticed when you first boot a Linux system that a message stating something to the effect of "Uncompressing Linux" is sometimes displayed on the screen. Now you know why!

FIGURE 11-4   The Linux kernel in /boot

After the kernel loads, several key things happen, including the following:

- The kernel initializes the basic hardware in your system using the various settings in your BIOS and your CMOS chips.
- The kernel searches for and uses the initrd file system to run the linuxrc program to set up the system.
- When linuxrc has finished executing, the initrd file system is dismounted and the ramdisk is destroyed.
- The kernel probes for new hardware and loads the appropriate driver modules.
- The real root (/) file system is mounted.
- The kernel loads the init process.

As you learned in the previous section, the init process is the key, critical process required to run the rest of the system. At this point in the boot process, init uses configuration parameters in the /etc/inittab file to load system processes and gets the system "up and running." When init is done, you can then log in and use the system.

An overview of the boot process is shown in Figure 11-5.

Now that you understand the Linux boot process, here are some possible scenario questions and their answers.

SCENARIO & SOLUTION

When you power on your Linux system, you see a message displayed on the screen that says "301 Keyboard Error." Where is this message coming from and how can you resolve the issue?	The message is being generated by the BIOS as a result of the power on self test (POST) routine. You can check the BIOS manufacturer's Web site to get more details about the error message. This message was most likely caused by something resting on the keyboard while system powered on.
Why does the Linux kernel create a ramdisk during the boot process?	The ramdisk is created to provide a temporary root file system that the kernel can use to load software needed to check and mount the real file system.
You need to check and see what version of the Linux kernel your system is using. Where can you look in your file system to determine this?	You can check the file name of the vmlinuz file in your /boot directory. The vmlinuz file name contains the kernel version.

An overview of the Linux boot process

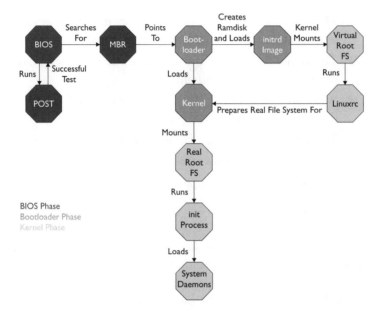

With this information in mind, you're ready to learn about configuring bootloaders. Let's discuss how this is done next.

CERTIFICATION OBJECTIVE 11.02

Configure Linux Bootloaders

As you can see, the bootlloaders play an extremely important role in the Linux boot process. Without a bootloader, the BIOS wouldn't be able to load an operating system off of the system's hard disk drive. Therefore, it's very important that you have a sound understanding of how to configure the bootloaders used by Linux.

As with so many aspects of Linux, you can choose from many different bootloaders to use with your Linux system. You can even use the Windows 2000/XP bootloader to load your Linux kernel! For your Linux+ exam, however, you only need to be familiar with two of the most widely used bootloaders: LILO and GRUB.

Therefore, in this part of this chapter we're going to spend some time looking at how to do the following:

- Configuring LILO
- Configuring GRUB
- Using a bootloader to create a dual-boot system

Let's begin by learning how to use the LILO bootloader.

Configuring LILO

The LILO bootloader has been around a very long time. LILO stands for *LInux LOader*. LILO is a very flexible bootloader that can be used to launch just about any operating system from your computer's hard drive, including Linux, Windows, or DOS.

When LILO is used as the default bootloader, the LILO boot menu is displayed to end users, allowing them to select which operating system kernel they want to boot. A sample LILO boot menu is shown in Figure 11-6.

Many Linux distributions may present the LILO menu graphically instead of the text menu shown in Figure 11-6.

| FIGURE 11-6 | The LILO boot menu |

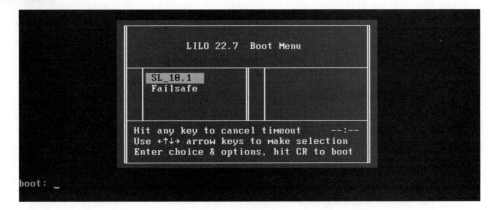

Most early Linux distributions used LILO as the default bootloader. Because of this, LILO is probably one of the most widely deployed Linux bootloaders. Therefore, a good Linux administrator needs to know how to work with LILO. We're going to look at the following LILO topics:

■ Installing LILO

■ Configuring LILO

■ About ELILO

Let's begin by discussing how to install the LILO bootloader.

Installing LILO

There are two different ways you can install the LILO bootloader. First, with most Linux distributions, you can specify that the LILO bootloader be used for the system being installed.

on the **Most current Linux distributions use the GRUB bootloader instead of LILO by**
Ⓙob **default.**

For example, in Figure 11-7, the SUSE Linux installer provides you with the option of changing the bootloader from the default of GRUB to LILO in the Boot Loader Settings screen.

In this screen, you can opt to install the LILO bootloader in either the MBR or within the boot partition itself. Either option seems to work just as well. In addition, you can also install the LILO bootloader on a system that's already configured with the GRUB bootloader by simply entering **lilo** at the shell prompt. This will overwrite the existing bootloader and install the LILO bootloader. However, before you can do this, you need to configure the LILO configuration file in /etc. Let's discuss how this is done next.

Configuring LILO

The LILO bootloader is configured using a file in /etc named lilo.conf. A sample lilo.conf file from a SUSE Linux system is shown in Figure 11-8.

Notice in Figure 11-8 that there are three sections of information within this file. The first section contains global options that apply to all other sections in the file. The last two sections contain options specific to each menu item. Let's run through the lines of the sample configuration file shown in Figure 11-8 and review what each one does in Table 11-1.

FIGURE 11-7 Configuring the LILO bootloader during installation

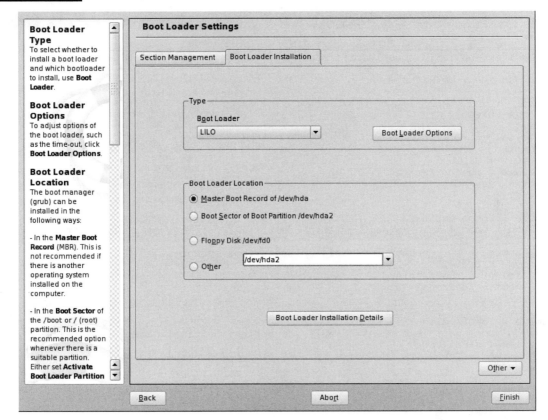

The options listed in Table 11-1 aren't all-inclusive. There are many more options you can use in your /etc/lilo.conf file. We don't have time or space to cover all of them here. For a complete listing, see the man page for lilo.conf.

The lilo.conf file is just a text file. You can use any Linux text editor to modify it. After modifying the file and exiting your editor, however, you must remember to run **lilo** from the shell prompt. If you don't, your changes to the configuration file won't be applied. This is shown in Figure 11-9.

Notice in Figure 11-9 that the output from the lilo command indicates that the two images were added. You may have noticed that the lilo command we just used here to update our configuration is the same command that is used to install LILO. It is exactly the same command. In effect, every time you make a change to the LILO configuration file, you have to reinstall it with the lilo command. We should point out here that you can use the –b option with the lilo command to specify where the

FIGURE 11-8   The LILO configuration file in /etc

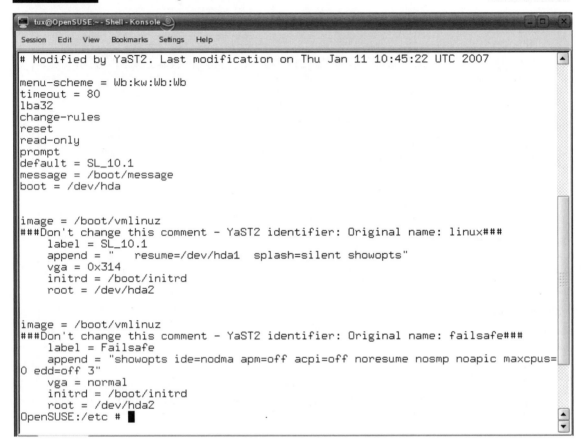

```
# Modified by YaST2. Last modification on Thu Jan 11 10:45:22 UTC 2007

menu-scheme = Wb:kw:Wb:Wb
timeout = 80
lba32
change-rules
reset
read-only
prompt
default = SL_10.1
message = /boot/message
boot = /dev/hda


image = /boot/vmlinuz
###Don't change this comment - YaST2 identifier: Original name: linux###
    label = SL_10.1
    append = "   resume=/dev/hda1  splash=silent showopts"
    vga = 0x314
    initrd = /boot/initrd
    root = /dev/hda2

image = /boot/vmlinuz
###Don't change this comment - YaST2 identifier: Original name: failsafe###
    label = Failsafe
    append = "showopts ide=nodma apm=off acpi=off noresume nosmp noapic maxcpus=
0 edd=off 3"
    vga = normal
    initrd = /boot/initrd
    root = /dev/hda2
OpenSUSE:/etc # █
```

bootloader should be installed. If you specify a device, such as /dev/hda, then the bootloader will be installed in that device's MBR. If you specify a partition, such as /dev/hda1, then it will be installed in that partition and a pointer placed in the MBR.

Before shifting gears and talking about the GRUB bootloader, we need to first review a variation of LILO called ELILO. Let's do that next.

About ELILO

If you look at the Linux+ objectives we're covering in this chapter, you'll notice that it mentions a variation of LILO called ELILO. ELILO works in pretty much

TABLE 11-1	/etc/lilo.conf Configuration Options	
Section	**Option**	**Description**
Global Options	menu-scheme	Describes the colors used in the LILO boot menu. The syntax is: *text_color:highlight_color:border_color:title_color* Notice in Figure 11-8 that two characters are used for each value. The first character is the foreground color while the second is the background color. See the lilo.conf man page for a listing of all the colors and their associated characters that can be used with this option.
	timeout	Sets the timeout period in 1/10th seconds before the default menu item is automatically run. In Figure 11-8, this option is set to 80, which gives the user 8 seconds to select a menu item.
	lba32	Tells lilo to ignore the hard drive's physical geometry and use logical block addressing. This allows LILO to work with disks that have more than 1023 cylinders (which all modern hard drives do).
	change-rules	Defines boot-time changes to partition type numbers.
	reset	Specifies that all default change-rules are removed.
	read-only	Specifies that the root (/) file system be mounted read-only at first. After checking the integrity of the file system, the kernel will usually remount the file system in read-write mode.
	prompt	Specifies that the boot: prompt be displayed.
	default	Specifies the default image that will be loaded if the user doesn't make a selection.
	message	Specifies the location of the image file that LILO will display.
	boot	Specifies the device that contains the boot sector. In Figure 11-8, LILO is configured to use the first IDE hard drive (/dev/hda).
Image Options	image	Specifies the path to the boot image of a Linux kernel.
	label	Specifies a name for the image.
	append	Appends the specified options to the parameters that are passed to the kernel by LILO. This is usually only used if the system uses hardware that the kernel is having a difficult time auto-detecting.
	vga	Specifies the VGA text mode that should be used while the system is booting.
	initrd	Specifies the initial ramdisk image to be loaded with the kernel. In Figure 11-8, the /boot/initrd image is to be used.
	root	Specifies the device that should be mounted as root. In Figure 11-8, the second partition on the first IDE hard drive (/dev/hda2) is specified as the partition that should be mounted as the root partition.

FIGURE 11-9 Running lilo to implement changes to the /etc/lilo.conf file

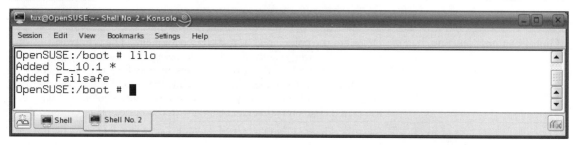

the same manner as LILO. However, it's designed to run on computer hardware that doesn't work well with the standard version of LILO. It's designed to boot a Linux kernel on the IA-64(IPF) and IA-32(x86) EFI-based hardware platforms.

ELILO is also backward-compatible with standard Intel x86 hardware. However, only a limited number of Linux distributions use it at this point.

Enough with LILO! It's time now to start working with GRUB!

Configuring GRUB

GRUB. What a name for a bootloader! The acronym GRUB doesn't sound very appealing, does it? However, as bootloaders go, GRUB is fantastic. GRUB stands for *GRand Unified Bootloader*. Like LILO, GRUB is a bootloader that can be used

SCENARIO & SOLUTION

Your Linux distribution installed the GRUB bootloader by default when it was installed. You want to use LILO instead. How can you overwrite GRUB with LILO?	First, create and configure your /etc/lilo.conf file. Then enter **lilo** at the shell prompt.
You want to configure your LILO menu to allow the user 15 seconds to select a menu item before loading the default menu selection. What parameter should you use in /etc/lilo.conf and what value should you set it to?	You need to modify the timeout parameter and set it to a value of 150.
You've just made several changes to your /etc/lilo.conf file. However, when you reboot, the changes haven't been applied. Why is this happening?	After making changes to the /etc/lilo.conf file, you need to re-install LILO by entering **lilo** at the shell prompt.

to boot a Linux kernel (or any other operating system kernel, for that matter) from your system's hard drive.

The LILO bootloader was very popular and very widely used for a number of years. However, in the last couple of years, there has been a steady shift away from LILO toward GRUB on the part of most distributions and many Linux administrators. Therefore, you need to have a solid understanding of how GRUB works and how to configure it.

In this part of this chapter, we're going to discuss the following GRUB topics:

■ How GRUB works
■ Installing GRUB
■ Configuring GRUB

Let's begin by discussing how GRUB works.

How GRUB Works

Remember when we discussed LILO that we said that it can be installed in either the MBR or the boot partition of the boot hard drive? GRUB is a little bit different. The GRUB bootloader is divided into separate chunks called *stages*. These include the following:

■ **Stage 1**   This stage of GRUB is usually stored in the MBR. Its only real job is to point to the location of Stage 2.

■ **Stage 2**   This stage of GRUB is stored in a disk partition. When loaded by Stage 1, Stage 2 presents a graphical menu on the screen that allows the user to select the kernel image that should be loaded. Like LILO, you can configure GRUB with a default image and a timeout value. If the user doesn't select an option within the timeout period, the system will automatically boot the default kernel image. A typical GRUB menu is shown in Figure 11-10.

on the job   *Like LILO, it's also possible to install Stage 1 in the boot partition. In addition, there may actually be a GRUB Stage 1.5 on some deployments. Stage 1 can either load Stage 2 directly, or it may point to Stage 1.5, which resides in the first 30KB after the MBR of the hard disk. Stage 1.5 then loads Stage 2.*

With this overview in mind, let's talk about installing GRUB.

The GRUB boot menu

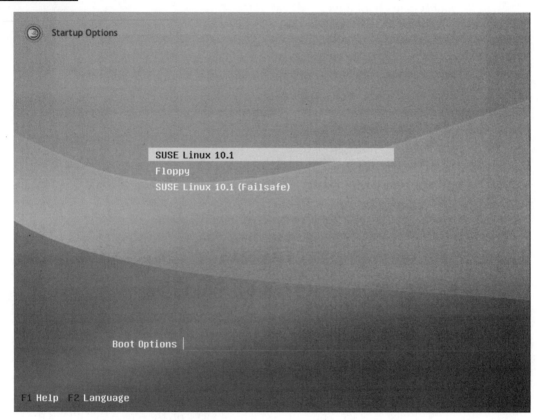

Installing GRUB

One of the things that I really like about GRUB is the fact that you don't have to re-install the bootloader every time you make a minor configuration change. After it's initially installed, you can modify your configuration files and the changes will be applied the next time GRUB is loaded because Stage 2 reads directly from the configuration file on disk.

To initially install GRUB, you enter **grub-install** *device* at the shell prompt. The *device* option is the name of the device whose MBR you want to install Stage 1 into. For example, if you wanted to install GRUB Stage 1 in the MBR of the first IDE hard drive in your system, you would enter **grub-install /dev/hda**. This is shown in Figure 11-11.

FIGURE 11-11	Installing GRUB

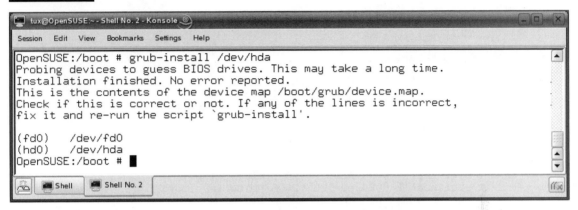

With GRUB installed, you're ready to configure it. Let's discuss how this is done next.

Configuring GRUB

To configure GRUB, you need to edit a text-based configuration file in much the same manner as the LILO boot manager we discussed earlier. However, with GRUB, the name of the file you need to edit can vary from distribution to distribution. Table 11-2 lists some common implementations by distribution.

Some distributions, such as Fedora, symbolically link /etc/grub.conf to the /boot/ grub/grub.conf file. The easiest way to find out which file you should use to configure grub is to simply switch to your /boot/grub directory and look for either a grub.conf or a menu.lst file, as shown in Figure 11-12.

Whichever file name your GRUB configuration file uses, it will use a standard structure. Remember that your LILO configuration file used a global section and

TABLE 11-2	GRUB Configuration Files

GRUB Configuration File	Distribution
/boot/grub/grub.conf	Fedora
/boot/grub/menu.lst	SUSE Linux, Debian

FIGURE 11-12   Identifying your GRUB configuration file

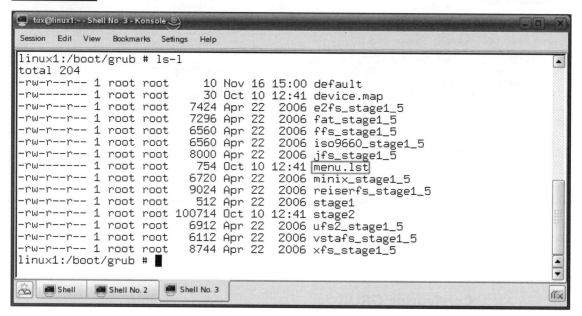

```
linux1:/boot/grub # ls-l
total 204
-rw-r--r-- 1 root root       10 Nov 16 15:00 default
-rw------- 1 root root       30 Oct 10 12:41 device.map
-rw-r--r-- 1 root root     7424 Apr 22  2006 e2fs_stage1_5
-rw-r--r-- 1 root root     7296 Apr 22  2006 fat_stage1_5
-rw-r--r-- 1 root root     6560 Apr 22  2006 ffs_stage1_5
-rw-r--r-- 1 root root     6560 Apr 22  2006 iso9660_stage1_5
-rw-r--r-- 1 root root     8000 Apr 22  2006 jfs_stage1_5
-rw------- 1 root root      754 Oct 10 12:41 menu.lst
-rw-r--r-- 1 root root     6720 Apr 22  2006 minix_stage1_5
-rw-r--r-- 1 root root     9024 Apr 22  2006 reiserfs_stage1_5
-rw-r--r-- 1 root root      512 Apr 22  2006 stage1
-rw-r--r-- 1 root root   100714 Oct 10 12:41 stage2
-rw-r--r-- 1 root root     6912 Apr 22  2006 ufs2_stage1_5
-rw-r--r-- 1 root root     6112 Apr 22  2006 vstafs_stage1_5
-rw-r--r-- 1 root root     8744 Apr 22  2006 xfs_stage1_5
linux1:/boot/grub # █
```

then one or more image-specific sections. The GRUB configuration file works in much the same manner. The first part of your GRUB configuration file contains global options that apply to all menu items. Then it has one or more title sections that are used to launch a specific operating system. This is shown in Figure 11-13.

Before we explore the entries in the sample GRUB configuration file in Figure 11-13, we need to review some GRUB nomenclature. First of all, GRUB references disks and partitions in your system in a manner that may be unfamiliar. When we worked with LILO, we used the entries in /dev to reference devices and partitions, such as /dev/hda1.

GRUB references these devices differently. Instead of using a /dev entry, GRUB uses the following syntax:

```
hddrive_number,partition_number
```

For example, the first partition on the first hard drive (/dev/hda1 or /dev/sda1) is referenced by GRUB as hd0,0. It doesn't matter if the first disk is an IDE or a SCSI drive, GRUB refers to it as hd0. This really threw me for a loop when I first started working with GRUB. In my mind, "hd" meant an IDE hard disk. After many

FIGURE 11-13   A typical GRUB configuration file

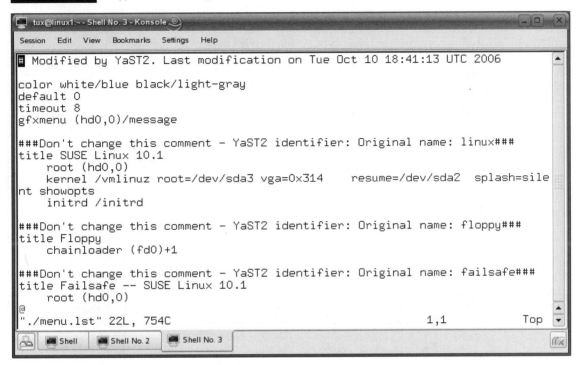

```
# Modified by YaST2. Last modification on Tue Oct 10 18:41:13 UTC 2006

color white/blue black/light-gray
default 0
timeout 8
gfxmenu (hd0,0)/message

###Don't change this comment - YaST2 identifier: Original name: linux###
title SUSE Linux 10.1
    root (hd0,0)
    kernel /vmlinuz root=/dev/sda3 vga=0x314    resume=/dev/sda2  splash=sile
nt showopts
    initrd /initrd

###Don't change this comment - YaST2 identifier: Original name: floppy###
title Floppy
    chainloader (fd0)+1

###Don't change this comment - YaST2 identifier: Original name: failsafe###
title Failsafe -- SUSE Linux 10.1
    root (hd0,0)
@
"./menu.lst" 22L, 754C                                      1,1        Top
```

misconfigured GRUB menus, I finally figured out that "hd" to GRUB means any hard drive, SCSI or IDE.

The other thing that really threw me was the fact that GRUB creates its own "root" called the GRUB root. This isn't necessarily the root file system mounted at /. Instead, it's the partition where the /boot directory resides (where Stage 2 is installed). Here's the confusing part: If you haven't created a separate partition for /boot when you first partitioned your hard drive, then GRUB will use the full path to refer to the GRUB root, which is usually /boot/grub. If, on the other hand, you have created a separate partition for /boot (a very common practice), then this partition becomes the GRUB root. GRUB then refers to files in the GRUB root *without* including /boot in path. This will drive you crazy until you get used to it.

Because the system used to create Figure 11-13 has a separate partition for /boot, I felt like we needed to review these two facts before proceeding. Otherwise, many of the entries in the menu.lst file won't make sense. With this in mind, let's step

TABLE 11-3   GRUB Configuration File Options

Section	Option	Description
Global	color	Specifies the colors to be used in the GRUB menu.
	default	Specifies the menu item that will be booted automatically if the user doesn't make a manual selection. In Figure 11-13, the first menu option (0) will be booted automatically if the user doesn't specify otherwise.
	timeout	Specifies the number of seconds to wait until the default menu item is automatically booted. In Figure 11-13, the timeout period is set to 8 seconds.
	gfxmenu	Specifies the location of the image file that will be used to display the graphical GRUB boot menu. In Figure 11-13, the message file on the first partition (0) of the first hard drive (hd0) will be used for the GRUB boot menu. Remember, because this system has a separate partition for /boot, /boot is omitted from the path to files, such as message, in the GRUB root. The true path to this file is /boot/message.
Title	title	Specifies the title of the menu item in the GRUB boot menu.
	root	Specifies the location of the partition that is to be mounted as the GRUB root. In Figure 11-13, this is hd0,0, which specifies the first partition (0) of the first hard drive (hd0). Remember in Figure 11-13 that the system has a separate partition (/dev/sda1) for /boot.
	kernel	Specifies the location of the Linux kernel. In Figure 11-13, the GRUB menu points to /boot/vmlinuz, which is actually a link that points to the actual Linux kernel file in /boot. The root= option specifies the partition that will be mounted as the root file system. The vga= option specifies the VGA mode the system should use during boot. The resume= option points to the system's swap partition.
	initrd	Specifies the initrd image that should be used by GRUB to create the initial ramdisk image during boot. In Figure 11-13, the /boot/initrd image is specified. Like vmlinuz, the initrd file in /boot is actually a link to the real initrd image file.

through each of the lines in the GRUB configuration file and discuss what each does in Table 11-3.

One of the cool things about GRUB is that you can manage the boot process interactively. This is something LILO can't do. Instead of being stuck with whatever is configured in the menu.lst or grub.conf file, you can customize your own boot process. To do this, complete the following:

1. In the GRUB menu, press the ESC key.

2. When prompted that you are leaving the graphical boot menu, select OK. When you do, the text-based GRUB menu is displayed, as shown in Figure 11-14.

3. If you want to edit the menu item, press E. When you do, the screen in Figure 11-15 is displayed.

FIGURE 11-14   The text-based GRUB menu

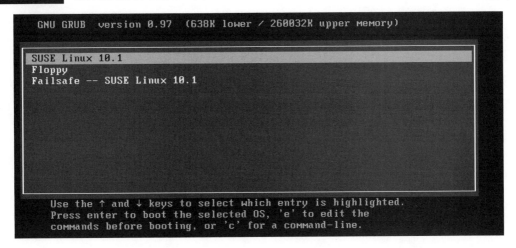

In this screen, you can arrow up or down to select the appropriate line and then press E again to edit. If you want to add a new line, press O. Press B when you're ready to start the boot process.

4. You can also access a GRUB prompt by pressing C. When you do, the screen shown in Figure 11-16 is displayed.

FIGURE 11-15   Editing a GRUB menu item

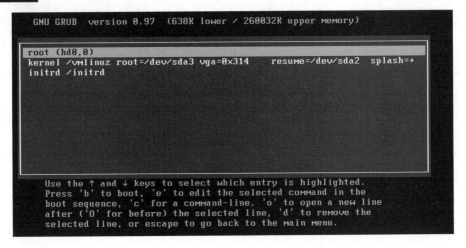

FIGURE 11-16   The GRUB prompt

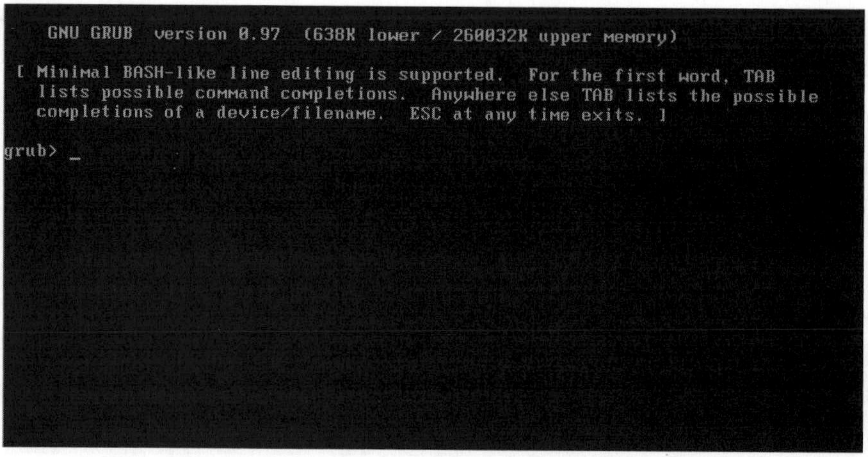

```
   GNU GRUB  version 0.97  (638K lower / 260032K upper memory)

 [ Minimal BASH-like line editing is supported.  For the first word, TAB
   lists possible command completions.  Anywhere else TAB lists the possible
   completions of a device/filename.  ESC at any time exits. ]

grub> _
```

You can enter **help** at the grub prompt to display information about creating GRUB menu lines from the grub> prompt. You can also press TAB to see a list of commands that you can enter at the grub> prompt. You can also press ESC to return to the GRUB menu.

Now that you understand how to configure the GRUB bootloader, here are some possible scenario questions and their answers.

SCENARIO & SOLUTION

Your Linux distribution installed the LILO bootloader by default when it was installed. You want to use GRUB instead. How can you overwrite LILO with GRUB?	You can enter **grub-install** *device_name* at the shell prompt. For example, if you want to install GRUB on your first IDE hard drive, you would enter **grub-install /dev/hda**.
You need to configure the GRUB bootloader on a SUSE Linux system. However, you can't find the grub.conf file in /boot/grub. Why is this?	Some distributions, including SUSE Linux, use /boot/grub/menu.lst instead of grub.conf to configure the GRUB bootloader.
You want to configure your GRUB bootloader on your Linux system such that the second menu item is the default item loaded if the user doesn't make a selection. What command would you need to enter in the GRUB configuration file?	You would need to add the following: `default 1`

Let's practice working with the GRUB bootloader in the following exercise.

EXERCISE 11-1

ON THE CD

Working with GRUB

In this exercise, you will practice customizing your GRUB menu. This exercise assumes that you've installed a distribution such as SUSE Linux or Fedora, which uses GRUB by default. Complete the following:

1. Boot your Linux system and log in as a standard user. If you used the lab exercise in Chapter 3 to install your system, you can log in as **tux** with a password of **M3linux273**.

2. Open a terminal session.

3. Switch to your root user account by entering **su –** followed by your root user's password.

4. At the shell prompt, enter **ls –l /boot/grub**. Identify whether your distribution uses the grub.conf or the menu.lst file to configure grub.

5. At the shell prompt, enter **vi /boot/grub/menu.lst** or **vi /boot/grub/ grub.conf**, depending on which file your system uses.

6. Press INSERT.

7. Scroll down to the timeout line.

8. Change the value of timeout to 12.

9. Press ESC.

10. Save your changes to the file and exit vi by entering **:exit**.

11. At the shell prompt, enter **reboot**. Wait while the system restarts.

12. Notice in the GRUB menu that you now have 12 seconds to make a selection before the default menu item is started.

Before we finish discussing bootloaders, we need to discuss how to create a dual-boot system. Let's do that next.

Using a Bootloader to Create a Dual-Boot System

If you take a look at the Linux+ objectives, you'll see that the objective covering bootloaders requires that you know how to create a dual-boot system. When we say dual-boot, we're talking about a system that can boot to either Linux or some other operating system, most likely a version of Windows.

Back in the late 1990s and early 2000, I used this option very frequently. However, I use it less and less as the years go by. The availability of virtualization software, such as VMware, makes the dual-boot option less desirable, in my opinion. However, you still have to know about dual-boot for Linux+, so we're going to spend some time reviewing how this is done here. We'll cover the following topics:

- Dual-boot considerations
- Configuring a dual-boot system with GRUB
- Configuring a dual-boot system with NTLOADER.EXE

Let's begin by discussing some considerations you need to keep in mind when creating a dual-boot system.

Dual-Boot Considerations

As we've progressed through this chapter, I've mentioned several times that the Linux bootloaders are capable of booting operating systems other than Linux, such as Windows. It also works the other way around. You can use the Windows bootloader to launch Linux. The first consideration you need to take into account is which bootloader you want to use.

Installing a dual-boot system using LILO or GRUB is really pretty easy. Most Linux installation routines will automatically detect the existing Windows OS and automatically create the appropriate menu item in GRUB or LILO for you.

Installing a dual-boot system using the Windows bootloader (NTLOADER.EXE) is a little more challenging. The problem is that the Windows installation routine doesn't detect Linux if it is installed first. You'll have to run through a series of steps (discussed later) to get NTLOADER to run the Linux kernel.

on the
① o b   *I suggest that, unless you have an overriding reason to do otherwise, you use GRUB or LILO as your bootloader when creating a dual-boot system. It's much easier and faster to set up.*

The second consideration you need to keep in mind is that of disk space. The key issue is that each operating system needs its own partition (or partitions). The problem is that whenever you install an operating system, the default behavior for most installation routines is to partition and format the entire disk for that OS. If this happens, and it usually does, then you don't have room on the disk for additional partitions for the new OS.

In this situation, you have several options. First, you could delete all partitions off the disk and reinstall everything from scratch. Usually, this isn't the most desirable option. It's a lot of work. Usually, critical data and applications have already been installed and created in the first operating system.

The second option is to use partition management software to shrink the existing partition on the disk enough to provide room for the second operating system's partition. For example, the YaST installer used by SUSE Linux has the capability of shrinking your Windows partition during the installation process. This process usually works. However, be warned that I have lost data in the past using these tools. The latest versions of these partition management utilities seem to be much more reliable, but I still don't trust them 100 percent.

Another option in this scenario is to use disk-imaging software (such as Ghost or MaxBlast) to create an image of the existing partition on the drive. Most of these utilities allow you to create the image file over a network connection on a remote computer. Then, you can wipe the disk clean, create a new smaller partition for the original operating system, and restore the image to the smaller partition. As long as the new partition isn't smaller than the amount of space consumed by the original operating system, this process works very smoothly. Once done, you can then create additional partitions in the free space on the disk for the second operating system you want to install.

The last option is to simply install a second hard drive in the system and use it for the second operating system. Hard disks used to be very expensive, making this option less desirable. Today, however, hard disks are very inexpensive when you consider how much space you get. If you don't want to go through the hassle of reinstalling, repartitioning, or shrinking partitions, then this is a great option.

With these considerations in mind, let's spend some time discussing how you actually go about creating a dual-boot system.

Configuring a Dual-Boot System Using GRUB

Creating a dual-boot system with GRUB isn't very difficult at all, once you've configured your system with enough free space for both operating systems. The overall process is as follows:

1. Install your Windows operating system first, if it hasn't already been done. Be sure to leave enough free (unpartitioned) space on the disk for the second operating system.

    The order in which you install operating systems is fairly critical. The key point to understand is that the bootloader of the last OS installed will be the one installed in the MBR when you're done. If you install Linux second, the LILO or GRUB bootloader will be the last one installed in the MBR (overwriting the Windows bootloader that was installed there first).

2. Install your Linux operating system. The installation routines for many Linux distributions will detect the existing operating system on the disk and automatically create a LILO or GRUB menu item for you that will launch it. For example, in Figure 11-17, the SUSE Linux YaST installer identified the Windows operating system installed in the first disk partition and automatically added a menu item to GRUB for you.

    However, the installer used by some distributions may not detect the presence of the other operating system in the existing partitions. If this is the case, then you can manually add the appropriate lines to your LILO or GRUB configuration files. I've provided some examples you can use as a starting point in the next step.

    Be warned, however, that some installers may try to *delete* the existing partition(s) by default in their partitioning proposals. If you want to keep the existing operating system, you need to create a custom partitioning proposal that preserves the existing partition.

3. Check your bootloader configuration file and verify that an entry for the new operating system has been created. If you're using GRUB, you should see an entry similar to the following:

```
title Windows
     chainloader (hd0,0)+1
```

This points the system to the Windows kernel files located in the first partition of the first hard disk in the system. The chainloader directive tells GRUB to turn control over to a different bootloader, which in this case,

FIGURE 11-17   Adding a Windows menu item to GRUB

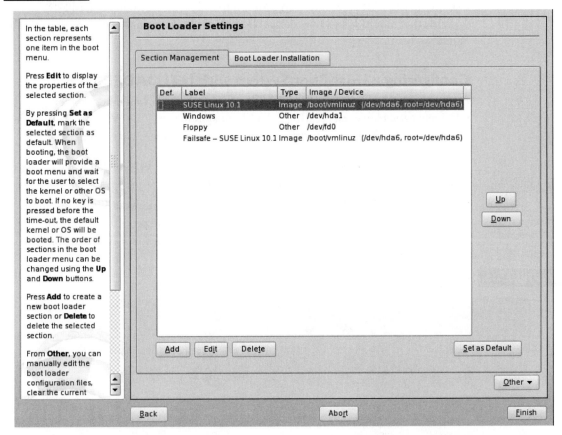

would be NTLOADER.EXE, located in the first partition of the first hard drive.

If your distribution uses LILO, you should see an entry similar to the following:

```
other=/dev/hda1
      label=WindowsXP
```

Like GRUB, the Windows bootloader is divided into two parts. One part is simply a pointer in the MBR. The main part of the Windows bootloader resides in the Windows boot partition. Using the configurations just specified, the GRUB or LILO bootloader simply points to the Windows bootloader in the Windows partition and turns control over to it to boot the system.

When you boot your system, you should see a new GRUB or LILO menu item added that allows you to boot Windows in addition to Linux, as shown in Figure 11-18.

With this in mind, let's now discuss how to configure a dual-boot system using the Windows bootloader.

Configuring a Dual-Boot System with **NTLOADER.EXE**

As I mentioned earlier, creating a dual-boot system with a Linux bootloader is relatively easy. However, creating a dual-boot system using the Windows bootloader (NTLOADER.EXE) is not nearly so straightforward. Here's what you need to do:

1. Install Windows first on the hard drive. As before, be sure you leave plenty of extra unpartitioned space on your drive for Linux.

2. Install Linux into the free space on the drive. Be sure your Linux installer doesn't try to delete your Windows partition in the process. In addition, be sure to install your Linux bootloader in the first sector of the partition that

FIGURE 11-18   Booting Windows using GRUB

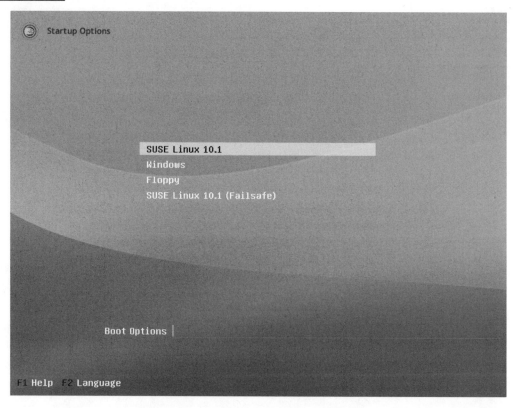

contains the /boot directory, as shown in Figure 11-19. It is very important that you do not install GRUB in the MBR of the drive. If you do, the Windows bootloader will be overwritten by GRUB.

Be sure to note the partition where GRUB was installed. In Figure 11-19, it was installed in /dev/hda3.

3. Wait while the system is installed.
4. When complete, make a copy of your Linux system's boot sector onto a floppy diskette by doing the following:
   a. Insert a blank, formatted floppy diskette into your system's floppy drive and mount it.
   b. At a shell prompt, enter **dd if=*boot_partition* of=*floppy_mount_point*/ linux.bin bs=512 count=1**.

      For the system in Figure 11-19, you would enter **dd if=/dev/hda3 of=media/ floppy/linbootl.bin bs=512 count=1**. This command copies your Linux boot sector to a file named linbootl.bin on your floppy diskette.
   c. Use umount to unmount your floppy diskette.
5. Restart your computer system and boot into your Windows operating system.
6. Configure your Windows bootloader by completing the following:
   a. Log in as Administrator or as a user who is a member of the Administrators group on your Windows system.
   b. Insert your floppy diskette and copy the linbootl.bin file from it to C:\ on your Windows partition.
   c. If not already done, click My Computer and open your C:\ drive.
   d. Select Tools | Folder Options | View.
   e. Select Show Hidden Files and Folders.
   f. Deselect Hide Protected Operating System Files and select Yes when prompted to confirm.
   g. Select OK. You should now see a file named boot.ini. This is the configuration file for your Windows bootloader.
   h. In My Computer, right-click boot.ini and select Properties.
   i. Make sure the Read-Only attribute is *not* marked, then select OK.
   j. Open C:\boot.ini in Notepad.

    k. At the end of the file, add the following line:

```
C:\linbootl.bin="Linux"
```

    l. Add a blank line to the file after the last line.

    m. Save the changes to the file and close Notepad.

7. Reboot your system. You should now have a menu item in your Windows bootloader that will allow you to boot your Linux operating system.

Now that you understand the Linux boot process and bootloaders, let's talk about managing runlevels.

FIGURE 11-19   Installing GRUB in the /boot partition

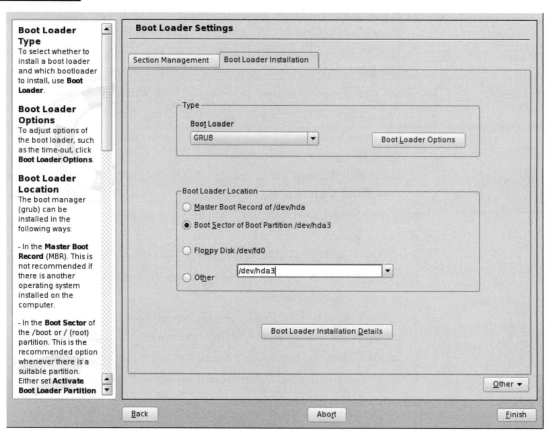

SCENARIO & SOLUTION

You're setting up a dual-boot system that will run both Windows and Fedora Linux. You want to use the GRUB bootloader to provide the user with a menu allowing them to select the operating system they want to use. Which operating system should be installed first on the hard drive?	You should install Windows first and Linux second. The Fedora installer should detect the Windows installation and automatically create a GRUB menu item for you.
You want to create a dual-boot system. Your computer already has Windows installed on it. When you try to install Linux, the installation routine generates an error indicating there isn't any free space on the drive. Why is this happening and how can you fix it?	The Windows partition (NTFS) uses the entire hard drive. To fix it, you must do one of the following: ■ Reinstall Windows with a smaller partition. ■ Resize the existing partition. ■ Image the existing partition and restore it to a smaller partition. ■ Add a second drive to the system.
You're installing a dual-boot system. You've already installed Windows and are now installing Linux. Given that you want to use the Windows bootloader, where should you install the GRUB bootloader for your Linux system?	You need to install GRUB into the boot partition, not into the MBR. If you install into the MBR, you will overwrite the existing Windows bootloader.

CERTIFICATION OBJECTIVE 11.03

Manage Linux Runlevels

If you've worked with Linux before, you may have heard the term "runlevel" used. I've noticed that the concept of a runlevel is difficult for many new Linux users to understand. In this part of this chapter, we'll review what a runlevel is and how you can manage runlevels on your system. The following topics will be covered:

■ How runlevels work
■ Managing runlevels

Let's begin by discussing how runlevels work.

How Runlevels Work

To manage a Linux system, you need to have a sound understanding of how runlevels work. In this part of this chapter, we'll discuss the following:

- What is a runlevel?
- Defining runlevels in /etc/inittab

Let's begin by discussing what a runlevel is.

What Is a Runlevel?

So what exactly is a "runlevel"? It sounds complicated, but when you get right down to it, it really isn't. A *runlevel* represents one of several different modes that your Linux system can run in. A runlevel on a Linux system is similar, in many ways, to a startup mode on a Windows system. If you've used Windows, you know that you can press the F8 key during system boot and select one of several startup modes, as shown in Figure 11-20.

For example, if you're having trouble with a particular device or driver in your Windows system, you can boot it in Safe Mode, which will load the operating system with only a minimal set of drivers so you can troubleshoot the problem.

FIGURE 11-20 Windows startup modes

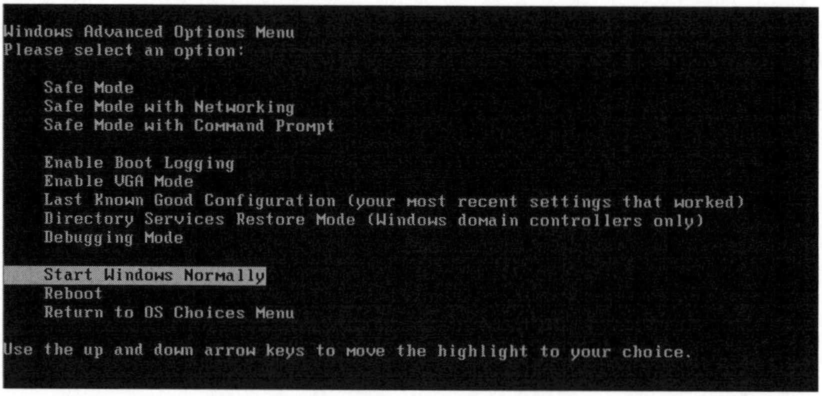

```
Windows Advanced Options Menu
Please select an option:

    Safe Mode
    Safe Mode with Networking
    Safe Mode with Command Prompt

    Enable Boot Logging
    Enable VGA Mode
    Last Known Good Configuration (your most recent settings that worked)
    Directory Services Restore Mode (Windows domain controllers only)
    Debugging Mode

    Start Windows Normally
    Reboot
    Return to OS Choices Menu

Use the up and down arrow keys to move the highlight to your choice.
```

Linux runlevels are similar. Like a Windows startup mode, Linux runlevels allow you to specify the mode in which you want your system to run. Linux uses seven default runlevels that you can choose from, as shown in Table 11-4.

As you can see in Table 11-4, there are some differences between Linux runlevels and Windows startup modes. First of all, runlevel 0 halts the system while runlevel 6 reboots the system. In addition, you can specify a default runlevel for your system as well dynamically switch between runlevels while the system is running. You can't do that with Windows!

These runlevels are defined through the /etc/inittab file. Let's review how this file works next.

Defining Runlevels with /etc/inittab

Remember from the previous chapter that the init process is the grandparent of all other processes. It is the process that is first run by the kernel and is responsible for loading the system processes that make Linux work. The init process is configured in the /etc/inittab file. A typical inittab file for a SUSE Linux system is shown in Figure 11-21.

The syntax of commands within the inittab file is *identifier:runlevel:action: command*. For example, as you can see in Figure 11-21, the first parameter defined in inittab specifies the default runlevel of the system. This parameter takes the form of id:5:initdefault. This command tells the init process to boot into runlevel 5 by default. Remember that runlevel 5 runs Linux in multi-user mode with networking and the GUI desktop enabled.

TABLE 11-4	Linux Runlevels

Runlevel	Description
0	Halts the system.
1	Runs Linux in single-user mode. The command-line interface is used.
2	Runs Linux in multi-user mode with networking disabled. The command-line interface is used.
3	Runs Linux in multi-user mode with networking enabled. The command-line interface is used.
4	Unused.
5	Runs Linux in multi-user mode with networking enabled. The graphical user interface is used.
6	Reboots the system.

FIGURE 11-21 The /etc/inittab file

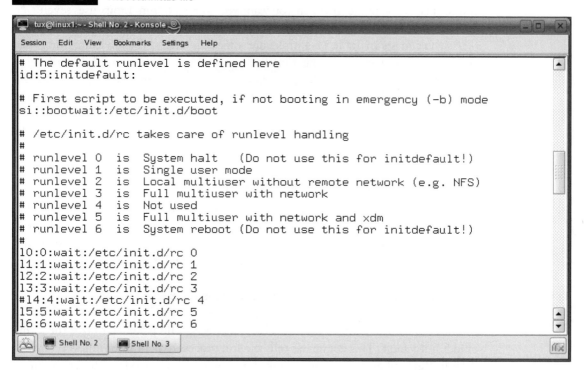

In addition, the inittab file also defines what init scripts are run in each runlevel. This is done using the following lines:

```
l0:0:wait:/etc/init.d/rc 0
l1:1:wait:/etc/init.d/rc 1
l2:2:wait:/etc/init.d/rc 2
l3:3:wait:/etc/init.d/rc 3
#l4:4:wait:/etc/init.d/rc 4
l5:5:wait:/etc/init.d/rc 5
l6:6:wait:/etc/init.d/rc 6
```

on the
ĵob

The syntax for commands within the inittab file is identifier:runlevel:action: command. *The wait action specified in these commands tells the init process to wait until the scripts for the specified runlevel have finished running before moving on.*
Also, notice that the definition for runlevel 4 is commented out. Runlevel 4 isn't implemented in Linux.

As we discussed in the previous chapter, all of the init scripts that start and stop services on your system are located in one of two directories, depending upon your distribution:

- **System V** Linux distributions that use System V init scripts store them in the /etc/rc.d directory. Within /etc/rc.d are a series of subdirectories named rc0.d through rc6.d. Each of these directories is associated with a particular runlevel. Within each of these subdirectories are symbolic links that point to the init scripts for your system daemons, which reside in /etc/rc.d/init.d. Red Hat Linux and Fedora use System V–type init scripts.

- **BSD** Linux distributions that use BSD-style init scripts store them in the /etc/init.d directory. Within /etc/init.d are a series of directories named rc0.d through rc6.d. As with System V init scripts, these directories are associated with a specific runlevel. These directories contain links that point to the init scripts in /etc/init.d. SUSE Linux uses this type of init script.

When the system boots up, init runs the scripts defined in /etc/inittab for the particular runlevel it's booting into. For example, if your system is configured to boot into runlevel 5, then init runs the scripts that are contained in /etc/rc.d/rc5.d or /etc/init.d/rc5.d, depending on your particular distribution. The runlevel 5 scripts for a typical SUSE Linux system are shown in Figure 11-22.

As you can see in Figure 11-22, these aren't the real scripts in this subdirectory. They are symbolic links to the real script files contained in the init directory (in this case /etc/init.d).

In addition to init scripts, there are several other important script files contained in /etc/init.d or /etc/rc.d/init.d that you need to be aware of for your Linux+ exam. These are listed in Table 11-5.

In summary, init completes the following tasks as it initializes a BSD-type system:

- Runs the /etc/init.d/boot script to prepare the system.
- Processes /etc/inittab to determine the appropriate runlevel and scripts.
- Runs the scripts in the appropriate runlevel directory in /etc/init.d.
- Runs the /etc/init.d/boot.local script.

FIGURE 11-22   Init scripts in /etc/init.d/rc5.d

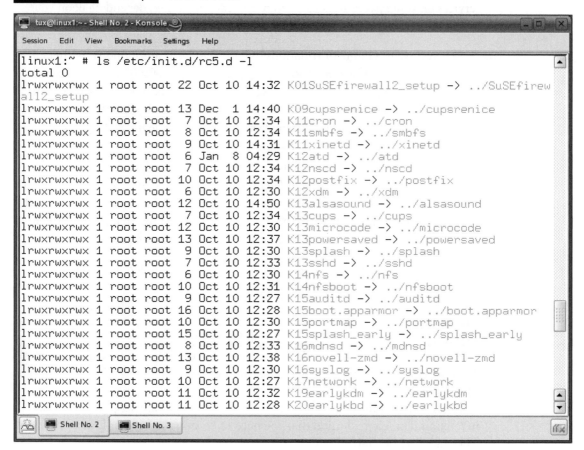

```
linux1:~ # ls /etc/init.d/rc5.d -l
total 0
lrwxrwxrwx 1 root root 22 Oct 10 14:32 K01SuSEfirewall2_setup -> ../SuSEfirew
all2_setup
lrwxrwxrwx 1 root root 13 Dec  1 14:40 K09cupsrenice -> ../cupsrenice
lrwxrwxrwx 1 root root  7 Oct 10 12:34 K11cron -> ../cron
lrwxrwxrwx 1 root root  8 Oct 10 12:34 K11smbfs -> ../smbfs
lrwxrwxrwx 1 root root  9 Oct 10 14:31 K11xinetd -> ../xinetd
lrwxrwxrwx 1 root root  6 Jan  8 04:29 K12atd -> ../atd
lrwxrwxrwx 1 root root  7 Oct 10 12:34 K12nscd -> ../nscd
lrwxrwxrwx 1 root root 10 Oct 10 12:34 K12postfix -> ../postfix
lrwxrwxrwx 1 root root  6 Oct 10 12:30 K12xdm -> ../xdm
lrwxrwxrwx 1 root root 12 Oct 10 14:50 K13alsasound -> ../alsasound
lrwxrwxrwx 1 root root  7 Oct 10 12:34 K13cups -> ../cups
lrwxrwxrwx 1 root root 12 Oct 10 12:30 K13microcode -> ../microcode
lrwxrwxrwx 1 root root 13 Oct 10 12:37 K13powersaved -> ../powersaved
lrwxrwxrwx 1 root root  9 Oct 10 12:30 K13splash -> ../splash
lrwxrwxrwx 1 root root  7 Oct 10 12:33 K13sshd -> ../sshd
lrwxrwxrwx 1 root root  6 Oct 10 12:30 K14nfs -> ../nfs
lrwxrwxrwx 1 root root 10 Oct 10 12:31 K14nfsboot -> ../nfsboot
lrwxrwxrwx 1 root root  9 Oct 10 12:27 K15auditd -> ../auditd
lrwxrwxrwx 1 root root 16 Oct 10 12:28 K15boot.apparmor -> ../boot.apparmor
lrwxrwxrwx 1 root root 10 Oct 10 12:30 K15portmap -> ../portmap
lrwxrwxrwx 1 root root 15 Oct 10 12:27 K15splash_early -> ../splash_early
lrwxrwxrwx 1 root root  8 Oct 10 12:33 K16mdnsd -> ../mdnsd
lrwxrwxrwx 1 root root 13 Oct 10 12:38 K16novell-zmd -> ../novell-zmd
lrwxrwxrwx 1 root root  9 Oct 10 12:30 K16syslog -> ../syslog
lrwxrwxrwx 1 root root 10 Oct 10 12:27 K17network -> ../network
lrwxrwxrwx 1 root root 11 Oct 10 12:32 K19earlykdm -> ../earlykdm
lrwxrwxrwx 1 root root 11 Oct 10 12:28 K20earlykbd -> ../earlykbd
```

On a System V–type system, init does the following as it gets the system up and running:

- Runs the /etc/rc.d/sysinit script to prepare the system.
- Processes /etc/inittab to determine the appropriate runlevel and scripts.
- Runs the scripts in the appropriate runlevel directory in /etc/rc.d/.
- Runs the /etc/rc.d/rc.local script.

TABLE 11-5		Important Files in /etc/init.d

File	Init Style	Function
Rc	BSD and System V	This script is used to switch between runlevels while the system is running.
Halt	BSD	This script can stop or reboot your system. It is run if the current runlevel is changed to 0 or 6.
Boot	BSD	This script is run by init when the system first starts. It runs the scripts contained in /etc/init.d/boot.d. These scripts accomplish a variety of startup tasks, such as loading kernel modules, verifying the file systems, and setting the system clock.
boot.local	BSD	This script is also run by init at startup. It contains additional startup commands. This script is extremely useful. If you want to run a particular command automatically at startup, you can insert the command into this file with a text editor.
rc.sysinit	System V	This script's function is similar to the boot script on a BSD-type system. It's used to set the path, check the file system for errors, set the system clock, etc.
rc.local	System V	This script's function is similar to that of the boot.local script on a BSD-type system. You can add your own commands to this script to ensure they are run every time the system boots.

SCENARIO & SOLUTION

The /etc/inittab file on your system contains the following line: `id:3:initdefault` What is your default runlevel?	Your system will boot into runlevel 3 by default.
You're using a Fedora Linux system. Where are the directories located that define which scripts will be run at each runlevel?	The Fedora distribution uses System V init scripts, so its runlevel directories are located in /etc/rc.d. These directories are named rc.0 through rc.6.
What process does the init process follow on a BSD-type distribution when the system is booting?	The init process completes the following tasks as it initializes a BSD-type system: ■ Runs the /etc/init.d/boot script to prepare the system. ■ Processes /etc/inittab to determine the appropriate runlevel and scripts. ■ Runs the scripts in the appropriate runlevel directory in /etc/init.d. ■ Runs the /etc/init.d/boot.local script.

With this background in mind, you're ready to learn how to manage runlevels on your system. Let's do that next.

Managing Runlevels

Managing runlevels is a very important aspect of administering a Linux system. You need to know how to configure the default runlevel as well as specify which system processes (daemons) are automatically started at a particular runlevel.

Recall in the preceding chapter that I mentioned that one of the first things I do after installing a new Linux system is to go through and turn off all of the unneeded services that run automatically. This saves memory and CPU utilization and also can plug up security holes in the system. In this part of the chapter, we're going to discuss how this is done. We'll cover the following topics:

- Configuring the default system runlevel
- Changing runlevels from the shell prompt
- Configuring services to run by default at a specified runlevel

Let's begin by learning how to configure the default system runlevel.

Configuring the Default System Runlevel

As you saw earlier in this chapter, the system's default runlevel is specified in the /etc/inittab file, shown in Figure 11-23.

You can change this by simply changing the second value in the command to the default runlevel you want to use. For example, suppose I wanted to change my system from the default runlevel of 5, shown in Figure 11-23, to a default runlevel of 3. I would simply open /etc/inittab in a text editor and change the value 5 to a value of 3. After saving the file and rebooting, the system would boot into runlevel 3.

In addition to changing runlevels at boot time, you can also change them on the fly as you're using the system. Let's discuss how this is done next.

Changing Runlevels from the Shell Prompt

If you think changing the default runlevel is easy, changing runlevels on the fly is even easier. This is done with the init command. The syntax for using init is init *runlevel*. For example, if my system is running in runlevel 5 and I want to switch to runlevel 3, I can simply enter **init 3** at the shell prompt.

on the
ⓘob

You have to switch to your root user before you can run the init command.

FIGURE 11-23   Setting the default runlevel

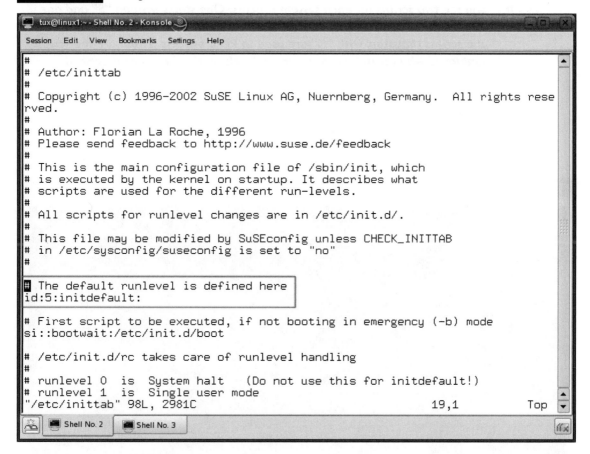

After entering the command, the system switches to runlevel 3, as shown in Figure 11-24.

When you change runlevels with the init command, the init process runs the rc script and tells it to switch to the appropriate level. The rc script reads /etc/inittab for the current runlevel and stops all of the services associated with that runlevel using the scripts in the appropriate runlevel directory in your init directory. The rc script reads /etc/inittab and runs the appropriate start scripts in the new runlevel's directory in the init directory.

on the

job

If you look inside an rcx.d directory within your distribution's init directory, you will see two scripts for each system process. One starts with an "S" and one starts with a "K." The scripts that start with S are used to start a process while the scripts that start with "K" are used to kill a process. These are the scripts employed when switching between runlevels on the fly as just described.

If you enter **init 0** or **init 6** at the shell prompt, the system will halt (init 0) or reboot (init 6).

Finally, let's review the process for configuring services to run at system boot.

FIGURE 11-24   Changing to runlevel 3 on the fly

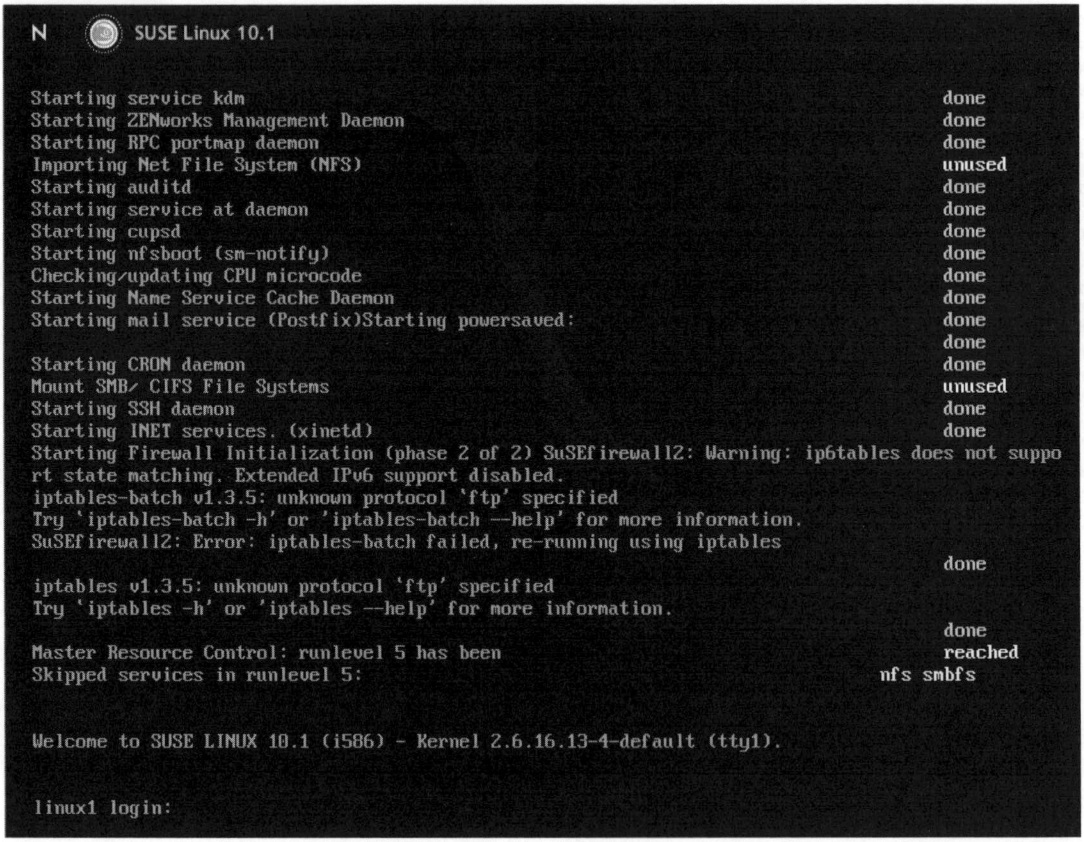

```
N        SUSE Linux 10.1

Starting service kdm                                                   done
Starting ZENworks Management Daemon                                    done
Starting RPC portmap daemon                                            done
Importing Net File System (NFS)                                        unused
Starting auditd                                                        done
Starting service at daemon                                             done
Starting cupsd                                                         done
Starting nfsboot (sm-notify)                                           done
Checking/updating CPU microcode                                        done
Starting Name Service Cache Daemon                                     done
Starting mail service (Postfix)Starting powersaved:                    done
                                                                       done
Starting CRON daemon                                                   done
Mount SMB/ CIFS File Systems                                           unused
Starting SSH daemon                                                    done
Starting INET services. (xinetd)                                       done
Starting Firewall Initialization (phase 2 of 2) SuSEfirewall2: Warning: ip6tables does not suppo
rt state matching. Extended IPv6 support disabled.
iptables-batch v1.3.5: unknown protocol 'ftp' specified
Try 'iptables-batch -h' or 'iptables-batch --help' for more information.
SuSEfirewall2: Error: iptables-batch failed, re-running using iptables
                                                                       done
iptables v1.3.5: unknown protocol 'ftp' specified
Try 'iptables -h' or 'iptables --help' for more information.
                                                                       done
Master Resource Control: runlevel 5 has been                           reached
Skipped services in runlevel 5:                                        nfs smbfs


Welcome to SUSE LINUX 10.1 (i586) - Kernel 2.6.16.13-4-default (tty1).


linux1 login:
```

Configuring Services to Run by Default at a Specified Runlevel

Earlier, we talked about using the boot.local and rc.local scripts to automatically run a command at system boot. Notice, however, that we said these scripts are used to run *commands,* not system services (daemons). If you want to configure a system service to run automatically at boot, you must associate it with a system runlevel and specify whether the service will be turned off or on.

Whenever you install a daemon, whether during system installation or by using the rpm utility, an init script is copied to your init directory (/etc/init.d or /etc/rc.d/init.d). You can use the chkconfig command to configure which runlevels each of your init scripts are associated with.

If you want to view a service's configuration, enter **chkconfig –l** *daemon_name* at the shell prompt. You can also enter **chkconfig –l** to see the status of all daemons installed on your system. For example, in Figure 11-25, the **chkconfig –l ntp** command has been issued.

As you can see in Figure 11-25, the ntp service has been configured to not automatically start at any runlevel. However, suppose we wanted the ntp daemon to run automatically at runlevels 3 and 5. We could make this happen by entering **chkconfig –s ntp 35**. This specifies that the ntp service (specified by the –s option) be enabled at runlevels 3 and 5. This is shown in Figure 11-26.

To disable a service, enter **chkconfig** *service_name* **off**. For example, to disable the ntp service enabled in Figure 11-26, you would enter **chkconfig ntp off**.

FIGURE 11-25   Checking a daemon's status with chkconfig

FIGURE 11-26 Enabling a daemon with chkconfig

```
linux1:~ # chkconfig -s ntp 35
linux1:~ # chkconfig -l ntp
ntp                     0:off  1:off  2:off  3:on   4:off  5:on   6:off
linux1:~ #
```

Shell No. 2   Shell No. 3

Let's practice working with Linux runlevels in the following exercise.

EXERCISE 11-2

Working with Linux Runlevels

In this exercise, you practice manipulating runlevels on your Linux system.
Complete the following:

1. Boot your Linux system and log in as a standard user. If you used the lab exercise
   in Chapter 3 to install your system, you can log in as **tux** with a password of
   M3linux273.

2. Open a terminal session.

3. Switch to your root user account by entering **su –** followed by your root user's
   password.

4. Practice changing your current runlevel from the shell prompt by doing the
   following:

   a. View your current runlevel by entering **runlevel** at the shell prompt.
      The first number displayed indicates your system's previous runlevel;
      the second number indicates your system's current runlevel.

      If you installed a graphical system, your current runlevel should be 5.

   b. Switch to runlevel 3 by entering **init 3** at the shell prompt.

   c. When prompted, log in as your root user.

   d. Switch back to runlevel 5 by entering **init 5** at the shell prompt.

5. Change your default runlevel to 3 by doing the following:

   a. Open a terminal session.

   b. At the shell prompt su to your root user account.

   c. At the shell prompt, enter **vi /etc/inittab**.

   d. Scroll down to the line that reads id:5:initdefault:.

   e. Press INSERT.

   f. Change the number 5 in this line to 3.

   g. Press ESC, then enter **:exit**.

   h. Reboot your system by entering **init 6** at the shell prompt.

      Your system should boot into a text-based login shell.

   i. Log in as your root user.

   j. At the shell prompt, use vi to edit /etc/inittab to change the default runlevel back to 5.

   k. Power off the system by entering **init 0** at the shell prompt.

   l. Power the system back on and log back in to your system as a normal user.

6. Practice enabling the ntp daemon at runlevels 3 and 5 on your system. The ntp daemon is used to synchronize your local Linux system's clock with the clock on other computer systems. Complete the following:

   a. Open a terminal session and su to your root user account.

   b. At the shell prompt, use the rpm utility to verify that the xntp package has been installed on your system. If it hasn't, use the steps presented earlier in this book to install the xntp package from your distribution CDs.

   c. At the shell prompt, enter **vi /etc/ntp.conf**.

   d. Scroll down to the lines that read:

```
server      127.127.1.0 #local clock (LCL)
fudge       127.127.1.0 stratum 10 #LCL is unsynchronized
```

   e. Press INSERT.

   f. Add a new line below the fudge line.

   g. Add the following directive on the new line:

```
server bigben.cac.washington.edu
```

This directive is used to configure the ntp service to synchronize your local computer's time with the time on the bigben.cac.washington.edu public ntp server on the Internet.

h. Press ESC; then enter **:exit**.

i. Start the ntp service by entering **/etc/init.d/ntp restart** or **/etc/rc.d/init .d/ntp restart** at the shell prompt. You should see messages that the daemon is starting and that it's getting its time from bigben.cac.washington.edu.

j. Configure the ntp daemon to automatically start at runlevels 3 and 5 by entering **chkconfig –s ntp 35** at the shell prompt.

k. Check the status of the ntp daemon by entering **chkconfig –l ntp** at the shell prompt. You should see runlevels 3 and 5 set to ON.

Excellent work! You're on your way to Linux+ certification! Let's review what we learned in this chapter.

CERTIFICATION SUMMARY

In this chapter, you learned how to manage the Linux boot process. We began this chapter by reviewing how the Linux boot process works. We broke the boot process down into three phases:

- The BIOS phase
- The bootloader phase
- The kernel phase

In the BIOS phase, the computer's BIOS chip has control of the system. Its main jobs are to set up the basic hardware in the system, test the hardware using the power on self test (POST) routine, and then locate a device with boot files on it.

In the bootloader phase, the BIOS turns control of the system over to a bootloader. The key job of the bootloader is to point to and load your operating system's kernel. The bootloader can reside in the master boot record (MBR) of the boot device or in the boot partition on the drive. Linux bootloaders can be configured with a menu that provides the end user with several options for booting the operating system. They can even be configured to point to and load non-Linux operating systems, such as Windows.

The Linux bootloader may also create a virtual hard drive in your system's RAM, called a ramdisk, and copy a basic root file system to it. This virtual file system can be used by your Linux kernel to load the software it needs to access your real storage devices, check them, and mount them. This virtual file system is called the initrd image.

In the kernel phase, the bootloader loads the operating system into your system RAM from the hard drive or other boot device. Your Linux kernel is located in /boot in the file system and is named vmlinuz-*version*.gz. After the kernel has been loaded, the following occurs in the kernel phase:

- The kernel initializes the basic hardware in your system using the various settings in your BIOS and your CMOS chips.
- The kernel searches for and uses the initrd file system to run the linuxrc program to set up the system.
- When linuxrc has finished executing, the initrd file system is dismounted and the ramdisk is destroyed.
- The kernel probes for new hardware and loads the appropriate driver modules.
- The real root (/) file system is mounted.
- The kernel loads the init process.

We then turned our attention to configuring Linux bootloaders. The first Linux bootloader we looked at was the LILO bootloader. LILO used to be the default bootloader used by most Linux distributions. Recently, most distributions have shifted away from LILO toward the GRUB bootloader. If your system currently uses GRUB and you want to switch to LILO, you must first create an /etc/lilo.conf configuration file. Then simply enter **lilo** at the shell prompt. By default, this will overwrite GRUB with LILO in the MBR of your boot device.

You can use the –b option with the lilo command to specify where LILO is installed. If you specify a storage device, such as /dev/hda, then LILO will be installed in the MBR of the specified device. If you specify a partition on a device, such as /dev/hda1, then LILO will be installed in that partition.

Once LILO has been installed, you can customize how it works using the /etc/lilo.conf file. After making any configuration changes in this file, you must re-install LILO by entering **lilo** at the shell prompt.

Some hardware will require you to use ELILO instead of LILO. ELILO is an enhanced version of LILO. ELILO is also backward-compatible with standard

Intel x86 hardware, so you can use it on your traditional Linux system instead of LILO as well.

After discussing LILO, we next discussed the GRUB bootloader. We pointed out that the GRUB bootloader is used by most current Linux distributions. We pointed out that GRUB is divided into several stages:

- **Stage 1** Usually stored in the MBR. It points to the location of Stage 1.5 or Stage 2.
- **Stage 1.5** Stored in the first 30KB after the MBR. It points to the location of Stage 2.
- **Stage 2** Stored within a disk partition. Presents the end user with a menu to select the operating system to boot.

We next pointed out that the file used to configure GRUB depends on your distribution. Some distributions use /boot/grub/grub.conf; others use /boot/grub/menu.lst. GRUB refers to hard disks in the system as hd$x$, where x is the number of the drive in the system. Both SCSI and IDE drives are referred to in this manner. Partitions on the drive are referred to as hd$x$,y, where y is the number of the partition on the drive.

If you've created a separate partition for your /boot directory in the file system, then GRUB will use this as the GRUB root and will refer to files within /boot/grub without including /boot in the path. If your /boot directory doesn't have its own partition, then GRUB will use the full path to refer to the /boot/grub/ files.

One of the cool features of GRUB is that it provides you with the ability to interactively manage the boot process. You can modify boot menu items at system startup to customize how the system boots. You can also create new boot menu items interactively by accessing the grub> prompt.

After working with GRUB, we were sufficiently prepared to discuss creating a dual-boot system. Most operating system bootloaders, including LILO, GRUB, and the Windows bootloader NTLOADER, are capable of booting operating systems other than their own native OS. This allows you to install two operating systems on the same hard drive and use the bootloader to select which one you want to use.

When creating a dual-boot system, keep the following considerations in mind:

- If creating a Windows/Linux dual-boot system, always install Windows first and Linux second.
- It's usually easier to use GRUB or LILO than NTLOADER as your dual-boot bootloader.
- You need to leave sufficient unpartitioned space on your hard drive for both operating systems. If you don't, you'll have to either re-install from scratch,

resize the existing partition to a smaller one and re-image the existing partition, or install additional hard drives to accommodate subsequent operating systems.

We then spent some time learning how to configure a dual-boot Windows/ Linux system using the GRUB bootloader. To do this, first install Windows. Then install Linux. Usually, most Linux installation routines will detect the Windows installation and automatically create a GRUB menu item for you. If not, you'll need to create a menu item manually by editing your GRUB configuration file that appears similar to the following:

```
title Windows
      chainloader (hdx,y)+1
```

Replace *x* with the number of the disk and *y* with the number of the partition on the disk where Windows is installed.

We then discussed how to use NTLOADER as your bootloader in a Linux/ Windows dual-boot system. To do this, first install Windows on the drive. Then install Linux in the free space on the drive. When you do, be sure that you install GRUB into the boot partition, not the MBR. Then you need to make a copy of your Linux system's bootloader on a floppy diskette using the dd command. Copy the resulting file to your Windows C:\ drive root directory. Then open your C:\boot.ini file in a text editor and add the following line:

```
C:\filename="Linux"
```

After saving the file and rebooting, you should see a menu item added that will load your Linux operating system.

After discussing how to create dual-boot systems, we then turned our attention to managing runlevels on Linux. We first discussed how runlevels work. Linux defines seven runlevels (0–6) that do the following:

- 0   Halts the system.
- 1   Runs Linux in single-user mode.
- 2   Runs Linux in multi-user mode with networking disabled.
- 3   Runs Linux in multi-user mode with networking enabled.
- 4   Unused.
- 5   Runs Linux in multi-user mode with networking enabled. The graphical user interface is used.
- 6   Reboots the system.

The /etc/inittab file is used to configure what happens in each runlevel. This file also defines the default runlevel that your system will boot into. Your system's init directory contains a series of subdirectories named rc.0 to rc.6 that each contains symbolic links to init scripts that should be run for the respective runlevel.

On a BSD-type system, the init process completes the following tasks as it initializes the system:

- Runs the /etc/init.d/boot script to prepare the system.
- Processes /etc/inittab to determine the appropriate runlevel and scripts.
- Runs the scripts in the appropriate runlevel directory in /etc/init.d.
- Runs the /etc/init.d/boot.local script.

On a System V–type system, the init process does the following as it gets the system up and running:

- Runs the /etc/rc.d/sysinit script to prepare the system.
- Processes /etc/inittab to determine the appropriate runlevel and scripts.
- Runs the scripts in the appropriate runlevel directory in /etc/rc.d/.
- Runs the /etc/rc.d/rc.local script.

We then shifted gears and discussed how to manage runlevels. We first discussed how to configure the default system runlevel in /etc/inittab. We then discussed how to change runlevels on the fly. This is done using the init command. You simply enter **init *runlevel*** from the shell prompt. When you do this, the init process runs the rc script, which shuts down services associated with the current runlevel and starts scripts associated with the runlevel you're switching to.

We ended the chapter by discussing how to specify which services run at each runlevel. This is done using the chkconfig command. Entering **chkconfig –l** will list each service and the runlevels they are configured to run at. To configure a service to start at a particular runlevel, enter **chkconfig –s *service_name runlevels***. To turn off a service, enter **chkconfig *service_name* off**.

✓ TWO-MINUTE DRILL

Explain How the Linux Boot Process Works

- ❑ In the BIOS phase, the computer's BIOS chip has control of the system.
- ❑ The BIOS tests the system hardware using the power on self test (POST) routine and then locates a storage device with boot files on it.
- ❑ In the bootloader phase, the BIOS turns control of the system over to a bootloader.
- ❑ The bootloader points to and loads your operating system's kernel.
- ❑ The bootloader can reside in the master boot record (MBR) of the boot device or in the boot partition on the drive.
- ❑ The Linux bootloader may also create a virtual hard drive in your system's RAM, called a ramdisk, and copy a basic root file system to it.
- ❑ This virtual file system (called the initrd image) is used by the Linux kernel to load the software it needs to access your real storage devices, check them, and mount them.
- ❑ In the kernel phase, the bootloader loads the operating system into your system RAM from the hard drive or other boot device.
- ❑ The Linux kernel is located in /boot and is named vmlinuz-*version*.gz.

Configure Linux Bootloaders

- ❑ LILO used to be the default bootloader used by most Linux distributions.
- ❑ If you want to install LILO, you must first create an /etc/lilo.conf configuration file; then enter **lilo** at the shell prompt.
- ❑ You can use the –b option with the lilo command to specify where GRUB is installed.
- ❑ You configure LILO using the /etc/lilo.conf file.
- ❑ After making any configuration changes in this file, you must re-install LILO by entering **lilo** at the shell prompt.
- ❑ If you're using Intel Itanium or Apple Macintosh hardware for your Linux system, you'll need to use ELILO instead of LILO.
- ❑ ELILO is also backward-compatible with standard Intel x86 hardware, so you can use it on your traditional Linux system instead of LILO as well.

❏ The GRUB bootloader is used by most current Linux distributions.

❏ GRUB is divided into several stages: Stage 1, Stage 1.5, and Stage 2.

❏ Some distributions use /boot/grub/grub.conf; others use /boot/grub/menu.lst to configure GRUB.

❏ GRUB refers to hard disks in the system as hd$x$, where x is the number of the drive in the system.

❏ Partitions on the drive are referred to as hd$x$,y, where y is the number of the partition on the drive.

❏ If you've created a separate partition for your /boot directory, GRUB will use this as the GRUB root and will refer to files within /boot/grub without including /boot in the path.

❏ If your /boot directory doesn't have its own partition, then GRUB will use the full path to refer to the /boot/grub/ files.

❏ GRUB allows you to modify boot menu items at system startup to customize how the system boots.

❏ GRUB allows you to create new boot menu items interactively by accessing the grub> prompt.

❏ Most operating system bootloaders are capable of booting operating systems other than their own native OS.

❏ This allows you to install two operating systems on the same hard drive and use the bootloader to select which one you want to load.

❏ If creating a Windows/Linux dual-boot system, you should always install Windows first and Linux second.

❏ It's usually easier to use GRUB or LILO than NTLOADER as your dual-boot bootloader.

❏ You need to leave sufficient unpartitioned space on your hard drive for both operating systems.

❏ Usually, most Linux installation routines will detect the Windows installation and automatically create a GRUB menu item for you.

❏ To use NTLOADER as your bootloader in a dual-boot system, you must use the dd command to make a copy of your Linux boot sector and copy it to the C:\ drive under Windows. Then you must manually edit C:\boot.ini to add a menu item that points to the boot sector file.

Manage Linux Runlevels

❑ Linux defines seven runlevels (0–6):

0 Halts the system.

1 Runs Linux in single-user mode.

2 Runs Linux in multi-user mode with networking disabled.

3 Runs Linux in multi-user mode with networking enabled.

4 Unused.

5 Runs Linux in multi-user mode with networking enabled. The graphical user interface is used.

6 Reboots the system.

❑ The /etc/inittab file is used to configure what happens in each runlevel.

❑ /etc/inittab also defines the default runlevel that your system will boot into.

❑ Your system's init directory contains a series of subdirectories named rc.0 to rc.6 that each contains symbolic links to init scripts that should be run for the respective runlevel.

❑ You can change runlevels on the fly using the init command by entering **init** *runlevel* from the shell prompt.

❑ When you change runlevels, the init process runs the rc script, which shuts down services associated with the current runlevel and starts scripts associated with the runlevel you're switching to.

❑ You can configure services to run a specific runlevel using the chkconfig command.

❑ Entering **chkconfig –l** will list each service and the runlevels they are configured to run at.

❑ To configure a service to start at a particular runlevel, enter **chkconfig –s** *service_name runlevels*.

❑ To turn off a service, enter **chkconfig** *service_name* **off**.

SELF TEST

Explain How the Linux Boot Process Works

1. What is the role of the BIOS during system boot? (Choose two.)

   A. It tests system hardware.

   B. It creates an initrd image in a ramdisk.

   C. It locates a bootable storage device.

   D. It provides a menu that lets you choose which operating system to boot.

   E. It points to your operating system kernel.

2. Where can your Linux bootloader reside? (Choose two.)

   A. In the BIOS.

   B. In an initrd image.

   C. In the MBR of a storage device.

   D. In the bootable partition.

   E. In the system chipset.

3. Where does the Linux kernel reside?

   A. In /boot.

   B. In the MBR.

   C. In /proc.

   D. In /kernel.

Configure Linux Bootloaders

4. Which directive within the /etc/lilo.conf file can be used to specify the menu item that will be automatically loaded if the user doesn't make a selection?

   A. prompt

   B. default

   C. image

   D. boot

5. Which directive within the /etc/lilo.conf file can be used to specify the device that should be mounted at / ?

   A. root

   B. initrd

    C. image

    D. default

6. You've just finished making several changes to your /etc/lilo.conf file. What should you do next?

    A. Reboot the system.

    B. Change to runlevel 3.

    C. Run lilo from the shell prompt.

    D. Restart the lilo service.

7. You want to install GRUB into the first partition on your first SCSI hard disk drive. Which shell command will do this?

    A. grub /dev/sda1

    B. grub-install /dev/sda1

    C. grub-install /dev/sda

    D. grub /dev/hda1

8. You're supporting a SUSE Linux system. Which file would you need to edit to configure the GRUB bootloader on this system?

    A. /etc/menu.lst

    B. /etc/grub.conf

    C. /boot/grub/grub.conf

    D. /boot/grub/menu.lst

9. Which of the following GRUB configuration file directives points to the partition on the hard drive where /boot resides?

    A. root

    B. boot

    C. kernel

    D. partition

10. When configuring your GRUB configuration file, which of the following uses the correct syntax that points to /dev/sda2?

    A. hd1,2

    B. hd0,2

    C. sd0,2

    D. hd0,1

11. When configuring a dual-boot system that will use the GRUB bootloader, which of the following tasks should be completed first?

 A. Install Windows.

 B. Install Linux.

 C. Make a copy of the hard drive's boot sector.

 D. Copy NTLOADER to a floppy diskette.

12. When configuring a dual-boot Windows/Linux system that will use the NTLOADER bootloader, where should the GRUB bootloader be installed?

 A. In the MBR.

 B. In the Windows boot partition.

 C. In the Linux boot partition.

 D. In the BIOS.

Manage Linux Runlevels

13. Which runlevel uses a graphical user interface by default?

 A. 2

 B. 3

 C. 4

 D. 5

14. Which runlevels use a command-line user interface by default? (Choose two.)

 A. 0

 B. 2

 C. 3

 D. 5

 E. 6

15. Which files can you use to add commands that you want executed each time the system boots? (Choose two.)

 A. rc

 B. boot.local

 C. rc.local

 D. rc.systinit

 E. boot

16. Which files can be used to set the default runlevel of a Linux system?

    A. /etc/inittab

    B. /etc/runlevel.conf

    C. /etc/init.conf

    D. /etc/sysconfig/init

17. Which command can be used to switch runlevels while the system is running?

    A. runlevel

    B. chrun

    C. mode

    D. init

LAB QUESTION

Your Linux system currently uses the LILO bootloader and has a default runlevel of 5. You want to switch to the GRUB bootloader and configure the system to run at runlevel 3 by default. In addition, you want the Apache Web server daemon (httpd) to run by default in runlevel 3. Outline the process you would follow to accomplish this.

SELF TEST ANSWERS

Explain How the Linux Boot Process Works

1. ☑ **A** and **C.** The BIOS tests your system hardware during the POST routine, then it locates a bootable storage device.
    ☒ **B, D,** and **E** are incorrect. **B, D,** and **E** are accomplished by the Linux bootloader.

2. ☑ **C** and **D.** The Linux bootloader can be stored in the MBR of the storage device and in the bootable partition on the disk.
    ☒ **A, B,** and **E** are incorrect. **A** is incorrect. You can't write data to the BIOS directly without flashing it. **B** is incorrect. The initrd image isn't created until after the bootloader has been loaded into memory. **E** is incorrect. You can't load software into your motherboard's chipset.

3. ☑ **A.** The Linux kernel resides in /boot in the file system.
    ☒ **B, C,** and **D** are incorrect. **B** usually holds the bootloader. **C** is a dynamic directory that is only created when accessed. **D** is a distracter and doesn't exist by default in the file system.

Configure Linux Bootloaders

4. ☑ **B.** The default directive can be used to specify the LILO menu label that will be loaded automatically if the user doesn't make a selection.
    ☒ **A, C,** and **D** are incorrect. **A** causes the boot: prompt to be displayed. **C** specifies the path to the boot image of a Linux kernel. **D** specifies the device that contains the system's boot sector.

5. ☑ **A.** The root directive in lilo.conf specifies the device that should be mounted at /.
    ☒ **B, C,** and **D** are incorrect. **B** specifies the initial ramdisk image to be loaded with the kernel. **C** specifies the path to the boot image of a Linux kernel. **D** specifies the LILO menu label that will be loaded automatically if the user doesn't make a selection.

6. ☑ **C.** After making changes to /etc/lilo.conf, you need to run **lilo** from the shell prompt to reinstall LILO.
    ☒ **A, B,** and **D** are incorrect. None of these options will apply the changes made in /etc/lilo.conf.

7. ☑ **B.** The grub-install /dev/sda1 command will install GRUB into the first partition on the first SCSI hard disk drive.
    ☒ **A, C,** and **D** are incorrect. **A** uses the incorrect command. **C** doesn't specify the partition and would cause GRUB to be installed in the disk's MBR. **D** uses the incorrect command and device.

8. ☑ **D.** The /boot/grub/menu.lst file is used to configure GRUB on a SUSE Linux system.
☒ **A, B,** and **C** are incorrect. **A** uses the wrong path. **B** works on some distributions that create a symbolic link from this file to the correct file in /boot/grub, but not on SUSE Linux. **C** is correct on some distributions, such as Fedora, but not on SUSE Linux.

9. ☑ **A.** The root directive in the GRUB configuration file specifies the partition on the hard drive where /boot resides.
☒ **B, C,** and **D** are incorrect. **B** is used with LILO, not GRUB. **C** specifies the location of the Linux kernel. **D** is a distracter that isn't used by GRUB.

10. ☑ **D.** The term hd0,1 in a GRUB configuration file points to the second partition on the first hard drive (SCSI or IDE) in the system.
☒ **A, B,** and **C** are incorrect. **A** points to the third partition on the second hard drive. **B** points to the third partition on the first hard drive. **C** uses incorrect syntax.

11. ☑ **A.** You should install Windows first when creating a Windows/Linux dual-boot system.
☒ **B, C,** and **D** are incorrect. **B** can be done first, but it will require extra effort to get the GRUB bootloader installed. **C** and **D** are distracters and are incorrect.

12. ☑ **C.** When using the NTLOADER bootloader, you should install the GRUB bootloader in the Linux boot partition.
☒ **A, B,** and **D** are incorrect. **A** and **B** will overwrite NTLOADER with GRUB. **D** is incorrect. You can't install a bootloader in the BIOS.

Manage Linux Runlevels

13. ☑ **D.** Runlevel 5 uses a graphical user interface by default.
☒ **A, B,** and **C** are incorrect. **A** doesn't offer a graphical user interface. **B** can be configured with a graphical user interface, but it must be launched manually with the startx command. **C** is incorrect because runlevel 4 isn't defined by default.

14. ☑ **B** and **C.** Runlevels 2 and 3 use a command-line interface by default.
☒ **A, D,** and **E** are incorrect. **A** causes the system to halt. **D** uses a graphical user interface by default. **E** causes the system to reboot.

15. ☑ **B** and **C.** You can enter commands in boot.local on BSD-type systems or rc.local on System V–type systems to have them automatically run each time the system boots.
☒ **A, D,** and **E** are incorrect. **A** is used to switch between runlevels while the system is running. **D** is used on System V systems to set the path, check for file system errors, and set the system clock. **E** is used on BSD-type systems to set the path, check for file system errors, and set the system clock.

16. ☑ **A.** The /etc/inittab file is used to set the default runlevel of a Linux system.
    ☒ **B, C,** and **D** are incorrect. **B, C,** and **D** are distracters and are incorrect.

17. ☑ **D.** The init command can be used to switch runlevels while the system is running.
    ☒ **A, B,** and **C** are incorrect. **A** can be used to display the current and past runlevels, but it can't be used to change runlevels. **B** and **C** are distracters and are incorrect.

LAB ANSWER

The first thing you should do is save or print a copy of your current /etc/lilo.conf file. Then run **grub-install** to install the GRUB bootloader. With GRUB installed, you can now use your old lilo.conf file to configure your /boot/grub/menu.lst or /boot/grub/grub.conf file with the appropriate parameters. Then test your new GRUB configuration and verify that it works correctly.

Once you've verified your new GRUB configuration, you can configure your default runlevel. To do this, open /etc/inittab in a text editor, such as vi. Change the value of 5 in the id:5:initdefault line to 3. Finally, enter **chkconfig –s httpd 3** at the shell prompt to cause the Web server daemon to run by default in runlevel 3. You can then reboot the system to have the new configuration applied.

12

Configuring Hardware

This is going to be a fun chapter! As I mentioned earlier in this book, I'm a true techie at heart. I love playing with PC hardware. I spend way too much time scouring hardware vendor catalogs and far too much money ordering new parts. (My local UPS delivery driver and I are on a first-name basis.) Every computer I own is a "Frankenstein" system made of a variety of parts from many different sources.

In this chapter, we're going to discuss how to install hardware in your system and configure Linux to support it. We're going to cover the following topics:

- Managing hardware and kernel modules
- Configuring power management
- Burning CDs and DVDs
- Implementing RAID
- Configuring X Windows

INSIDE THE EXAM

Configuring Hardware

For your Linux+ exam, you need to be very comfortable working with PC hardware in a Linux environment. Expect to see several questions about loading kernel modules and installing codecs. Be sure you know where kernel modules are stored in the system and the commands that are used to manage them.

You also need to know how to perform a variety of hardware-related tasks:

- Be prepared to answer a limited number of questions regarding power management. You should know the difference between APM and ACPI.
- Be sure you know how to burn CDs and DVDs on Linux.

- Be prepared to answer a number of questions about RAID levels. You should be familiar with the process of setting up a hardware-based RAID array and a software-based RAID array.
- Be very familiar with X Windows. Be sure you can identify which version of the X Server a particular system is using. You should know how to use Linux tools to configure X Windows to work with your video hardware. You should be familiar with video-related terms such as synchronization rate, resolution, and color depth. You also need to know how to specify which window manager your system should use.

Let's begin this chapter by discussing how to manage hardware and drivers.

CERTIFICATION OBJECTIVE 12.01

Manage Hardware and Kernel Modules

Back in the "old" days of Linux, working with hardware was hit and miss at best. If you were installing commonly used hardware from a well-known vendor, it would usually work. However, if you were installing specialty hardware or hardware from a less-visible vendor, chances were that the device wouldn't work under Linux.

Why? The key issue was one of driver support. Linux wasn't taken seriously in those days, so most hardware vendors didn't invest any time in developing a Linux driver for their hardware. Unless you were capable of writing your own driver, you had to rely on the good graces of a software developer somewhere in the world taking the time to write one that would support your hardware.

Fortunately, things have changed dramatically in today's IT environment. Linux is no longer viewed as a "plaything" for hobbyists. It's quickly gaining acceptance as a reliable, enterprise-level operating system. As a result, Linux driver support is relatively good. It isn't perfect yet, but it's getting better each year. I predict that it won't be much longer before Linux hardware drivers are as ubiquitous as Windows drivers currently are.

For your Linux+ exam, you need to be very familiar with how to manage hardware and drivers under Linux. In this section, we're going to discuss the following:

■ How drivers work under Linux
■ Managing kernel modules
■ Working with codecs

Let's begin by discussing how drivers work under Linux.

How Drivers Work Under Linux

If you are going to be responsible for managing Linux systems, it's very important that you understand how drivers work on the operating system. If you've used a Windows system, you're probably already familiar with the process required to load a driver to support a piece of hardware. However, the way drivers work under Linux is somewhat different.

To make sure you are proficient with Linux drivers, we're going to cover the following topics in this part of the chapter:

■ What exactly is a driver anyway?

■ How drivers are implemented under Linux

To effectively manage drivers under Linux, you first need to understand what a driver is in the first place. Let's start by defining what a driver is and how they work on Linux.

What Exactly Is a Driver Anyway?

The key idea you need to understand when discussing drivers is the fact that the CPU on your motherboard doesn't natively know how to communicate with other hardware devices installed in your system. It doesn't know how to send video data to the video board; it doesn't know how to save data on your hard drive; it doesn't know how to send data to the sound board.

To be able to do these things, the CPU needs instructions in the form of software that tell it how to communicate with these devices. The type of software and where it is stored depends on the type of device the CPU needs to communicate with. Generally speaking, PC hardware devices can be divided into three categories:

■ **Devices that are almost always present and don't have any configurable parameters.** Devices in this category are usually present in most PC systems. They have no configurable parameters and aren't likely to be upgraded. Devices in this category include your system speaker, your system clock, and your keyboard. The software needed for your CPU to communicate with devices in this category is stored in your motherboard's BIOS chip.

on the
job

You can't directly configure or modify this software. The only way to update this software is to download and install an update to the BIOS. This process is called flashing the BIOS. Your BIOS chip is composed of flash memory that is persistent when the system is powered off. However, it can be erased and rewritten with new information.

■ **Devices that are almost always present and have configurable parameters.** These devices include your system RAM, your hard disk drives, and your floppy diskette drive. The amount of RAM present in the system can vary, the size and geometry of your hard drives can vary, and the type of floppy diskette drive installed can vary. The BIOS alone can't handle these types of devices. Separate software for each and every type of device would have to be burned into the BIOS chip, which isn't practical.

Instead, we configure parameters for these devices in the complementary metal oxide semiconductor (CMOS) chip that is integrated into the BIOS. The CMOS chip is a RAM chip that can be dynamically written to and erased. One of the programs stored in your BIOS is the CMOS setup program. You press a particular keystroke at system startup to load the setup program, which allows you to specify parameters for hardware devices in this category, as shown in Figure 12-1.

Once configured, software in your BIOS can read the parameters stored in your CMOS chip to obtain the parameters it needs to allow the CPU to communicate with these devices.

■ **Devices that may or may not be present in a given system.**   Devices in this category include network boards, sound boards, FireWire boards, and so on. The CPU still needs software to communicate with these devices. However, there are so many different makes and models of these devices that it is completely unfeasible to store all the software needed for every last device within the BIOS chip. Instead, we store the software the CPU needs to communicate with on the system's hard drive. As the system boots, the operating system loads the software (called a *driver*) from the hard disk into RAM. Once done, the CPU has the instructions it needs to communicate with the associated hardware.

FIGURE 12-1

Accessing the
CMOS setup
program

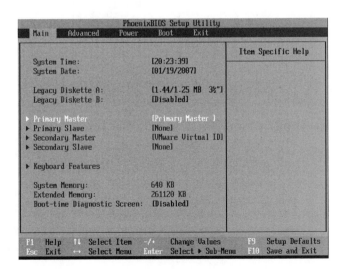

In this chapter, we're primarily concerned with drivers associated with this last category of hardware. There are two different ways in which these drivers can be implemented under Linux. Let's discuss how this is done next.

How Drivers Are Implemented Under Linux

There are two different ways in which Linux can implement a device driver for a particular piece of hardware in your PC system. First of all, the driver can be loaded as a *kernel module*. Once the Linux kernel has been loaded into memory during the boot process we reviewed in the previous chapter, it can be configured to load kernel modules, which allow the CPU and operating system to work with the hardware installed in the system.

Kernel modules have a .ko or .o extension and are stored within the /lib/modules/ *kernel_version*/kernel/drivers directory on your Linux system. Within this directory are a series of subdirectories where kernel modules for your hardware devices are actually stored. These are shown in Figure 12-2.

FIGURE 12-2	
Module subdirectories	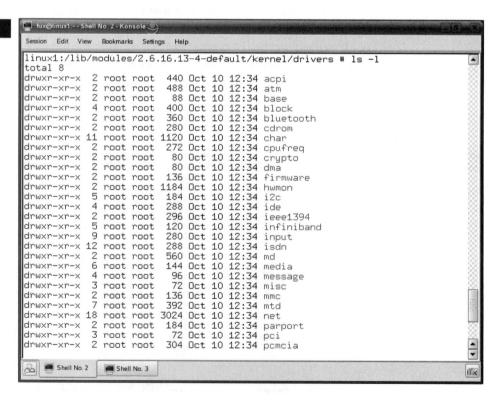

For example, the kernel modules used to support your IDE devices are stored in the ide subdirectory, as shown in Figure 12-3.

The second way hardware support can be implemented in Linux is to actually compile the necessary driver support directly within the kernel itself. Doing so requires that you manually recompile your kernel from its source code and specify which hardware support you want integrated directly within the kernel in the process. After doing so, kernel modules for those devices are no longer needed because the operating system now has all the software it needs within the kernel itself.

This sounds like a pretty great way to do things, right? So why don't we compile the drivers for all the hardware in the system directly into the kernel? It is a good strategy for some drivers; however, as a general rule of thumb, you should limit the drivers compiled into the kernel to only those drivers the system needs to boot up (keyboard drivers, hard disk drivers, floppy disk drivers, etc.). The rest should be loaded as kernel modules.

There are a couple of really good reasons for doing things this way. First of all, each driver you compile into the kernel increases the overall size of the kernel. You should try to keep your kernel as lean and clean as possible. Second, configuring a kernel is a more complex operation, requiring in-depth information about the hardware and what each configuration element provides.

Finally, the issue of modularity comes into play. If you never modify, upgrade, or reconfigure your computer system, then compiling more drivers directly into the kernel may make sense. However, it doesn't make sense for PC surgeons like me. I'm constantly adding, removing, and reconfiguring hardware in my PCs. Using kernel modules, I can load and unload support for my hardware devices very quickly from the command line. If I compiled them into the kernel, I may end up with a bloated kernel that contains support for hardware that is no longer in the system. Kernel modules allow your system to be much more dynamic.

FIGURE 12-3

IDE kernel
modules

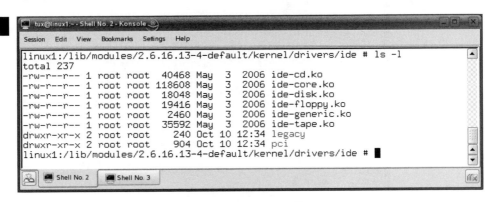

We'll be focusing primarily on kernel modules in this chapter. Let's discuss how to manage your kernel modules next.

Managing Kernel Modules

When I first started learning about managing kernel modules back when Linux was young, I was really intimidated. It sounded really difficult. Like many other aspects of Linux, however, it's really pretty easy. In this part of this chapter, we're going to discuss how to manage kernel modules on your system. We're going to cover the following topics:

- Viewing installed hardware
- Using shell commands to manage kernel modules

Let's start by discussing how to view the hardware installed on your system.

Viewing Installed Hardware

A key skill you need to have as a Linux system admin is to know how to view currently installed hardware in the system. One of the best tools for doing this is the good old /proc directory. We introduced you to /proc in Chapter 6. The /proc directory doesn't actually exist in the file system. Instead, it's a pseudo file system that is dynamically created whenever it is accessed. As you can see in Figure 12-4, the /proc directory contains a subdirectory for each process running on your system, as we discussed in Chapter 6.

FIGURE 12-4	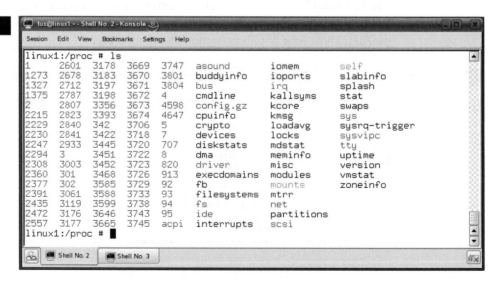
Using the /proc directory	

Viewing the
/proc/cpuinfo file

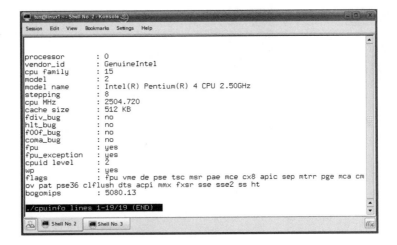

However, also notice in Figure 12-4 that /proc contains a number of other files. Some of the more useful files include the following:

- **cpuinfo** Contains details about the CPU installed in the system. You can use cat, less, more, or any text editor to view the contents of this file, as shown in Figure 12-5.

- **devices** Contains a list of devices installed in the system.

- **dma** Contains a list of DMA channel assignments in the system.

- **interrupts** Contains a list of IRQ assignments in the system. A sample is shown in Figure 12-6.

- **iomem** Contains a list of I/O port assignments in the system.

- **modules** Contains a list of all the kernel modules currently being used by the system. A sample is shown in Figure 12-7.

Viewing the
/proc/interrupts
file

FIGURE 12-7

Viewing the
/proc/modules file

- **version**   Contains the information about the version of the Linux kernel running on the system.
- **/scsi/**   Contains files that contain information about the SCSI devices in your system if you're using a SCSI adapter.
- **/bus/devices**   Contains information about the USB devices in the system.
- **/ide/**   Contains files that contain information about the IDE devices in your system.

Most Linux distributions also include a variety of command-line tools that you can use to view information about the hardware in your system. Some of these tools actually pull their information right out of the /proc directory we've been reviewing. You can use the following commands:

- **hdparm –a /dev/device**   Displays information about your hard drive. Replace *device* with hda, hdb, sda, sdb, etc.
- **sg_scan**   Scans your SCSI bus and lists all the devices connected to your SCSI controller. This is shown in Figure 12-8.
- **scsiinfo –l**   Lists your connected SCSI devices.
- **pnpdump**   Scans your ISA bus and lists any ISA plug-n-play cards found, if in use.
- **lsusb**   Displays information about USB devices connected to your Linux system.

With this information in hand, you're now ready to learn how to manage kernel modules from the shell prompt. Let's do that next.

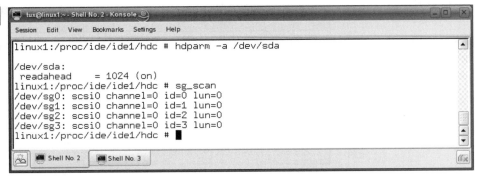

FIGURE 12-8

Using the hdparm
and sg_scan
utilities

Using Shell Commands to Manage Kernel Modules

As with most other operating systems, you can list, load, or unload Linux kernel modules. While there are many graphical utilities available that can do this, we're going to focus on accomplishing these tasks from the shell prompt.

To view all currently loaded kernel modules, you can use the lsmod command. This command actually pulls data from the /proc/modules file and reformats it for display on the screen. To use this command, simply enter **lsmod** at the shell prompt, as shown in Figure 12-9.

To view more information about a particular loaded module, you can use the modinfo command. Use lsmod to find out the name of the module, and then enter **modinfo *module_name*** at the shell prompt. For example, in Figure 12-9, one of the

FIGURE 12-9

Using the lsmod
command to view
loaded kernel
modules

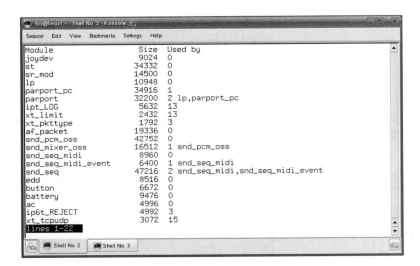

FIGURE 12-10

Using modinfo to
view details about
a loaded module

modules displayed by lsmod is joydev. This is your system's joystick kernel module.
To view more information about this particular module, you would enter **modinfo
joydev** at the shell prompt, as shown in Figure 12-10.

To load a kernel module, you first need to run the **depmod** command from the
shell prompt. This command is used to build a file named modules.dep that is stored
in /lib/modules/*kernel_version*/, as shown in Figure 12-11.

Within this file, depmod lists the dependencies between modules. This helps
other kernel module management utilities ensure that dependent modules are loaded
whenever you load a module.

With the modules.dep file created, you can now go ahead and load kernel
modules. You can use one of two different commands to do this. The first is the
insmod command. The syntax for insmod is insmod *module_filename*. The module
file name is usually a kernel module located in /lib/modules/*kernel_version*/kernel.
For example, if you wanted to load the driver for a standard PC parallel port, you
would enter **insmod /lib/modules/*version*/kernel/drivers/parport/parport_pc.ko** at
the shell prompt.

In addition to insmod, you can also use the modprobe command.

on the

!

i o b

*Most Linux admins prefer modprobe to insmod. The insmod command doesn't
take into account the dependencies identified by depmod.*

FIGURE 12-11

The modules.dep
file

The syntax for using modprobe is modprobe *module_name*. As with insmod, the module you load with modprobe resides in a subdirectory of /lib/modules/*kernel_version*/kernel. For example, the /lib/modules/*kernel_version*/kernel/net directory contains kernel modules for a variety of network boards, as shown in Figure 12-12.

If I wanted to load the kernel module for the 3c509 network board, I would enter **modprobe 3c509** at the shell prompt. For PCI and AGP plug-n-play boards, this command is usually sufficient. If, however, you're loading a kernel module for an older ISA board, you'll probably need to specify the IRQ and the I/O port the device has been configured to use. To do this, just add the irq and io options with the command. The syntax is modprobe *module_name* irq=*IRQ_number* io=*I/O_port*. The I/O_port parameter must be specified in hexadecimal notation.

You're probably wondering, at this point, if the module will be persistent across system restarts after it's been loaded with modprobe. The answer is no, it won't (unless the device is automatically detected during boot). However, modprobe is automatically run every time the kernel loads. It reads the information contained in your /etc/modprobe.conf file to determine what kernel modules should be loaded during startup. This file is shown in Figure 12-13.

on the
() o b

If the /etc/modprobe.conf file doesn't exist, then modprobe will use the files located in the /etc/modprobe.d directory to determine the kernel modules that will be loaded at boot.

FIGURE 12-12	
Network board kernel modules	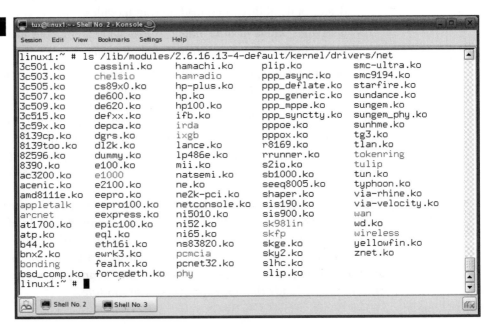

FIGURE 12-13

The /etc/
modprobe.conf
file

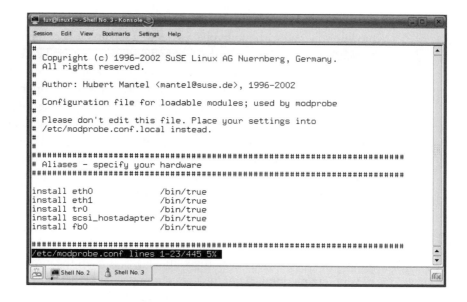

```
#
# Copyright (c) 1996-2002 SuSE Linux AG Nuernberg, Germany.
# All rights reserved.
#
# Author: Hubert Mantel <mantel@suse.de>, 1996-2002
#
# Configuration file for loadable modules; used by modprobe
#
# Please don't edit this file. Place your settings into
# /etc/modprobe.conf.local instead.
#
#
################################################################
# Aliases - specify your hardware
################################################################

install eth0            /bin/true
install eth1            /bin/true
install tr0             /bin/true
install scsi_hostadapter /bin/true
install fb0             /bin/true

################################################################
/etc/modprobe.conf lines 1-23/445 5%
```

The modprobe.conf file uses the following directives:

- **install** *module_name*   Tells modprobe to load the specified module. It can also be used to run any valid shell command, providing you with a high degree of flexibility when loading your modules.

- **alias** *alias_name module_name*   Gives a kernel module an alias name that can be used to reference it from the shell prompt.

- **options** *module_name options*   Gives modprobe a list of options, such as irq= or io=, that should be used when a particular kernel module loads.

Notice in Figure 12-13 that there is a big note at the beginning of the file that warns you not to modify /etc/modprobe.conf. Instead, if you need to manually specify that a particular kernel module be loaded at system startup, you should enter it in the /etc/modprobe.conf.local file using the modprobe.conf directives just specified.

on the
job

Alternatively, you could also insert the modprobe module_name command in your rc.local or boot.local file to ensure that the module is loaded at system startup. However, my experience has been that you will rarely need to do this. Most distributions run some kind of hardware detection routine, such as kudzu on Fedora Linux, at system boot that scans for new hardware and automatically loads the appropriate kernel module.

SCENARIO & SOLUTION

You need to see how interrupts have been assigned by the plug-n-play subsystem. What file in /proc can you use to view this information?	You can view /proc/interrupt.
You need to view information about the first IDE hard drive installed in your Linux system. What command can you enter at the shell prompt to do this?	You can enter **hdparm –a /dev/hda**.
You've just installed a 3Com 3C590 network board in your Linux system. The device wasn't detected at boot, so you need to manually load the kernel module (3c59x). What command would you enter?	You would enter **modprobe 3c59x** at the shell prompt.

What if you need to unload a currently loaded kernel module? You can use the **rmmod** *module_name* command at the shell prompt. Be warned that this command won't work if the device serviced by the module isn't in use. If it is, the command won't remove the module. Like insmod, rmmod doesn't take module dependencies into account and doesn't do anything with them. If you want to remove a module and take dependencies into account, then you should use modprobe instead. The syntax for removing a module with modprobe is modprobe –r *module_name*.

Let's practice working with kernel modules in the following exercise.

EXERCISE 12-1

Working with Kernel Modules

In this exercise, you will practice viewing information about kernel modules. Complete the following:

1. Boot your Linux system and log in as a standard user. If you used the lab exercise in Chapter 3 to install your system, you can log in as **tux** with a password of **M3linux273**.

2. Open a terminal session.

3. Switch to your root user account by entering **su** – followed by your root user's password.

4. View the status of your system's kernel modules by entering **lsmod | less** at the shell prompt.

5. Page through the list of kernel modules. When finished, press Q.

6. View information about the parport kernel module by entering **modinfo parport** at the shell prompt.

7. Create a list of module dependencies by entering **depmod** at the shell prompt.

8. Use the less or more utility to review the dependency file (modules.dep) you just built in /lib/modules/*kernel_version*/.

Now that you understand how to install and configure new hardware, we next need to discuss configuring power management on your Linux system. Let's discuss how this is done next.

CERTIFICATION OBJECTIVE 12.02

Configure Power Management

Managing the power consumed by computer systems is an important issue that you need to be aware of. In the old days, we didn't worry that much about power consumption. Few employees were allocated PCs at their desktops and only a limited number of servers were needed to support them.

Back in the late 1980s I put myself through my first year in college working as a security guard in the women's dormitory. (That was a great job, I might add!) The dorm administrative office staff consisted of three full-time employees and seven or eight part-timers, including me. For 11 staff members, we had only two 80286 computers. If you needed to type up a document, you had to wait your turn. The funny thing was, I don't remember ever having to wait very long to get on one of the computers. The organization didn't revolve around technology.

Today, all that has changed. Most organizations truly do revolve around their computers and their network. If you don't believe me, watch what happens if the power goes out or the network goes down. This is enough to bring most modern organizations to their knees. Nothing gets done until the computers come back up. Today, nearly every employee has a computer system on his or her desktop. Some employees may even have two or more computers.

What's the point? The dramatic influx of computers into the workplace in the last 15 years means most organizations are spending a lot of money on the electric bill. In fact, many of the power shortages of the late 1990s and early 2000s were blamed (in part) on the massive data centers that had been set up around the country to support the dot-com boom.

Remember, each desktop system you manage has a 350- to 450-watt power supply. Servers may have 500-watt or more power supplies implemented. That's equivalent to a light fixture containing five or more 75-watt light bulbs. Imagine how much power is consumed by 300 employees each running a 400-watt computer system for eight hours every day. That's a lot of juice! This level of power consumption represents a drain on the organization's budget and on the environment.

Fortunately, there's something you can do about it. You can implement power management on your computer systems to turn off devices within the computer that aren't currently in use. For example, if the hard drive isn't being used, it can be spun down. The same can be done with the CD or DVD drive. Doing so has a lot of benefits:

- It makes the computer system greener.
- It saves on the power bill.
- It reduces the amount of heat generated within the system.

In this part of this chapter, we're going to discuss how you can configure power management on a Linux system. We'll discuss the following:

- Power management implementations
- Configuring ACPI on Linux

Let's begin by discussing power management implementations.

Power Management Implementations

Currently, there are two power management schemes that you need to be aware of. The first is the Advanced Power Management (APM) scheme. APM is an older implementation and is being phased out. However, there are still a lot of systems around that use APM.

APM uses software within the BIOS to manage power consumption within the system. To do this APM uses device activity timeout periods to determine when to transition devices into lower power states. Because APM ran out of the BIOS, you would typically use your CMOS setup program to configure your parameters. A typical APM configuration screen is shown in Figure 12-14.

APM, however, had several shortcomings. First, because power management tasks were carried out by the BIOS, the operating system had no idea what was going on. It wasn't unusual to have a system go into standby and have the operating system completely freak out because it didn't know why everything was going down. The second problem was that APM was a "loose" standard. There were many different implementations by many different manufacturers, which resulted in a lack of uniformity. The third issue was that it was primarily used only in laptop/notebook computers.

As a result, APM was phased out in the late 1990s in favor a new, much more powerful power management scheme called the Advanced Configuration and Power Interface (ACPI). ACPI divides power management tasks between the BIOS and the operating system. This eliminates the problems experienced earlier where the BIOS would start shutting things down, leaving the operating system to wonder what's going on.

It's also a much tighter standard than APM. Programmers can easily create utilities that the end user can use to manage power settings within the system without having to enter the CMOS setup program. It also led to power management being widely implemented within desktop and server systems, not just in notebooks. With ACPI, the following can be done:

■ The user can specify when a device, such as a monitor or hard drive, is to be turned off.

FIGURE 12-14

Configuring APM power management settings

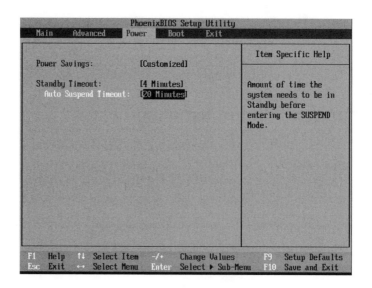

■ Notebook users can configure the system to use less power when running on batteries. This includes the ability to actually lower the clock speed of the CPU to conserve power.

■ Peripheral devices can be set to a low power consumption state until needed.

In addition, ACPI defines the following standard sleep states that the end user can configure his or her system to use:

■ **G0** This state is also called the *Working* or *Ready* state. In G0, the system is fully powered and ready for use.

■ **S1** This state is also called the *Stand-by* state In the S1 state, all peripheral devices are powered off, but the CPU and the system RAM continue to draw power.

■ **S3** This state is also called the *Suspend* state. All devices are shut down except for the system RAM, which continues to draw power and preserves your working data.

■ **S4** This state is also called *Hibernation.* This state saves the contents of the CPU registers and the system RAM to a file on the hard drive. Then, it powers off the system. When you resume from a hibernated sleep state, the BIOS performs the normal POST, and then reads the hibernation file to restore the system to the last state it was in before the computer entered hibernation mode.

Most of the computer systems you'll be working with today probably use ACPI. Let's spend some time learning how to use ACPI on a Linux system.

Configuring ACPI on Linux

By default, most Linux distributions should automatically detect ACPI support on your motherboard during installation and configure the operating system to use it. You can also enable either APM or ACPI power management on your Linux system manually by passing an option to the kernel in your GRUB configuration file. To enable ACPI, you would add the following to the kernel line:

```
apm=off acpi=on
```

To enable APM, you would add the following to the kernel line:

```
apm=on acpi=off
```

FIGURE 12-15

Manually enabling ACPI

```
# Modified by YaST2. Last modification on Tue Oct 10 18:41:13 UTC 2006

color white/blue black/light-gray
default 0
timeout 12
gfxmenu (hd0,0)/message

###Don't change this comment - YaST2 identifier: Original name: linux###
title SUSE Linux 10.1
    root (hd0,0)
    kernel /vmlinuz root=/dev/sda3 vga=0x314    resume=/dev/sda2  splash=sile
nt showopts apm=off acpi=on█
    initrd /initrd

###Don't change this comment - YaST2 identifier: Original name: floppy###
title Floppy
    chainloader (fd0)+1

###Don't change this comment - YaST2 identifier: Original name: failsafe###
title Failsafe -- SUSE Linux 10.1
    root (hd0,0)
    kernel /vmlinuz root=/dev/sda3 vga=normal showopts ide=nodma apm=off acpi
=off noresume nosmp noapic maxcpus=0 edd=off 3
-- INSERT --                                              11,105        Top
```

For example, in Figure 12-15, the /etc/grub/menu.lst file has been modified to enable ACPI at system boot.

on the
Job

If you're using the lilo bootloader, you can enable APM support by adding **append="apm=on"** *to your image definition in /etc/lilo.conf. You can enable ACPI support by adding* **append="acpi=on"** *in your image definition. Either way, remember to re-install lilo after making any changes to lilo.conf.*

Once ACPI has been enabled on your system, you can view ACPI information within files in the /proc/acpi directory, shown in Figure 12-16.

FIGURE 12-16

Viewing ACPI information in /proc/acpi

```
linux1:/proc/acpi # ls
ac_adapter   button              event   info            sleep
alarm        dsdt                fadt    power_resource  thermal_zone
battery      embedded_controller fan     processor       wakeup
linux1:/proc/acpi # █
```

With ACPI support enabled, you next need to configure a system daemon to manage power on your system. This daemon will be configured with a set of rules that specify what to do when specified power events occur. Two commonly used ACPI daemons on Linux include the following:

- **acpid**   This daemon uses the rules you specify in the /etc/acpi/events directory to control power events. All files found in this directory will be parsed to create ACPI rules that define power management events and what should happen as a result. For example, you can define an event for the power button being pushed, as shown here:

```
event=button/power.*
action=/sbin/shutdown -h now
```

  This tells the acpid daemon to run the shutdown –h now command when the power button is pushed. Check out the acpid man page to learn about other events you can define actions for.

- **powersaved**   This daemon uses the rules in /etc/powersave to control how it responds to various events, shown in Figure 12-17.

  The default configuration files used inside this directory include:

  - battery
  - common
  - cpufreq
  - disk
  - events
  - sleep
  - thermal

  Each of these files contains many directives that you can use to configure how your system responds to various power events. Each one is documented very well in the file. To learn how to use each option, just open the appropriate file in a text editor.

  In addition to configuration files, the powersaved daemon uses *scheme* files. These files contain sets of rules for a particular power state. The default scheme files include:

  - scheme_acoustic
  - scheme_performance

FIGURE 12-17

powersaved
daemon
configuration files

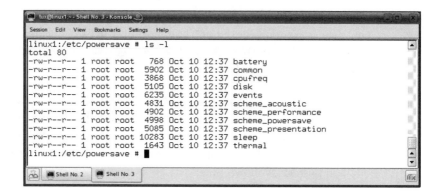

- scheme_powersave
- scheme_presentation

The scheme_powersave file is shown in Figure 12-18.

After making changes to any of the powersaved configuration files, you must restart the powersaved daemon using its init script in /etc/init.d or /etc/rc.d/init.d.

Be warned that these two daemons both use the same ACPI interface on the system, and this isn't allowed. In most cases, you will need to run either acpid or powersaved, but not both at the same time. On some distributions, such as SUSE Linux, you can run acpid with a blank rules file (saved as /etc/acpi/events/default). This causes acipd to

FIGURE 12-18

Configuring
powersave
schemes for
powersaved

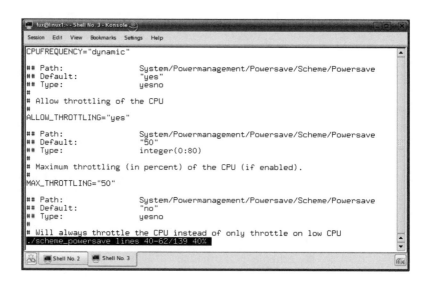

forward all ACPI events to another power management daemon running on the system, such as powersaved.

With the appropriate daemon running, you can view ACPI information by entering **acpi –V** from the shell prompt. You can also use a variety of command-line tools to manage power on your system. First, you can use the acpitool utility to manage ACPI actions on your system. You can use the following options with acpitool:

–a	Shows AC adapter information (notebooks only).
–B	Shows detailed battery status information (notebooks only).
–e	Shows everything.
–f	Shows fan status.
–l *x*	Sets the brightness of the LCD screen to level *x* (a value between 0 and 7).
–s	Puts the system in Suspend sleep state.
–S	Puts the system in Hibernation sleep state.
–t	Shows thermal information.
–w	Shows devices in the system that can be put into a sleep state.
–W *x*	Puts device *x* into a sleep state if it is awake or wakes it up if it's asleep. Use the –w option to determine the device number.

You can also use the powersave utility to manage power on your system. The powersave command is designed to work primarily with the powersaved daemon, but it can still accomplish a few tasks if acpid is in use instead of powersaved. Some of the more useful powersave options include the following:

–U	Puts the system into Hibernation sleep state.
–u	Puts the system into Suspend sleep state.
–m	Puts the system into Stand-by sleep state.
–x	Lists schemes.
–e *x*	Uses power scheme *x*.
–S	Detects whether APM or ACPI is supported by the system.
–B	Displays battery information.
–a	Displays AC status.
–T	Displays thermal information.
–F	Displays fan information.
–r	Displays CPU speed.

SCENARIO & SOLUTION

You need to disable APM and enable ACPI on your Linux system. What command could you enter in your GRUB boot menu's Boot Options field?	You can enter **apm=off apci=on**.
You need to configure power management rules for the powersaved daemon. Where are the files located that you need to edit?	The files are located in the /etc/powersave directory.

Depending on your distribution, you may need to install the acpi, acpitool, or powersave packages with the rpm utility before you can use these commands.

In addition to command-line utilities, you can also download and install a variety of power management front ends for either daemon. Being partial to SUSE Linux, I really like the YaST Power Management module, shown in Figure 12-19.

FIGURE 12-19

Using the YaST Power Management module

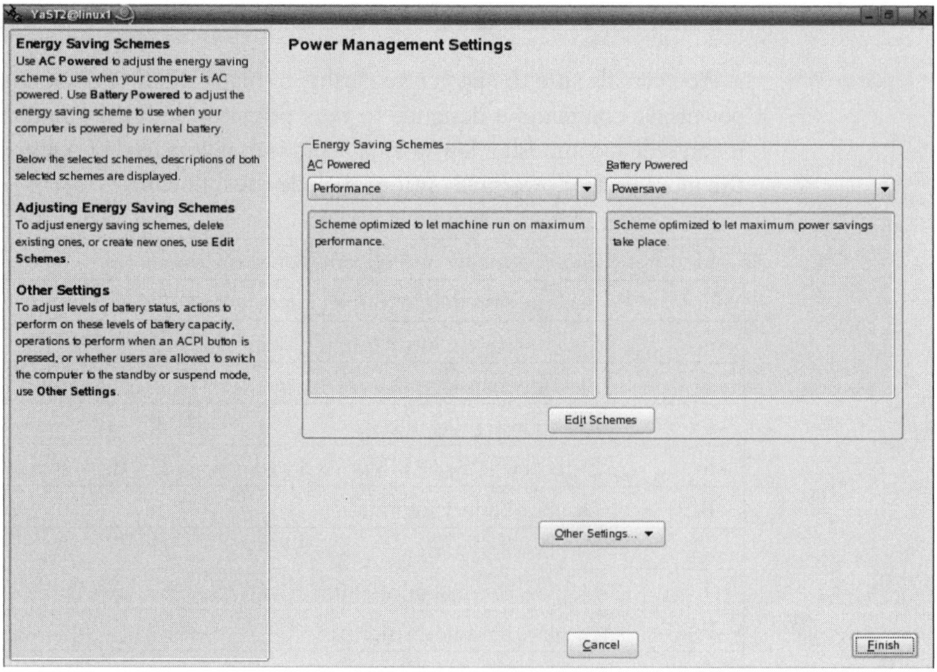

This utility provides an intuitive graphical interface that allows you to configure the powersaved daemon.

Let's practice working with power management in the following exercise.

EXERCISE 12-2

ON THE CD

Working with Power Management Utilities

In this exercise, you will practice working with power management utilities. This exercise assumes you are using a newer system that supports ACPI. If you're using a VMware virtual machine for your lab system, you won't be able to use Hibernation or Stand-by sleep states. Complete the following:

1. Log off and shut down your system.

2. Power your system back on.

3. In the Boot Options field in the GRUB menu screen, enter **apm=off acpi=on**.

4. Boot the system.

5. Log in as your standard user.

6. Open a terminal session.

7. Switch to your root user account by entering **su –** followed by your root user's password.

8. Use the rpm utility to install the acpitools and powersave packages from your distribution media. If these packages aren't available on your distribution CD, you can download them from http://www.sourceforge.net.

9. Use the rpm utility to query whether your system is using the acpid daemon, the powersaved daemon, or both.

10. If your system uses the acpid daemon, do the following:

    a. View all ACPI information for your system by entering **acpitool –e | less** at the shell prompt.

    b. Page through the output from acpitool.

    c. View devices that can be put into a sleep state by entering **acpitool –w** at the shell prompt.

     d. Select a device number from the output of the preceding command, then enter **acpitool –W** *x* at the shell prompt to put the device to sleep. Replace *x* with the number of the device.

     e. Wake the device back up by entering **acpitool –W** *x* again.

     f. Hibernate the system by entering **acpitool –S** at the shell prompt.

     g. When complete, power the system back on by pressing the power button.

11. If your system uses the powersaved daemon, do the following:

     a. Verify that your system supports ACPI by entering **powersave –S** at the shell prompt.

     b. List your available powersave schemes by entering **powersave –x** at the shell prompt.

     c. Pick a scheme from the powersave output.

     d. Change powersave schemes by entering **powersave –e** *x* at the shell prompt where *x* is the name of the scheme.

     e. Put the system into Stand-by by entering **powersave –m** at the shell prompt.

     f. When complete, power the system back on by pressing the power button.

Now that we have power management behind us, let's shift our attention to a new topic: burning CDs and DVDs.

CERTIFICATION OBJECTIVE 12.03

Burn CDs and DVDs

Let's face it; the ability to burn a CD or a DVD has gone from a high-end novelty to a daily necessity. Users expect to be able to burn data to optical discs. In this part of the chapter, we're going to discuss how to do this. We'll cover the following topics:

- Burning discs from the command line
- Using graphical utilities to burn discs

Let's begin by discussing how to burn optical discs on Linux from the command line.

Burning Discs from the Command Line

As with most aspects of Linux, you can burn discs either from the shell prompt or using a graphical utility. In this part of the chapter, we're going to discuss how to use the mkisofs and cdrecord utilities to burn discs from the command line.

Burning a disc from the shell prompt is a three-part task. First, you need to check your optical burning hardware and verify that it will work with Linux command-line burning utilities. It's important that you understand that all optical burners use standard SCSI commands to communicate with your CD or DVD burning utilities, even if it's an IDE/ATAPI device.

If your burner is a SCSI, USB, or FireWire drive, you're in good shape. The Linux cdrecord utility will work just fine with these devices. If your device is an IDE/ATAPI device (and many of them are), then things aren't quite so simple. The cdrecord utility can't natively communicate with these devices. To make things work, you need to make your IDE/ATAPI devices emulate a SCSI device. This can be done using the ide_scsi.ko kernel module. The exact steps for doing this vary from distribution to distribution. We don't have time or space to go through all the steps required enable ide_scsi.ko in this chapter. There's a great article on the Internet that will take you through the process step by step at http://www-128.ibm.com/developerworks/linux/library/l-cdburn.html.

After verifying that your hardware will work with the cdrecord utility, you next need to identify where your burner resides on the SCSI bus. You can use the cdrecord utility to do this by entering **cdrecord –scanbus** at the shell prompt. The cdrecord utility will print a list of SCSI devices on your system's SCSI bus. The output should appear similar to the following:

```
0,0,0      0) *
0,1,0      1) *
0,2,0      2) *
0,3,0      3) 'Sony' 'DRU-120A' '1.26' Removable CD-ROM
0,4,0      4) *
0,5,0      5) *
0,6,0      6) *
0,7,0      7) *
```

This output identifies the SCSI adapter (0), SCSI ID (3), and LUN (0) of your burner. Write this down; you'll need it later when we start the burning process.

Next, you need to use the mkisofs command to make an .iso image on your hard drive that contains the files you want to burn to the disc. The syntax for using mkisofs is mkisofs –o *file_name options* –V *disk_label files*. The –o option specifies the output file name, which should use an .iso extension. Some of the more useful *options* you can use with mkisofs include the following:

- **–J** Generates Joliet directory records in addition to regular iso9660 file names. Joliet extends the ISO 9660 file system to allow extended file names on the CDs you burn. This option should be used if the disc will be read on a Windows system.

- **–r** Generates Rock Ridge records in addition to iso9660 file names for Linux compatibility. Rock Ridge is also an extension to the ISO 9660 file system that allows longer file names and Linux permissions to be used with the files on the disc. This option will set the UID and the GID attribute of each file and directory to 0, allowing the files to be read by any user who mounts the disc after it's burned.

- **–udf** Includes UDF support in the generated file system image.

- **–ldots** Allows iso9660 file names to begin with a period. If not used, a leading dot is replaced with an underscore.

- **–allow-lowercase** Allows lowercase characters in iso9660 file names.

- **–allow-multidot** Allows more than one dot in iso9660 file names.

For example, if I want to create an .iso image named /tmp/tuxhome.iso that contains all of the files in the tux user's home directory, creates Joliet and Rock Ridge records, and sets the disk label to TUXHOME, I would enter **mkisofs –o /tmp/ tuxhome.iso –J –r –V TUXHOME /home/tux/**. The output from this command is shown in Figure 12-20.

Notice in Figure 12-20 that files whose name didn't match the ISO 9660 standard were renamed within the .iso file to bring them into compliance. After creating the .iso file, you're ready to burn it with the cdrecord utility. However, I strongly recommend that you check the integrity of the .iso file before you burn it. This can be done by mounting it into your file system. To do this, enter **mount –t iso9660 –o ro,loop=/dev/loop0** *iso_filename mount_point* at the shell prompt. For example, to mount the image created in Figure 12-20 in the /media/iso directory, you would enter **mount –t iso9660 –o ro,loop=/dev/loop0 /tmp/tuxhome.iso /media/iso** at the shell prompt. You can then view the files within the .iso file using the ls command, as shown in Figure 12-21.

Once you've verified your files, dismount the .iso image using the umount command. Now you're ready to burn the .iso image to disc using the cdrecord command. Insert a blank, recordable disc into your drive. Then, enter **cdrecord –eject dev=***SCSI_addr iso_filename*. The –eject option ejects the disc when it's done burning. The dev= option

FIGURE 12-20

Creating an ISO image with mkisofs

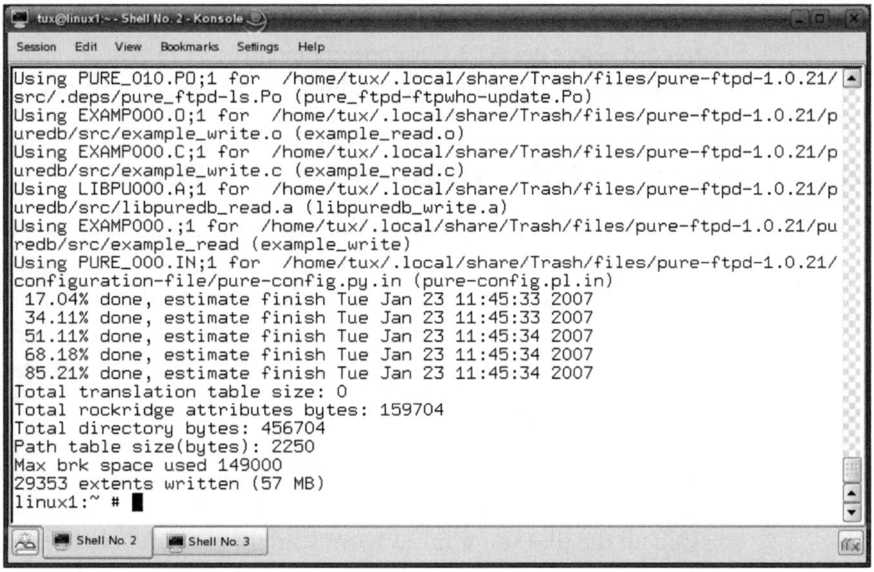

```
Using PURE_010.PO;1 for   /home/tux/.local/share/Trash/files/pure-ftpd-1.0.21/
src/.deps/pure_ftpd-ls.Po (pure_ftpd-ftpwho-update.Po)
Using EXAMP000.O;1 for   /home/tux/.local/share/Trash/files/pure-ftpd-1.0.21/p
uredb/src/example_write.o (example_read.o)
Using EXAMP000.C;1 for   /home/tux/.local/share/Trash/files/pure-ftpd-1.0.21/p
uredb/src/example_write.c (example_read.c)
Using LIBPU000.A;1 for   /home/tux/.local/share/Trash/files/pure-ftpd-1.0.21/p
uredb/src/libpuredb_read.a (libpuredb_write.a)
Using EXAMP000.;1 for   /home/tux/.local/share/Trash/files/pure-ftpd-1.0.21/pu
redb/src/example_read (example_write)
Using PURE_000.IN;1 for   /home/tux/.local/share/Trash/files/pure-ftpd-1.0.21/
configuration-file/pure-config.py.in (pure-config.pl.in)
 17.04% done, estimate finish Tue Jan 23 11:45:33 2007
 34.11% done, estimate finish Tue Jan 23 11:45:33 2007
 51.11% done, estimate finish Tue Jan 23 11:45:34 2007
 68.18% done, estimate finish Tue Jan 23 11:45:34 2007
 85.21% done, estimate finish Tue Jan 23 11:45:34 2007
Total translation table size: 0
Total rockridge attributes bytes: 159704
Total directory bytes: 456704
Path table size(bytes): 2250
Max brk space used 149000
29353 extents written (57 MB)
linux1:~ #
```

specifies the SCSI address of your burner. Recall earlier that we used the cdrecord –scanbus command to generate a list of the SCSI hardware in the system. Set the dev= option to the three numbers that identify your burner. The burner in my system has a SCSI address of 0,3,0 (which specifies that the device is on SCSI bus #0, has an ID of 3,

FIGURE 12-21

Mounting and viewing the contents of an ISO file

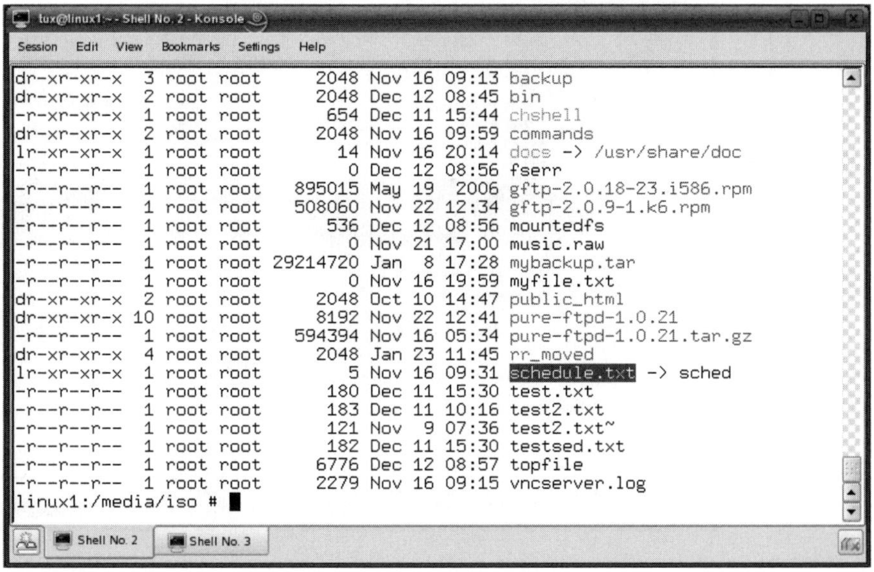

```
dr-xr-xr-x   3 root root     2048 Nov 16 09:13 backup
dr-xr-xr-x   2 root root     2048 Dec 12 08:45 bin
-r-xr-xr-x   1 root root      654 Dec 11 15:44 chshell
dr-xr-xr-x   2 root root     2048 Nov 16 09:59 commands
lr-xr-xr-x   1 root root       14 Nov 16 20:14 docs -> /usr/share/doc
-r--r--r--   1 root root        0 Dec 12 08:56 fserr
-r--r--r--   1 root root   895015 May 19  2006 gftp-2.0.18-23.i586.rpm
-r--r--r--   1 root root   508060 Nov 22 12:34 gftp-2.0.9-1.k6.rpm
-r--r--r--   1 root root      536 Dec 12 08:56 mountedfs
-r--r--r--   1 root root        0 Nov 21 17:00 music.raw
-r--r--r--   1 root root 29214720 Jan  8 17:28 mybackup.tar
-r--r--r--   1 root root        0 Nov 16 19:59 myfile.txt
dr-xr-xr-x   2 root root     2048 Oct 10 14:47 public_html
dr-xr-xr-x  10 root root     8192 Nov 22 12:41 pure-ftpd-1.0.21
-r--r--r--   1 root root   594394 Nov 16 05:34 pure-ftpd-1.0.21.tar.gz
dr-xr-xr-x   4 root root     2048 Jan 23 11:45 rr_moved
lr-xr-xr-x   1 root root        5 Nov 16 09:31 schedule.txt -> sched
-r--r--r--   1 root root      180 Dec 11 15:30 test.txt
-r--r--r--   1 root root      183 Dec 11 10:16 test2.txt
-r--r--r--   1 root root      121 Nov  9 07:36 test2.txt~
-r--r--r--   1 root root      182 Dec 11 15:30 testsed.txt
-r--r--r--   1 root root     6776 Dec 12 08:57 topfile
-r--r--r--   1 root root     2279 Nov 16 09:15 vncserver.log
linux1:/media/iso #
```

and a LUN of 0). Therefore, to burn the tuxhome.iso file to this burner, I would enter **cdrecord –eject dev=0,3,0 /tmp/tuxhome.iso**.

Let's next discuss how to burn discs using graphical utilities.

Using Graphical Utilities to Burn Optical Discs

I'll admit it; I don't like burning discs from the command line. As you can see in the previous topic, there are a lot of steps involved and it's easy to make a mistake. I much prefer the various graphical utilities provided with most distributions to burn optical discs. My favorite is the K3b utility, which runs in the KDE desktop environment. This utility provides an excellent graphical interface for burning discs, as shown in Figure 12-22.

As you can see in Figure 12-22, you simply drag and drop files and folders into the bottom frame. As you do, an indicator bar is displayed across the bottom of the screen indicating how much space your files will consume on the disc. When you've added all the files you want to burn, you just click the Burn button to write the information to the specified burner drive. Much easier and faster! I love K3b! If your

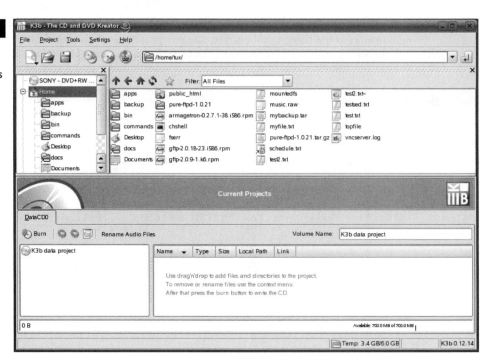

FIGURE 12-22

Using K3b to burn optical discs

SCENARIO & SOLUTION

You need to determine the device ID of your CD burner. What command can you enter at the shell prompt to do this?	You can enter **cdrecorder –scanbus**.
In preparation for burning a CD, you need to create an ISO file in /tmp named myfiles.iso that contains all of the files in your home directory. The ISO file must support the Joliet and Rock Ridge naming standards and have a volume name of MYFILES. What command would you enter to do this?	You would enter **mkisofs –o /tmp/myfiles.iso –J –r –V MYFILES ~/**.
You need to burn the /tmp/myfiles.iso file to a CD-R. Your CD burner is attached to your SCSI controller and has a SCSI ID of 5. What command would you enter?	You would enter **cdrecord dev=0,5,0 /tmp/myfiles.iso**.

distribution didn't include the K3b package, you can find a copy on the Internet, download it, and use the rpm utility to install it.

There are many other excellent graphical burning utilities available. Go to http://www.sourceforge.net and search for **burn CD**.

Let's practice burning CDs in the following exercise.

EXERCISE 12-3

ON THE CD

Burning CDs and DVDs

In this exercise, you will practice burning a CD from the shell prompt. This exercise requires that you have a CD or DVD burner installed in your system. If you're using VMware, you won't be able to complete this exercise. VMware doesn't allow the commands through its virtual disc interface needed to burn CDs. Complete the following:

1. Open a terminal session.
2. Switch to your root user account by entering **su –** followed by your root user's password.

3. At the shell prompt, enter **cdrecord –scanbus**.

4. Record the identifier for your optical burner.

5. Create an .iso file containing the contents of your root user's home directory by entering **mkisofs –o /tmp/roothome.iso –J –r –V ROOTHM /root/** at the shell prompt.

6. Verify your .iso file by doing the following:

   a. Make a directory named iso in /media.

   b. At the shell prompt, enter **mount –t iso9660 –o ro,loop=/dev/loop0 /tmp/roothome.iso /media/iso**.

   c. Use the ls command to view the files in /media/iso.

   d. When you're confident the .iso file has been created correctly, enter **umount /media/iso**.

7. Burn the .iso file by completing the following:

   a. Insert a blank CD in your optical burner's drive.

   b. At the shell prompt, enter **cdrecord –eject dev=*your_device_ID* /tmp/ roothome.iso**.

   c. Wait while the disc is burned.

   d. When complete, insert the CD in your drive and mount the disc.

   e. Use the ls command to view the files on the disc.

With burning discs under our belt, we're ready to move on and discuss RAID. Let's do that next.

CERTIFICATION OBJECTIVE 12.04

Implement RAID

RAID is a very cool, very powerful way of deploying hard disk drives in your Linux system. Using RAID allows you to:

■ Speed up your hard disk system.

■ Protect your data against hard disk failures.

Depending on how you implement your disks, RAID can do either of these things or both at the same time. Back when I first started working with computers in the late 1980s, RAID was something only the "server guys" were concerned with. RAID arrays were too expensive to be implemented in desktop systems. That has all changed, however. RAID is still the backbone of server hard disk storage systems. However, the price of RAID adapters and the price of hard disk drives have dropped enough to where it is feasible to implement a RAID solution in desktop systems as well. In this part of this chapter, we're going to introduce you to RAID. We'll cover the following concepts and tasks:

- An introduction to RAID
- Configuring a RAID array on Linux

Let's start by introducing you to basic RAID concepts.

An Introduction to RAID

Before you can effectively set up a RAID array, you need to be very familiar with basic RAID concepts. You'll also need to be familiar with these concepts for your Linux+ exam. To provide you with the background you need about RAID, we're going to discuss the following in this part of this chapter:

- Basic RAID concepts
- RAID levels
- Hardware vs. software RAID

Let's begin by reviewing some key RAID concepts.

Basic RAID Concepts

When RAID was first developed many years ago, the acronym stood for *redundant array of inexpensive disks*. Today, it's generally acknowledged to stand for *redundant array of independent disks*. Regardless of which definition you choose, RAID still works in the same way: you implement two or more hard disk drives in your system and then use a special hard disk controller or software in RAM to group the disks together into an *array*. The disk controller board (or software in RAM) presents the array to the operating system as a single hard disk drive. This is shown in Figure 12-23.

When grouping disks into an array, you can choose from a variety of schemes that define how the disks relate to each other and how data is stored on them. The first of

FIGURE 12-23

A RAID array

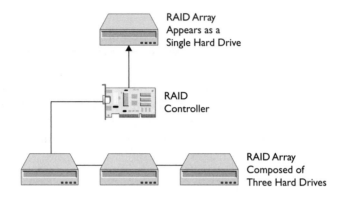

these schemes is called *striping*. When striping is employed, the hard drives in the array are joined together into one big disk. The size of the array is equal to the sum of the sizes of all the disks it contains. For example, if you have two 100GB hard disk drives in your array, the operating system would see the array as a single 200GB hard disk drive.

When striping is used, any data that is to be written to the array is split up and written to all the disks in the array at the same time. In Figure 12-24, a hypothetical file is being written to a striped RAID array.

The file is divided up into chunks determined by the *stripe size* of the array and written to all three disks in the array at the same time. Likewise, if the file were to be retrieved from the drive and loaded into RAM, its pieces would be read from all three drives in the array at the same time and reassembled by the RAID controller board and delivered to the operating system in its original, intact state.

Because of the way striping works, a striped array can dramatically increase the overall speed of your disk system. The more disks you stripe in the array, the faster it can read and write data. Striping is frequently used in server systems, video-editing systems, and so on. where large quantities of data need to be handled very quickly. The downside

FIGURE 12-24

Striping data
between disks in
an array

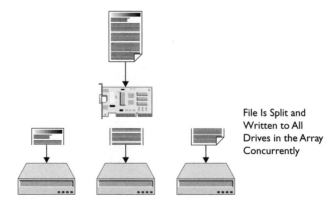

to striping is the fact that all of your files are spread across multiple hard drives. If one of the drives in the array fails, you will lose parts of all of your files, which isn't a good thing. Essentially, striping provides increased disk performance while increasing your risk of data loss.

Remember earlier that we said RAID arrays could also protect data in addition to making the disk system run faster. This is accomplished through another array scheme called *mirroring*. In a mirrored array, we group multiple hard drives together just like we did in the striped array. However, instead of spreading data across the drives, as striping does, mirroring writes complete data files redundantly to all of the drives in the array. This is shown in Figure 12-25.

Each disk in the array is a mirror copy of the others. The cool thing about mirroring is the fact that if one of the disks in the array fails, the others can immediately take over. There's no downtime; the data you need remains available. The downside of mirroring is that it doesn't provide any performance gain. The size of a mirrored array is equal to the size of the smallest disk in the array. For example, if you create a mirrored array that contains three 100MB hard drives, the total size of the array is 100MB.

on the
()ob

There's another version of mirroring called **duplexing. Notice in Figure 12-25** *that mirrored drives are connected to the same RAID controller board. Duplexing mirrors data between hard drives connected to two or more different RAID controllers. This protects the system from data loss if the RAID board itself were to fail.*

The last RAID concept you need to understand is *parity*. As we mentioned, one of the key weaknesses associated with striping is the fact that one failed disk in the array destroys all of the data in the array. That's a risky situation. Hard disk

FIGURE 12-25

Mirroring data in an array

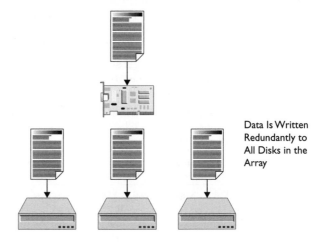

Data Is Written Redundantly to All Disks in the Array

drives fail and fail frequently. To add a degree of redundancy to a striped array, you can implement parity. Parity stores information in the array that can be used to reconstruct data in the event that one of the disks in the array fails. Parity requires a minimum of three disks in the array. Depending on the RAID level you choose, one disk in the array can be dedicated to storing parity information or parity information can be distributed equally across all disks in the array.

With these concepts in mind, let's review some common RAID levels next.

RAID Levels

These three concepts—striping, mirroring, and parity—can be deployed in a number of ways to create a variety of different RAID implementations called *levels*. There are many different RAID levels that you can choose from. Some of the more common ones are reviewed in Table 12-1.

TABLE 12-1	RAID Level	Description
RAID Levels	0	Mirrors data between two or more hard disk drives in an array.
	1	Stripes data between two or more hard disk drives in an array.
	3	Requires a minimum of three hard disk drives in the array. Data is striped between two or more of the hard disk drives. Parity information is stored on a dedicated hard disk drive. If one of the striped disks fails, it can be replaced and the data reconstructed from the parity drive. However, if the parity drive fails, the whole array fails.
	5	Requires a minimum of three hard disk drives in the array. Data is striped between all drives like RAID 3. However, parity information is evenly distributed among all drives in the array. This makes RAID 5 much more fault tolerant than RAID 3. Any failed drive in the array can be replaced and the data reconstructed from the parity information stored on the other drives in the array. This is a very widely used RAID level in server systems.
	0+1	This is a *nested* RAID array. In this configuration, a striped array is mirrored on one or more other striped arrays, making the very fast RAID 0 array more fault tolerant.
	1+0	This is also a nested RAID array. In this configuration, data is striped between two or more mirrored arrays. This speeds up the performance of a highly fault-tolerant mirrored array.
	5+0	This is also a nested RAID array. In this configuration, data is striped between two or more RAID 5 arrays.
	5+1	This is also a nested RAID array. In this configuration, data is mirrored between two or more RAID 5 arrays.

It's important to note that one RAID level isn't necessarily "better" than another. Many students new to RAID mistakenly assume that a RAID 1 array is better than a RAID 0 array and that a RAID 3 array is better than a RAID 1 array. This just isn't true. When selecting a RAID level, you should pick the one that fits your deployment best. If speed is the issue, then RAID 0 is a good choice, but remember that it doesn't offer any fault tolerance. In fact, it makes your systems more susceptible to disk failures. If fault tolerance is the issue, then RAID 1 is a good choice. If you need a balance between speed and fault tolerance, then RAID 3 or 5 are great options.

Finally, let's discuss the difference between hardware and software RAID.

Hardware vs. Software RAID

When implementing RAID, you can use either a RAID controller board to create and manage your array, or you can use RAID software provided with most Linux distributions. These options are called *hardware RAID* and *software RAID*.

With hardware RAID, you must purchase a dedicated RAID controller board and install it in an expansion slot in your motherboard. Most high-end RAID controller boards, more commonly used in server systems, use the SCSI or SATA hard disk interfaces. Low-end RAID boards, usually used in desktop systems, usually use the IDE/ATA disk interface. Once installed, you then connect your hard disks that will be members of your RAID array directly to the RAID controller. The RAID controller board has its own on-board BIOS and setup program that you use to configure the disks connected to the controller into an array. The RAID controller board then presents the array to the operating system as a single hard disk drive.

on the
Job

Nearly all RAID boards, including SATA and IDE/ATA, will be seen as SCSI controller boards by your operating system.

In addition to hardware RAID, you can also implement a RAID array using special software that's loaded into RAM by your Linux operating system. This is called software RAID. Software RAID is really cool. You don't need a RAID controller board to create an array. Instead, you connect your hard drives to your standard SCSI, IDE/ATA, or SATA interface. Then, you use your operating system software to group the drives together into an array. As with hardware RAID, the operating system then sees the array as a single hard disk drive.

You might be wondering at this point which RAID implementation is "best." Both hardware and software RAID have advantages and disadvantages. These are listed in Table 12-2.

TABLE 12-2	Type	Advantages	Disadvantages
Comparing Hardware and Software RAID	Hardware RAID	■ Usually offers more RAID levels to choose from. ■ Usually faster than software RAID. ■ Independent of the operating system.	■ More expensive than software RAID because you have to purchase a separate controller board. ■ Tends to be more difficult to set up. ■ You can only work with entire disks.
	Software RAID	■ Easier and faster to configure than hardware RAID. ■ Less expensive than hardware RAID. ■ Works with partitions on a disk, not the entire disk itself.	■ Usually offers fewer RAID levels. ■ Speed depends on the speed of your system RAM and your CPU. ■ Dependent upon the operating system.

on the
Ĵob

Because software RAID can work with partitions as well as entire disks, I've seen many new RAID students try to mirror or stripe two partitions on the same disk! Don't do this! You will lose the speed advantage when striping and you will lose the redundancy advantage when mirroring. Always work with partitions on separate disks.

When implementing a RAID solution, you'll need to weigh these factors against each other to determine which option is the best for your particular deployment. Let's now talk about how you go about configuring a RAID array on Linux.

Configuring a RAID Array on Linux

When configuring a RAID array on your Linux system, you can choose from either hardware RAID or software RAID, as discussed previously. If you choose to implement a hardware RAID board, make sure the board you select is supported by your distribution. Usually, higher-end SCSI RAID boards work very well in Linux systems. However, be very wary of low-end IDE/ATA RAID boards. Many, if not most, of them don't work properly under Linux. Instead of seeing your array as a single disk, the Linux kernel will probably see each disk in the array as a separate disk, just as if they were

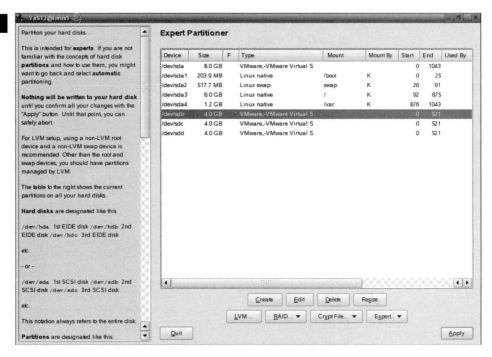

FIGURE 12-26

Using the
YaST partition
management
module

connected to a standard IDE/ATA interface. Before you buy, check the manufacturer's
Web site and your Linux vendor's Web site and see if the board you want to use is
supported.

The good news is that most Linux distributions support software RAID. In this
configuration, you simply connect your disks to your standard SCSI, IDE/ATA, or
SATA controller. Then you run your distribution's partitioning utility to create the
array. For example, in Figure 12-26, the YaST partition management module on a
SUSE Linux system has been loaded.

Notice in Figure 12-26 that I have three 4GB hard drives installed in the system
that don't have any partitions on them. If I wanted to create a RAID array with these
disks, I would do the following:

on the
ⓘ o b

*The steps here are written using the YaST Partitioner module. However, the
steps for creating a RAID array with other partition management utilities will
be very similar to those presented here.*

1. Create RAID partitions on each disk by doing the following:

   a. Select Create.

   b. Select the first *disk* to be included in the array, then select OK.

   c. Select Primary Partition, then select OK.

   d. In the Format field, select Do Not Format; then select 0xFD Linux RAID in the drop-down list.

   e. Set the size of the partition using the Start and End cylinder fields. This is shown in Figure 12-27.

   f. Select OK.

   g. Create RAID partitions of the same size on the other disks to be included in the array by repeating the preceding steps.

2. Create the RAID array by doing the following:

   a. Select RAID | Create RAID.

   b. Select your *RAID level*. With SUSE Linux, you can choose from RAID 0, RAID 1, or RAID 5, as shown in Figure 12-28.

   c. Select Next.

   d. Select each *partition* that should be included in the array and then select Add.

   e. Select Next.

   f. In the final screen, select Format and then configure the following:

     ■ File system type

     ■ Chunk (stripe) size

     ■ Mount point

FIGURE 12-27

Configuring a
RAID partition

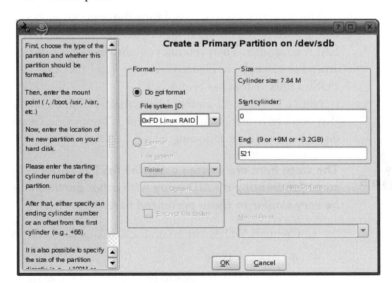

FIGURE 12-28

Selecting your RAID level

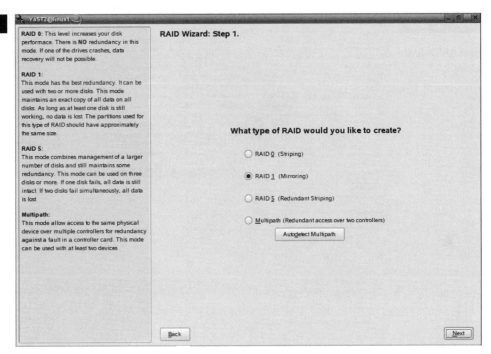

g. Select Finish. When you're done, you should see a new device named /dev/md0 added to your list of devices, as shown in Figure 12-29. This is your RAID device.

h. Select Apply.

i. Wait while the array is created and mounted. When complete, you should have a functioning RAID array mounted in your file system!

SCENARIO & SOLUTION

You need to make sure data is written redundantly on two hard drives in your system. What RAID level should you implement?	You need to create a RAID 1 array.
You have installed two extra IDE hard drives in your Linux system and want to use them to create a RAID 0 array. You don't own a RAID controller. Can you still do this?	Yes, you can create a software RAID array that will stripe data between the hard drives.

New RAID device added

Let's practice creating a software RAID array in the following exercise.

EXERCISE 12-4

Creating a Software RAID Array

In this exercise, you will practice creating a software RAID array. Be warned that this exercise requires additional hard disk drives to be installed in your system. Depending upon your lab system, you may or may not be able to complete this exercise. If you're using VMware, you can simply create two additional virtual hard drives. If you're using standard hardware, you will need to install two additional hard drives in the system. This exercise also assumes you're using SUSE Linux. Complete the following:

1. Install two extra hard drives in your computer. If you're using VMware, you can create two additional virtual hard drives in your virtual machine.

2. Boot your system and log in.

3. Open a terminal session.

4. Switch to your root user account by entering **su** – followed by your root user's password.

5. Make a directory named raid within /mnt.

6. At the shell prompt, enter **yast2**.

7. Create RAID partitions on each disk by doing the following:

   a. In YaST, select System | Partitioner.

   b. In the warning screen, select Yes.

   c. Select Create.

   d. Select the first *disk* to be included in the array, then select OK.

   e. Select Primary Partition, then select OK.

   f. In the Format field, select Do Not Format; then select 0xFD Linux RAID in the drop-down list.

   g. Set the size of the partition using the Start and End cylinder fields.

   h. Select OK.

   i. Create RAID partitions of the same size on the other disk to be included in the array by repeating the preceding steps.

8. Create the RAID array by doing the following:

   a. Select RAID | Create RAID.

   b. Select RAID 0, then select Next.

   c. Select each *partition* that should be included in the array and then select Add.

   d. Select Next.

   e. In the final screen, select Format and then configure the following:

      ■ File system type: Reiser

      ■ Chunk size: Use the default size

      ■ Mount point: /mnt/raid

   f. Select Finish. When you're done, you should see a new device named /dev/md0 added to your list of devices. This is your RAID device.

   g. Select Apply.

   h. Wait while the array is created and mounted.

Let's now move on and talk about the last topic for this chapter: configuring X Windows.

Configure X Windows

Let's face it, we live in a computing world dominated by graphical user interfaces (GUIs). As system admins, you and I are comfortable working with the Linux shell prompt. We're not intimidated by long shell commands that use a variety of options. However, I can promise you that your end users are not thrilled at all with the command-line interface. Frankly, most of them hate it and will probably refuse to use it.

To make Linux user-friendlier, you can use its graphical user interface. In this part of this chapter, we're going to part company with the shell prompt for a while and learn how to work with the Linux GUI. We're going to cover the following topics:

- How the Linux GUI works
- Configuring the graphical environment

Let's begin by discussing how the Linux GUI works.

How the Linux GUI Works

One of the great things about the Linux GUI is that it is very modular. It's composed of several different pieces that work together to create the graphical interface. Because the GUI is modular, you can mix and match different components together to customize the way it works. This provides a degree of flexibility that just isn't available with other operating systems. The Linux GUI is composed of the following components:

- **X Server** The heart of the Linux GUI is the X Server software. The X Server software is the component that draws windows graphically on the display screen. It's also responsible for managing your mouse and your keyboard. We call it a *server* because it is capable of displaying output not only on the local monitor, but also on any other system on the network that is also running X Server software. The location where the X Server software sends its output is controlled by the DISPLAY environment variable.

Over the years, two different X Server software packages have been implemented on Linux systems. These include:

- **X Windows**   X Windows is the oldest X Server software. It was developed back in the early 1980s and has been widely deployed on both UNIX and Linux. It is the default X Server (x.org) used on distributions such as SUSE Linux and Red Hat Fedora.

- **XFree86**   XFree86 is an open source version of X Windows. It works in pretty much the same manner as X Windows.

- **Window Manager**   While the X Server creates windows within the GUI environment, the window manager's job is to customize how the windows look and behave. A wide variety of window managers are currently available for Linux. Each one offers a different look and feel for your GUI environment. Some of the more popular window managers include the following:

  - enlightenment
  - fvwm
  - kwin
  - sawfish
  - twm
  - wmaker

  Which is best? None is best, really. It all depends on what you like. Some window managers are complex and full-featured, such as enlightenment, kwin, and sawfish. The enlightenment and sawfish window managers are commonly used with the GNOME desktop environment. The kwin window manager is commonly used with the KDE desktop environment.

  Other window managers are very basic. These include the feeble virtual window manager (fvwm), tab window manager (twm), and the window maker (wmaker) window manager.

  Depending on your users' preferences, I would suggest that you deploy a more full-featured window manager on your system, such as enlightenment, sawfish, or kwin. These window managers create a look and feel that is very similar to Microsoft Windows, making it easy for your users to transition over.

- **Desktop Environment**   The desktop environment leverages the look and feel created by the window manager and adds a series of tools and utilities that make the GUI truly useful. Basically, it ties all of your GUI components together into a cohesive environment. The desktop environment is optional, but highly recommended. As with X Server and window managers, the desktop environment is modular. You can try out the available environments and choose the one you like best. Two desktop environments are predominantly used with Linux systems today:

- **KDE**   KDE is an excellent desktop environment. It provides functionality that is very similar to Microsoft Windows. It's the default environment used on distributions such as SUSE Linux. A sample KDE desktop is shown in Figure 12-30.

- **GNOME**   As with KDE, the GNOME desktop environment is excellent. It also provides a look and feel that is reminiscent of Microsoft Windows. GNOME is the default environment used on distributions such as Red Hat Fedora. A typical GNOME desktop is shown in Figure 12-31.

These three components, the X Server software, the window manager, and the desktop environment all work hand in hand to create the GUI environment on

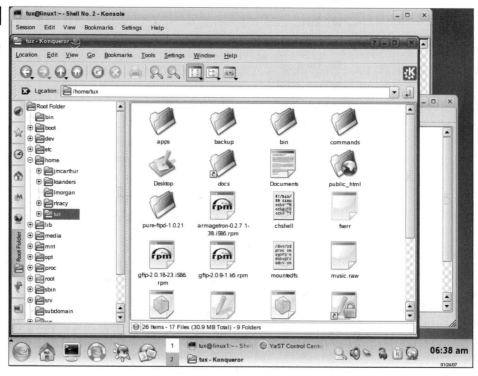

FIGURE 12-30

The KDE desktop environment

FIGURE 12-31

The GNOME desktop environment

a Windows system. You can mix and match between these three different components to customize the system to match your particular tastes and preferences.

Let's now discuss how you go about configuring your graphical environment.

Configuring the Graphical Environment

Because your graphical environment is composed of several modular components, you need to complete a variety of tasks to configure the GUI on a Linux system. In this part of the chapter, we're going to cover the following:

- Configuring the X Server
- Specifying a window manager and desktop environment

Let's begin by discussing how to configure the X Server.

Configuring the X Server

Because the X Server works directly with your video board and monitor, configuring it is the most critical and most difficult of all your GUI management tasks. It's imperative that you use the correct settings in your configuration. If done incorrectly, you could potentially damage your monitor.

on the

Job

I know this because I had it happen to me once. I configured my system to use a sync rate that was too fast for an older monitor I was using. It worked OK for a couple of weeks. However, one evening my monitor started hissing, sparking, and smoking. I pushed it too fast for too long and burned it up. Always check your video board and monitor documentation to obtain the correct specs!

Before you begin, you should pull out your video board and monitor documentation and identify the following information:

- Who's the manufacturer of the video board?
- What model number is the video board?
- How much memory is installed on the video board?
- What's the board's maximum resolution?
- What's the board's maximum color depth?
- What chipset is installed on the board?
- What's the maximum horizontal and vertical sync rate supported by your monitor?

Trust me, having this information in hand before you begin will save you a lot of trouble. Once you have this information gathered, you're ready to start configuring your X Server. If you're using X Windows, your configuration settings are saved in /etc/X11/xorg.conf. If you're using XFree86, your configuration settings are saved in /etc/X11/XF86Config. A sample xorg.conf file is shown in Figure 12-32.

FIGURE 12-32

The /etc/X11/ xorg.conf file

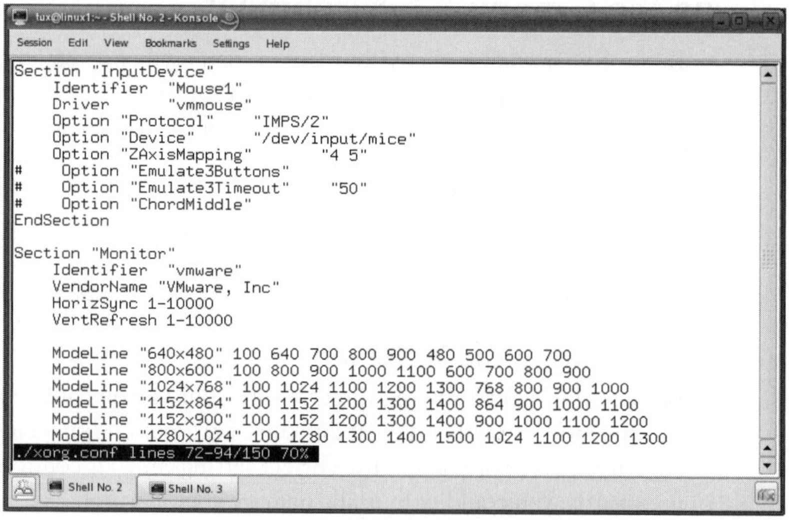

```
Session  Edit  View  Bookmarks  Settings  Help

Section "InputDevice"
    Identifier  "Mouse1"
    Driver      "vmmouse"
    Option "Protocol"      "IMPS/2"
    Option "Device"        "/dev/input/mice"
    Option "ZAxisMapping"      "4 5"
#   Option "Emulate3Buttons"
#   Option "Emulate3Timeout"    "50"
#   Option "ChordMiddle"
EndSection

Section "Monitor"
    Identifier  "vmware"
    VendorName "VMware, Inc"
    HorizSync 1-10000
    VertRefresh 1-10000

    ModeLine "640x480"  100 640 700 800 900 480 500 600 700
    ModeLine "800x600"  100 800 900 1000 1100 600 700 800 900
    ModeLine "1024x768"  100 1024 1100 1200 1300 768 800 900 1000
    ModeLine "1152x864"  100 1152 1200 1300 1400 864 900 1000 1100
    ModeLine "1152x900"  100 1152 1200 1300 1400 900 1000 1100 1200
    ModeLine "1280x1024"  100 1280 1300 1400 1500 1024 1100 1200 1300
./xorg.conf lines 72-94/150 70%
```

Shell No. 2   Shell No. 3

As with most Linux services, these are text-based files that can be modified with a simple text editor such as vi. However, I strongly suggest that you *do not* do this. These configuration files are very complex and a simple mistake can damage your hardware. You should instead use the configuration utility that came with your distribution to configure your X Server settings. On SUSE Linux, you can use the Graphics Card and Monitor YaST module, shown in Figure 12-33.

As you can see in Figure 12-33, this module allows you to configure your video board's make and model, your monitor parameters, your screen resolution, your color depth, your keyboard layout, and your mouse type. If your system isn't currently running in graphical mode, you can run **yast2** from the shell prompt and access the Graphics Card and Monitor module there. This is shown in Figure 12-34.

You can also access the configuration module directly by simply running **sax2** from the shell prompt.

On a Fedora system, you use the following shell commands to configure your X Server system:

- **system-config-display** Runs the Display Settings utility that you can use to configure your video board, monitor type, resolution, and color depth, as shown in Figure 12-35.

FIGURE 12-33

The YaST Graphics Card and Monitor module

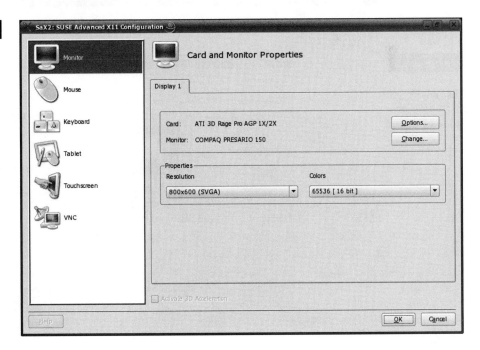

FIGURE 12-34

Running the YaST
Graphics Card
and Monitor
module in text
mode

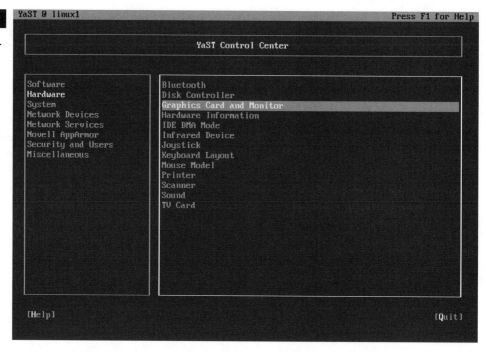

FIGURE 12-35

Using system-
config-display on
Fedora

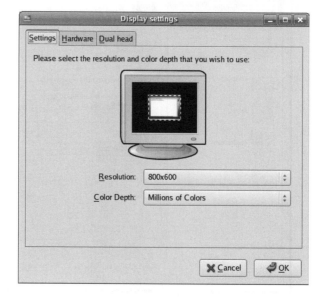

- **system-config-keyboard**   Runs the Keyboard utility, which allows you to select your keyboard layout.
- **system-config-mouse**   Runs the Mouse utility, which allows you to configure your mouse.

Be aware that the tools just mentioned are distribution-specific. You can't use YaST on Fedora (yet), nor can you use system-config-display on SUSE Linux. To provide cross-distribution functionality, X Windows and XFree86 provide several generic configuration utilities that you can also use to configure your X Server settings. On X Windows, you can use the xorgconfig utility in a text-based environment to configure your video board, monitor, resolution, color depth, and so on. This utility is shown in Figure 12-36.

The great thing about xorgconfig is that it tries to automatically detect your hardware for you. If you're a little hazy about what exactly is installed in the system, this can be a real lifesaver. In fact, if you enter **Xorg –configure** at the shell prompt, this utility will automatically detect all of your hardware and create a configuration file named /etc/X11/xorg.conf.new for you. You can then review the file and, if it looks to be correct, rename it as xorg.conf to use the new configuration.

X Windows also proves a graphical version of the xorgconfig utility that is launched by entering **xorgcfg** from the shell prompt. This utility diagrams your monitor, video board, keyboard, and mouse, as shown in Figure 12-37.

FIGURE 12-36

Using the
xorgconfig utility

```
N    (●) SUSE Linux 10.1




First specify a mouse protocol type. Choose one from the following list:

   1.  Auto [Auto detect]
   2.  SysMouse [SysMouse]
   3.  MouseSystems [Mouse Systems (3-button protocol)]
   4.  PS/2 [PS/2 Mouse]
   5.  Microsoft [Microsoft compatible (2-button protocol)]
   6.  Busmouse [Bus Mouse]
   7.  IMPS/2 [IntelliMouse PS/2]
   8.  ExplorerPS/2 [Explorer PS/2]
   9.  GlidePointPS/2 [GlidePoint PS/2]
  10.  MouseManPlusPS/2 [MouseManPlus PS/2]
  11.  NetMousePS/2 [NetMouse PS/2]
  12.  NetScrollPS/2 [NetScroll PS/2]
  13.  ThinkingMousePS/2 [ThinkingMouse PS/2]
  14.  AceCad [AceCad]

The recommended protocol is Auto. If you have a very old mouse
or don't want OS support or auto detection, and you have a two-button
or three-button serial mouse, it is most likely of type Microsoft.

Enter a protocol number: _
```

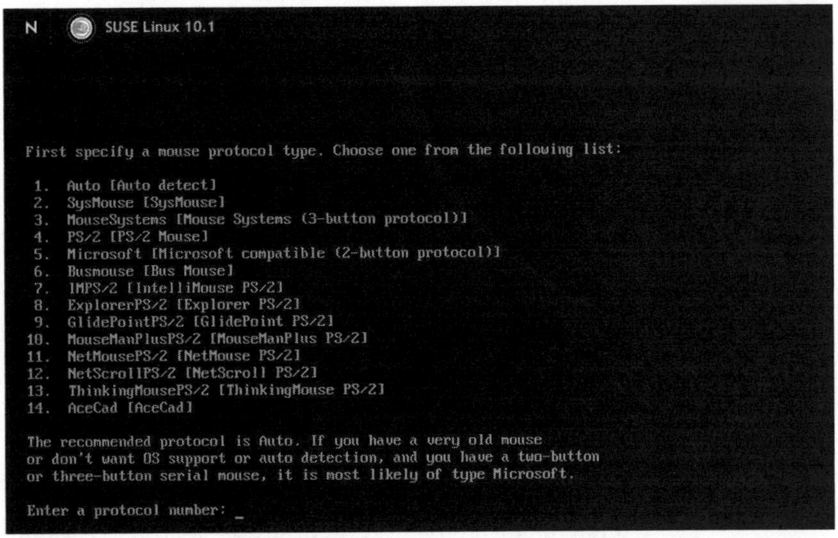

FIGURE 12-37

Using xorgcfg

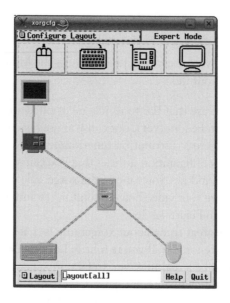

To modify a component, right-click on the appropriate icon and select Configure. If your distribution uses the XFree86 X Server, then you can use the following utilities to accomplish the same tasks:

■ **XFree-86 –configure**   Detects your hardware and creates a file named /etc/X11/XF86Config.new that you can rename to XF86Config.

■ **xf86config**   A text-based X Server configuration utility.

■ **xf86cfg**   A graphical X Server configuration utility.

After making any changes to your X Server configuration, keep the following in mind:

■ The configuration utility will prompt you to test the new settings to make sure they work. You should always do this. It will save a ton of time if you've made a mistake somewhere in the configuration.

■ After testing the configuration, you must restart your X Server to apply the changes. The easiest way to do this is to simply log out and then log back in.

■ If something is misconfigured and your X Server software gets hung, you can kill it by pressing CTRL-ALT-BACKSPACE.

■ If you want to fine-tune your X Server configuration, run the **xvidtune** utility from the shell prompt. This utility allows you to customize your monitor's horizontal and vertical synchronization. However, do so with extreme caution. Remember that using sync parameters that are beyond the monitor's capabilities will eventually fry it.

■ If you're in runlevel 3 and want to start the Linux GUI, simply enter **startx** at the shell prompt.

With this in mind, let's finish the chapter by discussing how to specify a particular window manager or desktop environment.

Specifying a Window Manager and Desktop Environment

Remember that we said the window manager and desktop environment components used by your Linux system are modular. You can try out the various window managers and desktop environments to see which one suits you. To do this, do the following:

1. Use the rpm utility (or other package installation utility) to install the window managers or desktop environments you want to try.

2. When complete, log out. In your login screen, you should see an option called Session Type. When you select this option, a list of window managers and desktop environments installed on the system is displayed. Select the window manager or desktop environment you want to use.

At this point, your system will load with the window manager or desktop environment you specified. If you like what you see, you can make it permanent. If your system boots to runlevel 3 by default and you use the startx command to load the Linux GUI, then you need to locate a hidden file named .xinitrc in your user's home directory (using ls –a). Open this file in a text editor and locate the line that reads "exec $WINDOWMANAGER," shown in Figure 12-38.

Replace $WINDOWMANAGER with the name of the window manager or desktop environment you want to use. Use the following:

■ KDE: **startkde**
■ GNOME: **gnome-session**
■ fvwm: **fvwm**
■ Window Maker: **wmaker**
■ Sawfish: **sawfish**
■ Tab Window Manager: **twm**

Save the file and run **startx**.

FIGURE 12-38

Editing the
.xinitrc file

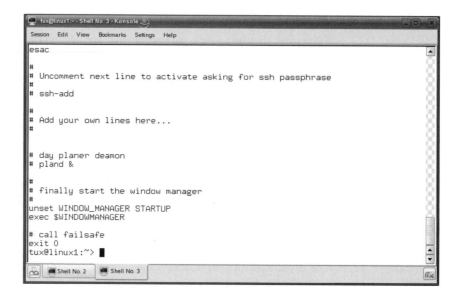

```
esac

#
# Uncomment next line to activate asking for ssh passphrase
#
# ssh-add

#
# Add your own lines here...
#


# day planer deamon
# pland &

#
# finally start the window manager
#
unset WINDOW_MANAGER STARTUP
exec $WINDOWMANAGER

# call failsafe
exit 0
tux@linux1:~>
```

If your system boots into runlevel 5 by default, then you make the same changes
to the .Xsession, .Xdefaults, or .Xclients file in your home directory, whichever one
is used by your particular distribution.

That's it for this chapter. Let's review what you learned.

SCENARIO & SOLUTION

You are configuring your GUI environment. You decide to use the Tab Window Manager (twm) without a desktop environment. Can you do this?	Yes, the desktop environment is optional. You can use a window manager such as twm alone.
You are implementing a new Linux system and need to configure your X Windows software. You open /etc/X11/xorg.conf in vi to do this. Are you following a proper procedure?	No, you really should avoid directly editing X Server configuration files. A small mistake can potentially damage your video hardware. Instead, you should use a configuration utility.
You've just installed a Fedora system and need to configure the video board, monitor, resolution, and color depth. What command should you enter at the shell prompt?	You would enter **system-config-display**.

CERTIFICATION SUMMARY

In this chapter, you learned how to manage and configure the hardware in your Linux system. We began by discussing how to configure kernel modules to enable the hardware in your system. We related that drivers are small programs that are loaded into RAM that enable the CPU to communicate with a particular hardware component. For basic components, this software is provided by the BIOS. For other components, the driver is stored on the hard disk and must be loaded into RAM by the operating system kernel.

On Linux, drivers can be loaded in two ways. First, they can be loaded as kernel modules after the operating system has started. Second, they can be compiled directly into the kernel itself. We related that, as a general rule of thumb, only drivers needed to boot the system should be compiled directly into the kernel. Drivers for other hardware should be loaded as kernel modules. This will keep your kernel lean and trim.

We then reviewed some of the tools you can use to view information about the hardware in your Linux system. Within the /proc directory, you can view hardware information in the following files and directories:

- cpuinfo
- devices
- dma
- interrupt
- iomem
- modules
- version
- /scsi/
- /bus/devices
- /ide/

You can also use the following command-line tools to view information about the hardware in your system:

- hdparm –a /dev/*device*
- sg_scan
- scsiinfo –l
- pnpdump
- lsusb

We then turned our attention to the shell commands that you can use to manage kernel modules. These include the following:

- **lsmod**   Views loaded kernel modules.
- **modinfo**   Views module information.
- **depmod**   Builds a module dependency list.
- **insmod**   Installs a kernel module, but doesn't factor in module dependencies.
- **modprobe**   Installs or removes a kernel module while taking module dependencies into account.
- **rmmod**   Removes a kernel module.

We pointed out that modprobe is run each time the system boots. It uses /etc/modprobe.conf to determine which kernel modules should be loaded at startup.

At this point, we shifted gears and talked about configuring power management in your Linux system. We reviewed the two management standards that have been used in PC systems. Advanced Power Management (APM) is an older standard that used the BIOS to manage power to hardware in the system. Today, most PCs use Advanced Configuration and Power Interface (ACPI). ACPI divides power management tasks between the BIOS and the operating system.

We then spent some time discussing how to configure ACPI on a Linux system. We pointed out that most distributions should automatically detect whether or not your motherboard supports ACPI during installation and enable ACPI support in the kernel. If not, you can add the acpi=on command to the kernel line in your GRUB configuration file. Once enabled, you can use either the acpid or the powersaved daemon to manage power in your system using rules you specify in the appropriate configuration file.

Next, we discussed how to burn CDs and DVDs on Linux. We pointed out that you can use the cdrecord command to burn CDs from the Linux command line. First, you enter **cdrecord –scanbus** to identify your burner hardware. Then you use the mkisofs command to create an .iso image file that contains all of the files you want to burn to the disc. Once created, you should mount the .iso file and review its contents to verify that the .iso file was created correctly. Then you use the cdrecord command to burn the .iso file to a recordable optical disc.

Next, we introduced you to the concept of RAID. We pointed out that RAID groups multiple disks together into an array using a RAID controller card or through software stored in RAM. To the operating system, the RAID array appears to be a single hard drive. RAID uses the following strategies to create arrays:

■ **Striping** Data is divided into chunks called stripes and saved on all the disks in the array. Striping significantly increases the speed of read and write operations. However, a failed disk in the array will corrupt all data in the array.

■ **Mirroring** Data is written redundantly to all of the drives in the array. Each drive contains exactly the same data. If one of the drives in the array fails, the other drives in the array can take over. Mirroring does not increase performance, however.

■ **Parity** Parity stores information on one or more drives in the array. If one drive fails, the data it contained can be reconstructed from the parity information.

We then reviewed some of the more commonly used RAID levels, such as RAID 0, RAID 1, RAID 3, and RAID 5. We also discussed nested RAID levels such as RAID 1+0, RAID 0+1, RAID 5+0, and RAID 5+1. We pointed out that one RAID level isn't inherently better than any other RAID level. You should review the strengths and weaknesses of each level to determine the one best suited to a particular implementation.

We also pointed out that RAID can be implemented using hardware RAID controllers or by using software included with most operating systems. Hardware RAID creates arrays from hard disks. Software RAID creates arrays from partitions on hard disks. Each option has advantages and disadvantages. We then presented the process you would follow to create a software RAID array.

We ended the chapter by discussing how to configure X Windows on your system. We pointed out that your Linux graphical environment is composed of the following components:

■ X Server
■ Window manager
■ Desktop environment

Each of these components is modular. You can choose from a variety of packages to customize your graphical environment to suit your tastes. We spent the rest of the chapter discussing how to configure your X Server software and your window manager. We pointed out that you should avoid directly editing your X Server configuration file. Instead, you should use a configuration utility to avoid mistakes that could potentially damage your hardware. Depending on your distribution, you can use one of the following utilities:

- YaST
- system-config-display
- system-config-keyboard
- system-config-mouse
- xorgconfig or xorgcfg
- xf86config or xf86cfg
- xvidtune

To specify your default window manager, you need to edit a hidden configuration file in your user's home directory. The name of the file depends on your distribution and your default runlevel:

- .xinitrc (runlevel 3)
- .Xsession (runlevel 5)
- .Xdefaults (runlevel 5)
- .Xclients (runlevel 5)

✓ TWO-MINUTE DRILL

Manage Hardware and Kernel Modules

❑ Drivers are small programs that are loaded into RAM that enable the CPU to communicate with a particular hardware component.

❑ For basic system components, driver software is stored in the BIOS.

❑ Other components require that a driver that is stored on the hard disk be loaded into RAM.

❑ On Linux, drivers can be loaded in two ways:

  ❑ Loaded as kernel modules after the operating system has started.

  ❑ Compiled directly into the kernel itself.

❑ You can view information about your system hardware within the /proc directory.

❑ You can use the following command-line tools to view information about the hardware in your system:

  ❑ hdparm –a /dev/device

  ❑ sg_scan

  ❑ scsiinfo –l

  ❑ pnpdump

  ❑ lsusb

❑ You can use the following command-line utilities to manage kernel modules:

  ❑ **lsmod**   Views loaded kernel modules.

  ❑ **modinfo**   Views module information.

  ❑ **depmod**   Builds a module dependency list.

  ❑ **insmod**   Installs a kernel module, but doesn't factor in module dependencies.

  ❑ **modprobe**   Installs or removes a kernel module while taking module dependencies into account.

  ❑ **rmmod**   Removes a kernel module.

❑ modprobe uses the /etc/modprobe.conf file to determine which kernel modules should be loaded at boot.

Configure Power Management

❑ Advanced Power Management (APM) is an older standard that used the BIOS to manage power to hardware in the system.

❑ Today, most PCs use Advanced Configuration and Power Interface (ACPI).

❑ ACPI divides power management tasks between the BIOS and the operating system.

❑ Linux automatically detects whether or not your motherboard supports ACPI during installation and enables ACPI support in the kernel.

❑ You can add the acpi=on command to the kernel line in your GRUB configuration file to manually enable ACPI support.

❑ You can use either the acpid or the powersaved daemon to configure power management using rules you specify in the appropriate configuration file.

Burn CDs and DVDs

❑ You can use the cdrecord command to burn CDs from the Linux command line.

❑ You can enter **cdrecord –scanbus** to identify your burner hardware.

❑ Use the mkisofs command to create an .iso image file that contains all of the files you want to burn to the disc.

❑ You should mount the .iso file you created and verify that it was created correctly.

❑ Use the cdrecord command to burn the .iso file to a recordable optical disc.

❑ You can also use a wide variety of graphical utilities, such as K3b, to burn CDs and DVDs.

Implement RAID

❑ RAID groups multiple disks together into an array using a RAID controller card or through software stored in RAM.

❑ The RAID array is presented to the operating system as a single hard drive.

❑ RAID uses the following strategies:
  ❑ Striping
  ❑ Mirroring
  ❑ Parity

❑ RAID implements these strategies in levels.

❑ Some of the more commonly used RAID levels include the following:

    ❑ **RAID 0** Striping

    ❑ **RAID 1** Mirroring

    ❑ **RAID 3** Parity

    ❑ **RAID 5** Parity

    ❑ **RAID 0+1** Mirroring two or more RAID 0 arrays.

    ❑ **RAID 1+0** Striping two or more RAID 1 arrays.

    ❑ **RAID 5+0** Striping two or more RAID 5 arrays.

    ❑ **RAID 5+1** Mirroring two or more RAID 5 arrays.

❑ One RAID level isn't inherently better than any other RAID level.

❑ RAID can be implemented using hardware RAID controllers or by using software included with most operating systems.

❑ Hardware RAID creates arrays from hard disks.

❑ Software RAID creates arrays from partitions on hard disks.

Configure X Windows

❑ The Linux graphical environment is composed of the following components:

    ❑ X Server

    ❑ Window manager

    ❑ Desktop environment

❑ You can choose from a variety of packages to customize your graphical environment.

❑ You should use a configuration utility to configure your X Server software to avoid mistakes that could potentially damage your hardware.

❑ You can use one of the following utilities to configure your X Server software:

    ❑ YaST

    ❑ system-config-display

    ❑ system-config-keyboard

    ❑ system-config-mouse

    ❑ xorgconfig or xorgcfg

❑ xf86config or xf86cfg

❑ xvidtune

❑ You can edit a hidden configuration file in your user's home directory to specify your default window manager:

❑ .xinitrc (runlevel 3)

❑ .Xsession (runlevel 5)

❑ .Xdefaults (runlevel 5)

❑ .Xclients (runlevel 5)

SELF TEST

Manage Hardware and Kernel Modules

1. You've just installed an older ISA network board in your Linux system. The kernel did not automatically detect the new device. How can you load a driver for this network board? (Choose two.)

   A. Load the appropriate driver from the BIOS.

   B. Insert the appropriate kernel module.

   C. Recompile the kernel and configure it to support the board.

   D. Load a Windows driver for the board using emulation mode.

   E. Embed the driver within a ROM chip on the board itself.

2. In which directory would you find your kernel modules?

   A. /lib/modules/*version*/kernel/drivers

   B. /lib/modules/*version*/drivers

   C. /boot/

   D. /usr/modules/*version*/drivers/kernel

3. In which directory would you find information about how IRQ channels have been assigned in your system?

   A. /proc/devices

   B. /proc/dma

   C. /proc/interrupt

   D. /proc/iomem

4. You need to get specific information about the IDE hard drive in your system. Which command could you use from the shell prompt to do this?

   A. hddump

   B. lsusb

   C. sg_scan

   D. hdparm

5. Which commands can be used to insert a kernel module? (Choose two.)

   A. insmod

   B. modinfo

   C. modprobe

   D. rmmod

   E. depmod

Configure Power Management

6. In which power management state are the contents of the CPU registers and the system RAM saved into a file on the hard drive?
   - A. Hibernation
   - B. Working
   - C. Stand-by
   - D. Ready

7. Which option can you add to the kernel line in your GRUB configuration file to enable ACPI support in the Linux kernel?
   - A. –acpi on
   - B. acpi=on
   - C. apm=on
   - D. set acpi on

8. Which command will put your system into Hibernation?
   - A. acpitool –S
   - B. acpitool –H
   - C. acpitool –s
   - D. acpitool –S4

9. Which command will put your system into Stand-by?
   - A. powersave –e 1
   - B. powersave –S
   - C. powersave –S1
   - D. powersave –m

Burn CDs and DVDs

10. You run cdrecord –scanbus and the following optical burning drive was detected: *1,2,0 2) 'Sony' 'DRU-120A' '1.26' Removable CD-ROM*. What is the SCSI ID assigned to this device?
    - A. 0
    - B. 2
    - C. 3
    - D. 4

11. Which command will create an .iso file in /tmp named backup.iso that will contain all of the files and subdirectories in /home using Rock Ridge naming and a volume label of HOMEBAK?

    A. mkisofs –o /tmp/backup.iso –J –V HOMEBAK /home/

    B. mkisofs –o /tmp/backup.iso –r –V HOMEBAK /home/

    C. mkisofs –o /tmp/backup.iso –r /home/

    D. mkisofs –o /tmp/backup.iso –r –V HOMEBAK

12. Which command will burn an .iso file in /tmp named backup.iso to a disc in an optical burning drive that has a SCSI ID of 2 on the first SCSI controller in your system?

    A. cdrecord dev=0,2,0 /tmp/backup.iso

    B. cdrecord dev=1,2,0 /tmp/backup.iso

    C. cdrecord dev=1,0,2 /tmp/backup.iso

    D. cdrecord –dev 0,2,0 /tmp/backup.iso

Implement RAID

13. Which RAID strategy writes data to two or more hard disks redundantly?

    A. Striping

    B. Parity

    C. Mirroring

    D. Nested RAID

14. You have three hard drives in your Linux system available for a RAID array. Which RAID levels can you use with three drives? (Choose two.)

    A. RAID 0

    B. RAID 5

    C. RAID 0+1

    D. RAID 1+0

    E. RAID 5+1

15. Which RAID levels use parity? (Choose two.)

    A. RAID 0

    B. RAID 1

    C. RAID 3

    D. RAID 5

    E. RAID 0+1

Configure X Windows

16. Which of the following draws graphical windows on the display?

A. KDE

B. fvwm

C. sawfish

D. X Windows

17. Your Linux system uses X Windows as its X Server. Which configuration file is used to configure this service?

A. /etc/X11/XF86Config

B. /etc/X11/xwindows.conf

C. /etc/X11/XFree86.conf

D. /etc/X11/xorg.conf

18. Which utility could you use on a Fedora Linux system to configure X Windows? (Choose two.)

A. system-config-display

B. xf86config

C. YaST

D. xorgcfg

E. xf86cfg

19. Your system is configured to boot to runlevel 3 by default. You use the startx command to start your graphical environment. What file can you edit in your home directory to specify your default window manager?

A. .xinitrc

B. .Xsession

C. .Xdefaults

D. .Xclients

LAB QUESTION

You've just installed three additional 200GB hard disks in your SUSE Linux system for editing digital videos. You want to use these disks to create a RAID array. This array needs to provide the performance provided by striping, but still provide a degree of fault tolerance. Outline the process you would go through to do this.

SELF TEST ANSWERS

Manage Hardware and Kernel Modules

1. ☑ **B** and **C.** You can insert the appropriate kernel module or you can recompile the kernel and include support for the board.
   ☒ **A, D,** and **E** are incorrect. **A** is incorrect because drivers for devices like network boards are not in the BIOS. **D** is incorrect because Windows drivers don't work on Linux. **E** is incorrect because drivers aren't stored in ROM chips on the device.

2. ☑ **A.** Your kernel modules are stored in /lib/modules/*version*/kernel/drivers.
   ☒ **B, C,** and **D** are incorrect. **B** and **C** use invalid paths. **D** is incorrect because kernel modules aren't stored in /boot.

3. ☑ **C.** Information about IRQ assignments are found in /proc/interrupt.
   ☒ **A, B,** and **D** are incorrect. **A** stores information about your hardware devices. **B** stores DMA information. **D** stores I/O port assignments.

4. ☑ **D.** The hdparm utility can be used to get hard disk information.
   ☒ **A, B,** and **C** are incorrect. **A** is an invalid command. **B** displays a list of USB devices connected to the system. **C** scans your SCSI bus.

5. ☑ **A** and **C.** You can use insmod or modprobe to insert a kernel module.
   ☒ **B, D,** and **E** are incorrect. **B** is used to display module information. **D** is used to remove a kernel module. **E** generates a list of module dependencies.

Configure Power Management

6. ☑ **A.** The Hibernation power management state writes the contents of your CPU registers and system RAM to a file on the hard drive.
   ☒ **B, C,** and **D** are incorrect. **B** and **D** are incorrect. Working and Ready are the same default state when the system is running normally. **C** is incorrect because Stand-by doesn't use a hibernation file.

7. ☑ **B.** The acpi=on option enables ACPI support in the kernel.
   ☒ **A, C,** and **D** are incorrect. **A** and **D** use incorrect syntax. **C** enables APM, not ACPI.

8. ☑ **A.** The acpitool –S command puts the system into the Hibernation sleep mode.
   ☒ **B, C,** and **D** are incorrect. **B** and **D** use incorrect syntax. **C** puts the system into the Suspend sleep state.

9. ☑ **D.** The powersave –m command will put the system into the Stand-by state.
   ☒ **A, B,** and **C** are incorrect. **A** specifies that the system use power scheme 1. **B** detects whether the system supports APM or ACPI. **C** uses incorrect syntax.

Burn CDs and DVDs

10. ☑ **B.** The burner drive uses SCSI ID 2.
☒ **A, C,** and **D** are incorrect. **A, C,** and **D** are SCSI IDs not used by the device.

11. ☑ **B.** The mkisofs –o /tmp/backup.iso –r –V HOMEBAK /home/ command will create an .iso file in /tmp named backup.iso that contains all of the files and subdirectories in /home using Rock Ridge naming and a volume label of HOMEBAK.
☒ **A, C,** and **D** are incorrect. **A** specifies Joliet instead of Rock Ridge support. **C** omits the volume label. **D** omits the path for files to be included in the .iso file.

12. ☑ **A.** The cdrecord dev=0,2,0 /tmp/backup.iso command will burn an .iso file in /tmp named backup.iso to a disc in an optical burning drive that has a SCSI ID of 2 on the first SCSI controller in the system.
☒ **B, C,** and **D** are incorrect. **B** specifies a device on the second SCSI controller in the system. **C** specifies a SCSI device with an ID of 5. **D** uses incorrect syntax.

Implement RAID

13. ☑ **C.** Mirroring writes data to two or more hard disks redundantly.
☒ **A, B,** and **D** are incorrect. **A** stripes data across multiple drives. **B** stores data reconstruction information on one or more drives in the array. **D** involves using two RAID levels in tandem.

14. ☑ **A** and **B.** You can use three drives in a RAID 0 or a RAID 5 array.
☒ **C, D,** and **E** are incorrect. **C** and **D** require a minimum of four drives. **E** requires a minimum of six drives.

15. ☑ **C** and **D.** RAID 3 and RAID 5 use parity to reconstruct data should a drive in the array fail.
☒ **A, B,** and **E** are incorrect. **A** uses striping, but not parity. **B** uses mirroring, but not parity. **E** uses striping and mirroring, but not parity.

Configure X Windows

16. ☑ **D.** X Windows is an X Server and draws graphical windows on the display.
☒ **A, B,** and **C** are incorrect. **A** is incorrect because KDE is a desktop environment. **B** and **C** are window managers.

17. ☑ **D.** X Windows uses the /etc/X11/xorg.conf configuration file.
☒ **A, B,** and **C** are incorrect. **A** is the configuration file for the XFree86 X Server. **B** and **C** are invalid files.

18. ☑ **A** and **D.** The system-config-display and the xorgcfg utilities can be used to configure X Windows on a Fedora Linux system.

    ☒ **B, C,** and **E** are incorrect. **B** and **E** are used by the XFree86 X Server. **C** is used on SUSE Linux systems.

19. ☑ **A.** The .xinitrc file in your home directory is used to specify your default window manager when the startx command is used.

    ☒ **B, C,** and **D** are incorrect. Each of these files is used when booting into runlevel 5.

LAB ANSWER

The first thing you need to decide is what RAID level you want to implement. Given the specifications listed here, RAID 5 would be a great choice. Data is striped across three or more drives in an array. Parity information is evenly distributed among all the drives in the array, providing a degree of fault tolerance.

Next, you need to determine how you will create the array. You could purchase a RAID board that supports RAID 5 or you could implement software RAID. In this scenario, a software RAID approach may be most appropriate due to the lower cost.

After making this decision, you would next need to boot the system. Create a directory in your file system where you want the array to be mounted, such as /mnt/raid. Then run your partition management utility. You should create a partition on each drive that spans the entire disk. The partitions should use a partition type of *0xFD Linux RAID* and not be formatted with any file system. Next, you would create a new RAID 5 device and specify that each of the new partitions be included within it. Specify your file system type, such as ext3 or Reiser, your stripe size, and your mount point to finish creating the array.

13

Configuring
Network Boards

U p to this point in this book, we've been focusing on configuring and using Linux as a standalone computer system. However, Linux also works extremely well in a networked environment. Unlike many operating systems, where networking is an afterthought, the Linux operating system was designed from the ground up with networking in mind.

One of the things that I love about Linux is the fact that you can take just about any distribution and configure it to fill a wide variety of roles on your computer network, all for little or no cost. For example, you can configure a Linux system as the following:

- A networked workstation
- A file and print server
- A database server
- A DHCP server
- A DNS server
- A gateway router
- A packet-filtering firewall
- A stateful firewall
- An application-level firewall

Isn't Linux fantastic? With other operating systems, you have to pay a lot of money to get this kind of functionality. With Linux, you've got just about everything you need to set up a very complex network. In this chapter, we're going to focus on enabling basic networking on your Linux system. In the next chapter, we'll discuss how to set up a variety of Linux services.

INSIDE THE EXAM

Configuring Network Boards

Be sure you are very comfortable with Linux networking basics before taking your Linux+ exam. The exam assumes you have a solid understanding of the Internet Protocol (IP). Be sure you understand how IP addressing works. You should be able to look at any given IP address and identify it as a class A, B, or C address. You should also be able to identify the network and node portions of the address using the subnet mask. You should know what the DNS server and default gateway router addresses are used for when configuring IP on a Linux system.

You should also know how to install a network interface in the system, including an Ethernet card and a modem. You should know how to use the ifconfig command to manage the network interfaces installed in your system. You should also know how to use the ping, netstat, and traceroute commands from the shell prompt to check the functionality of your network configuration. Finally, you should know to configure your Linux system as a router, connecting two different network segments.

Let's begin this chapter by discussing how to configure a network interface in your system.

CERTIFICATION OBJECTIVE 13.01

Configure a Network Interface

Obviously, before you can configure your Linux system to participate on a computer network, you have to first install some kind of network interface and then configure it to work on your particular network. Back in the old days of networking, there were a variety of network interfaces and network protocols that you could choose from to do this. For your network interface, you could select from the following:

- ARCnet
- Token Ring
- Ethernet

For protocols, you could choose from the Internetwork Packet Exchange (IPX) protocol or the Internet Protocol (IP) as well as some upper-layer protocols such as NetBIOS.

Today, ARCnet has completely disappeared from the network scene. I doubt you will ever encounter an ARCnet network. Likewise, Token Ring has almost disappeared, although you may find it still deployed on a very few networks. By far and away, most of the networks you will work with will be Ethernet networks.

The same holds true with networking protocols. There was a time when many networks ran the IPX protocol. Today, however, IPX has almost disappeared. If you're going to be working with a modern network, you will more than likely be working with the IP protocol.

In light of this situation, the Linux+ exam is heavily focused on using Ethernet boards configured with the IP protocol in Linux systems. We're going to spend the first part of this chapter learning how to do this. Let's begin by reviewing how the IP protocol works.

An Overview of the IP Protocol

For your Linux+ exam, you need to be proficient with the basics of the IP protocol. While not directly covered in the Linux+ objectives, the exam assumes that you know what an IP address is, what a subnet mask is, and how to configure the protocol such that a system can participate on the network. To make sure you have the information you need, we're going to briefly review IP addressing in this part of this chapter. We'll cover the following topics:

- What is a protocol?
- How IP addresses work
- How the subnet mask works
- Specifying the DNS server and default gateway router addresses

on the
Ĵob

This part of the chapter is intended only as a quick review. I'm assuming you already have some background with these topics. If you have no background whatsoever with networking hardware or protocols, you should purchase a book that covers the basics of networking and read it before attempting to take your Linux+ exam.

Let's begin by discussing what a protocol is.

What Is a Protocol?

So what exactly is a *protocol*? Strictly speaking, a protocol is a set of rules, and in the context of networking, a protocol is the set of rules that govern communication between two systems. A good analogy for a protocol is a human language. Before two people can communicate, they must speak the same language; otherwise, no information can be transferred between them. For example, suppose you were to call someone on the phone who doesn't speak your language. Even though they have picked up the receiver and are listening to the information you are sending, they don't understand what you are saying. Why? It's because you don't share a common language.

The same holds true with computer systems. Before they can share information, they must be configured to use the same language. Instead of calling it a "language," however, we call it a "protocol." The protocol specifies how the information is encoded and sent on the network so that that receiving system can interpret it and reconstruct the data that was originally sent.

As discussed previously, there are many different protocols you can use on a computer network. However, for your Linux+ exam, you need to be familiar with the IP protocol, which is the networking protocol used on the Internet. IP works in conjunction with other protocols, such as the Transmission Control Protocol (TCP) or the User Datagram Protocol (UDP) to divide information being transmitted on the network into chunks called *packets*. The IP protocol itself is used to only make sure each packet arrives at the destination system. The TCP or UDP protocol is used with IP to fragment the data from the sending host and then reassemble and re-sequence it when it arrives at the destination system. This is shown in Figure 13-1.

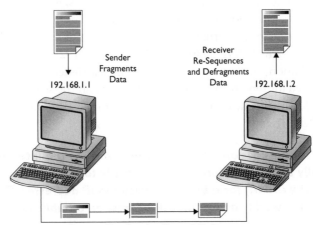

FIGURE 13-1

Transferring data with the IP protocol

To make all of this work, you need to assign each host on the network an IP address. Let's discuss how this is done next.

How IP Addresses Work

It's critical that you understand that every host on an IP-based network must have a *unique* IP address assigned to it. No two hosts on the same IP network can have the same IP address assigned.

The IP address is different than the MAC address. The MAC address is a hardware address that is burned into a ROM chip on every network board sold in the world. The MAC address is hard-coded and it can't be changed.

An IP address, on the other hand, is *logically* assigned to a host. That means you can assign any address to any host that you want. The assignment is not permanent. It can be changed at any time.

on the **Job**

The ARP protocol is used to map logical IP addresses assigned to systems to their hard-coded MAC addresses.

An IP address consists of four numbers, separated by periods. In decimal notation, each number must be between 0 and 255. For example, 192.168.1.1 is a typical IP address. Each number in the address is actually an 8-bit binary number called an *octet*. Because each octet is a binary number, it can be represented as 0's and 1's. For example, the address 192.168.1.1 can be represented in binary form as:

```
11000000.10101000.00000001.00000001
```

Some IP addresses are reserved and can't be assigned to a host. For example, the last octet in a host IP address can't be a 0. This is reserved for the address of the network segment itself that the host resides on. For example, the network address for the host assigned an IP address of 192.168.1.1 is 192.168.1.0.

In addition, the last octet of an IP address assigned to a host can't be 255. This is reserved for sending a broadcast to all hosts on the segment. In the preceding example, the broadcast address for a host with an IP address of 192.168.1.1 would be 192.168.1.255.

on the **Job**

If the host resides on a public network, such as the Internet, it must use a globally unique IP address. You can apply to the Internet Assigned Numbers Authority (IANA) for a block of registered IP addresses. Once assigned, no one else in the world can use that IP address on a public network.

In addition to assigning an IP address, you also need to assign a subnet mask when configuring the IP protocol on a Linux system. Let's discuss how this is done next.

How the Subnet Mask Works

If you've ever configured a system with an IP address, you probably noticed that you also had to assign a *subnet mask*. Have you ever wondered what this parameter is? Well, now is the time to learn.

To understand how a subnet mask works, you first need to understand that IP addresses are divided into two parts:

- Network address
- Node address

Part of the address is used to identify the network the host resides on. The rest uniquely identifies the particular host (node) on the network. Every system on the same network segment must have exactly the same numbers in the network portion of the address. However, they each must have a unique node portion. This is shown in Figure 13-2.

How much of the address is used for the network and how much is used for the node is defined by the subnet mask. Typical subnet masks include the following:

```
255.0.0.0
255.255.0.0
255.255.255.0
```

Any octet with a 255 in it indicates that that portion of the IP address is used for the network address. Remember that the operating system sees IP addresses in binary form. It also sees subnet masks in binary form as well. If you have an IP address of 192.168.1.1 and a subnet mask of 255.255.255.0, the subnet mask specifies that the first three octets of the address is network and the last octet is node. This is shown in Figure 13-3.

192.168.1.1

Network ¦ Node

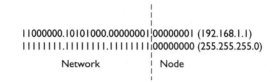

11000000.10101000.00000001!00000001 (192.168.1.1)
11111111.11111111.11111111!00000000 (255.255.255.0)

Network   Node

IP addresses are divided into five different classes. Each address class has its own default subnet mask. For our purposes here, we only need to be concerned with the first three address classes:

- **Class A** The decimal value of the first octet must be between 1 and 126. In a Class A address, the first octet is the network address and the last three octets are the node address. Therefore, the default subnet mask is 255.0.0.0.

- **Class B** The decimal value of the first octet must be between 128 and 191. In a Class B address, the first two octets are the network address and the last two octets are the node address. Therefore, the default subnet mask is 255.255.0.0.

- **Class C** The decimal value of the first octet must be between 192 and 223. In a Class C address, the first three octets are the network address while the last octet is the node address. Therefore, the default subnet mask is 255.255.255.0.

on the
Job
You don't have to use these default subnet masks, however. You could define a subnet mask of 255.255.0.0 for a Class A address, for example. You can also use only part of an octet for the network address. This is called partial subnetting. For example, you could define a subnet mask of 255.255.252.0 for a Class B address. This would cause only the first six of the eight bits in the third octet to be used for the network portion of the address.

The important thing to remember is that, for two hosts on the same network segment to communicate, they need to have exactly the same network address, which means they must have the same subnet mask. For example, suppose you have three systems as shown in Figure 13-4.

Host 1 and Host 2 both have the same network address and subnet mask. These two hosts can communicate on the IP network segment. However, Host 3 uses a subnet mask of 255.255.252.0 instead of 255.255.255.0. Therefore, Host 3 has a different network address than Host 1 and Host 2 and won't be able to communicate with them without the use of a network router.

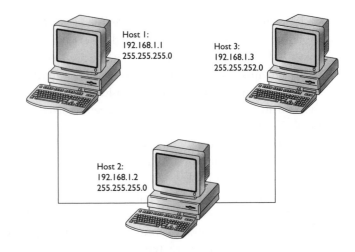

FIGURE 13-4

Hosts with wrong
subnet masks

*Within each address class are blocks of IP addresses that are non-routable,
called* private or reserved IP addresses. *These addresses are unallocated and
can be used by anyone. If you use private addresses, you can connect your
network to networks that require registered IP addresses using a Network
Address Translation (NAT) router. This allows you to use private addresses on
your local network and still be able to connect to the Internet. All traffic from
your private network appears to be originating from the registered IP address
configured on the public side of the NAT router.*
The private IP address ranges are:

10.0.0.0 – 10.255.255.255 (Class A)
172.16.0.0 – 172.31.255.255 (Class B)
192.168.0.0 – 192.168.255.255 (Class C)

Finally, let's discuss the DNS server address and the default gateway router address.

Specifying the DNS Server and Default Gateway Router Addresses

So far, we've discussed the IP address and subnet mask parameters that you need to
specify when configuring the IP stack on a Linux system. However, you should also
specify the DNS server address and the default gateway router address as well.

If you've used the Internet, you know that you can use domain names, such as
www.google.com, to navigate to particular hosts on the Web. However, your
system actually can't work with alphanumeric domain names. It has no idea where
www.google.com is or what it has to offer.

To make this work, your local system needs to resolve domain names into IP addresses. One of the ways this can be done is to submit the domain name to a DNS server. When a DNS server receives a name resolution request, it matches the domain name submitted with an IP address and returns it to the requesting system. Then your system can contact the specified host using its IP address. For example, in Figure 13-5, the domain name www.google.com has been resolved to an IP address of 66.102.7.99 by the DNS server.

To make this system work, you need to provide your system with the IP address of the DNS server you want it to use. We'll spend more time working with DNS in the next chapter of this book.

In addition, you also need to specify the IP address of your network's default gateway router. The IP protocol was designed from the ground up with internetworking in mind. In an internetwork, multiple network segments are connected together using routers. If a system on one segment tries to send data to

---

FIGURE 13-5   Resolving a domain name into an IP address

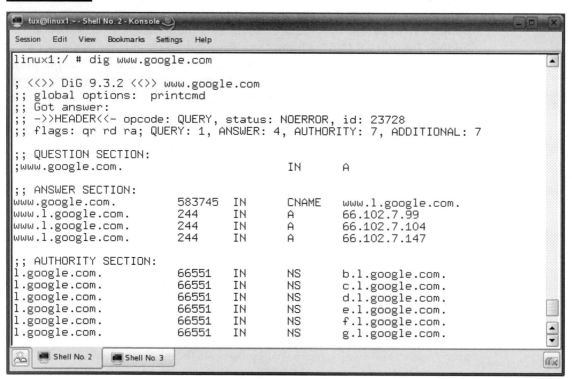

a host that doesn't reside on the same network, the IP protocol will redirect the packets to the default gateway router for its segment. The router will then use a variety of routing protocols to determine where the packets should be sent to get them to their destination. This is shown in Figure 13-6.

In Figure 13-6, the sending system 192.168.1.1 is sending data to 10.0.0.1. However, 10.0.0.1 resides on the 10.0.0.0 network segment, not the 192.168.1.0 network segment. Therefore, the IP stack on the sending system redirects the data to the router connecting the two segments together. The routing software on the router knows where the 10.0.0.0 network segment resides and forwards the packets on to that network where they are delivered to the receiving system.

This system is very powerful. It's what allows you to connect to the Internet and pull down files, such as Web pages, from a server somewhere else in the world. However, for it to work, your local system needs to know the IP address of the router where they should forward packets if they are addressed to a system that doesn't reside on the local network segment. You need to configure this parameter whenever you configure network settings on a Linux system. If you don't, the system will be able to communicate only with systems on the same local network segment.

Now that you understand how the IP protocol works, here are some possible scenario questions and their answers.

SCENARIO & SOLUTION

You need to assign an IP address to a newly installed Linux system in your network. You assign it an IP address of 192.168.1.255 and a subnet mask of 255.255.255.0. Have you configured it correctly?	No, 192.168.1.255 is a reserved address used for sending broadcasts on the local network segment.
Your network has three computers on it. Each one is assigned an IP address of 10.0.0.10 with a subnet mask of 255.0.0.0. Will this configuration work?	No, each host on the network segment must have a unique IP address assigned to it.
Your network has an IP address of 192.168.1.0 and your hosts are assigned IP addresses from 192.168.1.1 to 192.168.1.105. What's the default subnet mask for this network?	This network is a Class C network, so its default subnet mask is 255.255.255.0.
Your Linux workstation has an IP address of 10.0.0.17 and a subnet mask of 255.0.0.0. If you try to access a Web page using a Web browser from a server with an IP address of 172.16.3.1, where will your workstation send the request first?	Because the server doesn't reside on the local network, the IP stack on the Linux system will forward the request to the default gateway router for your network segment.

FIGURE 13-6

Using IP in a
routed network

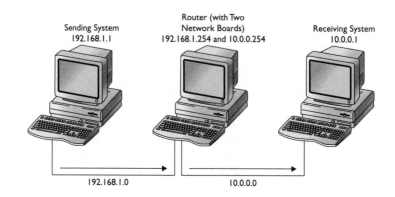

With this background in mind, let's now discuss how to configure an Ethernet interface in a Linux system.

Configuring an Ethernet Interface

One of the most common network interfaces you will work with in a Linux system is an Ethernet interface. To install this type of network interface in your system, you need to complete the following tasks:

■ Installing the Ethernet board
■ Configuring IP parameters

Let's begin by discussing how to install an Ethernet board in your system.

Installing the Ethernet Board

Obviously, the first thing you need to do when configuring an Ethernet interface is to install the card in the system. To do this, complete the following:

1. Power your system off.
2. Install your Ethernet board in an available expansion slot.
3. Connect the Ethernet board to your network switch or hub with a drop cable.
4. Power your system back on. If you installed a PCI Ethernet board, your Linux operating system will probably detect it as it boots. However, this will not always happen. Here are some general guidelines to keep in mind:

■ **PCI Ethernet Boards** If Linux recognizes the board, it will load the appropriate kernel module for you automatically. If not, you may have to download the appropriate module from the board manufacturer's Web site and load it manually.

■ **ISA Ethernet Boards** Linux probably won't automatically detect your board. You'll most likely need to manually load the appropriate kernel module using modprobe. You'll also need to specify the IRQ and the I/O port used by the board when you load the kernel module.

5. After the system has booted, you should check your /etc/modprobe.conf or /etc/modules.conf file and verify that the appropriate kernel module has been loaded and that an alias has been created for the new board. Ethernet adapters in your Linux system use the following aliases:

■ **eth0** The first Ethernet adapter in your system.

■ **eth1** The second Ethernet adapter in your system.

■ **eth2** The third Ethernet adapter in your system, and so on...

A sample /etc/modules.conf file is shown in Figure 13-7.

As you can see in Figure 13-7, the alias eth0 has been created that uses the pcnet32 kernel module. If this didn't happen automatically, you may need to manually edit this file and create the appropriate alias. If you don't, you'll lose your networking configuration when the system reboots.

FIGURE 13-7 Creating an alias for your Ethernet board

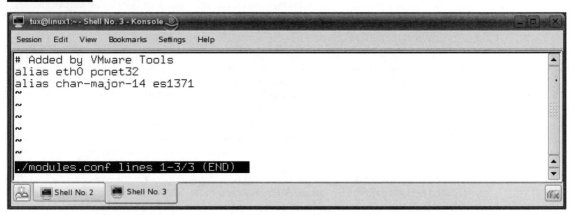

At this point, your network interface is loaded and active. However, before you can use it, you have to configure it with the IP protocol. Let's discuss how this is done next.

Configuring IP Parameters

Remember that you need to configure your network interface with four parameters in order for the system to participate on an IP-based computer network. These include the following:

- IP address
- Subnet mask
- Default gateway router address
- DNS server address

There are two different ways to do this. These are discussed in Table 13-1.

If you want to statically assign IP address parameters to a Linux system, you can use the ifconfig command. If **ifconfig** is entered without any options, it displays the current status of all network interfaces in the system, as shown in Figure 13-8.

TABLE 13-1   IP Address Assignment Options

Option	Description	Advantages	Disadvantages
Static address assignment	In this configuration, you manually configure a network host with IP address parameters.	The address used by a particular host never changes. This option is usually used by servers, routers, etc. in the network.	The host consumes the address regardless of whether the system is powered on or off. This strategy also requires a lot of legwork on the part of the system administrator. He or she has to visit each computer in the network and manually specify IP parameters.
Dynamic address assignment	In this configuration, a network host contacts a Dynamic Host Configuration Protocol (DHCP) server when it boots. The DHCP server dynamically assigns an IP address to the host for a specified period of time called a *lease*.	This option makes configuring IP parameters for a large number of network hosts very easy. Just power the system on and it gets its IP address information. It also conserves IP address usage. Addresses used by systems that are powered off can be reassigned to other network hosts.	You must have a DHCP server installed and configured before you can use this option. In addition, the address assigned to a particular host can change frequently, making it an unsuitable option for network infrastructure systems such as servers. Because of this, this option is usually used for workstations.

FIGURE 13-8   Using ifconfig to view network interface information

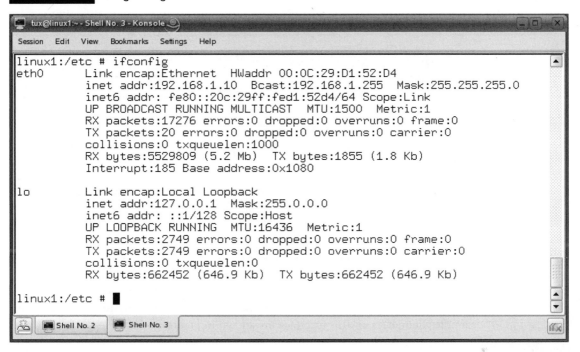

Notice in Figure 13-8 that two network interfaces are displayed, eth0 and lo. The eth0 interface is the Ethernet network interface installed in the system. The lo interface is the local loopback virtual network interface. The lo interface is required for many Linux services to run properly, so don't tinker with it. Notice in Figure 13-8 that ifconfig also displays extensive information about each network interface. Some of the more important parameters include those shown in Table 13-2.

In addition to displaying information about a particular network interface, ifconfig can also configure it with the IP address parameters discussed earlier. The syntax for using ifconfig is ifconfig *interface ip_address* netmask *subnet_mask* broadcast *broadcast_address*. For example, suppose I wanted to assign the eth0 interface an IP address of 192.168.1.1, a subnet mask of 255.255.255.0, and a broadcast address of 192.168.1.255. I would enter **ifconfig eth0 192.168.1.1 netmask 255.255.255.0 broadcast 192.168.1.255** at the shell prompt.

It's important to remember that this IP address assignment isn't persistent. If you reboot the system, it will be lost. To make it persistent, you need to configure a special file in the /etc/sysconfig/network directory, shown in Figure 13-9.

Notice in Figure 13-9 that there is a file in this directory named ifcfg-eth-id-00:0c:29:d1:52:d4. This is the configuration file for the Ethernet interface in the

TABLE 13-2   ifconfig Output

ifconfig Parameter	Description
HWaddr	The MAC address of the network board.
inet addr	The IP address assigned to the interface.
Bcast	The broadcast address of the network segment.
Mask	The subnet mask assigned to the interface.
RX packets	Statistics for received packets.
TX packets	Statistics for transmitted packets.
collisions	The number of Ethernet collisions detected.
RX bytes	The number of bytes of data received by the interface since it was brought up.
TX bytes	The number of bytes of data transmitted by the interface since it was brought up.

system with a MAC address of 00:0C:29:D1:52:D4, which in this case is the eth0 interface. Some distributions will name this file using the MAC address of the interface; others will name it using the alias assigned to the interface, such as eth0. Either way, this file is used to configure the interface when the system is powered on. Sample parameters for this interface are shown in Figure 13-10.

FIGURE 13-9   Contents of the /etc/sysconfig/network directory

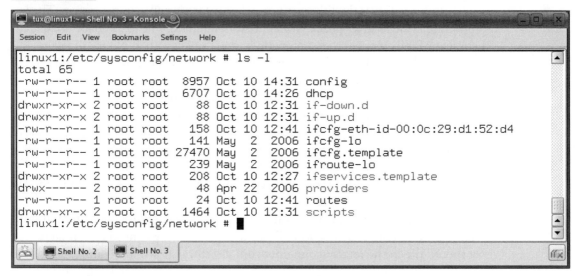

FIGURE 13-10   Configuring persistent settings for a network interface

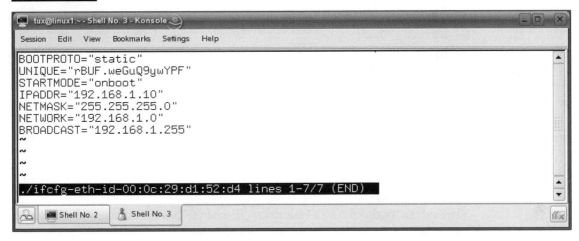

In Figure 13-10, the configuration options listed in Table 13-3 are used.

The lines for IPADDR, NETMASK, NETWORK, and BROADCAST are not required if BOOTPROTO set to "dhcp".

You may have noticed that we didn't configure two important IP parameters in the preceding examples: the default gateway router address and the DNS server address.

TABLE 13-3   Configuring Persistent Parameters for a Network Interface

Option	Description	Other Possible Values
BOOTPROTO="static"	This option specifies that the interface use a static IP address assignment.	Set to **dhcp** to dynamically assign an address.
STARTMODE="onboot"	This option specifies that the interface be brought online when the system is booted.	Set to **manual** to manually start the interface.
IPADDR="192.168.1.10"	Assigns an IP address of 192.168.1.10 to the interface.	
NETMASK="255.255.255.0"	Assigns a subnet mask of 255.255.255.0 to the interface.	
NETWORK="192.168.1.0"	Specifies the network address of the segment that the interface is connected to.	
BROADCAST="192.168.1.255"	Specifies the broadcast address of the segment the interface is connected to.	

FIGURE 13-11   Configuring a static route to the default gateway router

Your default gateway router address is stored in the /etc/sysconfig/network/routes file, shown in Figure 13-11.

The syntax for this file is default *router_IP_address*. Notice in Figure 13-11 that the default gateway router address is set to 192.168.1.1. You also need to specify the IP address of your DNS server. This is done using the /etc/resolv.conf file. The syntax for this file is nameserver *DNS_server_IP_address*. In Figure 13-12, the /etc/ resolve.conf file specifies a DNS server IP address of 205.171.3.65.

After making any changes to these files, you will need to restart your network interface to apply the changes. To do this, simply enter **ifdown** **interface** followed by **ifup** **interface**, where **interface** is the alias of the interface, such as **eth0**.

This is all well and good if you want to use a static address assignment, but what if you want to get an address dynamically from a DHCP server? You can configure your network interface to do this using the dhclient command at the shell prompt. The syntax for using this command is dhclient *interface*. For example, you could enter **dhclient eth0** to specify that your eth0 interface get its IP address information dynamically from a DHCP server. This is shown in Figure 13-13.

Notice in Figure 13-13 that the dhclient utility broadcasted a DHCPREQUEST packet on the eth0 interface. In response, the DHCP server with an IP address of 192.168.1.1 sent a DHCPACK packet back with an IP address of 192.168.1.100 that was assigned to the eth0 interface.

In addition to the command-line utilities discussed here, most Linux distributions provide some kind of graphical interface you can use to configure your network interfaces. For example, on SUSE Linux, you can use the Network Card YaST module to configure your network board as well as the IP address information assigned to it. This module is shown in Figure 13-14.

On the Red Hat Fedora distribution, you can use the Network Configuration utility to configure your network board and IP addressing information. This utility is shown in Figure 13-15.

FIGURE 13-12 Configuring the DNS server address

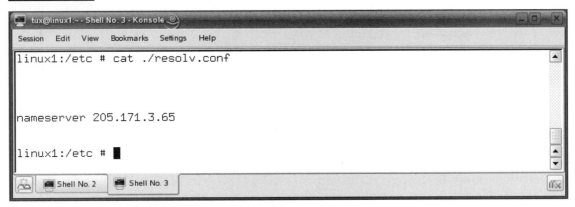

Now that you understand how to configure an Ethernet interface, here are some possible scenario questions and their answers.

SCENARIO & SOLUTION

You have one Ethernet board installed in your system. What alias will be assigned to it by default?	By default, the first Ethernet network interface card in the system is assigned an alias of eth0.
You manage a network for a small business. They only have five systems on the entire network. You decide to assign a static IP address to these systems. Is this an appropriate practice?	Yes, for networks that have less than 10–15 hosts, static IP addresses are manageable. If your network has more than 15 hosts, you should consider using dynamic IP address assignments.
You enter **ifconfig** at the shell prompt to view information about your eth0 network interface. What parameter in the output lists the MAC address of the network board?	The HWaddr parameter lists the MAC address of the network board.
You need to use ifconfig to statically assign an IP address of 10.200.200.10 and a subnet mask of 255.255.255.0 to the only Ethernet interface installed in a Linux system. What command would you enter?	You would enter **ifconfig eth0 10.200.200.10 netmask 255.255.255.0 broadcast 10.200.200.255** at the shell prompt.
You need to dynamically assign IP address information to the eth0 interface installed in a Linux system. What command would you enter to do this?	You would enter **dhclient eth0**.

FIGURE 13-13 Using dhclient to obtain an IP address lease

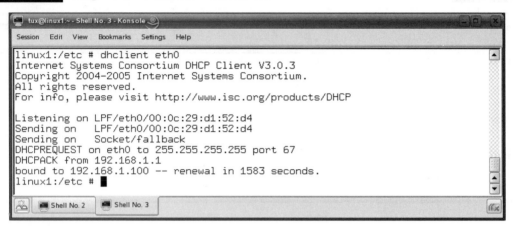

FIGURE 13-14 Using the YaST Network Card module

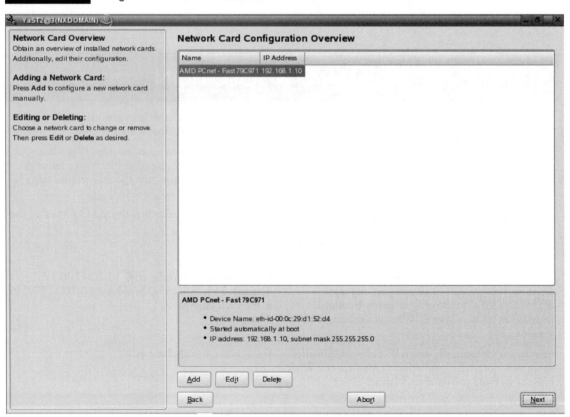

FIGURE 13-15

Using the
Network
Configuration
utility

Let's practice working with the ifconfig command in the following exercise.

EXERCISE 13-1

Working with Network Interfaces

In this exercise, you will practice using the ifconfig command to manage your
network interface. This exercise assumes that you have an Ethernet network board
installed in your Linux system. Complete the following:

1. Boot your Linux system and log in as a standard user. If you used the lab exercise
   in Chapter 3 to install your system, you can log in as **tux** with a password of
   M3linux273.

2. Open a terminal session.

3. Switch to your root user account by entering **su –** followed by your root user's
   password.

4. At the shell prompt, enter **ifconfig**. Record the following information about your Ethernet interface:

    ■ MAC address

    ■ IP address

    ■ Broadcast address

    ■ Subnet mask

5. At the shell prompt, change to the /etc/sysconfig/network directory.

6. Use the cat command to view the contents of the configuration file for your Ethernet network interface board.

7. Record the following information:

    ■ BOOTPROTO

    ■ Default gateway router

8. Use cat to view the contents of the /etc/resolve.conf file. Record your system's DNS server address.

9. Bring your interface down by entering **ifdown eth0** at the shell prompt.

10. Bring your interface back up by entering **ifup eth0** at the shell prompt.

11. Change the IP address assigned to your Ethernet network interface to 192.168.1.100 by entering **ifconfig eth0 192.168.1.100 netmask 255.255.255.0 broadcast 192.168.1.255** at the shell prompt.

12. Enter **ifconfig** again and verify that the change was applied.

13. Use ifconfig to change your IP configuration parameters back to their original values.

14. If you have a DHCP server on your network segment, dynamically assign an IP address to your Ethernet board by entering **dhclient eth0** at the shell prompt.

Let's shift gears now and discuss how to configure a modem interface.

Configuring a Modem Interface

Many users don't realize it, but a modem is also a network interface, just like an Ethernet network card. The difference is that a modem is used to establish a point-to-point connection between the host and just one other system through the public telephone lines. An Ethernet board, on the other hand, establishes a multi-point connection with many other computer systems using a shared network medium.

A modem connection will also use the Point-to-Point Protocol (PPP) to transfer data between the modem and the remote system it's connected to. Therefore, you need to make sure the pppd daemon is installed on your Linux system.

The good news is that the procedure for configuring a modem is much the same as that for configuring an Ethernet interface. First, power off your system and install the modem in an available expansion slot, if it is an internal modem. If it is an external modem, connect it to an available serial port in your system.

on the **job** *You may have to enable the serial port in the BIOS. I've encountered many systems where the serial port, because it is used infrequently these days, is set to disabled.*

When you power on the system, your Linux system should automatically detect the modem. If not, you'll need to manually load the appropriate kernel modules, just as with an Ethernet card. With the kernel modules loaded, you should now have a new network interface accessible through /dev/modem0. This interface is configured and managed using the ifcfg-modem0 file located in /etc/sysconfig/network, as shown in Figure 13-16.

Like your Ethernet interface, this file contains options that are used to configure how your modem interface works. A sample configuration file is shown in Figure 13-17.

Notice that this file uses a variety of modem-related options, such as DIALCOMMAND, DIALPREFIX, DIALPREFIXREGEX, INITx, PPPD_OPTIONS, and PROVIDER. These commands are modem- and ISP-specific. You'll need to check your modem documentation and your ISP's instructions to determine which of these options you need to use and what to set them to.

Also notice that this file sets the STARTMODE parameter to manual. That's because you usually dial in to an ISP when you need to access their network.

FIGURE 13-16   Using the ifcfg-modem0 file in /etc/sysconfig/network

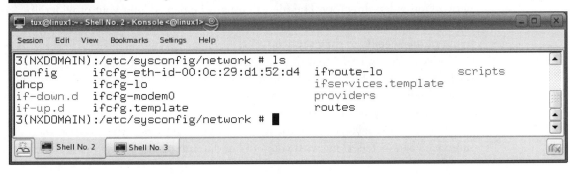

FIGURE 13-17   ifcfg-modem0 configuration options

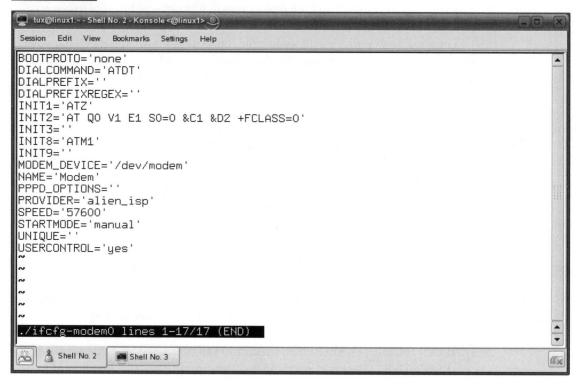

The rest of the time, the modem is inactive. To activate the connection, you enter **ifup modem0** at the shell prompt. This will bring the interface up, dial the connection, and get an IP address from the ISP. The number it should dial, as well as a variety of ISP-specific parameters, are stored in a file within the /etc/sysconfig/ network/providers directory. The file will usually be named after your provider. In Figure 13-18, a configuration file for the Alien ISP has been created and configured with options specific to their service.

Notice in Figure 13-18 that this file contains options that specify ISP-specific settings, such as USERNAME, PASSWORD, PROVIDER, PHONE, IPADDR, and so on. You'll need to contact your ISP to get their specific parameters to configure these options for your Linux system.

Once connected, you can use the ifconfig command to view the modem0 interface's parameters along with your eth0 and lo interfaces. When you're done

FIGURE 13-18 Configuring the provider file

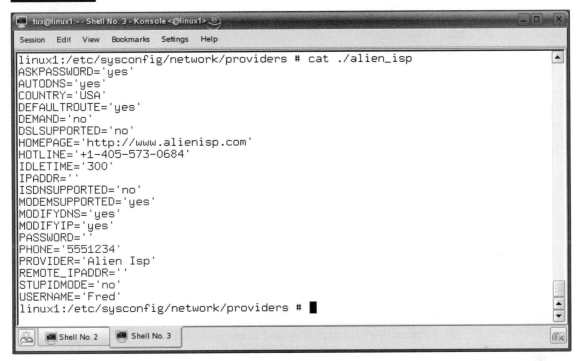

```
linux1:/etc/sysconfig/network/providers # cat ./alien_isp
ASKPASSWORD='yes'
AUTODNS='yes'
COUNTRY='USA'
DEFAULTROUTE='yes'
DEMAND='no'
DSLSUPPORTED='no'
HOMEPAGE='http://www.alienisp.com'
HOTLINE='+1-405-573-0684'
IDLETIME='300'
IPADDR=''
ISDNSUPPORTED='no'
MODEMSUPPORTED='yes'
MODIFYDNS='yes'
MODIFYIP='yes'
PASSWORD=''
PHONE='5551234'
PROVIDER='Alien Isp'
REMOTE_IPADDR=''
STUPIDMODE='no'
USERNAME='Fred'
linux1:/etc/sysconfig/network/providers #
```

using the connection, you can enter **ifdown modem0** at the shell prompt to close the connection.

Now that you know how to configure a network interface, we need to spend some time discussing how to test and monitor your network connection. Let's do that next.

CERTIFICATION OBJECTIVE 13.02

Test and Monitor the Network

Getting your network interface installed is only half the battle. To enable communications, you need to use a variety of testing and monitoring tools to make sure the network itself is working properly. We'll discuss how to do this in this part of the chapter. We'll cover the following topics:

- Using ping
- Using netstat
- Using traceroute

Let's begin by discussing how to use the ping utility.

Using ping

The ping utility is my best friend. It is one of the handiest tools in my networking virtual toolbox. I use ping all the time to test connectivity between hosts through the network. Ping works by sending an ICMP echo request packet from the source system to the destination system. The destination system then responds with an ICMP echo response packet. This process is shown in Figure 13-19.

If the ICMP echo response packet is received by the sending system, you know three things:

- Your network interface is working correctly.
- The destination system's up and working correctly.
- The network hardware between your system and the destination system is working correctly.

FIGURE 13-19

Using ping

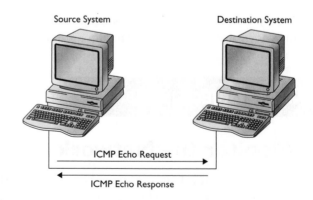

on the job *Be warned that many software host-based firewalls used by many operating systems, particularly Windows XP, are configured by default to not respond to ICMP echo request packets. This can give the false impression that the destination system is down. It's actually up and running just fine; it's just that the firewall on the host is stopping the ping packets from reaching the operating system.*

That is valuable information to know! The basic syntax for using ping is ping *destination_IP_address*. This causes ICMP echo request packets to be sent to the specified host. For example, you could enter **ping 192.168.1.1** to ping a host with this address. This is shown in Figure 13-20.

Notice in Figure 13-20 that the results of each ping sent are shown on a single line. Each line displays the size of the echo response packet (64 bytes), who it came from (192.168.1.1), its time to live value (127), and the round-trip time (0.594 ms to 5.68 ms).

on the job *The time to live (TTL) value specifies the number of routers the packet is allowed to cross before being thrown away.*

By default, the ping utility will continue sending ping requests to the specified host until you press CTRL-C to stop it. You can use the –c option with the ping command to specify a number of times to ping. For example, you can enter **ping –c 10 192.168.1.1** to ping ten times and then exit.

FIGURE 13-20   Pinging a host by IP address

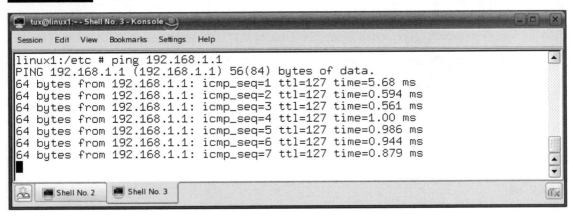

You can also ping by hostname instead of IP address. As long as you've configured your system with a valid DNS server address, ping will resolve the hostname into an IP address and send ping requests to it. This is shown in Figure 13-21.

Pinging with a host name can be a valuable troubleshooting tool. It lets you know if there is a problem with the DNS server. For example, if pinging by IP address works, but pinging by host name does not work, then you know that your basic network configuration and connectivity is working properly, but there is a problem with the DNS server.

In addition to ping, you should also be familiar with the netstat command. Let's look at it next.

Using netstat

The netstat utility is another powerful tool in your virtual toolbox. This utility can do the following:

- List network connections
- Display your routing table
- Display information about your network interface

FIGURE 13-21   Pinging by hostname

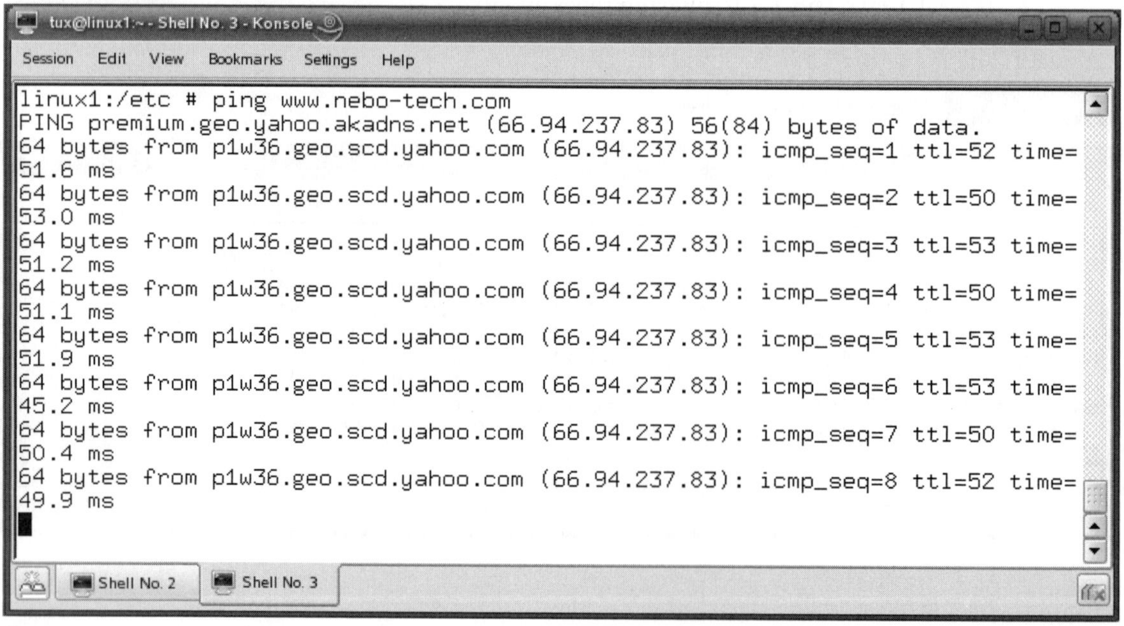

| TABLE 13-4 | netstat Options |

netstat Option	Description
–a	Lists all listening and non-listening sockets.
–i	Displays statistics for your network interfaces.
–l	Lists listening sockets.
–s	Displays summary information for each protocol.
–r	Displays your routing table.

The syntax for using netstat is to enter **netstat *option*** at the shell prompt. You can use the options listed in Table 13-4.

In addition to netstat, you should also be familiar with traceroute. Let's look at this utility next.

Using traceroute

The traceroute utility is really cool. Remember that if you try to send information to an IP host that doesn't reside on your local network segment, the packets will be sent to your default gateway router. This router will then use a variety of routing protocols to figure out how to get the packets to the destination system. In the process, the packets may have to be transferred from router to router to router to get them there. This is shown in Figure 13-22.

This is one of the beauties of an IP-based network. You can connect multiple networks together using routers and transfer data between them. It's this functionality that allows the Internet to exist. You can use a Web browser to send HTTP request packets to a Web server located somewhere in the world and have it respond with the Web page you want to view.

on the **job**

Routing protocols used by routers dynamically determine the best route for packets to take based on system load. The route taken can change as network conditions change.

The traceroute utility can be used to trace the route a packet must traverse through these routers to arrive at its destination. It does this using the same ICMP echo request and ICMP echo response packets used by the ping utility. An ICMP echo response packet is sent back to the source system each time packets cross a router, providing you with a list that comprises the route between the source and destination systems.

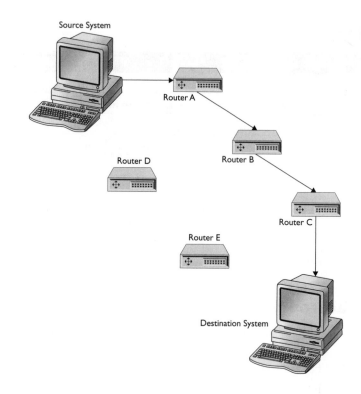

FIGURE 13-22

Routing in an IP
network

This utility can be a very useful tool if you're experiencing communication problems between networks. The traceroute utility can help you track down which router in the route isn't working correctly. The syntax for using this utility is traceroute *destination_hostname_or_IP_address*. When you do, traceroute creates one line for each router your packets cross as they make their way to the destination system. This is shown in Figure 13-23.

As you can see in Figure 13-23, the IP address of the router is displayed along with round-trip time statistics.

Now that you understand how to use command-line utilities to test and monitor your network, here are some possible scenario questions and their answers.

SCENARIO & SOLUTION

You need to test network connectivity between your system, which has an IP address of 192.168.1.10, and a system on a different network segment in your organization, which has an IP address of 192.168.2.56. You issue the **ping 192.168.2.56** command from your shell prompt and receive no responses from the remote system. What could be causing this?	It could be caused by a variety of causes, including: ■ The remote host is down. ■ The remote host is misconfigured. ■ The remote host's firewall is configured to not respond to ping requests. ■ There's a problem somewhere with the network media or network hardware.
What command can you enter at the shell prompt to display summary information about each IP protocol in use on your Linux system?	You can enter **netstat –s** at the shell prompt.
You want to verify that the router between your Linux system (192.168.1.10) and a remote system in your organization (192.168.2.56) is working correctly. What command can you issue at the shell prompt to do this?	You could enter **traceroute 192.168.2.56**.

FIGURE 13-23 Using traceroute

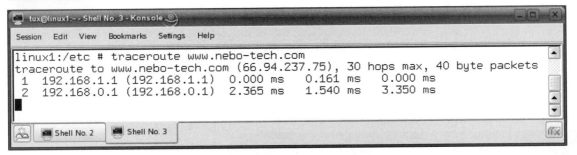

Let's practice working with network commands in the following exercise.

EXERCISE 13-2

Working with Network Commands

In this exercise, you will practice using network commands to manage and troubleshoot your network interface. This exercise assumes that you have an Ethernet network board installed in your Linux system and that it is connected to the Internet. Complete the following:

1. Boot your Linux system and log in as a standard user.

2. Open a terminal session.

3. Switch to your root user account by entering **su –** followed by your root user's password.

4. Test connectivity by entering **ping www.google.com** at the shell prompt. Your system should resolve the host name into an IP address and send ICMP echo request packets to it. (If your system isn't connected to the Internet, this step won't work.)

5. Display summary information about your network interface by entering **netstat –s | more** at the shell prompt. Review the information displayed.

6. Trace the route to www.google.com by entering traceroute **www.google.com** at the shell prompt. Note the various routers crossed as your packets traverse the Internet to www.google.com.

Before we end this chapter, let's spend a little more time talking about routing.

CERTIFICATION OBJECTIVE 13.03

Configure Routing

Earlier in this chapter, we reviewed in simple terms how the routing process works in an IP network. It's actually much more complex than what we've discussed here. Entire books have been written about IP routing and a full discussion is way beyond the scope of this chapter. However, the Linux+ exam expects you to know how to enable basic routing on a Linux system, so we're going to tackle the topic here.

The key thing to understand is that Linux, because of its extreme flexibility, can be used to create a software router that connects two or more networks together. However, most large organizations you encounter probably won't use Linux in this capacity. Instead, they will most likely use hardware routers from vendors such as Cisco to connect network segments together. These devices are dedicated to routing functions and don't do anything else.

However, many smaller organizations may implement Linux in this way. I've personally set up a number of systems in this manner. The great thing about using Linux as a router is the fact that it is very inexpensive to implement. A hardware router usually comes with a hefty price tag. A Linux router, on the other hand, costs very little to implement. In fact, if the system is only used for routing, you can get away with using very old hardware that wouldn't be usable for much else. If you've got an old 300 MHz Pentium II sitting in a closet somewhere, you can use it to configure a great Linux router! Let's talk about how this can be done. We'll cover the following topics:

- Configuring the hardware for routing
- Configuring the Linux kernel to support routing

Let's begin by discussing how to configure your routing hardware.

Configuring the Hardware for Routing

The first thing you need to do when configuring your Linux system as a router is to install and configure the necessary hardware. Linux can connect a number of network segments together; however, to keep things simple, we're going to discuss how to connect only two segments together.

Your Linux system needs to have one network interface installed for each network segment to be connected. To connect two Ethernet segments together, install a second Ethernet network board in your system using the steps presented earlier in this chapter. Connect your first network board (eth0) to your first network segment. Connect the second network board (eth1) to your second network segment. Because hosts on both networks need to know where to send packets that need to be routed, you should assign static IP addresses to both interfaces. Of course, you need to use an appropriate IP address and subnet mask for each segment. This is shown in Figure 13-24.

FIGURE 13-24

Configuring
Linux hardware
for routing

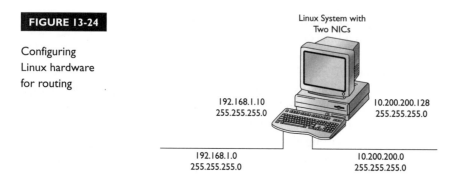

Linux System with
Two NICs

192.168.1.10
255.255.255.0

10.200.200.128
255.255.255.0

192.168.1.0
255.255.255.0

10.200.200.0
255.255.255.0

When you're done, you should have at least two network interfaces installed and working on your system (not including the lo interface). This is shown in Figure 13-25.

Now you need to configure the Linux kernel to route data between the two boards. Let's discuss how this is done next.

FIGURE 13-25 Installing two NICs in a Linux system

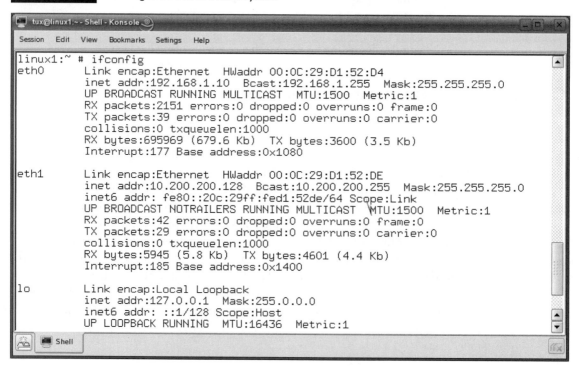

```
tux@linux1:~ - Shell - Konsole

Session  Edit  View  Bookmarks  Settings  Help

linux1:~ # ifconfig
eth0      Link encap:Ethernet  HWaddr 00:0C:29:D1:52:D4
          inet addr:192.168.1.10  Bcast:192.168.1.255  Mask:255.255.255.0
          UP BROADCAST RUNNING MULTICAST  MTU:1500  Metric:1
          RX packets:2151 errors:0 dropped:0 overruns:0 frame:0
          TX packets:39 errors:0 dropped:0 overruns:0 carrier:0
          collisions:0 txqueuelen:1000
          RX bytes:695969 (679.6 Kb)  TX bytes:3600 (3.5 Kb)
          Interrupt:177 Base address:0x1080

eth1      Link encap:Ethernet  HWaddr 00:0C:29:D1:52:DE
          inet addr:10.200.200.128  Bcast:10.200.200.255  Mask:255.255.255.0
          inet6 addr: fe80::20c:29ff:fed1:52de/64 Scope:Link
          UP BROADCAST NOTRAILERS RUNNING MULTICAST  MTU:1500  Metric:1
          RX packets:42 errors:0 dropped:0 overruns:0 frame:0
          TX packets:29 errors:0 dropped:0 overruns:0 carrier:0
          collisions:0 txqueuelen:1000
          RX bytes:5945 (5.8 Kb)  TX bytes:4601 (4.4 Kb)
          Interrupt:185 Base address:0x1400

lo        Link encap:Local Loopback
          inet addr:127.0.0.1  Mask:255.0.0.0
          inet6 addr: ::1/128 Scope:Host
          UP LOOPBACK RUNNING  MTU:16436  Metric:1

  Shell
```

Configuring the Linux Kernel to Support Routing

Every Linux system maintains a route table in RAM that it uses to determine where to send data on a network. You can view the route table on a given Linux system by entering either the **netstat –r** or the **route** command at the shell prompt. On a system with only one network interface, the output from the route command should appear similar to that shown in Figure 13-26.

As you can see in Figure 13-26, any data being sent to a host on the 192.168.1.0 network segment is sent out on the segment connected to eth0. Any information not addressed to a host on the local segment is forwarded to the default gateway router, which in this case is 192.168.1.1. The route command can also be used to manage the routes in your system's route table. You can use the options shown in Table 13-5 to do this.

Even though your Linux system has a route table in RAM and has two network interfaces installed, data can't pass between the interfaces. To make this happen, you have to enable routing in the Linux kernel. The Linux kernel itself has all the functionality required to configure routing. To make your Linux system route data between network boards, you need to enable IP forwarding. To do this, you need to manipulate the value of a file named ip_forward in the /proc/sys/net/ipv4/ directory. By default, this file contains only a single "0" character, as shown in Figure 13-27.

With a "0" in this file, the forwarding of IP packets between the network interfaces in the system is disabled. To enable it, you need to change the character in this file to a 1 instead of a 0. To do this, you can simply redirect output from the echo command to this file. For example, you can enter **echo 1 > /proc/sys/net/ipv4/ ip_forward** at the shell prompt. Doing so removes the 0 from the file and replaces it with a 1, as shown in Figure 13-28.

FIGURE 13-26   Using route to display the route table

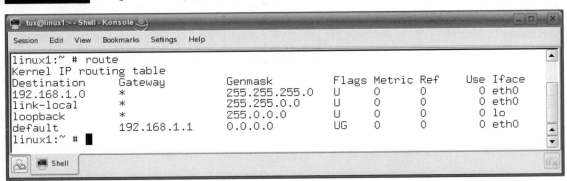

TABLE 13-5	Options Used with the route Command	

route Option	Description	Example
add –net	Adds a new route to a network to the route table.	route add –net 192.168.0.0 netmask 255.255.255.0 dev eth0
add default gw	Adds a default route to the route table.	route add default gw 192.168.0.1
del –net	Deletes a route from the route table.	route del –net 192.168.0.0 netmask 255.255.255.0 dev eth0

Be warned that this setting isn't persistent. If you reboot the system, the ip_forward file will revert to a value of 0, disabling IP forwarding. To make the setting persistent, you can edit the /etc/sysctl.conf file and add the following line:

```
net.ipv4.ip_forward = 1
```

This is shown in Figure 13-29.

FIGURE 13-27	Viewing the default value of ip_forward

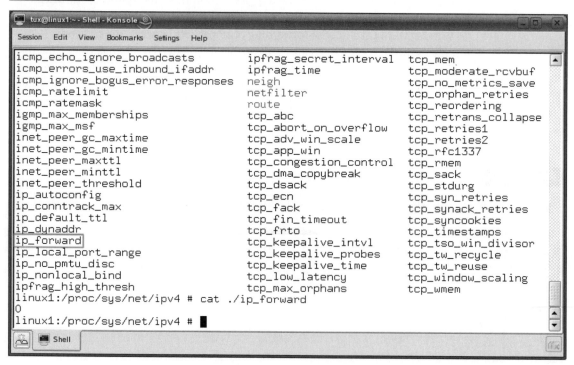

FIGURE 13-28   Setting the value of the ip_forward file

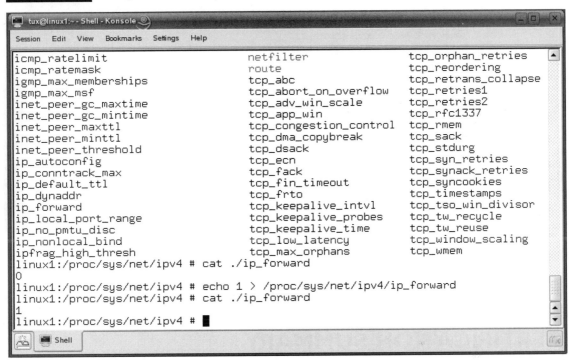

If your Linux system has a host-based firewall running, and most distributions do, you may need to create exceptions in the firewall or disable it completely to get routing to work correctly.

Now that you understand how to configure routing on your Linux system, here are some possible scenario questions and their answers.

SCENARIO & SOLUTION

What commands can you use to view the route table on your Linux system?	You can enter **netstat –r** or **route** at the shell prompt.
You want to enable packet forwarding between your eth1 and eth0 network interfaces. What command would you enter at the shell prompt to do this?	You need to remove the 0 and replace it with a 1 in the /proc/sys/net/ipv4/ip_forward file. To do this, you can enter **echo 1 > /proc/sys/net/ipv4/ip_forward** at the shell prompt.

FIGURE 13-29   Enabling IP forwarding in the /etc/sysctl.conf file

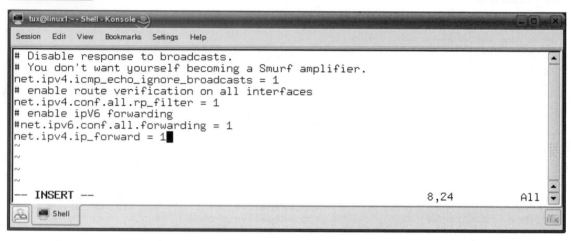

That's it for this chapter. Let's review what you learned.

CERTIFICATION SUMMARY

In this chapter, you learned how to set up networking on your Linux system. We first pointed out that you will most likely work with Ethernet network boards and the IP protocol in most modern organizations. We pointed out that a protocol is a common networking "language" that must be configured for two hosts to communicate. We pointed out that the Internet Protocol (IP) works in conjunction with the Transmission Control Protocol (TCP) or the User Datagram Protocol (UDP) to fragment, transmit, defragment, and resequence network data to enable communications between hosts.

For this process to work, each host on the network must have a correctly configured, unique IP address assigned to it. It must also have the correct subnet mask assigned. The subnet mask defines how much of a given host's IP address is the network address and how much is the IP address. When viewed in binary form, any bit in the subnet mask that has a 1 in it represents a network address bit in the IP address.

Any bit with a 0 in it represents host address. IP addresses are categorized into several classes. The first three classes each have a default subnet mask assigned:

- **Class A** 255.0.0.0
- **Class B** 255.255.0.0
- **Class C** 255.255.255.0

Hosts on the same network segment must have the same network address for them to communicate. Therefore, the same subnet mask must be assigned to each host.

To resolve domain names into IP addresses, your Linux system must also be configured with the IP address of your organization's DNS server. In addition, you must also configure it with the IP address of your network segment's default gateway router for it to communicate with hosts on other network segments.

We then shifted gears and discussed how to configure an Ethernet network interface in a Linux system. The first task you need to complete is to install the network board in the system and connect it to your network. Then you need to load the appropriate kernel modules for the board. For newer boards, this happens automatically. For older or uncommon network boards, you may have to do this manually. Once done, the network board should have an alias created for it named eth0. Subsequent network boards should have aliases of eth1, eth2, eth3, and so on created for them.

Once the board is installed, you need to use the ifconfig command or dhclient command to configure the network interface with the appropriate IP configuration parameters. When you enter **ifconfig** at the shell prompt without any parameters, the details of your installed network interfaces are displayed. To assign IP information, enter **ifconfig *interface ip_address* netmask *subnet_mask* broadcast *broadcast_address*** at the shell prompt. To make the assignment persistent, you need to enter your IP configuration parameters in the appropriate file located within /etc/sysconfig/network directory.

However, you can't use ifconfig to assign the DNS server address or the default gateway router address. To do this, you need to edit several configuration files:

- **DNS server address** /etc/resolv.conf
- **Default gateway router address** /etc/sysconfig/network/routes

To bring a network interface down, you can enter **ifdown** at the shell prompt. To bring it up, enter **ifup**. To use a DHCP server to dynamically assign IP address information to a Linux host, enter **dhclient *interface*** at the shell prompt.

Next, we discussed how to configure a modem interface. We pointed out that a modem is really a special type of network interface that uses a point-to-point connection with another computer system through the public telephone service. As such, you need the pppd daemon installed and running to use a modem interface.

A modem interface is installed in much the same manner as an Ethernet interface. Once done, you should have a new interface installed named modem0. You use the /etc/sysconfig/network/ifcfg-modem0 file to configure this device. You need to work with your ISP to determine how to configure this file. To dial the connection, you need to enter **ifup modem0** at the shell prompt. To close the connection, you need to enter **ifdown modem0**.

Next, we discussed several command-line utilities you can use to test and monitor the network. You can use the ping command to test connectivity between systems. The syntax is ping *destination_host*. You can use the netstat command to view a variety of network interface information using the –a, –i, –l, –s, and –r options. You can also use the traceroute utility to trace the route your packets must follow to reach a remote system. The syntax for using traceroute is traceroute *destination_host*.

We ended this chapter by discussing how to configure a Linux system to route data between two or more network boards. We pointed out that you use the route command or the netstat –r command to view your system's route table, which is stored in RAM. You can also use the route command to add or remove routes from the route table. To enable IP forwarding, you need to change the value of the /proc/sys/net/ipv4/ip_forward file from 0 to 1. This can be done using the echo command and redirecting the output to this file. To make the change persistent, set the value of the net.ipv4.ip_forward directive in the /etc/sysctl.conf file to 1.

✓ TWO-MINUTE DRILL

Configure a Network Interface

❑ You will most likely work with Ethernet network boards and the IP protocol when managing Linux systems.

❑ A protocol is a common networking language that must be configured for network hosts to communicate.

❑ The Internet Protocol (IP) works in conjunction with the TCP or the UDP to fragment, transmit, defragment, and resequence network data.

❑ Each host on the network must have a unique IP address assigned as well as the correct subnet mask.

❑ The subnet mask defines how much of a given host's IP address is the network address and how much is the IP address.

❑ IP addresses are categorized into several classes, each of which has a default subnet mask assigned:

   ❑ **Class A**   255.0.0.0
   ❑ **Class B**   255.255.0.0
   ❑ **Class C**   255.255.255.0

❑ Hosts on the same network segment must have the same subnet mask and must be assigned to each host.

❑ A network host must be configured with the IP address of a DNS server to resolve domain names into IP addresses.

❑ A network host must be configured with the IP address of the segment's default gateway router for it to communicate with hosts on other network segments.

❑ To install an Ethernet interface in a Linux system, you first need to install the network board in the system and connect it to the network medium.

❑ Next, you need to load the appropriate kernel modules for the board.

❑ The network board should have an alias created for it named eth0.

❑ Additional boards will have aliases of eth1, eth2, and so on assigned.

❑ You can enter **ifconfig** at the shell prompt to view the details of your installed network interfaces.

❏ To assign an IP address to a network interface, enter **ifconfig** *interface ip_address* **netmask** *subnet_mask* **broadcast** *broadcast_address* at the shell prompt.

❏ To make IP address assignments persistent, enter them in the appropriate file within the /etc/sysconfig/network directory.

❏ Enter your organization's DNS server address in the /etc/resolve.conf file.

❏ Enter your segment's default gateway router address in the /etc/systconfig/network/routes file.

❏ Enter **ifdown** at the shell prompt to bring a network interface down.

❏ Enter **ifup** to bring a network interface back up.

❏ To dynamically assign an IP address to a Linux host, enter **dhclient** *interface* at the shell prompt.

❏ A modem is a special type of network interface that uses a point-to-point connection with another computer system through the public telephone service.

❏ The pppd daemon must be installed and running to use a modem interface.

❏ After installing a modem, you will have a new interface installed named modem0.

❏ Use the /etc/sysconfig/network/ifcfg-modem0 file to configure the modem device.

❏ To dial the connection, you need to enter **ifup modem0** at the shell prompt.

❏ To close the connection, you need to enter **ifdown modem0**.

Test and Monitor the Network

❏ Linux includes a variety of command-line utilities you can use to test and monitor the network.

❏ Use ping to test connectivity between systems. The syntax is ping *destination_host*.

❏ Use the netstat command to view a variety of network interface information using the –a, –i, –l, –s, and –r options.

❏ Use the traceroute utility to trace the route your packets follow to reach a remote system. The syntax is traceroute *destination_host*.

Configure Routing

❏ Use the route command or the netstat –r command to view your system's route table.

❏ Use the route command to add or remove routes from the route table.

❏ To enable IP forwarding, change the value of the /proc/sys/net/ipv4/ip_forward file from 0 to 1.

❏ To make the change persistent, set the value of the net.ipv4.ip_forward directive in the /etc/sysctl.conf file to 1.

SELF TEST

Configure a Network Interface

1. Which of the following are true of the MAC address? (Choose two.)
   A. It's hard-coded in the network board.
   B. It's logically assigned by the operating system.
   C. MAC addresses are globally unique.
   D. The network administrator can configure its value.
   E. It is used by the DNS server to resolve domain names.

2. Which of the following are valid IP addresses that can be assigned to a network host? (Choose two.)
   A. 192.168.254.1
   B. 11.0.0.0
   C. 257.0.0.1
   D. 192.345.2.1
   E. 10.200.0.200

3. Which of the following is the default subnet mask for a class B network?
   A. 255.255.0.0
   B. 255.0.0.0
   C. 255.255.255.0
   D. 255.255.255.252

4. You've configured three hosts on your network with the following IP addresses and subnet masks:
   Host A IP = 23.0.0.1, Mask = 255.0.0.0
   Host B IP = 23.0.0.3, Mask = 255.255.0.0
   Host C IP = 23.0.0.4, Mask = 255.255.0.0
   Is this network configured properly?
   A. Yes, this network is configured properly.
   B. No, the 23.0.0.1 IP address used by Host A is a reserved IP address.
   C. No, Host A uses the wrong subnet mask.
   D. No, Host B and Host C must use the default Class A subnet mask.

5. Which files should you check to verify that a kernel module has been loaded and an alias created for a newly installed network board? (Choose two.)

  A. /etc/sysctl.conf

  B. /etc/modprobe.conf

  C. /etc/modules.conf

  D. /etc/drivers

  E. /etc/aliases

6. You have one Ethernet board installed in your Linux system. What alias is assigned to this interface by default?

  A. eth0

  B. eth1

  C. eth2

  D. eth3

7. You need to use ifconfig to assign an IP address of 176.23.0.12 and a subnet mask of 255.255.0.0 to your eth0 interface. Which of the following commands will do this?

  A. ifconfig eth0 176.23.0.12 netmask 255.255.0.0

  B. ifconfig 176.23.0.12 netmask 255.255.0.0

  C. ifconfig eth0 176.23.0.12 mask 255.255.0.0

  D. ifconfig dev=eth0 ipaddr=176.23.0.12 subnetmask=255.255.0.0

8. You need to make a permanent, static IP address assignment for your eth0 network interface, which has a MAC address of 00:0C:29:B1:50:A4. Which file do you need to edit to do this, depending upon your particular distribution? (Choose two.)

  A. /etc/sysconfig/network/eth0/ifcfg-eth-id-00:0C:29:B1:50:A4

  B. /etc/sysconfig/network/00:0C:29:B1:50:A4/eth0

  C. /etc/sysconfig/network/ifcfg-eth0

  D. /etc/sysconfig/network/ifcfg-eth-id-00:0C:29:B1:50:A4

  E. /etc/sysctl/network/ifcfg-eth-id-00:0C:29:B1:50:A4

9. Which option in your eth0 network interface configuration file should you use to get its IP address information dynamically from a DHCP server?

  A. STARTMODE

  B. BOOTPROTO

  C. IPADDR

  D. DHCP

10. You've opened your /etc/sysconfig/network/routes file in the vi editor. You want to specify a default gateway router address of 10.200.200.254. Which of the following directives would you enter in this file to do this?

   A. default 10.200.200.254

   B. gw_addr 10.200.200.254

   C. gateway 10.200.200.254

   D. router 10.200.200.254

11. You've opened your /etc/sysconfig/network/resolve.conf file in the vi editor. You want to specify a DNS server address of 10.200.200.1. Which of the following directives would you enter in this file to do this?

   A. host 10.200.200.1

   B. resolver 10.200.200.1

   C. dns_server 10.200.200.1

   D. nameserver 10.200.200.1

12. You want to use your organization's DHCP server to dynamically assign an IP address to your eth0 network interface. Which of the following commands would you enter at the shell prompt to do this?

   A. dhcp eth0

   B. dhclient eth0

   C. get address dynamic eth0

   D. ip address=dhcp dev=eth0

13. You want to temporarily disable the second interface in your Linux system. Which of the following commands would you enter at the shell prompt to do this?

   A. ifdown eth1

   B. ifdown eth0

   C. ifdown eth2

   D. ifconfig disable dev eth1

14. You've installed an internal 56 K modem in your Linux system. You now need to configure it to work with your ISP. Which of the following files would you edit to do this?

   A. /dev/modem0

   B. /etc/sysconfig/modems/ifcfg-modem0

   C. /etc/sysconfig/ppp/ifcfg-modem0

   D. /etc/sysconfig/network/ifcfg-modem0

Test and Monitor the Network

15. You need to verify that a remote host with a host name of fs1.mycorp.com is up and running. Which of the following commands would you enter at the shell prompt to do this?

 A. finger fs1.mycorp.com

 B. ping fs1.mycorp.com

 C. netstat –s fs1.mycorp.com

 D. verify fs1.mycorp.com

16. Your users can't access your organization's e-mail server, which is hosted by a third-party vendor. You suspect that a router may be down somewhere within your organization. Given that the host name of the e-mail server is pop.mymail.com, which of the following commands would you enter at the shell prompt to test this?

 A. traceroute pop.mymail.com

 B. netstat -r pop.mymail.com

 C. finger pop.mymail.com

 D. verify pop.mymail.com

Configure Routing

17. Which of the following commands will add a default gateway router address of 10.200.200.254 to your route table?

 A. route 10.200.200.254

 B. route add default gw 10.200.200.254

 C. netstat –a default 10.200.200.254

 D. gateway 10.200.200.254

18. Which of the following files can be used to enable routing on a Linux system? (Choose two.)

 A. /proc/sys/net/ipv4/ip_forward

 B. /proc/sys/net/ipv4/ip_routing

 C. /etc/sysctl.conf

 D. /etc/sysconfig/network/routes

 E. /etc/ip-forwarding

LAB QUESTION

You've just set up a new Linux workstation for a user. The workstation does not have a network interface card installed. Outline the process you would follow to configure this system to communicate on your organization's network.

SELF TEST ANSWERS

Configure a Network Interface

1. ☑ **A** and **C.** MAC addresses are hard-coded into the firmware of every Ethernet network board. Theoretically, no two network boards in the world should have the same MAC address.
   ☒ **B, D,** and **E** are incorrect. **B** is incorrect because the MAC address is hard-coded into the board itself. **D** is untrue for most network boards; however, a few Ethernet network boards do allow you to edit their MAC address using a special utility. **E** is incorrect because DNS servers only work with IP addresses and domain names.

2. ☑ **A** and **E.** 192.168.254.1 and 10.200.0.200 are both valid IP addresses that can be assigned to network hosts.
   ☒ **B, C,** and **D** are incorrect. **B** is a valid IP address, but is a network address that can't be assigned to a host. **C** isn't a valid IP address because the first octet is greater than 255. **D** is an invalid IP address because the value of the second octet exceeds 255.

3. ☑ **A.** 255.255.0.0 is the default subnet mask for a Class B network.
   ☒ **B, C,** and **D** are incorrect. **B** is the default subnet mask for a Class A network. **C** is the default subnet mask for a Class C network. **D** is a partial subnet mask that steals some network bits from the last octet of a Class C IP address.

4. ☑ **C.** The network isn't configured properly because Host A uses the wrong subnet mask.
   ☒ **A, B,** and **D** are incorrect. **A** is incorrect because Host A uses the wrong subnet mask. **B** is incorrect because 23.0.0.1 is a valid host address. **D** is incorrect. You could configure them with a Class A subnet mask, which would allow them to communicate with Host A; however, you're not required to use the default subnet mask for an address class.

5. ☑ **B** and **C.** You should check the /etc/modprobe.conf or the /etc/modules.conf file to verify that the correct module has been loaded and alias created.
   ☒ **A, D,** and **E** are incorrect. **A** can be used to enable IP forwarding, but not to load modules. **D** and **E** are distracters and are incorrect.

6. ☑ **A.** The first Ethernet board in your Linux system is assigned an alias of eth0 by default.
   ☒ **B, C,** and **D** are incorrect. **B** is assigned to the second Ethernet interface by default. **C** is assigned to the third Ethernet interface by default. **D** is assigned to the fourth Ethernet interface by default.

7. ☑ **A.** The ifconfig eth0 176.23.0.12 netmask 255.255.0.0 command will assign the IP address and subnet mask to the eth0 interface.
   ☒ **B, C,** and **D** are incorrect. **B** omits the network interface. **C** uses "mask" instead of "netmask." **D** uses incorrect syntax.

8. ☑ **C** and **D.** Depending upon which distribution you're using, you can make persistent IP address assignments using either the /etc/sysconfig/network/ifcfg-eth0 or the /etc/sysconfig/network/ifcfg-eth-id-00:0C:29:B1:50:A4 file.

☒ **A, B,** and **E** are incorrect. **A** uses the wrong directory (eth0). **B** uses the wrong directory (00:0C:29:B1:50:A4) and wrong file name (eth0). **E** uses the wrong directory (sysclt).

9. ☑ **B.** The BOOTPROTO option is used to specify whether the interface uses a static or dynamic IP address assignment.

☒ **A, C,** and **D** are incorrect. **A** is used to specify whether the interface is automatically or manually started. **C** is used to assign a static IP address. **D** is an invalid option.

10. ☑ **A.** The default 10.200.200.254 directive specifies a default gateway router address of 10.200.200.254.

☒ **B, C,** and **D** are incorrect. **B, C,** and **D** each use incorrect directives.

11. ☑ **D.** The nameserver 10.200.200.1 directive specifies a DNS server with an IP address of 10.200.200.1.

☒ **A, B,** and **C** are incorrect. **A, B,** and **C** each use incorrect directives.

12. ☑ **B.** The dhclient eth0 command will configure the eth0 interface with IP address information from a DHCP server.

☒ **A, C,** and **D** are incorrect. **A, C,** and **D** are distracters that use invalid commands.

13. ☑ **A.** The ifdown eth1 command will disable the second Ethernet interface in the system.

☒ **B, C,** and **D** are incorrect. **B** will disable the first Ethernet interface. **C** will disable the third Ethernet interface. **D** uses invalid syntax.

14. ☑ **D.** The /etc/sysconfig/network/ifcfg-modem0 file is used to configure your modem.

☒ **A, B,** and **C** are incorrect. **A** is the modem device, not its configuration file. **B** and **C** each use incorrect directories (modems and ppp).

Test and Monitor the Network

15. ☑ **B.** The ping fs1.mycorp.com command will test communications between your system and the specified host.

☒ **A, C,** and **D** are incorrect. **A** is incorrect because the finger command is used to get user information, not test communications. **C** is incorrect because the netstat –s command is used to display interface information, not test communications. **D** is distracter that uses an invalid command.

16. ☑ **A.** The traceroute pop.mymail.com command will list all of the routers between the source and destination hosts, allowing you to identify a router that isn't working correctly.
    ☒ **B, C,** and **D** are incorrect. **B** is incorrect. The netstat –r command will display your system's route table. **C** is incorrect because the finger command is used to get user information, not test communications. **D** is distracter that uses an invalid command.

Configure Routing

17. ☑ **B.** The route add default gw 10.200.200.254 command will add the specified IP address as the default gateway router.
    ☒ **A, C,** and **D** are incorrect. **A** doesn't add the route as a default gateway router. **C** is incorrect because the netstat –a command can't be used to add a route. **D** is a distracter that uses an invalid command.

18. ☑ **A** and **C.** The /proc/sys/net/ipv4/ip_forward file is used to enable or disable IP forwarding on the system. The /etc/sysctl.conf file is used to enable IP forwarding each time the system is booted.
    ☒ **B, D,** and **E** are incorrect. **B** is an invalid file. **D** is used to configure your default gateway router. **D** is a distracter that uses an invalid file name.

LAB ANSWER

The first task you need to complete is to power off the system and then install a network board in an available expansion slot in the motherboard. Assuming you're using a newer, common PCI network board, the Linux operating system should automatically detect the device on startup, load the appropriate kernel module, and assign it an alias of eth0. You can check your /etc/modprobe.conf or /etc/modules.conf files to verify that this has happened. You can also enter **ifconfig** at the shell prompt to verify that eth0 exists.

Next, you need to assign it an IP address. Because this system exists on a corporate network, it probably has a DHCP server in place that you can use to get IP addressing information from. To do this, you would enter **dhclient eth0** at the shell prompt. Watch the output from dhclient and verify that the correct IP addressing information was assigned.

Finally, you need to configure the system such that the eth0 interface is automatically assigned an IP address by the DHCP server whenever it boots. To do this, you need to edit the /etc/sysconfig/network/ifcfg-eth0 or the ifcfg-eth-id-MAC_*address* file, depending on which file your distribution uses. Configure the following directives in the file:

- BOOTPROTO="dhcp"
- STARTMODE="onboot"
- IPADDR=""
- NETMASK=""
- NETWORK=""
- BROADCAST=""

This will cause the system to enable the eth0 adapter each time the system boots and to get its IP addressing information dynamically from a DHCP server. After doing so, you should restart the system and verify that this is happening correctly. You should also check your /etc/resolv.conf file and make sure that the correct DNS server address is being delivered by the DHCP server. You should also use the route command to verify that the DHCP server is delivering the correct default gateway router address.

14

Configuring Linux Network Services

This is going to be a fantastic chapter! Get ready for a wild ride! We're going to teach you how to configure a variety of network services on your Linux system. In my opinion, this is where Linux really shines. You can take just about any Linux distribution and enable network services on it to configure it to fill a variety of powerful roles in your network. Do you need a Web server? No problem! Linux can do that. Do you need a Windows domain controller? Linux can do that as well. How about a firewall? Again, Linux can fill that role.

These roles are made possible using Linux daemons. To enable a service on your system, you need to first install the appropriate daemon from your distribution's installation media using the rpm utility. Once installed, you can use a text editor to modify the daemon's configuration file, usually saved in /etc/, to configure how it behaves. You can start, stop, or reload the service using the appropriate init script in the /etc/init.d or /etc/rc.d/init.d directory on your system.

Be warned that we need to cover a lot of topics in this chapter. Therefore, we're not going to go into depth on any one of them. Most of the network services we're going to cover in this chapter are quite complex. Entire books have been written about most of them. We don't have time or space to do that here. To get you ready for your Linux+ exam, we're going to introduce you to each topic and then teach you how to perform a basic configuration. We'll discuss the following topics:

- Configuring a DHCP server on Linux
- Configuring a DNS server on Linux
- Configuring the Apache Web server on Linux
- Configuring Samba on Linux
- Configuring printing on Linux
- Configuring basic network services with xinetd
- Configuring NFS on Linux
- Using NIS on Linux
- Accessing
- Configuring remote access on Linux

INSIDE THE EXAM

Configuring Linux Network Services

Try not to be overwhelmed by this chapter! We're going to cover a lot of network services, but you don't have to be an expert with them. Just familiarize yourself with the basics of each of the following services:

- DNS
- DHCP
- Apache Web server
- sendmail and postfix

- Samba
- CUPS and lpd
- NFS
- xinetd services
- ssh, rsh, and rlogin

Know what each service does, the name of the daemon that provides it, the port the daemon runs on, where its configuration file is saved, how to configure basic settings, and how to start and stop the service. You also need to be familiar with the basic NIS management commands presented in this chapter.

Let's begin this chapter by discussing how to configure a DHCP server on your Linux system.

CERTIFICATION OBJECTIVE 14.01

Configure a DHCP Server on Linux

In a modern organization, users expect to be able to come into the office at the beginning of the day, turn on their workstations, and have everything just "work." When it comes to configuring network settings, they don't want to have to configure anything (and you probably don't want them to).

Recall in the previous chapter that we reviewed how you use the dhclient utility to dynamically assign IP addressing information to your Linux system. For this to work, you need to have a Dynamic Host Configuration Protocol (DHCP) server on your local network segment. Just as Linux can function as a DHCP client, it can also function as a DHCP server, handing out IP addresses, subnet masks, gateway router addresses, and DNS server addresses to workstations when they boot on the network.

In this part of the chapter, we're going to discuss how to implement the dhcpd daemon on your Linux system. We're going to cover the following topics:

- How DHCP works
- Configuring the dhcpd daemon

Let's begin by talking about how DHCP works.

How DHCP Works

In the previous chapter, we talked about the two different options you have for assigning IP addresses to network hosts:

- Static assignment
- Dynamic assignment

Static address assignments work reasonably well if the network is very small. However, if you have more than about 15 workstations on the network, static address assignments quickly become unmanageable. In this situation, dynamic address assignments are preferable.

With a dynamic address assignment strategy, you configure a DHCP service on your network to automatically assign IP addresses to hosts when they boot up. The DHCP protocol is defined in RFC 2131. With the DHCP service running on a system in your network, hosts configured as DHCP clients broadcast a request for an IP address. The DHCP server responds to the broadcast and provides the client with an IP address assignment.

DHCP is widely implemented because it's very powerful. It eliminates the need for you to walk around to every system and manually configure IP address parameters. It's all taken care of automatically for you. In fact, the DHCP service can also configure more than just the IP address. You can configure the service to deliver an IP address, a subnet mask, and the IP addresses of DNS servers and the default gateway router.

To do this, you configure your DHCP server with a range of IP addresses that it can assign to network hosts. When it receives a request from a network host, the DHCP server takes the next available address from the range and assigns it to the host for a fixed period of time, called a *lease*. When the lease expires or when the host system is shut down, the IP address is released and can be assigned to another network host.

DHCP is a client-server protocol. In order for DHCP to work, you must have a DHCP service running on one of your network systems and a DHCP client running on the hosts that will request IP addresses from the DHCP server.

To obtain an IP address, the DHCP client and the DHCP server communicate with each other using the process shown in Figure 14-1.

When a host that is configured with the DHCP client is booted, it sends out a *DHCPDISCOVER* broadcast. The DHCP server receives the broadcast and selects an IP address from its range of available addresses that it can assign to the DHCP client.

The server sends a proposed IP address assignment back to the host in a *DHCPOFFER* message.

on the **Ϣ**ob *If there is more than one DHCP server on your network segment, the DHCP client may receive multiple DHCPOFFER messages, one from each server. Most DHCP clients opt for the first offer received.*

The DHCP client reviews the offers it has received and then selects the offer it wants to accept. The DHCP client then sends a *DHCPREQUEST* broadcast. This broadcast informs the DHCP server that it has accepted the addressing offer. If there are multiple DHCP servers on the same network segment, the broadcast also informs the other DHCP servers that their offer has been rejected and they can retract their offers.

on the **Ϣ**ob *Remember that the DHCPREQUEST message is a broadcast. That's why it can communicate with multiple DHCP servers at once.*

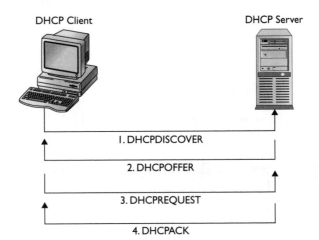

FIGURE 14-1

The DHCP protocol in action

The DHCP server whose offer was accepted responds to the client with a *DHCPACK* message, which contains the following:

- IP address
- Subnet mask
- Other options, including the default gateway router's IP address and the DNS server's IP address
- Lease information

With this background in mind, let's discuss how you go about configuring the dhcpd daemon.

Configuring the dhcpd Daemon

To configure the dhpcd daemon, you need to complete the following tasks:

- Installing the dhcpd daemon
- Configuring the dhcpd daemon

Let's begin by discussing how to install the dhcpd daemon.

Installing the dhpcd Daemon

Before you can configure the dhcpd daemon, you must first install it on your Linux system. Most distributions won't install the dhcp packages by default during system installation. You must locate the following packages on your installation media and install them using the rpm utility:

- dhcp
- dhcp-server
- dhcptools

These packages are shown in Figure 14-2.

```
linux1:/media/cdrom/suse/i586 # ls dh*
dhcdbd-1.12-14.i586.rpm          dhcp-server-3.0.3-21.i586.rpm
dhcp-3.0.3-21.i586.rpm           dhcp-tools-1.6-41.i586.rpm
dhcp-client-3.0.3-21.i586.rpm    dhcpcd-1.3.22p14-221.i586.rpm
linux1:/media/cdrom/suse/i586 #
```

FIGURE 14-3

The dhcpd
daemon's init
script

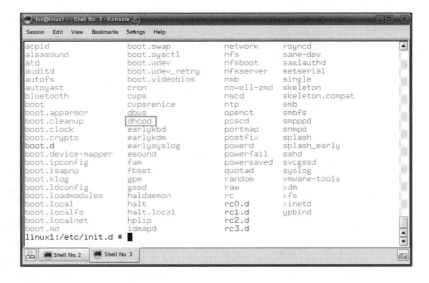

The binary that provides the DHCP service is the dhcpd executable located in
/usr/sbin. The dhcpd daemon is started and stopped using the dhcpd init script in
/etc/init.d or /etc/rc.d/init.d, as shown in Figure 14-3.

*In the field, you may hear the dhcpd daemon referred to as a **DHCP** server.
This term actually refers to the dhcp service running on the system, not to
the hardware or operating system.*

Once the DHCP service is installed on your system, you're ready to configure and
start the daemon on your server. Let's discuss how to do this next.

Configuring the dhcpd Daemon

To configure the dhcpd daemon, you need to open the /etc/dhcpd.conf file in a text
editor such as vi. This file is the primary configuration file for the dhcpd daemon on
your server. A sample dhcpd.conf file is shown in Figure 14-4.

The key element in this file is the *subnet* declaration. This is used to define the
IP addresses that can be distributed by the daemon, which is probably one of your
foremost concerns when configuring the DHCP service. The syntax of the subnet
declaration is as follows:

```
subnet network_address netmask subnet_mask {
     range start_address end_address;
     default-lease-time lease_duration;
     max-lease-time maximum_lease_duration;
}
```

FIGURE 14-4

The dhpcd.conf
file

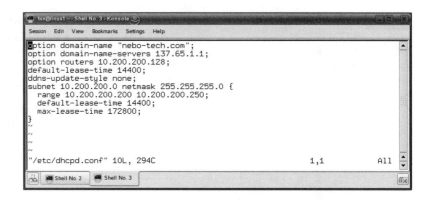

The *network_address* and *subnet_mask* parameters are used to specify the network address and the subnet mask of the network segment where dhcpd will deliver addresses. In Figure 14-4, the dhcpd daemon is configured to operate on the 10.200.200.0 network segment with a subnet mask of 255.255.255.0.

The *range* option identifies which IP addresses dhcpd can assign. The *start_address* parameter identifies the first address it can assign. The *end_address* parameter identifies the last address in the range it can assign. In Figure 14-4, the dhcpd daemon has been configured to assign addresses within the range of 10.200.200.200 to 10.200.200.250.

The last two options specify the lease time for assigned IP addresses. The *default-lease-time* option sets the default lease time in seconds for the address range. In Figure 14-4, the default-lease-time has been set to four hours. You probably noticed in Figure 14-4 that there are actually two default-lease-time options in the configuration file. One is within the subnet declaration; the other is placed earlier in the file. The one within the subnet declaration is specific to the address range. It overrides the default-lease-time parameter that is listed earlier in the file, which only is applied if a default-lease-time isn't specified within a particular subnet declaration.

If, for some reason, the DHCP client that requests an address from this service has been configured to request a specific amount of time in its address lease, then the *max-lease-time* option is used instead of the default-lease-time. This option specifies the maximum lease length the daemon can assign. In Figure 14-4, the maximum-lease-time has been set to 48 hours.

In addition to configuring the subnet, you can also configure options that can be delivered to DHCP clients in the /etc/dhcpd.conf file. These options allow you to configure DHCP clients with a variety of IP protocol-related parameters. There are many options defined in the DHCP protocol that you can deliver to clients. Some of the more useful options are shown in Table 14-1.

TABLE 14-1	Option	Delivers
DHCP Options	subnet-mask	The subnet mask
	routers	The IP address of the default gateway router
	domain-name-servers	The IP address of your DNS server
	domain-name	The DNS domain for the client
	broadcast-address	The broadcast address for the client

For a full list of DHCP options, look up RFC 2132 at http:// www.faqs.org/rfcs/ rfc2132.html. In Figure 14-4, three options have been defined. Because these appear outside of the subnet declaration, these options would apply to all DHCP clients if there were more than one subnet defined in the file. The syntax for defining options is as follows:

```
option option_name option_value
```

The first option defined in Figure 14-4 sets the domain name for the client to nebo-tech.com. The next option delivers the IP address of the network's DNS server (137.65.1.1). The last option delivers the IP address of the network segment's default gateway router, which is 10.200.200.128.

With the dhcpd.conf file configured, you're ready to start your dhcpd daemon. To do this, enter **/etc/init.d/dhcpd start** or **/etc/rc.d/init.d/dhcpd start** at the shell prompt. Now, you can configure your workstations to get their IP addressing

SCENARIO & SOLUTION

Your organization has two network segments separated by a router. The router is configured to not forward broadcasts. You set up your organization's DHCP server on one of the segments. Will this configuration work?	No, the DHCP protocol uses broadcasts to communicate between DHCP clients and the DHCP server. Clients on the same network segment as the server will be able to get an address from the server. Clients on the other segment won't.

You want to configure the dhcpd daemon on your Linux system to deliver IP addresses from 10.0.0.100 to 10.0.0.200, a subnet mask of 255.0.0.0, a router address of 10.0.0.254, and a DNS server address of 10.0.0.1. The IP address lease should last four days. What lines would you need to add to your dhcpd.conf file to make this happen?	You would enter the following lines:
	```option domain-name-servers 10.0.0.1```
	```option routers 10.0.0.254```
	```subnet 10.0.0.0 netmask 255.0.0.0 {```
	``` range 10.0.0.100 10.0.0.200;```
	``` default-lease-time 14400;```
	``` max-lease-time 172800;```
	```}```

FIGURE 14-5

Configuring a
Windows XP
system to use
DHCP

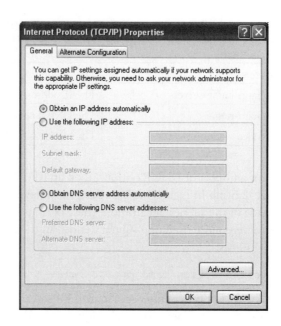

information from a DHCP server. This can be done with Linux workstations,
Macintosh workstations, or Windows workstations, as shown in Figure 14-5.

*You'll need to create an exception in your Linux system's host firewall for the
dhcpd daemon to work.*

Let's create a DHCP server in the following exercise.

EXERCISE 14-1

Configuring a DHCP Server

In this exercise, you will install and configure the dhcpd daemon on your Linux
system. This exercise assumes you have an Ethernet network board installed and
configured in your system. To test your configuration, you'll also need a second
workstation configured to use DHCP to get its IP address information.

In addition, you should not complete this exercise on a system that is connected
to a production computer network. It will be possible for other client systems to get

their IP addressing information from your DHCP server instead of your company's DHCP server, which could make some folks mighty unhappy.

With this in mind, complete the following:

1. Boot your Linux system and log in as a standard user. If you used the lab exercise in Chapter 3 to install your system, you can log in as **tux** with a password of **M3linux273**.

2. Open a terminal session.

3. Switch to your root user account by entering **su –** followed by your root user's password.

4. Using the RPM utility, install the following packages on your system:

   ■ dhcp

   ■ dhcp-server

   ■ dhcptools

5. Open /etc/dhcpd.conf in a text editor.

6. Add the following lines:

```
option domain-name-servers your_Linux_system's_IP_address
option routers your_segment's_default_gateway_router_address
subnet your_network_address netmask your_subnet_mask {
        range beginning_address ending_address;
        default-lease-time 14400;
        max-lease-time 172800;
}
```

7. Save your changes to the /etc/dhcpd.conf file.

8. At the shell prompt, start the dhcdp daemon using its init script in /etc/init.d or /etc/rc.d/init.d.

9. If you have a second workstation available for testing, verify that you can get an IP address lease from your DHCP server.

10. At the shell prompt, use the dhcpd init script to stop the service.

Let's next look at how you can configure your Linux system to function as a DNS server.

Configure a DNS Server on Linux

On an IP network, users today take for granted that they can access local network and Internet resources using *domain names* instead of IP addresses. I doubt that a single workday goes by that the typical employee doesn't access a Web site using a domain name such as http://www.google.com. However, the IP stack on your Linux system doesn't understand domain names. It has no idea who www.google.com is. For communications to occur, your system must convert the domain name into an IP address. This is done by sending domain names to a *Domain Name Service* (DNS) server. In this section, you'll learn how to install a DNS service on your Linux system that other systems in your network can use to resolve domain names into IP addresses. We're going to cover the following topics:

- How DNS works
- Installing the named daemon
- Configuring the named daemon
- Using dig and nslookup

Let's begin by discussing how DNS works.

How DNS Works

DNS is a network service that allows you to map easy-to-remember host and domain names to IP addresses. Early IP networks didn't have DNS servers. Instead, each network computer was configured with a hosts file that contained a simple mapping of IP addresses to host names. On Linux, the hosts file is stored in /etc. A typical hosts file is shown in Figure 14-6.

Notice in Figure 14-6 that the hosts file contains one line per host record. The syntax for a record in your hosts file is:

```
IP_address   host_name    alias
```

For example, in Figure 14-6:

```
192.168.1.10     linux1.nebo-tech.com     linux1
```

Your system can use these mappings in the hosts file to resolve a host name or alias into an IP address. For example, if I were to enter **ping linux1** at the shell

FIGURE 14-6

A typical hosts
file

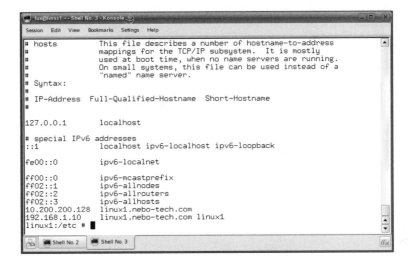

```
# hosts          This file describes a number of hostname-to-address
#                mappings for the TCP/IP subsystem.  It is mostly
#                used at boot time, when no name servers are running.
#                On small systems, this file can be used instead of a
#                "named" name server.
# Syntax:
#
# IP-Address  Full-Qualified-Hostname  Short-Hostname
#

127.0.0.1      localhost

# special IPv6 addresses
::1            localhost ipv6-localhost ipv6-loopback

fe00::0        ipv6-localnet

ff00::0        ipv6-mcastprefix
ff02::1        ipv6-allnodes
ff02::2        ipv6-allrouters
ff02::3        ipv6-allhosts
10.200.200.128 linux1.nebo-tech.com
192.168.1.10   linux1.nebo-tech.com linux1
linux1:/etc #
```

prompt, the system can use the linux1 record in the hosts file to resolve the alias
into an IP address of 192.168.1.10.

However, we don't use the hosts file much anymore. That's because DNS makes
name resolution on your IP network much easier. The main weakness with hosts files
is the fact that name resolution is decentralized. You must manually maintain the
hosts file on every system. On a small network, this isn't a big deal. But on a large
network or on a network that's connected to the Internet, using a hosts file for name
resolution just doesn't cut it.

DNS works much better. Most modern IP networks use one or more DNS servers
to resolve domain names. Instead of relying on the hosts file, computers on your
network can send requests for resolving host names into IP addresses (and vice
versa) to the DNS server.

on the
  Job

*Even though your system is configured to use a DNS server for name
resolution, you can still manually enter a host name-to-IP address mapping in
the hosts file.*

One of the key differences between DNS and hosts files is the fact that DNS
employs a hierarchy of domains and zones. This hierarchy is referred to as the *DNS
namespace*. DNS organizes hosts into a highly structured domain structure. Think of
this structure as an inverted tree, as depicted in Figure 14-7.

To understand how DNS domains organize host names, let's analyze a sample
domain name: www.nebo-tech.com.

FIGURE 14-7

The DNS domain structure

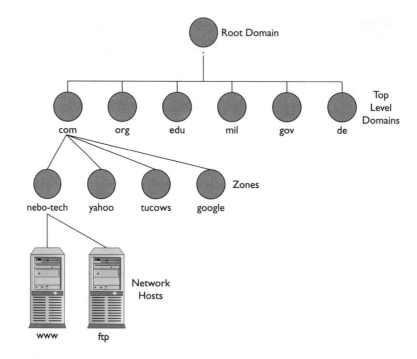

At the top of the DNS hierarchy is the *root* domain. It's denoted by a simple period, as shown in Figure 14-7. This will be the right-most domain in any DNS domain name. Notice the period at the end of www.nebo-tech.com.. This period represents the root domain. However, you probably don't include the trailing period whenever you use a domain name in a URL. Most people don't. However, you should always remember that a properly written domain name always ends with a trailing period, denoting the root domain. As an experiment, try opening a Web browser and navigating to your favorite Web sites using a trailing period after the domain name. You'll find that it works!

The root domain contains a number of top-level domains (TLDs). If you've visited Web sites on the Internet, you're probably already familiar with these top-level domain names. Some of the more commonly used TLDs include those shown in Table 14-2.

In recent years, new top-level domains have been added, including tv, biz, and info. There are also top-level domains for specific countries. For example, the top-level domain for Australia is au. The top-level domain for Spain is es.

In our www.nebo-tech.com. example, the TLD after the root domain is com. Within these TLDs reside thousands of sub-domains called *zones*. Zones are usually specific to a particular organization. Zones can contain either sub-zones or specific hosts. In our

TABLE 14-2	TLD	Description
	com	Used by commercial organizations
Common TLDs	edu	Used by educational organizations
	org	Used by non-profit organizations
	gov	Used by United States government organizations

example, the zone comes immediately to the left of the top-level domain, which in this case is nebo-tech.

In Figure 14-7, you'll notice that the nebo-tech zone contains two specific records, one for www and one for ftp. These records contain mappings that map the host name to an IP address. In our example, www specifies a host within the nebo-tech zone.

This record can be used by the DNS server to resolve the host name into an IP address. A computer system that needs to resolve a host name into an IP address sends a resolution request to the DNS server it's been configured to use. Here's how the resolution process works:

1. The system that needs to resolve a host name sends a request to the DNS server it's been configured to use on IP port 53. If the DNS server has a record for the host name being requested, it returns the corresponding IP address. If not, the process continues to step 2.

on the
Job

The DNS server is said to be **authoritative** *if it has a record for the domain name being requested in its local database.*

2. If the DNS server doesn't have a record for the requested host name, it sends a request to a *root-level DNS server*. There are thirteen root-level DNS servers on the Internet. When you install the DNS daemon on your Linux system, it's automatically configured with the IP addresses of these servers in the /var/lib/named/root.hint file, shown in Figure 14-8.

3. The root-level DNS server responds to your DNS server with the IP address of a DNS server that's authoritative for the TLD of the host name in question.

4. Your DNS server sends a resolution request for the host name the TLD DNS server specified by the root-level DNS server.

5. The TLD DNS server responds with the IP address of the DNS server that's authoritative for the DNS zone of the host name that you need to resolve.

6. Your DNS server sends a request to the DNS server that's authoritative for the zone where the host name resides.

FIGURE 14-8

Root-level DNS
servers

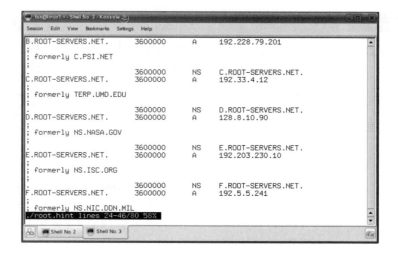

7. The authoritative DNS server for the host name responds to your DNS server with the appropriate IP address.

8. Your DNS server responds to the system that originated the request with the IP address.

9. Your system contacts the host using its IP address.

When your DNS server resolves a host name for which it is not authoritative, it saves that address in its *name cache*. If it receives a request to resolve the same host name again in the future, it simply pulls the IP address out of its cache and responds to the requesting system directly instead of going through the entire resolution process again.

One of the problems with current DNS implementations is fault tolerance. If you had your DNS daemon running on a particular Linux system and it were to go down, name resolution for your network is gone.

To provide a degree of redundancy, you can configure *master* and *slave* DNS servers. A master server is a DNS server that hosts zone files. Any changes made to the zone are made to the zone files on the master server. A slave DNS server, on the other hand, is configured to get its zone data from a master DNS server. A slave DNS server can resolve host names just like a master DNS server. To make this possible, the slave server contacts the master server and downloads its zone data. This is called a *zone transfer*.

By configuring both a master and a slave server in your network, you provide a degree of fault tolerance. If your master server were to go down, network hosts can still use the slave server for name resolution as long as they have been configured with its IP address.

on the
○○b

Most operating systems allow you to configure up to three DNS server IP addresses that the host can use to resolve domain names in IP addresses.

DNS servers can perform two types of lookups for name resolution tasks. The first type is called a *forward lookup*. When performing a forward lookup, the client system sends a request to the DNS server asking it to resolve a host name into an IP address. However, this process can also work in reverse. These are called *reverse lookups*. In a reverse lookup, the DNS server resolves an IP address into a host name.

If you want a DNS server to provide forward and reverse lookups, you have to create two different zones—a *forward zone* and a *reverse zone*. Both zones contain the same data, they're just formatted in a slightly different fashion.

Installing the named Daemon

To turn your Linux system into a DNS server, you need to install, configure, and run a DNS daemon. There are many DNS server packages you can choose from, but the one most commonly used is the Berkeley Internet Name Domain (BIND) package. This package includes the *named* daemon, which is the heart of your DNS system. Most Linux distributions don't install the BIND daemon by default during installation, so you'll need to install it manually using rpm. You'll need to install the following BIND packages:

- bind
- bind-libs
- bind-chrootenv
- bind-utils

Your distribution media should include the BIND packages, as shown in Figure 14-9.

The binary that provides the DNS service is the named executable located in /usr/sbin. You can start and stop your DNS service using the named init script in /etc/init.d or /etc/rc.d/init.d, shown in Figure 14-10.

Once BIND is installed on your system, you're ready to configure and start the service on your server. Let's discuss how this is done next.

FIGURE 14-9

Installing the BIND daemon package

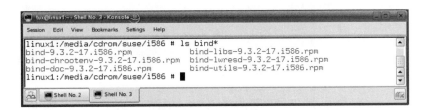

FIGURE 14-10

The named init script

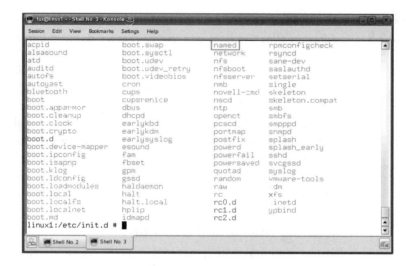

Configuring the named Daemon

As with many other daemons, the named daemon is configured using several configuration files in /etc. The first file you need to be familiar with is named.conf, shown in Figure 14-11.

The named.conf file is the main configuration file for the named daemon. This file comprises directives along with blocks of information associated with those directives. A block is composed of lines of data enclosed in curly brackets. After the last curly bracket is a semi-colon.

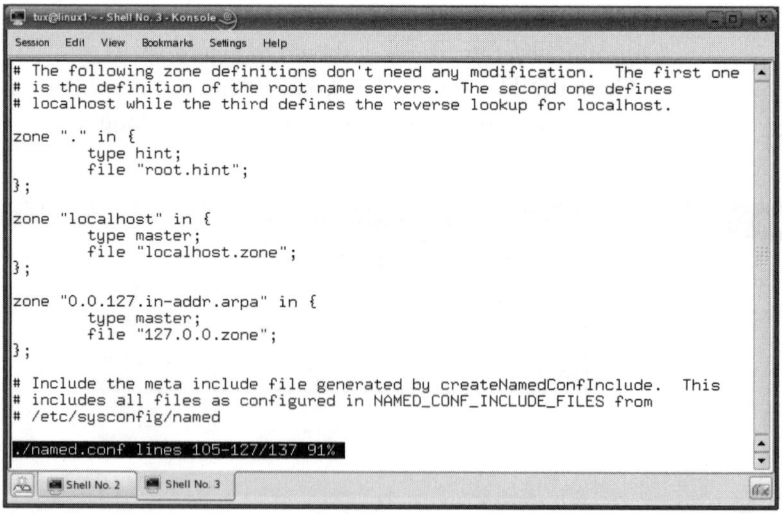

FIGURE 14-11

Configuring named with the /etc/named.conf file

TABLE 14-3	Directive	Description
	options	Defines general configuration options for the named service.
named.conf Directives	logging	Configures logging for the named service.
	zone	Defines the zones serviced by named.

The directives within the named.conf file include those shown in Table 14-3.

The first parameter you need to be aware of is the directory parameter within the options directive, shown in Figure 14-12.

This parameter specifies the working directory for the named daemon. This is where the zone files used by the named service reside. By default, this parameter is set to /var/lib/named. Any time a file name is specified in any directive that follows the directory parameter in the named.conf file, it is assumed to reside in the working directory specified.

The second set of parameters you need to be familiar with are the zone directives. These are found further down in the file after the options directive, as shown in Figure 14-11. The zone directives in named.conf define the zones that will be serviced by the named daemon. The syntax for a zone directive is as follows:

```
zone    zone_name name_space {
        type zone_type;
        file zone_filename;
};
```

A sample zone directive is shown in Figure 14-13.

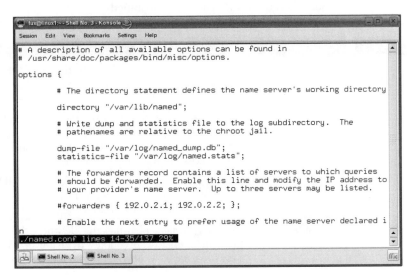

FIGURE 14-12

Setting the named working directory

```
                  file "root.hint";
};

zone "localhost" in {
        type master;
        file "localhost.zone";
};

zone "0.0.127.in-addr.arpa" in {
        type master;
        file "127.0.0.zone";
};

# Include the meta include file generated by createNamedConfInclude.  This
# includes all files as configured in NAMED_CONF_INCLUDE_FILES from
# /etc/sysconfig/named

include "/etc/named.conf.include";
zone "nebo-tech.com" in {
        file "master/nebo-tech.com";
        type master;
};
./named.conf lines 111-133/137 94%
```

Table 14-4 defines the components of the zone directive.

In Figure 14-11, you can see that three other zones are also defined in named.conf. These zones are automatically created when the BIND package is installed. The first zone is the . zone and is configured as a hint file. The records in this zone point to the root-level name servers on the Internet. This zone is used by named when it receives a request to resolve a host name residing in a zone for which it isn't authoritative. The IP address for these root-level name servers is contained in the root.hint file, shown earlier in Figure 14-8. The root.hint file is automatically copied to /var/lib/named when the BIND package is installed.

TABLE 14-4	Component	Description
Defining a Zone in named.conf	*zone_name*	The *zone_name* comes right after the zone directive. The zone name is enclosed in quotes. In Figure 14-13, the nebo-tech.com zone has been created.
	name_space	The *name_space* comes after the zone name. In Figure 14-13, the Internet namespace (in) is being used. The Internet namespace is used almost exclusively. It's very unlikely that you will encounter any other namespaces when implementing a DNS server.
	zone_type	The *zone_type* identifies whether the server will be a master DNS server or a slave DNS server for the zone. In Figure 14-13, the DNS server will be a master server for the nebo-tech.com zone.
	zone_filename	The *zone_filename* identifies the file where the zone data is stored. The file name is enclosed in quotes. In Figure 14-13, the nebo-tech.com zone file is saved as nebo-tech.com in the master subdirectory.

The next default zone defined in named.conf is localhost. This zone only contains a single record that simply maps localhost to the IP address 127.0.0.1. The last default zone defined in named.conf is named 0.0.127.in-addr.arpa. That name may sound a little confusing, but it actually isn't. This zone is a reverse zone. It maps the IP address 127.0.0.1 to the localhost host name.

As you may have noticed, these three default zones don't define real DNS zones, as the nebo-tech zone does. You may be surprised that you can configure a fairly powerful DNS server without configuring any zones beyond the three default zones. In this configuration, the named daemon operates as a *caching-only name server*.

Remember that a DNS server will query root-level name servers when it's asked to resolve a host name that it isn't authoritative for. The DNS server will use the information supplied by the root-level DNS server to locate an authoritative DNS server for the requested host name. When the host name is finally resolved, the DNS server then stores that information in its cache. The next time it receives a request to resolve the same host name, it simply pulls the information out of its cache.

This type of configuration is appropriate for situations where you don't have your own domain and you simply want to provide users with access to Internet resources. If, on the other hand, you want to set up a DNS server for your organization's own zone, then you will need to create your own zone files and configure named to use them.

To do this, you first need to edit your /etc/named.conf file and add a new zone directive, such as the nebo-tech.com zone shown in Figure 14-13. The next thing you need to do is to create a zone file for the zone. Notice in Figure 14-13 that I've specified a file name of master/nebo-tech.com for my nebo-tech.com zone. Because the directory parameter in /etc/named.conf specifies that the working directory is /var/lib/named, the zone file for my zone will be /var/lib/named/master/nebo-tech.com.

After saving the /etc/named.conf file, the next thing you need to do is open the zone file you specified and add the appropriate host name and IP address information. This is where things get a little more complicated. A basic zone file I've created for the nebo-tech.com zone is shown in Figure 14-14.

In this zone, there are two hosts: linux1 and gateway. Let's explore each element of the zone file in a little more depth in Table 14-5.

In addition to a forward-lookup zone, you can also create reverse-lookup zones. A reverse-lookup zone operates in the opposite manner of a forward-lookup zone. Instead of resolving host names into IP addresses, a reverse-lookup zone resolves IP addresses into host names.

Before your named daemon can perform this type of lookup, you need to create a companion reverse-lookup zone for your forward-lookup zone. An example of a reverse-lookup zone for the nebo-tech.com zone is shown in Figure 14-15.

FIGURE 14-14

A sample zone
file

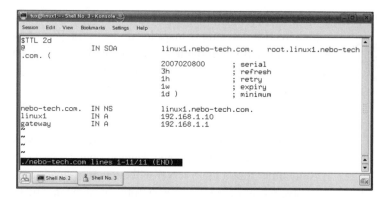

```
$TTL 2d
@                IN SOA         linux1.nebo-tech.com.    root.linux1.nebo-tech
.com. (
                                2007020800     ; serial
                                3h             ; refresh
                                1h             ; retry
                                1w )           ; expiry
                                1d )           ; minimum

nebo-tech.com.   IN NS         linux1.nebo-tech.com.
linux1           IN A          192.168.1.10
gateway          IN A          192.168.1.1
~
~
~
~
./nebo-tech.com lines 1-11/11 (END)
```

TABLE 14-5   Zone File Components

Zone File Component	Description
$TTL	Stands for *time to live*. This value specifies the default time to live for each record. If a record has an explicit time to live value, it takes precedence over the TTL value specified here. If no unit is specified, the value is assumed to reference seconds. The example in Figure 14-14 shows a TTL value of two days.
IN	Specifies that the zone use the Internet namespace.
SOA	Stands for *start of authority*. The SOA is a zone record, just like the other records in the file. However, the SOA record has a special purpose. It must be placed immediately after the $TTL parameter. The SOA record identifies: ■ The DNS server that is the authoritative server for the zone. In Figure 14-14, linux1.nebo-tech.com. is identified as the authoritative DNS server for the nebo-tech.com zone. Remember to use trailing periods! ■ The e-mail address of the system administrator who maintains the zone. In this example, it is root@linux1.nebo-tech.com. ■ The zone's serial number. This number is used by slave DNS servers for this zone to determine if they should update their databases. You can actually use any initial value you wish in this field; however, the general practice is to use the date the zone file was created concatenated with a couple of zeros. In Figure 14-14, the zone file was created on February 8, 2007. If you update your zone, you should increment the last digit of this number by 1 (that's why zeros are added to the end). This tells any slave DNS servers that the zone file has changed and that they need to update their database from the master server. ■ The interval (refresh) in which slave DNS servers should update their databases from the master server. In Figure 14-14, the refresh interval is set to three hours. ■ The number of attempts (retry) slave servers should make before giving up when trying to update their database from the master server. In Figure 14-14, this is set to one hour. ■ The amount of time allowed before data on slave servers expires (expiry). In Figure 14-14, this is set to one week. ■ The amount of time failed name resolution requests should be stored in the cache of slave servers (minimum). In Figure 14-14, this is set to one day.

TABLE 14-5	Zone File Components (*Continued*)

Zone File Component	Description
Host Name Records	After the SOA record are the host records used for name resolution. The general syntax for host records is:
	`host_name   namespace   record_type   IP_address or host_name`
	Here's a description of each of these parameters:
	host_name Specifies the host name of the system.
	namespace Specifies the namespace used for the record (usually IN).
	record_type Specifies the DNS record. The following types are used:
	■ **NS** Specifies the host name of the DNS server that hosts the specified zone.
	■ **A** Maps a host name to an IP address.
	■ **CNAME** A CNAME record is an alias. It maps an alias name to another host name in the zone.
	■ **MX** Represents a mail server. It maps a host name to another host name in the zone.
	IP_address* or *host_name Specifies the IP address or host name you are mapping the host name to.

Notice in Figure 14-15 that the $TTL parameter and the SOA record are pretty much the same as in the forward-lookup zone we reviewed earlier. Locate the NS record in Figure 14-15. Notice the odd zone name used. Instead of nebo-tech.com, the zone's name is 1.168.192.in-addr.arpa. Reverse-lookup zone names are constructed in the following way:

`reversed_network_address.in-addr.arpa.`

FIGURE 14-15	

Creating a reverse-lookup zone

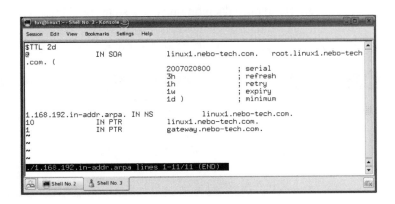

For example, in Figure 14-15, the network address for the hosts in the zone is 192.168.1.0. Therefore, the zone name is 1.168.192.in-addr.arpa. Accordingly, the hosts in the zone are referenced by the last octet of their IP address, for example:

```
10      IN      PTR      linux1.nebo-tech.com
```

This record points the host 10.1.168.192-in-addr.arpa (192.168.1.10) to linux1.nebo-tech.com. With the reverse-lookup zone configured, you can use the DNS server to resolve IP addresses into domain names instead of the other way around.

With your zones defined, you can now start your named daemon using its init script. You should also configure your workstations to use your new DNS server to resolve host names. On a Linux system, you need to edit the /etc/host.conf or the /etc/resolv.conf file and add the IP address of the system running the named daemon. On a Windows system, you use the Network applet to specify the DNS server address.

on the

job

You must open port 53 in your system's firewall for clients to be able to send requests to your DNS server.

Once that's done, you can use a variety of Linux command-line tools to test your system. Let's discuss how this is done next.

Using dig and nslookup

Linux provides you with several tools that you can use to send name resolution requests to your named daemon. The first is the nslookup utility. To use this utility to send a name resolution request, complete the following:

1. At the shell prompt, enter **nslookup**.

2. At the > prompt, enter the *hostname* or *IP address* you want your DNS server to resolve.

3. The named daemon on your system should respond with the requested mapping. For example, in Figure 14-16, the linux1 host name has been sent

---

FIGURE 14-16

Using nslookup

for resolution to the DNS server at 127.0.0.1 (the localhost) on port 53. The named daemon on the local host returned an IP address for the host of 192.168.1.10.

4. When you are done, enter **exit** at the > prompt.

Another utility you can use is dig. The dig utility works much like nslookup, but it provides more extensive information about the requested host name or IP address. In Figure 14-17, the dig linux1.nebo-tech.com command was issued at the shell prompt.

Notice that the output from dig is considerably more extensive than that displayed by nslookup. It returns the IP address associated with the host name in the ANSWER SECTION. It also lists the authoritative name server for the host name and zone in the AUTHORITY SECTION.

Now that you understand how DNS works, here are some possible scenario questions and their answers.

SCENARIO & SOLUTION

Your workstation sends a name resolution request for www.nebo-tech.com to your organization's DNS server. This server is not authoritative for the nebo-tech.com zone. How will your DNS server resolve this domain name into an IP address?	Your DNS server will send a request to a root-level DNS server. The root-level DNS server responds to your DNS server with the IP address of a DNS server that's authoritative for nebo-tech.com zone. Your DNS server sends a resolution request for the .com TLD to the DNS server specified by the root-level DNS server. The DNS server responds with the IP address of the DNS server that's authoritative for the nebo-tech.com zone. Then your DNS server sends a request for the www host to the authoritative DNS server for the nebo-tech.com zone where the host name resides. The authoritative DNS server responds to your DNS server with the appropriate IP address. Your DNS server returns this address to your workstation, which then contacts the host using its IP address.
You're configuring a DNS server for your network. Your network address is 192.168.1.0. What would the name of your reverse-lookup zone be?	Your reverse-lookup zone would be named 1.168.192.in-addr.arpa.

FIGURE 14-17

Using dig

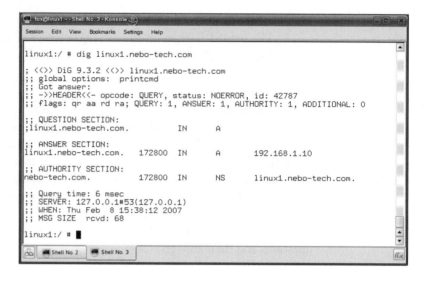

```
linux1:/ # dig linux1.nebo-tech.com

; <<>> DiG 9.3.2 <<>> linux1.nebo-tech.com
;; global options:  printcmd
;; Got answer:
;; ->>HEADER<<- opcode: QUERY, status: NOERROR, id: 42787
;; flags: qr aa rd ra; QUERY: 1, ANSWER: 1, AUTHORITY: 1, ADDITIONAL: 0

;; QUESTION SECTION:
;linux1.nebo-tech.com.          IN      A

;; ANSWER SECTION:
linux1.nebo-tech.com.   172800  IN      A       192.168.1.10

;; AUTHORITY SECTION:
nebo-tech.com.          172800  IN      NS      linux1.nebo-tech.com.

;; Query time: 6 msec
;; SERVER: 127.0.0.1#53(127.0.0.1)
;; WHEN: Thu Feb  8 15:38:12 2007
;; MSG SIZE  rcvd: 68

linux1:/ #
```

Let's create a DNS server in the following exercise.

EXERCISE 14-2

Configuring a DNS Server

In this exercise, you will install and configure the named daemon on your Linux system. This exercise assumes you have an Ethernet network board installed and configured in your system. Complete the following:

1. Boot your Linux system and log in as a standard user. If you used the lab exercise in Chapter 3 to install your system, you can log in as **tux** with a password of **M3linux273**.

2. Open a terminal session.

3. Switch to your root user account by entering **su –** followed by your root user's password.

4. Using the rpm utility, install the following packages on your system:
   - bind
   - bind-libs
   - bind-chrootenv
   - bind-utils

5. Open /etc/named.conf in a text editor.
6. Add the following lines:

```
zone "my-zone.com' in {
        file "master/my-zone.com";
        type master;
}
```

7. Save your changes to the /etc/named.conf file.
8. Using a text editor, open a new file named /var/lib/named/master/my-zone.com.
9. Add the following lines to your my-zone.com file:

```
$TTL 2d
@      IN SOA     your_hostname.my-zone.com.    root.your_hostname.my-zone.com. (
                  2007020800 ; serial
                  3h         ; refresh
                  1h         ; retry
                  1w         ; expiry
                  1d )       ; minimum

my-zone.com.      IN NS      your_hostname.my-zone.com.
your_host         IN A       your_host_IP_address
```

10. Save your changes to the file.
11. Open /etc/resolve.conf in a text editor.
12. Add the following lines to the file:

```
domain my-zone.com
nameserver your_host_IP_address
```

13. If your system has a host-based firewall running, create an exception for IP port 53.
14. At the shell prompt, start the named daemon using its init script in /etc/init.d or /etc/rc.d/init.d.
15. Use the dig command to resolve your system's host name. Verify that the correct IP address is returned.
16. Use dig to resolve a domain name on the Internet, such as www.yahoo.com.

It's time to shift gears and look at another network service you can install and configure on your Linux system: the Apache Web server!

Configure the Apache Web Server on Linux

In addition to functioning as a DHCP server and a DNS server, your Linux system can also function as a Web server. There are a variety of Web server packages that you can use on Linux, but by far and away, the most popular is the Apache Web server. Most of the Web servers you access on the Internet are actually running some version of Apache. Therefore, this is the Web server you need to be familiar with for your Linux+ exam. In this part of this chapter, we're going to discuss the following topics:

■ How a Web server works

■ Installing the Apache Web server daemon

■ Configuring the Apache Web server

Let's begin by reviewing how a Web server works.

How a Web Server Works

Twenty years ago, few could have foreseen the changes that the widespread adoption of the Internet would have on the world and its various peoples and cultures. Information that was unavailable to the average person in the 1980s is only a click away now.

Web servers provide much of the functionality we associate with the Internet today. When we use the term *Web server*, we're referring to the network service running on your system, not the hardware itself. The hardware the Web server runs on may be an appliance dedicated to providing only Web services or it may be a standard network server that has been configured to provide Web services. A Web server can even run on a networked desktop computer system.

A Web server's job is to send Web pages, graphics, and other files to clients requesting them. A Web server can transfer just about any type of computer file between the server and the client. However, the most common type of file used with a Web server is a Web page. A Web page is simply a text document written using a special markup coding system (called *Hypertext Markup Language* or HTML) that instructs the Web browser how the information should be formatted and displayed. A simple HTML file is shown in Figure 14-18.

To view this file properly, the user needs a *Web browser*. A Web browser is an application that runs on the client computer that is used to request Web pages

FIGURE 14-18

A simple HTML
Web page file

```
<!DOCTYPE html PUBLIC "-//W3C//DTD HTML 4.01 Transitional//EN">
<html>
<head>
  <meta content="text/html; charset=ISO-8859-1"
 http-equiv="content-type">
  <title>HTML Sample Web Page</title>
</head>
<body>
<h1>HTML Sample</h1>
This is a sample web page. It uses HTML to format the text and layout
of the document. A web page can include elements such as:<br>
<ul>
  <li>Text</li>
  <li>Graphics</li>
  <li>Hyperlinks</li>
  <li>Forms</li>
</ul>
<br>
</body>
</html>
```

from a Web server, format them, and display them on screen. There are a variety of different Web browsers currently in use. These include the following:

- Konqueror
- Mozilla Firefox
- Netscape Navigator
- Opera
- Safari
- Microsoft Internet Explorer (IE)

When the user's Web browser receives this file from the Web server, it interprets the marked-up text from the file and displays it on the screen. For example, the file in Figure 14-18 is displayed as shown in Figure 14-19 when it is opened in a Web browser.

The information in the text file is reformatted and displayed according to the markup information it contains.

The files that comprise a Web site are saved in a special directory in the file system of the system running the Web server daemon. This directory is called the

FIGURE 14-19

Viewing an HTML
file in a browser

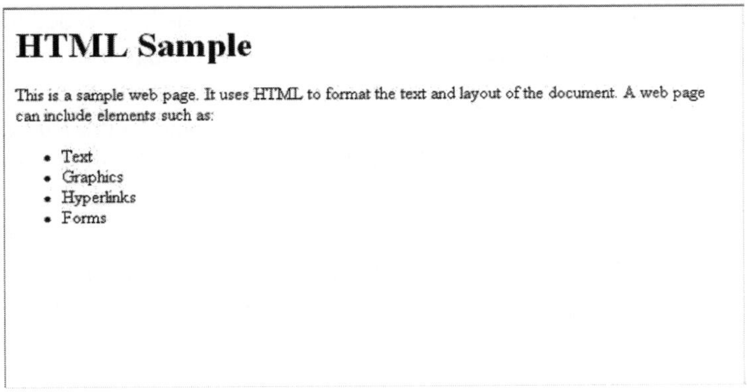

HTML Sample

This is a sample web page. It uses HTML to format the text and layout of the document. A web page can include elements such as:

- Text
- Graphics
- Hyperlinks
- Forms

document root or *root directory*. The Apache Web server's document root is the /srv/www/htdocs directory.

Communications between the Web browser and the Web server are accomplished using the IP protocol in conjunction with the *Hypertext Transfer Protocol* (HTTP). HTTP is a request/response protocol used by the Web browser to get information from the Web server. The browser initiates the request by establishing a TCP/IP communication session between the client system and the Web server, which runs on IP port 80 by default. The Web server then listens for the browser to tell it what information it wants. The browser does this by sending a GET message to the Web server, which responds with the requested files.

When using a Web browser, you use a *Uniform Resource Locator* (URL) to access information on the Web server. A URL is used by your browser to specify the exact information you need from the Web server as well as how it is to be retrieved. The syntax for a URL is as shown here:

```
protocol://domain_name or IP_address:port/filename
```

The *protocol* portion of the URL specifies the protocol the browser will use to retrieve information. If you're accessing a Web server, you will be using the HTTP or HTTPS protocol, so the first part of the URL will be http or https.

The HTTP protocol is used to transfer information from the Web server using unencrypted transmissions. This level of security is acceptable for many Web pages. However, if you are transferring sensitive information, this could present a problem. Someone using sniffing software could potentially capture the information being transferred between your browser and the Web server.

For sensitive information, such as credit card numbers or personal information, we use the HTTPS protocol. The HTTPS protocol uses standard HTTP, but it also uses the Secure Sockets Layer (SSL) protocol to encrypt the data before sending it. Only the sender and receiver have the keys that can decrypt the information. Sniffers on the Internet can still capture the information being transferred, but they won't be able to decode the data because they don't have the key needed to decipher it.

After specifying the protocol, you next add a :// to the URL. After these characters, you specify the domain name or IP address of the Web server you want to access. After the domain name or IP address, you add a : to the end of the URL. Then you (optionally) specify the IP port where the Web server is running. For example:

```
http://www.nebo-tech.com:80
```

This tells the browser to access port 80 on www.nebo-tech.com. However, we don't usually specify a port at the end of URLs when browsing the Web. That's because Web browsers default to port 80 if you don't specify a port number in the URL.

(HTTPS requests default to port 443.) Because most Web servers are configured to use port 80, this convention works most of the time. If, for some reason, the Web server you're accessing has been configured to use a different port number, however, you will need to explicitly include it in the URL.

After the port number, you add a / to the end of the URL. Then you specify the file name that you wish to retrieve from the Web server, for example:

```
http://www.nebo-tech.com:80/index.html
```

As with ports, you also don't have to always explicitly include the name of the file you want to retrieve from the Web server. That's because Web servers are usually configured such that, if no file name is specified in the URL, it sends a file named index.html by default. If the file you're requesting has a name other than index.html, then you will need to explicitly specify it in the URL.

With this background in mind, let's next discuss how you go about installing the Apache Web server daemon on your system.

Installing the Apache Web Server Daemon

Depending upon your distribution and the options you selected during installation, you may or may not have the Apache Web server daemon installed on your Linux system. To install a simple Apache Web server on your Linux system, you need to install the following packages:

- apache2
- apache2-doc
- apache2-example-pages
- apache2-prefork

These packages should be available on your distribution media, as shown in Figure 14-20.

FIGURE 14-20

Apache Web server packages

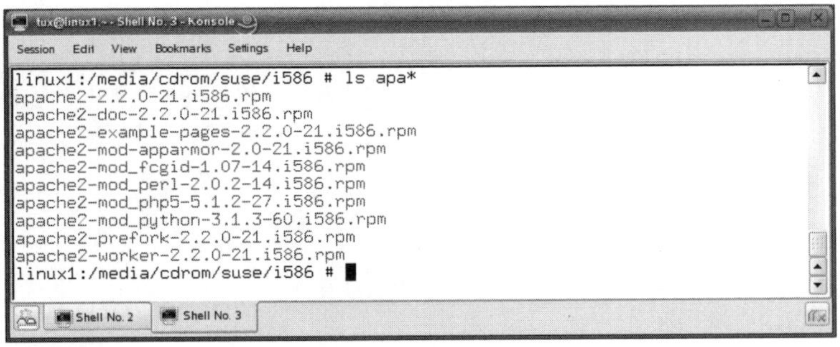
Session Edit View Bookmarks Settings Help
linux1:/media/cdrom/suse/i586 # ls apa*
apache2-2.2.0-21.i586.rpm
apache2-doc-2.2.0-21.i586.rpm
apache2-example-pages-2.2.0-21.i586.rpm
apache2-mod-apparmor-2.0-21.i586.rpm
apache2-mod_fcgid-1.07-14.i586.rpm
apache2-mod_perl-2.0.2-14.i586.rpm
apache2-mod_php5-5.1.2-27.i586.rpm
apache2-mod_python-3.1.3-60.i586.rpm
apache2-prefork-2.2.0-21.i586.rpm
apache2-worker-2.2.0-21.i586.rpm
linux1:/media/cdrom/suse/i586 #
Shell No. 2
Shell No. 3

on the **Job**

The apache2 packages have many dependencies. Depending upon your distribution and how it was originally installed, you may have to install these packages with rpm as well. If you want to save yourself the hassle, you can use a graphical installation utility, such as YaST, to install all the required packages.

After installation, you can use the apache2 init script in your /etc/init.d or /etc/rc.d/init.d directory to start, stop, or reload the Apache Web server daemon. This script is shown in Figure 14-21.

After installing the daemon on your system, it is configured to listen for HTTP requests on all installed network interfaces, including your lo interface. You can initially test the functionality of the daemon by entering **/etc/init.d/apache2 start** or **/etc/rc.d/init.d/apache2 start** at the shell prompt to enable the daemon. Then open a Web browser on your Linux system and navigate to http://127.0.0.1. You should see the default Apache2 Web server home page, shown in Figure 14-22.

With the daemon up and running, we now need to configure how it works. Let's discuss how this is done next.

Configuring the Apache Web Server

The Apache Web server is a very powerful Web server that can be configured in a variety of ways. Entire books have been written about advanced Apache Web server configuration options. We don't have time or space to go into that kind of detail here. Instead, we're going to focus on some common configuration options used to set up a basic Apache Web server.

FIGURE 14-21

The apache2 init script

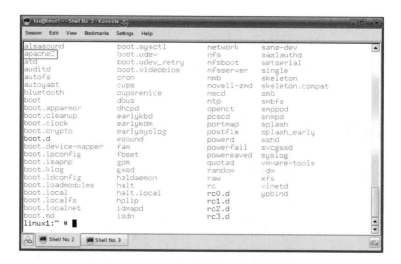

FIGURE 14-22

The default
Apache Web
server page

After installation, the default document root used by Apache is /srv/www/htdocs, shown in Figure 14-23.

As you can see in Figure 14-23, some basic Web files are installed in the document root by default during installation. The index.html file in Figure 14-23 is the file displayed in Figure 14-22. At this point, your Web server is up, running, and available for use by clients. You can copy your own Web files into the document root to set up your Web site.

You can also customize the way the Apache Web server behaves. The /etc/apache2 directory on your Linux system contains a large number of files that are used to configure the Web server. Some of the more frequently used configuration files are listed in Table 14-6.

There are actually many other configuration files in this directory. The good news is that most of them work just fine using their default settings. The main configuration file for Apache is the /etc/apache2/httpd.conf file, shown in Figure 14-24.

As you can see in Figure 14-24, the httpd.conf file actually links to all of the other configuration files in /etc/apache2 using Include directives. You should avoid directly editing httpd.conf. Instead, make your changes in the include files. Directives within the include files will override directives within httpd.conf. For example, if you wanted to change your document root directory, you would edit the default-server.conf file, shown in Figure 14-25.

If you wanted to change the IP address and port number used by the Web server, you would edit the listen.conf file, shown in Figure 14-26.

FIGURE 14-23

The Apache Web
server document
root

TABLE 14-6   Apache Web Server Configuration Files

Configuration File	Description
/etc/apache2/httpd.conf	This is the main configuration file for the Apache Web server.
/etc/apache2/default-server.conf	This file is used to configure basic Web server settings.
/etc/apache2/uid.conf	This file is used to specify the user and group that the Apache daemon will run under.
/etc/apache2/listen.conf	This file is used to specify the IP addresses and ports that the Web server will listen for HTTP requests on.
/etc/apache2/error.conf	This file is used to configure how the Web server will handle errors.
/etc/apache2/vhost.d/	This directory contains configuration files that can be used to configure virtual Web hosts.

on the job   *You must open ports 80 and 443 in your system's firewall for clients to be able to connect to your Web server.*

FIGURE 14-24

The /etc/apache2/
httpd.conf
configuration file

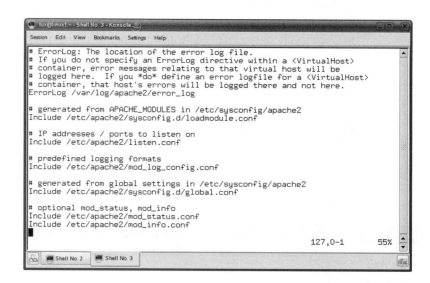

FIGURE 14-25

Setting the
document root
directory

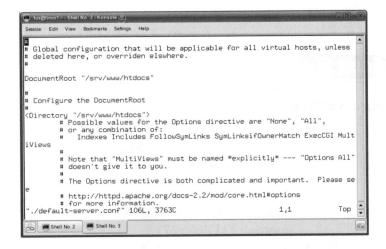

FIGURE 14-26

Configuring the
listen port

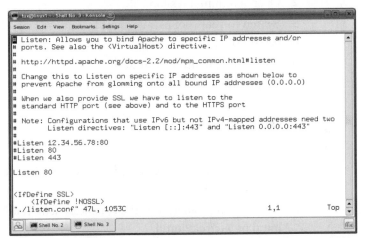

SCENARIO & SOLUTION

Your Linux system has the Apache Web server installed and has a domain name of apps.my-zone.com. A workstation opens a browser and accesses the http://apps.my-zone.com/schedule.html URL. What file in your file system is sent to the workstation's browser?	Assuming you're using a default configuration, the /srv/www/htdocs/schedule.html file is sent to the browser.
A workstation opens a browser and accesses the http://apps.my-zone.com/schedule.html URL. What IP port is the browser sending this request on?	Because no zone was explicitly included in the URL, the request is automatically sent on IP port 80.

Let's configure a Web server in the following exercise.

EXERCISE 14-3

Configuring a Web Server

In this exercise, you will install and configure the apache2 daemon on your Linux system. This exercise assumes you have an Ethernet network board installed and configured in your system. Complete the following:

1. Boot your Linux system and log in as a standard user. If you used the lab exercise in Chapter 3 to install your system, you can log in as **tux** with a password of **M3linux273**.

2. Open a terminal session.

3. Switch to your root user account by entering **su –** followed by your root user's password.

4. Using the rpm utility, install the following packages on your system:
   - apache2
   - apache2-doc
   - apache2-example-pages
   - apache2-prefork

5. If your system has a host-based firewall running, create an exception for IP ports 80 and 443.

6. At the shell prompt, start the apache2 daemon using its init script in /etc/init.d or /etc/rc.d/init.d.

7. Run a Web browser and navigate to http://*your_system_address*/index.html. You should see the "It works!" message displayed.

8. If you know how to use HTML, experiment with customizing your /srv/www/htdocs/index.html file.

Let's shift gears yet again and discuss working with Samba on Linux.

CERTIFICATION OBJECTIVE 14.04

Configure Samba on Linux

One of the coolest network services, in my opinion, that you can install on a Linux system is a product called Samba. In a nutshell, Samba allows your Linux system to emulate a Windows server system. Users can access shared directories and printers just as they would on a Windows server.

This is a really powerful solution. I've installed many Linux servers for a variety of small businesses. When I tell my clients that I can set up a file and print server that is perfectly compatible with their Windows workstations without having to buy an expensive copy of Windows NT, 2000 Server, or Server 2003, they get a big grin on their faces. In this part of this chapter, you'll learn how to set up a basic Samba server and create a shared directory. To do this, you need to understand the following:

- How Samba works
- Installing the Samba daemon
- Configuring Samba

Let's begin by reviewing how Samba works.

How Samba Works

Using only the Microsoft Client for Microsoft Networks client and the File and Printer Sharing for Microsoft Networks service, shown in Figure 14-27, Samba allows Windows users to browse to shared directories and connect to printers on your Linux system.

In addition, Samba can turn your Linux system into a Primary Domain Controller (PDC). A PDC is used to host a Windows domain and provide authentication services for your Windows desktop systems. Instead of logging in using a local Windows user account, you can add your Windows workstations to the domain hosted by the Samba service on your Linux system. Then, when a user needs to log in to his or her Windows workstation, their username and password are sent to your Linux system for authentication.

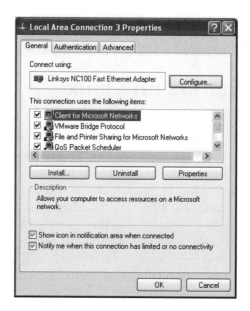

FIGURE 14-27

Configuring a
Windows client
to connect to
Samba

In addition to providing domain, file, and print services, Samba can also do the
following:

- Participate in a Microsoft Active Directory tree.
- Use a Windows-based domain controller to authenticate users.
- Run a Windows Internet Naming Service (WINS) server.

on the
◉ o b
*You can also connect to a Samba share from another Linux system using the
smbclient and smbmount commands at the shell prompt.*

The key to making all this work is the protocol that Samba uses. Samba is based
on the Server Message Block (SMB) protocol. The earliest version of SMB was
developed by IBM in the mid-1980s. In the early 1990s, Andrew Tridgell developed
an SMB version that would run on UNIX. The SMB protocol was later adopted and
widely deployed by Microsoft beginning with Windows 95 and Windows NT. It is
now the backbone of the Windows networking infrastructure.

on the
◉ o b
*Microsoft's SMB implementation is called the Common Internet File System
(CIFS). Because CIFS is based on SMB, it is compatible with Samba.*

The SMB protocol makes directories and printers available to SMB clients
through a process called *sharing*. Shared resources on a Samba server are referenced

using the Universal Naming Convention (UNC). The syntax for using UNC names is as follows:

```
\\server_name\share_name
```

For example, if I had a Linux system named linux1 with Samba configured, I could access a share on the system named myfiles using a UNC of \\linux1\myfiles. Let's discuss how you install Samba on your Linux system.

Installing the Samba Daemon

As with the other products we've reviewed in this chapter, the Samba packages may or may not have been installed by default when you installed your Linux distribution. Therefore, you'll probably need to install them manually using the rpm utility. You'll need to install the following packages from your distribution media:

- kdebase3-samba (for systems using the KDE desktop environment)
- libsmbclient
- samba
- samba-client
- samba-doc
- samba-pdb
- samba-winbind

The samba-client and libsmbclient packages are only needed if you want your Linux system to function as both a Samba server and as a Samba client. If you only want it to be a Samba server, you can omit these packages.

After installation, the following daemons are used on your Linux system to provide the Samba service:

- **/usr/sbin/smbd**   This daemon is the heart of the SMB server. It allows you to share local directories and printers with SMB-based clients.
- **/usr/sbin/nmbd**   This daemon is a Linux-based WINS server. It provides NetBIOS-to-IP address name resolution for SMB-based systems on your network.
- **/usr/sbin/winbindd**   This daemon connects your Samba server to a Microsoft Windows server network.

After the Samba packages are installed, you can start, stop, and restart the Samba services using the smb, nmbd, and winbind init scripts in the /etc/init.d or /etc/rc.d/ init.d directory, as shown in Figure 14-28.

FIGURE 14-28

Samba init scripts

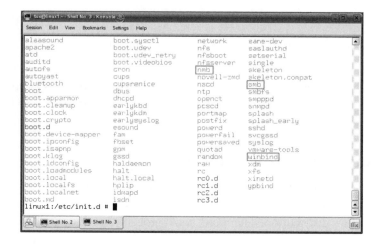

With the Samba package installed on your system, you're ready to configure and start the service. Let's review how this is done next.

Configuring Samba

As with the Apache Web server, the Samba server is a very powerful, very extensive product. We don't have time or space in this chapter to make you a Samba expert (nor does the Linux+ exam expect you to be one). Instead, we're going to focus on creating a basic Samba server that can be used to share directories and printers. To do this, we're going to discuss the following topics:

- Configuring Samba
- Samba-enabling Linux users

Let's begin by discussing how to configure the Samba service on your Linux system.

Configuring Samba

As with the other services we've discussed in this chapter, the Samba service is configured by editing text files. The files you need to be familiar with to do this reside in the /etc/samba directory.

The first is the /etc/samba/lmhosts file. This functions in a way very similar to your /etc/hosts file on your Linux system. In the absence of a WINS server, lmhosts can be used to provide simple NetBIOS name resolution. The lmhosts file, shown in Figure 14-29, provides a static mapping of NetBIOS names to IP addresses.

FIGURE 14-29

The /etc/samba/
lmhosts file

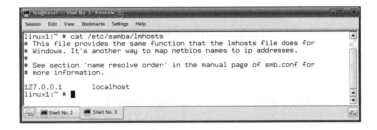

You can implement the nmbd daemon on your Linux system as a part of your Samba implementation. This daemon provides a WINS server that reduces the need for the lmhosts file.

The next file you need to be familiar with is /etc/samba/smbfstab. This file is used when configuring the Samba client on your system. It's not required when configuring your system as a Samba server. The smbfstab file is used to automatically mount a shared directory on a remote system when the system is booted. A sample smbfstab file is shown in Figure 14-30.

To do this, you specify the share, the local directory where it's to be mounted, the remote file system type (cifs or smbfs), and various options, such as the username and password needed to authenticate to the remote server.

The next file we need to look at is the /etc/samba/smbpasswd file. The smbd daemon uses this file to store Samba user accounts. It's important to remember that the Samba service uses a *separate* set of user accounts from your Linux user accounts. You have to import and configure your standard Linux users as Samba users before anyone can access shared directories and printers on the system.

FIGURE 14-30

The /etc/samba/
smbfstab file

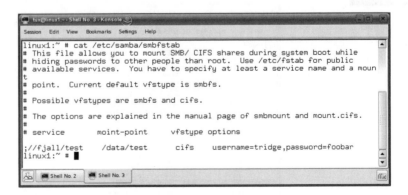

The next file you need to be familiar with is /etc/samba/smbusers. This file is used by Samba to map usernames from client systems to user accounts on the local server. You use the following syntax:

```
Samba_server_username = client_username
```

The configuration file that you need to spend most of your time with is the /etc/samba/smb.conf file. This file is the heart of your Samba configuration. It's divided into two parts: *global options* and *shared resources*. The [global] section is used to define options that apply server-wide. The shared resources section is used to define resources on the server that can be accessed by SMB clients. A portion of an smb.conf file is shown in Figure 14-31.

There are a ton of options that you can configure in the [global] section of smb.conf, most of which we don't have time to cover here. If you want to see a list of all possible parameters, see the man page for smb.conf. For your Linux+ certification, you need to be familiar with the global options in Table 14-7.

The next section of smb.conf that you need to know about is [homes] (see Figure 14-31). The [homes] section of the configuration file is used to define shared resources and share the home directories of the user accounts on your system.

In addition to sharing home directories, you can also use smb.conf to create your own shared directories. To do this, you add a section to the smb.conf file using the following syntax:

```
[share_name]
        comment = share_description
        path = path to shared directory
        other_smb_options
```

FIGURE 14-31

The /etc/samba/smb.conf file

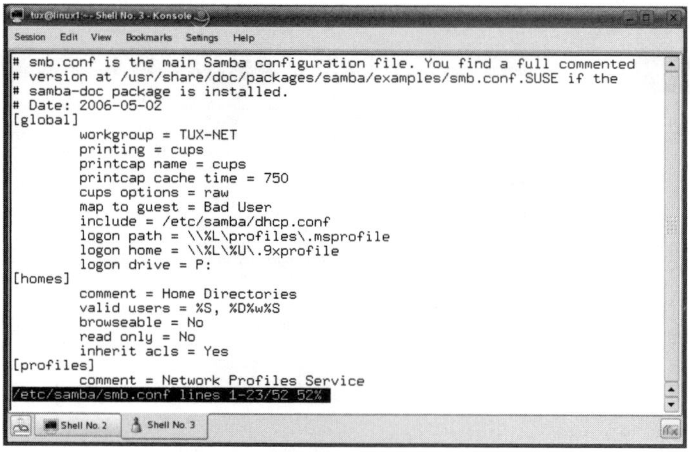

| TABLE 14-7 | Global Samba Options |

Global Option	Description
workgroup	Defines the name of the workgroup or domain the Samba server will participate in.
netbios name	Sets the NetBIOS name of the Samba server.
server string	Provides a description of the Samba server that will be displayed in My Network Places for Windows clients.
encrypt passwords	Configures smbd to use encrypted passwords. This should be enabled as every version of Windows since Windows 98 requires encrypted passwords.
passdb backend	Identifies where Samba user accounts are stored.
wins server	Specifies the IP address of your network's WINS server.
wins support	If your network doesn't already have a WINS server, set this parameter to yes. This will enable a WINS service by running the nmbd daemon on your system.
load printers	If you include this parameter in your smb.conf file, all printers defined in the /etc/printcap file will be automatically shared.
security	Determines how smbd will authenticate users. There are several different values you can use with this parameter: ■ **user** Authentication is handled on a per-user basis. An SMB client must first authenticate with a valid username and password to the Samba server before it is allowed to access shared resources on the server. This is the default value if the security option isn't explicitly included in smb.conf. ■ **share** Authentication is handled on a per-share basis. Each share in the system is assigned its own password. Client systems can access the share by simply providing the share's password. User names are not checked. ■ **domain** All authentication processes are handled by a primary domain controller or a backup domain controller.
printing	Defines the type of printing system that will be shared by Samba. The possible values are CUPS, LPRNG, PLP, SYSV, AIX, HPUX, QNX, SOFTQ, and BSD. Usually you will use CUPS for this parameter.

The *share_name* parameter specifies the name of the share. The *comment* parameter is used to provide a description of the share. The *path* parameter specifies the full path to the shared directory. Of course, you'll need to configure the directory with the appropriate permissions to provide users with access to the share.

In addition, you can also configure several other optional share parameters, shown in Table 14-8.

Once you have your smb.conf file configured, you need to Samba-enable your users. Let's discuss how to do that next.

Samba-Enabling Linux Users

This is one of the key tasks that many Linux admins new to Samba forget! It's critical that you remember that Samba doesn't use the user accounts in the /etc/passwd file. Instead, it uses /etc/samba/smbpasswd. By default, the smbpasswd file doesn't have any users listed in it. To populate the smbpasswd file with user accounts, you must use the smbpasswd utility from the shell prompt. To do this, complete the following:

1. Open a terminal session.
2. At the shell prompt, **su –** to root. If you run smbpasswd as any user other than root, it can only be used to manage the smbpasswd account for the currently logged-in user. If you want to manage other users' accounts, you must be logged in as root.
3. At the shell prompt, enter **smbpasswd –a** *username*.
4. When prompted, enter a *password* for the Samba user account. While not required, most Samba administrators use the same password for the SMB user account as for the Linux user account.
5. When prompted, re-enter the *password*. You will be prompted that the user account as been added, as shown in Figure 14-32.

TABLE 14-8   Samba Share Options

Share Option	Description
browseable	Specifies whether or not the share can be browsed in My Network Places or Network Neighborhood. If you don't include this parameter, a default value of yes is assumed.
read only	If set to yes (default), users cannot create or edit files in the shared directory.
writeable	If set to yes, users may create or edit files in the shared directory, as long as the file system permissions assigned to the directory allow it.
public	If set to yes, users can connect to the shared directory without a password using the "nobody" system user account. This is only used with share-level security. The default value for this parameter is no.
valid users	Restricts access to the share to a specified list of users. Separate user names with a comma (,).
guest ok	When set to yes, users don't need to supply a password to access the shared resource. The default value is no.

FIGURE 14-32

Adding the tux
user to the
smbpasswd file

This user account is now in the /etc/samba/smbpasswd file, as shown in Figure 14-33.
After starting the smbd daemon using its init script in /etc/init.d or /etc/rc.d/init.d,
the user will now be able to access shared resources provided by the Samba server.
You can map a drive to a Samba share from a Windows workstation by doing the
following:

1. Right-click on My Computer, then select Map Network Drive.

2. Select a *drive letter* to map to the share.

3. In the Folder field, enter the **UNC** to the share. You can use the Browse
   button, if necessary, to browse to the Samba server and share.

4. If you've logged in to the local workstation using a username and password
   that are different from your Samba username and password, select Connect
   Using a Different User Name and enter your Samba **username** and **password**.

5. Select Finish. The shared directory is displayed in a new Explorer window.
   In Figure 14-34, the tux user has mapped the Z:\ drive to his home directory
   shared through Samba.

You can also access shared Samba resources from a Linux client system.
You can view shared resources available on a Samba server by entering
smbclient –L *Samba_servername*. For example, in Figure 14-35, the smbclient

FIGURE 14-33

Viewing the tux
user account in
smbpasswd

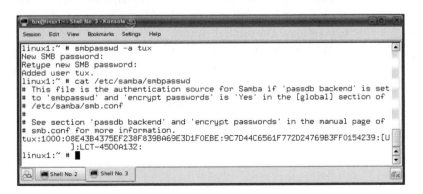

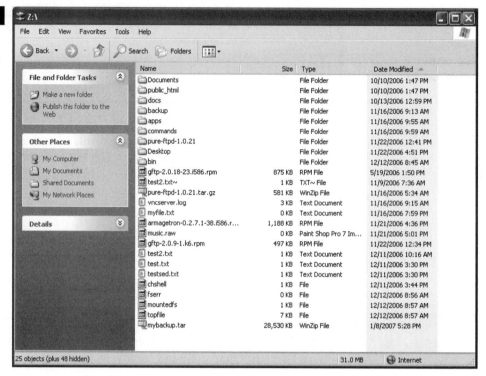

FIGURE 14-34

Mapping a drive
to a Samba share

utility has been used to display shared resources available on the LINUX1 Samba
server.

To mount a shared directory on a Samba server, you can use the smbmount
command. The syntax is smbmount *share_name mount_point* user=*username*. For
example, to mount a share on the LINUX1 server named resources in /mnt/smb
as a user named tux, you would enter **smbmount //LINUX1/resources /mnt/smb
user=tux**. You can then access the files in the remote shared directory by switching
to your local /mnt/smb directory.

You can also use the good old mount command to do the same thing. The syntax
is mount –t smbfs *share_name mount_point*. Note that the value of your USER
environment variable will be used as the username to authenticate to the remote
Samba server. To dismount a mounted share, just use the umount command as you
would with any mounted file system.

FIGURE 14-35

Viewing shares
with smbclient

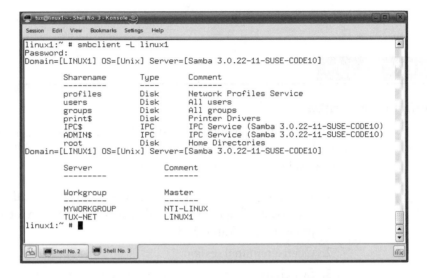

<table>
<thead>
<tr><th colspan="5">SCENARIO & SOLUTION</th></tr>
</thead>
<tbody>
<tr>
<td>You're implementing Samba on your Linux system. You've created a directory named /data and you want to share this directory. Users need to be able to read and write data to this directory. How would you define this share in the smb.conf file?</td>
<td>You could define it using the following:

<code>[Data]
    comment = "Data Directory"
    path = /data
    writable = yes</code></td>
</tr>
<tr>
<td>You have implemented shared directories using Samba. You've used the smbpasswd utility to add your users to the smbpasswd file. Your users are able to map network drives from their Windows systems to the shared directories without any problems. However, when you try to map a network drive using your root user account, you're unable to do so. Why did this happen?</td>
<td>To access Samba shared resources, users, including root, need to be added to the smbpasswd file. You can do this by entering **smbpasswd –a root** at the shell prompt.</td>
</tr>
</tbody>
</table>

Let's create a simple Samba server in the following exercise.

EXERCISE 14-4

Configuring Samba

In this exercise, you will install and configure the Samba daemon on your Linux system. This exercise assumes you have an Ethernet network board installed and configured in your system. Complete the following:

1. Boot your Linux system and log in as a standard user. If you used the lab exercise in Chapter 3 to install your system, you can log in as **tux** with a password of **M3linux273**.

2. Open a terminal session.

3. Switch to your root user account by entering **su –** followed by your root user's password.

4. Using the rpm utility, install the following packages on your system:
   - libsmbclient
   - samba
   - samba-client
   - samba-doc
   - samba-pdb
   - samba-winbind

5. Open /etc/samba/smb.conf in a text editor.

6. Set the *workgroup=* parameter to a workgroup name of your choice.

7. Set the *netbios name=* parameter to the host name of your Linux system.

8. Verify that the [homes] share is listed.

9. Share your /tmp directory by adding the following lines:

   ```
   [Temp]
           comment = "Temporary Directory"
           path = /tmp
           writable = yes
   ```

10. Save your changes to the /etc/samba/smb.conf file.

11. Samba-enable your tux user account by entering **smbpasswd –a tux** at the shell prompt.

12. When prompted, enter a password for the tux Samba account.

13. Start the Samba service using the smb init script in /etc/rc.d/init.d or /etc/init.d.

14. Using a text editor, open a new file named /var/lib/named/master/my-zone.com.

15. View the shares available on your system by entering **smbclient –L** **your_netbios_name** at the shell prompt. Verify that the homes and Temp shares are listed.

16. If you have a Windows system available, map a network drive to the Temp share on your Samba server by right-clicking My Computer and selecting Map Network Drive. You'll need to connect as your tux user with the password you specified in step 12.

It's time to shift gears once again and talk about printing on Linux.

CERTIFICATION OBJECTIVE 14.05

Configure Printing on Linux

No matter what operating system you're using, one of the most important services it offers is the ability to send print jobs to a printer. If you don't believe me, just unplug your office's printer for an hour and observe the mayhem that results. OK, don't really unplug your office's printer. Your co-workers may cause you significant bodily harm.

The point is, printing is vital to most users. Because of this, you need to be very familiar with Linux printing. In this part of this chapter, we're going to cover the following topics:

- How Linux printing works
- Installing CUPS
- Configuring CUPS
- Using the Line Printer Daemon (LPD)

Let's begin by discussing how Linux printing works.

How Linux Printing Works

The most common Linux printing system in use today is the Common UNIX Printing System (CUPS). CUPS was designed from the ground up to make Linux printing as easy as possible, whether printing to a locally attached printer or to a remote network printer. The CUPS service is provided by the cupsd daemon, which automatically announces the availability of its print queues on the local network. CUPS client systems listen to these announcements, allowing the user to select the printer he or she wants with little networking knowledge. In addition, CUPS supports network printing over the *Internet Printing Protocol* (IPP) on port 631.

The CUPS system is composed of several component parts. The first is the *CUPS scheduler*. The CUPS scheduler is a Web server that is used solely to handle IPP printing requests from CUPS clients. Because the CUPS scheduler runs on IP port 631, it can co-exist with the Apache Web server running on the same system. In fact, the CUPS configuration file even looks like the Apache Web server's configuration file. In addition to processing print jobs, the CUPS scheduler also functions as a typical Web server, providing documentation as well a CUPS administration tool in a browser interface.

The next components you need to be familiar with are the CUPS filters. Modern printers use a variety of different *page description languages* (PDLs). In a Linux system, most applications generate print jobs using Adobe's PostScript PDL. This works well if you have a PostScript-compatible printer. However, not all printers include PostScript support due to the fact that the printer manufacturer must pay licensing fees to Adobe, which can dramatically increase the price of the unit. Instead, many printer manufacturers, such as Hewlett-Packard, use the Printer Control Language (PCL) PDL. Other manufacturers, such as Epson, use the ESC/P PDL.

If your printer isn't PostScript-compatible, you use CUPS filters to convert print jobs from PostScript into the appropriate format using the PDL of the printer to which it is being sent. These filters are located in /usr/lib/cups/filter.

The next components you need to know about are the CUPS backends. Backends are responsible for providing the interface between the scheduler and the actual printer hardware. The CUPS backends are located in /usr/lib/cups/backend. CUPS provides backends for a variety of different printer interfaces, including parallel, serial, USB, and so on. Each time cupsd starts, it queries each backend installed on the system. The backends respond to the daemon, reporting whether or not a printer is connected. If a printer is connected, they report information about the printer, such as the make and model.

The next CUPS components you need to be familiar with are the PPD (PostScript Printer Description) files. PPDs are used by cupsd to determine the capabilities of your printer. These PPD files are stored in /etc/cups/ppd.

The last CUPS component you need to be familiar with is the Web-based administration utility. The CUPS scheduler provides the Web-based administrative interface. The CUPS administration utility can be used to set up printers and manage print jobs. To access the CUPS Web-based administration utility, just open a Web browser and navigate to http://*your_server_address*:631. When you do, the screen in Figure 14-36 is displayed.

When a print job is submitted to a CUPS server, the process depicted in Figure 14-37 occurs.

First, an application on the client system generates a print job and sends it to the cupsd daemon on the server. The daemon saves the job in the spooling directory. Print queue and filter information from the print job are saved in /var/spool/cups. The file is named with a "c," concatenated with a print job number assigned by cupsd. The document to be printed is also saved in /var/spool/cups. This time, however, the file is named with a "d," concatenated with the print job number assigned by cupsd.

Next, the print job is sent to the filter for conversion to the appropriate PDL. Once that's done, the converted print job is sent from the filter to the backend, which forwards the job to its connected printer. After sending the job to the printer, the backend notifies the cupsd daemon and the print job is deleted from the print queue.

Now that you know how CUPS printing works, we need to discuss how to install the service on your Linux system. Let's do that next.

FIGURE 14-36

Using the CUPS administration utility

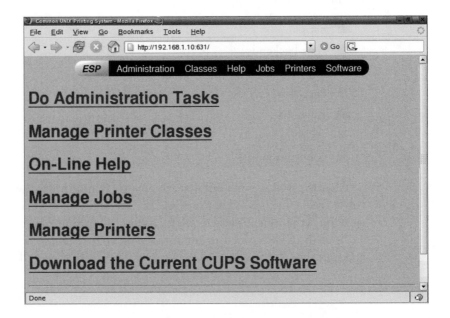

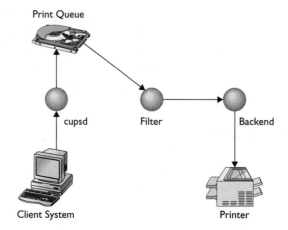

FIGURE 14-37

Sending a print job

Installing CUPS

Unlike the services we reviewed earlier in this chapter, there's a pretty good chance that your Linux distribution installed the packages required to provide CUPS printing by default. As we said earlier, CUPS is the default printing system used by most modern Linux distributions.

If your distribution didn't install CUPS for some reason, use the rpm utility to install the following packages:

- cups
- cups-backends
- cups-client (optional)
- cups-drivers
- cups-libs
- gtklp (optional)
- xpp (optional)

After the packages are installed, the binary that provides the CUPS service is the cupsd executable located in /usr/sbin. The service is started and stopped using the cups init script in /etc/init.d or /etc/rc.d/init.d, shown in Figure 14-38.

Once the CUPS packages are installed on your system, you're ready to configure and start the CUPS service on your server. Let's learn how to do that next.

FIGURE 14-38

FIGURE 14-38

The CUPS init
script

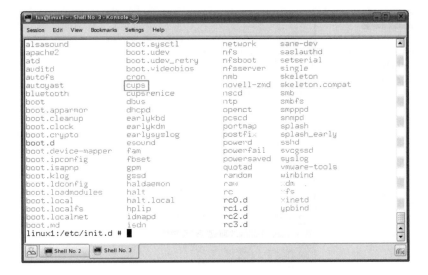

Configuring CUPS

The CUPS service appears complicated and, under the hood, it is. Fortunately, the developers who wrote CUPS made it very easy for you and me to configure and manage. In this part of this chapter, we're going learn how to configure CUPS by learning about the following topics:

- Configuring the CUPS service
- Configuring a CUPS printer
- Using command-line tools to manage CUPS

Let's begin by learning how to configure the cupsd daemon.

Configuring the CUPS Service

The CUPS service is configured using several text files within the /etc/cups directory. The /etc/cups/cupsd.conf file is the main configuration file you will use to configure the cupsd daemon. Remember that cupsd is also an HTTP server, like Apache. Accordingly, the cupsd.conf file is very similar to the Apache Web server configuration file. A sample cupsd.conf file is shown in Figure 14-39.

Figure 14-39 only shows a very small portion of the cupsd.conf file, which is quite long. The cupsd.conf file is composed of several server directives, which specify

Using the
cupsd.conf file to
configure CUPS

how cupsd operates. As with Apache, we don't have time or space in this book to cover all the configuration options in cupsd.conf. We're just going to cover the most important ones here. For more information, see the man page for cupsd.conf. You can also open http://localhost:631/sam.html in a browser on your Linux system to see an extensive list of cupsd.conf directives.

If you look at the cupsd.conf file, you'll notice that it is divided into several logical groupings of directives, listed here:

- Server Identity
- Server Options
- Fax Support
- Encryption Support
- Filter Options
- Network Options
- Security Options

Organizing this file in this manner makes it relatively easy to locate a particular directive you need to modify. Some of the more useful cupsd.conf directives within these groups include those shown in Table 14-9.

The way you configure cupsd.conf will largely depend on the particular network you are implementing the system in. The good news is that you don't need to do much with cupsd.conf to configure a basic implementation that provides local printing.

TABLE 14-9	cupsd.conf Configuration Directives	
Section	**Directive**	**Description**
Server Identity	ServerName	Specifies the server name that is announced to CUPS clients.
	ServerAdmin	Specifies the e-mail address users can use to contact the CUPS administrator.
Server Options	DocumentRoot	Specifies the directory where documents cupsd serves to clients are located. By default, this is /usr/share/doc/packages/cups.
	LogLevel	Specifies the level of detail stored in log files. You must use one of the following values: ■ **none** No logging. ■ **error** Log errors only. ■ **warn** Log errors and warnings. ■ **info** Log errors, warnings, and print requests. (Default) ■ **debug** Log nearly all cupsd messages. ■ **debug2** Log all cupsd messages.
	MaxCopies	Sets a limit on the number of copies for a single print job. The default is 100.
	MaxJobsPerUser	Limits the number of active print jobs per user.
Filter Options	User	Specifies the user cupsd runs as. By default, cupsd runs as lp.
	Group	Specifies the cupsd group. By default, this is the lp group.
Network Options	MaxClients	Sets a limit on the number of concurrent client connections. By default this is set to 100.
Browsing Options	Browsing	Specifies whether or not cupsd will announce its printers using broadcasts on the network. The default value is on.
	BrowseAddress	Specifies the broadcast address cupsd should use to announce its printers. You should set this directive to the broadcast address of your network segment. This directive is disabled by default. Until you enable it, cupsd won't announce its printers. If your clients can't see your CUPS printers, this directive should be the first thing you check.
	BrowseInterval	Specifies the interval between printer announcements. The default is 30 seconds.

However, if you want other Linux systems to be able to print through your CUPS printer, you must enable BrowseAddress or else CUPS won't announce its printers on the network. This directive is *not* enabled by default. This is a very common mistake made by Linux admins when setting up network CUPS printing. The BrowseAddress directive is usually set to a value of @LOCAL for most implementations. This causes CUPS to send printer announcement broadcasts to all local interfaces in the system except for PPP connections. A sample cupsd.conf file with the BrowseAddress directive enabled is shown in Figure 14-40.

After making any changes to cupds.conf, be sure to restart the cupsd daemon using its init script.

After configuring your cupsd.conf file, you next need to set up a Linux user account that will be used as the CUPS administrator. As with Samba, CUPS does not use the same user accounts that your Linux system uses. Instead, CUPS is configured to use the /etc/cups/passwd.md5 file to store user accounts. To create an administrative user in the passwd.md5 file named root that is a member of the CUPS administration group named sys, you would enter **lppasswd –g sys –a root**. Until you do this, you won't be able to use the CUPS Web-based administration utility.

Now that you've configured an administrative user, your next task is to configure a CUPS printer and queue. Let's discuss how to do that next.

Configuring a CUPS Printer

All CUPS printers are defined in the /etc/cups/printers.conf file. While you can manually edit this file, you really should use the CUPS Web-based administration

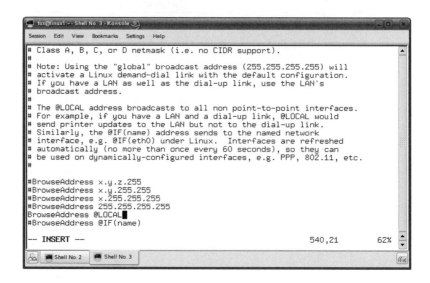

FIGURE 14-40

Enabling
local printer
announcement

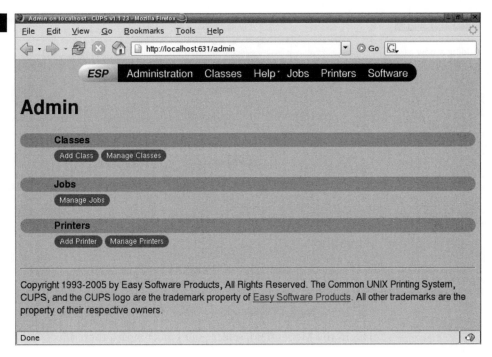

FIGURE 14-41

The CUPS administration screen

utility instead. Configuring a CUPS printer is a snap when you use this utility. Do the following:

1. On your Linux system, start a Web browser and navigate to http://localhost:631.

2. Select Administration.

3. When prompted, authenticate as the *user* you configured earlier using lppasswd. The screen in Figure 14-41 is displayed.

4. Under Printers, select Add Printer. The screen in Figure 14-42 is displayed.

5. In the Name field, enter a ***name*** for the printer.

6. In the Location field, enter a ***location*** for the printer.

7. In the Description field, enter a ***description*** of the printer.

8. Select Continue.

9. In the Device drop-down list, select the *interface* where the printer is connected, then select Continue.

FIGURE 14-42

Adding a new
CUPS printer

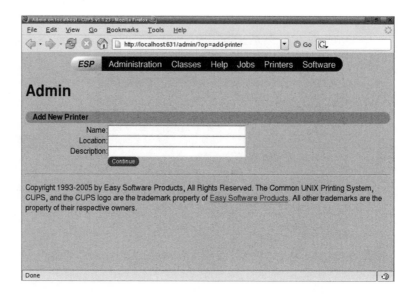

10. In the Model/Driver screen, select the *printer manufacturer*, then select Continue.

11. In the Model field, select your *printer model*; then select Continue.

At this point, a page is displayed indicating your printer has been added. To see the current status of your printer, select the link for the printer. A screen similar to that shown in Figure 14-43 is displayed.

FIGURE 14-43

Viewing the
printer status

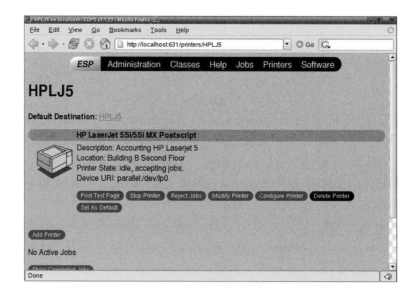

From the Printer Status page, you can manage your CUPS printer. You can send a test page, stop the printer, kill a print job, modify the printer configuration, or delete the printer altogether.

At this point, you can send print jobs to the printer. If you're using a graphical X Windows application, you can simply select File | Print, then select the printer and click OK. You can also send print jobs from the command line to the printer. This is done using the lp command, which will send a specified file to the printer. The syntax for using lp is lp –d *printer_name filename*. For example, if I wanted to print the myfiles file in the current directory to the HPLJ5 printer I just created, I would enter **lp –d HPLJ5 ./myfiles** at the shell prompt, as shown in Figure 14-44.

As you can see in Figure 14-44, the job is created and assigned an ID, in this case HPLJ5-2. The lp utility includes a variety of options besides –d that you can use to create print jobs, including the following:

- **–n *x*** Prints *x* number of copies.
- **–m** E-mails a confirmation message to my local user account when the job is finished printing.
- **–q** Sets the priority of the print job.
- **–o landscape** Prints the file landscape instead of portrait.
- **–o sides=2** Prints the file double-sided on a printer that supports duplexing.

You can also configure other Linux systems to print to the CUPS printer. Simply configure a new printer, but specify that it listen for CUPS announcements. The CUPS printer you configured should be displayed within 30 seconds. After selecting it, all print jobs sent to that printer will be redirected over the network connection to your CUPS printer.

In addition, if you've installed Samba on your system, then your CUPS printers are automatically shared. You can connect to them from Windows workstations and submit print jobs. Now that's cool!

Let's next discuss how to use command-line tools to manage your CUPS printers.

FIGURE 14-44

Sending a print job from the shell prompt

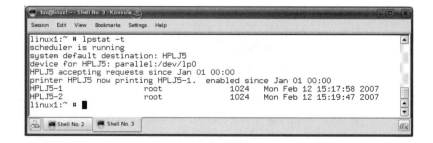

Using Command-Line Tools to Manage CUPS

In addition to the CUPS Web-based administration utility, you can also use a variety of command-line tools to configure CUPS. To view CUPS printer information, you can use the lpstat utility. One of the most useful options you can use with lpstat is –t. This will cause lpstat to display all information about all CUPS printers on the system. This is shown in Figure 14-45.

This shows the default CUPS printer (HPLJ5), how it's connected (/dev/lp0), the print job currently being processed (HPLJ5-1), and a list of pending print jobs.

To cancel a pending print job, you can use the cancel command. The syntax is cancel *job_ID*. For example, in Figure 14-46, the HPLJ5-2 print job has been removed from the print queue.

If you have more than one CUPS printer connected, you can use the lpoptions –d *printer* command to specify the default printer. For example, to set the HPLJ5 printer as the default, I would enter **lpoptions –d HPLJ5**. This sets the default printer for all users on the system. Individual users can override this setting, however, by creating

```
linux1:~ # lpstat -t
scheduler is running
system default destination: HPLJ5
device for HPLJ5: parallel:/dev/lp0
HPLJ5 accepting requests since Jan 01 00:00
printer HPLJ5 now printing HPLJ5-1.  enabled since Jan 01 00:00
HPLJ5-1                  root              1024   Mon Feb 12 15:17:58 2007
HPLJ5-2                  root              1024   Mon Feb 12 15:19:47 2007
linux1:~ # cancel HPLJ5-2
linux1:~ # lpstat -t
scheduler is running
system default destination: HPLJ5
device for HPLJ5: parallel:/dev/lp0
HPLJ5 accepting requests since Jan 01 00:00
printer HPLJ5 now printing HPLJ5-1.  enabled since Jan 01 00:00
HPLJ5-1                  root              1024   Mon Feb 12 15:17:58 2007
linux1:~ #
```

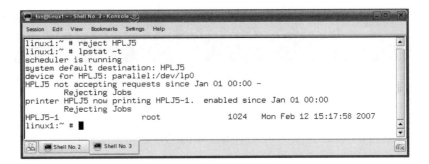

FIGURE 14-47

Disabling a print
queue

a file named .lpoptions in his or her home directory and adding the following
directive:

```
default printer_name
```

If you want to view your printer's configuration settings, you can enter **lpoptions –l**
at the shell prompt.

In addition to the lpoptions command, you can also use the accept *printer_name*
and reject *printer_name* commands to enable or disable a printer's print queue. For
example, I could enter **reject HPLJ5** at the shell prompt to disable the printer's
print queue. This is shown in Figure 14-47.

The printer itself will continue processing queued print jobs, but cupsd will not
allow any new jobs to enter the queue. To enable the queue again, I would enter
accept HPLJ5 at the shell prompt.

To disable the printer itself, not the queue, I could enter **disable HPLJ5** at the
shell prompt. This is shown in Figure 14-48.

The print queue will continue to accept jobs, but none of them will be printed
until I enter **/usr/bin/enable HPLJ5** at the shell prompt. Notice that I had to use

FIGURE 14-48

Disabling a
printer

SCENARIO & SOLUTION	
You want to create a CUPS administrative user named cupsboss for your CUPS system. What command would you use to do this?	You would enter **lppasswd –g sys –a cupsboss** at the shell prompt.
You want to send a file named /var/log/messages to a CUPS printer named Lex1000 on your system. What shell command would you use to do this?	You would enter **lp –d Lex1000 /var/log/messages** at the shell prompt.

the full path to the enable executable. This is because there is an internal shell command called "enable" and the shell defaults to this before looking for an external command called "enable."

Using the Line Printer Daemon (lpd)

By far and away, CUPS is the preferred printing system for modern Linux distributions. Many years ago, however, the preferred printing system was the *Line Printer Daemon* (lpd). You probably won't work much with lpd, but the Linux+ exam still expects you to know some of the commands used to manage this daemon. Most of the lpd commands have functionality similar to that offered by a CUPS command, as shown in Table 14-10.

As an interesting side note, these commands will also work with cupsd. For example, you can enter **lpc status** at the shell prompt and it will return the status of your CUPS printers, if CUPS is installed instead of lpd.

TABLE 14-10	Task	lpd Command-Line Utility
	Print a document.	lpr –P *printer_name filename*
lpd Commands	View printer status.	lpc status
	View pending print jobs.	lpq
	Delete a pending print job from the queue.	lprm *job_number*

Let's configure CUPS in the following exercise.

EXERCISE 14-5

Configuring CUPS

In this exercise, you will install and configure CUPS on your Linux system. This exercise assumes you have an Ethernet network board installed and configured in your system. It also assumes you have a printer available to connect to a USB or parallel port in the system. Complete the following:

1. Power down your Linux system and physically connect your printer.

2. Boot your Linux system and log in as a standard user. If you used the lab exercise in Chapter 3 to install your system, you can log in as **tux** with a password of **M3linux273**.

3. Open a terminal session.

4. Switch to your root user account by entering **su –** followed by your root user's password.

5. Using the rpm utility, install the following packages on your system

   ■ cups   ■ cups-libs

   ■ cups-backends   ■ gtklp

   ■ cups-client   ■ xpp

   ■ cups-drivers

6. Open your /etc/cups/cupsd.conf file in a text editor.

7. Enable broadcasting by deleting the **#** character from the beginning of the BrowseAddress @LOCAL line.

8. Save your changes to the file.

9. At the shell prompt, restart your cupsd daemon using its init script in /etc/rc.d/init.d/ or /etc/init.d.

10. Create a CUPS administrative user named boss by completing the following:

    a. At the shell prompt, enter **lppasswd –g sys –a boss**.

    b. When prompted for a password, enter **penguin**.

11. Create a CUPS printer by completing the following:

    a. Open a Web browser and navigate to http://localhost:631.

    b. Select Administration.

    c. When prompted to authenticate, log in as **boss** with a password of **penguin**.

      d. Under Printers, select Add Printer.

      e. In the Name field, enter a *name* for your printer.

      f. In the Location field, enter a *location* for your printer.

      g. In the Description field, enter a *description* of your printer; then select Continue.

      h. In the Device drop-down list, select the *interface* to which your printer is connected; then select Continue.

      i. In the Make field, select your printer's *manufacturer*; then select Continue.

      j. In the Model field, select your printer's *model*; then select Continue. You should be prompted that the printer has been successfully added.

      k. Select the link for your printer.

12. Send a print job to the printer by doing the following:

      a. Open a terminal session and generate a list of files in your user's home directory.

      b. Select a text file for printing.

      c. At the shell prompt, enter **lp –d** *printer_name filename*.

      d. Verify that the document is printed on your printer.

It's time once again to shift gears. The next topic we're going to discuss in this chapter is configuring network services with xinetd.

CERTIFICATION OBJECTIVE 14.06

Configure Basic Network Services with xinetd

Your Linux system includes a special daemon called xinetd that can be used to provide a number of different network services. Most Linux distributions install this daemon by default, so you shouldn't need to install it manually. In this part of this chapter, you will learn how to configure and use xinetd. We'll discuss the following topics:

- How xinetd works
- Configuring xinetd network services

Let's begin by discussing how the xinetd daemon works.

How xinetd Works

The xinetd daemon is a special type of network service called a *super daemon*. Understand that most Linux distributions install a wide variety of network services during the system installation process. Most of these services, such as Telnet, are very handy and provide a valuable service. However, they aren't needed much of the time. We need a way to provide these services when requested, but then unload them when they aren't needed, saving memory and reducing CPU utilization.

This is done using the xinetd daemon. It's called a super daemon because it acts as an intermediary between the user requesting network services and the daemons on the system that provide the actual service. This is shown in Figure 14-49.

When a request for one of the network services managed by xinetd arrives at the system, it is received and processed by xinetd, not the network daemon being requested. The xinetd daemon then starts the daemon for the requested service and forwards the request to it. When the request has been fulfilled and the network service is no longer needed, xinetd unloads the daemon from memory.

Some of the network services managed by xinetd include the following:

- chargen
- daytime
- echo
- ftp
- pop3
- rsync

- smtp
- telnet
- tftp
- time
- vnc

FIGURE 14-49

How xinetd
works

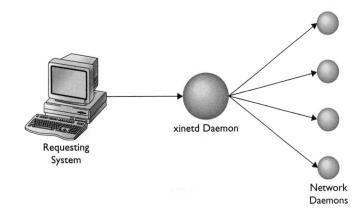

Requesting
System

xinetd Daemon

Network
Daemons

on the **! **Job

Some distributions use the inetd daemon instead of xinetd. This daemon works in much the same manner as xinetd.

Let's discuss how you configure services managed by xinetd next.

Configuring xinetd Network Services

As with all of the network services we've discussed in this chapter so far, the xinetd configuration files are stored in /etc. The xinetd daemon itself is configured using the /etc/xinetd.conf file, shown in Figure 14-50.

Generally speaking, you won't need to make many changes to this file. The default configuration usually works very well. Notice that the last directive in the file reads:

```
includedir /etc/xinetd.d
```

This line tells the xinetd daemon to use the files in /etc/xinetd.d. These files tell xinetd how to start each service when requested. The files in this directory are shown in Figure 14-51.

Each of these files is used to configure the startup of a particular service managed by xinetd. For example, the vsftpd file is used to configure the vsftpd FTP server daemon, shown in Figure 14-52.

Notice that this file doesn't configure the daemon itself. It only tells xinetd how to start up the daemon. As noted in the file, the actual configuration file for the vsftpd daemon is in /etc/vsftpd.conf. One of the most important parameters in the /etc/xinetd.d/vsftpd file is the disable directive. This directive specifies whether

FIGURE 14-50

The /etc/
xinetd.conf file

```
# Copyright (c) 1998-2001 SuSE GmbH Nuernberg, Germany.
# Copyright (c) 2002 SuSE Linux AG, Nuernberg, Germany.
#

defaults
{
        log_type        = FILE /var/log/xinetd.log
        log_on_success  = HOST EXIT DURATION
        log_on_failure  = HOST ATTEMPT
#       only_from       = localhost
        instances       = 30
        cps             = 50 10


# The specification of an interface is interesting, if we are on a firewall.
# For example, if you only want to provide services from an internal
# network interface, you may specify your internal interfaces IP-Address.
#
#       interface       = 127.0.0.1

}

includedir /etc/xinetd.d
./xinetd.conf lines 4-26/26 (END)
```

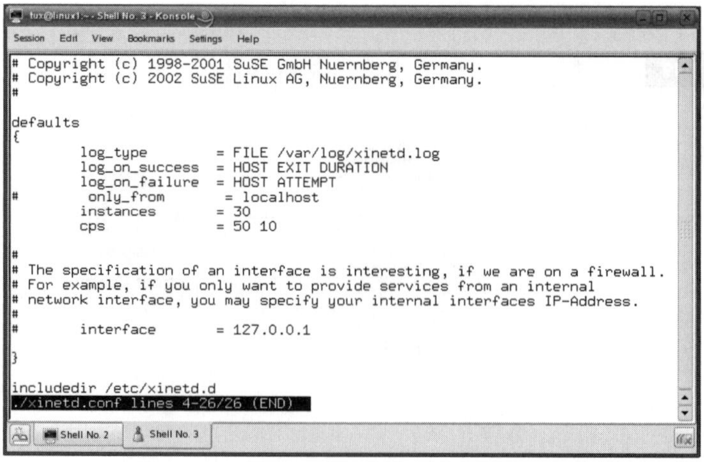

FIGURE 14-51

Configuration files in /etc/ xinetd.d

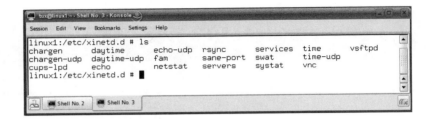

or not xinetd is allowed to start the daemon when requested. In Figure 14-52, this directive is set to yes, which means the daemon will not be started when requested. To enable this daemon, you need to edit this file and change the disable parameter to a value of no. After changing a value in any of the files in /etc/xinetd.d, you need to restart the xinetd daemon using its init script in /etc/rc.d/init.d or /etc/init.d.

on the
Job

As with the other services we've discussed in this chapter, if you enable a service provided by xinetd, you'll need to create an exception in your Linux system's host-based firewall to allow traffic for the IP port used by the daemon.

FIGURE 14-52

The /etc/ xinetd.d/vsftpd file

```
# default: off
# description:
#   The vsftpd FTP server serves FTP connections. It uses
#   normal, unencrypted usernames and passwords for authentication.
# vsftpd is designed to be secure.
#
# NOTE: This file contains the configuration for xinetd to start vsftpd.
#       the configuration file for vsftp itself is in /etc/vsftpd.conf
#
service ftp
{
        socket_type             = stream
        protocol                = tcp
        wait                    = no
        user                    = root
        server                  = /usr/sbin/vsftpd
#       server_args             =
#       log_on_success          += DURATION USERID
#       log_on_failure          += USERID
#       nice                    = 10
        disable                 = yes
}

./vsftpd lines 1-23/23 (END)
```

SCENARIO & SOLUTION

A user on a client system opens a Telnet session with your Linux system. How is this request processed?	First, the xinetd daemon receives the request for the Telnet service. The xinetd daemon starts the Telnet server daemon and forwards the request to it. When the user closes the Telnet session, the xinetd daemon unloads the Telnet server daemon.
You've installed the vsftpd package on your Linux system, but users are unable to connect to your system using the FTP protocol. Why did this happen?	Most likely, you neglected to enable the service. To do this, you would edit the /etc/xinetd.d/vsftpd file and set the disable directive to a value of no.

Let's next discuss using NFS on Linux.

CERTIFICATION OBJECTIVE 14.07

Configure NFS on Linux

Earlier in this chapter, you learned how to use the Samba service to share directories in your local file system with remote client systems. You can accomplish a similar task using the Network File System (NFS) service on your Linux system. In this part of this chapter, you'll learn how to export and mount a directory using NFS. We'll cover the following topics:

- How NFS works
- Exporting a directory using NFS
- Mounting an exported directory using NFS

Let's begin by learning how NFS works.

How NFS Works

Like Samba, NFS makes specified directories in your Linux file system available to network clients. Unlike Samba, NFS is only concerned with directories in the file system. It can't be used to share other resources, such as printers. It also doesn't provide user authentication services as Samba does.

NFS operates on a client-server model, like most of the network services we've covered thus far in this book. The NFS server provides shared directories (called *exports*). The NFS client mounts these shared directories into a mount point in the local file system. For example, an NFS server could export the /data directory in its file system. An NFS client could mount this export in the /mnt/nfs directory in its local file system.

Let's review how this can be done by learning how to configure an NFS export.

Exporting a Directory Using NFS

You can export a directory using the /etc/exports file. Each exported directory is listed on a single line. The syntax is as follows:

```
directory_name allowed_hosts(options)
```

A sample export is shown in Figure 14-53.

In Figure 14-53, the /data directory is being made available to remote NFS clients. All remote hosts are allowed to connect to the export, as denoted by *. If I wanted to restrict access to the export, I could list the allowed host's domain name or IP address instead of a *. If I wanted to allow all hosts on a particular network, then I could have listed the network address, such as 192.168.1.0, where the hosts reside. For options, I've specified the following:

- **ro**   The directory is exported read-only. NFS clients can open files in the directory, but they aren't allowed to modify files or create new ones. If you want to allow remote NFS clients to modify or create files, you should use rw (read-write) instead of ro.

- **root_squash**   This option maps remote root user accounts to the nobody account on the NFS server. This prevents someone from logging in to their local Linux system and gaining root-level access to the exported directory on the NFS server. If you want to allow remote root user accounts to have root-level access to the exported directory on the NFS server, then you should use the no_root_squash option instead.

FIGURE 14-53

Creating an NFS export in /etc/exports.

With NFS, you can also specify different options for different hosts. For example, if I wanted 192.168.1.2 to have read-write access to the export but 192.168.1.3 to have read-only access, I could create an export that reads:

```
/data        192.168.1.2(rw) 192.168.1.3(ro)
```

After entering or modifying an export in /etc/exports, you need to restart NFS. This is done using the nfsserver init script in /etc/init.d or /etc/rc.d/init.d, shown in Figure 14-54.

You can check your export by entering **showmount –e *NFS_server_address*** at the shell prompt. For example, in Figure 14-55, this command displays the /data export defined earlier.

You will also need to configure your host-based firewall to allow NFS traffic on IP port 2049. With the export defined, you can now mount it from a remote NFS client. Let's review how this is done next.

Mounting an Exported Directory Using NFS

Before you do anything from the client NFS system, you first need to configure its host-based firewall to allow NFS traffic on IP port 2049. If you don't, you'll spend hours banging your head on the wall wondering why it doesn't work. (Trust me, I know this from experience.)

You can mount an NFS export in two different ways. First, you can mount it from the shell prompt using the mount command. To do this, you first need to verify that

FIGURE 14-54

The nfsserver init script

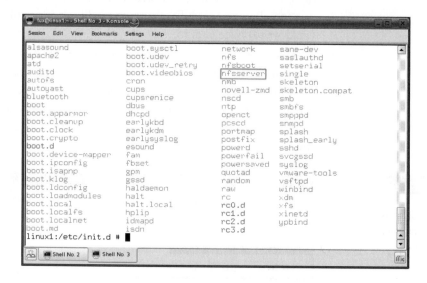

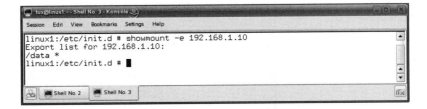

FIGURE 14-55

Using showmount
to view available
exports

the portmap service is running. The portmap daemon is started using the portmap
init script in your init directory, as shown in Figure 14-54. Once that's done, you can
then use mount to mount the remote export. The syntax for doing this is mount –t
nfs *NFS_server_address:export_path mount_point*. For example, to mount the /data
export defined earlier in /mnt/nfs, you would enter **mount –t nfs 192.168.1.10:/
data /mnt/nfs** at the shell prompt. You can then use the mount command to verify
that the export has been mounted, as shown in Figure 14-56.

Second, you can create an entry in your /etc/fstab file that will automatically
mount the exported directory every time the system boots. The syntax for doing this
is as follows:

```
NFS_server_address:/export_path    mount_point  nfs  0 0
```

Now that you understand how NFS works, here are some possible scenario
questions and their answers.

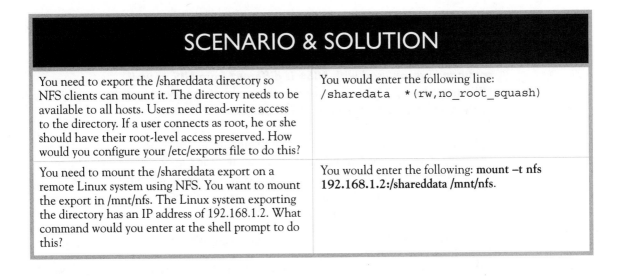

SCENARIO & SOLUTION

You need to export the /shareddata directory so NFS clients can mount it. The directory needs to be available to all hosts. Users need read-write access to the directory. If a user connects as root, he or she should have their root-level access preserved. How would you configure your /etc/exports file to do this?	You would enter the following line: `/shareddata  *(rw,no_root_squash)`
You need to mount the /shareddata export on a remote Linux system using NFS. You want to mount the export in /mnt/nfs. The Linux system exporting the directory has an IP address of 192.168.1.2. What command would you enter at the shell prompt to do this?	You would enter the following: **mount –t nfs 192.168.1.2:/shareddata /mnt/nfs**.

FIGURE 14-56

Mounting an NFS export

```
lux@linux1 ~ Shell No. 3 Konsole
Session  Edit  View  Bookmarks  Settings  Help
linux1:/etc/init.d # mount -t nfs 192.168.1.10:/data /mnt/nfs
linux1:/etc/init.d # mount
/dev/sda3 on / type reiserfs (rw,acl,user_xattr,usrquota,grpquota)
proc on /proc type proc (rw)
sysfs on /sys type sysfs (rw)
debugfs on /sys/kernel/debug type debugfs (rw)
udev on /dev type tmpfs (rw)
devpts on /dev/pts type devpts (rw,mode=0620,gid=5)
/dev/sda1 on /boot type reiserfs (rw,acl,user_xattr)
/dev/sda4 on /var type reiserfs (rw,acl,user_xattr)
/dev/md0 on /mnt/raid type reiserfs (rw,acl,user_xattr)
securityfs on /sys/kernel/security type securityfs (rw)
nfsd on /proc/fs/nfsd type nfsd (rw)
192.168.1.10:/data on /mnt/nfs type nfs (rw,addr=192.168.1.10)
linux1:/etc/init.d #
         Shell No. 2    Shell No. 3
```

Next, let's discuss working with NIS on Linux.

CERTIFICATION OBJECTIVE 14.08

Use NIS on Linux

The Network Information Service (NIS) daemon is an interesting network service. NIS is designed to help you, the Linux admin, more efficiently manage a network of Linux computer systems. NIS was implemented widely in the early days of Linux. Lately, I'm seeing it used less and less. Other network services, such as OpenLDAP, are being used more and more instead of NIS.

on the
Job

A newer version of NIS called NIS+ is also available. NIS+ was redesigned from the ground up as a NIS replacement. It can support older NIS clients using YP compatibility mode. The overall structure of NIS+ is different from NIS. The command syntax used with NIS+ is different from NIS as well.
NIS+ is a powerful directory service that uses directory objects, table objects, entry objects, group objects, and link objects.

However, there are still a lot of NIS implementations around, so the Linux+ exam expects you to be familiar with it. That said, the Linux+ exam doesn't expect you to be a NIS expert. It only expects you to know how to use NIS commands to manage a NIS domain. Therefore, in this part of this chapter, we're going to cover the following topics so you can do just that:

■ How NIS works   ■ Using NIS commands

Before you can manage a NIS domain, you must first understand how NIS works. Let's discuss this topic first.

How NIS Works

As stated earlier, NIS is designed to help you manage a large network of Linux systems. The issue here is that Linux configuration files are stored and managed separately on each local computer system. That's not a problem if you're working in a single-computer environment. However, if you're working in a large environment with lots of Linux systems, managing all of these configuration files can be very cumbersome.

For example, suppose you have six Linux systems in your network. You want users to be able to connect to various services offered by each of these systems using their own username and password. The problem in this scenario is that each Linux system has its own database of usernames and passwords in /etc/passwd and /etc/shadow. For users to connect to other Linux systems and use their resources, a separate username and password for each user must be manually created and kept current on each of the six Linux systems. That's a lot of work. On a very large network, it's almost impossible.

That's where NIS comes into play. With NIS, a common set of configuration files is stored centrally on the network and copied out to all the network hosts. This saves you a ton of work. Instead of having to visit each machine and manually make the same change over and over, your network hosts can simply download a new copy of the updated configuration file. The system's configuration files are automatically brought up to date and your work is done.

To make this work, NIS uses the following components:

- ■ **Maps**   Maps are database files that are created from Linux configuration files. These maps are the components that are distributed around the network that Linux systems can use instead of their local configuration files.

- ■ **Domain**   The NIS domain is different from a DNS domain. A NIS domain is a group of Linux systems that will share a common set of configuration files in the form of maps.

- ■ **Master Server**   The master NIS server is the system where all maps are stored. The master server is responsible for sending maps out to NIS slave servers and NIS clients. The ypserv daemon creates the master NIS server.

- ■ **Slave Server**   The job of the slave NIS server is to take the load off of the master server. Slave servers receive a copy of the NIS maps from the master server and then distribute them to NIS clients. The slave server is optional, but recommended.

- ■ **Clients**   The NIS clients are the Linux systems that connect to a master or slave server, download map files, and then use the map files for their configuration. NIS clients can be configured to use local configuration files or NIS maps, or a combination of both. The NIS client daemon is ypbind.

NIS is really cool. Using NIS, you can create a set of configuration files and copy them around automatically, allowing all of your Linux systems to share the same configuration parameters. For example, you can create map files from your /etc/passwd and /etc/shadow files. After distributing the map file, each system on your network will have exactly the same user accounts with exactly the same passwords. That's handy!

To make NIS work you need to install the following packages on your system:

- **portmap** The portmap daemon is required on all systems in the domain.
- **ypserv** The NIS server daemon is only required on the Linux system that will function as a NIS server.
- **ypbind** The NIS client daemon is required on all systems in the domain.
- **yp-tools** This package provides the command-line tools needed to manage the NIS domain. It should be installed on all systems in the domain.

The process of installing and configuring NIS is somewhat complex. The Linux+ exam doesn't expect you to know how to set up a NIS domain, so we're not going to address the steps here. Instead, we're going to focus on managing an existing NIS domain using command-line utilities. Let's do that next.

Using NIS Commands

When managing a NIS domain, you can use the tools in Table 14-11 to customize how NIS works. Be aware that you need to specify the full path to these utilities on many distributions.

TABLE 14-11   NIS Command-Line Utilities

Command	Purpose
/bin/ypdomainname	Displays or sets the current NIS domain. To view the current domain, just enter **ypdomainname**. To set the domain, enter **ypdomainname** domain at the shell prompt.
/usr/bin/ypwhich	Displays the name of the NIS server a NIS client has been configured to use.
/usr/bin/ypcat	Displays the contents of a NIS map file. For example, if you're using maps of the /etc/passwd file, you would enter **/usr/bin/ypcat passwd** at the shell prompt.
/usr/bin/yppasswd	Changes the password of a user on the NIS server. It's important to remember that you need to use this utility instead of the password utilities covered earlier in this book to change the password; otherwise, you will only change the password in the local /etc/shadow file. When you use yppasswd, the /etc/shadow file on the NIS master server is updated and new maps are automatically generated.
/usr/sbin/yppoll	Displays the ID number of a NIS map on your NIS server. The syntax for using yppoll is /usr/sbin/yppoll –h NIS_server_address –d NIS_domain map_name.
ypbind	Starts the NIS client.

In addition to NIS commands, you also need to know how to configure remote access services on your Linux system for your Linux+ exam. Let's review how to do this next.

CERTIFICATION OBJECTIVE 14.09

Configure Remote Access on Linux

In addition to the network services discussed previously in this chapter, you also need to know how to configure remote access to a Linux system for your Linux+ exam. Remote access can be a real lifesaver for the Linux administrator. I've developed a new Law of the Universe for system administrators that I call "Tracy's Law." Simply put, Tracy's Law states, "A system problem will occur at the most inopportune time." It never fails that a major issue manifests itself while you're away at a conference, on vacation, or at home asleep. Without a remote access solution in place, you have to change out of your pajamas, drive in to work, slap yourself three or four times to stay awake, and fix the problem. What a waste of time!

on the
job   *It's often said that Linux administrators are more effective at solving problems with bed head while wearing pajamas.*

A better approach is to configure your Linux systems such that you can access them remotely through a network connection. Using remote access, a system problem in the middle of the night goes from a major trial to a minor inconvenience. Let's spend some time reviewing the remote access tools you can use with Linux. We're going to hit the following topics:

- Configuring Telnet
- Configuring SSH
- Using remote command-line utilities

Let's begin by discussing how to use Telnet.

Configuring Telnet

Telnet has been around for a very long time. It's the traditional means of accessing a Linux system's shell prompt from a remote computer system. The Telnet protocol is a client-server protocol. The Telnet service must be running on the system that

FIGURE 14-57

Linux Telnet
packages

is being accessed remotely. A Telnet client is run on the remote client computer system and is used to access the Telnet service on the first system.

On Linux, the Telnet service is provided by the telnet-server package. The Telnet client is provided by the telnet package. These are shown in Figure 14-57.

Depending upon which Linux distribution you installed, these packages may or may not have been installed by default on your system. If they haven't, you can install them using the rpm utility. Once installed, the Telnet service is managed by the xinetd daemon. You enable the Telnet service by editing the /etc/xinetd.d/telnet file and changing the disable directive to no, as shown in Figure 14-58.

After making this change, restart the xinetd daemon. The Telent service will then be available. However, before remote Telnet clients can connect to your system, you will need to open IP port 23 in your system's host-based firewall. Once that's done, you can connect using any Telnet client. Most operating systems, including Linux and Windows, provide a command-line Telnet client that you can use to connect to a Telnet service.

For example, in Figure 14-59, I've connected to my Linux server from a Windows workstation by opening a command window and entering **telnet 192.168.1.10** at the command prompt. After connecting, the Telnet service on the Linux system prompts for a Linux username and password. Upon authentication, you have access to the Linux shell prompt through the Telnet service on the system.

FIGURE 14-58

Enabling the
Telnet service

```
# default: off
# description: Telnet is the old login server which is INSECURE and should \
#              therefore not be used. Use secure shell (openssh).
#              If you need telnetd not to "keep-alives" (e.g. if it runs over a ISDN \
#              uplink), add "-n". See 'man telnetd' for more details.
service telnet
{
        socket_type     = stream
        protocol        = tcp
        wait            = no
        user            = root
        server          = /usr/sbin/in.telnetd
        disable         = no
}
~
~
~
~
-- INSERT --                                              13,15-29      All
```

FIGURE 14-59

Using the
Windows Telnet
client to connect
to a Linux Telnet
service

At this point, you can manage the system from the shell prompt as if you were sitting in front of your Linux system. When you're done, you can close the Telnet session by entering **exit** at the shell prompt.

Telnet works great as a remote access solution. However, it's got one key weakness that has made it fall out of favor with most Linux administrators. All the data transmitted between the Telnet client and the Telnet service is sent unencrypted. If someone were to "sniff" your network media, they could easily capture all the data being sent between the client and the service, including your username and password.

To make remote access more secure, you should consider using ssh instead of Telnet. Let's review how ssh works next.

Configuring SSH

The Secure Shell (ssh) service on your Linux system works in almost the same manner as Telnet. Like Telnet, it allows you to access the shell prompt on your Linux system from a remote computer system. Also like Telnet, ssh is a client-server system. You run the sshd daemon on the Linux system you want to connect to. You run an ssh client on the remote client system.

However, unlike Telnet, ssh uses encryption to scramble that data being transmitted between the ssh client and the sshd daemon. This scrambling is accomplished using encryption keys. An eavesdropper can still capture data begin transferred between the client and the server, but because they don't have the encryption key, it's just gibberish to them.

To use ssh, you must first install the openssh package on your system from your distribution media, shown in Figure 14-60.

FIGURE 14-60

Installing the
openssh package

FIGURE 14-61

FIGURE 14-61

The sshd
configuration file

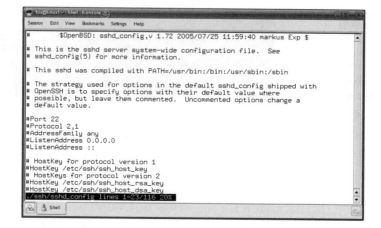

This package includes both the sshd daemon and the ssh client. After installation, you can configure the sshd daemon using the /etc/ssh/sshd_config file, shown in Figure 14-61.

There are many directives within this file. The good news is that after installing the openssh package the default parameters work very well in most circumstances. To get sshd up and running, you shouldn't have to make any changes to the sshd_config file.

The ssh client on a Linux system is configured using the /etc/ssh/ssh_config file, shown in Figure 14-62.

The /etc/ssh/ssh_config file is used to specify default parameters for all users running ssh on the system. A user can override these defaults using the ~/ssh/ssh_config file in his or her home directory.

As with the sshd daemon, the default parameters used in this file usually work without any customization. Of course, before you can connect to the sshd daemon

FIGURE 14-62

The ssh client
configuration file

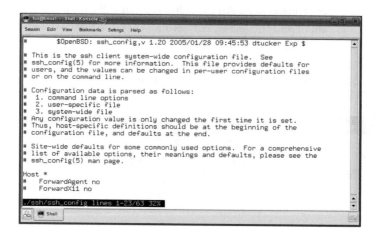

on your Linux system, you must open up IP port 22 in your host-based firewall. After doing so, you can load the ssh client on the remote computer and connect to the sshd daemon on your Linux system by entering **ssh –l** *user_name ip_address*. For example, if I wanted to connect to my remote Linux system (which has an IP address of 192.168.1.10) as the user tux using the ssh client on a local computer system, I would enter **ssh –l tux 192.168.1.10** at the shell prompt. This is shown in Figure 14-63.

As with Telnet, ssh allows you full access to the shell prompt. You can manage your Linux system as if you were sitting in front of it. To close the connection, just enter **exit** at the shell prompt.

on the
Job

Because the ssh client uses an encryption key to encrypt and decrypt transmissions, you may be prompted to accept the key the first time you connect to a given sshd daemon. If you see this prompt, enter yes *to accept the key. Windows workstations don't provide an ssh client. You can download the PuTTY ssh client from the Internet to connect to a Linux sshd daemon from a Windows workstation.*

Next, let's review some other command-line utilities you can use to remotely manage a Linux system.

Using Remote Command-Line Utilities

In addition to Telnet and ssh, you also need to know how to use several other remote management utilities for your Linux+ exam. These include the following:

- rsh
- rlogin
- rcp

These utilities are frequently referred to as the "r" utilities. Frankly, the "r" utilities aren't used much any more. Nearly everything they can do can be done more securely using ssh. Like Telnet, the "r" utilities don't use encryption; an eavesdropper sniffing the network can capture all data transmissions, including usernames and passwords.

FIGURE 14-63

Connecting using
the ssh client

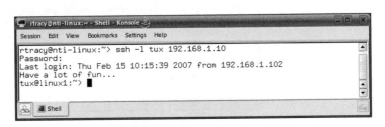

FIGURE 14-64

The "r" packages

The "r" services are provided by daemons in the rsh-server package. Before you can connect to a Linux system using these utilities, the system must have this package installed. You can install the rsh-server package from your distribution media using the rpm utility. In addition, you need to have the rsh package installed on the system you will be connecting from. These are shown in Figure 14-64.

Like Telnet, the "r" daemons are managed using the xinetd daemon. You must edit the appropriate configuration file in /etc/xinetd.d directory for the particular "r" service you want to run and enable it. Then restart the xinetd daemon.

It's important that you understand that the "r" utilities allow access *without* a password. Therefore, you must configure trusted access on the system to be managed for these utilities to work. This is done using the /etc/hosts.equiv file. The syntax for this file is:

```
hostname
```

Any host listed in the file is considered to be logically equivalent to the local computer system. Any user logged into the hostname specified in the file is considered to be the same as a like-named user account on the local system. For example, if the local system and the system specified in the hosts.equiv file both have a user account named tux, the user on the remote system can access the local system using an "r" utility as the local tux user without supplying a password.

The root user account is never trusted, however, when using the /etc/ hosts.equiv file.

In Figure 14-65, the host nti-linux has been made a trusted host for the local system.

FIGURE 14-65

Configuring the /etc/hosts.equiv file

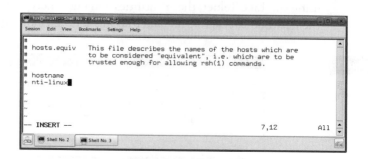

FIGURE 14-66

Using rlogin

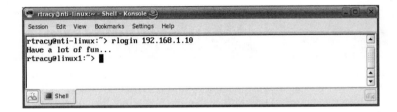

Once done, you can use the "r" utilities to perform management tasks. The Remote Login (rlogin) utility is used to open a shell prompt on the remote Linux system. It communicates with the rlogind daemon running on the remote system. The syntax for using rlogin is to enter **rlogin IP_address** at the shell prompt. For example, in Figure 14-66, I've used rlogin to open a terminal session on a remote Linux system with an IP address of 192.168.1.10.

For this to work, you need to open IP port 513 in your host-based firewall. Once connected, you can enter commands as if you were sitting at the remote Linux system. When done, you can enter **exit** to close the connection.

You can also use the Remote Shell (rsh) utility to run a command on the Linux system remotely. The local system uses the rsh utility to send the command to the rshd daemon running on the remote computer. The output from the command is displayed in the local terminal session. IP port 514 must be opened in your host-based firewall for rsh to work. The syntax for rsh is rsh *IP_address shell_command*.

Finally, you can use the Remote File Copy (rcp) command to copy files between the local computer system and the remote system. The syntax for using rcp is rcp *remote_IP_address:file_name local_path*. For example, to copy the /tmp/myfile file from a system with an IP address of 192.168.1.10 to /tmp on the local system, you would enter **rcp 192.168.1.10:/tmp/myfile /tmp** at the shell prompt. This is shown in Figure 14-67.

FIGURE 14-67

Using rcp

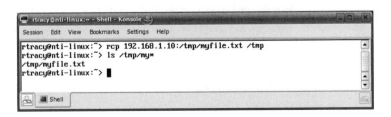

SCENARIO & SOLUTION

You need to enable the Telnet service on your Linux system, which has an IP address of 10.200.200.1. Outline the process you would follow to enable Telnet on your system and connect to it from a remote Windows client workstation.	First, you need to install the telnet-server package on your system. Then, you would edit the /etc/xinetd/ telnet file and set the disable directive to no. After saving the file, you would restart the xinetd daemon. Then you could initiate a connection to the Telnet service on your Linux system by opening a command prompt on the remote Windows system and entering **telnet 10.200.200.1**.
You need to connect to a remote Linux system with an IP address of 192.168.1.2 as a user named ksanders. What command would you enter at your shell prompt to do this?	You would enter **ssh –l ksanders 192.168.1.2**.
You need to copy a file named /tmp/new_config.txt on your local computer to the /tmp directory on another Linux system with an IP address of 192.168.1.201. What command would you use to do this?	You would enter **rcp /tmp/new_config.txt 192.168.1.201:/tmp**.

Let's configure remote access in the following exercise.

EXERCISE 14-6

Configuring Remote Access

In this exercise, you will install and configure Telnet and ssh on your Linux system. This exercise assumes you have an Ethernet network board installed and configured in your system. It also assumes you have a second system to test the configuration with. Complete the following:

1. Boot your Linux system and log in as a standard user. If you used the lab exercise in Chapter 3 to install your system, you can log in as **tux** with a password of **M3linux273**.

2. Open a terminal session.

3. Switch to your root user account by entering **su –** followed by your root user's password.

4. Using the rpm utility, install the following packages on your system:
   - telnet-server
   - telnet
   - openssh

5. Configure Telnet on your system by doing the following:

   a. Open your /etc/xinetd.d/telnet file in a text editor.

   b. Set the disable directive to a value of no.

   c. Restart your xinetd daemon using its init script in /etc/rc.d/init.d/ or /etc/initd.d.

   d. From another system on your network, enter **telnet** *Linux_system_IP_address*.

   e. When prompted, log in as your **tux** user.

   f. Try out a few shell commands from the Telnet shell prompt. When you're done, close the connection by entering **exit** at the shell prompt.

6. Configure ssh on your system by doing the following:

   a. Verify that the openssh package has been installed on your Linux system and on the remote system you will test the connection from.

   b. On your Linux system, start the sshd daemon using its init script in /etc/rc.d/init.d or /etc/init.d.

   c. On your remote system, enter **ssh –l tux** *Linux_system_IP_address*.

   d. When prompted to accept the encryption key, enter **yes**.

   e. Authenticate as your tux user.

   f. Try out a few shell commands from the ssh shell prompt. When you're done, close the connection by entering **exit** at the shell prompt.

Let's end this chapter by discussing how to access local e-mail accounts.

CERTIFICATION OBJECTIVE 14.10

Access Local E-Mail

E-mail has become the backbone of communications in modern organizations. If you've ever had your e-mail server at work go down, you know how true this statement is. Everything grinds to a halt. I find it humorous when two employees who sit in adjacent cubicles e-mail each other instead of standing up and talking over the cubicle wall.

Because e-mail is so integral to the modern organization, the Linux+ exam expects you to have a degree of familiarity with this service. Be warned, however, that setting up a full-blown e-mail server is a complicated task that is beyond the scope of the Linux+ certification. In this part of the chapter, we're going to discuss the basics of how e-mail works and how you can access mail messages on a Linux system. We'll cover the following topics:

- How e-mail works
- Accessing mail

Let's begin by discussing how e-mail works.

How E-Mail Works

To manage an e-mail system, it's critical that you first understand how the e-mail process itself works. An e-mail system is composed of several modular components. Each component plays a different role in delivering messages from the sender to the recipient. These components and the e-mail message delivery process are shown in Figure 14-68.

FIGURE 14-68

The message delivery process

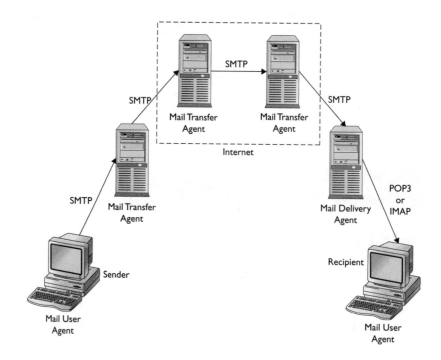

The following steps occur as an e-mail message is originated at the sender and sent to the recipient.

First, the user composes a message using an e-mail client at the sending workstation. The e-mail client software is called the *Mail User Agent* (MUA). Common MUAs include Outlook Express, Evolution, Mozilla Thunderbird, and Mutt.

The MUA doesn't know how to get the e-mail message to the intended recipient. Therefore, it sends outgoing messages to an e-mail server. When the user selects Send in the MUA, it uses the *Simple Mail Transfer Protocol* (SMTP) to transfer the message from the MUA to the e-mail server. SMTP is an IP-based protocol that runs on port 25. Its job is to transfer e-mail messages between mail agents.

on the ! Job *When you configure your e-mail client software, you specify the IP address or host name of your SMTP server.*

Using SMTP, the message is transferred from the MUA on the sender's workstation to the *Mail Transfer Agent* (MTA) on the e-mail server. After receiving the message, the MTA decides what to do with the message. If the message is intended for another user in your same domain, the message is held by the local MTA for delivery to the recipient's MUA. If it's intended for a recipient in a different domain, the MTA forwards the message through a series of MTAs on the network and Internet until it arrives at the MTA used by the message's recipient. Inter-MTA transfers use the SMTP protocol.

The destination MTA transfers the message to the *Message Delivery Agent* (MDA) for the recipient. The MDA is sometimes called a *Message Store*. The MDA stores the message until the MUA of the recipient requests it. The recipient uses e-mail client software (MUA) on his or her workstation to connect to the MDA and pull down the message.

The recipient's MUA can use either the *Post Office Protocol* (POP) version 3 or the *Internet Message Access Protocol* (IMAP) to download messages from the MDA. Most MDAs and MUAs can use either protocol. POP3 is the simpler of the two protocols. POP3 uses port 110 and is designed to pull messages down from the MDA. The message is deleted from the MDA after the MUA downloads it.

IMAP is a more powerful mail protocol. IMAP uses port 143. IMAP allows you to download the entire message from the MDA or only pull down the message headers, allowing you to determine the messages to be downloaded. IMAP also allows you to retain a copy of downloaded messages on the MDA, and to create your own folders on the MDA for organizing messages.

Your Linux distribution includes an MTA that runs by default on the system. Two MTAs are commonly implemented on Linux:

- Postfix
- sendmail

These MTAs can be used to receive sent e-mail messages from MUAs. However, MUAs can't download messages from them using the POP3 or IMAP protocols. To add this functionality, you can install the imap package on your Linux system. This package installs IMAP and POP3 daemons that you can use to transfer e-mail messages from your Postfix or sendmail MTAs to your e-mail client software. Both of these daemons are managed using the xinetd super daemon. You enable these daemons using the /etc/xinetd.d/imap file. Both of these daemons are disabled by default, as shown in Figure 14-69.

If you want to provide POP3 and IMAP support, you will need to enable these daemons in the imap file and then restart the xinetd daemon.

Let's discuss how you access your mail next.

Accessing Mail

You may have noticed a message indicating a user has new mail in many of the images shown in this chapter. You may have wondered how you go about accessing and reading these mail messages. You have several options.

FIGURE 14-69

POP3 and IMAP support

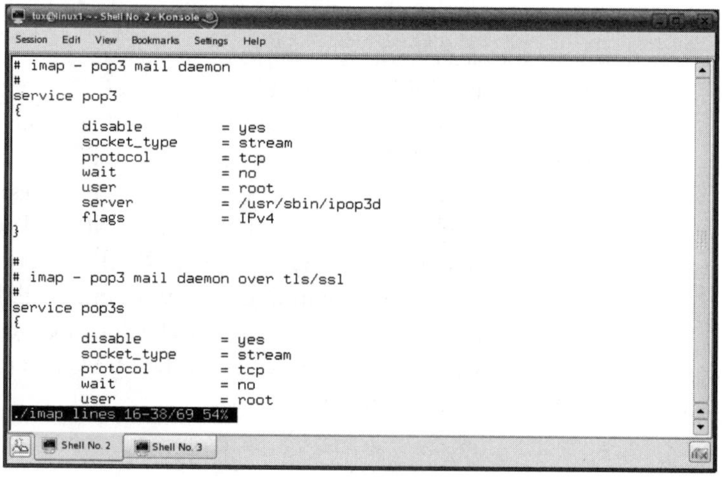

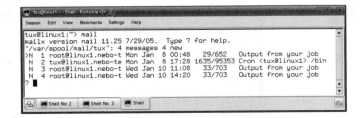

FIGURE 14-70

Using mail to
read messages

First, you can read them directly from the command line by entering **mail** at the shell prompt. When you do, a list of messages is displayed, as shown in Figure 14-70.

These messages are stored in your user's mail queue, which is in the /var/spool/mail/ directory. The mail utility reads your messages directly out of this queue file. Because you're running the mail utility on the same system where the queue resides, you don't need POP3 or IMAP support configured to access your messages. To read a message, simply enter the message number at the ? prompt. You can delete a message by entering **d** *message_number* at the ? prompt. You can quit mail by entering **q**.

To send a message, you can invoke mail from the shell prompt by entering **mail** *recipient_address*. You can then enter a subject line and the body text of your message, as shown in Figure 14-71.

Press CTRL-D to send the message. When you do, the message is delivered to the other user's mail queue by the MTA on your system. In Figure 14-72, the message composed in Figure 14-71 has been delivered to the ksanders user.

In addition to mail, you can also use the mutt utility to read mail. The mutt utility is a little easier to use than mail for many end users. To use mutt, you must first install the mutt package with rpm. After doing so, you can start mutt by entering **mutt** at the shell prompt. The messages for the currently logged-in user are displayed in the mutt interface, as shown in Figure 14-73.

In addition to mutt, there are many other packages available that you can install to read mail from the shell prompt.

The key thing to remember about these command-line utilities is that the user must run them from the shell prompt. If the user isn't using the local computer

FIGURE 14-71

Using mail to
send a message

FIGURE 14-72

Viewing a sent
message

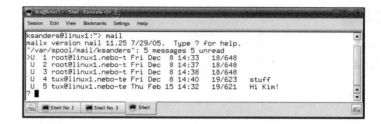

system, then he or she has to ssh into the system to read mail. If you want users to
be able to download mail, then you need to enable the POP3 and IMAP daemons
using xinetd, as discussed earlier. Then you can choose from a wide variety of e-mail
clients to download and read e-mail. For example:

- Evolution
- Mozilla Thunderbird
- Kmail

When you run one of these clients for the first time, you'll be prompted to
configure an incoming POP3 or IMAP server IP address, user account, and password.
You'll also be prompted to configure an SMTP outgoing server IP address, user
account, and password. After doing so, you can then use the remote e-mail client
to download, read, compose, and send e-mail messages through your Linux system's
MTA. For example, in Figure 14-74, the Kmail utility has been configured to send
and receive e-mail through the Linux system's Postfix MTA.

FIGURE 14-73

Using mutt to
read mail

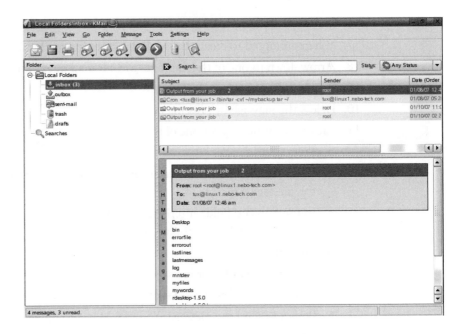

FIGURE 14-74

Using Kmail to
read e-mail

Let's practice accessing mail in the following exercise.

EXERCISE 14-7

Accessing Mail

In this exercise, you will install mutt and use it to read and send mail. Complete the
following:

1. Boot your Linux system and log in as a standard user. If you used the lab
   exercise in Chapter 3 to install your system, you can log in as **tux** with a
   password of **M3linux273**.

2. Open a terminal session.

3. Switch to your root user account by entering **su –** followed by your root user's
   password.

4. Using the rpm utility, install the mutt package on your system.

5. Return to your tux user account by entering **exit** at the shell prompt.

6. At the shell prompt, enter **mutt**.

7. When prompted to create the Mail directory in your home directory, press Y.

8. Arrow down to one of the messages in your mail queue and press ENTER.

9. Read the message.

10. Delete the message by pressing D.

11. Create a new message for one of the users on your system by doing the following:

   a. Press M.

   b. In the To: field, enter the *username* on your system that you want to send the message to.

   c. In the Subject: field, enter a *subject line* for your message. After pressing ENTER, the vi editor is displayed.

   d. Press INSERT.

   e. Enter the text of your message.

   f. When you're done, press ESC, then enter **:exit**.

   g. Press Y to send the message. You should be prompted that the message was sent.

   h. Press Q to quit mutt.

   i. When prompted to delete the purged message, enter Y.

   j. Use the **su – *username*** command to change to the user you sent the message to. For example, to change to the ksanders account, you would enter **su – ksanders** at the shell prompt.

   k. Enter **mutt** at the shell prompt.

   l. Create the Mail directory in the user's home directory by pressing Y.

   m. Arrow down to and select the message you just sent the user.

   n. Exit the message by pressing I.

   o. Exit mutt by pressing Q.

   p. When prompted to move read messages to /home/*user*/mbox, press Y.

That's it for this chapter. Let's review what you learned.

CERTIFICATION SUMMARY

In this chapter, we reviewed the basic setup and configuration of a variety of Linux network services. We started this chapter by discussing how to configure the dhcpd daemon on your Linux system. DHCP is used to automatically assign IP addressing information to network systems when they boot. To do this, the DHCP client sends a DHCPDISCOVER broadcast. The DHCP server receives the broadcast and sends an IP address assignment proposal in the form of a DHCPOFFER. The client selects an offer and sends a DHCPREQUEST back to the server and the address is assigned.

The DHCP protocol can be used to assign a variety of IP addressing information including an IP address, a subnet mask, a default gateway router address, and the DNS server address. To configure the dhcpd daemon on your system, you need to install the dhcp, dhcp-server, and dhcptools packages on your system. The daemon is configured using the /etc/dhcpd.conf file. You define IP address ranges and DHCP options to be delivered to client systems in this file. The dhcpd daemon is started and stopped using the dhcpd init script in your init directory. After making any changes to the dhcpd.conf file, you need to restart the dhcpd daemon.

Next, we discussed how to configure a DNS service on your Linux system. DNS servers allow you to map easy-to-remember domain names to IP addresses. DNS eliminates the need for long /etc/hosts files. Instead of using flat-file mappings, DNS organizes hosts into a highly structured domain hierarchy. The . root domain exists at the top of the hierarchy. Beneath the root are the top-level domains, such as .com, .edu, .gov, and so on. Beneath the top-level domains are organization-specific zones. Within the zones are sub-zones or individual hosts.

DNS runs on IP port 53. DNS clients send name resolution requests to the DNS server. If a DNS server doesn't have the record for a host being requested, it can send a series of requests to a variety of different DNS servers to locate the DNS server that is authoritative for the host in question, allowing it to resolve the host name into an IP address. To make DNS fault-tolerant, you can implement master and slave DNS servers. Slave DNS servers use zone transfers to download records from the master DNS server.

You can configure forward-lookup zones and reverse-lookup zones on your DNS server. Forward-lookup zones resolve domain names into IP addresses. Reverse-lookup zones resolve IP addresses into domain names. Forward-lookup zones are named using the domain name, such as nebo-tech.com. Reverse-lookup zone names are constructed using the following syntax:

```
reversed_network_address.in-addr.arpa.
```

To install DNS on your Linux system, you need to install the bind, bind-libs, bind-chrootenv, and bind-utils packages. The DNS service is provided by the named daemon. The daemon itself is configured using the /etc/named.conf file. Zones are configured using files in the /var/lib/named directory. After making any changes, you need to restart the named daemon using its init script in your init directory.

You configure your DNS resolver by editing the /etc/host.conf or the /etc/resolve.conf file and entering the IP address of the Linux system running the named daemon. You can test your DNS server using the dig and nslookup utilities.

We next discussed how to configure the Apache Web server on a Linux system. Web servers communicate with Web browsers using the HTTP and HTTPS protocols. By default, the HTTP protocol uses port 80. The HTTPS protocol uses port 443. The Apache Web server serves Web pages written using HTML in the /srv/www/htdocs directory.

To install the Apache Web server on your Linux system, you need to install the apache2, apache2-doc, apache2-example-pages, and apache2-prefork packages. After installation, the Apache Web server can be run using its default configuration parameters. If you want to customize the way it works, you need to edit the files in /etc/apache2. After doing so, you'll need to restart the apache2 daemon using its init script in your init script directory.

Then we learned how to configure Samba on Linux. The Samba service allows your Linux system to emulate a Windows NT server on your network using the SMB protocol. It can share directories and printers. It can also provide authentication services by hosting a domain. It can resolve NetBIOS names into IP addresses by providing a WINS server.

To install Samba on your system, you need to install the libsmbclient, samba, samba-client, samba-doc, samba-pdb, and samba-winbind packages. Samba stores its user accounts in the /etc/samba/smbpasswd file. You can Samba-enable user accounts using the smbpasswd –a *username* command. The service is configured using the /etc/samba/smb.conf file. You can define global options as well as shared directories and printers in this file. Shared Samba resources can be accessed by Windows and Linux systems.

We next discussed how to set up Linux printing with CUPS. The CUPS service is provided using the cupsd daemon. CUPS can announce the availability of its printers on the local network. Other Linux systems can listen for these announcements, connect to the CUPS service, and send print jobs to its printers. The CUPS system is made up of the following components:

- CUPS scheduler
- CUPS filters
- CUPS backends

- PPD files
- Web-based configuration utility
- Print queue (/var/spool/cups)

To install CUPS on your Linux system, you need to install the cups, cups-backends, cups-client, cups-drivers, cups-libs, gtklp, and xpp packages. The CUPS service is configured using the /etc/cups/cupsd.conf file. To enable other Linux systems to print through your CUPS printers, you must uncomment the BrowseAddress directive in this file.

One of the tasks you need to complete when setting up CUPS is to configure a CUPS administrator. To do this, enter **lppasswd –g sys –a *user_name*** at the shell prompt. After doing so, you can use the Web-based configuration utility to create your printers. You do this by opening a Web browser and navigating to http://localhost:631.

After creating your printer, you can send print jobs by selecting File | Print in your graphical Linux applications. You can also send print jobs from the shell prompt using the lp command. You can using the following command-line utilities to manage your CUPS system:

- **lpstat –t** Displays information about CUPS printers on the system.
- **cancel** Cancels a print job.
- **lpoptions –d** Sets the default printer for the system.
- **accept/reject** Enables or disables a CUPS print queue.
- **enable/disable** Enables or disables a CUPS printer.

We next discussed configuring basic network services with the xinetd daemon. The xinetd daemon is a super daemon. It manages other network service daemons on the system. When a network service is requested, the xinetd daemon starts the service and forwards the request to it. When the request has been completed and the service is no longer needed, xinetd unloads it from memory.

The xinetd daemon is configured using the /etc/xinetd.conf file. Individual services managed by xinetd can be enabled or disabled using the appropriate configuration file located in the /etc/xinetd.d directory.

Next, we reviewed NFS. NFS allows remote Linux systems to mount exported directories in your file system. NFS exports are defined in the /etc/exports file. After defining an export in the /etc/exports file, you need to restart the NFS service using the nfsserver init script in /etc/init.d or /etc/rc.d/init.d.

After doing so, you can use the showmount command to view available exports on a particular system. You can mount an exported NFS directory from a remote system by entering **mount –t nfs** *address:exported_directory mount_point* at the shell prompt. You can also create an entry in /etc/fstab to automatically mount the exported directory at boot.

Next, we looked at NIS. NIS is designed to manage large Linux networks. Using NIS, you can convert Linux configuration files into NIS map files that can be distributed to other Linux systems participating in the NIS domain. This allows multiple Linux systems to use the same configuration files, including the /etc/passwd and /etc/shadow files.

To install NIS on your system, you need to install the portmap, ypserv, ypbind, and yp-tools packages. Once installed and configured, you can use the following commands to manage the NIS system:

- **/bin/ypdomainname** Displays or sets the current NIS domain.
- **/usr/bin/ypwhich** Displays the name of the NIS server a NIS client has been configured to use.
- **/usr/bin/ypcat** Displays the contents of a NIS map file.
- **/usr/bin/yppasswd** Changes the password of a user on the NIS server.
- **/usr/sbin/yppoll** Displays the ID number of a NIS map on your NIS server.
- **ypbind** Starts the NIS client.

We then spent some time discussing how to configure remote access to your Linux system. The first solution we looked at was Telnet. If you configure the Telnet service on your Linux system, you can connect to it from another system using a Telnet client. You need to install the telnet-server and telnet packages on your system to enable Telnet. Once installed, Telnet is managed by the xinetd daemon. You must enable the Telnet service using the /etc/xinetd.d/telnet configuration file.

One of the key problems with Telnet is that it doesn't encrypt data being transmitted, allowing sniffers to capture usernames and passwords. Therefore, you should consider using ssh instead. The sshd daemon provides similar functionality as Telnet, but it encrypts all data being exchanged. To use ssh, you must first install the openssh package on your system. The sshd daemon is configured using the /etc/ssh/sshd_config file. The ssh client is configured using the /etc/ssh/ssh_config file. To connect to the sshd daemon using an ssh client on a Linux system, enter **ssh –l** *username IP_address* at the shell prompt.

In addition to Telnet and ssh, there are a variety of older "r" utilities that you can use to accomplish similar tasks. These include rsh, rlogin, and rcp. Be warned that these utilities, like Telnet, do not encrypt transmissions. To use the "r" utilities, you need to first install the rsh-server package on the Linux system you want to connect to. You also need to install the rsh package on the Linux system you want to connect from. You enable these services using the appropriate configuration file in the /etc/xinetd.d directory. You access these services using the following commands:

- **rlogin** Provides a remote terminal session, much like Telnet.
- **rsh** Allows you to run a command on the remote system.
- **rcp** Allows you to copy a file between systems.

We ended this chapter by discussing several utilities you can use to access e-mail. For messages to be delivered, an e-mail system is composed of the following components:

- **MUA** Client software used to read and compose e-mail.
- **SMTP** Protocol used to transfer mail from MUAs to MTAs and to transfer mail between MTAs.
- **MTA** Holds mail for local delivery or forwards to the next MTA to get a message to its destination.
- **MDA** Holds mail waiting for client MUAs to access it.
- **POP3** and **IMAP** Protocols used to transfer messages from an MDA to a client MUA.

Most Linux distributions install an MTA by default. Common Linux MTAs include sendmail and Postfix. To enable a full e-mail system, you need to install and configure a POP3 or IMAP daemon to work with your sendmail or Postfix daemons.

Mail for local user accounts is stored in the /var/spool/mail directory on your Linux system. You can access your message using a variety of mail reader tools. You can use mail or mutt from the command line. You can also configure a graphical utility such as Evolution or Kmail.

✓ **TWO-MINUTE DRILL**

Configure a DHCP Server on Linux

❑ DHCP is used to automatically assign IP addressing information to network systems when they boot.

❑ The DHCP client sends a DHCPDISCOVER broadcast.

❑ The DHCP server receives the broadcast and sends a DHCPOFFER.

❑ The client selects an offer and sends a DHCPREQUEST to assign the address.

❑ The DHCP protocol can deliver an IP address, a subnet mask, a default gateway router address, and the DNS server address.

❑ You need to install the dhcp, dhcp-server, and dhcptools packages to configure a DHCP server.

❑ The dhcpd daemon is configured using the /etc/dhcpd.conf file.

❑ You define IP address ranges and DHCP options to be delivered to client systems in the /etc/dhcpd.conf file.

❑ The dhcpd daemon is started and stopped using the dhcpd init script.

❑ After making any changes to the dhcpd.conf file, you need to restart the dhcpd daemon.

Configure a DNS Server on Linux

❑ DNS servers map domain names to IP addresses.

❑ DNS organizes hosts into a highly structured domain hierarchy.

❑ The . root domain exists at the top of the hierarchy.

❑ Beneath the root are the top-level domains, such as .com, .edu, .gov, etc.

❑ Beneath the top-level domains are organization-specific zones.

❑ Within the zones are sub-zones or individual hosts.

❑ DNS runs on port 53.

❑ DNS clients send name resolution requests to the DNS server.

❑ If a DNS server doesn't have the record for a host being requested, it can send requests to a variety of different DNS servers to locate the DNS server that is authoritative for the host in question.

❑ You can implement master and slave DNS servers.

❑ Slave DNS servers use zone transfers to download records from the master DNS server.

❑ You can configure forward-lookup zones and reverse-lookup zones on your DNS server.

❑ Forward-lookup zones resolve domain names into IP addresses.

❑ Reverse-lookup zones resolve IP addresses into domain names.

❑ Forward-lookup zones are named using the domain name.

❑ Reverse-lookup zone names are constructed as follows: *reversed_network_address*.in-addr.arpa.

❑ You need to install the bind, bind-libs, bind-chrootenv, and bind-utils packages to configure a DNS server on your Linux system.

❑ The DNS service is provided by the named daemon.

❑ The named daemon is configured using the /etc/named.conf file.

❑ Zones are configured using files in the /var/lib/named directory.

❑ After making any changes, you need to restart the named daemon.

❑ You configure your DNS resolver by editing the /etc/host.conf or the /etc/resolve.conf file.

❑ You can test your DNS server using the dig and nslookup utilities.

Configure the Apache Web Server on Linux

❑ Web servers communicate with Web browsers using the HTTP and HTTPS protocols.

❑ The HTTP protocol uses port 80.

❑ The HTTPS protocol uses port 443.

❑ The Apache Web server serves Web pages written using HTML in the /srv/www/htdocs directory.

❑ To install the Apache Web server, you need to install the apache2, apache2-doc, apache2-example-pages, and apache2-prefork packages.

❑ The Apache Web server can be configured using the files in /etc/apache2.

Configure Samba on Linux

❑ The Samba service allows your Linux system to emulate a Windows NT server using the SMB protocol.

❑ Samba can share directories and printers.

❑ Samba can also authenticate users by hosting a domain.

❑ Samba provides an optional WINS service that can resolve NetBIOS names into IP addresses.

❑ Your need to install the libsmbclient, samba, samba-client, samba-doc, samba-pdb, and samba-winbind packages to use Samba.

❑ Samba stores its user accounts in the /etc/samba/smbpasswd file.

❑ You Samba-enable user accounts using the smbpasswd –a *username* command.

❑ Samba is configured with the /etc/samba/smb.conf file.

❑ You define shared directories and printers in the /etc/samba/smb.conf file.

❑ Shared Samba resources can be accessed by Windows and Linux systems.

Configure Printing on Linux

❑ Most Linux distributions use CUPS to provide local and network printing.

❑ The CUPS service is provided by the cupsd daemon.

❑ CUPS can announce the availability of its printers on the local network.

❑ Other Linux systems can listen for these announcements, connect to the CUPS service, and send print jobs to its printers.

❑ The CUPS system is made up of the CUPS scheduler, CUPS filters, CUPS backends, PPD files, Web-based configuration utility, and the Print queue (/var/spool/cups).

❑ To enable CUPS, you need to install the cups, cups-backends, cups-client, cups-drivers, cups-libs, gtklp, and xpp packages.

❑ The CUPS service is configured with the /etc/cups/cupsd.conf file.

❑ To enable other Linux systems to print through your CUPS printers, you must uncomment the BrowseAddress directive in the /etc/cups/cupsd.conf file.

❑ Use the **lppasswd –g sys –a *user_name*** command at the shell prompt to create a CUPS administrative user.

❑ You use the Web-based configuration utility to configure your printers. It is accessed at http://localhost:631.

❑ After creating your CUPS printer, you can send print jobs by selecting File | Print in a graphical Linux application.

❑ You can send print jobs from the shell prompt using the lp command.

❑ You can use the following command-line utilities to manage your CUPS system:

  ❑ lpstat –t
  ❑ cancel
  ❑ lpoptions –d
  ❑ accept/reject
  ❑ enable/disable

Configure Basic Network Services with xinetd

❑ The xinetd daemon is a super daemon.

❑ It manages other network service daemons on the system.

❑ When a network service is requested, the xinetd daemon starts the service and forwards the request to it.

❑ When the request has been completed and the service is no longer needed, xinetd unloads it from memory.

❑ The xinetd daemon is configured using the /etc/xinetd.conf file.

❑ Services managed by xinetd can be enabled or disabled using the configuration files located in the /etc/xinetd.d directory.

Configure NFS on Linux

❑ NFS allows remote Linux systems to mount exported directories in your file system.

❑ NFS exports are defined in the /etc/exports file.

❑ You can use the showmount command to view available exports on a system.

❑ You can mount an export by entering **mount –t nfs** *address:exported_ directory mount_point* at the shell prompt.

❑ You can create an entry in /etc/fstab to automatically mount an NFS export at boot.

Use NIS on Linux

❑ NIS is designed to manage large Linux networks.

❑ NIS converts Linux configuration files into NIS map files that can be distributed to other Linux systems participating in a NIS domain.

❑ NIS allows multiple Linux systems to use the same configuration files, including the /etc/passwd and /etc/shadow files.

❑ To install NIS on your system, you need to install the portmap, ypserv, ypbind, and yp-tools packages.

❑ You can use the following commands to mange the NIS system:

  ❑ /bin/ypdomainname

  ❑ /usr/bin/ypwhich

  ❑ /usr/bin/ypcat

  ❑ /usr/bin/yppasswd

  ❑ /usr/sbin/yppoll

  ❑ ypbind

Configure Remote Access on Linux

❑ Telnet allows you to access a shell prompt on a Linux system from a remote system using a Telnet client.

❑ You need to install the telnet-server and telnet packages on your system to enable Telnet.

❑ Telnet is managed by the xinetd daemon

❑ You enable the Telnet service using the /etc/xinetd.d/telnet configuration file.

❑ Telnet doesn't encrypt data, allowing sniffers to capture usernames and passwords.

❑ You should consider using ssh instead of Telnet.

❑ The sshd daemon provides similar functionality as Telnet, but it encrypts all data transmissions.

❑ To use ssh, you must install the openssh package on your system.

❑ The sshd daemon is configured using the /etc/ssh/sshd_config file.

❑ The ssh client is configured using the /etc/ssh/ssh_config file.

❑ To connect to the sshd daemon using an ssh client, you enter **ssh –l** *username IP_address* at the shell prompt.

❑ You can use rsh, rlogin, and rcp to remotely access a Linux system.

❑ These utilities do not encrypt transmissions.

❑ To use the "r" utilities, you need to first install the rsh-server package on the Linux system you want to connect to.

❑ You need to install the rsh package on the Linux system you want to connect from.

❑ You enable the "r" services using the appropriate configuration file in the /etc/xinetd.d directory.

❑ The rlogin utility provides a remote terminal session, much like Telnet.

❑ The rsh utility allows you to run a command on the remote system.

❑ The rcp utility allows you to copy a file between systems.

Access Local E-Mail

❑ An e-mail system is composed of MUAs, the SMTP protocol, MTAs, MDAs, and the POP3 and/or IMAP protocol.

❑ Most Linux distributions install an MTA by default.

❑ Common Linux MTAs include sendmail and Postfix.

❑ To enable a full e-mail system, you need to install and configure a POP3 or IMAP daemon to work with your sendmail or Postfix daemon.

❑ Mail for local user accounts is stored in the /var/spool/mail directory.

❑ You can access your messages using a variety of command-line mail reader tools such as mail or mutt.

❑ You can also configure a graphical utility such as Evolution or Kmail.

SELF TEST

Configure a DHCP Server on Linux

1. What is contained in a DHCPOFFER message?

   A. A request for an IP address from the DHCP client.

   B. A discovery packet used to locate the DHCP server.

   C. An IP address assignment proposal from the DHCP server.

   D. Acceptance of an IP address assignment from the DHCP client.

2. Which of the following will configure a subnet range declaration to use an IP address range of 10.0.0.100 to 10.0.0.190?

   A. range 10.0.0.100 10.0.0.190

   B. address range 10.0.0.100 10.0.0.190

   C. range 10.0.0.100 – 10.0.0.190

   D. lease 10.0.0.100 10.0.0.190

Configure a DNS Server on Linux

3. Which file is used to configure the named daemon?

   A. /var/lib/named/named.conf

   B. /etc/named.d/named.conf

   C. /etc/named.conf

   D. /var/lib/named/localhost.zone

4. What type of DNS record is used to map a host name to an IP address?

   A. NS   **B.** A

   C. PTR   **D.** MX

Configure the Apache Web Server on Linux

5. Which of the following is the default document root used by the Apache 2 Web server?

   A. /tmp   **B.** /home/httpd

   C. /var/lib/httpd/htdocs   **D.** /srv/www/htdocs

6. What IP ports does your Apache 2 Web server listen on by default? (Choose two.)

   A. 80   **B.** 25

   C. 21   **D.** 443

   E. 631

Configure Samba on Linux

7. What protocol is used by the Samba service on a Linux system to communicate with Samba clients?

   A. FTP

   B. HTTP

   C. SMB

   D. NCP

8. Which of the following commands will add a user named tux to the smbpasswd file?

   A. smbpasswd –a tux

   B. smbuseradd tux

   C. smbpasswd tux

   D. useradd –a tux

9. Which of the following commands will mount a Samba share named Data, located on the mylinux server, in the /mnt/samba directory as a user named ksanders?

   A. smbmount //mylinux/Data –u ksanders

   B. smbmount //mylinux/Data /mnt/samba –u ksanders

   C. smbmount //Data /mnt/samba user=ksanders

   D. smbmount //mylinux/Data /mnt/samba user=ksanders

Configure Printing on Linux

10. Which of the following commands will print two copies of the /home/tux/employees.txt file to a CUPS printer named MIN2300W?

    A. –d MIN2300W –n 2 /home/tux/employees.txt

    B. –p MIN2300W –c 2 /home/tux/employees.txt

    C. /home/tux/employees.txt

    D. –d MIN2300W /home/tux/employees.txt

11. Which of the following commands sets the default printer on a Linux system to a printer named MIN2300W?

    A. lpoptions MIN2300W

    B. lpstat –d MIN2300W

    C. lp default = MIN2300W

    D. lpoptions –d MIN2300W

Configure Basic Network Services with xinetd

12. Which of the following directories contains configuration files that the xinetd daemon uses to manage network daemons (by default)?

    A. /var/lib/xinetd.d   B. /etc/xinetd.d

    C. /etc/xinetd   D. /srv/xinetd.d

Configure NFS on Linux

13. Which of the following files contains exported NFS directories?

    A. /etc/exports   B. /etc/nfs.d/export

    C. /srv/nfs/export   D. /var/lib/nfs/exports

Use NIS on Linux

14. Which of the following commands is used to display the name of the NIS server a NIS client has been configured to use?

    A. /bin/ypdomainname   B. /usr/bin/ypwhich

    C. /usr/bin/ypcat   D. ypbind

15. Which of the following commands is used to display the contents of a NIS map?

    A. /bin/ypdomainname

    B. /usr/bin/ypwhich

    C. /usr/bin/ypcat

    D. /usr/sbin/yppoll

Configure Remote Access on Linux

16. Which of the following files is used to enable the Telnet service on a Linux system?

    A. /etc/xinitd.d/telnet

    B. /etc/telnetd.conf

    C. /etc/telnetd.d/telnet.conf

    D. /var/lib/telnet/telnet.conf

17. Which of the following commands will load the ssh client and connect as the user ksanders to an sshd daemon running on a host with an IP address of 10.0.0.254?

    A. sshd –l ksanders 10.0.0.254

    B. ssh –u ksanders 10.0.0.254

    C. ssh –l ksanders 10.0.0.254

    D. ssh user=ksanders 10.0.0.254

18. Which of the following utilities provides a shell prompt on a remote system?

    A. rlogin   **B.** rsh

    C. rcp   **D.** rshell

Access Local E-Mail

19. Which of the following protocols can be used to download e-mail messages from a Mail Delivery Agent? (Choose two.)

    A. POP3   **B.** SMTP

    C. IMAP   **D.** HTTP

    E. FTP

20. Which of the following shell commands will send an e-mail message to a user named rtracy?

    A. mail –s –u rtracy

    B. mail user=rtracy

    C. mail –s rtracy

    D. mail rtracy

LAB QUESTION

You need to set up a DNS server on your system. The host name of the DNS server is resolve.myzone.com. This DNS server must resolve the following host names and IP addresses:

- linux1.my-zone.com: 10.200.200.1
- linux2.my-zone.com: 10.200.200.2
- linux3.my-zone.com: 10.200.200.3

    You also need to configure an existing DHCP service on the same system to deliver the DNS server IP address of 10.200.200.254 to clients when they get their IP address. Outline the process you will follow to accomplish this.

SELF TEST ANSWERS

Configure a DHCP Server on Linux

1. ☑ **C.** The DHCPOFFER message contains an IP address proposal from the DHCP server.
   ☒ **A, B,** and **D** are incorrect. **A** and **B** re contained in a DHCPDISCOVER message. **D** is contained in a DHCPREQUEST message.

2. ☑ **A.** The range 10.0.0.100 10.0.0.190 line will configure the DHCP server to hand out addresses in this range.
   ☒ **B, C,** and **D** are incorrect. **B** uses the invalid term "address." **C** incorrectly places a hyphen between range ends. **D** incorrectly uses "lease" instead of "range."

Configure a DNS Server on Linux

3. ☑ **C.** The /etc/named.conf file is used to configure the named daemon.
   ☒ **A, B,** and **D** are incorrect. **A** and **B** used invalid paths or file names. **D** is used to configure the localhost zone.

4. ☑ **B.** An A record maps a host name to an IP address.
   ☒ **A, C,** and **D** are incorrect. **A** is used to map a name server name to a domain name. **C** is used to map an IP address to a domain name. **D** is used to map a mail server name to a domain name or IP address.

Configure the Apache Web Server on Linux

5. ☑ **D.** The /srv/www/htdocs directory is the default document root used by the Apache 2 Web server.
   ☒ **A, B,** and **C** are incorrect. **A** is used for temporary files. **B** doesn't exist unless a user account named http is created. **C** was used as the document root by older versions of Apache.

6. ☑ **A** and **D.** Port 80 (HTTP) and port 443 (HTTPS) are used by default by the Apache Web server.
   ☒ **B, C,** and **E** are incorrect. **B** is incorrect. Port 25 is used by the SMTP protocol. **C** is incorrect. Port 21 is used by the FTP protocol. **E** is incorrect. Port 631 is used by the IPP protocol.

Configure Samba on Linux

7. ☑ **C.** Samba uses the SMB protocol.
   ☒ **A, B,** and **D** are incorrect. **A** is incorrect because the FTP protocol is used by FTP servers.

B is incorrect because Web servers use the HTTP protocol. D is incorrect because NetWare servers use the NCP protocol.

8. ☑ **A.** The smbpasswd –a tux command will add the tux user to the smbpasswd file.
   ☒ **B, C,** and **D** are incorrect. **B** omits the "–a" option and uses an invalid command. **C** omits the "–a" option. **D** is incorrect because the useradd command adds users to the passwd file.

9. ☑ **D.** The smbmount //mylinux/Data /mnt/samba user=ksanders command will mount a Samba share named Data, located on the mylinux server, in the /mnt/samba directory as a user named ksanders.
   ☒ **A, B,** and **C** are incorrect. **A** uses the incorrect "–u" option and omits the mount point. **B** uses the incorrect "–u" option. **C** omits the Linux system name "mylinux."

Configure Printing on Linux

10. ☑ **A.** The lp –d MIN2300W –n 2 /home/tux/employees.txt command will print two copies of the /home/tux/employees.txt file to a CUPS printer named MIN2300W.
    ☒ **B, C,** and **D** are incorrect. **B** uses the incorrect "–c" option. **C** omits the CUPS printer name. **D** only prints one copy of the document.

11. ☑ **D.** The lpoptions –d MIN2300W command will set the default printer on a Linux system to a printer named MIN2300W.
    ☒ **A, B,** and **C** are incorrect. **A** omits the "–d" option. **B** and **C** use the incorrect commands.

Configure Basic Network Services with xinetd

12. ☑ **B.** The /etc/xinetd.d directory contains the configuration files that the xinetd daemon uses to manage network daemons?
    ☒ **A, C,** and **D** are incorrect. Each of these responses specifies an invalid directory.

Configure NFS on Linux

13. ☑ **A.** The /etc/exports file contains NFS exported directories.
    ☒ **B, C,** and **D** are incorrect. These responses specify invalid directories.

Use NIS on Linux

14. ☑ **B.** The /usr/bin/ypwhich command is used to display the name of the NIS server a NIS client has been configured to use.
    ☒ **A, C,** and **D** are incorrect. **A** is used to view or set the NIS domain name. **C** is used to view the contents of a NIS map file. **D** is used to start the NIS client.

15. ☑ **C.** The /usr/bin/ypcat command is used to display the contents of a NIS map file.
☒ **A, B,** and **D** are incorrect. **A** is used to view or set the NIS domain name. **B** is used to display the name of the NIS server a NIS client has been configured to use. **D** is used to display the ID number of a NIS map on your NIS server.

Configure Remote Access on Linux

16. ☑ **A.** The /etc/xinetd.d/telnet file is used to enable the Telnet service on a Linux system.
☒ **B, C,** and **D** are incorrect. These responses specify invalid files and directories.

17. ☑ **C.** The ssh –l ksanders 10.0.0.254 command is used to load the ssh client and connect as the user ksanders to the sshd daemon running on a host with an IP address of 10.0.0.254.
☒ **A, B,** and **D** are incorrect. **A** uses "sshd" instead of "ssh." **B** uses the incorrect "–u" option. **D** uses the incorrect "user=" option.

18. ☑ **A.** The rlogin utility provides a shell prompt on a remote system.
☒ **B, C,** and **D** are incorrect. **B** is used to run a command on a remote system. **C** is used to copy files between systems. **D** is an invalid command.

Access Local E-Mail

19. ☑ **A** and **C.** The POP3 and IMAP protocols are used by MUAs to download messages from an MDA.
☒ **B, D,** and **E** are incorrect. **B** is used to send e-mail from an MUA to an MTA and between MTAs. **D** is used by Web servers and Web browsers. **E** is used by FTP servers and FTP clients.

20. ☑ **D.** The mail rtracy command will allow you to compose and send a message to the rttracy user.
☒ **A, B,** and **C** are incorrect. **A** uses the incorrect "–u" and "–s" options. **B** uses the incorrect "user" option. **C** uses the incorrect "–s" option.

LAB ANSWER

First, you should install the bind, bind-libs, bind-chrootenv, and bind-utils packages on your server. Then you would need to edit your named.conf file and add a zone directive for the my-zone.com zone, as shown here:

```
zone my-zone.com in {
type master;
file "master/my-zone.com";
};
```

Next, you need to create a zone file named /var/lib/named/master/my-zone.com and insert the following A records that resolve to the specified host names:

```
$TTL 2d
@       IN  SOA      resolve.my-zone.com.      root.resolve.my-zone.com. (
                     2007020800  ; serial
                     3h          ; refresh
                     1h          ; retry
                     1w          ; expiry
                     1d )        ; minimum

my-zone.com.         IN NS       resolve.my-zone.com.
resolve              IN A        10.200.200.254
linux1               IN A        10.200.200.1
linux2               IN A        10.200.200.2
linux3               IN A        10.200.200.3
```

After configuring these files, you would then start the named daemon using its init script in your init directory.

To deliver your DNS server IP address to DHCP clients, you would edit your /etc/dhcpd.conf file and add the following line:

```
option domain-name-servers 10.200.200.254
```

After restarting your dhcpd daemon, clients will receive the new DNS server address the next time they request or renew their DHCP lease.

15

Configuring Linux Security

I n today's networked world, security is a key issue in nearly every organization. As a Linux system administrator, you need to be very aware of the security issues affecting your implementation. In this chapter, we're going to spend some time discussing how you can increase the security of your Linux systems and network. We'll discuss the following topics:

- Securing the system
- Controlling user access
- Defending against network attacks
- Detecting intrusion attempts

INSIDE THE EXAM

Configuring Linux Security

Security-related questions will comprise a large part of your Linux+ exam! According to the folks at CompTIA, roughly one in five questions on the exam will cover some aspect of Linux security. Computer and network security are evolving, ever-changing topics. The security issues of last year are ancient history. You will see this reflected in your Linux+ exam. Don't be concerned with specific security threats. Instead, focus on security principles and skills. You should know how to:

- Physically secure the computer.
- Use the right user account at the right time.

- Use a strong-password policy.
- Stay current on the latest security threats.
- Identify unneeded network services and shut them down.
- Control access to network services.
- Implement a basic firewall.
- Identify when someone is trying to hack into your system.

Let's begin this chapter by discussing how to physically secure your Linux system.

CERTIFICATION OBJECTIVE 15.01

Secure the System

One of the most important, and most frequently overlooked, aspects of Linux security is securing the system itself. We'll address the following topics here:

- Securing the physical environment
- Securing access to the operating system

Let's begin by discussing how to secure the physical environment.

Securing the Physical Environment

As a consultant, I work with a variety of different clients. In any given week, I may visit three or four different organizations to help them with their network or to help them develop training materials for computing products (such as this book). In this capacity, I've had the opportunity to observe a wide range of system implementations. One of the most common mistakes I see over and over is the failure to properly secure physical access to the organization's computer systems.

Most of the larger organizations I work with are very security conscious and do properly secure access to their systems. However, many of the smaller organizations I work for do not. You would be surprised how many organizations place computer systems that contain sensitive or mission-critical data in areas that are easily accessible.

For example, one client I did work for a few years ago kept their server in an unoccupied cubicle in the back of the office where it was "out of the way." There was no door to the cubicle. Anyone with access to the office could have simply picked up the server and walked out the door with it. Because it was kept in an out-of-the-way location, no one in the organization would have ever seen the perpetrator walking off with the server. No firewall in the world can protect you from this kind of threat.

As a Linux administrator, one of the most important things you can do is to limit who can access your systems. The level of access depends on the type of system involved. Keep the following points in mind:

- **Servers** The server should have the highest degree of physical security. No one (and I mean NO ONE) from the general public should have physical access to your organization's servers. In fact, only a very limited number of employees within the organization should have access to your servers. Servers should not be kept in an unoccupied cubicle or on the network administrator's desk. Instead, they should be kept in a locked server room that only the system administrator and very few other people have access to.

  You should evaluate your situation and see how hard it would be for someone to get access to your servers. I've heard of instances where intruders have dressed up as copier technicians, plumbers, electricians, and even vending machine repairmen to gain access to an organization. Once inside, they had free run of the place and were able to walk off with critical computing equipment. Because they looked "official" no one questioned what they were doing.

  The key idea is that an intruder should have to defeat several layers of security to get at the server system. At a minimum, someone should have to get through a secured front door, past a receptionist or security guard, and through a locked door to get to your servers. Most of the larger organizations I work with use a proximity lock that requires an ID card on their server rooms to limit access to specific people in the organization.

  I walked into a small store just last month and the door to the server room in the back was wide open. Even worse, the server room door was right next to the rear emergency exit. If I had wanted to, I could have grabbed the server and ran out the emergency exit before anyone in the store could have known what was going on.

- **Workstations** Securing access to workstations is much more difficult. The key problem is the broad use of cubicles in the modern working environment. If you've ever worked in a sea of cubicles, you can probably already guess what the issue is. Yep, you're right. There are no doors in cubicles. Anyone with access to the office has access to just about everyone's computer system. As with servers, this allows an intruder to fake his or her way into the office and walk out with a workstation system. If done correctly, they won't even be challenged as they walk out the front door. The best you can do is to secure access to the office itself. Again, proximity locks and ID cards work well in this scenario. Only someone with an authorized card can gain access to the work area.

on the **j o b** *There are some cool biometric systems available that scan retinas, fingerprints, or even your voice to control access to a room.*

In addition to controlling access to the office, you can further protect your organization's workstations and servers by securing access to the operating system.

Securing Access to the Operating System

After physically securing access to your computer systems, your next line of defense is the access controls built into the Linux operating system itself. Of course, Linux uses user accounts and passwords to control who can do what with the system. This is a very good thing. In fact, we'll talk about using strong passwords later in this chapter.

However, there is a key problem that occurs daily in most organizations. During the course of the day, users constantly come and go from their cubicles or offices. It's very common to find one or more workstations logged in and unattended at any given point in the day. Users have meetings, take breaks, go to lunch, and use the restroom. During these times, the data on their systems is highly vulnerable. An intruder who managed to get access into the office (remember the copier tech and vending machine repairperson mentioned earlier) now has access to everything the given user account has access to on the system and the network. This window of opportunity may last only a few minutes or may even last several hours. It doesn't take long to copy a lot of critical, sensitive data to a flash drive! Even worse, the intruder could load any one of a number of programs onto the system that compromise security, such as key-logging software or a virus.

So what can you do to protect your systems? First of all, you can implement screen-saver passwords. This will require an intruder to supply a password to gain access to the system console. This helps, but it still leaves the system vulnerable for a period of time, depending on how long the screen-saver inactivity period is set for.

Better yet, you should train your users to log out or lock their workstations before leaving them for even the shortest period of time. Most Linux graphical desktop environments provide the option of locking the operating system. For example, within KDE, you can select K Menu | Lock Session to lock the system. You must then re-authenticate before you can use the system again. This is shown in Figure 15-1.

If you're using a text-based environment, your users should log out when they leave their desks and then log back in when they return.

on the **j o b** *You should never leave a server logged in. If you're not using the server console, log out!*

Locking the
desktop

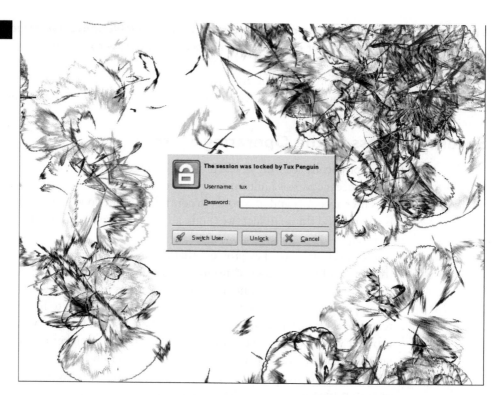

Many users, especially software developers, like to take a break while the Linux
system is working on a big task, such as compiling a program, downloading a
database update, etc. If the user logs out from the shell prompt while these processes
are running, they will be automatically stopped. To allow the user to log out and
leave without killing an important process, you can use the nohup command to
initially load it. Any process loaded by nohup will ignore any hang-up signals it
receives, such as those sent when logging out from a shell prompt. The syntax for
using nohup is nohup *command* &. For example, in Figure 15-2, the find –name

Using nohup

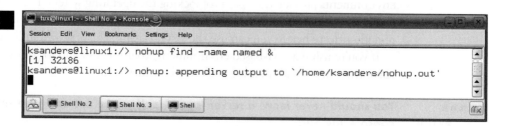

SCENARIO & SOLUTION

You need to implement a Linux server for a small startup company. They've told you to put the server in an unoccupied office. Is this a secure place for it?	If the office door has a lock, it may be a good option. You should verify who has keys to the office.
You notice that your users frequently leave their Linux systems logged in when going to meetings, going to lunch, or taking a break. What can you do to protect the unattended systems?	You should train users to lock or log out from their systems before leaving them unattended. You should also configure screen-saver passwords.

named & command has been loaded using nohup, allowing it to run even if the shell were logged out.

My experience is that this issue mostly comes down to end-user training. There's only so much you can do as the system administrator to secure individual workstations. If the end user doesn't cooperate, it won't make much difference. Educate your users as to the danger and teach them how to mitigate it.

Along these lines, you also need to configure user access controls to secure your Linux systems. Let's discuss how this is done next.

CERTIFICATION OBJECTIVE 15.02

Control User Access

A key aspect of both Linux workstation and Linux server security is to implement and use user access controls to constrain what users can do with the system. Earlier in this book, we discussed how to create and manage users, groups, and permissions to do this. However, there are additional measures that you can take to increase the security of your systems. In this part of the chapter, we'll review the following:

- ■ To root or not to root?
- ■ Implementing a strong password policy
- ■ Using a GRUB password

Let's begin by discussing the proper care and feeding of the root user account.

To root Or Not to root?

As we've already discussed earlier in this book, every Linux system, whether a workstation or a server, includes a default super-user account named root. This account has full access to every aspect of the system. As such it should be used with great care. In this part of this chapter, we'll discuss the following:

- Proper use of the root user account
- Using su
- Using sudo

Let's begin by discussing the proper way to use the root user account.

Proper Use of the root User Account

One of the key mistakes made by new Linux users is excessive use of the root user account. There's a time and a place when the root user account should be used. However, most of your work on a Linux system should be done as a non-root user account. The rule of thumb that you should follow is this: Only use root when absolutely necessary. If a task can be completed as a non-root user, then it should be done so.

Why is the proper use of the root user account of concern? A few pages back, we discussed the risks of leaving a logged-in system unattended. Imagine the havoc an intruder could wreak if he or she were to happen upon an unattended system that was logged in as root! All of the data on the system could be accessed and copied. Major configuration changes could be made to the daemons running on the system. Heaven only knows what kind of malware could be installed.

In a nutshell, a system logged in as root represents a serious security risk. Leaving such a system unattended represents a critical security risk. Everyone, including the system administrator (that's you!), should have a standard user account that he or she *always* uses to log in to the system.

If you find that you need root-level access while working on the system, you can use the su command. Let's discuss how this is done next.

Using su

By now, you should already know how su works. We've used it countless times in this book's exercises. This command allows you to change to a different user account at the shell prompt. The syntax for using su is su *options user_account*. If no user account is specified in the command, su assumes you want to switch to the root user account. Some of the more useful options you can use with su include the following:

- **–** Loads the user's environment variables. Notice that we've always used the su – command to switch to the root user account. This changes to root and loads root's environment variables.
- **–c** *command* Switches to the user account and runs the specified *command*.
- **–m** Switches to the user account but preserves the existing environment variables.

The su command will be your best friend as a Linux administrator. However, there are times when other users may need root-level access. You can use sudo to give them limited root access. Let's discuss how sudo works next.

Using sudo

Suppose you have a power user on your Linux system. This user may be a programmer, a project manager, or a database administrator. Users in this category may frequently need to run some root-level commands. But do you really want to give them your root password? Probably not. You want them to be able to run a limited number of commands that require root privileges, but you don't want them to have full root access. This can be done using the sudo command.

The sudo command allows a given user to run a command as a different user account. As with su, it could be any user account on the system; however, it's most frequently used to run commands as root. The sudo command uses the /etc/sudoers file to determine what user is authorized to run which commands. This file uses the following aliases to define who can do what:

- **User_Alias** Specifies the users who are allowed to run commands.
- **Cmnd_Alias** Specifies the commands that users are allowed to run.
- **Host_Alias** Specifies the hosts users are allowed to run the commands on.
- **Runas_Alias** Specifies the usernames that commands may be run as.

To edit your /etc/sudoers file, you need to run the visudo command as your root user. The /etc/sudoers file is loaded in your default editor, which is usually vi. Your changes are written to /etc/sudoers.tmp until committed. This is shown in Figure 15-3.

FIGURE 15-3

Editing /etc/
sudoers with
visudo

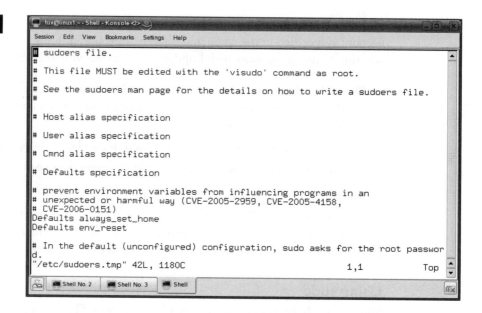

To configure your sudoers file, you need to use User_Alias to define an alias containing the user accounts (separated by commas) you want to allow to run commands. The syntax is:

```
User_Alias alias = users
```

For example, to create an alias named PWRUSRS that contains the tux and ksanders user accounts, you would enter the following in the /etc/sudoers file:

```
User_Alias PWRUSRS = tux, ksanders
```

on the **ı̇ob**

All alias names must start with a capital letter!

You next need to use Cmnd_Alias to define an alias that contains the commands (using the full path) that you want the users you just defined to be able to run. Separate multiple commands with commas. For example, if your users were programmers who need to be able to kill processes, you could define an alias named KILLPROCS that contained your kill command, as shown here:

```
Cmnd_Alias KILLPROCS = /bin/kill, /usr/bin/killall
```

Then you need to use Host_Alias to specify what systems the users can run the commands on. For example, to let them run the commands on a system named linux1, you would use the following:

```
Host_Alias MYHSTS = linux1
```

Finally, you need to glue these aliases together to define exactly what will happen. The syntax is:

```
User_Alias Host_Alias = (user) Cmnd_Alias
```

Using the aliases just defined, you could allow the specified users to run the specified commands on the specified hosts as root by entering:

```
PWRUSRS      MYHSTS = (root) KILLPROCS
```

This entire configuration is shown in Figure 15-4.

To exit the editor, press ESC and then enter **:exit**. The visudo utility will check your syntax and inform you if you've made any errors. At this point, the users you defined can execute the commands you specified as root by entering **sudo *command*** at the shell prompt. For example, the tux user could kill a process named vmware-toolbox owned by root by entering **sudo killall vmware-toolbox** at the shell prompt.

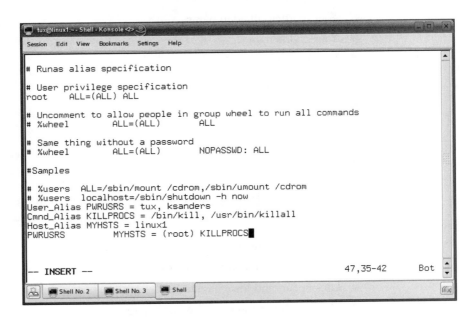

FIGURE 15-4

Configuring /etc/ sudoers

After supplying the tux user's password, the process will be killed. This is shown in Figure 15-5.

In addition to using the root user account properly, you also should implement a strong password policy. Let's discuss how this is done next.

Implementing a Strong Password Policy

Another serious security weakness I've observed over the years is the use of weak passwords. A weak password is one that can be easily guessed or cracked. Here are some examples:

- Your last name
- Your spouse's name
- Your mother's maiden name
- Your child's name
- Your birthday
- Your pet's name
- Any word that can be found in the dictionary
- Using "password" for your password
- Single-character passwords
- Blank passwords

You would be surprised how often users use these types of words for passwords. You need to train your users to use strong passwords. A strong password:

- Uses six or more characters
- Uses numbers in addition to letters
- Uses upper- and lowercase letters
- Uses words not found in the dictionary

For example, the password we created for our tux user early on in this book, **M3linux273**, is a relatively strong password because it meets the preceding criteria. You can test the relative strength of your users' passwords using one of the many password-cracking programs available on the Internet. These programs can throw thousands of words at your user accounts using a word list to see if it can guess the password and gain access to the system. One of my favorites is John the Ripper, available at http://www.openwall.com/john/. I strongly recommend that you run a cracker against your password database from time to time to identify user accounts that are using weak passwords.

In addition, you should also configure your user accounts such that passwords expire after a certain period of time. This is called *password aging*. Why age passwords? The longer a user has the same password, the more likely it is to be compromised. By forcing users to periodically rotate passwords, you keep intruders guessing. Even if they do manage to get a user's password, it will be rendered useless at some point. The length of time allowed for a given password varies from organization to organization. More security-minded organizations may mandate a password age of 30 days. Less paranoid organizations may use an age of 60 or even 90 days.

You can configure aging for your passwords using the chage command. The syntax for using chage is chage *option user*. You use the following options with chage:

- **–m *days*** Specifies the minimum number of days between password changes.
- **–M *days*** Specifies the maximum number of days between password changes.
- **–W *days*** Specifies the number of warning days before a password change is required.

For example, in Figure 15-6, the chage command has been used to specify a minimum password age of five days, a maximum password age of 90 days, and seven warning days for the user ksanders.

FIGURE 15-6

Using chage to set password aging

In addition, your Linux systems should not be configured to store passwords within the /etc/passwd file. Many processes running in a Linux system need access to /etc/passwd to complete various tasks. Storing your passwords in that file exposes them to these processes and opens a serious security hole. Most system implementers realize that storing passwords within /etc/passwd is a very bad idea, so you probably won't run into many systems configured this way any more. However, if you do run into such a system, you can use the pwconv command to move user passwords out of /etc/passwd and into /etc/shadow.

You should also train your users to use good common sense when working with passwords. One security breach I see all too often is users writing their password on a sticky note and sticking it somewhere on their desk. I've even seen system passwords written on a sticky note right on the monitor or keyboard. I know the thought of passwords written down and displayed in plain sight makes you cringe, but I see it over and over and over. Some users try to hide their sticky note under the keyboard or in a drawer, but it's still a significant security issue. All the intruder has to do is watch the user at login and note where they have hidden their password, making his or her job a cakewalk.

on the Job

The "sticky note phenomenon" is yet another reason for enforcing good physical security. A ne'er-do-well can gain easy access to corporate information using a password that's posted in plain sight. Once done, there's no way to trace the breach back to the intruder.

Finally, you should train your users how to deal with social engineering attempts. This is actually one of the easiest and most effective tools in the intruder's toolbox. Social engineering exploits human weaknesses instead of technical weaknesses in the system. Here's how a typical social engineering exploit works.

The intruder calls an employee of an organization posing as another employee. The intruder tells the employee that he is "Fred" from accounting and is on the road at a client site. He needs to get a very important file from the server and can't remember his password. He then asks the employee if he can use his or her password "just this once" to get the files he needs.

Most employees want to be team players and help out in an emergency. They are all too willing to hand out their password, granting the intruder easy access to the system. Some social engineering attempts are less direct. Instead of calling and asking for passwords, the intruder sifts through the company garbage looking for little yellow sticky notes with users' passwords written on them. Some social engineering attempts are more "in your face." The intruder sifts through the trash to find the name of a high-ranking person in the company. He then calls an employee posing as that person and demands that the employee divulge his or her password, threatening to fire them if they don't comply. Pretty sneaky, huh?

The best way to combat social engineering is to, again, train your users. Teach them to not write down passwords. Teach them to not throw sensitive data in the trash—shred it instead! Teach them about social engineering phone calls and how to deal with them. Most organizations simply tell their employees to forward any calls asking for a password to the Help Desk (that's you). Chances are, all they will hear is a click on the other end.

You can also increase the security of your systems by implementing a boot menu password. Let's discuss how this is done next.

Using a GRUB Password

You should also consider implementing a GRUB password on your Linux system. One of the security weaknesses of GRUB is the fact that an unauthorized person could manipulate and customize the GRUB menu, using the steps we discussed earlier in this book, to boot the system into runlevel 1 (single-user mode). With some distributions, this will boot the system and open a login shell as root, without requiring a password! You don't want that!

on the *job*

Not all distributions behave in this manner. Some will require you to enter your root password. Others allow you to log in using any user account in runlevel 1.

With a GRUB password in place, users must authenticate before they can use custom boot options in the GRUB boot menu. You can even require them to enter a password to select a menu item. To add a GRUB password, complete the following:

1. Open a terminal session and su – to root.
2. At the shell prompt, enter **grub**.
3. Encrypt the password in the GRUB shell by entering **md5crypt** at the grub prompt.
4. At the Password prompt, enter the ***password*** you want to use. You will be presented with a hashed version of the password.
5. Enter **quit** at the grub prompt.
6. Open your /boot/grub/menu.lst file in a text editor.
7. Beneath the gfxmenu directive, add the following:

   ```
   password --md5 hashed_password
   ```

8. Save the file and exit the editor.

Now users will have to press P and enter a password in the GRUB menu screen in order to configure any boot options. You can also configure GRUB to require a password in order to boot from any GRUB menu option. This is done by adding **lock** to the end of every menu item you want to lock down, as shown in the following example:

```
title linux
      kernel (hd0,4)/boot/vmlinuz root=/dev/sda5 vga=791
      initrd (hd0,4)/boot/initrd
      lock
```

Let's practice controlling user access to a Linux system in the following exercise.

EXERCISE 15-1

Controlling User Access

In this exercise, you will practice setting age limits on user passwords and implementing a GRUB password. Complete the following:

1. Boot your Linux system and log in as a standard user. If you used the lab exercise in Chapter 3 to install your system, you can log in as **tux** with a password of **M3linux273**.

2. Open a terminal session.

3. Switch to your root user account by entering **su –** followed by your root user's password.

4. Practice configuring age limits by completing the following:
   a. Use the cat or less utility to view the /etc/passwd file. Identify a user on your system that you want to configure password age limits for.
   b. Set the minimum password age to three days, the maximum password age to 60 days, and the number of warning days before expiration to seven by entering **chage –m 3 –M 60 –W 7 *username*** at the shell prompt.

5. Set a password on your GRUB menu by completing the following:
   a. At the shell prompt, enter **grub**.
   b. Encrypt the password in the GRUB shell by entering **md5crypt** at the grub prompt.

c. At the Password prompt, enter the **password** you want to use. A password hash is displayed.

d. Write down both the unencrypted and encrypted forms of the password. If you forget it, you won't be able to get into your system!

e. Enter **quit** at the grub prompt.

f. Open your /boot/grub/menu.lst file in a text editor.

g. Beneath the gfxmenu directive, add the following:

```
password --md5 hashed_password
```

h. Save the file and exit the editor.

i. Reboot the system. Notice that GRUB doesn't use the graphical menu when a password has been applied.

j. Press P and enter the password you configured.

k. Experiment with what you can and can't do with the GRUB password in place. When done, boot your system as per normal.

Now that you've got your users secured, let's next discuss how to defend against network attacks.

SCENARIO & SOLUTION

Throughout the course of a given day, you need to complete many root-level tasks on your Linux system. You log in to the system as root each morning. Are you following proper security guidelines?	No. You should log in using a regular user account. When you need to perform a task that requires root-level privileges, you can switch to the root account using su.
One of your users has created a password of mary for his password. Mary is the name of the user's oldest child. Is this a strong password?	No. The password can be easily guessed. It's too short (less than six characters), doesn't use uppercase letters, and doesn't include numbers.
A user receives an instant message from your company's CFO wanting to temporarily use her password. How should she respond to the message?	She should respond that she's not allowed to do that according your company's security policy and direct the CFO to call your organization's help desk.

Defend Against Network Attacks

It would be nice if we lived in a world where we could connect networks together and be able to trust others to respect our systems. Unfortunately, such a world doesn't exist. If your Linux systems are connected to a network, then you need to be concerned about network attacks. If your network is connected to a public network, such as the Internet, then you need to be extremely concerned about network attacks.

As with most of the topics discussed in this book, network security is a huge topic that can fill many volumes. We really don't have time or space here to really do the topic justice. Instead, we're going to discuss some basic things you can do to defend against network attacks. We'll discuss the following:

- Mitigating network vulnerabilities
- Using TCP Wrappers
- Implementing encryption
- Implementing a firewall with iptables

Let's begin by discussing some things you can do to mitigate network vulnerabilities.

Mitigating Network Vulnerabilities

The good news is that there are some simple things that you can do to mitigate the threat to your Linux systems from network attacks. These include the following:

- Staying abreast of current threats
- Unloading unneeded services
- Installing updates

Let's first discuss staying abreast of current network threats.

Staying Abreast of Current Threats

One of the biggest problems with network security threats is the fact that we're always one step behind the guys wearing black hats. No sooner do we implement a fix to protect our systems from the latest exploit, than they hit us with a new one. Therefore, it's critical that you stay up to date with the latest network threats. You'll soon see that they change week to week, sometimes even day to day! The only way you can keep your systems safe is to be aware of what the current threats are.

The best way to do this is to visit security-related Web sites on a regular basis. These sites inform you of the latest exploits and how to defend yourself against them. One of the best sites to visit is http://www.cert.org, which is maintained by the Computer Emergency Response Team (CERT) at the Carnegie Mellon Software Engineering Institute. The CERT Web site contains links to the latest security advisories.

Another excellent resource is http://www.us-cert.gov. Maintained by the United States government's Computer Emergency Readiness Team, the US-CERT Web site provides tons of information about current cyber-attacks.

Of course, there are hundreds of other security-related Web sites out there. However, those I've listed here are among the most authoritative sites around. Most of the other security-related Web sites derive their content from these sites. If you visit these sites religiously, you can stay abreast of what's happening in the security world and hopefully prevent an attack on your systems.

In addition to staying current with these sites, you should also review your systems to see if all the services they provide are really necessary. Let's talk about how to do that next.

Unloading Unneeded Services

One of the easiest things you can do to mitigate the threat from a network attack is to simply unload network services running on your system that aren't needed. Depending upon your distribution and how you installed it, you probably have a number of services running on your system that you didn't know were there and that you don't need. You can view a list of installed services and whether they are running or not by entering **chkconfig** at the shell prompt. This command will list each service and its status, as shown in Figure 15-7.

on the
j o b
Chkconfig is not available on all distributions. It was originally a Red Hat utility and has been ported to many other distributions, such as SUSE Linux. If you're using Debian, however, you'll find that it isn't available.

FIGURE 15-7

Viewing installed
services

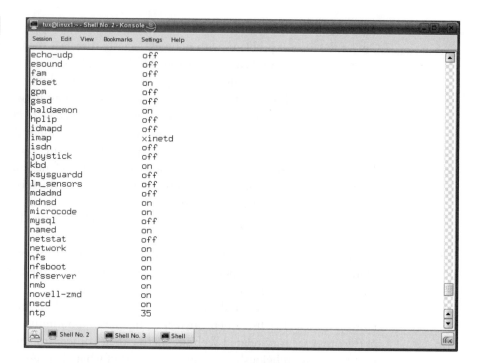

A word of caution: don't disable a service unless you know what it actually does.
Some daemons are required for the system to run properly. If you don't know what a
particular service is, use the Internet to look it up and determine if it is necessary or not.

In addition to chkconfig, you can also use the nmap command to view open
IP ports on your Linux system. This information is really useful. Each port that is
open on your Linux system represents a potential vulnerability. Some open ports
are necessary. Others, however, may not be necessary. You can close the port by
unloading the service that is using it. The syntax for using nmap is nmap –sT
host_IP_address for a TCP port scan and nmap –sU *host_IP_address* for a UDP port
scan. In Figure 15-8, the nmap utility has been used to scan for open TCP ports.

As you can see in Figure 15-8, a number of services are running on the host
scanned. You can use this output to determine what should and shouldn't be left
running on the system. To disable a service, you can use its init script in your init
directory to shut it down. You should also use the chkconfig command to configure
the service to not automatically start.

In addition to unloading unneeded services, you should also install operating
system updates. Let's discuss how this is done next.

FIGURE 15-8

Using nmap to
scan for open
ports

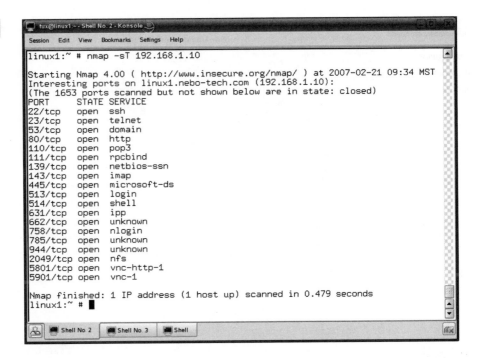

Installing Updates

One of the most important things you can do to defend against network attacks is
to regularly install operating system updates. A simple fact of life that we have to
deal with in the IT world is that software isn't written perfectly. Most programs and
services have some defects. Even your Linux kernel has defects in it. Some of these
defects are inconsequential, some are just annoying, and others represent serious
security risks.

As software is released and used, these defects are discovered by system administrators,
users, and (unfortunately) hackers. As they are discovered, updates are written and
released that fix the defects. With most distributions, you can configure the operating
system to automatically go out on the Internet and periodically check for the availability
of updates. For example, with SUSE Linux, you can use the YaST Online Update
module, shown in Figure 15-9, to do this.

After registering with Novell, your system will periodically check for updates. You
can configure the system to either automatically install them for you or prompt you
to install them.

Next, lets discuss using TCP Wrappers to secure your Linux services.

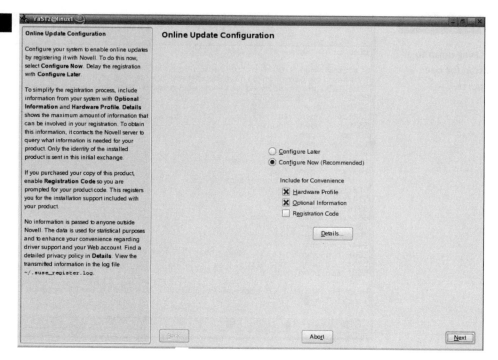

FIGURE 15-9

Configuring automatic updates

Using TCP Wrappers

Recall in the previous chapter that you learned how to use the xinetd daemon. This daemon is a super daemon that manages access to other network services on the system, such as Telnet and FTP. If you enable a particular service using its configuration file in the /etc/xinetd.d/ directory, any host can connect to it through xinetd.

Depending upon how your system is deployed, you may need to control access to these network services. You may want to limit access to only a specific set of hosts and deny access to everyone else. If this is the case, then you need to configure these services to use TCP Wrappers. TCP Wrappers are used by xinetd to start and run the network services using a set of configuration files that specify who can and who can't access the service.

To use TCP Wrappers, you first need to enable the functionality in each service's configuration file in /etc/xinetd.d. Do the following:

1. Verify that the tcpd package has been installed on your Linux system.

2. Open the appropriate configuration file in a text editor.

3. Comment out the existing server = line from the file.

4. Add following line:

```
server      = /usr/sbin/tcpd
```

This will cause xinetd to start the tcpd daemon instead of the service daemon.

5. Add the following line:

server_args   =*path_to_daemon*

This tells the tcpd daemon to run the specified network daemon. In Figure 15-10, the /etc/xinetd.d/telnet file has been configured to run the Telnet daemon within a TCP wrapper.

6. Save the file and restart the xinetd daemon.

Next, you need to create access controls. The tcpd daemon uses the /etc/hosts.allow and /etc/hosts.deny files to specify who can access the services it manages. Entries in /etc/hosts.allow are allowed access; hosts in /etc/hosts.deny are not allowed access. The syntax for both of these files is:

```
service: host_addresses
```

The best strategy for controlling access is to first explicitly deny all access to the service to all hosts in the /etc/hosts.deny file. For example, to deny access to all hosts for the Telnet service, you would make the entry shown in Figure 15-11.

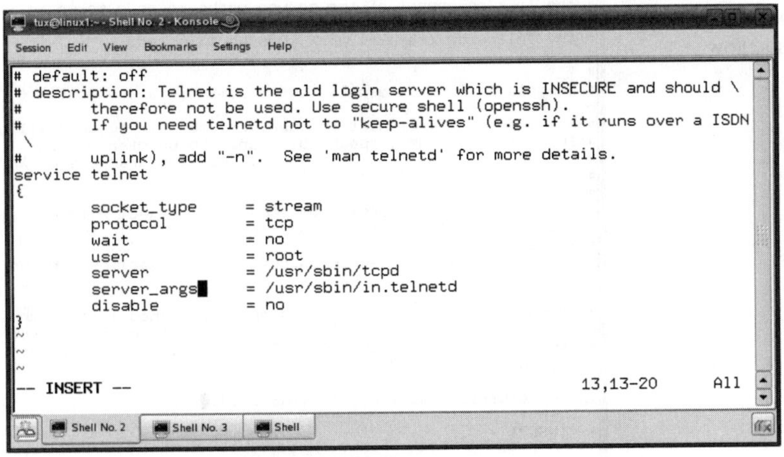

FIGURE 15-10

Enabling TCP Wrappers

FIGURE 15-11

Configuring the
/etc/hosts.deny
file

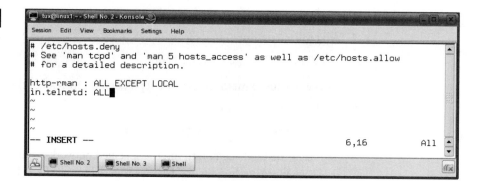

Next, you need configure the /etc/hosts.allow file to allow access to specific hosts. For example, in Figure 15-12, access has been granted to the Telnet service to hosts with the IP addresses of 192.168.1.10 and 192.168.1.102.

Be aware that hosts.deny is read and applied first, followed by hosts.allow. That means any directive in hosts.allow will trump any conflicting directive in hosts.deny.

If an unauthorized host tries to connect, the request fails, as shown in Figure 15-13.

Now that you understand how to use TCP Wrappers, we need to turn to a discussion of using encryption on your Linux system. Let's do that next.

FIGURE 15-12

Configuring the
/etc/hosts.allow
file

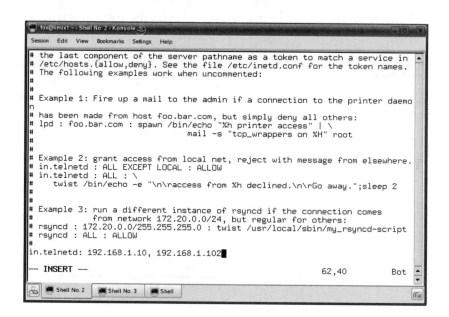

FIGURE 15-13

Denied access by tcpd

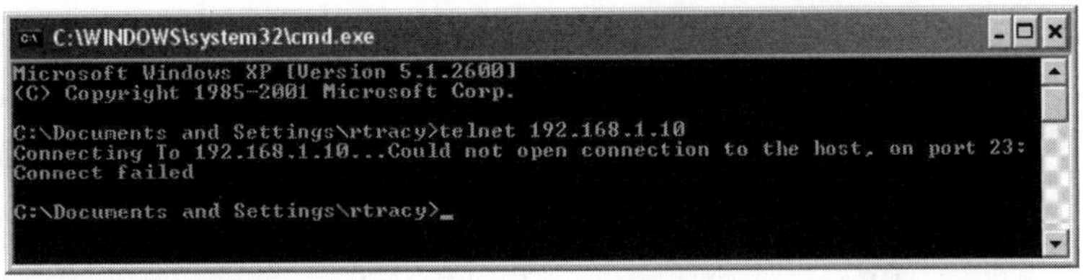

Using Encryption

Remember that one of the problems with network services such as Telnet, rlogin, rcp, rshell, and FTP is the fact that they transmit data as clear text. Anyone running a sniffer can easily capture usernames, passwords, and contents of transmissions. Not a good thing.

As an alternative, you can employ encryption to encrypt transmissions. Although the data can still be sniffed, it is scrambled and the hacker can't read it. In order to transmit or receive encrypted data, you need to have an encryption key. Keys are used to scramble and descramble encrypted data. Some encryption systems use a single key to encrypt and decrypt data. This is called *symmetric encryption*. Other encryption systems use two keys, a public key and a private key. Data encrypted with the private key can only be decrypted with the public key. Data encrypted with the public key can only be decrypted with the private key. This type of system is called *asymmetric encryption*. An important point to remember when working with encryption is that the longer the key is, the more difficult it is to crack the code and, hence, the stronger the encryption.

There are a variety of encryption methods that you can use to encrypt data between two Linux systems. These include the following:

- **Triple Data Encryption Standard (3DES)**   3DES is commonly used by many Linux services. 3DES encrypts data in three stages. It uses either a 112-bit or a 168-bit key.
- **Advanced Encryption Standard (AES)**   AES is an improved version of 3DES. It supports 128-bit, 192-bit, and 256-bit keys.
- **Blowfish**   Blowfish uses variable key lengths up to 448 bits.

You can use the OpenSSH package to accomplish management tasks using encryption. OpenSSH offers the following encryption-enabled utilities:

- **sshd**   This is the ssh daemon that allows remote access to the shell prompt.
- **ssh**   This is the ssh client used to connect to the sshd daemon on another system.

- ■ **scp** This utility can be used to copy files between systems, much like rcp.
- ■ **sftp** This utility can be used to securely FTP files between systems.
- ■ **slogin** This utility can also be used to access the shell prompt remotely, much like rlogin.

It's important to remember that when you are using a utility from the OpenSSH package that uses encryption, the client system must be configured to use the same encryption method as the server system. For example, you configure the encryption used by the sshd daemon in the /etc/ssh/sshd_config file. The ssh client, on the other hand, is configured using the /etc/ssh/ssh_config file or the ~/ssh/ssh_config file.

In addition to using encryption, you should also implement a firewall to protect your Linux systems. Let's discuss how this is done next.

Implementing a Firewall with iptables

Today, most organizations connect their corporate networks to the Internet. Doing so enhances communications and provides access to a wealth of information. Unfortunately, it also exposes your network to a serious security threat. If your users can go out on the Internet, then an uninvited person from the Internet can also get into your network unless you take measures to keep this from happening. To do this, you need to implement a network firewall.

A network firewall is very different from the host-based firewalls we've been discussing in this book. A host-based firewall controls traffic in and out of a single computer system. A network firewall, on the other hand, is used to control traffic in and out of a network segment or an entire network.

In this part of the chapter, we're going to spend some time learning how to use Linux as a network firewall. We'll discuss the following topics:

- ■ How firewalls work
- ■ Implementing a packet-filtering firewall

Let's begin by discussing how firewalls work.

How Firewalls Work

So what exactly is a firewall? A firewall is a combination of hardware and software that acts like a gatekeeper between your network and another network. Usually, a router has two or more network interfaces installed. One is connected to the internal network; the other; connected to the public network, much like a router.

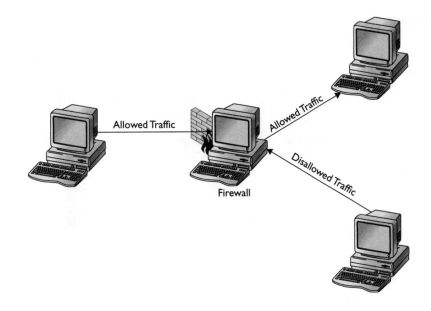

FIGURE 15-14

How a firewall
works

However, a firewall is not a router (although it may be implemented in conjunction with one).

The job of a firewall is to monitor the traffic that flows between the networks, both inbound and outbound. You configure the firewall with rules that define the type of traffic that is allowed through. Any traffic that violates the rules is not allowed, as shown in Figure 15-14.

Firewalls can be implemented in a variety of ways. However, for your Linux+ exam, you need to be familiar with a *packet-filtering firewall*. In a packet-filtering firewall, all traffic moving between the private and the public network must go through the firewall. As it does, the firewall captures all incoming and outgoing packets and compares them against the rules you've configured.

The firewall can filter traffic based on the origin address, the destination address, the origin port, the destination port, the protocol used, or the type of packet. If a packet abides by the rules, it is forwarded on to the next network. If it doesn't, it is dropped, as shown in Figure 15-15.

on the
job

Packet-filtering firewalls don't necessarily have to be implemented between your network and the Internet. They can also be implemented between a network segment and a backbone segment to increase your internal network security.

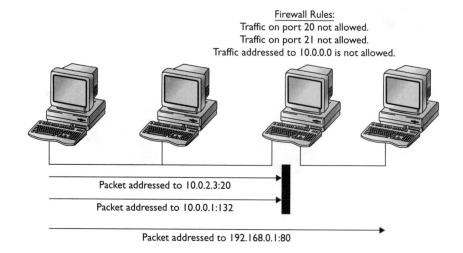

FIGURE 15-15

Using a packet-
filtering firewall

To use a packet-filtering firewall, you must be familiar with which port numbers are used by default by specific services. IP ports 0 through 1023 are assigned by the IANA organization to network services and are called *well-known ports*. Some of the more common port assignments that you need to be familiar with are shown in Table 15-1.

TABLE 15-1	Port	Service
	20, 21	FTP
Common Port	22	ssh
Assignments	23	Telnet
	25	SMTP
	53	DNS
	80, 443	HTTP and HTTPS
	110	POP3
	119	NNTP
	137, 138, and 139	SMB and NetBIOS (used by Samba)
	143	IMAP
	161 and 162	SNMP
	177	X Display Manager Control Protocol (xdmcp)
	389, 636	LDAP (insecure and secure)
	631	IPP

Packet-filtering firewalls are widely used. They cost less than other types of firewalls. They also require relatively little processing. Data moves through very quickly, making them much faster than other firewalls.

With this background in mind, let's review how to implement a packet-filtering firewall on Linux.

Implementing a Packet-Filtering Firewall

Just as Linux can act as a router (as we discussed earlier in this book), it can also be configured to function as a firewall. In fact, it can be used to configure a very robust, very powerful firewall.

The first step in setting up a packet-filtering firewall on a Linux system is to design your implementation. You should answer the following questions in your firewall design:

- Will you allow all incoming traffic by default, establishing rules for specific types of traffic that you don't want to allow in?

- Will your firewall deny all incoming traffic except for specific types of traffic that you want to allow?

- Will you allow all outgoing traffic by default, blocking only specific types or destinations?

- Will you block all outgoing traffic except for specific types or destinations?

- What ports must be opened on the firewall to allow traffic through from the outside? For example, are you going to implement a Web server that needs to be publicly accessible behind the firewall? If so, then you will need to open up ports 80 and probably 443 on your boundary firewall.

How you decide to configure your firewall depends on your organization's security policy. However, I recommend that you err on the side of caution. Given a choice, I'd rather deal with a user who's upset because the firewall won't let him share music files over the Internet than deal with a major attack that worked its way deep into my network.

Once your firewall has been designed, you're ready to implement it. After installing and configuring the required network boards, you can configure a firewall on your Linux system using the iptables utility.

on the job *Many Linux distributions include graphical front-ends for iptables that you can use to build your firewall. These front-ends are usually not as flexible as the command-line utility, but they make the setup process much faster and easier!*

The heart of the Linux firewall is the iptables package. Most distributions include it. If yours didn't, it can be downloaded from http://www.netfilter.org. Versions of the Linux kernel prior to 2.4 used ipfwadm or ipchains instead of iptables. If you visit The Linux Documentation Project at http://www.tldp.org, you'll see that many of the firewall HOWTOs are written to these older packages.

The Linux kernel itself completes packet-filtering tasks on Linux. In order to use iptables, your kernel must comply with the netfilter infrastructure included. The netfilter infrastructure is included by default when installing most distributions.

The netfilter infrastructure uses the concept of *tables* and *chains* to create firewall rules. A chain is simply a rule that you implement to determine what the firewall will do with an incoming packet. The netfilter infrastructure uses the *filter table* to create packet-filtering rules. Within the filter table are three default chains:

- **FORWARD**   The FORWARD chain contains rules for packets being transferred between networks through the Linux system.
- **INPUT**   The INPUT chain contains rules for packets that are being sent to the local Linux system.
- **OUTPUT**   The OUTPUT chain contains rules for packets that are being sent from the local Linux system.

If you don't explicitly specify a table name when using the iptables utility, it will default to the filter table. Each chain in the filter table has four policies that you can configure:

- ACCEPT
- DROP
- QUEUE
- REJECT

You can use iptables to create rules within a chain. A chain can contain multiple rules. Each rule in a chain is assigned a number. The first rule you add is assigned the number 1. The iptables utility can add rules, delete rules, insert rules, and append rules. The syntax for using iptables is iptables –t *table command chain options*. You can use the following commands with iptables:

- **–L**   Lists all rules in the chain.
- **–N**   Creates a new chain.

You can work with either the default chains listed previously or create your own chain. You create your own chain by entering **iptables –N** *chain_name*. You can add rules to a chain by simply using the **–A** option. You can also use one of the other options listed here:

- **–I** Inserts a rule into the chain.
- **–R** Replaces a rule in the chain.
- **–D** Deletes a rule from the chain.
- **–F** Deletes all the rules from the chain (called *flushing*).
- **–P** Sets the default policy for the chain.

You can also use the following options with iptables:

- **–p** Specifies the protocol to be checked by the rule. You can specify all, tcp, udp, or icmp. If you specify tcp or udp, you can also use the following extensions for matching:
  - **–sports** Specifies the source port to match on.
  - **–dports** Specifies the destination port to match on.
- **–s** *ip_address/mask* Specifies the source address to be checked. If you want to check all IP addresses, use 0/0.
- **–d** *ip_address/mask* Specifies the destination address to be checked. If you want to check all IP addresses, use 0/0.
- **–j** *target* Specifies what to do if the packet matches the rule. You can specify ACCEPT, REJECT, DROP, or LOG actions.
- **–i** *interface* Specifies the interface where a packet is received. This only applies to INPUT and FORWARD chains.
- **–o** *interface* Specifies the interface where a packet is to be sent. This only applies to OUPUT and FORWARD chains.

on the ❶o b   *The options presented here represent only a sampling of what you can do with iptables. To see all the options available, see the iptables man page.*

TABLE 15-2   iptables Commands

iptables Command	Function
iptables –L	Lists existing rules.
iptables –D FORWARD 1	Deletes the first rule in the FORWARD chain.
iptables –t filter –F	Deletes all rules from the filter table.
iptables –P INPUT DROP	Sets a default policy for the INPUT chain that drops all incoming packets.
iptables –P FORWARD DROP	Configures your FORWARD chain to drop all packets.
iptables –A INPUT –s 0/0 –p icmp –j DROP	Configures the firewall to disregard all incoming PING packets addressed to the local Linux system.
iptables –A FORWARD –p tcp –s 0/0 –sport 80 –j ACCEPT	Configures the firewall to allow HTTP traffic.
iptables –A INPUT –i eth0 –s 192.168.2.0/24 –j DROP	Configures the firewall to accept all incoming packets on eth0 coming from the 192.168.2.0 network.

The best way to learn how to use iptables is to look at some examples. Table 15-2 has some sample iptables commands that you can start with.

You can use iptables to create a sophisticated array of rules that control how data flows through the firewall. Most administrators use the –P option with iptables to set up the firewall's default filtering rules. Once the default is in place, then use iptables to configure exceptions to the default behavior needed by your particular network.

Remember that any rules you create with iptables are not persistent. If you reboot the system, they will be lost by default. To save your rules, you use the iptables-save command to write your tables out to a file. You can then use the iptables-restore command to restore the tables from the file you created.

Let's practice implementing network security measures on a Linux system in the following exercise.

EXERCISE 15-2

Implementing Network Security Measures on Linux

In this exercise, you will practice scanning for open IP ports, configuring TCP Wrappers, and implementing a simple firewall. This exercise assumes that you have successfully completed the exercises in the previous chapter. You will also need a second system to test your configuration with.

With this in mind, complete the following:

1. Boot your Linux system and log in as a standard user. If you used the lab exercise in Chapter 3 to install your system, you can log in as **tux** with a password of **M3linux273**.

2. Open a terminal session.

3. Switch to your root user account by entering **su –** followed by your root user's password.

4. Scan your system for open ports by completing the following:

   a. At the shell prompt, use the rpm utility to verify that the nmap package has been installed. If it hasn't, install it from your distribution media.

   b. At the shell prompt, enter **nmap –sT *your_IP_address***. What TCP/IP ports are in use on your system?

   c. At the shell prompt, enter **nmap –sU *your_IP_address***. What UDP/IP ports are in use on your system?

5. Configure the Telnet service on your system to use TCP Wrappers by completing the following:

   a. Use the rpm utility to verify that the tcpd package has been installed on your system. If it hasn't, install it from your distribution media.

   b. Open the /etc/xinetd.d/telnet file in a text editor.

   c. Add following line:

   ```
   server      = /usr/sbin/tcpd
   ```

   d. Change the server = /usr/sbin/in.telnetd line to:

   ```
   server_args      = /usr/sbin/in.telnetd
   ```

   e. Save the file and exit your editor.

   f. Restart the xinetd daemon using its init script in your init directory.

   g. Open the /etc/hosts.deny file in a text editor.

   h. Add the following line:

   ```
   in.telnetd ALL EXCEPT LOCAL
   ```

   i. Save the file and exit your editor.

    j. Try to access the Telnet daemon from a remote computer system. Can you get in?

    k. At the shell prompt of your local Linux system, enter **telnet localhost**. Are you able to get in?

6. Configure a simple firewall with iptables by doing the following:

    a. Use the rpm utility to verify that the iptables package has been installed on your system.

    b. From a remote Windows or Linux system, ping your Linux system and verify that it responds.

    c. Open a terminal session.

    d. At the shell prompt su – to root.

    e. Configure the kernel to use the iptables filter by entering **modprobe iptable_filter** at the shell prompt.

    f. List the current rules for the filter table by entering **iptables –t filter –L** at the shell prompt.

    g. At the shell prompt, enter **iptables –t filter –A INPUT –s 0/0 -p icmp –j DROP**.

    This command creates a rule that will drop all incoming packets using the ICMP protocol from any source destined for the local system.

    h. View your new rule by entering **iptables –t filter –L | more** at the shell prompt. You should see the following rule added to your INPUT chain:

```
DROP        icmp --  anywhere             anywhere
```

    i. Using your remote Windows or Linux system, ping your Linux system's IP address. The packets should be dropped, as shown in this sample output:

```
Microsoft Windows XP [Version 5.1.2600]
(C) Copyright 1985-2001 Microsoft Corp.
C:\Documents and Settings\rtracy>ping 192.168.1.10
Pinging 192.168.1.10 with 32 bytes of data:
Request timed out.
Request timed out.
Request timed out.
Request timed out.
Ping statistics for 192.168.1.10:
    Packets: Sent = 4, Received = 0, Lost = 4 (100% loss),
C:\Documents and Settings\rtracy>
```

SCENARIO & SOLUTION

After running nmap on your Linux system, you notice that the Apache Web server is running. You don't need this service. What can you do to disable it?	First, you should stop the service using the apache2 init script. Then you should enter **chkconfig apache2 off** at the shell prompt to prevent it from being loaded the next time the system is booted.
You want to configure the firewall on a Linux system to block all Web server traffic addressed to port 80 on the local system. What command would you enter at the shell prompt to do this?	You would enter **iptables –t filter –A INPUT –s 0/0 –p tcp ––dport 80 –j DROP** at the shell prompt.

Now that you understand how to defend your network, let's spend some time learning how to detect intrusion attempts.

CERTIFICATION OBJECTIVE 15.04

Detect Intrusion Attempts

In addition to a firewall, you should consider taking steps to detect any intruders on your system should someone break through your firewall or instigate an attack from behind the firewall. This is called *intrusion detection*. Intrusion detection sounds high-tech, but it actually involves a lot of relatively simple and sometimes mundane system monitoring. It also involves a fair amount of intuition as you try to discern something that appears out of place or unusual. In this part of the chapter, we're going to discuss how we can detect intruders by doing the following:

- Analyzing Linux log files
- Implementing an intrusion detection system (IDS)
- Implementing security auditing with Tripwire

Let's start by reviewing how to analyze log files.

Analyzing Linux Log Files

Much like a scene from CSI, detecting intruders involves looking for clues they left behind in the system. One of your best resources in this regard are the log files your Linux system maintains for you. Much like a CSI detective, you need practice and experience to develop an intuitive sense that lets you know when something looks suspicious. The best way to develop this intuition is to spend a lot of time reviewing your log files. This will help you develop a feel for what is "normal" for your system. Once you know what is normal, you can spot that which is not normal.

With this in mind, let's look at several log files you can analyze to identify suspicious activities. The first is the /var/log/wtmp file. This log file contains a list of all users who have authenticated to the system. The file is saved in binary format. You can't use cat, less, or a text editor, such as vi, to view it. Instead, you must use the last command at the shell prompt. Output from the last utility is shown in Figure 15-16.

The last utility displays the user account, login time, logout time, and where they authenticated from. When you review this file, look for anything that appears unusual—for example, logins that occurred in the middle of the night when no one is at work is suspicious.

You can also view the /var/log/faillog file. This log file contains a list of failed authentication attempts. This file is very effective at detecting *dictionary attacks*, which run through a list of dictionary terms, trying them as passwords for user accounts.

FIGURE 15-16

Using last to review login history

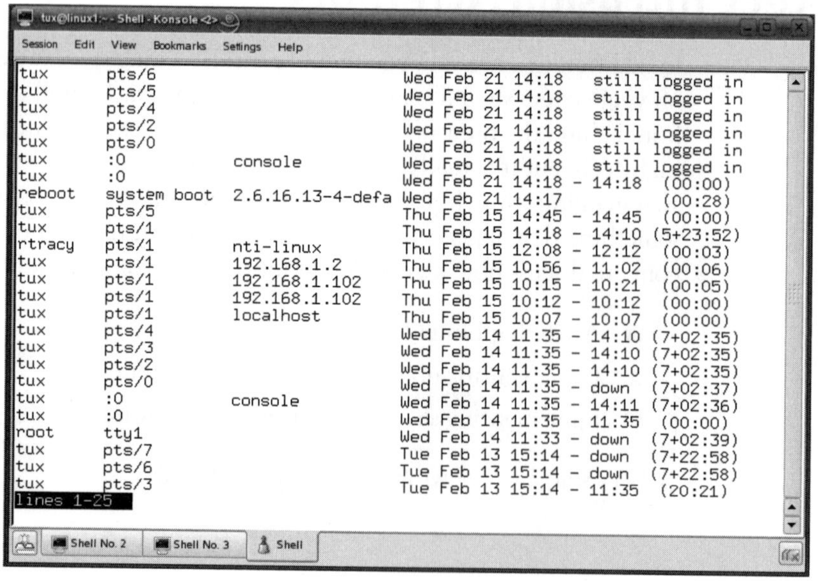

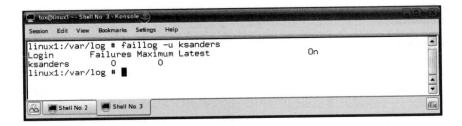

FIGURE 15-17

Using faillog to view failed login attempts

Like wtmp, faillog is a binary file. To view it, you need to use the faillog utility. This utility displays the user who tried to authenticate, how many times they failed to log in, and when the last unsuccessful attempt occurred. You can use the –u option to view login attempts for a specific user account, as shown in Figure 15-17.

When reviewing this log file, look at unusual login attempts, such as an abnormally high number of failed logins, especially if they occurred late at night. You can also use the faillog utility to specify how the system handles failed login attempts. This is done using the following options with the faillog command:

- **–l *seconds*** Locks the account for the specified number of seconds after a failed login attempt.
- **–m *number*** Sets the maximum number of failed login attempts before the user account is disabled.

The next log file is /var/log/lastlog. This file contains a list of all the users in the system and when they last logged in. Like the other log files we've looked at, you can't view lastlog with less, cat, or a text editor. To view lastlog, you must use the lastlog utility from the shell prompt, as shown in Figure 15-18.

The last log file we're going to review here is /var/log/messages. This log file contains messages from all services running on the system. As such it contains a lot of data that may or may not be related to intrusion attempts. You can use grep to isolate the relevant entries. For example, you could use the cat /var/log/messages | grep login command to view login-related entries in the file. This is shown in Figure 15-19.

In addition to viewing log files, you can also use a variety of command-line tools to see who is currently using the system. The first is the who command. You can use who to see who is currently logged in to your system. In Figure 15-20, you can see that the tux user is logged in to the system from four different terminals.

FIGURE 15-18

Using lastlog to view last login times

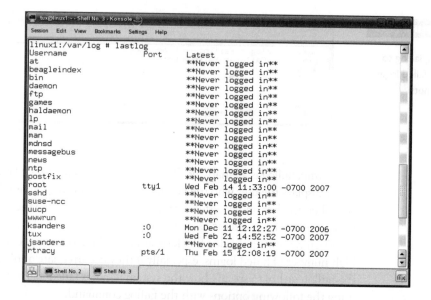

FIGURE 15-19

Viewing authentication-related entries in /var/log/messages

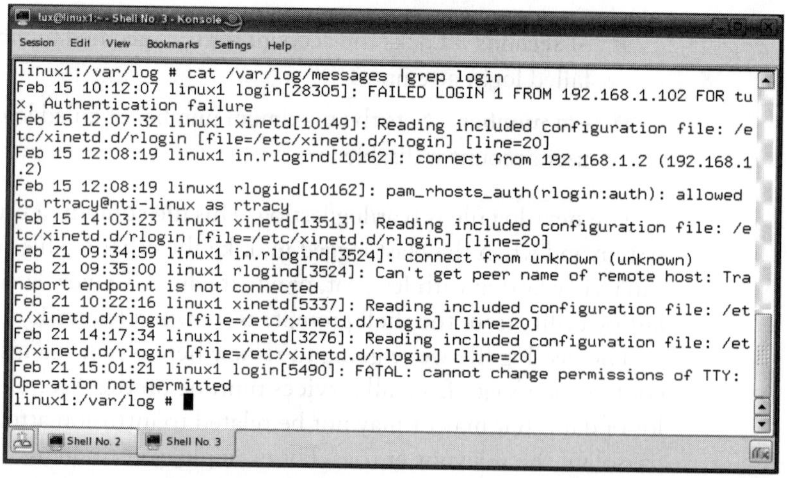

FIGURE 15-20

Using who

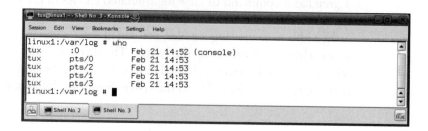

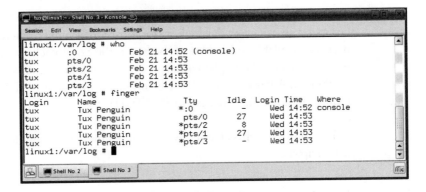

FIGURE 15-21

Using finger

You can also use the finger utility to see who's currently logged in to the system, as shown in Figure 15-21.

In addition to analyzing log files, you can also implement an intrusion detection system (IDS) on your server to catch intruders in the act when they try to infiltrate your system. Let's talk about how to implement an IDS next.

Implementing an Intrusion Detection System (IDS)

Intrusion detection systems are fantastic! An IDS operates by monitoring network traffic looking for patterns in the data that could indicate suspicious activity. For your Linux+ exam, you don't need to know how to set up an IDS. You only need to know what it is and how it works.

Some IDS systems function in much the same manner as anti-virus software, which looks for virus patterns in files. The IDS has a database of intrusion definitions that it uses to detect intrusion attempts. Just as virus definitions need to be updated regularly, these IDS systems must have their intrusion definitions updated regularly to be effective.

Some IDS systems don't use predefined patterns. Instead, they monitor the system for a period of time, developing a baseline of activity. Once the baseline is complete, they look for traffic that doesn't fit the baseline and analyze it to see if an attack is in progress. Some IDS systems can be linked into your network firewall. When these systems detect an intrusion, they can contact your firewall and immediately shut down a communication session. That's powerful stuff!

IDS systems are becoming more and more popular due to the insidious nature of intrusion attempts. They can be so stealthy that administrators don't even realize they are happening until it's too late. Many system administrators are both amazed and scared to death when they realize how many attacks are regularly detected on their systems after implementing an IDS.

An IDS is usually implemented on a dedicated computer system that does nothing but spend all day every day looking for intrusion attempts. There are a variety of IDS packages available today. One of the best is the Snort package, which is open source software that can be implemented on a Linux system. Other popular packages include PortSentry, Advanced Intrusion Detection Environment (AIDE), Integrity Checking Utility (ICU), Simple Watcher (SWATCH), and Linux Intrusion Detection System (LIDS).

Let's finish out this chapter by discussing how you can implement security auditing with Tripwire.

Implementing Security Auditing with Tripwire

Some intruders, if they manage to gain access to a system, are fairly benign. They just want to poke around and see what's there. Others, unfortunately, aren't so friendly. Their goal is to wreak havoc with your system. To do this, they may make a variety of changes to your critical system files. Tracking down these changes after an intrusion can be almost impossible. It's like throwing feathers into the wind. The odds of tracking down every one as it blows away are remote.

To remedy this situation, you can implement an auditing system. An auditing system monitors your critical system files to ensure that they haven't been tampered with. There are many auditing packages available, but for your Linux+ exam, you need to be familiar with Tripwire. Therefore, that's the package we're going to discuss here.

When you first set up Tripwire, it creates a baseline shapshot of your system by creating a database of your critical system files. Then, Tripwire automatically runs checks on your critical system files periodically. It then uses data in its database to identify any changes. It can also identify files that have been added to or deleted from the system using its database. Notifications are logged any time Tripwire finds that a system file has been altered, created, or deleted.

To configure Tripwire on your system, complete the following:

1. Download the latest tripwire tarball from http://www.tripwire.org.
2. Switch to your root user account.
3. Extract and install the Tripwire tarball.
4. Open /etc/tripwire/twpol.txt in a text editor.
5. Set the HOSTNAME variable equal to your system's host name.
6. Save your changes to the file and exit the editor.

SCENARIO & SOLUTION

You suspect that an intruder may be invading your system in the night when everyone is gone from your office. Where could you check to see if this is the case?	You could check the /var/log/wtmp file using the last command to see when a user logged in and where they logged in from. You could also check the /var/log/lastlog file using the lastlog utility.
What command would you use to see who is currently logged in to your Linux system?	You could use either the who or the finger utilities.

7. Run the /etc/tripwire/twinstall.sh script from the shell prompt.

8. When prompted, enter your site and local **passwords**. These passwords will be used to generate encryption keys that will be used to encrypt the Tripwire database files.

9. Create your initial Tripwire database by entering **tripwire --init** at the shell prompt.

10. Configure cron to run the tripwire-check command at least once a day.

At this point, Tripwire is ready to roll. You can wait for cron to run tripwire-check each day or you can manually run tripwire-check at the shell prompt. If tripwire-check finds any anomalies, it logs them to encrypted report files in /var/lib/tripwire/report/. Because it's encrypted, you can't view it directly with less, cat, or vi. Instead, you need to use the **twprint −m r --twfile** *filename* command at the shell prompt. Replace *filename* with the name of the Tripwire report you want to view.

That's it for this chapter. Let's review what you learned.

CERTIFICATION SUMMARY

In this chapter, you were introduced to a variety of security issues affecting Linux systems. We started this chapter by discussing the importance of physically securing your Linux system. We pointed out that many organizations overlook this very important issue. Many organizations leave their systems in unsecured areas, allowing an intruder to easily snatch the system and walk away.

We pointed out that servers need the highest degree of physical security. Servers should be locked in a server room. Access to the server room should be strictly controlled. Workstations, by their very nature, demand a higher degree of access than servers. Access to the work area itself should be secured to prevent unauthorized persons from accessing users' workstations.

We then discussed measures you can take to secure the operating system itself. One of the problems with workstations in most organizations is that users tend to leave them logged in while the system is unattended. To prevent unauthorized access, you should consider implementing screen-saver passwords. You should also train your users to lock their workstations or log out completely before leaving their systems. To facilitate this, users can use the nohup command to load processes. This will allow the processes to continue running even if the user logs out from the shell prompt.

We then discussed user access controls you can use to constrain what users can and can't do in the system. Users, groups, and permissions are the main means of controlling access to the system. However, there are other things you can do to increase the security of the system. First of all, you need to use your root user account judiciously. The root user should be used only to complete root tasks. All other tasks should be completed using a standard user account. The system should never be left unattended while the root user is logged in. You can use the su command to switch to the root user account when you need to complete tasks that require root-level access. You can use the exit command to switch back to your regular user account when done.

If you have users who occasionally need to run commands as root, but you don't want to give them your root password, you can use the sudo command. You use the /etc/sudoers file to specify which users can run which commands as root. You edit this file using the visudo utility. This utility will load the /etc/sudoers file in the vi editor. When you exit vi, it will check your syntax to make sure you didn't make syntax errors in the file.

Next, we talked about implementing a strong password policy. Users need to be trained to avoid using passwords that can be easily guessed, such as spouses' names, children's names, or pets' names. Users need to be trained to use strong passwords, which use:

- Six or more characters.
- Numbers in addition to letters.
- Upper- and lowercase letters.
- Words not found in the dictionary.

You should also configure password aging with the chage command. You can specify the minimum number of days between password changes, the maximum number of days between password changes, and the number of warning days before a password change is required.

You should also verify that your Linux systems use shadow passwords. Storing passwords in /etc/passwd is highly insecure. You can use the pwconv command to migrate passwords from /etc/passwd to /etc/shadow.

In addition, you need to train your users to follow proper security procedures. You should not allow them to write their passwords down. You should also train them how to handle social engineering attempts. Users should also shred important documents rather than just throw them in the common trash.

We also discussed how to set a password for your GRUB bootloader. Doing so will prevent an unauthorized user from customizing GRUB to boot into runlevel 1. This is done by creating an encrypted password and then configuring your /boot/grub/menu.lst file to use the password.

We then shifted our focus to the threat from network attacks. We pointed out that connecting your network to the Internet exposes your Linux systems to a host of network attacks. To mitigate these threats, you need to stay abreast of current threats. Two excellent resources to do this include the http://www.cert.org and http://us-cert.gov Web sites.

You should also check your system to see if any unneeded daemons are running. You can do this using the chkconfig and the nmap utilities. Unnecessary services can be easily unloaded using the appropriate init script. You should also use chkconfig to prevent the unneeded services from being loaded at system boot.

To further protect your system from network attacks, you should regularly install operating system updates that patch security holes. Most distributions provide some type of online update functionality that you can use to automate the task.

To add additional security, you can use TCP Wrappers to control access to your network services. Using TCP Wrappers, the xinetd daemon runs the tcpd daemon instead of the network service itself. The tcpd daemon checks the /etc/hosts.deny and /etc/hosts.allow files to determine if the requesting host is allowed to use the service. If it is, tcpd loads the requested daemon.

We also discussed the important role of encryption on a Linux system. We pointed out that older utilities, such as Telnet, rlogin, and rshell, send data unencrypted (using plain text). This could potentially allow usernames, passwords, and other sensitive information to be captured by a sniffer. To prevent this, you should use utilities that can encrypt transmissions. Encryption methods available on Linux include:

- 3DES
- AES
- Blowfish

The OpenSSH package offers a variety of utilities that you can use to manage your system securely using encryption, including:

- sshd
- ssh
- scp
- sftp
- slogin

When using these utilities, you need to make sure that the client system has been configured to use the same encryption method as the server system.

We then took a giant leap forward and discussed how to implement a simple packet-filtering firewall with iptables. We pointed out that firewalls are a critical security component in your network. A firewall sits between your network and another network. It captures all network traffic and compares it against a set of rules that you define. If the traffic meets the conditions in the rules, it is allowed through. If it doesn't, it is denied. Rules can be based on the origin address, the destination address, the origin port, the destination port, the protocol used, or the type of packet.

We then discussed how you can use a Linux system to implement a firewall. The first step is to design how it will work. Once you've determined what type of traffic will be allowed and what traffic will be denied, you can implement the firewall using the netfilter infrastructure, which is usually compiled into your Linux kernel by default. The netfilter infrastructure uses the concepts of tables, chains, and rules. The filter table is used to create packet-filtering rules. The filter table includes the FORWARD, INPUT, and OUTPUT chains. Each chain in the filter table can be configured with ACCEPT, DROP, QUEUE, and REJECT policies. This is done using the iptables command. The general practice when creating a firewall with iptables is to use the –P option to set the default rules, which are usually quite restrictive. Then you use iptables to configure exceptions to the default rules.

We then discussed how to detect intrusion attempts. Some of the best tools at your disposal for doing this are your Linux log files. You should periodically review your log files, looking for anomalies that indicate an intrusion attempt. The log files best suited to this task include:

- /var/log/wtmp
- /var/log/faillog
- /var/log/lastlog
- /var/log/messages

You can also use the who and finger utilities to see who is currently using the Linux system.

In addition to log files, you can also implement an intrusion detection system (IDS). IDS systems watch traffic on your network and look for patterns that indicate an intrusion attempt. Common IDS packages include:

- Snort
- PortSentry
- Advanced Intrusion Detection Environment (AIDE)
- Integrity Checking Utility (ICU)
- Simple Watcher (SWATCH)
- Linux Intrusion Detection System (LIDS)

We ended this chapter by discussing how to implement security auditing with Tripwire. This software takes a shapshot of your critical system files when it is first installed. Then it monitors these files and alerts you if they are modified. It also lets you know when files are created or deleted.

TWO-MINUTE DRILL

Secure the System

❑ Many organizations overlook physical security and leave their systems in unsecured areas.

❑ This allows an intruder to easily steal a system.

❑ Servers need the highest degree of physical security.

❑ Servers should be locked in a server room.

❑ Access to the server room should be strictly controlled.

❑ Workstations require a higher degree of access than servers.

❑ Access to the work area itself should be secured to prevent unauthorized persons from accessing users' workstations.

❑ Users tend to leave workstations logged in while the system is unattended.

❑ You should implement screen-saver passwords.

❑ You should train your users to lock their workstations or log out completely before leaving their systems.

❑ Users can use the nohup command to load processes, allowing the processes to continue running even if the user logs out from a shell prompt.

Control User Access

❑ Users, groups, and permissions are the main means of controlling access to the system.

❑ The root user should be used only to complete root tasks.

❑ All other tasks should be completed using a standard user account.

❑ The system should never be left unattended while the root user is logged in.

❑ You can use the su command to switch to the root user account when you need to complete tasks that require root-level access.

❑ You can use the exit command to switch back to your regular user account.

❑ You can use the sudo command to allow specific users to run commands as root without giving them your root password.

❑ You use the /etc/sudoers file to specify which users can run what commands as root.

❑ You edit /etc/sudoers using the visudo utility.

❑ The visudo utility will check your syntax to make sure you didn't make syntax errors in the file.

❑ Users need to be trained to avoid using passwords that can be easily guessed.

❑ Users should be trained to use strong passwords, which use:

    ❑ Six or more characters.

    ❑ Numbers in addition to letters.

    ❑ Upper- and lowercase letters.

    ❑ Words not found in the dictionary.

❑ You can configure password aging with the chage command.

❑ The chage utility allows you to specify the minimum number of days between password changes, the maximum number of days between password changes, and the number of warning days before a password change is required.

❑ Verify that your Linux systems use shadow passwords.

❑ Storing passwords in /etc/passwd is highly insecure.

❑ You can use the pwconv command to migrate passwords from /etc/passwd to /etc/shadow.

❑ You should not allow users to write their passwords down.

❑ You should train users how to handle social engineering attempts.

❑ Users should shred important documents rather than throw them in the common trash.

❑ You should consider setting a password for your GRUB bootloader. This will prevent an unauthorized user from customizing GRUB to boot into runlevel 1.

Defend Against Network Attacks

❑ Connecting your network to the Internet exposes your Linux systems to a number of network attacks.

❑ You need to stay abreast of current threats.

❑ You should regularly visit the http://www.cert.org and http://us-cert.gov Web sites to see the latest issues.

❑ You should check your system to see if any unneeded daemons are running using the chkconfig and the nmap utilities.

❑ Unnecessary services can be unloaded using the appropriate init script.

❑ You should also use chkconfig to prevent the unneeded services from being loaded at system boot.

❑ You should regularly install operating system updates to patch security holes.

❑ Most distributions provide some type of online update functionality that you can use to automatically install patches.

❑ You can use TCP Wrappers to control access to your network services.

❑ With TCP Wrappers, the xinetd daemon runs the tcpd daemon instead of the network service.

❑ The tcpd daemon checks the /etc/hosts.deny and /etc/hosts.allow files to determine if the requesting host is allowed to use the service. If it is, tcpd loads the requested daemon.

❑ Older Linux utilities, such as Telnet, rlogin, and rshell, send data as clear text.

❑ This could potentially allow usernames, passwords, and other sensitive information to be captured by a sniffer.

❑ You should use utilities that can encrypt transmissions.

❑ Encryption methods available on Linux include:
  ❑ 3DES
  ❑ AES
  ❑ Blowfish

❑ The OpenSSH package offers a variety of utilities that you can use to manage your system securely using encryption.

❑ When using OpenSSH utilities, you need to make sure that the client system has been configured to use the same encryption method as the server system.

❑ Firewalls are a critical security component in your network.

❑ A firewall sits between your network and another network.

❑ A firewall captures all network traffic and compares it against a set of rules that you define.

❑ If the traffic meets the conditions in the rules, it is allowed through.

❑ If the traffic doesn't meet the rules, it is denied.

❑ Rules can be based on the origin address, the destination address, the origin port, the destination port, the protocol used, or the type of packet.

❑ Linux can be configured to function as a firewall.

❑ You should first design how the firewall will work.

❑ You can implement the firewall using the netfilter infrastructure, which is usually compiled into your Linux kernel by default.

❑ The netfilter infrastructure uses the concepts of tables, chains, and rules.

❑ The filter table is used to create packet-filtering rules.

❑ The filter table includes the FORWARD, INPUT, and OUTPUT chains.

❑ Each chain in the filter table can be configured with ACCEPT, DROP, QUEUE, and REJECT policies using the iptables command.

❑ The general practice when creating a firewall with iptables is to use the –P option to set the default rules, then configure exceptions to the default rules.

Detect Intrusion Attempts

❑ Linux can be used to detect intrusion attempts.

❑ Some of the best tools for detecting intrusion attempts are your Linux log files.

❑ You should periodically review your log files, looking for anomalies that indicate an intrusion attempt:

   ❑ /var/log/wtmp

   ❑ /var/log/faillog

   ❑ /var/log/lastlog

   ❑ /var/log/messages

❑ You can use the who and finger utilities to see who is currently using the Linux system.

❑ You can also implement an intrusion detection system (IDS).

❑ IDS systems watch traffic on your network and look for patterns that indicate an intrusion attempt.

❑ Common IDS packages include:

   ❑ Snort

   ❑ PortSentry

   ❑ Advanced Intrusion Detection Environment (AIDE)

   ❑ Integrity Checking Utility (ICU)

❑ Simple Watcher (SWATCH)

❑ Linux Intrusion Detection System (LIDS)

❑ You can implement security auditing with Tripwire.

❑ Tripwire takes a shapshot of your critical system files when it is first installed.

❑ Tripwire then monitors these files and alerts you if they are modified.

❑ Tripwire also lets you know when files are created or deleted.

SELF TEST

Secure the System

1. Which of the following would be a secure place to locate a Linux server?
   A. On the receptionist's front desk.
   B. In the CIO's office.
   C. In an unoccupied cubicle.
   D. In a locked room.

2. Which of the following can be used to secure users' workstations? (Choose two.)
   A. Screen-saver password
   B. Session lock
   C. Long screen-saver timeout period
   D. Passwords written on sticky notes and hidden in a drawer
   E. Easy-to-remember passwords

3. Which of the following commands will load the updatedb process and leave it running even if the user logs out of the shell?
   A. updatedb
   B. updatedb &
   C. updatedb –nohup
   D. nohup udatedb &

Control User Access

4. Which of the following commands can be used to switch to the root user account and load root's environment variables?
   A. su –
   B. su root
   C. su root –e
   D. su –env

5. Which of the following is a strong password?
   A. Bob3
   B. TuxP3nguin

    C. penguin

    D. Castle

6. You need to set password age limits for the ksanders user account. You want the minimum password age to be one day, the maximum password age to be 45 days, and the user to be warned five days prior to password expiration. Which command will do this?

    A. usermod –m 1 –M 45 –W 5 ksanders

    B. useradd –m 1 –M 45 –W 5 ksanders

    C. chage –M 1 –m 45 –W 5 ksanders

    D. chage –m 1 –M 45 –W 5 ksanders

Defend Against Network Attacks

7. You need to scan a Linux system with an IP address of 10.200.200.1 to determine what services are currently running on it. What commands could you use at the shell prompt to do this? (Choose two.)

    A. nmap –sT 10.200.200.1

    B. scan 10.200.200.1 –TCP

    C. scan 10.200.200.1 –UDP

    D. nmap –sU 10.200.200.1

    E. nmap 10.200.200.1 –scan

8. You need to configure your /etc/hosts.allow file to allow the linux1, linux2, and linux3 systems to access the vsftpd daemon on your system. Which of the following lines in the file will do this?

    A. vsftpd: ALL

    B. vsftpd: linux1, linux2, linux3

    C. vsftpd: ALL EXCEPT linux1, linux2, linux3

    D. vsftpd linux1, linux2, linux3

9. You need to configure your Linux firewall to block all network traffic addressed to the DNS service on the local system. Which command will do this?

    A. iptables –t filter –A INPUT –s 0/0 –p tcp –dport 53 –j DROP

    B. iptables –t filter –A OUTPUT –s 0/0 –p tcp –dport 53 –j DROP

    C. iptables –t filter –A INPUT –s 0/0 –p tcp –dport 80 –j DROP

    D. iptables –t filter –A INPUT –s 0/0 –p tcp –dport 53 –j ACCEPT

Detect Intrusion Attempts

10. Which log file contains a list of all users who have authenticated to the Linux system, when they logged in, when they logged out, and where they logged in from?
    A. /var/log/faillog
    B. /var/log/last
    C. /var/log/wtmp
    D. /var/log/login

11. Which log file contains a list of failed login attempts?
    A. /var/log/faillog
    B. /var/log/last
    C. /var/log/wtmp
    D. /var/log/login

12. Which log file contains messages from all services running on the system?
    A. /var/log/faillog
    B. /var/log/messages
    C. /var/log/wtmp
    D. /var/log/services

13. Which utility can you use to view your /var/log/lastlog file?
    A. cat
    B. last
    C. grep
    D. lastlog

14. Which command is used at the shell prompt to initially build Tripwire's database of critical system files?
    A. twinstall.sh
    B. tripwire --init
    C. tripwire-check
    D. twprint –m r --twfile *database_file_name*

LAB QUESTION

You've been asked to develop a security plan for your organization's Linux systems. Outline the process you would follow to do this.

SELF TEST ANSWERS

Secure the System

1. ☑ **D.** A locked room would be the most secure place to locate a Linux server.

   ☒ **A, B,** and **C** are incorrect. **A** would leave the server highly vulnerable to theft through the front door. **B** would leave the server vulnerable if the CIO were to leave her office door open. It would also leave the server vulnerable to visitors to the CIO's office. **C** isn't a secure option because cubicles don't have locking doors.

2. ☑ **A** and **B.** Screen-saver passwords and the session lock function offered by KDE and GNOME can be used to secure users' workstations.

   ☒ **C, D,** and **E** are incorrect. **C, D,** and **E** each reduce the security of the users' workstations.

3. ☑ **D.** The nohup udatedb & command will load the updatedb process and leave it running even if the user logs out of the shell.

   ☒ **A, B,** and **C** are incorrect. **A** loads updatedb normally. **B** runs updatedb in the background. **C** uses an invalid option.

Control User Access

4. ☑ **A.** The su – command switches to the root user account and loads root's environment variables.

   ☒ **B, C,** and **D** are incorrect. **B** switches to the root user's account, but it doesn't load root's environment variables. **C** and **D** use invalid options (–e and –env).

5. ☑ **B.** The TuxP3nguin password is a strong password.

   ☒ **A, C,** and **D** are incorrect. **A** uses uppercase letters and a number, but it is too short. **C** is long enough, but it doesn't use uppercase letters or numbers. It also uses a common word from the dictionary. **D** Doesn't use numbers and also is a common word from the dictionary.

6. ☑ **D.** The chage –m 1 –M 45 –W 5 ksanders command will set the minimum password age to be one day, the maximum password age to be 45 days, and the user to be warned five days prior to password expiration.

   ☒ **A, B,** and **C** are incorrect. **A** and **B** are incorrect. You can't use usermod or useradd to age passwords. **C** uses incorrect values for the –m and –M options.

Defend Against Network Attacks

7. ☑ **A** and **D.** The nmap –sT 10.200.200.1 command scans for open TCP ports. The nmap –sU 10.200.200.1 command scans for open UDP ports.

   ☒ **B, C,** and **E** are incorrect. **B** and **C** use an invalid command (scan). **E** uses an invalid option (–scan).

8. ☑ **B.** The vsftpd: linux1, linux2, linux3 line in /etc/hosts.allow will configure the tcpd daemon to allow these hosts access to the vsftpd daemon.

☒ **A, C,** and **D** are incorrect. **A** grants access to all hosts. **C** grants access to all hosts except those specified. **D** is missing the colon (:) after the service name.

9. ☑ **A.** The iptables –t filter –A INPUT –s 0/0 –p tcp –dport 53 –j DROP command configures your Linux firewall to block all network traffic addressed to the DNS service on the local system.

☒ **B, C,** and **D** are incorrect. **B** specifies the OUTPUT chain instead of the INPUT chain. **C** specifies the incorrect destination port (80). DNS runs on port 53. **D** specifies that the packets be accepted, not dropped.

Detect Intrusion Attempts

10. ☑ **C.** The /var/log/wtmp log file contains a list of all users who have authenticated to the Linux system, when they logged in, when they logged out, and where they logged in from.

☒ **A, B,** and **D** are incorrect. **A** contains a list of failed login attempts. **B** and **D** are distracters and don't exist in the system.

11. ☑ **A.** The /var/log/faillog log file contains a list of failed login attempts.

☒ **B, C,** and **D** are incorrect. **B** and **D** are distracters and don't exist in the system. **C** contains a list of all users who have authenticated to the Linux system, when they logged in, when they logged out, and where they logged in from.

12. ☑ **B.** The /var/log/messages log file contains messages from all services running on the system.

☒ **A, C,** and **D** are incorrect. **A** contains a list of failed login attempts. **C** contains a list of all users who have authenticated to the Linux system, when they logged in, when they logged out, and where they logged in from. **D** is a distracter that doesn't exist in the system.

13. ☑ **D.** The lastlog command can be used to view your /var/log/lastlog file.

☒ **A, B,** and **C** are incorrect. **A** and **C** are incorrect. The lastlog file is a binary file that can't be read by text manipulation utilities. **B** is a distracter and is incorrect.

14. ☑ **B.** The tripwire --init command is used at the shell prompt to initially build Tripwire's database of critical system files.

☒ **A, C,** and **D** are incorrect. **A** is used to generate encryption keys. **C** is used to check the current state of your system files against the Tripwire database. **D** is used to view Tripwire database or report files.

LAB ANSWER

To implement a security plan, you should objectively evaluate your organization's current security situation. You should answer the following questions:

- Are my servers kept in a locked room?
- Who has keys to the server room?
- Who has access to user workstations on any given day? Employees, contractors, vendors, service personnel, the public?
- Have users, groups, and permissions been implemented to control access to the file system?
- Have screen-saver passwords been implemented?
- Do users leave their systems logged in while unattended?
- Do system administrators log in using superuser accounts or regular user accounts?
- Do any regular users need to run root-level commands?
- Are users using strong passwords?
- Do users write their passwords down? If so, are they left in plain sight?
- Are passwords aged?
- How do users respond to social engineering attempts? You may want to try calling some of your users asking for passwords and see how they respond.
- Have bootloader passwords been implemented?
- Are any systems running unnecessary services?
- Are security updates regularly downloaded and installed?
- Should some network services be restricted to specific hosts?
- Do system administrators use secure remote management utilities?
- Has a firewall been implemented between the organization's network and the Internet? If so, what rules have been defined? Are there any other kinds of traffic that need to be blocked, both incoming and outgoing?
- Has an IDS system been implemented?

By answering these questions, you will have the data you need to formulate a plan for action that will mitigate security threats.

16

Documenting and Troubleshooting the System

W e're on the last chapter! It's time to wrap things up by talking about two very important, often-overlooked topics: documentation and troubleshooting. A good system administrator doesn't manage his or her systems "by the seat of the pants." Instead, a good system administrator follows proven, established procedures and documents everything he or she does. We're going to teach you how to do this in this chapter. We'll discuss the following topics:

- Documenting the system
- Troubleshooting system problems

Let's begin this chapter by discussing how to document your system.

CERTIFICATION OBJECTIVE 16.01

Document the System

I'm sure you're probably tempted to skip this part of the chapter. I've yet to meet a system or network administrator who likes to document things. In fact, just about everyone I know who works in the field *hates* to document their systems.

However, documenting your systems is one of the most important things you can do. There are two main reasons for doing this. First, what seems perfectly clear and apparent to you right now will not be 6–12 months down the road. I can't tell you how many times I've encountered a problem, spent hours troubleshooting and resolving the issues, and could not for the life of me remember how I did it when I encountered the same problem again months later.

The same thing happens to me when I implement a new system. I spend hours installing hardware, configuring the operating system, and installing drivers. Everything I've done is fresh in my mind right after I finish working on a system. Many times, for particularly troublesome deployments, it seems that the systems and their configuration parameters are indelibly burned into my brain. However, I work on so many projects that, within about nine months, I've usually forgotten everything about the project.

The second reason for documenting your systems is the fact that you will probably move on to new responsibilities at some point. You may get a new job with a different company. You may get promoted to a new position within your own company. When this happens, someone else will need to take over the systems you have been managing. Trust me, this can be one of the most challenging tasks in a system administrator's career if the prior occupant of the position didn't document their network and system configurations. It can take weeks or month to try and figure out what the guy before you was doing.

As a consultant, I am frequently hired by small companies to come in and fix problems with their networks and systems. These companies hire a consultant to come in and initially implement their systems, but they usually don't keep an IT person on staff full time. Instead, when a problem arises, they simply call someone like me to come and fix the current problem at hand. If the person who originally set up the network took the time to document what they did, my job is easy. I can get in and out very quickly. However, if the consultant who worked on the system before me didn't document their work, it can take me days to figure out how things were set up. That costs my clients money and it wastes my time. A word to the wise: Document what you do!

With that in mind, we need to discuss what to document and how to do it. In this part of this chapter, we're going to review the following topics:

- Documenting the system configuration
- Documenting changes and maintenance
- Creating a system baseline
- Using standardized procedures

Let's begin by discussing how to document your system configuration.

Documenting the System Configuration

After you initially deploy a new Linux system, you should carefully document your system configuration. How you store this information is up to you. Some system administrators record system information by hand using a simple, spiral-bound notebook. This method is inexpensive, portable, and doesn't require electricity to use it. Unlike an electronic method, this system works very well in an emergency when the power has gone off. The disadvantage is that it can be tedious to record this much information by hand. In addition, some of us, ahem, don't have the best handwriting, making it difficult for others to read the documentation. Also, this information can become dated quickly, requiring constant updates.

Many administrators opt instead for an electronic method for storing system documentation. Many use templates that can be filled in with a word processor. Others use a database system that stores all of your system information centrally. In fact, there are a variety of agents you can install on networked Linux systems that can automatically update a central database with information about all of your systems. That's pretty slick. If you choose an electronic method, you should still consider printing a hard copy of the information occasionally and storing it in a big three-ring binder. As I mentioned, sometimes this information is needed in an emergency situation. If the power is out or your system that stores the information is inaccessible, that hard copy may come in very handy.

So what should you document? Consider the information shown in Table 16-1 to be the minimum information you should document.

TABLE 16-1	System Parameters to Be Documented

Category of Information	Parameter to Be Documented
Hardware	System manufacturer and model number
	Vendor purchased from and date purchased
	Warranty information
	Motherboard make and model number
	BIOS make and version number
	CPU make and model number
	RAM manufacturer, size, type, and installed amount
	Hard drive make, model, size, and geometry

TABLE 16-1	System Parameters to Be Documented (*Contiuned*)
Category of Information	**Parameter to Be Documented**
	CD/DVD drive make and model number
	List of installed expansion boards
	Video board and monitor information, including: ■ Video card make and model number ■ Installed video memory ■ Chipset ■ Maximum screen resolution supported by the monitor ■ Monitor refresh rates
Operating System	Distribution installed, including version number
	Date installed
	Disk partitions and mount points
	Additional kernel modules loaded
	Operating system parameters such as: ■ Keyboard type and language ■ Mouse type ■ Time zone
	Packages installed
Network Settings	Network board make and model
	Dynamic or static IP address. If static, record: ■ IP address ■ Subnet mask ■ Default gateway router address ■ DNS server address
	Network services installed
	Network service configuration parameters. (You may want to simply print out the appropriate .conf files from /etc.)

I know it sounds tedious to maintain this amount of information. Trust me, you'll find your system documentation to be an extremely valuable resource down the road.

In addition to documenting your system after it was initially deployed, you should also maintain a change log and a maintenance log. Let's discuss how this is done next.

Documenting Changes and Maintenance

If you've managed a large number of systems, you know that things change over time. Updated operating system versions are installed; new hardware is installed; new software is installed; networking parameters change. To keep track of these changes, you should also maintain a *change log* and a *maintenance log*. You should make an entry in your change log every time you make a significant change to the system. For example, if you were to replace a network board in one of your systems, you should record the information in Table 16-2.

In addition to documenting changes, you should also document your routine maintenance activities. I know it seems like a lot of paperwork, but maintaining a maintenance log can really help you organize your maintenance efforts. In addition, it can help you make sure your organization's maintenance plan is actually being implemented. Your maintenance log could include information such as that listed in Table 16-3.

In addition to documenting your systems, you should also consider developing and using standardized procedures for your systems. Let's talk about how this is done next.

Using Standardized Procedures

In addition to documenting your systems' configuration parameters and your maintenance activities, you should also consider documenting the procedures *you* will use to install, configure, and manage your systems. Again, I know most system administrators recoil at the very thought of using documented procedures in their

TABLE 16-2	Component Changed:	
	Reason for Change:	
Sample Change Log Template	Date Change Was Made:	
	New Component Information:	Make: Model: Vendor: Driver File:

TABLE 16-3	Category of Information	Parameter to Be Documented
Suggested Activities to Include in a Maintenance Log	Backup	Date the backup was run
		Type of backup (incremental, differential, or full)
		Media name
	Case Cleaning	Date interior was checked for excessive dust buildup
	Baselining	Date baseline test was run
	Updates	Type of update (BIOS, kernel, driver, or package)
		Name of update installed
		Date update was installed

day-to-day work. I've been there and I know how you feel. I worked for a large operating system vendor in the 1990s that decided to seek ISO 9001 certification. To get this certification, everyone in the organization had to document the procedures they used each and every day. It was painful. It took months to get all of the documentation created and organized. No one was happy with the process. I was perhaps one of the biggest naysayers about the whole idea.

However, an amazing thing happened as a result. First of all, we noticed that there were multiple disconnects between functional groups. One group would do things one way while another would do the same task in a completely different way. As I mentioned earlier in this book, we discovered that one team in our organization had implemented their own Windows NT server without telling anyone and was using it to store my team's critical work files (that were literally worth millions of dollars). This server was completely unknown to the Information Systems department. No one ever backed it up, installed updates, or maintained it in any way.

Second, with documented procedures in place, it was much easier when new employees were hired. Prior to using documented procedures, my organization's training procedures consisted mostly of giving new employees a desk, a computer, a phone, and wishing them the best of luck (that's how I was trained). Now, we could give new employees a binder that described exactly how to do the tasks expected of them.

Finally, this process can also identify areas of redundancy. Many times, you will discover that two or more groups within the organization are doing exactly the same tasks. Streamlining these processes can produce potential cost savings.

Was it a lot of work to document our procedures? Yes. Was it worth it in the end? As much as I didn't want to admit it at the time, yes it was. Workflow was streamlined, consistency was obtained, and new employees could ramp up much faster. You should also consider documenting your procedures for managing your organization's Linux systems. How you create your procedures will depend on your organization's values and preferences. The first company I worked for after graduating from college stored procedures in hardcopy format in filing cabinets. Most of the companies I've worked for since then have maintained their procedures electronically on a Web server.

The actual procedures that you document will also vary from organization to organization. However, there are some procedures that are regularly documented by just about everyone. These include the procedures listed in Table 16-4.

TABLE 16-4	Procedure	What to Document
Documenting Procedures	Procurement	■ Vendors that have been approved for hardware and software purchases ■ Procedure for approving purchases ■ Procedure for ordering new hardware and software ■ Procedure for returns

	Installation	■ Hardware approved for new deployments
		 ■ Distributions approved for new deployments
		 ■ Applications approved for new deployments
		 ■ Procedure for approving a new server or workstation in the network
		 ■ Procedure for installing the operating system, including:
		   ■ Disk partitions and mount points
		   ■ File system types
		   ■ Installed packages
		   ■ Networking parameters

	Configuration	■ Procedure for configuring network parameters on a server ■ Procedure for configuring network parameters on a workstation ■ Procedure for installing and configuring a service ■ Procedure for installing and configuring an application

TABLE 16-4	Procedure	What to Document
Documenting Procedures (*Continued*)		■ Procedure for upgrading an expansion board ■ Procedure for upgrading a hard drive ■ Procedure for upgrading a CD/DVD drive ■ Procedure for adding RAM ■ Procedure for adding users ■ Procedure for adding groups ■ Procedure for modifying permissions
	Security	■ Procedure for installing operating system updates ■ Procedure for staying abreast of current threats and exploits ■ Procedure for configuring and using remote access ■ Firewall configuration parameters ■ Procedure for detecting intruders ■ IDS configuration parameters
	Management	■ Procedure for proper system shutdown ■ Procedure and frequency for backing up the file system ■ Procedure and frequency for cleaning case interiors ■ Procedure for creating system baselines

This list isn't all-inclusive. You'll probably need to document many other procedures, depending upon which organization you work for.

I hope I've properly emphasized the importance of documentation in your role of Linux system administrator. It's one of those things that most system administrators hate to do, but readily recognize its importance. My advice to you is to just do it! Get the wheels turning and pretty soon it will become second nature to you.

It's time to shift gears and discuss how to troubleshoot problems on a Linux system. Let's do this next.

SCENARIO & SOLUTION

You've just installed a new Linux system for a user in your organization. What system parameters should you document?	You should consider documenting the following parameters: ■ System manufacturer and model number ■ Purchase date and vendor ■ Warranty information ■ Motherboard manufacturer and model number ■ BIOS firmware revision number ■ CPU manufacturer and model number ■ Memory module manufacturer, size, type, and installed quantity ■ Hard drive make, model, size, and geometry ■ CD/DVD drive manufacturer and model number ■ List of installed expansion boards ■ Video board and monitor information ■ Linux distribution installed ■ Disk partitions and mount points ■ Additional kernel modules loaded ■ Packages installed ■ Network interface make and model ■ IP addressing information ■ Network services installed and their configuration parameters
You've just disabled the apache2 daemon on a user's Linux system. What information should you document in your change log?	You should document the following: ■ The component that was changed ■ The reason for the change ■ The date the change was made

CERTIFICATION OBJECTIVE 16.02

Troubleshoot System Problems

Being a good troubleshooter is a key part of being an effective Linux system administrator. I've been teaching new system administrators for 11 years now and this is one of the hardest skills for many to master. Some new admins seem to just have an intrinsic "sense" for how to troubleshoot problems; others don't. The reason for this, in my opinion, is that troubleshooting is part art form. Just as it's difficult for some of us (me included) to learn how to draw, sculpt, or paint, it's also difficult for some of us to learn how to troubleshoot.

However, I've noticed that, with a little training and a lot of practice, most new administrators can eventually learn how to troubleshoot effectively. There are three keys to doing this:

■ A solid troubleshooting procedure

■ A good knowledge of troubleshooting tools

■ A lot of experience troubleshooting problems

The last point is beyond the scope of this book. The only way to gain troubleshooting experience is to spend a couple of years in the field. However, we can work with the first two points. In this chapter, we're going to discuss the following:

■ Using a standardized troubleshooting model

■ Creating a system baseline

■ Using log files to troubleshoot errors

■ Troubleshooting network and hardware issues

Let's begin by discussing how to use a standardized troubleshooting model.

Using a Standardized Troubleshooting Model

Many new system administrators make a key mistake when they troubleshoot system or network problems. Instead of using a methodical troubleshooting approach, they go off half-cocked and start trying to implement fixes before they really know what the problem is. I call it "shotgun troubleshooting." The administrator tries one fix after another, hoping that one of them will repair the problem.

This is a very dangerous practice. I've watched system administrators do this and cause more problems than they solve. Sometimes they can cause absolutely horrendous problems. Case in point: Several years ago I was working with a client to set up several servers in a network. One of the servers was misconfigured and was having trouble synchronizing information with the other systems. While I was trying to figure out the source of the problem, my client's system administrator started implementing fixes trying to get the server to sync data with the other servers. In the process he managed to mess up all of the other servers. The actual issue was relatively minor and would have only required about 20 minutes to fix. Instead, we had to spend the rest of the day and part of the night re-installing the servers from scratch and restoring their data.

Instead of using shotgun troubleshooting, you should use a standardized troubleshooting model. The goal of a troubleshooting model is to concretely identify the source of the problem *before* you start fixing things. I know that sounds simple, but many system administrators struggle with this concept. Here's a suggested troubleshooting model that you can use to develop your own personal troubleshooting methodology:

1. **Step 1: Gather information.** This is a critical step. You need to determine exactly what has happened. What are the symptoms? Were any error messages displayed? What did they say? How extensive is the problem? Is it isolated to a single system, or are many systems experiencing the same problem?

2. **Step 2: Identify what has changed.** In this step, you should identify what has changed in the system. Has new software been installed? Has new hardware been installed? Did a user change something? Did you change something?

3. **Step 3: Create a hypothesis.** With the information gathered in the preceding steps, develop several hypotheses that could explain the problem. To do this, you may need to do some research. You should check FAQs and knowledgebases available on the Internet. You should also consult with peers to validate your hypotheses. Using the information you gain, narrow your results down to the one or two most likely causes.

4. **Step 4: Determine the appropriate fix.** The next step is to use peers, FAQs, knowledgebases, and your own experience to identify the steps needed to fix the problem. As you do this, be sure to identify the possible ramifications of implementing the fix and account for them. Many times, the fix may have side effects that are as bad as or worse than the original problem.

5. **Step 5: Implement the fix.**   At this point, you're ready to implement the fix. Notice that in this troubleshooting model, we did a ton of research before implementing a fix! Doing so greatly increases the likelihood of success. After implementing the fix, be sure to verify that the fix actually repaired the problem and that the issue doesn't reappear.

6. **Step 6: Ensure user satisfaction.**   This is a key mistake made by many system administrators. I like to teach students the adage "If the user isn't happy, you aren't happy." We system admins are notoriously poor communicators. If the problem affects users, you need to communicate the nature of the problem with them and make sure they are aware that it has been fixed. If applicable, you should also educate them as to how to keep the problem from occurring in the future. You should also communicate with your users' supervisors and ensure they know that the problem has been fixed.

7. **Step 7: Document the solution.**   As we discussed earlier in this chapter, you need to document the solution to your problem. That way, when it occurs again a year or two down the road, you or other system administrators can quickly identify the problem and how to fix it.

If you use this methodology, you can learn to be a very effective troubleshooter as you gain hands-on experience in the real world.

In addition to using a troubleshooting methodology, you also need to know how to use a variety of troubleshooting tools for your Linux+ exam. We're going to spend the rest of the chapter creating a system baseline to be an effective troubleshooter. Let's discuss how you do this next.

Creating a System Baseline

System *baselines* are an invaluable resource when monitoring and troubleshooting Linux systems. Baselining involves taking a snapshot of a system's performance when it's in a pristine state, such as right after it is initially deployed. This is your *initial baseline*. As the weeks and months go by, you take subsequent baselines at regular intervals and compare the results to your initial baseline. Over time, this process will give you a picture of what's happening with your system. For example, you may see that CPU utilization is gradually increasing as the weeks pass, indicating that you may need to upgrade to a faster CPU. Or, you may see that your system RAM or swap partition is over-utilized, indicating that you need to install more memory.

You may see that disk I/O operations are slowing the system down, indicating that you need to upgrade to a faster disk system.

To create a system baseline, you can monitor and document a variety of system parameters. The actual parameters you choose to monitor may vary from organization to organization. Some suggested parameters to monitor include the following:

- Processor utilization
- Memory utilization
- Swap partition utilization
- Free disk space
- Disk write performance
- Disk read performance
- Network throughput

Your Linux system includes a variety of utilities that you can use to measure these parameters to create a system baseline. One that is very useful is the top utility, which we discussed in depth earlier in this book. There are also a number of other utilities that you can use. We're going to discuss the following here:

- Using sar
- Using vmstat
- Using pstree

Let's begin by discussing how to use sar.

Using sar

The System Activity Reports (sar) utility is contained in the sysstat package, which you can install on your Linux system using the rpm utility. This package contains a number of extremely useful utilities that you can use to create a server baseline, the most useful of which is the sar utility. You configure cron to run sar on a regular basis, usually every ten minutes. Each time it runs, it writes its output to a log file in the /var/log/sa directory. A different log file is used each day of the month, allowing you to keep a month's worth of sar logs at a time.

To configure sar on your system, do the following:

1. If necessary, install the sysstat package on your system using the rpm utility.
2. Use su – to change to root.

3. At the shell prompt, enter **crontab –e**.

4. Add the following lines to the file:

```
#crontab for sysstat
#activity reports every 10 minutes everyday
*/10   *      *      *      *   root /usr/lib/sa/sa1
#update reports every 6 hours
0      */6    *      *      *   root /usr/lib/sa/sa2 -A
```

on the

job *You can use the /etc/sysstat/sysstat.cron file as a template for creating this cron entry.*

5. Save the file and exit the editor.

At this point, cron will run the sa1 script every ten minutes. You can view data gathered by the script by entering **sar** at the shell prompt. Entering **sar** without any options will display sar CPU metrics for the current date. You can also force sar to take a quick snapshot of current metrics. For example, to take ten CPU measurements every five seconds, you would enter **sar 5 10** at the shell prompt. The results are displayed on screen, as shown in Figure 16-1.

Table 16-5 explains the output of sar.

In addition to CPU metrics, the sar utility can report I/O stats using the –b option. Enter **sar –b** *interval measurements* at the shell prompt. For example, to take five measurements three seconds apart, you would enter **sar –b 3 5** at the shell prompt. The output is shown in Figure 16-2.

FIGURE 16-1

Using sar to take a snapshot of CPU performance

```
tux@linux1:~ - Shell No. 3 - Konsole

Session   Edit   View   Bookmarks   Settings   Help

linux1:~ # sar 5 10
Linux 2.6.16.13-4-default (linux1)        02/23/07

12:58:23        CPU     %user    %nice    %system    %iowait    %idle
12:58:28        all      2.39     0.00       5.38       0.00     92.23
12:58:33        all      2.00     0.00       5.41       0.00     92.59
12:58:38        all      1.80     0.00       5.59       0.00     92.61
12:58:43        all      2.20     0.00       4.39       0.00     93.41
12:58:48        all      1.80     0.00       6.81       0.00     91.38
12:58:53        all      1.80     0.00       4.99       0.00     93.21
12:58:58        all      1.80     0.00       4.79       0.00     93.41
12:59:03        all      2.20     0.00       4.80       0.00     93.00
12:59:08        all      2.59     0.00       4.79       0.00     92.61
12:59:13        all      2.20     0.00       4.80       0.00     93.00
Average:        all      2.08     0.00       5.17       0.00     92.75
linux1:~ # 

Shell No. 2    Shell No. 3    Shell
```

TABLE 16-5	Column	Description
sar Output	Time	Time the measurement was taken.
	CPU	The CPU being measured. In Figure 16-1, only one CPU was installed in the system.
	%user	The percentage of CPU cycles spent working on user processes.
	%nice	The percentage of CPU cycles spent working on processes with a custom nice value.
	%system	The percentage of CPU cycles spent working on kernel processes.
	%iowait	The percentage of time that the CPU was idle waiting for a disk I/O request to complete.
	%ide	Percentage of time that the CPU was idle.

Table 16-6 explains the columns in the output.

In addition to CPU and I/O metrics, you can use sar to measure many other metrics on a Linux system. You can use the following options:

- **–B**   Displays paging statistics.
- **–c**   Displays the number of processes created each second.
- **–d**   Displays I/O stats for each block device in your system.
- **–I**   Displays stats for interrupts on your system.
- **–n**   Displays network statistics.
- **–p**   Displays processor queue lengths and load averages.

FIGURE 16-2	
Taking a snapshot of I/O performance with sar	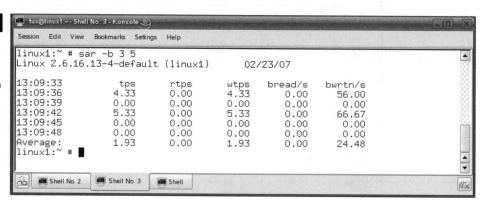

TABLE 16-6	Column	Description
I/O Output Columns	Rtps	Read requests per second
	Wtps	Write requests per second
	Bread/s	Total data read in blocks per second
	Bwrtn/s	Total data written in blocks per second

- **–r** Displays memory and swap partition utilization stats.
- **–R** Displays memory stats.
- **–u** Displays CPU utilization stats (default).
- **–v** Displays kernel stats.
- **–W** Displays swap partition stats.

As you can see, sar is an excellent tool for developing a system baseline. In addition to sar, you can also use the vmstat utility to gather data for a system baseline. Let's discuss how to do this next.

Using vmstat

The vmstat utility is used to report virtual machine statistics such as processes, memory, paging, and CPU activity. To use vmstat, simply enter **vmstat** at the shell prompt. This is shown in Figure 16-3.

Table 16-7 describes the output of vmstat.

You also need to know how to use the pstree utility to create system baselines for your Linux+ exam. Let's discuss this utility next.

FIGURE 16-3   Using vmstat

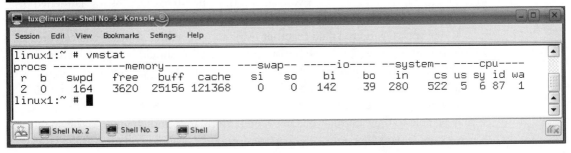

TABLE 16-7	Column	Description
vmstat Columns	r	Processes waiting to be run
	b	Sleeping processes
	swpd	Virtual (swap partition) memory in use (in KB)
	free	Free RAM
	buff	Amount of memory used for buffers
	cache	Amount of memory used for cache
	si	Amount of memory in KB swapped in from disk per second
	so	Amount of memory in KB swapped out to disk per second
	bi	Blocks read per second
	bo	Blocks written per second
	in	Interrupt requests per second
	cs	Context switches per second
	us	CPU time spent running user processes
	sy	CPU time spent running kernel processes
	id	CPU idle time
	wa	CPU time spent waiting for I/O operations

Using pstree

The pstree utility is a simple, yet handy utility. Recall that we discussed the hierarchy of processes earlier in this book. We said that one process could launch another process. When this happens, the first process is the *parent* and the launched process is the *child*. We also pointed out that the init process is the grandparent of all other processes. You can use the pstree utility to view this hierarchy, as shown in Figure 16-4.

For example, in Figure 16-4 you can see that the firefox process was launched by the kdeinit process, which was launched by the init process.

Once you've gathered data together using the preceding utilities, you can create your baselines. As we said earlier, your initial baseline should be created when the system is in its most pristine state, such as right after initial deployment. Then you need to create subsequent baselines that will be compared to the initial and prior baselines. By comparing baseline data with your system documentation, you may be able to draw correlations between performance and changes in the system. For example, you may notice network performance dropping off after an updated network board driver was installed. As you can see, a baseline can be an invaluable troubleshooting tool!

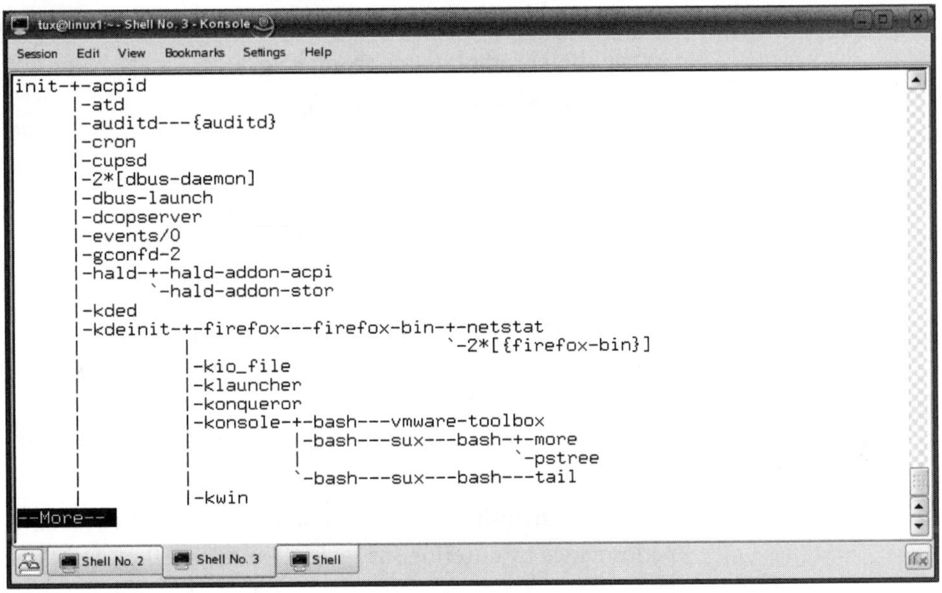

FIGURE 16-4

Viewing the hierarchy of processes with pstree

```
init-+-acpid
     |-atd
     |-auditd---{auditd}
     |-cron
     |-cupsd
     |-2*[dbus-daemon]
     |-dbus-launch
     |-dcopserver
     |-events/0
     |-gconfd-2
     |-hald-+-hald-addon-acpi
     |      `-hald-addon-stor
     |-kded
     |-kdeinit-+-firefox---firefox-bin-+-netstat
     |         |                       `-2*[{firefox-bin}]
     |         |-kio_file
     |         |-klauncher
     |         |-konqueror
     |         |-konsole-+-bash---vmware-toolbox
     |         |         |-bash---sux---bash-+-more
     |         |         |                   `-pstree
     |         |         `-bash---sux---bash---tail
     |         |-kwin
--More--
```

The interval for taking baselines will vary from organization to organization and from system to system. For example, a Linux server contains mission-critical information and must remain available 24/7. Therefore, it's a good idea to take baselines very frequently, such as weekly or bi-weekly. Workstations, on the other hand, can probably handle a much longer interval between baselines.

Let's practice creating a baseline for your Linux system in the following exercise.

EXERCISE 16-1

ON THE CD

Generating a System Baseline

In this exercise, you will practice creating a baseline for your Linux system using the sar utility. Complete the following:

1. Boot your Linux system and log in as a standard user. If you used the lab exercise in Chapter 3 to install your system, you can log in as **tux** with a password of **M3linux273**.

2. Open a terminal session.

3. Switch to your root user account by entering **su –** followed by your root user's password.

4. If necessary, install the sysstat package on your system using the rpm utility.

5. At the shell prompt, enter **crontab –e**.

6. Add the following lines to the file:

```
#crontab for sysstat
#activity reports every 10 minutes everyday
*/10 * * * * root /usr/lib/sa/sa1
#update reports every 6 hours
0 */6 * * * root /usr/lib/sa/sa2 -A
```

7. Save the file and exit the editor.

8. Generate a snapshot of your CPU performance by entering **sar 5 10** at the shell prompt. Record the average.

9. Generate a snapshot of your system's I/O performance by entering **sar –b 5 10** at the shell prompt. Record the average.

10. Generate a snapshot of your system's memory and virtual memory performance by entering **sar –r 5 10** at the shell prompt. Record the average.

11. Generate a snapshot of your system's kernel performance by entering **sar –v 5 10** at the shell prompt. Record the average.

12. Use a word processor or spreadsheet application, such as OpenOffice.org, to compile the information gathered in the preceding steps into a system baseline document.

That's it for baselines. Now we need to discuss using log files to troubleshoot problems.

Using Log Files to Troubleshoot Errors

In the previous chapter, we discussed how you could use your log files to detect intruders into your system. Log files can also be used to troubleshoot problems with your system. In fact, they can be a key tool when troubleshooting Linux problems. In this part of the chapter, we'll teach you how to manage and use your system log files. We'll cover the following topics:

■ Configuring log files

■ Using log files to troubleshoot problems

Let's begin by discussing how to configure your log files.

Configuring Log Files

As you learned in the previous chapter, your system log files are stored in the /var/log directory, shown in Figure 16-5.

Notice in Figure 16-5 that there are a number of subdirectories in /var/log where system daemons, such as apache2, apparmor, audit, and cups, store their log files. As we learned in the previous chapter, some of these log files are simple text files that can be read with text manipulation utilities. Others are binary files that require the use of a special utility, such as lastlog. As you can see in Figure 16-5, there are quite a number of files within /var/log and its subdirectories. As with anything, some log files are much more useful than others. Table 16-8 contains a list of some of the more important log files.

on the **job**

These are the log files used on a SUSE Linux system. Other distributions, such as Fedora, may use different files by default. You can customize your logging using the syslog.conf file, discussed next.

FIGURE 16-5
Contents of the /var/log directory

```
tux@linux1:~ - Shell No. 3 - Konsole

Session  Edit  View  Bookmarks  Settings  Help

linux1:/var/log # ls -l |more
total 24794
-rw-r----- 1 root root      278837 Feb  2 12:13 NetworkManager
-rw-r--r-- 1 root root       38963 Jan 24 07:35 SaX.log
lrwxrwxrwx 1 root root          10 Oct 10 12:34 XFree86.0.log -> Xorg.0.log
lrwxrwxrwx 1 root root          14 Oct 10 12:34 XFree86.0.log.old -> Xorg.0.log.o
ld
-rw-r--r-- 1 root root       26865 Feb 23 12:08 Xorg.0.log
-rw-r--r-- 1 root root       26865 Feb 23 11:37 Xorg.0.log.old
drwx------ 3 root root         800 Feb 21 11:09 YaST2
-rw-r----- 1 root root       21283 Feb 23 12:08 acpid
drwxr-x--- 2 root root         144 Feb  9 13:35 apache2
drwx------ 5 root root         136 Oct 10 12:38 apparmor
drwx------ 2 root root          80 Feb 22 12:16 audit
-rw-r----- 1 root root           0 Oct 10 12:30 boot.log
-rw-r--r-- 1 root root       34889 Feb 23 12:27 boot.msg
-rw-r--r-- 1 root root       40055 Feb 23 12:06 boot.omsg
drwxr-xr-x 2 lp   lp          136 Feb 12 15:17 cups
-rw------- 1 root root       24168 Feb  9 13:24 faillog
-rw-r----- 1 root root     1671161 Feb 23 14:41 firewall
-rw-r--r-- 1 root root       75177 Feb 23 12:08 kdm.log
drwx------ 2 root root          48 May  2  2006 krb5
-rw-r--r-- 1 root tty       294044 Feb 23 12:26 lastlog
-rw-r----- 1 root root         126 Feb  2 13:13 localmessages
-rw-r----- 1 root root       28948 Feb 23 13:10 mail
-rw-r----- 1 root root         184 Oct 10 14:48 mail.err
-rw-r----- 1 root root       26172 Feb 23 13:10 mail.info
-rw-r----- 1 root root        2023 Oct 10 14:26 mail.warn
-rw-r----- 1 root root    14541724 Feb 23 14:41 messages
lrwxrwxrwx 1 root root          23 Feb  9 13:25 mysqld.log -> ../lib/mysql/mysqld

Shell No. 2   Shell No. 3   Shell
```

	Log File	Description
TABLE 16-8 Useful Log Files	boot.log	Contains log entries from daemons as they were started during bootup.
	boot.msg	Contains all of the messages displayed on screen during system boot. This can be a very valuable troubleshooting tool when trying to rectify startup problems. The messages displayed on screen usually fly by too quickly to be read.
	faillog	Contains failed authentication attempts.
	firewall	Contains firewall log entries.
	lastlog	Contains last login information for users.
	mail	Contains messages generated by the postfix or sendmail daemons.
	messages	Contains messages from most running processes. This is probably one of the most useful of all log files. You can use it to troubleshoot services that won't start, services that don't appear to work properly, etc.
	warn	Contains warning messages.
	wtmp	Contains a list of users who have authenticated to the system.
	xinetd.log	Contains log entries from the xinetd daemon.

Logging on a Linux system is handled by the syslogd daemon. Instead of each daemon maintaining its own individual log file, most of your Linux services are configured to write log entries to /dev/log by default. This device file is maintained by the syslogd daemon. When a service writes to this socket, the input is captured by syslogd. The syslogd daemon then uses the entries in the /etc/syslog.conf file, shown in Figure 16-6, to determine where the information should go.

on the
ⓙob

The SUSE Linux distributions version 10 and later use syslog-ng instead of syslogd to manage logging.

The syntax for the syslog.conf file is:

```
service.priority        file
```

The syslogd daemon uses the following priority levels:

■ **debug** All information
■ **info** Informational messages

FIGURE 16-6

The /etc/
syslog.conf file

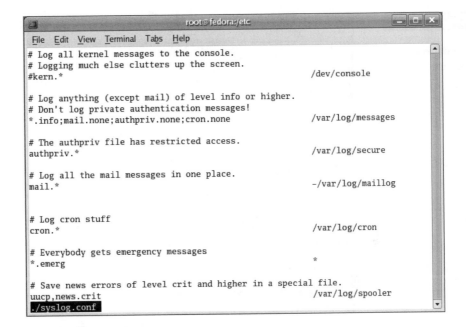

```
                                    root@fedora:/etc
File  Edit  View  Terminal  Tabs  Help
# Log all kernel messages to the console.
# Logging much else clutters up the screen.
#kern.*                                              /dev/console

# Log anything (except mail) of level info or higher.
# Don't log private authentication messages!
*.info;mail.none;authpriv.none;cron.none             /var/log/messages

# The authpriv file has restricted access.
authpriv.*                                           /var/log/secure

# Log all the mail messages in one place.
mail.*                                              -/var/log/maillog


# Log cron stuff
cron.*                                               /var/log/cron

# Everybody gets emergency messages
*.emerg                                                   *

# Save news errors of level crit and higher in a special file.
uucp,news.crit                                       /var/log/spooler
./syslog.conf
```

- **notice** Issues of concern, but not yet a problem
- **warn** Non-critical errors
- **err** Serious errors
- **crit**, **alert**, or **emerg** Critical errors

For example, in Figure 16-6, the syslog.conf file directs messages of all priority levels (*) from the cron daemon to the /var/log/cron file. If desired, you could customize your syslog.conf file to split messages of different priority levels to different files.

Your Linux distribution should also include a utility named logrotate. The logrotate utility is run daily, by default, by the cron daemon on your system. You can customize how your log files are rotated using the /etc/logrotate.conf file, shown in Figure 16-7.

This file contains default global parameters used by logrotate to determine how and when log files are rotated. However, these defaults can be overridden for specific daemons using the configuration files located in the /etc/logrotate.d/ directory. For example, in Figure 16-8, the /etc/logrotate.d/apache2 file is used to customize logging for the apache2 daemon.

FIGURE 16-7

Configuring log
file rotation
in /etc/
logrotate.conf

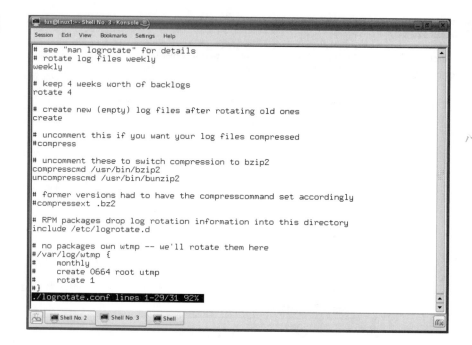

```
# see "man logrotate" for details
# rotate log files weekly
weekly

# keep 4 weeks worth of backlogs
rotate 4

# create new (empty) log files after rotating old ones
create

# uncomment this if you want your log files compressed
#compress

# uncomment these to switch compression to bzip2
compresscmd /usr/bin/bzip2
uncompresscmd /usr/bin/bunzip2

# former versions had to have the compresscommand set accordingly
#compressext .bz2

# RPM packages drop log rotation information into this directory
include /etc/logrotate.d

# no packages own wtmp -- we'll rotate them here
#/var/log/wtmp {
#    monthly
#    create 0664 root utmp
#    rotate 1
#}
./logrotate.conf lines 1-29/31 92%
```

FIGURE 16-8

Configuring
Apache Web
server logging

```
linux1:/etc/logrotate.d # ls
apache2       net-snmp      samba          syslog       wtmp       zmd-backend
i41-isdnlog   ntp           samba-winbind  syslog-ng    xdm
mysql         rsync         scpm           vsftpd       xinetd
linux1:/etc/logrotate.d # cat ./apache2
/var/log/apache2/access_log {
    compress
    dateext
    maxage 365
    rotate 99
    size=+4096k
    notifempty
    missingok
    create 644 root root
    postrotate
     /etc/init.d/apache2 reload
    endscript
}

/var/log/apache2/error_log {
    compress
    dateext
    maxage 365
    rotate 99
    size=+1024k
    notifempty
    missingok
    create 644 root root
    postrotate
     /etc/init.d/apache2 reload
```

In Figure 16-8, the /var/log/apache2/access_log file will be compressed. It can have a maximum age of 365 days after which it will be removed (maxage 365). Old versions of the file will be archived using a date extension (dateext). The log file will go through 99 rotations before being removed (rotate 99). If the file grows larger than 4096KB, it will be rotated (size=+4096k). The file will not be rotated if it is empty (notifempty). No error message will be generated if the file is missing (missingok). The file will be created with 644 permissions, the root user will be the owner, and will be associated with the root group (create 644 root root). After rotating a log file, the /etc/init.d/apache2 reload command will be run (postrotate /etc/init.d/apache2 reload).

on the job

There are many other directives that can be used in a logrotate configuration file. See the logrotate man page.

One of the cool features of the syslogd daemon is that it supports logging to a remote host. Moving your log files from the local system to a different computer on the network can be a very valuable administrative and security measure. For example, you could redirect all logging by Linux systems on your network to a single log host. Then, if a user calls with a problem, you have instant access to their log files on the log host.

In addition, remote logging increases the security of your systems. As you learned in the previous chapter, inexperienced intruders will leave footprints all over in your log files. However, a savvy intruder will try to erase his or her tracks by altering the log files after accessing the system, making it very difficult to detect the intrusion. If you redirect your logging however, the intruder can't cover his tracks nearly so easily. To redirect logging, complete the following:

1. Open a terminal session and su – to root.
2. Open /etc/syslog.conf in a text editor.
3. Add the following line to the beginning of the file:

   ```
   *.*          @IP_address_of_loghost
   ```

   For example, in Figure 16-9, all messages are redirected to a host with an IP address of 192.168.1.10.
4. Save the file and exit your editor.
5. Restart the syslogd daemon.

FIGURE 16-9

Configuring
remote logging

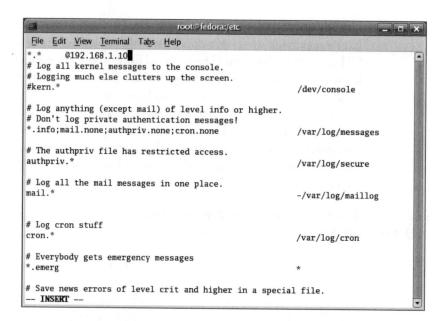

6. To configure the loghost system to receive log messages from the other systems, complete the following:

   a. In a text editor, open /etc/sysconfig/syslog.

   b. Locate to the SYSLOGD_PARAMS directive.

   c. Set the value of the SYSLOGD_PARAMS directive to –r.

   d. Save the changes and exit the file.

   e. Restart syslogd.

With this background in mind, let's next discuss how to actually view and use your log files.

Using Log Files to Troubleshoot Problems

As I mentioned earlier in this chapter, your log files can be an invaluable resource when troubleshooting Linux problems. If the kernel or a service encounters a problem, it will be logged in a log file. Reviewing these log files can provide you with a wealth of information that may not necessarily be displayed on the screen.

Some log files, as we discussed in the previous chapter, are binary files that must be read with a special utility. However, most of your log files are simple text files that you can view with standard text manipulation utilities. Earlier in this book,

FIGURE 16-10

Viewing a log file
with less

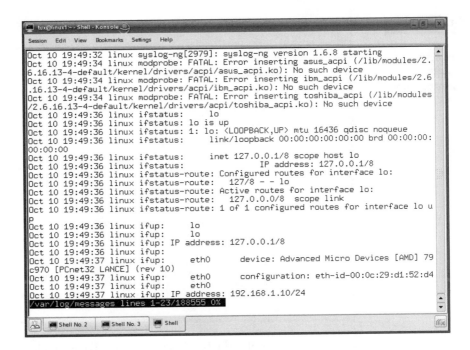

```
Oct 10 19:49:32 linux syslog-ng[2979]: syslog-ng version 1.6.8 starting
Oct 10 19:49:34 linux modprobe: FATAL: Error inserting asus_acpi (/lib/modules/2.
6.16.13-4-default/kernel/drivers/acpi/asus_acpi.ko): No such device
Oct 10 19:49:34 linux modprobe: FATAL: Error inserting ibm_acpi (/lib/modules/2.6
.16.13-4-default/kernel/drivers/acpi/ibm_acpi.ko): No such device
Oct 10 19:49:34 linux modprobe: FATAL: Error inserting toshiba_acpi (/lib/modules
/2.6.16.13-4-default/kernel/drivers/acpi/toshiba_acpi.ko): No such device
Oct 10 19:49:36 linux ifstatus:      lo
Oct 10 19:49:36 linux ifstatus: lo is up
Oct 10 19:49:36 linux ifstatus: 1: lo: <LOOPBACK,UP> mtu 16436 qdisc noqueue
Oct 10 19:49:36 linux ifstatus:      link/loopback 00:00:00:00:00:00 brd 00:00:00:
00:00:00
Oct 10 19:49:36 linux ifstatus:      inet 127.0.0.1/8 scope host lo
Oct 10 19:49:36 linux ifstatus:              IP address: 127.0.0.1/8
Oct 10 19:49:36 linux ifstatus-route: Configured routes for interface lo:
Oct 10 19:49:36 linux ifstatus-route:   127/8 - - lo
Oct 10 19:49:36 linux ifstatus-route: Active routes for interface lo:
Oct 10 19:49:36 linux ifstatus-route:   127.0.0.0/8  scope link
Oct 10 19:49:36 linux ifstatus-route: 1 of 1 configured routes for interface lo u
p
Oct 10 19:49:36 linux ifup:      lo
Oct 10 19:49:36 linux ifup:      lo
Oct 10 19:49:36 linux ifup: IP address: 127.0.0.1/8
Oct 10 19:49:36 linux ifup:
Oct 10 19:49:37 linux ifup:      eth0      device: Advanced Micro Devices [AMD] 79
c970 [PCnet32 LANCE] (rev 10)
Oct 10 19:49:37 linux ifup:      eth0      configuration: eth-id-00:0c:29:d1:52:d4
Oct 10 19:49:37 linux ifup:      eth0
Oct 10 19:49:37 linux ifup: IP address: 192.168.1.10/24
/var/log/messages lines 1-23/188555 0%
```

you learned how to use the cat, less, and more utilities to view text files on a Linux
system. These utilities can, of course, be used to view log files as well. However,
there's a problem with these utilities: Log files are usually way too long to be viewed
effectively with these utilities. For example, in Figure 16-10, the less /var/log/
messages command has been issued at the shell prompt.

Notice the line reference displayed at the bottom of the screen. The /var/log/
messages file has 188,555 lines in it! That's a lot of text! The less utility only displays
24 lines at a time. You're going to have to press the SPACEBAR a lot of times to get to
the end of the file!

There are two strategies you can use to get around this. We presented the first
one to you already in the previous chapter. You can redirect the output of the cat
command to the grep command to locate a specific term within a log file. For
example, suppose you wanted to locate information within /var/log/messages related
to the rlogin utility. You could enter **cat /var/log/messages | grep rlogin** at the shell
prompt. Then, only entries containing the term "rlogin" are displayed, as shown in
Figure 16-11.

In addition to grep, you can also use the head and tail utilities to view log file
entries. Understand that most log files record entries chronologically, usually oldest to
newest. If you want to view the beginning of a log file, you can enter **head** *filename* at

FIGURE 16-11

Using grep to locate information in a log file

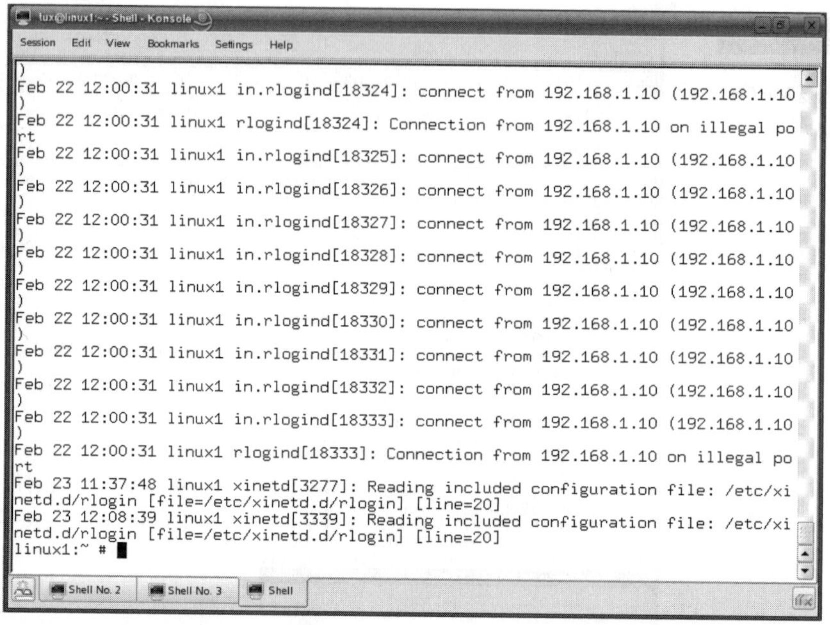

the shell prompt to display the first lines of the file. For example, in Figure 16-12, the beginning of the /var/log/messages file has been displayed with head.

The tail utility works in a manner opposite of head. Instead of displaying the first lines of a file, it displays the last lines. This is very useful. Usually, when troubleshooting, you need to see only the last few lines of a log file. To do this, enter **tail *filename*** at the shell prompt. In Figure 16-13, the /var/log/messages file is being viewed using tail.

FIGURE 16-12

Using head to view a log file

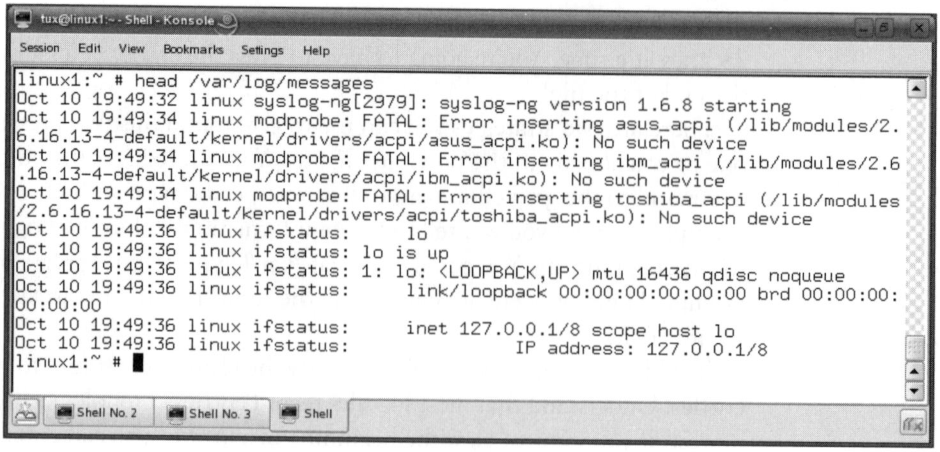

FIGURE 16-13

Using tail to view a log file

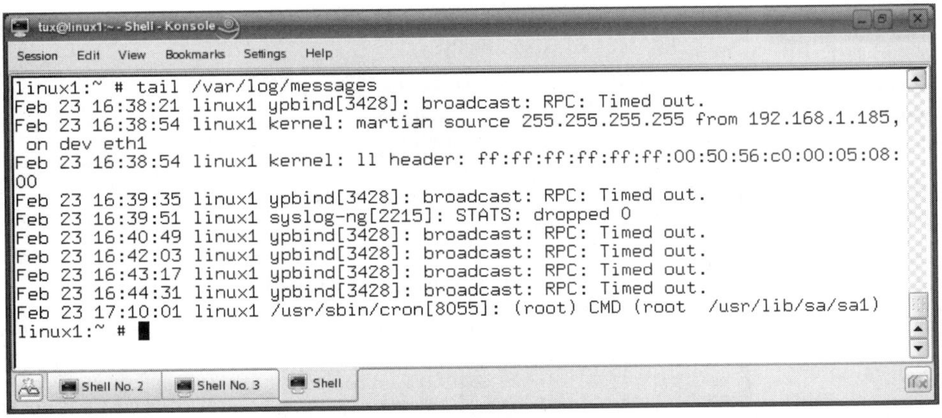
tux@linux1:~ - Shell - Konsole
Session Edit View Bookmarks Settings Help
linux1:~ # tail /var/log/messages
Feb 23 16:38:21 linux1 ypbind[3428]: broadcast: RPC: Timed out.
Feb 23 16:38:54 linux1 kernel: martian source 255.255.255.255 from 192.168.1.185, on dev eth1
Feb 23 16:38:54 linux1 kernel: ll header: ff:ff:ff:ff:ff:ff:00:50:56:c0:00:05:08:00
Feb 23 16:39:35 linux1 ypbind[3428]: broadcast: RPC: Timed out.
Feb 23 16:39:51 linux1 syslog-ng[2215]: STATS: dropped 0
Feb 23 16:40:49 linux1 ypbind[3428]: broadcast: RPC: Timed out.
Feb 23 16:42:03 linux1 ypbind[3428]: broadcast: RPC: Timed out.
Feb 23 16:43:17 linux1 ypbind[3428]: broadcast: RPC: Timed out.
Feb 23 16:44:31 linux1 ypbind[3428]: broadcast: RPC: Timed out.
Feb 23 17:10:01 linux1 /usr/sbin/cron[8055]: (root) CMD (root /usr/lib/sa/sa1)
linux1:~ #
Shell No. 2
Shell No. 3
Shell

The tail utility provides the –f option, which I use all of the time when troubleshooting. When you use the –f option, tail will display the last lines of a log file as per normal. However, it doesn't exit after it initially displays the text on the screen. Instead, it monitors the file being displayed and displays new lines as they are added to the log file. For example, in Figure 16-14, the tail –f /var/log/messages command has been issued at the shell prompt.

The tail command now monitors the /var/log/messages file waiting for new lines to be added. If something happens on the system that generates messages, such as stopping and then restarting a network interface, the results are instantly displayed on the screen without having to run tail again. This is shown in Figure 16-15.

You can quit monitoring the file by pressing CTRL+C.

FIGURE 16-14

Using the –f option with tail

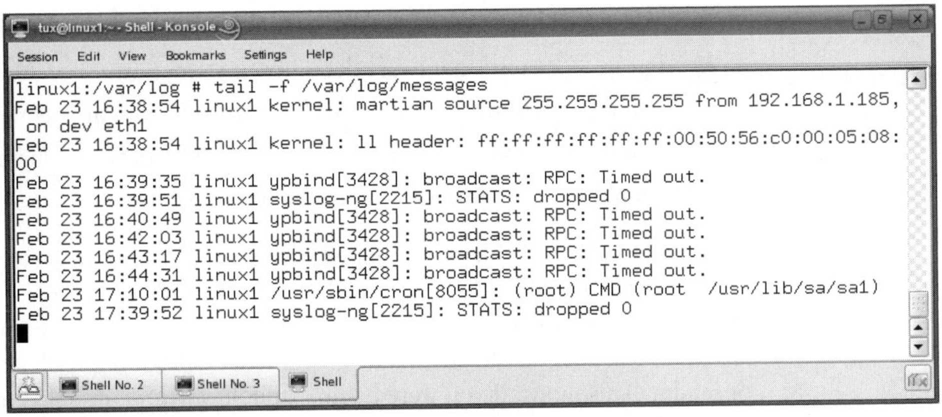
tux@linux1:~ - Shell - Konsole
Session Edit View Bookmarks Settings Help
linux1:/var/log # tail -f /var/log/messages
Feb 23 16:38:54 linux1 kernel: martian source 255.255.255.255 from 192.168.1.185, on dev eth1
Feb 23 16:38:54 linux1 kernel: ll header: ff:ff:ff:ff:ff:ff:00:50:56:c0:00:05:08:00
Feb 23 16:39:35 linux1 ypbind[3428]: broadcast: RPC: Timed out.
Feb 23 16:39:51 linux1 syslog-ng[2215]: STATS: dropped 0
Feb 23 16:40:49 linux1 ypbind[3428]: broadcast: RPC: Timed out.
Feb 23 16:42:03 linux1 ypbind[3428]: broadcast: RPC: Timed out.
Feb 23 16:43:17 linux1 ypbind[3428]: broadcast: RPC: Timed out.
Feb 23 16:44:31 linux1 ypbind[3428]: broadcast: RPC: Timed out.
Feb 23 17:10:01 linux1 /usr/sbin/cron[8055]: (root) CMD (root /usr/lib/sa/sa1)
Feb 23 17:39:52 linux1 syslog-ng[2215]: STATS: dropped 0
Shell No. 2
Shell No. 3
Shell

FIGURE 16-15

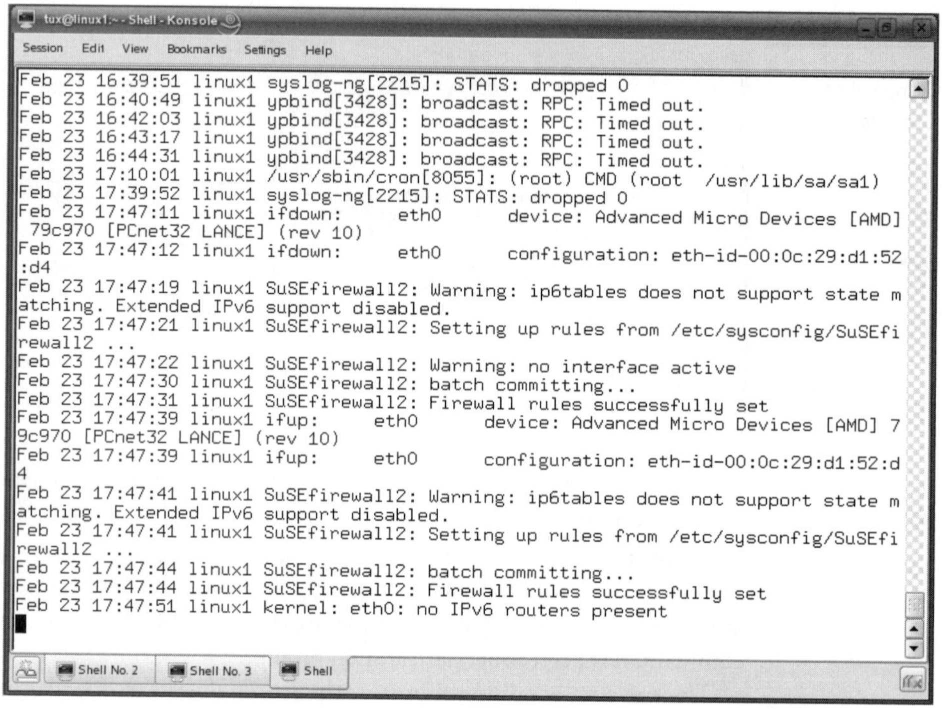

Changes displayed
by tail –f

To troubleshoot system-related problems with one of these utilities, you can check one of the system log files listed previously in Table 16-8. Note that the files in Table 16-8 are the default log files used with SUSE Linux. On other distributions, such as Fedora, you may need to look at other log files, including:

- **cron**   Contains entries from the cron daemon.
- **dmesg**   Contains hardware detection information.
- **maillog**   Contains entries generated by the sendmail daemon.
- **secure**   Contains information about access to network daemons.
- **rpmpkgs**   Contains a list of installed rpm packages.

To troubleshoot problems associated with an application or service, you may need to check for a log file maintained specifically for that service. For example, you would check the mail, mail.err, mail.info, or mail.warn files on a SUSE Linux system or the maillog file on Fedora system to troubleshoot problems with the postfix or sendmail daemons. If you were having trouble with the mysqld daemon (a very powerful database service), you would look in the mysqld.log file. To troubleshoot problems with the Apache Web server, you would investigate the various log files within the /var/log/apache2 directory.

Before we end this chapter, we need to hit one more troubleshooting topic: troubleshooting hardware issues. Let's do that next.

Troubleshooting Network and Hardware Issues

Troubleshooting network and hardware issues is a very broad topic. There's no way we can cover every possible problem with all the various distributions and the wide range of hardware that can be installed in your system. Instead we're going to address some general topics necessary for you to pass your Linux+ exam. Specifically, we'll look at the following:

- Troubleshooting basic network issues
- Troubleshooting basic hardware issues
- Rescuing a system

Let's begin by discussing basic network troubleshooting.

Basic Network Troubleshooting

If you're having problems with your network connection, the ifconfig and ping commands are your best friends. To troubleshoot network issues, you should follow the methodical troubleshooting approach we discussed earlier in this chapter. Start with the basics. Verify that the drop cable is connected to the wall and that the link light is lit on the network hub or switch. There's no point troubleshooting anything else until the basic infrastructure is working correctly.

Next, you should first verify your networking configuration using ifconfig. You should check for the following:

- Is the network interface enabled? If not, you should enable it with ifup.
- Are the IP address and subnet mask assigned appropriate for your network? If the interface gets its configuration from a DHCP server, you can use the ifdown and ifup commands to renew the DHCP lease.
- Use the route command to verify that the correct gateway router address has been configured.
- Check your /etc/resolv.conf file and verify that the correct DNS server address has been assigned.

Once you've verified the configuration, you can use the ping command to start checking communication. Do the following:

- Ping localhost and verify that your system responds to itself.
- Ping your system's IP address and verify that the system responds to itself.
- Ping another system on your same network segment. Verify that it responds. This verifies that your network cabling and hub or switch are working and that communications are occurring correctly on the local network segment.
- Ping your default gateway router. Verify that it responds.
- Ping a host on the other side of the router. This verifies that the router itself is working correctly.
- Ping a host on the Internet using its domain name. This verifies that routing is working, your firewall is working, and that the DNS server is working.

Next, let's discuss how to troubleshoot basic hardware issues.

Troubleshooting Basic Hardware Issues

Troubleshooting hardware issues can be challenging. There are so many hardware devices of so many different types that the possible issues are innumerable. However, there are several basic problems that commonly occur. These are listed in Table 16-9.

Remember that you can use /proc to view a great deal of information about the hardware in your system. We reviewed how to view information in /proc in Chapter 12.

Occasionally, you will encounter problems with the file systems on your hard disk drives. When this happens, you need to rescue the system. Let's end this chapter by learning how to do this.

Rescuing a System

Over time, it's possible for problems to develop with the disks in your Linux system. Sometimes the problems are due to corrupted file systems. Sometimes the problem is with the hard disk itself. The key to being able to rescue a system is to have a good set of backups readily available. There's a chance you can fix your system. However, chances are that you will need to restore data from a backup device at some point. Remember that hard disk drives are mechanical devices that slowly wear out and eventually fail completely.

If a file system other than the one mounted at the root directory (for example, /home) system gets corrupted, you can attempt to repair it. This is done by

TABLE 16-9   Common Hardware Issues

Problem	Resolution
Faulty hardware	Sometimes hardware components simply fail. If this happens, you will need to replace the defective part. If the part is an expansion board that is integrated into your motherboard, such as a network or video board, you will need to disable it in the CMOS setup program before installing a replacement in an expansion slot.
Outdated BIOS firmware doesn't support newer hardware	Your motherboard's BIOS was designed to support hardware that was available at the time it was released. As time passes and newer components become available, your BIOS may not support them properly. This is particularly true of hard disk drives. Usually your BIOS manufacturer will release firmware updates that you can download and "flash" into your BIOS chip that will enable it to support the latest hardware.
Unsupported hardware	Linux hardware support is getting better and better each year. However, there is still a lot of hardware out there that simply won't work with Linux. Check your distribution's HCL to see if your hardware is supported.
Misconfigured hardware	Hardware devices can be misconfigured in a variety of ways. SCSI devices may have termination set incorrectly. IDE devices may have the master/slave relationship set incorrectly. Plug-n-play devices could have been configured to share interrupts with non-PnP devices. Verify that you have set up your hardware correctly.
Buggy or missing drivers	Most distributions automatically detect new hardware when the system initially boots. However, if your distribution does not include a kernel module for a particular device, you'll need to locate one on the Internet, download it, and install it manually.
	In addition, drivers sometimes don't work correctly after they are installed. Again, your best bet is to check the Internet for a newer version, download it, and install it manually.
	You can check your /var/log/boot.msg file to view boot messages to diagnose bad or missing drivers. You can also use the dmesg command to print out your boot messages.

umounting the file system and then running fsck on the appropriate device in /dev to fix the errors. If you cross your fingers and place your left thumb on the right side of your nose, there's a chance that this may fix the corruption and restore the file system to normal operation.

My experience has been, however, that you will usually need to re-create the file system and restore data from a backup to achieve reliable performance. To do this, first use the fdisk utility to re-create the partition. If the disk itself has gone bad (and they do so regularly), then you may need to replace the disk itself and re-create the partition on the new disk. Then use mkfs to re-create the file system. Mount the new partition in its appropriate mount point and restore the data from backup.

If, however, it's the root file system that is corrupt, then things get a little more interesting. If the root file system is corrupt, you may not be able to get at the utilities you need to check the file system. In fact, the system may not be able to finish booting. In this situation, you're going to need to rescue the system.

To do this, you need an alternative way to boot the system. One option is to use a floppy diskette as a boot disk. *Before* you start having problems with your system, you should create a boot disk and keep it in a safe place in the event you need it to boot the system and repair a problem that couldn't be fixed otherwise. To make a boot disk, do the following:

1. Change to your root user account with su –.
2. At the shell prompt, enter **uname –r**. This utility returns your kernel version. Make note of the kernel version. You will need to use it later on and you must enter it *exactly*.
3. At the shell prompt, enter **umount /dev/fd0**.
4. Insert a blank floppy diskette into your system's floppy drive.
5. At the shell prompt, enter **/sbin/mkbootdisk** *kernel_version*.

Another option is to boot your system from your distribution's installation CD. In the first installation screen, select Rescue System, as shown in Figure 16-16.

on the **Job**

On a Fedora system, you can enter linux rescue **at the boot: prompt.**

The system will boot to a rescue login shell in runlevel 1. Most distributions will require you to authenticate as root to proceed. However, many distributions will not require you to supply root's password. This is shown in Figure 16-17.

At this point, you can try using fsck to repair a corrupt file system. If that doesn't work, then you can use fdisk and mkfs to re-create the file system. Then you can restore data from backup.

FIGURE 16-16

Rescuing the
system

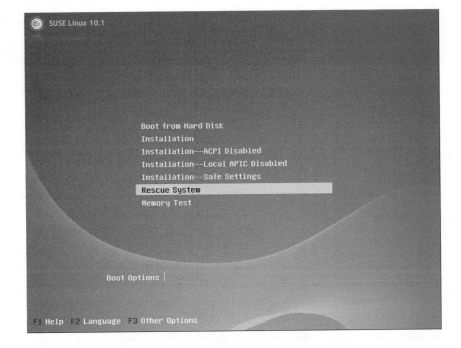

FIGURE 16-17

Using the rescue
shell

```
Setting up hostname 'Rescue'                                                    done
Setting up loopback interface      lo
    lo       IP address: 127.0.0.1/8                                            done
Retry device configuration                                                      done
Creating /var/log/boot.msg                                                      done
Setting up the hardware clock                                                   done
Activating remaining swap-devices in /etc/fstab...                              done
Setting up linker cache (/etc/ld.so.cache) using ldconfig                       done
System Boot Control: The system has been                                        set up
System Boot Control: Running /etc/init.d/boot.local                             done
INIT: Entering runlevel: 3
Boot logging started on /dev/tty1(/dev/console) at Sat Feb 24 06:49:12 2007
Master Resource Control: previous runlevel: N, switching to runlevel:           3
Starting D-BUS daemon                                                           done
Initializing random number generator                                           done
Starting HAL daemon                                                             done
Setting up network interfaces:
    lo
    lo       IP address: 127.0.0.1/8                                            done
    eth0     device: Advanced Micro Devices [AMD] 79c970 [PCnet32 LANCE] (rev 10)
             No configuration found for eth0                                    unused
    eth1     device: Advanced Micro Devices [AMD] 79c970 [PCnet32 LANCE] (rev 10)
             No configuration found for eth1                                    unused
Setting up service network  .  .  .  .  .  .  .  .  .  .  .  .  .  .            done
Starting syslog services                                                        done
Starting RPC portmap daemon                                                     done
Importing Net File System (NFS)                                                 unused
Master Resource Control: runlevel 3 has been                                    reached
Skipped services in runlevel 3:                                        nfs nfsboot

Rescue login: root
Rescue:~ # _
```

SCENARIO & SOLUTION

You want to use the sar utility to generate a snapshot of your system's memory performance. You want to take five measurements five seconds apart. What command would you use to do this?	You would enter **sar –R 5 5** at the shell prompt.
You want to continually monitor the /var/log/messages file for changes. What command would you use to do this?	You would enter **tail –f /var/log/messages** at the shell prompt.
As your Linux system boots, you notice an error message displayed in the startup screen. Unfortunately, it scrolls off the screen before you can read it. What file could you view to read the text of the error message?	You could view the /var/log/boot.msg file with a utility such as cat or less.
The log file for the Samba service running on your Linux system (/var/log/samba/log/smbd) is currently set to rotate if the size of the file grows beyond 1024KB. This rotates the log file too quickly. You want the file to grow to 4096KB before being rotated. What file and parameter would you modify to do this?	You would modify the /etc/logrotate.d/samba file and set the size= parameter to +4096K.

That's it for this chapter. Let's review what you learned.

CERTIFICATION SUMMARY

In this chapter, you learned how to document and complete basic troubleshooting tasks on a Linux system. We began this chapter by emphasizing how important it is for you to document everything you do with your systems. Proper documentation will help you when you're troubleshooting problems with your systems. It will also be an invaluable resource should you move on and someone else is hired to fill your position.

We then discussed the types of information that you should document. First, you should extensively document new systems as soon as they are deployed. You could consider documenting the following:

- System manufacturer and model number
- Vendor purchased from and date purchased
- Warranty information
- Motherboard make and model number

- BIOS make and version number
- CPU make and model number
- RAM manufacturer, size, type, and installed amount
- Hard drive make, model, size, and geometry
- CD/DVD drive make and model number
- List of installed expansion boards
- Video board and monitor information
- Operating system distribution installed, including version number
- Date installed
- Disk partitions and mount points
- Additional kernel modules loaded
- Operating system parameters such as:
  - Keyboard type and language
  - Mouse type
  - Time zone
- Packages installed
- Network board make and model
- Dynamic or static IP address. If static, record:
  - IP address
  - Subnet mask
  - Default gateway router address
  - DNS server address
- Network services installed
- Network service configuration parameters

In addition, you should also consider documenting changes you make to your systems. If you upgrade a component, install a new application, or enable a network service, you should document it. You should document the following information:

- Component changed
- Reason for change
- Date change was made

- New component information:
  - Make
  - Model
  - Vendor
  - Driver file

Maintenance activities should also be documented. You should consider documenting information such as:

- Backup
  - Date the backup was run
  - Type of backup (incremental, differential, or full)
  - Media name
- Date interior was checked for excessive dust buildup
- Date baseline test was run and the results
- Updates
  - Type of update
  - Name of update installed
  - Date update was installed

Next, you should document the procedures you follow in your day-to-day work. Documenting procedures is not an exciting task to complete, but can be very beneficial. It can help you identify problems and disconnects in your work. It can also make it very easy for new hires to ramp up. The actual procedures you document will vary from organization to organization. Here are some suggested procedures to include in your documentation:

- Procurement
- Installation
- Configuration
- Security
- Management

At this point, we changed the focus of the chapter from documentation to troubleshooting. We pointed out that troubleshooting is part skill and part art form. To be a good troubleshooter, you need the following:

- A solid troubleshooting procedure
- A good knowledge of troubleshooting tools
- A lot of experience troubleshooting problems

To develop a solid troubleshooting procedure, you need to learn how to use a standardized troubleshooting model. Instead of guessing at the cause of problems and then implementing fixes based on your guesses, you should use a standardized troubleshooting model to extensively research problems with your systems and concretely identify the cause. Once you know what the real problem is, you can research the solution and implement a fix. A basic troubleshooting model consists of the following steps:

- **Step 1** Gather information.
- **Step 2** Identify what has changed.
- **Step 3** Create a hypothesis.
- **Step 4** Determine the appropriate fix.
- **Step 5** Implement the fix.
- **Step 6** Ensure user satisfaction.
- **Step 7** Document the solution.

We then discussed the importance of using system baselines. A baseline is a snapshot of your system's performance. The first baseline should be taken when a system is initially deployed. Then subsequent baselines should be taken on a regular schedule. You can compare baselines against each other to identify trends. You can also compare your baselines to your system documentation to identify what has changed that could account for changes in your baseline trends. You should consider including the following parameters in your system baselines:

- Processor utilization
- Memory utilization
- Swap partition utilization
- Free disk space
- Disk write performance
- Disk read performance
- Network throughput

You can use the sar, vmstat, and pstree utilities to gather the information you need for your baselines.

In addition to baselines, you can also use system log files to troubleshoot problems with your system. Your system log files are stored in /var/log. Some of the more important log files in this directory include:

- boot.log
- boot.msg
- faillog
- firewall
- lastlog
- mail
- messages
- warn
- wtmp
- xinetd.log
- cron
- dmesg
- maillog
- secure
- rpmpkgs

Not all distributions will use the same log files. Logging is handled by the syslogd daemon on a Linux system. The way syslogd manages log files can be customized using the /etc/syslog.conf file. Most Linux distributions are configured to automatically rotate your log files periodically, preventing them from growing too large. The cron daemon periodically runs the logrotate utility to do this. How logrotate rotates specific log files is configured using the /etc/logrotate.conf file and the configuration files for individual services located in /etc/logrotate.d/.

You can configure syslogd to send all logging events to a syslogd daemon running on a different Linux system. Many administrators will set up a single system in their network to function as a log host where all Linux administrators will send their log files. Doing so centralizes your log files and also makes it harder for intruders to modify log files to cover their tracks. You configure remote logging by adding the following command to the beginning of your /etc/syslog.conf file:

```
*.*    @IP_address_of_loghost
```

You also need to set the value of the SYSLOGD_PARAMS directive in the /etc/sysconfig/syslog file on the log host to –r.

We then discussed the utilities that can be used to view text-based log files. While you can use less, cat, and more, the tail and head utilities can be used to view log files more effectively. The tail utility displays the last few lines of a file. The head utility will display the first few lines of a file. You can also use grep to search for content within a log file. You can use the –f option with tail to monitor a log file for new entries.

We then changed gears and discussed some simple troubleshooting measures you can use to diagnose and repair specific issues. To troubleshoot network issues, you should check the obvious first, such as unplugged cables. Then you should use ifconfig and route to verify that the network interface has been configured correctly. Then you can use ping to verify that network communications are working correctly.

We next discussed troubleshooting hardware issues. Because of the wide range of hardware components that you can use in a Linux system, the range of possible problems is expansive. Some basic issues you can check for include the following:

- Faulty hardware
- Outdated BIOS firmware
- Unsupported hardware
- Misconfigured hardware
- Buggy or missing drivers

We ended this chapter by discussing how you can rescue a system with corrupted file systems. You must first have a valid set of backups to do this. If the corrupt file system isn't the root file system, you can dismount it and run fsck on it to try to fix the errors. If that doesn't work, then you will need to repartition the disk and restore data from backup.

If the root file system is corrupt, you will need to boot from an alternative boot medium. You can create a boot diskette using the mkbootdisk command. You can also boot from your distribution's installation CD and select Rescue System in the welcome screen. Once done, you can try to run fsck on the root file system. If that fails, you can repartition the disk and restore data from backup.

✓ TWO-MINUTE DRILL

Document the System

- ❏ It is important that you document everything you do with your systems.
- ❏ Documentation will help when you're troubleshooting problems with your systems.
- ❏ Documentation will be an invaluable resource when someone is hired to fill your position after you have left the organization.
- ❏ You should extensively document new systems as soon as they are deployed.
- ❏ You should document changes you make to your systems after they are deployed.
- ❏ If you upgrade a component, install a new application, or enable a network service, you should document it.
- ❏ Maintenance activities should also be documented.
- ❏ You should also document the procedures you follow in your day-to-day work.
- ❏ Documenting procedures can be very beneficial.
- ❏ It can help you identify problems and disconnects in your work.
- ❏ It can also make it very easy for new hires to ramp up.
- ❏ The actual procedures you document will vary from organization to organization.

Troubleshoot System Problems

- ❏ Troubleshooting is part skill and part art form.
- ❏ To be a good troubleshooter, you need the following:
  - ❏ A solid troubleshooting procedure
  - ❏ A good knowledge of troubleshooting tools
  - ❏ A lot of experience troubleshooting problems
- ❏ To develop a solid troubleshooting procedure, you need to learn how to use a standardized troubleshooting model.
- ❏ You should use a standardized troubleshooting model to extensively research problems with your systems and concretely identify the cause.

❑ Once you know what the real problem is, you can research the solution and implement a fix.

❑ A basic troubleshooting model consists of the following steps:

  ❑ **Step 1** Gather information.

  ❑ **Step 2** Identify what has changed.

  ❑ **Step 3** Create a hypothesis.

  ❑ **Step 4** Determine the appropriate fix.

  ❑ **Step 5** Implement the fix.

  ❑ **Step 6** Ensure user satisfaction.

  ❑ **Step 7** Document the solution.

❑ You should use baselines to troubleshoot system problems.

❑ A baseline is a snapshot of your system's performance.

❑ The first baseline should be taken when a system is initially deployed.

❑ Then subsequent baselines should be taken on a regular schedule.

❑ You can compare baselines against each other to identify trends.

❑ You can also compare your baselines to your system documentation to identify what has changed that could account for changes in your baseline trends.

❑ You should consider including the following parameters in your system baselines:

  ❑ Processor utilization

  ❑ Memory utilization

  ❑ Swap partition utilization

  ❑ Free disk space

  ❑ Disk write performance

  ❑ Disk read performance

  ❑ Network throughput

❑ You can use the sar, vmstat, and pstree utilities to gather the information you need for your baselines.

❑ You can also use system log files to troubleshoot problems with your system.

❑ Your system log files are stored in /var/log.

❑ Some of the more important log files in this directory include boot.log, boot.msg, faillog, firewall, lastlog, mail, messages, warn, wtmp, xinetd.log, cron, dmesg, maillog, secure, and rpmpkgs.

❑ Not all distributions use the same log files.

❑ Logging is handled by the syslogd daemon.

❑ The syslogd daemon can be customized using the /etc/syslog.conf file.

❑ Most Linux distributions are configured to automatically rotate your log files periodically, preventing them from growing too large.

❑ The cron daemon periodically runs the logrotate utility to rotate log files.

❑ How logrotate rotates specific log files is configured using the /etc/logrotate.conf file and the configuration files for individual services located in /etc/logrotate.d/.

❑ You can configure syslogd to send all logging events to a syslogd daemon running on a different Linux system.

❑ Many administrators will set up a single system in their network to function as a log host where all Linux administrators will send their log files.

❑ You configure remote logging by adding the following command to the beginning of your /etc/syslog.conf file:

```
*.*     @IP_address_of_loghost
```

❑ You also need to set the value of the SYSLOGD_PARAMS directive in the /etc/sysconfig/syslog file on the log host to –r.

❑ While you can use less, cat, and more, the tail and head utilities can be used to view log files more effectively.

❑ The tail utility displays the last few lines of a file.

❑ The head utility will display the first few lines of a file.

❑ You can also use grep to search for content within a log file.

❑ You can use the –f option with tail to monitor a log file for new entries.

❑ To troubleshoot network issues, you should check the obvious first, such as unplugged cables.

❑ Then you should use ifconfig and route to verify that the network interface has been configured correctly.

❑ Then you can use ping to verify that network communications are working correctly.

❑ Because of the wide range of hardware components that you can use in a Linux system, the range of possible problems is expansive.

❑ Some basic issues you can check for include faulty hardware, outdated BIOS firmware, unsupported hardware, misconfigured hardware, and buggy or missing drivers.

❑ You need to know how to rescue a system with corrupted file systems.

❑ You must first have a valid set of backups to do this.

❑ If the corrupt file system isn't the root file system, you can dismount it and run fsck on it to try to fix the errors.

❑ If that doesn't work, then you will need to repartition the disk and restore data from backup.

❑ If the root file system is corrupt, you will need to boot from an alternative boot medium.

❑ You can create a boot diskette using the mkbootdisk command.

❑ You can also boot from your distribution's installation CD and select Rescue System in the welcome screen.

❑ Once done, you can try to run fsck on the root file system. If that fails, you can repartition the disk and restore data from backup.

SELF TEST

Document the System

1. Which of the following should be included when documenting a newly installed Linux system? (Choose two.)
   A. The amount of RAM installed in the system
   B. The color of the system case
   C. Your assessment of the system's quality
   D. The make and model of the hard disk drive
   E. The time of day when the system was first powered on

2. You've just upgraded the RAM in a Linux system from 512MB to 1GB. What should you document?
   A. The reason for the change
   B. When the last backup was run
   C. When the interior of the case was last vacuumed
   D. The name of the last security updates installed

3. You just ran a differential backup on a Linux system to magnetic tape. What information should you document?
   A. The reason the backup was run
   B. The hard drive's geometry
   C. The name of security updates installed
   D. The name of the tape where the backup is stored

Troubleshoot System Problems

4. A Linux system won't boot. An error message is displayed on the screen that reads "NTLDR is missing, press any key to restart." You determine that the MBR of the disk is corrupt and decide to re-install the system from scratch and restore data from a backup. Did you follow a proper troubleshooting model?
   A. Yes, a proper troubleshooting process was followed.
   B. No, you should have simply re-installed GRUB in the MBR.
   C. No, you should have replaced the hard disk drive before re-installing.
   D. No, you failed to diagnose the cause of the error message.

5. You're creating a system baseline using the sar utility. You want to generate a snapshot of your system's CPU performance using five measurements 60 seconds apart. Which of the following commands will do this? (Choose two.)

   A. sar 5 60

   B. sar –b 60 5

   C. sar –r 5 60

   D. sar 60 5

   E. sar –u 60 5

6. You're creating a system baseline using the vmstat utility. What information does the "us" column contain?

   A. Sleeping processes

   B. Free RAM

   C. CPU time spent running user processes

   D. Processes waiting to be run

7. You need to view the first few lines of the /var/log/boot.msg file. Which of the following commands will do this? (Choose two.)

   A. head /var/log/messages

   B. tail /var/log/messages

   C. grep –l 10 /var/log/boot.msg

   D. less /var/log/boot.msg

   E. cat /var/log/boot.msg

8. You're configuring the /etc/logrotate.d/ntp file to customize logging from the Network Time Protocol daemon on your system. You want old, archived logs to be saved using the current date in the file name extension. Which directive in the ntp file will do this?

   A. notifempty

   B. dateext

   C. rotate

   D. create

9. Which option, when used with the tail command, will cause the utility to monitor a log file for new entries?

   A. –

   B. –l

   C. –m

   D. –f

10. You're troubleshooting a Linux system that can't open Web pages from the Internet. You've used ifconfig to verify the configuration and have determined that you can ping hosts on the Internet using IP addresses. Which of the following is the most likely cause of the problem?

    A. The system has been configured with an incorrect default gateway router address.

    B. The DNS server is down.

    C. The system has been configured with an incorrect subnet mask.

    D. Your firewall is blocking ICMP traffic.

11. You've just installed a new 250GB IDE hard drive in a Linux system. However, your CMOS setup program only detects the drive as having 130GB. Which of the following is the most likely cause?

    A. You need to update your kernel to the latest version.

    B. You need to load an updated kernel module for the new disk.

    C. The BIOS firmware is outdated.

    D. The drive is configured to be a master drive when it should be configured as a slave.

LAB QUESTION

You have a Linux system that won't boot. A message is displayed on the screen indicating that the root file system (/) is corrupted and can't be mounted. Outline the process you would follow to fix this problem.

SELF TEST ANSWERS

Document the System

1. ☑ **A and D.** You should document the amount of RAM as well as the make and model of hard drive in the system, among other things.
   ☒ **B, C,** and **E** are incorrect. The information in **B, C,** and **E** is inconsequential.

2. ☑ **A.** You should document the reason for the change.
   ☒ **B, C,** and **D** are incorrect. **B, C,** and **D** are items to be included in your maintenance log, not the change log.

3. ☑ **D.** You should document the name of the magnetic tape where the backup is stored.
   ☒ **A, B,** and **C** are incorrect. **A** would be more appropriate in the change log. **B** would be more appropriate in an installation or change log. **C** would be entered in a change log.

Troubleshoot System Problems

4. ☑ **D.** No, you failed to diagnose the cause of the error message. The most likely cause of the problem is simply a floppy diskette advertently left in a floppy drive and the system is trying to boot from it.
   ☒ **A, B,** and **C** are incorrect. **A** is incorrect because you didn't identify the cause of the problem before trying to fix it. **B** is incorrect. There's probably nothing wrong with the GRUB bootloader on the hard disk. **C** is incorrect. There's probably nothing wrong with the hard drive.

5. ☑ **D and E.** The sar 60 5 and sar –u 60 5 commands generate a snapshot of your system's CPU performance using five measurements 60 seconds apart.
   ☒ **A, B,** and **C** are incorrect. **A** takes a snapshot of CPU performance using 60 measurements five seconds apart. **B** takes a snapshot of I/O performance. **C** would take a snapshot of RAM and virtual memory performance using 60 measurements five seconds apart.

6. ☑ **C.** The "us" column in the vmstat output lists CPU time spent running user processes.
   ☒ **A, B,** and **D** are incorrect. **A** is displayed in the "b" column. **B** is displayed in the "free" column. **D** is displayed in the "r" column.

7. ☑ **A and D.** The head /var/log/messages and the less /var/log/boot.msg commands will display the first few lines of the file on screen.
   ☒ **B, C,** and **E** are incorrect. **B** will display the last few lines of the file. **C** uses incorrect syntax (–l). **E** will not pause the output to allow you to view the first lines of the file.

8. ☑ **B.** The dateext directive will cause old, archived log files to be saved using the current date in the file name extension.

☒ **A, C,** and **D** are incorrect. **A** will cause the file to not be rotated if it is empty. **C** specifies the number of days between rotations. **D** is used to specify the permissions to be applied when creating the log file.

9. ☑ **D.** The –f option, when used with tail, will cause it to monitor a file for changes and display them on the screen.

☒ **A, B,** and **C** are incorrect. Each of these options is invalid when used with tail.

10. ☑ **B.** The most likely cause is that the DNS server is down or the wrong address has been entered in /etc/resolv.conf.

☒ **A, C,** and **D** are incorrect. **A** is incorrect. If the system can ping Internet hosts by IP address, then routing is working correctly. **C** is incorrect. If the host can route out correctly and ping Internet hosts, then the correct subnet mask has probably been used. **D** is incorrect. If the firewall were blocking ICMP traffic, the ping packets wouldn't be allowed through.

11. ☑ **C.** The most likely cause of the problem is outdated BIOS firmware that won't allow the system to address a disk larger than 130GB.

☒ **A, B,** and **D** are incorrect. **A** and **B** are incorrect because the operating system hasn't been loaded yet. **D** is incorrect. A misconfigured master/slave jumper won't cause part of the disk to be unaddressable.

LAB ANSWER

The issue in this scenario is a corrupted root partition. You should first try to repair the file system using fsck. To do this, you would first boot the system from the installation CD. In the welcome screen, you need to select Linux Rescue. When the system has booted, log in as root. Then run fsck on the / partition.

If this doesn't work, you'll need to use fdisk to repartition the disk (or create a partition on a new disk if the disk itself is bad). Then use mkfs to re-create the file system. Mount the file system in / and then restore files from your backup.

Alternatively, you could simply re-install the system from scratch and restore the data from backup.

GLOSSARY

absolute path   The full path to a file or directory in the Linux file system starting from the root directory. For example, to refer to a file named myfile.txt in the tmp directory, you would use an absolute path of /tmp/myfile.txt.

Accelerated Graphics Port (AGP)   AGP is a special type of expansion bus used only for video expansion boards in many PC systems.

Advanced Configuration and Power Interface (ACPI)   ACPI is a power management standard used in modern PC systems. Using ACPI, power consumption by system devices can be managed to reduce power consumption. ACPI divides power management tasks between the BIOS and the operating system.

Advanced Power Management (APM)   APM is an older power management implementation that is being phased out. APM uses software within the BIOS to manage power consumption within the system. To do this, APM uses device activity timeout periods to determine when to transition devices into lower power states.

AGP   *See* Accelerated Graphics Port.

alias   An alias is a shortcut to a different file or command on a Linux system. Many aliases are automatically defined when the Linux system is booted. For example, the md alias actually runs the mkdir –p command. You can also define your own custom aliases.

APM   *See* Advanced Power Management.

application   An application is computer software designed to perform a specific function. Applications are usually designed to be used by end users. Commonly used applications include word processors, database programs, graphics/drawing programs, Web browsers, and e-mail programs. Application is also the process of choice, demonstration, performing a procedure, solving, plotting, calculation, changing, interpretation, and operation.

asymmetric encryption   Asymmetric encryption systems use two keys, a public key and a private key. Data encrypted with the private key can only be decrypted with the public key. Data encrypted with the public key can only be decrypted with the private key.

authentication   Authentication occurs when a user supplies credentials, usually a username and password, that match those stored in the Linux username and password store, allowing the user access to the system.

background   When a command is launched in the background, the program will run normally. However, control will be returned immediately to the shell. You can use the shell to launch other programs or perform other shell tasks.

backup   A backup is the process of creating a copy of the data in a Linux file system on a secondary storage device. You can create three different types of backups with most Linux backup utilities:

- **Full**   In a full backup, all specified files are backed up, regardless of whether or not they've been modified since the last backup. After being backed up, each file is flagged as having been backed up.
- **Incremental**   During an incremental backup, only the files that have been modified since the last backup (full or incremental) are backed up. After being backed up, each file is flagged as having been backed up.
- **Differential**   During a differential backup, only the files that have been modified since the last full backup are backed up. Even though they have been backed up during a differential backup, the files involved are not flagged as having been backed up.

baseline   Baselining involves taking a snapshot of a system's performance. To create a system baseline, you can monitor and document a variety of system parameters, including:

- Processor utilization
- Memory utilization
- Swap partition utilization
- Free disk space
- Disk write performance
- Disk read performance
- Network throughput

bash   The Bourne-Again Shell (bash) is an improved version of the sh shell and is one of the most popular shells today. It's the default shell used by most Linux distributions.

basic input/output system (BIOS)   The system BIOS is a ROM chip integrated in the motherboard that contains a series of very small programs and drivers that allow the CPU to communicate with basic system devices, such as the keyboard, I/O ports, the system speaker, system RAM, floppy disk drives, and hard drives.

BIOS   *See* basic input/output system.

boot   The process of loading the Linux operating system kernel into RAM.

boot sector   On a hard disk drive, the boot sector contains the Master Boot Record (MBR).

bootloader   The bootloader is software that the BIOS can load from the MBR of the hard drive that allows the CPU to load the Linux kernel into RAM. To do this, the bootloader is configured with the location of the operating system files on the hard disk drive. The bootloader software itself may or may not actually be in the MBR. You can install some bootloaders within the MBR or you can install them within a partition somewhere else on the hard drive and place a pointer in the MBR. Other bootloaders install components in both places. The LILO and GRUB bootloaders are commonly used with most Linux distributions.

cache   Static RAM implemented within the CPU itself to store frequently accessed data.

central processing unit (CPU)   The central processing unit is the component in a PC that interprets computer program instructions and processes data.

change log   A log maintained by the Linux system administrator that contains an entry each time a change is made to the system, such as an operating system upgrade or a hard drive replacement.

checksum   A value generated by calculating the contents of a file using a Message Digest 5 (MD5) algorithm. You can run a checksum on a downloaded file and compare the results with the checksum value of the original file on the download source site. Identical values indicate that the file arrived intact. Differing values indicate corruption occurred during transfer.

command-line interface (CLI)   A command-line interface uses keyboard commands to send input to the operating system.

complementary metal oxide semiconductor (CMOS)   A rewritable chip on a PC motherboard that works in conjunction with the BIOS to store system parameters such as the type of floppy drive installed in the system, the type of hard drive(s) installed in the system, power management features of the motherboard, and the order of boot devices in the system.

control structures   Control structures are decision-making routines that can be added to shell scripts. Samples of control structures include if/then/else, case, while loops, and until loop structures.

Common UNIX Printing System (CUPS)   CUPS is a Linux printing system. The CUPS service is provided by the cupsd daemon, which automatically announces the availability of its print queues on the local network. CUPS client systems listen to these announcements, allowing the user to select the printer he or she wants with little networking knowledge. In addition, CUPS supports network printing over the Internet Printing Protocol (IPP) on port 631.

CUPS backends   CUPS backends are responsible for providing the interface between the scheduler and the actual printer hardware. The CUPS backends are located in /usr/lib/cups/backend. CUPS provides backends for a variety of different printer interfaces, including parallel, serial, USB, etc.

CUPS filters   If your printer isn't PostScript-compatible, you use CUPS filters to convert print jobs from PostScript into the appropriate format using the PDL of the printer to which it is being sent.

CUPS scheduler   The CUPS scheduler is a Web server that is used solely to handle IPP printing requests from CUPS clients.

daemon   Software that runs in the background on a Linux system and usually doesn't provide any kind of user interface. Also called a *system process*. Examples of common Linux daemons include named, httpd, and dhcpd.

dependency   A Linux software package may be dependent upon another package being installed on the system before it can work properly. If this is the case, the dependent package is called a dependency.

DHCP   *See* Dynamic Host Configuration Protocol.

direct memory access (DMA)   DMA is a chip on the motherboard that transfers data between the system RAM and a device in the system without the intervention of the CPU.

distribution   A customized version of Linux. Currently hundreds of Linux distributions are available.

DMA   *See* direct memory access.

DNS   *See* Domain Name System.

Domain Name System (DNS)   DNS is a system used on an IP network to resolve alpha-numeric domain names into IP addresses. DNS is a client-server system. DNS clients send resolution requests to DNS servers. DNS servers resolve domain names into IP addresses and return the results to the DNS client.

driver   The CPU needs software to communicate with hardware devices installed in the system. As the system boots, the operating system loads driver software from the hard disk into RAM. Once done, the CPU has the instructions it needs to communicate with the associated hardware.

Dynamic Host Configuration Protocol (DHCP)   DHCP is a protocol used to automatically assign IP addresses, subnet masks, router addresses, and DNS server addresses to network hosts. DHCP is a client-server protocol. When a DHCP client is booted, it sends out a DHCPDISCOVER broadcast. The DHCP server receives the broadcast and selects an IP address from its range of available addresses that it can assign to the DHCP client.

The server sends a proposed IP address assignment back to the host in a DHCPOFFER message. The DHCP client reviews the offers it has received and then selects the offer it wants to accept. The DHCP client then sends a DHCPREQUEST broadcast. This broadcast informs the DHCP server that it has accepted the addressing offer. The DHCP server responds to the client with a DHCPACK message, which contains the IP address assignment.

Emacs   Emacs is a commonly used Linux text editor that uses a menu-driven user interface.

environment variable   Environment variables are created, named, and populated by the operating system. Environment variables are used to configure the system's computing environment. Common environment variables used on a Linux system include MANPATH, HOST, SHELL, and DISPLAY.

ext2   Stands for Second Extended File System. It stores data in the standard hierarchical fashion used by most other file systems. Data is stored in files; files are stored in directories. A directory can contain either files or other directories called subdirectories. The maximum file size supported in the ext2 file system is 2 terabytes (TB). An ext2 volume can be up to 4TB. File names can be up to 255 characters long. The ext2 file system supports Linux file system users, groups, and permissions (called POSIX permissions). It also supports file compression.

ext3   Stands for Third Extended File System. It is an updated version of ext2. The ext3 file system offers journaling. Before committing a transaction to the hard disk drive, the ext3 file system records the transaction to a journal and marks it as incomplete. After the disk transaction is complete, the ext3 file system marks the transaction as complete in the journal. By doing this, the ext3 file system can keep a log of the most recent file transactions and whether or not they were actually completed.

file descriptors   There are three file descriptors that are available for every command entered at a Linux shell prompt:

- **stdin**   This file descriptor stands for standard input. Standard input is the input provided to a particular command to process. The stdin for a command is represented by the number 0.
- **stdout**   This file descriptor stands for standard output. Standard output is simply the output from a particular command. The stdout for a command is represented by the number 1.
- **stderr**   This file descriptor stands for standard error. Standard error is the error code generated, if any, by a command. The stderr for a command is represented by the number 2.

file system   When conducting disk I/O operations, the operating system needs to know where data is stored, how to access it, and where it is safe to write new information. The role of the file system is to reliably store data on the hard drive and organize it in such a way that it is easily accessible.

Filesystem Hierarchy Standard (FHS)   The Filesystem Hierarchy Standard defines the directories that must exist under the root directory on a Linux system.

firewall   A firewall is a combination of hardware and software that acts like a gatekeeper between your network and another network. It monitors traffic that flows between the networks, both inbound and outbound. You configure the firewall with rules that define the type of traffic that is allowed through. Any traffic that violates the rules is not allowed.

FireWire   FireWire is also known as IEEE 1394 and i.Link. FireWire devices are PnP-compatible and hot-swappable. It is frequently used for external hard drives, external CD and DVD drives, digital cameras, and digital video cameras. FireWire can transfer data at 400 Mbps. FireWire connects devices in true bus fashion by running a cable from device to device to device, forming a chain. A maximum of 63 devices can be connected together in this manner.

first in first out (FIFO) A FIFO is a special file used to move data from one running process on the system to another. A FIFO file is basically a queue where the first piece of data added to the queue is the first piece of data removed from the queue. Data can only move in one direction through a FIFO.

floppy diskette drive Floppy diskette drives are older storage devices in PCs. Floppy diskettes use an oxide-coated Mylar disk to store data. Floppy diskette drives are slowly being phased out.

foreground When a command is entered at the Linux shell prompt, a subshell is created and the process is run within it. As soon as the process exits, the subshell is destroyed. During the time that the process is running, the shell prompt of the parent shell disappears.

forward lookup In a forward lookup, a DNS client system sends a request to the DNS server asking it to resolve a host name into an IP address.

GNU General Public License (GPL) The GNU General Public License is a free software license used by the GNU Project. The source code for software governed by the GPL is freely distributable and modifiable.

GNU Project The GNU Project is a free software project launched by Richard Stallman in 1983. The goal of the project was to develop a body of freely available software.

graphical user interface (GUI) A graphical user interface displays information on the computer screen graphically. The user interacts with the system using a pointing device, such as a mouse, as well as keyboard input. A graphical user interface usually includes pull-down menus, dialog boxes, buttons, graphics, and icons.

GRUB Stands for GRand Unified Bootloader. GRUB is a bootloader that can be used to boot a Linux kernel from your system's hard drive. Recently, there has been a steady shift away from LILO toward GRUB on the part of most distributions and many Linux administrators.

GUI *See* graphical user interface.

hard disk drive Hard disk drives are the primary type of persistent storage used in PC systems. Hard disk drives read and write magnetic information to and from spinning aluminum disks called platters.

Hardware Compatibility List (HCL)   Most Linux distributions publish a Hardware Compatibility List that lists hardware that is supported by the software in the distribution.

HCL   *See* Hardware Compatibility List.

HTTP   *See* Hypertext Transfer Protocol.

Hypertext Transfer Protocol (HTTP)   HTTP is a request/response protocol used by a Web browser to get information from a Web server. The browser initiates the request by establishing a TCP/IP communication session between the client system and the Web server, which runs on IP port 80 by default. The Web server then listens for the browser to tell it what information it wants. The browser does this by sending a GET message to the Web server, which responds with the requested files.

IDE   *See* Integrated Drive Electronics.

Industry Standard Architecture (ISA)   The Industry Standard Architecture (ISA) bus was the earliest type of expansion bus used in the PC. The earliest version of the ISA bus was 8 bits wide. A 16-bit version of the ISA bus was introduced in the mid-1980s with the Intel 80286 CPU that ran at a clock speed of 8.33 MHz and used a 98-pin expansion slot.

info   You can use the info utility to view documentation for commands, utilities, services, and files on your Linux system. Most info nodes contain the same information as a man page. However, info nodes are usually more verbose and can actually teach you how to use a particular Linux tool.

initrd image   The initrd image contains a basic file system that can be used to complete a variety of startup tasks. The kernel can't mount some Linux file systems, such as RAID, Samba, and NFS, until special software is loaded. To make the system boot correctly, the bootloader creates a small, virtual hard drive in memory called a ramdisk and transfers a temporary root file system from the initrd image to it. The Linux kernel can then use this temporary file system to load the software and complete the tasks required for it to mount the file systems on these types of devices.

input/output port   I/O addresses allow communications between the devices in the PC and the operating system. They serve as mailboxes for the devices installed in the system. Data can be left for a device in its I/O address. Data from the device can be left in the I/O address for the operating system to pick up.

Integrated Drive Electronics (IDE) IDE is a standard for connecting storage devices to a PC system. IDE drives implement the hard disk drive controller hardware on the drive itself instead of a separate expansion board. A single controller on one drive can control a total of two different IDE devices. Most desktop motherboards available today include two separate IDE channels called the Primary and the Secondary channels. Because one controller can manage two IDE devices, you can install a maximum of two IDE drives on each channel. Each channel is configured using a 40-pin, 80-wire ribbon cable that connects each device to the motherboard.

Internet Control Message Protocol (ICMP) A commonly used IP protocol. This protocol provides data transfers between systems for diagnostic purposes. The ping command is an example of a utility that uses the ICMP protocol.

Internet Message Access Protocol (IMAP) IMAP is used by MUAs to download messages from an MDA. IMAP uses port 143. IMAP allows you to download the entire message from the MDA or only pull down the message headers, allowing you to determine the messages to be downloaded. IMAP also allows you to retain a copy of downloaded messages on the MDA and to create your own folders on the MDA for organizing messages.

interrupt request (IRQ) An IRQ is an electrical signal that a device in the system sends to the computer's CPU requesting the processor's attention.

Intrusion Detection System (IDS) An IDS operates by monitoring network traffic looking for patterns in the data that could indicate suspicious activity. Some IDS systems use pattern files to detect intrusion attempts. These IDS systems must have their intrusion definitions updated regularly to be effective. Some IDS systems monitor the system for a period of time, developing a baseline of activity. Once the baseline is complete, they look for traffic that doesn't fit the baseline and analyze it to see if an attack is in progress.

IP address An IP address is an address that is logically assigned to a network host. In IP version 4, an IP address consists of four numbers, separated by periods. In decimal notation, each number must be between 0 and 255. For example, 192.168.1.1 is a typical IP address. Each number in the address is actually an 8-bit binary number called an *octet*.

IRQ *See* interrupt request.

ISA *See* Industry Standard Architecture.

ISO image   An ISO image is a disk image of an optical disc, such as a CD or DVD. All data files, folders, and file system metadata are contained within a single file.

kernel   This is the central software component of the Linux operating system.

kernel module   A kernel module is a file that contains code to extend the running kernel. Kernel modules are typically used to add support for new hardware to the kernel.

LILO   Stands for *LInux LOader*. LILO is a flexible bootloader that can be used to launch just about any operating system from your computer's hard drive, including Linux, Windows, or DOS.

Line Printer Daemon (LPD)   An older printing daemon used by Linux distributions.

link   A link file in the Linux file system is a pointer that points to another file. You can create two different types of link files:

- **Hard**   A hard link is a file that points directly to the inode of another file. An inode stores basic information about a file in the Linux file system, including its size, device, owner, and permissions. Because the two files use the same inode, you can't tell which file is the pointer and which is the pointee after the hard link is created.
- **Symbolic**   A symbolic link file also points to another file in the file system. However, a file that is a symbolic link has its own inode. Because the pointer file has its own inode, the pointer and the pointee in the file system can be easily identified.

login shell   A login shell is in use if your Linux system boots to a text-based login screen in runlevel 3 and you use it to log in to the system.

MAC address   The MAC address is a hardware address that is burned into a ROM chip on every network board sold in the world. The MAC address is written using hexadecimal notation—for example, 00-08-74-4C-7F-1D. The MAC address is hard-coded into the network board and can't be changed.

Mail Transfer Agent (MTA)   An MTA is a software agent that transfers e-mail messages from one computer system to another. The postfix and sendmail daemons commonly used on Linux systems are examples of MTAs.

Mail User Agent (MUA)   The MUA is e-mail client software, such as Outlook Express, Evolution, Mozilla Mail, and Mutt.

maintenance log   A log maintained by the Linux system administrator that contains entries for each maintenance action taken.

makefile   A makefile file contains specific instructions for how an executable should be compiled to run on your platform.

man pages   One of the primary means used by the Linux operating system to maintain system documentation is through the use of manual (man) pages. These manual pages contain documentation about the operating system itself as well as any applications installed on the system. These man pages are viewed using the man utility.

Master Boot Record (MBR)   The MBR resides in the boot sector of your system's hard disk drive. It plays a key role in the process of booting your Linux system. The MBR tells the system where a bootloader resides.

Message Delivery Agent (MDA)   The MDA is sometimes called a Message Store. The MDA stores e-mail messages until the MUA of the recipient requests them. The recipient uses e-mail client software (MUA) on his or her workstation to connect to the MDA and pull down the messages.

mirroring   Mirroring is also called RAID 1. In a mirrored RAID array, data is written redundantly to two or more identical hard drives. If one drive in the array fails, the other drive(s) take over, preserving data and keeping the system up and running until the failed drive can be replaced.

multiplier   The multiplier allows the CPU to perform multiple cycles during a single cycle of the front side bus.

multitasking   The Linux operating system uses multitasking to quickly switch between the various processes running on the CPU, making it appear as if the CPU is working on multiple processes concurrently. However, the CPU actually only executes a single process at a time. All other currently running processes wait in the background for their turn. The operating system maintains a schedule that determines when each process is allowed access to the CPU.

needs assessment   A needs assessment is the process of determining why the Linux deployment is being undertaken and what outcomes are expected when it is complete.

network   A network is two or more computers connected together by cable or wireless media for the purpose of sharing data, hardware peripherals, and other resources.

Network File System (NFS)   NFS is a file sharing service used on Linux systems. NFS operates on a client-server model. The NFS server provides shared directories called exports. The NFS client mounts these shared directories into a mount point in the local file system.

Network Information Service (NIS)   NIS is designed to help you manage large networks of Linux systems. With NIS, a common set of configuration files is stored centrally on the network and copied out to all the network hosts. The system's configuration files are automatically brought up to date. To make this work, NIS uses the following components:

- Maps
- Domain
- Master server
- Slave server
- Clients

network interface card (NIC)   An NIC is an expansion board installed in a computer system. It connects the system to the network medium, allowing data to be sent and received on the network.

NIC   *See* network interface card.

operating system (OS)   The operating system is a set of programs that manage a computer's hardware and software resources.

owner   By default, the owner of a file or directory is the Linux user and group account that created it.

package   A bundle of one or more files that are necessary for the installation and execution of a service or application on a Linux system.

Packet Inter-Network Groper (PING)   Ping is a very useful utility that can be used to test communications between two network hosts. Ping works by sending ICMP echo requests to a remote host. The remote host responds with an ICMP echo response message.

parent process ID (PPID)   The PPID is the PID of a process' parent process.

parity   Parity works in conjunction with striping in a RAID array. To prevent data loss associated with the loss of a disk in a striped array, parity is stored on one or more disks in the array that will allow data to be reconstructed in the event of a failure.

partition   A partition is a logical division of your hard disk drive. Using the read-write heads inside the hard disk drive, an operating system can create magnetic divisions on the drive platter to divide it into separate sections. A hard drive can have a single partition that encompasses the entire hard drive or it can have many partitions.

password aging   Password aging involves specifying a finite lifetime for user passwords. After passwords reach the specified age, they expire and must be changed.

PCI   *See* Peripheral Component Interconnect.

PCMCIA   *See* Personal Computer Memory Card International Association.

Peripheral Component Interconnect (PCI)   PCI is a common expansion bus used in most PC systems today. The PCI bus is 32 bits wide and runs at 33 MHz, allowing it to transfer data at a rate around 66 MB/s.

permissions   Permissions are used to specify exactly what a particular user may do with files and directories in the file system. Each file or directory in your Linux file system stores the specific permissions assigned to it, called the mode of the file. Any file or directory can have the following permissions in its mode:

- Read
- Write
- Execute

These permissions are assigned to each of three different entities for each file and directory in the file system:

- Owner
- Group
- Others

Personal Computer Memory Card International Association (PCMCIA)   PCMCIA is an association of 300 industry manufacturers that has defined a set of standards for credit card–sized expansion boards used in notebook PCs. These cards function much like expansion boards in a desktop PC system. PCMCIA cards are PnP-compatible and hot-swappable.

piping   The process of chaining the output of one Linux command to the input of another Linux command. For example, you can pipe the output of the ls command to the grep command by entering **ls** | **grep** *search_term* at the shell prompt.

plug-n-play (PnP)   The plug-n-play (PnP) standard was introduced in the late 1990s. It is designed to automatically configure the system resources used by your expansion boards for you every time you boot the system. A PnP system requires three components to be present in your system:

- A PnP-compatible BIOS
- A PnP-compatible operating system
- A PnP-compatible device

When the system is powered on, the PnP BIOS negotiates with the PnP expansion board to determine what interrupt, I/O addresses, and DMA channels it will use. If necessary, the operating system can also add its input as to what resources it thinks should be assigned.

PnP   *See* plug-n-play.

Point-to-Point Protocol (PPP)   PPP is a serial communication protocol used to connect a computer system to a network using a modem and standard telephone lines.

Post Office Protocol version 3 (POP3)   POP3 is an IP protocol that operates on port 110. POP3 is used by MUAs to download e-mail messages from an MDA.

power on selftest (POST)   The POST happens when the BIOS tests the various system components and makes sure they are working properly when the system is first powered. If the POST encounters a problem with system devices, it will either display an error message on the screen or sound a series of beeps in code.

power supply   The power supply in a PC system converts 110-volt AC current from the wall outlet into 12-volt, 5-volt, and 3.3-volt DC current.

PPP   *See* Point-to-Point Protocol.

process   A process is a program that has been loaded from a long-term storage device, usually a hard disk drive, into system RAM and is currently being processed by the CPU on the motherboard.

process heredity   Any process running on a Linux system can launch additional processes. The process that launched the new process is called a *parent process*. The new process that was created is called the *child process*. This parent/child relationship constitutes the heredity of processes.

process ID (PID)   The PID is a number assigned to each process that uniquely identifies it on the system.

protocol   A protocol is a set of rules that computers use to communicate with one another.

quota   Quotas establish disk space limitations for users on a Linux system.

RAID   *See* redundant array of inexpensive disks.

random access memory (RAM)   Random access memory is used to store data in PC systems. RAM uses memory chips that allow any storage cell to be accessed at random, regardless of its physical location and whether or not it is related to the previous storage location.

redundant array of inexpensive disks (RAID)   RAID allows you to implement two or more hard disk drives in your system and then use a special hard disk controller or software in RAM to group the disks together into an array.

The disk controller board (or software in RAM) presents the array to the operating system as a single hard disk drive.

Reiser The Reiser file system is an alternative to the ext3 file system. Like ext3, Reiser utilizes journaling to make crash recovery very fast. However, Reiser is a completely different file system from ext2 and ext3, using a dramatically different internal structure. This allows the Reiser file system to support a larger maximum file size of 8TB and maximum volume size of 16TB. In addition, the different structure of Reiser allows it to perform much faster than ext2 or ext3.

relative path A relative path used in a Linux command is relative to some other point in the file system.

reverse lookup In a reverse lookup, a DNS server resolves an IP address into a host name.

root The root user account is the superuser account on a Linux system.

root directory The root directory is the topmost directory in the Linux file system hierarchy and is denoted as the **/** directory.

routing Routing involves connecting multiple network segments together using special network devices called routers. Routing forwards IP packets from the source network to a destination network. This may involve forwarding the packets through intermediary networks. Routers use routing tables to determine the best routes to remote networks.

runlevel A runlevel represents one of seven different modes that a Linux system can run in.

Samba Samba is a Linux service that can be used to configure a Linux system to communicate over the network using the Server Message Block (SMB) protocol. Effectively, this allows the system to emulate a Windows server or a Windows client.

script A shell script is a text file that contains a series of commands and control structures that are executed by the shell. Shell scripts can be used to run multiple commands at once. They can also be used to read input from the end user or from shell commands and make decisions based on the input.

SCSI *See* Small Computer System Interface.

Secure Shell (ssh) The Secure Shell (ssh) service works in almost the same manner as Telnet. It allows you to access the shell prompt on a remote Linux system. ssh is a client-server system. The sshd daemon runs on the Linux system you want to connect to. You run an ssh client on the remote client system. ssh uses encryption to scramble that data being transmitted between the ssh client and the sshd daemon.

SGID   Set Group ID. This permission can be applied to binary executable files (not shell scripts). When a user runs an executable file with SGID set, the user temporarily becomes a member of the file's owning group. When a user creates a file in a directory that has SGID set, the file's owner is set to the user's account (as per normal). However, the owning group assigned to the new file is set to the owning group of the parent directory.

sh   The Bourne Shell (sh) was the earliest shell; it was developed for UNIX back in the late 1970s. While not widely used on Linux systems, it is still very widely used on UNIX systems.

shell   Software that provides a command-line user interface on a Linux system.

Simple Mail Transfer Protocol (SMTP)   SMTP is an IP protocol that operates on port 25. It is used to transfer e-mail messages from MUAs to MTAs and between MTAs.

Small Computer System Interface (SCSI)   SCSI is a general-purpose interface that can be used to connect a variety of different types of devices to a PC system, including:

- Hard disk drives
- CD/DVD drives
- Tape drives
- Scanners
- RAID arrays
- Printers

socket   Sockets are a type of file similar to FIFO files in the Linux file system. They are used to transfer information bi-directionally between sockets.

sticky bit   When the sticky bit is assigned to a directory, users can only delete files within the directory for which they are the owner of the file or the directory itself. This negates the effect of having the write permission to a directory, which could allow a user to delete files in a directory that he or she doesn't own.

striping   Striping is a RAID concept that allows data to be divided up into chunks and written to two or more drives concurrently. Striping increases the speed of the disk system, but it does not protect data. If one of the disks in a striped array fails, all of the data on all disks is lost.

SUID   Set User ID. This permission can only be applied to binary executable files (not shell scripts). When an executable file with the SUID set is run, the user who ran the file temporarily becomes the file's owner.

symmetric encryption   Symmetric encryption systems use a single encryption key to encrypt and decrypt data.

tape drive   Tape drives use magnetic tape, much like the tape used in an 8mm video camera, to store data. Tape drives can store a lot of data and are relatively inexpensive. They are commonly used to back up data on a Linux system.

tarball   An archive file containing one or more files created with the tar utility. The archive file may or may not be compressed with the gzip utility.

TCP Wrappers   TCP Wrappers are used by xinetd to start and run the network services using a set of configuration files that specify who can and who can't access the service.

Telnet   The Telnet protocol and utilities are used on a Linux system to access the shell prompt on a remote Linux system. Telnet does not encrypt transmissions, making it insecure. The ssh protocol and utility is usually used in place of Telnet today to access the shell prompt of a remote system.

UID   A unique number assigned to every Linux user account when it is created. No two user accounts on a Linux system can have the same UID.

UNC   *See* Universal Naming Convention.

Uniform Resource Locator (URL)   A URL is used by your browser to specify the exact information you need from the Web server as well as how it is to be retrieved. The syntax for a URL is: protocol://domain_name or IP_address:port/ filename.

Universal Naming Convention (UNC)   UNC is a standard for addressing systems on an SMB network. The syntax for using UNC names is: \ \ server_name \ share_name.

universal serial bus (USB)   Universal serial bus (USB) is a high-speed removable hardware interface. Most PC systems today include an integrated USB interface in the motherboard. USB can be used to connect a wide variety of external devices, including external hard drives, external CD and DVD drives, printers, scanners, digital cameras, mice, keyboards, and flash drives. A single USB bus can support up to 127 external devices. USB devices are self configuring, self-identifying, and hot-swappable. USB has been implemented in two different versions:

- ■ **USB 1.1**   This is the oldest USB version. It transfers data at a rate of 12 Mbps.
- ■ **USB 2.0**   This is the current version of USB. It can transfer data at 480 Mbps.

USB   *See* universal serial bus.

user account   The user account is the information that defines a particular user on a network, which includes the username, password, group memberships, and rights and permissions assigned to the user.

user process   Processes created by end users when they execute a command from the shell prompt or though the X Windows graphical interface.

vi   vi is a common text editor used by most Linux distributions.

Virtual Network Computing (VNC)   Virtual Network Computing is a GUI desktop sharing system that allows you to remotely control another computer.

Web server   A Web server sends Web pages, graphics, and other files to Web clients requesting them. A Web server can transfer just about any type of computer file between the server and the client. However, the most common type of file used with a Web server is a Web page. A Web page is simply a text document written using a special markup coding system (called Hypertext Markup Language, or HTML) that instructs the Web browser how the information should be formatted and displayed.

window manager   The window manager's job is to customize how the windows in the Linux GUI appear and behave. It works in conjunction with the X Server. A wide variety of window managers are currently available for Linux.

X Server   The X Server is the heart of the Linux GUI. It draws windows graphically on the display screen. It's also responsible for managing the mouse and the keyboard.

xinetd   The xinetd daemon is a special type of network service called a super daemon. It acts as an intermediary between the user requesting network services and the daemons on the system that provide the actual services. When a request for one of the network services managed by xinetd arrives at the system, it is received and processed by xinetd, not the network daemon being requested. The xinetd daemon then starts the daemon for the requested service and forwards the request to it. When the request has been fulfilled and the network service is no longer needed, xinetd unloads the daemon from memory.

YaST   YaST stands for Yet Another Setup Tool. It's a powerful installation and configuration utility used by the SUSE Linux distribution.

zone transfer   The transfer of DNS zone information from a master DNS server to a slave DNS server.

The CD-ROM included with this book comes complete with MasterExam and the electronic version of the book. The software is easy to install on any Windows 98/NT/2000/XP/Vista computer and must be installed to access the MasterExam feature. You may, however, browse the electronic book and CertCam files directly from the CD without installation. To register for a second bonus MasterExam, simply click the Online Training link on the Main Page and follow the directions to the free online registration.

System Requirements

Software requires Windows 98 or higher and Internet Explorer 5.0 or above and 20MB of hard disk space for full installation. The electronic book requires Adobe Acrobat Reader.

Installing and Running MasterExam

If your computer CD-ROM drive is configured to auto-run, the CD-ROM will automatically start upon inserting the disk. From the opening screen you may install MasterExam by clicking the MasterExam button. This will begin the installation process and create a program group named "LearnKey." To run MasterExam, select Start | Programs | LearnKey. If the auto-run feature did not launch your CD, browse to the CD and click on the LaunchTraining.exe icon.

MasterExam

MasterExam provides you with a simulation of the actual exam. The number of questions, the type of questions, and the time allowed are intended to be an accurate representation of the exam environment. You have the option to take an open book exam, including hints, references, and answers; a closed book exam; or the timed MasterExam simulation.

When you launch MasterExam, a digital clock display will appear in the upper-left corner of your screen. The clock will continue to count down to zero unless you choose to end the exam before the time expires.

CertCam Video Training

CertCam .AVI clips provide detailed examples of key certification objectives in audio/video format direct from the author of the book. These clips walk you step by step through various system configurations. You can access the clips directly from the CertCam table of contents by selecting the CertCam link on the Main Page.

The CertCam .AVI clips are recorded and produced using TechSmith's Camtasia Producer. Since .AVI clips can be very large, we use TechSmith's special AVI Codec to compress the clips. The file named tsccvid.dll is copied to your Windows\System folder during the first auto-run. If the .AVI clip runs with audio but no video, you may need to re-install the file from the CD-ROM. Browse to the PROGRAMS\ CERTCAMS folder, and run TSCC.

Electronic Book

The entire contents of the Study Guide are provided in a PDF file. Adobe's Acrobat Reader has been included on the CD.

Help

A help file is provided through the Help button on the Main Page in the lower-left corner. An individual help feature is also available through MasterExam.

Removing Installation(s)

MasterExam is installed to your hard drive. For best results in removing the programs, select Start | Programs | Learnkey | Uninstall to remove MasterExam.

Technical Support

For questions regarding the technical content of the electronic book or MasterExam, please visit www.osborne.com or e-mail customer.service@mcgraw-hill.com. For customers outside the 50 United States, e-mail international_cs@mcgraw-hill.com.

LearnKey Technical Support

For help with technical problems with the software (installation, operation, removing installations), please visit www.learnkey.com or e-mail techsupport@learnkey.com.

INDEX

J

K

L

T

U

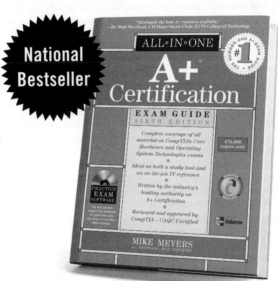